Northcliffe

Northcliffe

Press Baron in Politics, 1865–1922

———————◆———————

J. LEE THOMPSON

JOHN MURRAY
Albemarle Street, London

© J. Lee Thompson 2000

First published in 2000
by John Murray (Publishers) Ltd,
50 Albemarle Street, London W1X 4BD

A catalogue record for this book is available from the British
Library

ISBN 0–7195–5725 9

Typeset in 11.75/13pt Garamond by Servis Filmsetting Ltd,
Manchester

Printed and bound in Great Britain by The University Press
Cambridge

To Quince Adams

Contents

Contents

Illustrations

———————◆———————

The author and publisher would like to thank the following for permission to reproduce illustrations: Plates 1–3, 5–25 and 27–30, the Harmsworth Archive; Plate 4, The British Library; Plate 26, Hulton Getty.

Preface

L ORD NORTHCLIFFE DID not like the one biography of him published
before his death, William Carson's *Northcliffe: England's Man of Power*.
Released in 1918, and only in the United States, the book was inaccurate
and sketchy, written to capitalize on the press lord's visit as head of the
British War Mission the previous year. Though he was not lacking in
ego, Northcliffe was rather uncomfortable with the idea of a biography
of himself. However, he realized such books were inevitable, and after
the Great War he permitted the *Daily Mail* writer H. W. Wilson to begin
an authorized life, opening his papers to the effort. When the publisher,
Herbert Jenkins, told Northcliffe that the writer reckoned it would take
three volumes to encapsulate his life, he responded, 'Gott in Himmel!'
The manuscript delivered in 1921 did not meet Jenkins's approval. He
wrote to its subject that the work was 'not biography' and did not show
the 'real' Northcliffe, spending too much time on the press, the *Daily
Mail* and the Great War. What the publisher wanted was a 'biography,
vital, impressionistic, and full of personality'. Jenkins envisioned a book
which would 'be for biographies what the *Daily Mail* was to its contemporaries when it first appeared'.[1] This large order has never and probably will never be fulfilled.

   This has not, however, stopped writers from trying. Since his death
in 1922, many works have recorded Northcliffe's life and even his after-
life, from Hannen Swaffer's 1925 *Northcliffe's Return*, with its spiritual
musings on existence in the great beyond, to the massive 1959 official
biography by Reginald Pound and Geoffrey Harmsworth. Too often the

books either were written by former employees and friends or were based on the memoirs of the many enemies who survived him. Had he published them, Northcliffe's recollections of events would have radically challenged Lloyd George, Beaverbrook, Churchill and a host of others who surely breathed a sigh of relief that he was unable to do so. Of the more recent works concerned with him, such as Tom Ferris's *House of Northcliffe* (1972), Richard Bourne's *Lords of Fleet Street: The Harmsworth Dynasty* (1990) and S.J. Taylor's *The Great Outsiders: Northcliffe, Rothermere and the Daily Mail* (1996), none has placed Northcliffe in his era, or considered his political or imperial connections, which were myriad. The author of the most ambitious survey of the nineteenth- and twentieth-century British political press, Stephen Koss, noted that 'neither Harmsworth's panegyrists nor his debunkers have taken the trouble to unravel his political entanglements'.[2]

Northcliffe has been variously hated, dismissed and elevated to sainthood. A.J.P. Taylor summed him up as 'newsman first, last and all the time' and he holds a prominent place in accounts of the rise of the new journalism, the press barons and the political press in the late nineteenth and early twentieth centuries. He also has been widely criticized as a prime example of the dangers of press 'power without responsibility'. E.T. Raymond warned in 1919 that his 'present indirect power was one of the chief dangers of the State'. Winston Churchill's very personal account of events, *The World Crisis* (1927), criticized Northcliffe's wartime role, stating that he 'wielded power without official responsibility, enjoyed secret knowledge without the general view, and disturbed the fortunes of national leaders without being willing to bear their burdens'. More recent authors have been equally hostile. In *The Prerogative of the Harlot: Press Barons and Power* (1980), Hugh Cudlipp described Northcliffe as a man corrupted by power and wealth, who desecrated journalistic standards and became dominated by 'the pursuit of political power, unguided by political prescience'.

Alfred Harmsworth, the later Lord Northcliffe, was born near the midpoint of the Victorian age, two years before Disraeli's 1867 Reform Bill ushered in the modern era of mass politics, abetted before the turn of the century by the franchise extension and redistribution of 1884–5. It is fitting for a biography of the press lord to mention Disraeli, who cajoled Queen Victoria into accepting that she become the embodiment of Empire. Although the two never met, the Prime Minister's actions profoundly affected Alfred Harmsworth, who would take advantage of both mass politics and imperial enthusiasms to create the age's greatest media enterprise. Like many of his time, he saw the greatness of Britain and her possessions as indivisible. The world's greatest imperial nation fought a constant battle to maintain and extend her domain. Northcliffe judged politicians on the measures they were willing to take to defend and strengthen the 'bond of empire'.

Northcliffe was also able to take advantage of another development of his age – the growth in importance of public opinion. More and more during the nineteenth and into the twentieth century, if one could claim to tap opinion, influence followed. From at least the time when Britain became involved in the Crimean War, under pressure from the public and *The Times*, newspapers were given an unprecedented influence by the fear of the governing class that journalism, by mastering the temper of the masses, somehow drove events. By the 1880s, when Alfred Harmsworth entered Fleet Street as a journalist, politics had become 'something of a permanent campaign', which needed constant newspaper support.[3] A new and more powerful popular political press targeted the increasingly literate and affluent millions who had benefited from government-sponsored education and the repeal, in the mid nineteenth century, of the various taxes on paper and daily journals. Once he became a newspaper proprietor, Harmsworth used a system of 'ferrets and spies', took polls long before Gallup, and made up his mind on the great and minor issues of his day according to the number of letters his journals received. In the final years of his life, during Lloyd George's reign as head of the 1918–22 coalition, one historian has described the political atmosphere as 'one long press conference'.[4]

The following work focuses on political and imperial connections, revealing Northcliffe largely through his correspondence and the letters of those who wrote about him, without overwhelming authorial prodding and comment. Compared with the previously published accounts, relatively little attention is given to the founding of the publishing empire and more is placed upon the press lord's career once he began to shape a newspaper voice for his ambitions and started to be regularly mentioned in the political correspondence of his contemporaries. Even with these limitations, putting the events of Northcliffe's life into a reasonably sized single volume has proved a formidable challenge. From the 1890s he carried on what was perhaps the largest private correspondence of his day, in an age before letter writing was replaced by telephone conversations. He was among the first to make regular use of the new instrument (and many other technological innovations), but, fortunately for the biographer, a squad of stenographers and secretaries, armed with typewriters, often recaptured his conversations and thoughts.

There is voluminous manuscript evidence available of the courtship of Northcliffe by the British political and military elite. Most of his public papers and diaries are in 245 volumes designated as the Northcliffe Additional Manuscripts in the British Library. Significant material can also be found at the Archive of *The Times*, London, which also holds the most recently discovered Northcliffe material available to scholars, allowing this work to be based partly on evidence not previously published. A final repository examined, the private Harmsworth Archive, includes much political and family correspondence which had hitherto been unavailable for several decades. More than fifty other sets of papers consulted for this study, encompassing many of the principal political, military and press figures of the period, leave no doubt as to the influence of Northcliffe in the calculations and policy decisions of the nation's leadership.

The record of his personal life is more tenuous. There is little remaining correspondence between Northcliffe and his wife, who left no papers that can be located. His relationship with his long-time mistress, Mrs Wrohan, who bore him three children, is, understandably, even less well documented. The following is therefore a biography largely of the public man, based on his letters and the words of others about him and to him. It is hoped that from this the reader will gain a new perspective on the life and career of one of the most remarkable figures in British press, political or imperial history.

I must express my thanks to the following individuals and institutions who made materials available to me without which this study could not have been completed: Mr Vyvyan Harmsworth, Associated Newspaper Holdings Limited; Ms Katharine Bligh, the House of Lords Record Office; Dr Piers Brendon, the Churchill Archives Centre, Churchill College, Cambridge; Mr Eamon Dyas, Archive of *The Times*, News International plc; Mr Robin Harcourt Williams, librarian and archivist to the Marquess of Salisbury; the British Library, Great Russell Street, Oriental and India Office Collections and the Colindale Newspapers Library; the Imperial War Museum; the Bodleian Library, Oxford; the Cambridge University Library; the National Library of Scotland; the Public Record Office; the British Library of Political and Economic Science; the Liddell Hart Centre for Military Archives, King's College, London; the Library of Congress; and Ms Judith Ann Schiff, the Yale

Preface

University Library. For much-needed photographic assistance I thank Jan and Sim Seckbach and Felicity Swan.

For permission to quote materials for which they hold copyright, I wish to thank Ms Alison Kagamaster Bullock, granddaughter of Walter Frederick Bullock; Lord Burnham; Mr Rupert Murdoch; Mr John Grigg; Mr Vyvyan Harmsworth; Lord Rothermere; Mr A.J. Maxse; the British Library Board; the Science Museum Library; the Clerk of the Records of the House of Lords Record Office, on behalf of the Beaverbrook Foundation; Lord Salisbury; Lord Rosebery; Lord Fisher; Mr and Mrs William Bell; Lord Derby; Lord Scarsdale; Thomas Arthur and Caroline Kenny; the Mariam Coffin Canaday Library, Bryn Mawr College; Milton Gendel; Edward Rory Carson; Professor A.K.S. Lambton; Lord Coleraine; the Wardens and Fellows, New College, Oxford; the *Spectator*, David McKenna; Leo Amery; Lady Patricia Kingsbury; News International plc; Lt Col. J.A. Charteris; A.P. Watt Ltd, on behalf of the Literary Executors of the Estate of H.G. Wells; the National Library of Scotland; the Syndics of Cambridge University Library; the Controller of HM Stationery Office; and the Yale University Library. If I have unwittingly infringed on the copyright of any persons or institutions, I hope they will accept my sincerest apologies and notify me of the oversight.

Special thanks are due to Mr John Grigg and Professor James Startt, who both read the manuscript and offered valuable criticisms and guidance. Professor Startt was also kind enough to provide transcripts of the Josephus Daniels and Roy Howard papers at the Library of Congress. I also wish to thank my publisher and editor, Mr Grant McIntyre and Mr Bob Davenport, and my literary agent, Mr Andrew Lownie, for their help and encouragement in this project. My wife, Diane, read every word of the manuscript and has with good humour shared her husband with Alfred Harmsworth for six years. Without her loving support and understanding this project would never have been completed. Finally, I wish to thank Professor R.J.Q. Adams, my teacher and valued friend, to whom I dedicate this work.

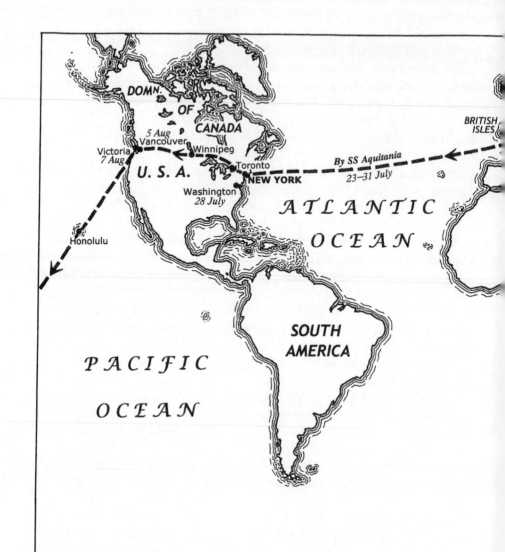

DOMN. OF CANADA

BRITISH ISLES

5 Aug
Vancouver
Victoria
7 Aug
Winnipeg

U. S. A.

Toronto
NEW YORK

By SS Aquitania
23–31 July

Washington
28 July

ATLANTIC OCEAN

Honolulu

PACIFIC

OCEAN

SOUTH AMERICA

LORD NORTHCLIFFE'S JOURNEY

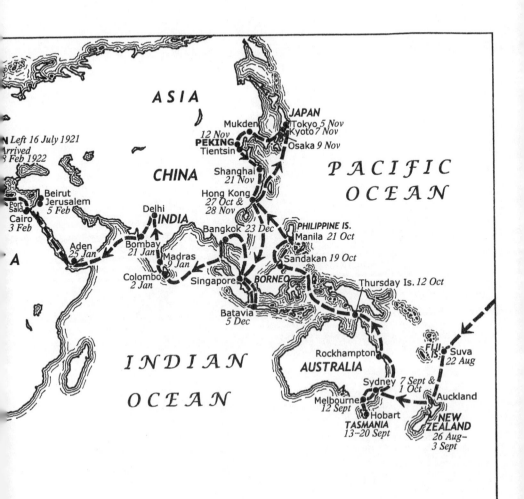

ASIA

Mukden *12 Nov*
PEKING
Tientsin

JAPAN
Tokyo *5 Nov*
Kyoto *7 Nov*
Osaka *9 Nov*

N *Left 16 July 1921*
Arrived
3 Feb 1922

Beirut
Jerusalem
5 Feb
Port
Said
Cairo
3 Feb

CHINA

Shanghai
21 Nov

PACIFIC
OCEAN

Delhi
INDIA

Hong Kong
27 Oct &
28 Nov

A

Aden
25 Jan

Bombay
21 Jan
Madras
9 Jan
Colombo
2 Jan

Bangkok *23 Dec*

PHILIPPINE IS.
Manila *21 Oct*

Sandakan *19 Oct*

Singapore
BORNEO

Thursday Is. *12 Oct*

Batavia
5 Dec

INDIAN

OCEAN

Rockhampton
AUSTRALIA

FIJI
IS.
Suva
22 Aug

Sydney *7 Sept &*
1 Oct

Melbourne
12 Sept
Hobart
TASMANIA
13–20 Sept

Auckland

NEW
ZEALAND
26 Aug–
3 Sept

AROUND THE WORLD, 1921–1922

I

From Adonis to Answers, *1865–1894*

IN THE SUMMER of 1922, Lord Northcliffe, who towered over Fleet Street as has no other figure, lost his mind and then his life. Only recently turned fifty-seven, the exertion of building an unparalleled press empire and the mental and physical effort put forth in the Great War finally took a mortal toll. The official diagnosis of a parade of noted medical attendants was malignant endocarditis, the symptoms of which in this case included periods of delirium. The final stage of the illness had descended upon him on the Continent, and he had been bundled back to London in a special train arranged by the French premier, Raymond Poincaré.

From time to time the mental fog which shrouded Northcliffe in his last months cleared sufficiently for him to recognize those about him, including family and physicians. One of the latter, Sir Thomas Horder, had recently been knighted by the Lloyd George coalition. When Horder entered Northcliffe's bedroom to perform an examination, his patient greeted him as 'one of George's bloody knights', pulled a pistol from underneath his pillow, and made ready to fire.[1] Unbeknown to the terrified doctor, the weapon had been unloaded by a male nurse. Not long after this episode, on 14 August 1922, Northcliffe's life ended. Two months later so did the government of his great enemy, David Lloyd George, hoist in part with the petard of a scandal over the sale of honours. It is fitting that Northcliffe and Lloyd George should each have gone to his respective physical and political oblivion so close to the other. Though he lived another two decades, the Welshman would never again hold office. Their co-operation and conflict had spanned more than a decade, and the Great War marked the high point of both men's careers. Before their sometime alliance ended in late 1918, Northcliffe had aided 'The Man Who Won the War' more than Lloyd George would ever care to admit.

On Tuesday 17 August 1922, after a service at Westminster Abbey, the funeral cortège slowly wound its way towards the St Marylebone Cemetery in East Finchley. As it passed through central London, the procession was observed by thousands lining its route, silently paying their final respects to the first media giant of Britain, whose popular newspaper campaigns had made the people consider him one of their own. He left behind a print kingdom of unprecedented size and scope which would not long survive him. While he lived, however, Northcliffe had remade Fleet Street, and in the process had touched all of British society, from the ruling élite to the middle- and working-class audience to which his publications appealed.

Alfred Charles William Harmsworth was born on 15 July 1865 at Sunnybank Cottage on the river Liffey in Chapelizod, near Dublin. The family name, or slight variations on it, can be traced back for five hundred years in Middlesex.[2] More recently, young Alfred's paternal grandfather and namesake, Charles Harmsworth, born in Odiham in Hampshire, had married one of the more mysterious and colourful members of the family, Hannah, née Carter. The lineage of Charles's bride, family lore would have it, included blood royal through Frederick, Duke of York, a son of George III. Hannah had a sufficiently powerful personality to keep the stories alive, and it did not hurt the legend that in old age she came to resemble the court portraits of her reputed grandfather. Her husband, Charles, followed a more pedestrian occupation as a London shopkeeper dealing in greengroceries and coal. Charles succumbed to the physical ravages of alcoholism while in his early fifties. He passed on a weakness for drink to his son Alfred, born in London in 1837.

The father of the future press lord was sent to boarding school at Kensal Green, and then at age fourteen to St Mark's College, Chelsea, where, it had been decided by his mother that he should prepare himself for a career as a teacher. Three years later Alfred took up his first post, a junior grammar-school mastership at Truro in Cornwall. After two undistinguished years he returned to London, taking temporary positions until 1861, when he won the position of fourth master at the Royal Hibernian Military School in Phoenix Park, Dublin.

By the time he took up his duties in Ireland, Alfred had matured into a lanky, rather handsome man who combed his dark hair across his forehead in a single lock and kept his whiskers stylishly thick. In Dublin he met and fell in love with Geraldine Maffett. A year younger than Alfred, she was auburn-haired and pretty, in a plump Victorian way. The Maffett family, of long-transplanted Protestant Scottish stock, had lived for many years in County Down. William Maffett, Geraldine's father, was a gruff disciplinarian, successful enough as a land agent to afford trips to the Continent and governesses for the education of his daughters, who were taught, among other lessons, how to sing and to moderate their Irish accents. Though the Maffetts were decidedly more prosperous than the Harmsworth clan, Geraldine was willing to overlook Alfred's present status. The pair complemented each other. The rather serious-minded Geraldine was attracted to his romantic affability and easy laughter. He sensed in her traits which he lacked – ambition, drive and an indomitable will. After a courtship of two years, the couple married on 22 September 1864 at St Stephen's Church, Dublin.

Geraldine took up Alfred, and his promotion, as her life's work. Believing a career at law a much superior path to advancement than teaching, she pushed her husband to become a barrister. He obediently travelled to London and was formally admitted as a student of the Middle Temple in 1864, but continued his studies in Ireland. The next year the couple's first child, Alfred Charles William, was born. Baby Alfred – called 'Sunny' by a family fond of nicknames – was described as a 'strangely quiet child' with 'solemn blue eyes'. His head was considered to be too large for his body. Later, the press lord would judge others by their cranial capacity, and be dismissive of those he imagined not so well endowed as himself. He also would refer to salmon splashing in an Irish stream as his earliest childhood memory – extraordinary given that he was not yet two when the family departed for London so that his father could complete his legal training and begin his new career at the centre of the British Empire.[3]

The Harmsworths embarked for England in March 1867 with the infant Alfred and a new daughter, Geraldine Adelaide Hamilton Harmsworth. Their first London residence was at 6 Alexandra Terrace, St John's Wood. Alfred Senior found temporary employment with a government commission examining the finances of the Church of England. In England, baby Alfred was subject to many illnesses and periodic 'fits', which doctors attributed to 'congestion of the brain'. A second son, Harold, later Lord Rothermere and dubbed 'Bunny', was born in London on 26 April 1868. The next year a third boy arrived, Cecil Bisshopp. Cecil, the future Lord Harmsworth, was assigned the pet name 'Buffles' for his thick mane of buffalo-like hair.

In 1869 Alfred Harmsworth completed his studies at the Middle Temple and was called to the bar. Though not without skill in the court-room, he lacked determination. Despite his wife's constant attempts to 'stir him up', he was too often found in taverns, where, in his cups, he would proclaim his royal lineage. In this period he also helped to found the Sylvan Debating Club, displaying his genial eloquence at its meeting place, the tavern adjoining Lord's Cricket Ground.[4] Fondness for drink and failure to find success in his profession combined to the detriment of his career and the family's fortunes. Reduced circumstances forced the Harmsworths to relocate into successively less comfortable dwellings more distant from central London, and by April 1870 they had descended to a residence called Rose Cottage in the Vale of Health at Hampstead Heath. There the family continued to increase in numbers. Robert Leicester was born on 1 November 1870, Hildebrand Aubrey on 15 March 1872, and Violet Grace on 11 April 1873. While the children enjoyed the outdoor activities of the more rural setting, their father battled with a growing stack of overdue accounts, worries over which often drove him to visit the King of Bohemia in Hampstead High Street, a favourite drinking establishment.

With his father often absent, the eldest son formed a strong – some would later say fanatical – bond with his mother, who became the anchor of the family, holding it together in a struggle to keep up respectable, middle-class appearances, even as their income fell perilously closer to working-class level. Following her upright example, in later life he did not swear or gamble. A lifelong disgust for drunkenness was undoubtedly a reaction to his father's weakness and addiction. The young man's aloof temperament was also more attuned to the maternal influence.[5] Since neither parent held fervent religious beliefs, he escaped strict instruction, although the family did attend Church of England services. At Hampstead, Geraldine Harmsworth's sisters, Grace and Caroline, paid visits with their German husbands. Later, during the Great War, Northcliffe, at the behest of his mother, would support his aunts with funds sent by clandestine methods into enemy territory.

In the summer of 1873, young Alfred made the acquaintance of George Samuel Jealous, a friend of the family who was also owner and editor of the *Hampstead and Highgate Express*. The lad enjoyed poking about the newspaper premises, and Jealous became a close example of the relative prestige the press could afford. On one such visit, the editor gave the boy a bag of used type and perhaps thus set in motion the greatest career Fleet Street has known. Alfred later recalled how on that occasion, though still a small boy, he had declared that he would start his own newspaper one day.[6] The future press lord used the worn type to learn his letters. The cost of school fees, and his father's determination that formal education should not start too early, meant that Alfred was not sent to school until age eight. In the main, his early education came from observation, the uncanny use of which faculty, whether developed as a child or inherent, proved invaluable to his later endeavours.

Once at a local school, Wykeham House in Boundary Road, Alfred was not a good student, particularly in arithmetic, and was easily distracted. Brother Harold, on the other hand, displayed a real acumen for figures. Alfred had some skill in composition, but from an early age he distinguished himself most by his blond good looks – one admirer dubbed him 'the Adonis of Hampstead'. He also displayed natural leadership abilities, defending some of the younger boys from bullies at times. One of those whom he protected grew to become the banker Henry Arnholz, who recollected his champion as an 'extraordinarily attractive' boy whose golden hair and blue eyes caused people to turn and 'look at him in the street'.[7]

The family relocated once again, to a house at 94 Boundary Road, next door to Alfred's school. More children arrived: Charles Harmondsworth, William Albert St John, Christabel Rose, Vyvyan George and Harry Stanley Giffard. In all, Geraldine Harmsworth delivered fourteen children, eleven of whom survived. As the eldest, Alfred helped to maintain discipline (and peace and quiet) among the noisy tribe. His future sensitivity to loud noises undoubtedly springs from this period.

After a brief and unhappy tenure at Browne's School, at Stamford in Lincolnshire, Alfred returned to attend a school closer to home, Henley House, in St John's Wood. The proprietor of this new school, John Vine Milne, considered the likeable Alfred (called 'Billy' by the other boys) one of the brighter pupils. Milne noted his natural leadership of the others in field sports, but viewed him, as many others would in future, as 'something of a puzzle'.[8]

In addition to involvement in the usual athletic endeavours, cricket and football, Alfred courted novelty. He joined those swept up in the

English craze for bicycling, and acquired part ownership of a high-front-wheeled, forty-eight-inch Coventry. His leadership soon extended to the local cycle club, whose enthusiastic members, led by a bugler, would rally for excursions as far afield as Bournemouth (100 miles) and Eastbourne (60 miles), terrorizing those they came upon on the roads. Alfred used cycling to build his strength and stamina, but often overtaxed himself and was bedridden after overambitious sorties in cold and rainy conditions. A friend, Max Pemberton, later recalled the first occasion on which he, literally, ran into the future press lord when both were schoolboys in the summer of 1879. He described Alfred as 'a handsome and well built boy of fourteen', who on this occasion was mounted on a Timberlake with fifty-two-inch front and nineteen-inch rear wheels. The rider was 'dressed in a grey knickerbocker suit and wore a polo hat so placed that an obstinate forelock, almost golden in colour, could not fail to obtrude itself on the notice of an observer'.[9]

When not on the road, Alfred gained his first practical experience of the press at his school, where he hounded Milne until allowed to estab- lish and edit the *Henley House School Magazine*. The editor's identity, 'Alfred C. Harmsworth', was displayed prominently below the title in the first issue, dated March 1881. This schoolboy enterprise revealed to Alfred and others his talent, and helped to determine the direction his life would take. Further early press experience came from George Jealous, who, when Alfred had free time during holidays, gave the lad reporting jobs for the *Hampstead and Highgate Express*. At the end of the Christmas term 1881, aged sixteen and a half, Alfred left school for good, to pursue a career as a freelance journalist. The rest of his educa- tion would come from Fleet Street, not Oxford or Cambridge. Alfred Senior, disappointed that his eldest son was not following him into the law, tried to discourage him from entering such a disreputable profes- sion as journalism, telling him that 'none of my friends will have any- thing to do with you'.[10] This advice was seconded by none other than the venerable George Augustus Sala of the *Daily Telegraph*. It was all to no avail: the young man had made up his mind.

In addition to ascertaining his life's calling, by age seventeen Alfred had also discovered and explored the opposite sex. Succumbing to its attraction would become a lifelong habit and one of his few vices. Cecil King, Northcliffe's nephew, later revealed that his uncle was forced to leave home because he 'got the family servant in the family way'.[11] The girl in question, Louisa Jane Smith, was a village lass from Essex. She returned to her family and delivered a son, called Alfred Benjamin, on 5

November 1882. The birth certificate showed no father.[12] Nevertheless, Alfred's parents were furious over the indiscretion, particularly the strict and highly moral Geraldine. He found himself expelled from the house.

When Alfred left home in 1882, he moved to lodgings in Hampstead with an old friend, Herbert Ward, who was often absent on adventures abroad. The two had an unsteady income and apparently shared one suit of evening clothes. Unable to afford public transport or the Royal Mail, Alfred walked everywhere and delivered his contributions to editors by hand. When Ward joined Henry Morton Stanley's expedition to the Congo, his place in lodgings was taken by Max Pemberton, recently down from Cambridge. Pemberton, who would later gain a considerable reputation as a novelist, was making ends meet by contributing short articles to periodicals. He and Alfred became reacquainted by chance outside the British Museum Reading Room. Pemberton later recalled Alfred's preoccupation with keeping up appearances, believing it the key to first impressions and possible future contacts. When the two impoverished, yet properly frock-coated and top-hatted, authors were hailed by a hansom-cab driver, Alfred told Pemberton, 'We are all right, the cabbies want us for a fare.'[13] In London the two continued to share a mania for cycling. Among Alfred's earliest accepted contributions were articles on the sport to the *Cyclist* and *Wheeling*.

Besides articles on cycling, through sheer perseverance Alfred managed to have other, unrelated, work accepted by such worthy journals as the *Weekly Budget, Young Folks' Tales* and *Youth*. The last, a paper aimed at young men like himself, was owned by the Ingrams, a family with several popular publications, and was produced from their *Illustrated London News* office. *Youth*'s editorial policy was opposed to that of the more vulgar and shoddy publications of the time, which appealed to the lowest tastes with violent and risqué stories. The future Lord Northcliffe would follow the same, more elevated, path in his own publications. He contributed several improving rags-to-riches serials, and his hard work and talent so impressed the owner that he was offered the editorship, which he accepted at two pounds a week. Only nineteen, this apprenticeship represented a golden opportunity for the young man to gain practical knowledge. He gleaned invaluable business knowledge from the other Ingram employees, from artists to advertising men. However, within a year, *Youth* was sold and its neophyte editor was forced to move on. Nevertheless, he took with him a new polish and sophistication in publishing matters.

Besides journalism and cycling, Alfred also had other interests. He had taught himself to play the piano, and while lodging with Pemberton he tried his hand at composing music. One effort, 'The Ellen Terry Waltz', was something of a success – perhaps more because of the renown of its actress namesake than for its own merit. Alfred also had developed a deep affection for the brown-eyed Mary Milner, called 'Molly' by family and friends. He had known the girl for some years; her brother, Harry, had been a boyhood friend. The Milner patriarch, Robert, was a partner in an importing firm, and, though not wealthy, the family stood several financial levels above the struggling Harmsworth clan. While he continued his freelance existence, young Alfred, badly smitten, spent as much time as possible at the Milner home, 'St Vincent', in the company of the vivacious and graceful Mary.

Meanwhile, their articles turned down elsewhere, Pemberton suggested a visit to the Farringdon Street offices of George Newnes's *Tit-Bits*, which, it was rumoured, paid a pound a column. Newnes had become wealthy and *Tit-Bits* a success by compiling scraps of interesting and entertaining information for offer to a new market, Britain's increasingly educated, literate and more affluent lower middle class. This audience had not previously had the time, money or inclination to read periodicals. In the initial interview with Newnes, the two young men bluffed their way through, offering articles on 'Jerrybuilders' and 'Curious Butterflies'. Newnes later recorded that before long Harmsworth, now aged twenty, was 'almost daily in the building . . . bringing in most interesting copy'.[14] Given his curious and observant nature, the format of *Tit-Bits* was heaven-sent for Alfred Harmsworth, who recognized opportunity when he saw it, telling Pemberton that Newnes

has got hold of a bigger thing than he imagines. He is only at the very beginning of a development which is going to change the whole face of journalism. I shall try to get in with him. We could start one of these papers for a couple of thousand pounds, and we ought to be able to find the money. At any rate, I am going to make the attempt.[15]

Raising a 'couple of thousand' proved more difficult and time-consuming than Alfred foresaw. Few investors would even listen to such a youthful principal when he proposed what sounded like a very risky venture.

To survive until he could afford to start a business of his own, Alfred accepted an offer from William Iliffe to edit the ailing *Bicycling News*, one of the Iliffe family's many cycling papers. The Iliffes were impressed by his knowledge, of both the press and the sport, and by his contributions to their leading periodical, the *Cyclist*.[16] In April 1886, at the age of twenty, Alfred relocated to Coventry, centre of English bicycle manu-facture and home of the *Bicycling News* office. The efforts of the new editor succeeded in reversing the fortunes of the venture, despite some bad feeling and a minor revolt among the staff over the hiring of such a young upstart to head the revival. Contributors whose work he often edited heavily dubbed him 'the Yellow Headed Worm'.

Harmsworth's success came in part because he recognized the social implications of the new cycling boom and linked it with other, hitherto unrelated, fields such as photography. While he increased advertising revenue with publicity stunts, he also brought in a female correspon-dent, Lillias Campbell Davidson, to appeal to a new, overlooked, read-ership. The results were striking. Sales, which had dwindled to a few hundred an issue before his arrival, threatened to overtake those of the *Cyclist* – a prospect the owners did not find pleasing. Annoyed by his detractors' criticism and a bit full of himself over the paper's success, Alfred agreed to a parting of the ways from the Iliffes. William Iliffe later commented that the younger man was 'too hot for me'.[17] Alfred also had a romantic motivation for departing Coventry. Mary Milner was much on his mind, and he had decided to ask for her hand in marriage.

With a provincial success to his credit, in early 1888 Alfred returned to London determined to publish his own journal. The road to success, he had decided, lay in the 'Answers' section of *Tit-Bits*, one of the paper's most popular features and one Alfred had used himself in the *Henley House School Magazine* and *Bicycling News*. His bid to match Newnes's great commercial success would be called *Answers to Correspondents on Every Subject Under the Sun*. Before Alfred left Coventry, William Iliffe had listened with some interest to his proposal for the new weekly, but in the end had not been persuaded to back the venture. The impetuous youth had a rare talent, Iliffe had to admit, but the twenty-two-year-old's passion frightened the more careful and senior man. Alfred did not leave completely empty-handed, however. Iliffe hedged his bets by offering the services of the Coventry printing plant on credit terms if other backers could be found to cover start-up costs. Consequently, even before he was again in the metropolis, Alfred resumed his search for financial aid.

Money for the purpose was finally forthcoming that year from an unlikely source: the dowry of one of Geraldine Harmsworth's girlhood friends in Ireland. The husband of the lady in question, Dargaville Carr, came to England in search of a promising investment. He interviewed Alfred in Coventry and, after further discussion in London, committed to a partnership. With the capital came naming rights. The new Carr & Co. had its first tiny offices at 26 Paternoster Square, London. Harmsworth became editor and Carr business manager. Two others were included in the partnership agreement: Edward Markwick, a barrister friend of the Harmsworth family, and Markwick's half-sister, Annie Rose Rowley, assigned to handle the typing duties.[18] Before attempting a weekly paper, the company began with a variety of brief offerings, many signed 'A.C. Harmsworth'. One example was the shilling pamphlet *A Thousand Ways to Earn a Living*, the author of which was not being overly successful himself. Further capital was unearthed by Markwick, who convinced a wealthy acquaintance, Captain Alexander Spink Beaumont, to invest £1,000. Alfred, meanwhile, longed to launch his original idea, *Answers to Correspondents*. For the time being, however, the fledgling organization remained unable to shoulder such a venture.

Despite the unsteadiness of the partnership, Alfred forged ahead with his marriage plans. Mary Milner accepted his engagement ring, bought with money borrowed from Markwick. The barrister also acted as best man at the wedding, on 11 April 1888. During the service and reception, both the groom and Markwick displayed dummy copies of *Answers to Correspondents* in their suit pockets. George Jealous's *Hampstead and Highgate Express* described the charming bride, the many presents and the customary dance given the same evening for the unmarried friends of the couple. Though the paper mentioned a Continental honeymoon, the newly-weds could afford to go on no further than Folkestone. Afterwards, they moved to their first London home, at 31 Pandora Road, West Hampstead. The groom's mother, who had been against the marriage, predicted that they would have 'so many children and no money' and was wrong on both counts. The childless union would last until Northcliffe's death.

While the happy couple celebrated at Folkestone, Markwick travelled to the Beaumont family villa in Italy, where he gained assurances of a further £1,000 investment. This sum made possible the publication of the first edition of *Answers to Correspondents*. Printed on cream-coloured paper, the penny weekly borrowed from *Tit-Bits* and also was heavily influenced in its features by American periodicals. The inaugural edition, numbered 3, was dated 2 June 1888. Max Pemberton bought the first copy at the Paternoster Square office, and, as 'Mr. Answers', became a roving correspondent for the paper. Hawked by street vendors, mostly in the environs of Fleet Street, 12,000 of the 60,000 copies printed were sold. The remainder were given away – an expedient method of advertising that would become a mainstay for future Harmsworth efforts.

In these early years Alfred and Mary worked side by side, at home and the office, doing everything from writing articles to clipping interesting material from any likely source – much of it from American newspapers and magazines. Both would look back upon this time as a period of great happiness. Sales of their creation, whose title was soon shortened simply to *Answers*, varied in the first months from 8,000 to 20,000 – figures that did not make a profit. The editor of *Answers* blamed the low circulation on several causes, from a depressing and long-lasting fog to the Jack the Ripper scare that kept people indoors. To stimulate sales, various remedies were tried. *Answers* added interviews with notables, and soon after adventure stories as well. A number of contests and prizes were offered, including a junior editorship. Open to both sexes, this drew 10,000 entries and in the end a female contestant won the position.

To increase revenues the journal also sold advertising, directly as well as through commission agents such as T.R. Browne, who helped keep the venture afloat through its early hard times.[19] From the beginning Alfred limited the size, type and number of advertisements allowed in his publications, and he would never be comfortable relying on such revenue. For the rest of his career he bemoaned the problems that advertising brought and the limitations he believed it placed on his freedom of action. Despite all efforts, after eight months circulation stood at 30,000 – still below the break-even point. Adrift among the approximately 200 new British periodicals of 1888, it seemed that *Answers* was destined to join most of them in failure. That autumn the cover colour was changed to bright orange, meant to be gold. It was not until the weekly made this association more concrete in the mind of the public that sales of *Answers* would boom.

Sizeable prizes, including buried gold, had been used by *Tit-Bits* and other journals to build circulations. In early 1889 Newnes upped the ante by offering £100 to the beneficiary of anyone found killed in a rail accident with a copy of *Tit-Bits* in their pocket. The scheme made a considerable publicity success, despite questions from the Inland Revenue as to its legality. Alfred Harmsworth wrote to his chief investor,

Beaumont, that 'We cannot cope with the enemy if they are to have such a material advantage.'[20] *Answers* retaliated with coverage of its own worth £200. In addition, the Harmsworths tried a variety of puzzles to stimulate circulation. One became a sensation. It consisted of a tiny glass-covered box containing seven balls that, if properly shaken, fell into spaces spelling 'Answers'. The puzzle mania became so widespread that the manager of one of London's largest banks sent a letter to the proprietor complaining that when his back was turned his clerks spent all their time 'shaking up the little boxes to get the balls in their right places'.[21] Sales of the novelty stimulated weekly circulation to 45,000.

Harold Harmsworth, who had already been helping out at night with bookkeeping, joined the publishing business full time in June 1889, only a few weeks after his twenty-first birthday. This risky course had been embarked upon only after severe soul-searching by the serious-minded Harold, who left a secure position at the Mercantile Marine Office of the Board of Trade. He suggested that *Answers* should be separated from Carr & Co. and assumed the position of company secretary for Answers Company Limited.[22] Harold's financial and organizational acumen balanced Alfred's more flamboyant talents, and he played a central role in the subsequent startling growth of the Harmsworth publishing empire. Before long his management skills and cost-cutting genius proved their worth and, to ensure his continued services, he was rewarded with 130 shares of his own, transferred from Carr and Beaumont. A year after the first issue of *Answers*, its company secretary was able to report weekly sales of 48,000 and a gross profit for the first year of a little more than £1,000.

That same month the family had some less happy news. In mid-July, after being well enough to attend a garden party with friends, Alfred Harmsworth Senior fell ill and died within days. As had his own father, he had succumbed to the ravages of alcohol – specifically, cirrhosis of the liver. Alfred and Mary had been at Broadstairs when the news arrived. Never as close to his dreamy father as to his practical-minded mother, at twenty-four Alfred found himself the head of the family, the members of which had to scrape together the cost of their father's burial.

With a renewed purpose, Alfred turned his energies back to business. Though the *Answers* ship had been steadied, the real success of the weekly was not sealed until in October 1889 a new contest was announced which promised 'A Pound a Week for Life!' The idea for this latest publicity stunt came from a conversation Alfred and Harold had with a vagabond on the banks of the Thames, who shared his modest dream of riches with the young men. Magnified into 'The Most Gigantic Competition the World Has Ever Seen!', the contest offered a pound a week for life to the person who came closest to guessing the amount of gold coinage in the Bank of England at the close of business on 4 December 1889. Entries had to be on postcards and include the signatures and addresses of five 'witnesses' who were not relatives or living at the same address.

This contest caught the fancy of the nation and became a popular sensation. Twenty temporary clerks were hired to deal with the deluge of entries. The Harmsworth family also pitched in: sister Geraldine and brothers Leicester and Cecil aided the effort. They joined their seventeen-year-old brother Hildebrand, who had been working in the firm's circulation department for some months. In all, 718,218 postcards were received.[23] Even allowing for dishonesty, the five witnesses involved brought *Answers* to the attention of millions of possible subscribers. On the day the gold coinage figure was posted outside the Bank of England in Threadneedle Street, police had to be called to control the crowds. The prize was won by Sapper C.D. Austin, on the staff of the Ordnance Survey at Southampton, who guessed within two pounds of the correct sum. His new wealth enabled him to marry ahead of schedule. The Christmas 1889 *Answers* issue that reviewed the results sold more than 200,000 copies. Alfred Harmsworth had arrived in Fleet Street and, despite the predictions of the detractors he had already collected, he would stay for some time.

Flushed with success, the firm announced that it had outgrown its Paternoster Square location (it had already added number 27 to number 26) and would move to 'handsome' new premises at 108 Fleet Street. The new space included 'luxurious' offices for its editor, who had a view of the spire of St Bride's and the bustle of Fleet Street at Ludgate Circus. There also was much change in staff at this time. New arrivals included a young Irish peer, Lord Mountmorres. A friend of Pemberton, Mountmorres supplemented his inadequate income with journalism. He gave a certain legitimacy to *Answers* and, as Pemberton's replacement, would win interviews with figures who would otherwise have been unapproachable, such as William Ewart Gladstone, the living embodiment of British Liberalism. Alfred's new prosperity allowed him the luxury of a private secretary in the person of George Augustus Sutton. Formerly on the staff of the *Star*, Sutton became an invaluable aide to the editor of *Answers* and would remain on board, in a variety of increasingly important posts, until Northcliffe's death. Dargaville Carr, who had not proved a talented businessman, decided to return to Ireland. He much preferred Dublin society and became the Irish representative for *Answers* and future Harmsworth efforts.

To keep up the interest of the public – and sales – in 1890 *Answers* advertised a variety of novelties, including an *Answers* pipe, a waltz, cigarettes, dogs, fountain pens, toothache cures and coffee. The rail insurance offered grew to £500 and then to £1,000. Despite all this, circulation languished at 200,000 while *Titbits* continued regularly to hit 500,000. When sales refused to reach a quarter of a million as he wished, Alfred announced a new *Answers* prize: '£2 a Week for Life'. At this point a concerned Treasury stepped in to quash the scheme on the basis of the recent Lotteries Act, which made prizes for guesswork illegal. This setback prompted some to predict that it would not be long before the Harmsworths would fall back into the obscurity from which they had come. Among those who questioned the future was an insider, Edward Markwick. Many years older than Alfred and much more conservative in his business outlook, the barrister decided to sell his 140 shares in Answers Company Limited to the Harmsworths and Beaumont. This would prove a very costly decision indeed.

One of the 1890 Harmsworth gambles which prompted Markwick to leave the concern was the Pandora Publishing Company, named after the street of Alfred and Mary's first residence. Launched with £500 of capital, Alfred and Harold Harmsworth's new creation targeted the humour market with a halfpenny journal called *Comic Cuts*.[24] The slogan 'Amusing Without Being Vulgar' summarized the aim of the magazine, which purposefully took a higher moral tone than the usual inexpensive 'penny dreadfuls', which had aimed at the lowest tastes and were often, in Alfred's view at least, vulgar and obscene. The 17 May 1890 first edition sold 118,864 copies. As had *Answers*, the new publication borrowed features of *Tit-Bits* and American journals. Sustained publicity in *Answers* – including a report that the humour magazine had been spotted in the House of Commons – helped ensure its continued success. As the periodical list grew, this pattern of support would be repeated many times in future. Before long *Comic Cuts* had an average circulation of 300,000 and outstripped *Answers* as the Harmsworth publishing mainstay.

Seeking further to exploit this auspicious beginning, other periodicals aimed at the *Comic Cuts* market followed. The first edition of *Illustrated Chips* – soon simply *Chips* – was published on 26 July 1890. To the formula, it added a cartoon character, Chips, as a continuing feature. This early comic strip also caught on with readers, who could buy both Harmsworth humour magazines for a penny. In each case, the Harmsworths strove to price their products below the competition. They produced inexpensive 'reading matter for the masses' by using new mass-production techniques. Before long, combined circulation topped 500,000.

The profits of such success allowed Alfred and Mary to add a residence outside London. Several childhood excursions had developed in him a love of the area near Broadstairs which was associated with Charles Dickens, perhaps Alfred's favourite author. In summer 1890 a property called 'Elmwood' at St Peter's, Kent, became available. After a short negotiation the rambling house, the core of which dated back to Tudor times, was purchased for £4,000. Aged twenty-five, Alfred had bought the home which he would prefer over the many other, grander, residences he would acquire over the years. He and Mary moved into the premises, which had been furnished by Liberty's of London, in April 1891. The decorations reflected the taste of the late Victorian age. The dining room was a black oak-panelled reproduction of the Palace of Holyroodhouse. Potted palms graced the drawing room, where the furniture, as in much of the rest of the house, was covered with scarlet-flowered chintzes. Elmwood also displayed many of the most modern conveniences, including a telephone. At this time Alfred was also able to buy a London home for his mother, at 112 Maida Vale. The rest of the family benefited too. Although Alfred dismissed Oxford and Cambridge for himself, he fully realized the value, in British society, of such an education and the connections it would bring. Leicester and Hildebrand, the brothers of college age, were sent off to Oxford. St John would soon follow them, while Vyvyan went up to Cambridge. Arrangements were also made for the education and security of the Harmsworth sisters.[25]

In November 1891 the Harmsworths unveiled *Forget-Me-Not*, subtitled 'A Pictorial Journal for Ladies'. This penny weekly was aimed at the growing – and, the brothers believed, neglected – female market. The journal was advertised as better value than more expensive rivals such as the *Lady's Pictorial* and the *Queen*. *Forget-Me-Not*'s outlook was improving, stressing etiquette and propriety, well in step with the moral tone prevalent in the fifty-fourth year of Queen Victoria's reign. Though the magazine began modestly, before long it grew to dominate its competitors. In the fourth anniversary issue of *Answers*, Alfred called *Forget-Me-Not* 'far and away the most successful of the Answers

publications'.[26] Amid all this effort, Alfred found some time for entertainment. He and Mary enjoyed the theatre, and saw many productions,
including Gilbert and Sullivan's *The Mikado*. But, despite taking some
recreation, he often complained in his diary of overwork.[27]

In part because of the strain of his many responsibilities, in March
1892 Alfred and his wife took their first extended trip, to the Holy Land.
Surviving seasickness, which would be the bane of many subsequent
voyages, the couple arrived at Cyprus via Sicily on 14 March. They
toured Beirut and its environs two days later. Though they skipped
Jerusalem, they visited Damascus and Port Said on their way to Cairo,
where they spent a very pleasant week sightseeing and shopping. The
exotic pyramids, museums and bazaars made a lasting impression.
Alfred recorded in his diary of 2 April, 'today left Cairo with severe
regrets having enjoyed the stay here as much as any period in our
lives'.[28] At Malta, on the way home, the couple gave a successful ship-
board party for the local regiments. Alfred was heartened that the
soldier in charge of the visitor's book at Gibraltar was reading *Answers*,
which had also been in evidence at Sicily and Port Said. Back at
Plymouth on 16 April, after a rough final leg, he recorded that he had
'had quite enough of the Bay of Biscay which I hope never to cross
again. It was rather strange to come back to the snow and cold.'[29]

The editor of *Answers* returned to find circulation at 300,000. The
weekly described itself in 1892 as 'A Journal of Instruction, Literature
and Amusement for Home and Train'. Sales had been boosted in
recent issues by a serial story by Arthur Conan Doyle, 'The Doings of
Raffles Haw'. Alfred recognized the power of the serial, and exploited
this feature beyond any other proprietor. The company sometimes
began a series in one paper, only to continue it elsewhere – to the
annoyance of the newsagents, who had to field the complaints and
questions of the public. By mid-1892 the Harmsworth publications
claimed net sales of 1,009,067. This announcement instituted the practice of issuing net-sales certificates, signed by independent accountants,
which would become an industry standard. The *Manchester Guardian*
noted that, though Americans claimed to be dominating English-language publishing, it was Alfred C. Harmsworth who led the world in
periodical circulation.

Sales of this magnitude began to attract the attention of the British
political world, not unaware of the power of the press in a new age of
mass politics. During the 1892 general-election campaign, Lord
Mountmorres, 'Mr. Answers', was able to gain an audience in Scotland

with Gladstone, who would soon be Liberal prime minister for a fourth time. In the resulting article, Gladstone remarked that he considered the 'gigantic circulation of *Answers* an undeniable proof of the growth of a sound public taste for healthy and instructive reading. The journal must have vast influence.'[30] Apropos the interview with Gladstone, the editor noted that the paper employed reporters of 'all political persuasions', but in the main left politics to the daily press. However, to amuse its readers, the journal did 'talk to great figures in all walks of life'. Taking care not to alienate Opposition readers, the same issue repeated a declaration from the Conservative side made in March of the previous year by Lord Randolph Churchill that 'I do not believe that literature would do anything but gain by the existence of *Answers*. I am inclined to think that it will continue to flourish, and that, far from being evanescent, it will become – as it practically has – a permanent feature of the journalism of the day.'[31] The editor of *Answers* revealed that in the near future the paper hoped to print an interview with the Conservative premier, Lord Salisbury, who had been too busy with 'pressing affairs' when approached. All this was heady wine for the twenty-seven-year-old proprietor, who, in September 1892, was able to lunch with his former employer, William Illife, to discuss whether he would purchase Illife's Coventry newspapers.

Answers and its editor had also become successful enough to draw the fire of competitors. When the weekly joined the 'Missing Words' publishing fad started by *Pearson's Weekly*, the Liberal *Daily News* attacked it for abetting national degeneration, beginning an anti-Harmsworth crusade in this particular journal which would continue until Northcliffe's death. 'Missing Words' competitions offered a prize for the entrants who could guess the word or words left out of a sentence. Entries had to be accompanied by a shilling postal order. The public response rivalled that of the *Answers* 'Pound a Week for Life' contest and made the fortune of Cyril Arthur Pearson, who had started his career with Newnes at *Tit-Bits*. On this success *Pearson's Weekly* grew into a serious rival of *Answers* and *Tit-Bits*. The government crackdown on 'Missing Words' contests as illegal lotteries brought an end to this fad, which was not mourned by Alfred Harmsworth and gave him the theme for his first recorded after-dinner speech. To the 'Ye Sette of Odde Volumes' literary dining club he quipped, 'While I am always ready with my "Answers" every Tuesday, I regret that I am unable to produce them tonight. I have never made a speech in my life before and most of my words are missing.'[32]

Alfred and his brother Harold had proved a formidable duo, but by 1893 the differences in their temperaments had already become apparent in their business attitudes. The younger brother's feet remained firmly on the ground and his eye for cost-cutting and economy continued unabated, while the astounding profits they had begun to realize made Alfred want to expand even further. On more than one occasion, Harold vetoed the acquisition of a publishing property that Alfred coveted. One project that passed Harold's muster in 1893 was a new offering for boys called the *Halfpenny Marvel*, filled with stories of nature, exploration and travel. It joined another paper for boys, *Funny Wonder*, which had been added the year before. (These titles were later shortened simply to *Marvel* and *Wonder*.) Several other such journals would follow over the next fourteen months, including the *Union Jack* and, the most influential, the *Boy's Friend*. These all published 'pure, healthy stories' and were advertised as 'one more nail in the coffin of the penny dreadful'.[33] To keep more of the profits of their labours in-house, a Harmsworth subsidiary was formed to take over the printing work. The Geraldine Press, named after their matriarch, ensured further expansion of circulations at ever lower costs.

While the businesses grew by appealing to the youth market, Alfred and Mary remained childless. Both wanted a family, and physicians were consulted. Numerous attempts were made to solve the problem. Mary followed several courses of treatment, including surgery in April 1893. Though the couple expected 'great things' from the procedure, they would remain without issue. Much to their disappointment, the children that would enjoy their many houses over the years would only be visitors – multitudes from the orphanages the Harmsworth fortune helped to support, or nieces and nephews, many of whom Alfred would stand by as godfather over the years, beginning with Harold's first-born in September 1894.

This failure at home was counterbalanced by unbridled success in the business sphere. By June 1893 the total circulation numbers neared 1,500,000 and, despite some advice to the contrary, the decision was made to float a public offering of the company. That month Answers Limited (later Answers Publications Limited) was formed. The offering – 50,000 ordinary £1 shares and 125,000 7 per cent preference £1 shares – quickly sold out. New financing brought more luxurious offices, at 24 Tudor Street, where the editor's spacious room was hung with reproduction Pre-Raphaelites. George Sutton was installed in one corner behind a curtain. At the end of 1893, Alfred summarized the year as a good one. Though circulations were not up as much as he had wished, the year had seen one new paper, making seven in all. The new printing facility was practically completed. His investments had also increased.

The new year began with Alfred's first trip to North America. This combined business with leisure, and lasted more than three months. On 3 January he and Mary left from Liverpool on the 10,000-ton *Teutonic*, which he described as the 'most comfortable of floating hotels'.[34] The first destination was New York, with accommodations at the Waldorf. Surprised to see 'mud in the streets', he regarded the city with disappointment. The United States was equally unimpressed by him. He was ignored by interviewers, but in compensation he received the good news from Harold, by cable, that the circulation of *Answers* had reached 350,000. Alfred visited several newspaper offices, paying close attention to their printing and distribution organizations. After two weeks in New York, mixing sightseeing with making contacts in publishing and business circles, Alfred and Mary travelled to Niagara Falls. From that romantic spot they crossed into Canada, bound for Montreal. In early February Alfred returned to the United States, spending time at the publishing establishments of Boston. This brought an end to the business portion of the trip.

Outfitted with the latest equipment in New York, the Harmsworths departed for the fishing grounds of Florida on 8 February. At Jacksonville, Alfred described the climate as 'exactly like that of Cairo at the beginning of March'. From the Atlantic coast, he travelled west to Tampa, on the Gulf of Mexico, where he tried his hand at pier fishing. From Naples, just south of Tampa, he went after tarpon, angling from a boat as recommended by his friend R.B. Marston, editor of the *Fishing Gazette*. The expedition included a day at Marco Island, where Alfred spent the night at a small store frequented by the local Seminole Indians. He was successful in reeling in several tarpon and a seven-foot shark as well. Souvenirs of the trip included a number of mounted tarpon and a walking stick fashioned from the shark's backbone. After two weeks of fresh air and sport, the Harmsworths returned to New York, where they boarded a White Star liner bound for England. He called this time the 'pleasantest holiday of our lives'.[35]

Alfred Harmsworth returned from America ready for new challenges; however, his attention was first focused on the periodical publishing list, which continued to grow in size and variety.[36] By the end of 1894 the various journals enjoyed a total circulation of 2 million – then the world's largest. The revenues generated by such numbers allowed Alfred to emulate the stories in his own adventure magazines and support the British side in the international contest to reach the North Pole. Polar explorers were the astronauts of their day; however, after several notable and deadly failures in the 1870s the British government withdrew funding from the risky ventures.[37] While in the United States early in 1894, Alfred had learned of plans for an American expedition. To arrange a British counter, in New York he had cabled Archangel to locate the British adventurer Frederick George Jackson, who had trekked the wilds from Australia to Siberia and was eager to try his hand at polar exploration. As a result, the proprietor of *Answers* financed the Jackson–Harmsworth expedition to Franz Josef Land (named in the 1870s by Austrian explorers after their emperor) and points north. To transport the team north, the steamship *Windward* was purchased and refitted inside and out for Arctic duty. Amenities were not neglected. Jackson noted in his diary that Mary Harmsworth had 'made my cabin and the saloon very pretty with the pictures she has so kindly put on the walls for me, which give them a very home-like appearance'.[38] The *Windward* sailed from England on 12 July 1894, depositing the expedition at Cape Flora (the southernmost point of Franz Josef Land) several months later. The base camp was dubbed 'Elmwood'. London expedition headquarters was set up at 119 Pall Mall.

At the time, the proprietor of *Answers* downplayed talk of the venture being a 'stunt' to publicize his publications. An interview described the expedition as 'in no way connected' to the paper, even though two writers travelled as far as Archangel on the *Windward* and sent back stories.[39] Later, on the anniversary of the expedition's departure, Alfred commented that he had always been 'fascinated by the great mystery of the North' and that Franz Josef Land was the 'best road to the North Pole'.[40] He claimed not to know Jackson's chances of reaching the Pole, but asserted simply that he would like to see the Union Jack planted further north than the Americans had progressed. However, he continued that he would be happy enough with any new knowledge brought back about Arctic geography and flora and fauna, adding that if Jackson reached the North Pole but brought back no scientific knowledge he would 'regard the venture as a failure'.[41] Despite this noble disclaimer, there were undoubtedly other, more selfish and non-scientific, considerations behind the considerable financial investment involved. Wealth had not brought with it the respectability for himself and his family that

Alfred Harmsworth desired. Financing the Harmsworth-Jackson expedition was only a first instalment in the monetary and personal accounts which would need to be settled in order for him to rise out of the anonymous middle class from which he came and to garner the honours and position Alfred believed were his due.

2

Newspapers and Politics, 1894–1897

THE CONQUEST OF Britain's periodical market had brought Alfred Harmsworth wealth, yet magazine publishing could not satisfy a growing appetite for influence. There were, it was true, a handful of important small-circulation journals that mattered to the political elite of Britain, but the owner of *Answers* sought a mass outlet for his ambitions in weekly and daily newspapers.[1] In August 1894 the chance presented itself to purchase a London daily, the *Evening News and Post*, at what was considered a bargain price, and the Harmsworths took the leap into the, for them, uncharted waters of daily newspaper publication.

The *Evening News*, established in 1881 in the Conservative interest, had developed one of the largest circulations in its market. This was insufficient, however, to make the paper pay. By 1894 the owner, Coleridge Kennard, had lost over £90,000 in the venture. Though it was at present a losing proposition, the paper maintained a circulation of 100,000, and Alfred, looking to the future, decided it could be made profitable. Harold was hesitant to become associated with it, warning his older brother that an open attachment to the Conservative Party would not suit their purposes. Alfred, not as inclined to Liberalism as the rest of the family, forged ahead.

The *Evening News* opportunity was first brought to the attention of the Harmsworths by John Boyle, manager of the *Westminster Gazette*, who acted as an intermediary for Louis Tracy, assistant editor at the *Sun*. Tracy and William Kennedy Jones, chief sub-editor at the same paper, had obtained an option on the *Evening News* and, with only a few days remaining on the contract, turned to the owner of *Answers* for financial backing.[2]

After a brief negotiation, on 28 August an agreement was signed to purchase the *Evening News* for £25,000; possession was taken two days later. Tracy eventually became business manager and Kennedy Jones editor. Each was assigned 7½ per cent of the profits of the new company formed to acquire the property.[3] The 31 August *Evening News* announced the ownership change along with its positions on the great issues of the day. The newspaper pledged that it would 'preach the gospel of loyalty to the Empire and faith in the combined efforts of the peoples united under the British flag'. The declaration of principles continued that, in politics, the paper would be 'strongly and unfalteringly' Conservative and Unionist in imperial matters, while sympathetic to labour at home. On social issues the paper vowed to 'occupy an advanced democratic platform' and to be 'progressive in municipal reform'. Concerning Church matters, it would be non-sectarian.

The Harmsworth team used the *Evening News* as a prototype and laboratory for their future newspaper endeavours. In this process Alfred applied the knowledge of American newspaper methods gathered earlier in the year. However, having no previous direct experience, the new proprietor listened closely to the advice of others, particularly Kennedy Jones, whose gruff manner, acid tongue and inability to suffer fools gladly had made him one of the most hated men in Fleet Street. As chief sub-editor at the *Sun*, Jones held an important position, overseeing the assistant sub-editors, distributing assignments, and deciding which news items from the morning papers were important enough to publish. A chief sub-editor's duties also included writing news summaries of domestic and foreign news, as well as miscellaneous tasks such as writing obituaries. This experience would prove invaluable in developing the new paper.

The *Evening News* would reflect many of the changes since the 1880s in the new popular journalism, which continued to transform the face of daily newspapers. A decade earlier, as editor of the *Pall Mall Gazette*, W.T. Stead had begun a trend toward a more concise, lively and personal newspaper style which would soon revolutionize the trade. Stead also brought in typographical changes, such as informative cross-heads which broke up the previously solid pages. He used illustrations as a matter of course – something not previously a feature of daily journalism.[4] T.P. O'Connor, the editor of the *Sun*, had also been an advocate of this new style and had written an influential article on the subject for the October 1889 *New Review*.

Following the path blazed by Stead and O'Connor, the revitalized *Evening News* had fresh typography, a more open format, simplified news reporting and a women's column. The paper also widened its appeal with improved news gathering. Though its proprietor previously had condemned sensational press coverage of crime stories, the *Evening News* exploited several of the more lurid domestic murder trials of the time. In international news, on 1 November it was the first out with the death of the Tsar. Though initially sales disappointed, advertisers soon flocked to the publication. By year's end, the growing profits led Alfred to describe the purchase of the newspaper as 'a most fortunate investment'.[5] In three years it had returned its purchase price.

As he had hoped, the acquisition and successful rehabilitation of the *Evening News* brought its owner into the political spotlight and, for the first time, into a direct party alliance. The three nineteenth-century extensions of the franchise had made all politicians more sensitive to the vexed issue of 'public opinion', and each party struggled to find the best way in which to harness it.[6] In 1894, the Conservatives, led by Lord Salisbury, had feared the *Evening News* might be sold to a Gladstonian group. Richard Middleton, the Conservative Party's principal agent, told Schomberg McDonnell, Salisbury's private secretary, that 'it would be a great blow to us if the other side got the control of our only ½d evening newspaper of wide circulation we possess in London'. Middleton counted the Harmsworths 'real good friends' for saving the *Evening News*.[7]

Despite Harold's misgivings, the Harmsworth press and the Conservatives were a good match. Both looked to the same middle-class core constituency of 'Villa Toryism' for support, and both successfully appealed to imperial patriotism to sell their wares to a wider mass audience. Also, the party of Disraeli sought to attract new men of means, like Alfred Harmsworth, who did not need the financial assistance of Conservative Central Office. The owner of the *Evening News* reported the rebound in the fortunes of the paper to Salisbury, who responded that he was 'very glad to hear of the good prospects which have opened before the Evening News . . . I believe that such organs of opinion may be of great value if they can be made financially to succeed, but a paper which does not in the end pay its own way is generally too much crippled to have an effective influence.'[8]

Robert Arthur Talbot Gascoyne-Cecil, third Marquess of Salisbury, was the last prime minister to sit in the House of Lords, and lived in grand style at Hatfield House, since Elizabethan times the seat of the Cecil Family. On the death of Lord Beaconsfield (Disraeli) in 1881, Salisbury had succeeded to the Conservative leadership in the Lords. The contrast between the two men could hardly have been greater, and it was unfortunate for his future reputation that the untidy Salisbury, with his massive beard and depressive and negative demeanour, followed the colourful Disraeli. A deeply religious champion of the hereditary aristocracy, Salisbury nevertheless successfully led his party during years in which it was forced to broaden its appeal to the new mass electorate created by the 1884–5 franchise extension and redistribution. His expertise and interest in diplomacy meant that in eleven of the fourteen years in which Salisbury was premier he also took charge of the Foreign Office. Known as an isolationist, it is probably closer to the truth to say that Salisbury wished Britain to keep a flexible course in foreign policy. Not as flamboyant in the imperial sphere as had been Disraeli, he was a pragmatic champion of the Empire and of the strong British navy necessary to defend it. By the time Salisbury began his correspondence with Alfred Harmsworth in 1894, he had already been Prime Minister twice (1885 and 1886–92). A third term seemed imminent as the Liberal government appeared to be on its last legs, with the Prime Minister, Lord Rosebery, seeking an opportunity to lay down his burden.

Alfred Harmsworth was drawn to the Conservative standard; however, he was never a strict follower of any party line. His political philosophy combined Tory populism, Disraelian imperialism and a firm belief in 'the Anglo-Saxon future'. Cecil Harmsworth, who would later be elected to the House of Commons as a Liberal Imperialist, wrote that he 'often wondered what Alfred's politics really were'.[9] One bedrock tenet was sympathy for any group which preached support of the Empire and a continued bond with Ireland. Alfred was therefore attracted to Joseph Chamberlain's Liberal Unionist Party, which had been born in 1886 out of the failed effort towards Irish Home Rule. In the following years Chamberlain's party aligned itself with the Conservatives and both carried the Unionist political label, until officially merged a few years before the Great War. The *Evening News* promoted Chamberlain's idea of a bigger and better Britain. Its owner also sought to animate imperialist sentiment within the remnants of the old Liberal Party and would, for a time, be captivated by Lord Rosebery's Liberal Imperialism.

In an increasingly threatening international climate, the safety of Britain and the Empire was of paramount concern to Alfred, who became involved with the many imperial organizations which multiplied in late-Victorian Britain. Since the 1880s, numerous groups – the conservative Primrose League being one of the more successful and lasting – had made patriotic appeals for England to look to the defence of her Empire against the economic and military threats of the other great powers. Alfred consulted Primrose League officials and representatives of the newly created Navy League, which campaigned for British preparedness and shipbuilding. A true believer that Britain was in peril, Harmsworth gave monetary support to these organizations, and others, up to the outbreak of the Great War.

Answers underlined the menace to the country with one of the earliest serials to have a war theme. William Le Queux's 1894 'The Poisoned Bullet', set three years later, had Russia and France (which had recently signed a naval treaty) combining to invade England. Sales boomed as the instalments chronicled the 'Massacre of Eastbourne' and the 'Battle of Beachy Head'.[10] This warning that England's day of reckoning was hourly advancing was published as *The Great War in England in 1897*. The preface of the first edition included a letter from Lord Roberts of Kandahar, in which the former Commander-in-Chief of Britain's Indian Army stated, 'I entirely concur with you in thinking it most desirable to bring home to the British public in every possible way the dangers to which the nation is exposed, unless it maintains a Navy and Army sufficiently strong and well organised to meet the defensive requirements of the Empire.'[11]

As the proprietor of a newspaper which supported the Empire, Alfred came to the attention of Cecil Rhodes, creator of Rhodesia, gold and diamond magnate, and also Prime Minister of the Cape Colony. At the end of November 1894, Rhodes was fresh from a stay at Windsor with the Queen and newly installed as a privy counsellor. He cultivated the support of influential newspaper men, and was described by W.T. Stead as being at the 'zenith of his power' in 1894–5. The Cape premier and the proprietor of the *Evening News* met for breakfast.[12] They were joined by Dr Leander Starr Jameson, a Rhodes lieutenant who was at that moment being hailed in London as the 'conqueror of Matabeleland'. Jameson, made a Companion of the Order of the Bath for his efforts in Africa, would soon loom even larger, and more infamously, in Britain's imperial story. Their meeting left Alfred greatly impressed with the charismatic Rhodes, a self-made man like himself, who had followed his own path and helped to paint Africa red in the maps of empire the newspapers were fond of printing. Indeed, the esteem in which he held him bordered on hero worship. On 17 December, at the Sylvan Debating Club, Alfred spoke in support of Rhodes's expansionist policy – a vision of British dominion from the Cape to Cairo. The next month he again met the great man. The two had an interview of an hour and a half in London, during which an invitation was extended to travel to the Cape for a visit.[13]

Emboldened by his growing wealth and influence, Alfred Harmsworth decided to try his hand at parliamentary politics. He had declined a nomination for Folkestone; however, in March 1895, a few months before his thirtieth birthday, he answered the call of Richard Middleton, and took the plunge as Conservative candidate for one of Portsmouth's seats in the Commons. In an age of 'new men' of wealth in many industries, the Conservatives were always on the lookout for candidates who could pay their own way. Harmsworth's newspaper connections were an added bonus. Mirroring the national pattern of coalition with the Liberal Unionists, he campaigned alongside Evelyn Ashley, who stood for the other Portsmouth seat. Ashley had been Lord Palmerston's personal secretary and was well connected within Britain's aristocracy. Beginning with a Constitutional Club meeting in late March, for the next four months the Conservative candidate divided his time between London and Portsmouth, where he addressed an endless number of meetings and dinners. His excursion into politics gained the attention of *Vanity Fair*, which in April dispatched its artist, Leslie Ward, to execute a 'Spy' caricature of the 'Conservative Candidate for Portsmouth'. This effort – the first of many political cartoons to come – bore scant resemblance to its subject.

Campaigning did not suit Alfred. He had not inherited his father's gift for public speaking or his love of the activity. In addition, his voice was rather weak, and throat problems plagued him. Often he would answer questions, rather than give a set address. Nevertheless, he gamely carried on the fight before mostly Conservative audiences, for example at several Primrose League meetings. These often were long and boring, despite attempts to divert the audience. He described one Primrose Concert as 'the most terrible entertainment I have ever attended'.[14] The candidate's wife was also pressed into service. Mary Harmsworth dutifully accompanied him to several meetings, and on one occasion spoke when he fell ill.

Alfred railed against the Liberal government's naval policy, calling for increased spending and modernization. He dutifully visited the Portsmouth dockyard, and listened attentively to the concerns of varied deputations, from warrant and petty officers to 'labourers and navvies'. At the invitation of its commander, he took an excursion on the torpedo destroyer *Charing*. To strengthen local ties, he joined several fraternal organizations, becoming a Freemason, an Oddfellow, a Druid and a Buffalo. His wife was made a Forester. The two also gave donations to forty-seven causes, from the roof fund of an Anglican church to educational classes in Hebrew.

Alfred's party made some attempts to support him. Schomberg McDonnell advised Salisbury that Harmsworth 'should be encouraged'.[15] The Conservative leader scheduled a trip to Portsmouth to speak at a mass meeting at the Drill Hall. The candidate wrote to Salisbury:

> Now that I am able to judge the effect of the announcement of your visit on June 25th I take the opportunity of thanking you very sincerely on behalf of my colleague Mr. Evelyn Ashley & the whole of your party here. The stimulus given the work in the borough would I feel sure greatly gratify you. The party is disorganised & there is a feeling that Portsmouth has been neglected. The stir made by the announcement of the great gathering . . . has cheered us all immensely.[16]

Unfortunately, Salisbury had to cancel his trip when the Liberal government resigned and he was called on by the Queen to form a Cabinet a few days before his scheduled visit. The new Prime Minister sent a last-minute cable of apology. Several other distinguished figures did speak in Alfred's support, including Lord Onslow, Lord Edmund Field, Sir George Willis and Sir Edward Clarke, MP for Plymouth and a former Solicitor-General. Besides these notables, during the campaign Alfred also made the acquaintance of the Under-Secretary for War, William St John Brodrick (the future Lord Midleton), and of G.J. Goschen, First Lord of the Admiralty.

To combat the local Liberal newspaper, with a month to go before the general election set for mid-July, the Harmsworths acquired the Portsmouth *Evening Mail*, renaming it simply the *Mail* (and later the *Southern Daily Mail*). In its pages 'The Siege of Portsmouth', a serial tale of French and Russian perfidy, sensationalized Britain's lack of preparedness and laid the blame squarely on Liberal neglect. On 16 June the first instalment recounted the 'Startling Appearance of a French Man

O'War at Spithead' on 3 September 1897. Over the next weeks the series chronicled dire events such as the 'Battle of Eddystone' and the capture of the Army's Commander-in-Chief, Lord Wolseley. The finale recounted the glorious British victory at 'The Battle of Spithead', despite the muddling of a failed Liberal government headed by Lord Rosebery, with Henry Campbell-Bannerman at the War Office.[17] The last instalment ran on the day of the poll, 16 July.

Besides the 'Siege of Portsmouth' effort, the *Mail* also publicized the varied campaign activities of Harmsworth and Ashley and battered their Liberal opponents, Sir John Baker and Walter Clough. In addition to verbal attacks, political cartoons ridiculed the enemy. On 29 June the paper depicted the four candidates lined up on a starting line in foot-racing attire. Harmsworth and Ashley appear tall, youthful and athletic, while their opponents are short, old and portly. Another drawing showed Baker's long career as that of a political turncoat, first Tory, then Radical, then back.[18] On the anniversary of the departure of the Harmsworth–Jackson polar expedition the *Mail* carried an interview which congratulated the patriotic spirit of the Conservative candidate, who had stepped in when the government balked at funding the venture.[19]

While Alfred tried his hand at politics, the *Windward* returned to Port Flora to resupply the Harmsworth–Jackson expedition. In 1895 Jackson put the Harmsworth name on several pieces of frozen terrain. Alfred Harmsworth Island, Capes Mary and Cecil Harmsworth and the Harold Harmsworth Straits joined Salisbury Island and the Chamberlain and Cecil Rhodes Fjords on the map of Franz Josef Land. Rather than meeting American competition, Jackson had, quite by chance, run across the trail of the Norwegian explorer Fridtjof Nansen, who was near exhaustion, attempting to find his way out of the ice fields. Nansen returned on the *Windward*, to European acclaim.[20] Meanwhile, in Portsmouth, the final *Mail* cartoon of the campaign displayed Harmsworth and Ashley as 'The Men For Portsmouth!' and urged the populace to 'Vote for Them Today'.[21]

In the country at large, during the 1895 election campaign the Liberals remained as divided out of power as they had been in office. Rosebery's splintered party had no unifying scheme. The Liberal leader sought to bring the obstructionism of the House of Lords to the fore, while his bitter rival Sir William Harcourt promoted the radical Newcastle Programme. At the same time, John Morley carried on Gladstone's moral crusade for Home Rule.[22] In London, the

Harmsworth *Evening News* chose to attack the Liberal enemy over Home Rule and imperial defence and to prey on middle-class fears of radical socialism. On 1 July the paper laid out a political map of the city which displayed the constituencies of 'socialists and labour' as darkened areas and those of the Conservatives and Liberal Unionists in white. The paper exhorted its readers to 'wipe out those black patches in darkest London, so that our metropolis may be the brightest and most pure spot on earth'. Even with the Liberals in disarray, the Conservatives were surprised by their crushing victory, returning 340 Members – 73 more than 1892, and a majority even without the 70 seats won by their Liberal Unionist allies. At the end of the campaign the *Evening News* congratulated the city on the Conservative majority with the headlines 'Bravo London!' and 'A Glorious Victory'.[23]

Unfortunately for Alfred Harmsworth's political aspirations, Portsmouth did not follow the national pattern. Though the *Mail* series and its other election articles succeeded in selling newspapers, the campaign did not build enough sentiment to elect either the Conservative or the Liberal Unionist candidate. Harmsworth consoled himself with the fact that he had received more votes than the winner in the 1892 election.[24] He was magnanimous in defeat, admitting that, though he had done his best, 'There is no doubt we got a good, square licking.' Asked if he would run again, Alfred declared that, 'given good health and strength, most undoubtedly, and perhaps very shortly'. He continued that he would endeavour to carry out his naval-reform scheme from some platform, if not from Portsmouth. A final comment on the loss was that 'At my age defeat does one good. Too much success in life is bad for one.'[25]

Though not elected, Harmsworth was still considered a viable and valuable Conservative asset, and he did not immediately turn his back on the House of Commons as has been suggested previously. Salisbury reportedly promised him that he would soon have another opportunity, and at the end of 1895 the Brixton Conservative Association visited to sound out Alfred's interest. However, he decided not to pursue the opening. After some consideration, he concluded from his losing sortie into electoral politics at Portsmouth that 'my place is in the House of Lords where they don't fight elections'.[26]

Losing at Portsmouth did not lead Alfred to retire from an interest in national and imperial issues, particularly the situation in South Africa, which had been uneasy since the 1881 British defeat by the Transvaal Boers at Majuba Hill. After this disaster, Gladstone's government had agreed to terms which many found humiliating, rather than engage the tough Boer settlers in a war. In the decade and a half since, many thousands of new immigrants, predominantly British, had been drawn to South Africa by the prospect of making their fortunes in the gold and diamond fields north of the Cape Colony. If these 'Uitlanders' (Outlanders) were given the franchise rights which they demanded, the Boers rightly feared that their country would soon be voted out of existence. These descendants of Dutch Calvinist separatists, who had trekked north from the Cape Colony to the Transvaal and the Orange Free State to escape British interference, were not a people to give up to the Empire without a fight. The combative President of the Transvaal, Paul Kruger, who as a boy had been among the trekkers, was an especially sharp thorn in the side of British aspirations.

Alfred Harmsworth's imperial hero Cecil Rhodes plotted to end this South African dilemma with two bold strokes: an invasion of the Transvaal, co-ordinated with an Outlander rising in its capital, Johannesburg. The second part of the plan had little popular support and was severely disorganized from the start. Realizing he had problems, on the eve of the scheduled invasion and rising, Rhodes called for delay. Nevertheless, a force of 500 Rhodesian troops, led by Dr Leander Starr Jameson, crossed the border from British territory into the Transvaal on 29 December 1895.

In London, Joseph Chamberlain, who might have had any post he wished in the June 1895 Salisbury government, had taken the Colonial Office. Like Rhodes's, Chamberlain's imperial vision also included a unified British South Africa. In an attempt to have some control of events, he had been in touch with the Prime Minister of the Cape Colony and knew much more than a colonial secretary should about the illegal invasion plan. At age sixty-six, the former 'Radical Joe', who had made a fortune in the Birmingham metal-screw trade, dreamed of using his ministry to tie the self-governing colonies – Canada, New Zealand, Australia, Natal and the Cape – to Britain in a union of mutual self-defence and trade. Since his entry into politics at Birmingham, Chamberlain had realized the value of newspaper publicity and, unlike the other ministries, who treated newsmen as unwelcome interlopers, the Colonial Office fed the press with information.[27] When the news of Jameson's incursion from British-held territory was cabled to Chamberlain, he immediately repudiated the raid in statements from the Colonial Office.

On New Year's Day 1896, the *Evening News* questioned whether Chamberlain was 'blundering' in not supporting the invasion. Accounts had been received that Dr Jameson had entered Kruger's territory, but the paper reported that 'Kruger has cut the wire and we do not know what is going on in Johannesburg.' It fears 'unarmed Englishman' were at the 'mercy of the Boers', and called for the immediate response of the government as 'the last chance for British prestige in South Africa'. The next day's edition lauded 'Brave Dr. Jim' and added, 'May his march to the relief of our brothers and sisters in the Transvaal be crowned with success.' After Jameson's surrender at Doornkoop, fourteen miles from Johannesburg, the 3 January paper reported 'Dr. Jim's Defeat'. In the *Evening News* version of events, 5 had been killed and 22 wounded by the Boers, who had lain in wait for the attack and had 'crushed' his mission. With Johannesburg now at the mercy of Kruger, the paper asked, 'What Was the End to Be?' The end was rather an anticlimax. Jameson and his raiders were marched to prison in Pretoria, there to be joined by those involved in the stillborn Johannesburg rising. Cecil Rhodes resigned as premier of the Cape Colony in answer to charges that he was responsible for the disaster.[28]

Those who planned and carried out the raid were saved from the consequences of their embarrassing failure by outside, international events. Germany had taken the side of the Transvaal against Britain in the months before the incursion. This had only stiffened Salisbury's resolve to deal 'firmly' with the recalcitrant Boers.[29] On 3 January, Kaiser Wilhelm sent Kruger a cable of congratulations for having defeated the British invasion. As nothing else could have done, this action rallied public support for the failed effort and for Rhodes and Jameson. 'News From Berlin' in the *Evening News* revealed (incorrectly) that in his message the Kaiser had congratulated Kruger not only on repulsing the raid, but also on having 'killed Englishmen'.[30] This was not only a paper crisis; before cooler heads prevailed and the international tempest subsided, the British fleet was mobilized. Humiliated by her impotence when faced by the world's strongest navy, Germany, led by the Kaiser and his naval adviser Alfred von Tirpitz, in the following years passed a series of naval laws which authorized the construction of a battle fleet capable of challenging Britain's.[31]

Still feeling the effects of his long political campaign and disturbed by the events in South Africa, Alfred retired to Elmwood for a rest. He had been unable to visit his favourite home for many months, and recorded in his diary that he was 'very glad to get there again'.[32] For the remainder of his life, he preferred to work at Elmwood whenever possible. He had a bungalow built in the garden, to which he often retreated for solitude. The main house was fitted with all the latest technological marvels, including one of the first 'portable' telephones – a heavy sewing-machine-sized device that had to be hauled from room to room. Alfred was also fond of playing recordings on the gramophone, often driving his acquaintances and secretaries to distraction by repeating the same selection for hours at a time. As usual, his personal interests were intertwined with his business life: the Harmsworth publications were among the first to review new gramophone releases.

While Alfred recovered at Elmwood, Cecil Rhodes travelled to London in an attempt at damage control. He was particularly worried that sanctions might be imposed on his British South Africa Company.[33] Rhodes courted newspaper support as usual, and before he left England on 10 February he had a two-hour interview with the proprietor of the *Evening News*. Alfred also met 'Dr Jim' on his return to London after the Boers had shipped their prisoners home for trial in England. The two dined on 20 April, but Alfred noted in his diary only that he 'met some interesting people'. Three months later a special jury in London sentenced Jameson to fifteen months in prison. However, because of illness, he was released in December 1896 and served no more of his term.

The aftermath of the Jameson Raid shook the Colonial Office. Joseph Chamberlain was accused by some of criminal collusion, of being a partner in the plan to use British troops from the Crown Colony of Rhodesia to overthrow a friendly neighbour, the Transvaal. A parliamentary committee – soon dubbed 'the Lying-in-State at Westminster' – was convened in January 1897 to look into the matter. Chamberlain was included in the all-party inquiry, whose members took his word when he swore he had had no idea of the plans for the raid. Strong evidence suggests otherwise: that he did, at least, agree to allow Jameson to use a base in the Bechuanaland protectorate as a staging area. To forestall any chance of this coming to light, the Colonial Secretary struck a deal with Rhodes in which he agreed to shield the diamond magnate in return for the suppression of a series of telegrams which clearly implicated Chamberlain and have since been uncovered.[34]

By the time Rhodes returned to England to appear before the parliamentary committee, Alfred Harmsworth had a new and powerful voice with which to defend both his imperial allies. On 1 May 1896, Middleton informed Salisbury's private secretary:

On Monday next Harmsworth is producing his new paper, *The Daily Mail*, a morning ½d paper, and I think it ought to prove of very great value to our Party. I understand that a copy will be sent, together with a letter, to Lord Salisbury and I should be very glad if a suitable reply could be made so as to encourage the undertaking, as I am very anxious this should be run on the same valuable lines that Harmsworth is running the *Evening News*.[35]

Since he considered Harmsworth 'such a loyal supporter of ours', to aid the new venture Middleton did all he could to make high and authentic sources of information available to the *Daily Mail*. He needn't have worried: the new journal tapped the same popular vein as had the Conservative Party. The first edition, on 4 May 1896, sold over 300,000 copies, doubling the best hopes of its proprietor. After he had signed it, Alfred had the first copy to come off the presses sent to his mother.

Letters and cables of congratulations on the latest Harmsworth success flooded the office. These included a message from Salisbury, to which Alfred replied that the Prime Minister's kind telegram 'had given very great pleasure to my staff & me. Fortune has placed us in possession of a most sudden & almost unexpected success & we shall spare no pains to maintain & increase it.'[36] Arthur James Balfour, Salisbury's nephew and the Conservative leader in the Commons, sent a private, handwritten note on a 10 Downing Street card:

> Though it is impossible for me, for obvious reasons, to appear among the list of those who publish congratulatory comments in the columns of the 'Daily Mail' perhaps you will allow me privately to express my appreciation of your new undertaking. That, if it succeeds, it will greatly conduce to the wide dissemination of sound political principles, I feel assured; and I cannot doubt, that it *will* succeed, knowing the skill, the energy, the resource, with which it is conducted. You have taken the lead in the newspaper enterprise, and both you and the Party are to be heartily congratulated.[37]

Though the philosophically inclined Balfour claimed not to read the press, as this letter shows he appreciated its usefulness to the Party, and during the following six years before he succeeded his uncle in the premiership the politician had frequent contact with the proprietor of the *Daily Mail*.

In the pages of the *Daily Mail* the new popular journalism found its highest form. Priced at only a halfpenny, the paper distinguished itself from the competition by being printed on more expensive white newsprint, with its front page devoted to advertisements, in the style of the penny journals. White paper was also needed for the reproduction of illustrations, which would play a more and more important role. At the top corners of the front page, the 'ears' of the journal sported the slogans 'The Busy Man's Paper' and 'A Penny Paper for a Half-Penny'. Inside, concise leaders on parliamentary affairs appealed to the new voters created by the Third Reform Bill of 1884. For this mass audience, the sub-editors were instructed to construct their stories of many brief paragraphs, to 'explain, simplify and clarify'.[38] The paper combined innovative features with the latest technology, including new folding and Linotype machines. Overseas news-gathering offices opened in New York and Paris were aided by advances in cable transmission speed at the General Post Office, which had reached 600 words per minute by 1896. The Harmsworths also exploited the expanding British railway system to distribute the *Daily Mail* throughout the relatively compact home market so that readers all over Britain could peruse the paper over their breakfasts. Thus it can be argued that the *Daily Mail* was the first truly national newspaper. In the early years Alfred himself acted as editor, directly overseeing the newspaper's policy. Kennedy Jones stood in when the proprietor was abroad or otherwise occupied.

The national audience which Alfred courted also included women – the first issue contained a section called 'Women's Realm'. But, though he hoped to, and did, lure a female readership, the majority of the original audience was male, and the journal deliberately courted the aspirations of those who envisioned themselves as 'tomorrow's £1000 a year men'. The purchasers of the *Daily Mail* have been described as 'not so much the newly educated as the recently better-off . . . clerks . . . willing to spend a halfpenny, where they might balk at a penny'.[39] Despite the oft-repeated, but unattributed, jibe of Salisbury that the *Daily Mail* was 'run by office boys for office boys',[40] many on the staff had university educations. These included, from Oxford, the leader writer H.W. Wilson, Mayson Beeton and G.A.B. Dewar. One of the reasons the paper sported so many graduates was that Harmsworth had revolutionized salaries, sending them sharply higher. He was also widely admired by young, ambitious men, who dreamed of duplicating his success.

The *Daily Mail* halfpennies added up handsomely. Before the first edition was published, its owner had predicted that the enterprise would lead to either 'Bankruptcy or Berkeley Square'. One year later, Mary and Alfred Harmsworth, as he had predicted, moved to number 36 of that prestigious address. This was only a brisk walk from the Conservative Party's club, the Carlton, to which Salisbury's nomination had ensured his election.[41] This was a necessary step for any coming man in the Party, although, as Balfour had warned another new member a few years before, it was 'a beastly club infested by the worst of the species . . . the bore political'.[42]

Three days after the birth of the *Daily Mail*, its proprietor spoke as guest of honour at the Anglo-Saxon Club in praise of Cecil Rhodes. Another British imperial figure, Sir Charles Dilke MP, author of the influential *Greater Britain* among other works, attended the affair. Dilke wrote to G.W. Steevens, a reporter at the *Pall Mall Gazette* who would soon find employment with the *Daily Mail*:

> I met last night perhaps the most remarkable man I have ever seen – though I know Bismarck and knew Gambetta well. It is Harmsworth. The similarity of ideas between this Bonaparte First Consul and yourself suggests to me that it is possible that he might like to catch for some of his journalistic undertakings so cultivated, so intelligent, and so modern a journalist.
>
> He is very young and his speech showed that he rates Rhodes too high. Rhodes is as strong as Bismarck, and youth rates strength too high, but Rhodes was never sharp and has become stupid. Harmsworth himself is superior, in that he is (probably) both strong and sharp.[43]

Steevens and the owner of the *Daily Mail* soon developed a business relationship and became friends. One commentator wrote that the 'schoolboy in Alfred went out to meet the schoolboy in Steevens'.[44] The writer's first important commission for the paper was a series of articles chronicling his touring the United States. These were published as a successful book, *The Land of the Dollar*.

Unparalleled success in the publishing sphere led Alfred to aim for honours to match those given to other press figures, such as the baronetcy awarded Sir George Newnes in 1895. This afforded the owner of *Tit-Bits* a decided advantage in raising capital, of which his competitors, including the Harmsworths, were well aware. In July 1896 Lady Bulkley sent a letter to Sidney Greville, one of Salisbury's secretaries, which confided that Harmsworth believed a baronetcy was not too much to ask in reward for his services to the nation and the Party. An enclosed list of accomplishments (in what appears to be Alfred's hand) included the Portsmouth candidacy, the proprietorship of Conservative papers there and in Glasgow (the *Echo*), and the Jackson–Harmsworth expedition. Lady Bulkley's letter also noted 'the Daily Mail he has just started as a Conservative morning paper at a cost of near £100,000'.[45] Asked for his opinion, Middleton wrote from Conservative Central Office to

Greville that 'there are reasons why you should be very careful what you reply to Lady Bulkley's letter – the best course would be to write nothing and say as little as possible . . . anyhow I advise the greatest caution'.[46] Under Salisbury, the Party was not ready to confer such a distinction. A knighthood offered instead was declined.

Fresh from this rebuff by the Conservatives, in the autumn of that year the proprietor of the *Daily Mail* travelled to Scotland in an attempt to gain an interview with Lord Rosebery, who had been much in the political headlines over reports that he would resign the Liberal leadership. Since the 1895 election débâcle Rosebery had remained as the titular head of his factious colleagues, but his rather vague ambition to form a 'national' party through 'concentration' on a few major issues, such as the Empire, had not rallied the Liberals, who in the main followed a negative policy of waiting for the Conservatives to choose the political battlegrounds. Rosebery, already exhausted by politics, was further put upon in late 1896 by Gladstone's public pronouncements on Turkish 'atrocities' in Armenia, recalling his Bulgarian campaign of 1876 and in opposition to Rosebery's stated position. The Liberal leader consequently decided to resign until his party purged itself of such Gladstonian remnants as its Newcastle Programme, anti-imperialism and support for Irish Home Rule.[47] Though a body of Liberal Imperialists rallied to the Earl, the rest of the Party was never willing to change itself sufficiently to suit Rosebery's taste.

Alfred was successful in gaining an interview at Dalmeny, the Earl's Scottish seat. Rosebery recorded that there had been a 'good deal of fuss over his resignation' and that 'Mr. Harmsworth came to interview me. I lunched him instead. An interesting young man.'[48] As he left, Alfred met Herbert Henry Asquith, a Rosebery partisan who had been Home Secretary in Gladstone's 1892 government. The future Liberal prime minister arrived with another party leader, Sir Henry Fowler. The day after the audience, Alfred attended Rosebery's resignation meeting at the Empire Palace, Edinburgh. He called Rosebery's address, 'about the best speech I ever heard'.[49] The next morning's *Daily Mail* editorial, 'Well Done Rosebery', extended congratulations on his 'patriotic' resignation. A separate article, 'By Our Special Correspondent', described the personal interview of the day before and assigned the immediate cause of the resignation to differences with Gladstone. During the talk, Rosebery had commented that he thought the *Daily Mail*, 'came from the other camp'.[50] Its proprietor had responded that the paper was 'independent and imperial'. The two men – who would be neighbours in Berkeley Square within a year – then spoke on a number of affairs, including polar exploration, journalism and angling.

Fishing was among the diversions which Alfred – worn down by work – was ordered to pursue by his doctors soon after his return to London. When in town, he sought further relaxation at the theatre, sometimes meeting the players. After seeing her in *Cymbeline*, Alfred chatted with the renowned actress Ellen Terry, for whom he had named his waltz composition years before. Other popular productions attended included *The Importance of Being Earnest* and *The Geisha*. To escape business he sometimes returned to cycling, but he characteristically overexerted himself in a 120-mile ride from Norwich to London. His cycling days, however, would soon be behind him for ever. A new means of locomotion, the automobile, had caught Alfred's fancy.

On the cold, wet Saturday morning of 14 November 1896 the owner of the *Daily Mail* attended the start of the London-to-Brighton 'Emancipation Run' motor-car rally. That day marked the end of the four-miles-per-hour rural speed limit and of the archaic 1865 rule – previously still enforced in some places – that a man had to walk before vehicles waving a red flag.[51] More than thirty self-propelled conveyances of varying sizes, shapes and colours departed from the Hôtel Métropole, at Northumberland Avenue and Whitehall Place. The police, surprised by the turnout of spectators, struggled to make a path for the motley procession of noisy, fume-spewing contraptions. Somehow, despite the crowds, the mechanical delicacy of the machines and the state of the roads, ten vehicles completed the journey, whose route was littered with the remainder. This result led the *Daily Mail* to call the run a 'comparative fiasco' and its proprietor to remark, 'the less said the better'.[52]

Nevertheless, Alfred became an unabashed enthusiast of the new sport. Because of the restrictions at home, his previous automobile touring had been undertaken on the Continent. The first such excursion, he would later claim, had taken place in 1891. Within a year of the 1896 revision in British law, several hundred drivers were travelling, and degrading, the British roadways. Using statutes originally drawn up for horses and coaches, the police were soon regularly issuing summonses for 'furious' driving to those who exceeded the twelve-miles-per-hour limit.[53] Britain's relative backwardness in things automotive had greatly hindered the domestic industry, while France and Germany forged ahead in the new technology. The first issue of the *Daily Mail* questioned the future of the automobile in comparison with the tried and true horse-powered alternative; however, subsequent articles and editorials soon complained of Britain's handicap in this new and revolutionary mode of travel in comparison with the Continent, where there were no speed limits and, consequently, many more automobile manufacturers, with superior products.

Two weeks after the Emancipation Run, the Harmsworths embarked on another trip ordered by Alfred's doctors for complete rest, away from England. Their destination was India, the Jewel in the Crown of the British Empire. Reginald Nicholson, a friend from Broadstairs, had spent some time working for the Bengal–Nagpur Railway Company and came along as companion and guide. The party left London for Dover on 10 December, reaching Brindisi three days later by train. From there they took ship for Egypt. Having passed through the Suez Canal – the first time for Alfred and Mary – the travellers reached Aden on the 22nd and had a rough and uncomfortable crossing of the Indian Ocean. At sea for Christmas, Alfred noted in his diary that he had received a gold cigarette case from his wife, but that he did not like his first Yuletide away from home.

Two days later the party were in Bombay, where they dined at the Yacht Club. The following week was taken up by sightseeing, although Alfred could not stay away from work completely. He made a call at the *Times of India* office and visited the local *Daily Mail* representative. The first days of 1897 found him fishing near Poona. On the journey to Nagpore, he recorded that he heard the jackals wailing at night. The travellers rode an elephant, and enjoyed very much the tiger beat they joined, although Alfred did not bag a trophy. On 18 January the couple arrived in Delhi, and two nights later he noted they had seen the romantic 'Taj by moonlight'. At Cawnpore Alfred inspected various infamous sites of the Great Mutiny of forty years before. The party also visited the Holy Man of Benares and toured the Monkey Temple and many other of the more celebrated destinations.

It was probably not completely coincidental that the Harmsworths visited the subcontinent at the same time as it was undergoing a severe food crisis which had led to outbreaks of bubonic plague. The owner of the *Daily Mail* was unable to resist the tremendous story at hand. As the travellers viewed the scenic wonders of India, Alfred also visited suffering areas, collected famine statistics, and called on the law courts. His articles on the widespread disease and starvation were published in the *Daily Mail* as the series 'Hard Facts from India'. The proprietor reported in part one, 'Through the Plague and Famine Districts', that going out he had been told that all the talk of dire conditions was simply 'food for newspapers and globetrotters'. However, during his first morning in Bombay he had 'met more than a dozen of those hurried little processions bearing an obvious Something under a cloth'.[54] Though the first two accounts tended to downplay the crisis, for the third Alfred visited a 'Starvation Camp', where he witnessed shocking scenes he hoped never to see again. In Lucknow, healthy natives were in stark contrast to 'the spectres, the gaunt, shrivelled old men and women, the babies who seem all head and staring eyes' seen at a 'Poorhouse'.[55] After a month in the countryside, Alfred and Mary returned on 5 February to the 'deserted, reeking streets' of Bombay, which, in his opinion, needed more government aid and did not reflect the newspaper reports which minimized the gravity of the situation. He was told by Surgeon-Major-General Clegham that 300,000 had fled the city.

The travellers returned to Europe in a vessel flying a yellow quarantine flag.[56] At Aden, the ship was left severely alone except for the visits of doctors, and it was hurried through the Suez Canal. Alfred called the 'whole thing a hideous farce', since it was 'well known' that plague showed itself in nine days, and that period had expired since they left Bombay. At Marseilles, fear of the Indian epidemic resulted in the party not being allowed to proceed by train and, instead, having to travel for days in heavy seas to Plymouth, which they reached on 26 February.

Alfred returned home with a new appreciation for the immensity of the Empire, but also with a strong sense of its vulnerability. Though the scenes he had witnessed left in him no love for India, for the rest of his life the owner of the *Daily Mail* would look to the defence of the imperial idea which that country represented in the minds of most Englishmen.

3

Upbuilder of Empire, 1897–1899

T HE EXHAUSTED VOYAGERS returned to England from India just as the parliamentary committee looking into the Jameson Raid finished taking the testimony of Cecil Rhodes. The previous month, the *Daily Mail* had noted the arrival in London of 'The Great Man of Africa'. The 23 January editorial commented that he had returned 'to face the music', but that the music had 'all gone out of tune'. The newspaper wondered aloud what exactly the committee was seeking, since a Cape Committee had already assigned the blame to Jameson and since the command of the Rhodesian troops had been put under control of the Queen's High Commissioner, making no more raids possible. Consequently, it called for the parliamentarians to 'cut the farce short' and to allow Rhodes to 'go back to Africa to redeem his one great error by a further addition to his many great services to the Empire'.

The testimony of Rhodes before the committee in February 1897 was attended by a raft of notables, including the Prince of Wales and many members of both Houses of Parliament. The *Daily Mail* recorded that Rhodes appeared 'at bay' on his first day of testimony, but more relaxed by the second. He stood his ground unapologetically and, when asked, claimed that he never wrote letters of instruction and that any cables to Chamberlain were confidential and could not be produced.[1] By the second week of testimony, the *Daily Mail* declared, 'Mr. Rhodes Holds the Field.' The great man appeared to be enjoying himself before the committee, even when seated next to Jameson. The paper reported that, when asked if he communicated anything to the press, his reply,

'No; I never go near the Press', drew loud laughter from the audience.[2] As soon as possible, the imperturbable proconsul returned to South Africa to await the foregone verdict.[3] The *Daily Mail* declared that it was for posterity to judge Rhodes in the 'whole melancholy story'. He had 'played for a great stake and played for it badly', it continued, 'his actions created international complications of the gravest kind, and went near to involve the country in war . . . but . . . he has served his country nobly, and taken his place for all time amongst the makers of the British Empire'. The article concluded that if 'we must condemn his methods as unsuited to an age of peaceful regard to international duties, we must admit that in the earlier days of rugged carving of Empire his only fault would have been his failure'.[4]

With the Rhodes spectacle over, the *Daily Mail* prepared for its first anniversary. Quotes for publication were gathered from a variety of sources. The proprietor wrote to Lord Salisbury, anxious for some 'greeting or sentiment, or an expression of your opinion concerning the paper'.[5] The letter went on that the *Daily Mail* 'appeals, as you will see from the number I send you, to all classes, and is now circulating over 300,000 copies. The largest day-by-day circulation ever attained by a newspaper in England.' Salisbury's Secretary, Schomberg McDonnell, suggested that the Prime Minister should 'write privately to Mr. Harmsworth & say that Your Lordship cannot say anything for publication: congratulate him personally on his success'.[6] On this note Salisbury wrote, 'Is that Safe?' A personal message was sent.

The year 1897 marked Queen Victoria's sixtieth year of rule – her Diamond Jubilee. For the million and a half visitors expected to view the Jubilee Procession and to attend the countless other celebratory activities, London was scrubbed, repainted and bedecked with countless 'VR' symbols and banners. So that Alfred's mother and twenty friends could watch the cavalcade in comfort, a room was rented on the route, at 66 St James's Street. The 22 June event was truly awe-inspiring. Two separate columns totalling 50,000 troops – the largest military force ever assembled in London – converged on St Paul's for the thanksgiving service. The Colonial Procession was made up of contingents from around the Empire, each led by its respective premier, beginning with Sir Wilfrid Laurier of Canada, who had been knighted on Jubilee morning. Mile after mile of the Empire's warriors marched past the cheering multitude, from the Dyaks of Borneo to the Sikhs of India, each carrying Her Majesty's rifle, bayonet fixed. Among the colonial cavalry, the Rhodesian Horse, who had ridden in the Jameson Raid, received the loudest welcome. A banner in St James's proclaimed in English and Hindustani that Victoria alone was the Queen of Earthly Queens. 'When the Queen caught the view of the scene down St James's Street,' said the *Daily Mail*, 'delight was pictured on her face. Never before had that thoroughfare presented a scene so beautiful; all that flowers and flags and brilliant costumes and immense variety of colours could supply was here combined. The wave of applause gradually drifted into the singing of the national anthem.'[7]

The proprietor of the *Daily Mail* described the scene as 'the most magnificent spectacle I ever beheld, or can ever behold'.[8] An eight-page 'Golden Extra' souvenir edition was sold for sixpence. This gold-inked issue proclaimed 'The Greatness of the British Race' that the sight of the parading colonials affirmed. The 23 June editorial summed up the significance of the event:

> It is over. The great pageant has unrolled itself majestically before our eyes, and passed on till all its gold and steel have faded, its clash of brass and drums died in the distance. It is over and we rub our eyes and ears and try to tell ourselves what it meant.
>
> It meant that we ought to be a proud nation today. Proud of our fathers that founded this Empire, proud of ourselves who have . . . increased it, proud of our sons, who we can trust to keep what we had . . . and increase it for their sons in turn and their sons's sons. Until we saw it all passing through our city we never quite realised what Empire meant . . . It makes life newly worth living . . . better and more strenuously to feel that one is a part of this enormous, this wondrous machine, the greatest organisation the world ever saw.

The closing events of the Jubilee included a 'Great Naval Review' at Portsmouth, where Alfred spent a day on the destroyer *Lightning*. He called it 'a delightful and novel experience'.[9]

Joseph Chamberlain took advantage of the Jubilee to convene the colonial premiers in an Imperial Conference, the first since 1887. However, even in the euphoria of the Jubilee celebration, the Colonial Secretary was unable to sway the visitors towards any of his proposals for imperial unity. The premiers were widely fêted in London society, and among the many invitations they accepted was one from Alfred Harmsworth, whose position had become such that he was able to host a party for the dignitaries at 36 Berkeley Square, his new London home. The proprietor of the *Daily Mail* met the premiers on 20 June, and on the next day – only a little more than a month after he and Mary had moved in – he recorded that the home was 'pulled to pieces, in consequence of our party tonight . . . The House was beautifully decorated and party was, I think, a great success.'[10] Certainly no expense was spared. A Parisian chef and his staff were imported to prepare dinner, while the company was entertained by the pianist Ignace Paderewski and the Australian prima donna Nellie Melba.

In common with many others, Harmsworth considered Canada the key to any scheme of imperial co-operation, and a recent extension of Canadian preference to some British goods made Sir Wilfrid Laurier the most popular figure in attendance.[11] The day after the first conference session, Alfred met Laurier for an hour to discuss imperial affairs. The *Daily Mail* proclaimed that 'For the first time on record, a politician of our New World has been recognised as the equal of the great men of the Old Country.'[12] The newspaper described Laurier's address to the conference delegates as 'the first practical attempt on the part of a public man to deal in detail with the various difficulties in the way of closer unity between Great Britain and Greater Britain'.[13]

Laurier, who emerged as the leader of the premiers, made many speeches praising the value of the imperial connection; however, he would not commit to sharing the cost of imperial defence. Chamberlain was embarrassed further by the premiers' acceptance of Canada's proposal to extend imperial preference only if Britain would in return renounce her trade agreements with Germany and Belgium. Only the premiers of New Zealand and Tasmania – Richard Seddon and Edward Braddon – gave any support to Chamberlain's suggestion for the creation of an Imperial Council. The conference ended without the passage of anything more substantial than a weak resolution that further 'periodical' meetings should be held.[14] The disappointed owner of the *Daily Mail* attended a farewell reception for the visiting dignitaries.

The same month, during a speech at the annual shareholders meeting, Alfred declared that he and his newspapers had no use for old-fashioned Conservatism or radicalism. 'We are Unionist and Imperialist,' he continued, and felt 'no sympathy whatever with the politicians of the 'sixties, the 'seventies or the 'eighties'. He and the newspapers would stand, instead, for the 'unwritten alliance of the English-speaking peoples', underpinned by a strong British navy. It was apparent to the owner of the *Daily Mail* that the Navy was vital and would be needed. More and more Germany appeared to be replacing France as Britain's most likely future foe, and the second half of 1897 was marked by heightened tensions between the two nations. During the Jubilee Procession, Victoria's grandson Kaiser Wilhelm had been booed at places along the route, because of his telegram of support to Kruger at the time of the Jameson Raid. As long as the Queen, whom he deeply loved and revered, lived, 'Willy' was kept in check. After her passing, things would be more problematic. The Kaiser viewed his Uncle 'Bertie', the future Edward VII, with only slightly veiled contempt, as a weak womanizer.

In addition to the instability of its sovereign, Germany's growing industrial power and threatening militarism also had begun to make many observers nervous. For the past year one of the best-selling books in Britain had been E.E. Williams's *Made in Germany*, which outlined the economic threat and specified a series of remedies to meet the challenge of the industrial giant across the North Sea. The solutions offered included implementing reciprocal 'Fair Trade' policies against foreign tariffs, federation of the Empire to develop a market comparable in size to the competition, increased technical education, and greater use of commercial agents to further British interests. The *Daily Mail* supported Williams, who during the next years contributed a number of leaders which kept the problem in the public eye. On 24 September 1897 the paper began a series by G.W. Steevens meant further to expose the Teutonic menace. The first of sixteen instalments, 'Under the Iron Heel', warned Britain 'for the next ten years fix your eyes very hard on Germany'. Consciousness was also awakening in regard to Britain's relative decline in relation to another emerging power, the United States, involved in the recent Venezuela border dispute with Britain. The owner of the *Daily Mail* believed the USA would be needed as a counter to the German menace, and worked to better relations between the two great Anglo-Saxon powers.

With the Jubilee celebration and the Imperial Conference concluded, Alfred Harmsworth returned to publishing matters, meeting the American magazine proprietor Frank Munsey. In July, as the owner of the *Daily Mail*, he was almost marched to jail for contempt of court. In the end the newspaper was forced to pay a £50 fine, and print an apology, for an inaccurate story on a financial syndicate. Minor problems aside, the fantastic success of Harmsworth Brothers Limited continued: 1897 net profits grew to £178,000. Prospects for Alfred and Mary blossomed socially as well, with introductions to the Dukes of Edinburgh and Abercorn. During a levee at St James's Palace, the couple were presented to the Prince of Wales. The society of plutocrats with which the soon-to-be King surrounded himself was widely emulated and set its own moral standards. Like Edward with his Mrs Keppell, Alfred also took a long-term mistress, Mrs Wrohan, who would bear him two sons and a daughter. Succumbing to temptation in dalliances with women outside marriage, whether with Mrs Wrohan or many others over the years, was one of the few vices of the age to which Alfred was subject. He did not gamble or share his father's taste for alcohol, but had a fondness for German cigars, smoked with the band on. At the same time, Mary Harmsworth – lonely, and frustrated by the couple's failure to have children – liberally applied her husband's fortune to launching herself into British society. Mary also took lovers, with Reggie Nicholson later listed among them.[15]

At the recommendation of his doctors for increased recreation, in September 1897 Alfred tried golf for the first time and found that he liked it. The sport replaced cycling as his main form of exercise, and he had several courses built, including one near Elmwood. A golf professional, Sandy Thomson, often travelled with him. The same month the Jackson–Harmsworth expedition returned from Franz Josef Land. The explorer had not reached the North Pole, but did add useful new information to the store of northern data. The expedition disproved the idea that Franz Josef Land was a solid mass, showing it to be an archipelago of islands combined by an ice cover. Jackson also mapped previously unknown areas, and returned with numerous specimens of flora and fauna. One of these trophies, a polar bear, was mounted and placed in the hall at Elmwood. The disappointed financial backer of the expedition afterwards often joked with visitors that the specimen had cost £30,000. He had at least done better than George Newnes, who had staked a similar expedition to £38,000 and later remarked that all he had got in return for his money was 'one stuffed penguin'.[16] One of the *Windward* lifeboats, the *Mary Harmsworth*, was installed as a decoration in Elmwood's garden. Though his own expedition fell short, by presenting the *Windward* to Lieutenant Robert Peary of the United States Navy, Alfred contributed to the explorer who finally did reach the North Pole. The ship was used in survey work preliminary to the successful attempt. For this aid, Alfred was made a member of the American Geographical Society.

Aristocratic society continued to beckon as well. The Harmsworths found themselves included on the guest lists for weekends at the country homes of the nobility, such as the Earl of Onslow, Under-Secretary of State for India, who had given his support at Portsmouth two years before. In mid-November the couple accepted an invitation to The Priory, a Georgian house near Reigate, home to George Curzon, Under-Secretary for Foreign Affairs in the Commons and considered a 'coming man' among the Conservatives. He had travelled widely, written several books, and become an expert on matters Asiatic. With little chance to replace the Prime Minister as Foreign Secretary, Curzon desired to be made Viceroy of India, and gained the appointment within a year. The viceroy's palace at Calcutta had been modelled on his family's ancestral home, Kedleston. Six years older than Alfred, Curzon was the son and heir of Lord Scarsdale and in public often assumed an attitude of stiff arrogance which caused widespread resentment. Since his days at Balliol, he had been plagued by what he called the 'accursed doggerel':

My name is George Nathaniel Curzon,
I am a most superior person,
My cheek is pink, my hair is sleek,
I dine at Blenheim once a week.[17]

Despite this reputation, on social occasions and among his friends Curzon could be extremely charming. During the year, Alfred had made many calls on the Under-Secretary and Schomberg McDonnell at the Foreign Office.

In addition to McDonnell, at The Priory the same weekend were a number of rising political figures. These included Herbert Asquith, with his wife, Margot; Alfred Lyttelton; and Joseph Chamberlain's son, Austen. These three men were destined to be prime minister, colonial secretary and Chancellor of the Exchequer, respectively. It was an era in which Curzon could count Asquith, his unceasing Liberal parliamentary antagonist, among his friends. Margot Asquith and Alfred Lyttelton were old acquaintances of Curzon's and fellow members of the 'Souls', a loose group of politicians, writers and wits who regularly entertained each other at weekend parties and other social gatherings. Some said Curzon was their leader, others Arthur Balfour, who was not present on this occasion. Alfred Harmsworth described the weekend 'as very interesting party' at which he heard 'a great many interesting things about the inner life of politics and much about Gladstone and Rosebery'.[18] He spoke for some time with Margot Asquith, a renowned political gossip, in particular discussing the quarrel between Rosebery and the Liberal leader Sir William Harcourt.

Alfred enjoyed the novelty of his stay at The Priory; however, he was

ill-suited to the verbal swordplay and out of his element among the educated élite, exemplified by Curzon, who had honed his debating skills at
the Oxford Union. Before long he considered such diversions a waste
of time and, much to Mary's displeasure, turned down most of the
mounting number of invitations. She was forced to build her social connections independently.

In addition to gleaning domestic political information from a widen-
ing circle of acquaintances, Alfred was also building an independent
intelligence network. The thousands of letters addressed to his newspapers by its readers, which the proprietor solicited and encouraged,
gave insight into British public opinion on home and foreign policy. His
overseas correspondents, and other contacts abroad, made him privy to
sometimes valuable tit-bits concerning developments from the
Continent to the Far East. By 1897 he began to share interesting information with the government. Since Salisbury acted as Foreign Secretary,
Alfred passed along what he believed might be important through
Schomberg McDonnell.[19] Salisbury would before too long complain to
the influential clergyman Canon Malcolm MacColl that the 'diplomacy
of nations is now conducted quite as much in the letters of foreign correspondents as in the dispatches of the Foreign Office . . . I wish it were
otherwise, but wishing is no good.'[20]

For Alfred and Mary 1898 began with renewed foreign travels in
search of rest and relaxation. They planned a trip to Egypt, but, since
they had never made a proper Continental tour, their route also
included stops in Paris, Genoa, Florence and Rome. Two days in Rome
included viewing the major attractions, such as St Peter's, the Vatican,
the Colosseum and, according to Alfred, 'other of the splendid ruins'.[21]
On 8 January they sailed from Brindisi on the *China* for Port Said, arriving in Cairo two days later. Alfred recorded that the city reminded them
of India, perhaps because he and his wife were joined on the trip, as
they had been on the Indian voyage, by Reggie Nicholson, who had
recently joined the businesses as a solicitor for the *Evening News*.

While in Egypt, Alfred spent some time looking to newspaper affairs,
in particular *Daily Mail* coverage of the British campaign against the
Mahdi's successor, the Khalifa. For more than a year, a combined force
under Major-General Sir Horatio Herbert Kitchener, the Egyptian
Sirdar, had been making its way south in deliberate stages to face the
enemy. To ensure their supply line, the methodical British built and
maintained a railway along the route. As Sirdar, Kitchener commanded
the Egyptian army, and his fervent desire was to avenge the death of

General Gordon at Khartoum thirteen years before. It was expected that in 1898 vengeance would at last be meted out and the stain on Britain's imperial prestige removed. Only very grudgingly did Kitchener allow a contingent of reporters to accompany the force. He had nothing but contempt for the journalists, whom he called a bunch of 'drunken swabs'.[22] Two papers for which he made an exception were *The Times* and the *Daily Mail*, and this favouritism only caused further problems.

In Cairo, Alfred talked of press coverage at the front with Colonel Frank Rhodes, who two years before, under a death sentence for his part in the Jameson Raid affair, had been ransomed out of captivity in the Transvaal by his brother Cecil. The Colonel wrote dispatches for *The Times*, while G.W. Steevens became the principal *Daily Mail* correspondent. Alfred also met the British Governor-General in Egypt, Lord Cromer, and his aide Rennell Rodd, to gain the official view of the situation. Alfred liked Cromer and described him as a 'strong, practical man'.[23] Unofficial sightseeing included viewing the whirling dervishes and a visit to the pyramids at Giza, along with a tour of the Museum of Egyptian Antiquities in the old Khedival palace. After a shopping expedition for souvenirs and supplies at the famous Cairo bazaars, Alfred, Mary and Reggie embarked on a cruise down the Nile.

For their leisurely journey, the travellers engaged the dahabeeyah *Horus*. Dahabeeyahs were floating residences, comfortably furnished in European style, many even including a piano. Such an enterprise required a guide and organizer – the dragoman – who would make all the necessary arrangements and oversee the servants, as well as appoint the captain and crew needed to man the lateen-sailed vessel.[24] A dahabeeyah cruise down the Nile was a slow progression which could be as full of activities or as unplanned as the traveller wished. Along the way, the *Horus* stopped for minor ancient sites in addition to the larger temples, as well as for bird-shooting parties. In between there was plenty of time to read or simply to relax and do nothing – a pursuit Alfred gradually came to appreciate. At Abydos, the trio toured the temple of Seti I and the more dilapidated temple of Rameses II. The second stop of note for the Harmsworth expedition was the massive ruin at Karnak, with its great temple of Amen-Re and imposing avenue of sphinxes leading to the temple of Mut. A short donkey ride took the party to the smaller temple of Luxor. On 8 February the party reached Edfu. Alfred described its temple of Horus as 'the most beautifully preserved thing we have seen'. Here a sandstorm forced them to lay up for the night. Reggie and Alfred spent the time playing cards and dominoes.

The month on the Nile was a tonic for Harmsworth, who recorded that he felt 'fitter than I remember for years'.[25] From Aswan, he wrote to an old friend of his father's, Frederick Wood:

> This is the existence you would enjoy. We are living the classics. You must let me pack you off here one day. To be able to survey thirty civilizations in three or four weeks, to look upon works and records of folks who had put in four thousand years of culture B.C., makes one regard the Greeks and Romans, whose work is as plentiful here as anywhere, as people who lived the day before yesterday.
>
> We live in a kind of glorified houseboat and sail thirty or forty miles a day, shooting, exploring, photographing, as we choose. That piece of brown stuff I enclose I took from a tomb 4,000 years old. It is a piece of mummy cloth. As my dear father would have said, from journalism to robbing the dead is but a natural and brief step.[26]

Even hundreds of miles down the Nile, it was impossible for Alfred to escape completely from business. G.W. Steevens and his chief had a rendezvous at Aswan on 12 February, and the two bought camels for Steevens's adventure. After the writer departed to join Kitchener's force, the next stage of the cruise included being towed up the rapids of the first cataract, after which the *Horus* stopped at the island of Philae. Called 'the pearl of Egypt' by the 1898 *Baedeker's Guide*, Philae was the furthest point in their progress. After a tour of the island's temple of Isis, the party came back down the rapids. On the 16th, the craft began its return journey to Cairo, stopping during the following ten days at other points of interest along the way.

Alfred enjoyed this experience on the great river thoroughly, calling the trip 'a boon and a blessing'.[27] He wrote to his brother Cecil that it had been 'the most surprisingly delightful trip of our lives. As for dahabieh life, with companions one loves and a goodly store of books, I know nothing like it.'[28]

In the first days of March, before leaving Cairo for home, Alfred had another interview with Lord Cromer, and also spoke with Colonel John Hay, the American ambassador to Britain. Hay, a future United States Secretary of State, was also on vacation and in no hurry to return to his duties in London, despite the war clouds that were gathering between Spain and the USA in the wake of the sinking of the American battleship *Maine* in Havana harbour two weeks before.

Once again the passage to Europe, on the *Clyde*, was a rough one for Alfred, who vowed in his 8 March diary, after landing at Marseilles, that he would 'never to go to sea again'. By the time he had arrived back at Berkeley Square, at midnight on 15 March, he had recovered sufficiently to sum up the holiday as 'most enjoyable'.

The next month the Spanish-American War – the 'Splendid Little War', as John Hay described it – began after declarations of war first by Spain and then retroactively by the US Congress, so as to beat the Spanish to the punch. The *Daily Mail* commented that France, Italy and Austria were denouncing US aggression as they had condemned Britain in similar circumstances. The two Anglo-Saxon powers, said the paper, shared the same mission – civilizing the world. The time might not be too distant, it went on, when the USA and Britain might have to stand together against Germany and other European 'barbarians'.[29] The *Daily Mail* scrambled to cover the great event, sending out Charles Hands, one of the proprietor's favourites. However, Alfred found the war a disappointment. The Harmsworth newspapers, unlike those of Hearst and Pulitzer, did not reap significant profits from the story. Later in the year Alfred complained that 'Journalistically speaking, the American War was not a source of increase of revenue for the Press' and challenged those, like Henry Labouchère MP, editor of the radical *Truth*, who asserted that war was beneficial to newspapers.[30] 'The actual facts' Alfred revealed, were that the organization which Kennedy Jones put in the field cost £300 a week – which the increase in sales was insufficient to cover. In the first excitement, circulation had increased by 100,000 copies, but within three weeks sales had fallen back to normal. Even the 'smash of the Spanish fleet at Santiago', he went on, failed to move the circulation 'by one copy'. On the other hand, the death of Gladstone in May, which the paper covered in depth though it disagreed with him politically, increased sales greatly. After a four-month conflict, the United States emerged a true imperial power, relieving Spain of her imperial possessions from the Philippines to Cuba and Puerto Rico. The last annexation guarded the approaches to the isthmian canal which the Americans became determined to build with or without British approval.

Disappointment in the Spanish–American War did not deter the *Daily Mail* from continuing its coverage of military developments on the Nile. G.W. Steevens returned to London on 2 May with a report from Egypt. Kitchener's forces had defeated one of the Khalifa's armies under Mahmud a month before at the Atbara river and were soon to begin the final leg of the advance to Khartoum. The proprietor dined with Steevens before the writer returned to the front. To gain the latest intelligence, Alfred met an impressive variety of imperial and military figures. Among these was Sir Charles Dilke, who, with the writer Spenser Wilkinson, had recently co-authored a cautionary volume entitled *Imperial Defence*. Alfred discussed the fleet and the Far East with Lord Charles Beresford, before the Admiral departed for the Far East – a tour he chronicled the following year in *The Break-up of China*. Army readiness was mooted with Sir Henry Evelyn Wood, in 1898 the Adjutant-General. Alfred, accompanied by brother Leicester, also visited Hatfield for lunch with Salisbury. On 13 May he had breakfast with Cecil Rhodes, for whom he had given a dinner party at Berkeley Square earlier in the month.[31] At the same time, changes were taking place at Alfred's favourite residence. The purchase of Joss Farm, which adjoined Elmwood, expanded the grounds down to the North Foreland seashore and added several cottages to the estate.

In this period, Alfred made the first tentative explorations towards purchasing *The Times*, the most prestigious British journal. The founding Walter family continued to control the paper, which had been embroiled for years in legal disputes with the shareholders, who wished to sell their interests to outsiders. Alfred's diary records that on 22 June he spent two hours at *The Times* office 'discussing with Mr. [Arthur] Walter negotiations in regard to that paper'. (The same evening he relaxed by going to see Sarah Bernhardt perform.) A month later, Charles Frederick Moberly Bell, long-time manager of *The Times*, dined with Alfred.[32] These talks came to nothing when the lawyers advised that buying the one-fortieth interest in *The Times* on offer by a Walter granddaughter would bring only troublesome litigation.

An interesting and somewhat mysterious relationship developed after July 1898 between Alfred Harmsworth and Lord Rosebery, his neighbour for the previous year in Berkeley Square. Though their houses were side by side, the Earl's London mansion at number 38 dwarfed the more modest Harmsworth residence. The backgrounds of the two men were equally disparate. Archibald Philip Primrose, fifth Earl of Rosebery, had led a truly charmed existence. Thirty years before, aged twenty-one, he had inherited his grandfather's title and a considerable income. When given the choice between horse racing and completing his degree at Christ Church, Oxford, his love for the turf led him to choose the former. A decade later he married Hannah, daughter of Baron Meyer de Rothschild. Among other benefits, the connection carried with it the magnificent Rothschild house, Mentmore. Rosebery's political fortune was made when he managed Gladstone's 1879–80

Midlothian campaign, although the two men would never see eye to eye. A world voyage in 1883–4 led Rosebery to become champion of the Empire in opposition to his leader. Though he had been talked of as a possible prime minister from that time, the charismatic younger man had to wait until 1894 to accept what had become for him by that time a poisoned chalice. The experience of fifteen months in office led him later to write that there were 'two supreme pleasures in life. One is ideal the other real. The ideal is when a man receives the seals of office from his sovereign. The real pleasure comes when he hands them back.' Ironically, he would win the Derby twice during his otherwise unpleasant tenure as Prime Minister.

Despite the fact that he had declared himself tired of politics and had given up the leadership of his party, there developed around Rosebery a cult of followers who were fervent in their belief that he would, at some point, emerge from his tent to reclaim the leadership of the nation at the head of a Liberal or centrist coalition government. This sentiment was abetted by the fact that, in an age of famous speakers, the Earl was blessed with oratorical gifts which exceeded those of almost all others. His every utterance was eagerly awaited and dissected for its true message by the faithful. Meanwhile, the Earl spent his time writing books – in 1898 a biography of Peel published the next year.

For whatever reason, Rosebery appeared genuinely to like and to be fascinated by his unlikely neighbour, who had risen from the middle class by forecasting the reading preferences of the masses. The younger man raised the spirits of the Earl, who was subject to depression and insomnia after the death of his wife eight years before. When both were in town, the pair began to take walks to Hyde Park and back, chatting about various topics, imperial and ordinary. After July 1898, Rosebery often dropped in on his neighbour. Unfortunately, Alfred's diary does not reveal the particulars of their many conversations.

In the following months, while Alfred spent considerable time with the former Liberal prime minister, he also met Conservative figures, including Salisbury's heir apparent and nephew, Arthur Balfour. In August, Balfour's comrade in the 'Souls', George Curzon, was appointed Viceroy of India. For a viceregal title, and so that he would not be forced into the House of Lords before his father's death, he was created Baron Curzon of Kedleston in the Irish peerage. The *Daily Mail* applauded the appointment, and would be generally supportive of Curzon almost until the end of his tenure in the subcontinent.

At the same time, Kitchener and his army arrived at Omdurman, the gateway to Khartoum. On the first day of September 1898 the *Daily Mail* trumpeted the 'Plan of Attack on Omdurman'. In the following issues, the newspaper unfolded the story of the battle. Printed alongside was news of a French incursion into Fashoda, a marshy outpost on the Nile 400 miles further south of Khartoum – territory claimed by Egypt and, by extension, Britain. This represented the latest skirmish in the so-called 'Scramble for Africa', in which the country had competed with France and Germany for two decades. On 3 September the *Daily Mail* noted that Germany had recognized the legitimacy of Britain's role in Egypt, in return for a lease of Delgoa Bay in Portuguese East Africa and for giving the 'Kaiser a Free Hand in Asia Minor'. France, for a season, became the greater rival.

Two days later, the editorial 'Well Done Sirdar' acclaimed Kitchener's victory at Omdurman, which finally had avenged the death of Gordon. The same issue began Steevens's series 'With Kitchener at Khartum', which described the utter rout of the Khalifa's army, while at the same time praising the 'Magnificent Heroism of the Doomed Dervishes'. Although the Khalifa escaped, Kitchener crushed his army at a tiny cost. In a 26,000-man force, only 48 officers and men were lost, with another 382 wounded. Kaiser Wilhelm sent his grandmother a letter of congratulations on the victory.[33] The *Daily Mail*, in addition to lauding the Sirdar, also warned that in 'France there seems to be a certain inclination in foolish talk respecting one M. Marchand and certain curious suzerain rights on behalf of France which he is said to have established South of Khartoum. Jocularity is not always timely.'[34]

In the next weeks international focus shifted from Khartoum to Fashoda, where Captain Marchand, to plant an imperial claim, had led an intrepid band of Frenchmen and natives across the continent from France's equatorial possessions. Kitchener carried with him sealed orders from Salisbury, to be opened after recapturing Khartoum, which instructed the Sirdar to travel down the Nile and to deal sharply with any incursion, French or otherwise. The *Daily Mail* appraised the dispatch of Marchand as 'the last hope of the French in opposing England's policy of expansion in Africa'.[35] On 12 September the paper declared that a captured dervish gunboat had confirmed a 'white expedition', believed to be French, at Fashoda and that France's government was 'Resolved to Defend Its Claims'. In fact Marchand's tiny command had beaten off an attack by dervish gunboats, which, had not the British intervened by destroying the power of the Khalifa, would almost certainly have returned with reinforcements to finish the job. Instead of the dervishes, the interlopers now faced Kitchener, who started south with a force ten times their size.

The press was not included in this excursion. In the opinion of the *Daily Mail*, this demonstrated that 'grave complications' were possible and that the curiosity of correspondents 'might be inconvenient' in the circumstances. The journal was, however, quick to point out that it trusted the Sirdar to take the best course without press supervision. It warned France that 'England will stand no more tricks of the kind that have been played upon her by the Quai D'Orsay in West Africa and Siam [Thailand]. She means to have a clear road from the Cape to the Mediterranean, and no Fashoda in the hands of the French will be allowed to break the continuance of the Strip of Red.'[36] In the following days of heightened international tension, while the Paris papers demanded 'No Surrender to England', the *Daily Mail* warned that 'the French have got to go and the sooner they make up their minds the better'.[37] On 19 September the 'unmuzzled' *Daily Mail* revealed that Kitchener had arrived at Fashoda, met Marchand the day before, and extended to him 'British Hospitality'. The journal was reassured by news that the French government did not consider Marchand's expedition 'official', despite the cries of the Paris press. The report went on to congratulate Kitchener for his handling of the affair, and Marchand and his 'intrepid band of explorers' for surviving their adventure. This optimism proved premature, however. The Fashoda stalemate, and the accompanying press war, continued into October. The *Daily Mail* blamed the situation on the plans of the French Foreign Minister, Théophile Delcassé, and on Britain's lack of firmness in the past. It opined that France 'has come to think that she has only to make preposterous demands to gain part, at least, of what she wants'. The editorial went on, 'the time has come for France to be plainly told of the folly and danger of an Anglophobe policy, which presumes upon British . . . peacefulness to divert attention from scandals at home'.[38]

Had France wished to provoke a conflict with Britain, her timing could not have been worse. Since before the beginning of the crisis, coverage of the French 'Dreyfus Affair' had shared the *Daily Mail* and other European newspaper headlines with the events at Khartoum and Fashoda. From the January 1898 publication of Émile Zola's 'J'Accuse' letter to French President François Faure in George Clemenceau's *L'Aurore*, France was divided into two warring camps. One supported the French Army against charges that it had falsely convicted the Jewish Captain Dreyfus of treason, and turned a blind eye to compelling new evidence of his innocence. The other side wanted the case reopened and justice served, regardless of the embarrassment and demoralization it might cause. On 27 September a majority of the French Cabinet voted to reopen the Dreyfus case. This national division, along with the reality that the British navy would undoubtedly decimate the French fleet as easily as Kitchener would overrun Marchand's outpost, made a stand-down by France inevitable. However, before this, some face-saving arrangement had to be found.

In Britain, to foster public support for his government's course, Salisbury published a Blue Book on the negotiations. The 10 October *Daily Mail* revealed 'The Fashoda Dispatches' of 27 September, which instructed Kitchener that 'Her Majesty's Government considers that there could be no discussion on such questions as the right of Egypt to Fashoda.' This agreed with the newspaper's assertions throughout that Marchand was 'trespassing on Egyptian soil'. Meanwhile, it was reported, the French government awaited Marchand's report. Over the next week, the journal recounted Lord Rosebery's assertion that the people of Britain were united behind the government, as well as the 'vast scheme of mobilization' of the French armed services and the 'Precautions Necessary' in response.[39] *Daily Mail* maps traced the relative positions of the British and French forces. By the third week in October the Reserve Fleet had been readied and war orders had been drafted for the active fleets.

On 22 October the *Daily Mail* editorial, 'A Grave Situation', revealed that Marchand's report was now in Paris. In the paper's opinion, this ended the first stage of the crisis, yet the French government was still procrastinating. The editorial continued with the warning that 'Thus the nation may be approaching the hour of trial . . . for years France has engaged in what can only be described as a veiled war upon British interests and trade in every quarter of the globe . . . yielding now we should only have to face more preposterous demands tomorrow.' It was the duty of the British, the paper went on, to trust in the Navy, which stood 'at the ready', and to prove to the world that the English were not 'degenerate descendants of glorious stock'. This bellicose rhetoric aside, the newspaper's proprietor apparently did not believe there was a serious possibility that war would break out. Alfred and his mother took their usual Continental vacation that week. They visited Germany, Amsterdam and Paris. In the French capital he noted the excitement over the 'Dreyfus revision' rather than the stand-off in Africa.

Despite the nonchalant attitude of its proprietor, international tensions mounted and the *Daily Mail* carried 'France's Reply' – that Fashoda was hers by conquest – and Salisbury's 'No Wavering' response that France would be allowed 'No Outlet on the Nile'. Articles by G.W. Steevens gave voice to the opinion of the British public: that England had backed down too often in the past and that the French should clear out. The newspaper also reported the fall of M. Brisson's government.[40] On the 27th it revealed a possible settlement, and two days later reported that Marchand was at Khartoum and that an evacuation appeared at hand.

At this delicate time, the British government asked the newspapers to withhold coverage of military matters. In 'The Press and the Crisis', the *Daily Mail* reported that a letter from the War Office three days before had asked the paper not to publish anything which might be 'of aid to the enemy'.[41] It added that the editor would call that day at the War Office and the Admiralty to ascertain what sort of news it was possible to print. On 29 October the *Daily Mail* announced that, without compensation, 'France Submits' and that Marchand's mission would retire. At the Mansion House on 4 November, with the newly created Lord Kitchener of Khartoum at his side, Salisbury announced that the French would withdraw from Fashoda.

Some commentators – Kennedy Jones among them – have seen the Fashoda crisis as a dividing line after which the government was more forthcoming in its co-operation with the press. Others at the time decried the unhealthy influence of newspapers. After a tour of the Continent in 1898, W.T. Stead commented that the

> fact is that the intervention of the Press in international disputes tends daily to become more and more hostile to peace and civilization . . . our modern journalism is the most potent weapon yet invented by the devil for banishing peace and goodwill from the earth. Sooner or later the nations will in self-defence have to provide some means of silencing newspaper comment when international questions are in debate, in the same way as English newspapers are promptly forbidden by law to express an opinion upon any case that is before the courts.[42]

Stead and others would continue this criticism, to no avail, over the following years.

On 1 November Alfred spent his first day in the new Harmsworth Building, a five-storey structure of red brick and stone on Carmelite Street. The £500,000 building brought all the Harmsworth papers under one roof. One commentator referred to it as 'a factory in

Bohemia'. The proprietor moved into his luxurious quarters before the rest of the premises – soon dubbed Carmelite House – were quite complete. 'Room One', on the first floor, was panelled in mahogany, its bookcases filled with leather-bound volumes. Each end of the rectangular room contained a fireplace, with a mahogany overmantel. On one of these rested a bust of Napoleon, a hero of Alfred's. The furniture was solid Empire, on a thick pile carpet which reportedly cost a thousand pounds. The owners' private secretary, George Sutton, was installed next door. Sutton and brother St John Harmsworth, just down from Oxford, were both added to the board of directors at this time. It was also after the move to Carmelite House that the proprietor began to be called 'the chief', in the American manner, by his employees, in place of 'Mr Alfred'. Among the many visitors to the new office was Winston Churchill, the as yet unproven son of Lord Randolph Churchill, and grandson of the seventh Duke of Marlborough. The twenty-three-year-old political hopeful had managed to attach himself to the 21st Lancers and had been at Omdurman. His account of the campaign, *The River War*, helped gain him considerable notoriety. The next month, at a lunch with Churchill, Alfred was introduced to Consuelo, the young and beautiful Duchess of Marlborough.

Besides the new Harmsworth Building, a £40,000 printing works across the Thames in Lavington Street, Southwark, began operations at this time. This was a complement to the printing operation at Gravesend, which devoted itself to the more substantial periodicals, such as the recently launched *Harmsworth Magazine*. The addition meant that the Harmsworth press owned and operated more rotary presses than any other. Such economies of scale helped the businesses to pay a 30 per cent dividend, while the company of Sir George Newnes, including *Tit-Bits* among other publications, paid 10. Much of Alfred's career can be viewed, and he himself certainly viewed it, as a competition with Newnes, who in 1895 had been created a baronet. Alfred complained in October 1898 to Lord Onslow:

> My opponent and friend Sir George Newnes started the *Westminster Gazette* and Lord Rosebery promptly recognised his journal by a reward that in the formation of his company this year proved of enormous commercial advantage to him.
>
>   On our side, owners of newspapers of comparatively slight influence are rewarded and my predecessor in the *Evening News* received recognition, though the journal was a failure.

However, I would rather say nothing more on the subject: the Party leaders are no doubt quite ignorant of the revolution which the *Daily Mail,* in its infancy at present, is making in London journalism. They have never even enquired into the new provincial offshoots I am preparing. The Government has an enormous majority and can dispense with young men and, moreover, such of the leaders as know me are aware that I would never sacrifice any belief in the need for a strong imperial and Foreign policy to any personal dis-appointments and annoyance at the favouring of opponents.[43]

Within a few weeks of this letter being sent, J.W. Lowther MP recommended Alfred to Lord Salisbury, who was also Warden of the Cinque Ports, as an addition to the Cinque Ports Peace Commission. Lowther noted that

Harmsworth has built a large house at Broadstairs ... being very well off, and socially fully up to the standard for County beaks. As I mentioned previously, Harmsworth has never, as yet, taken any prominent local part, but it is with an eye to his position elsewhere (Press &c &c) that it strikes me that the Lord Warden might think it expedient to afford him some local recognition ... now that he is fully established as a resident freeholder upon a large scale.[44]

Accordingly, an invitation was extended by Salisbury, to which the pro-prietor of the *Daily Mail* replied that he scarcely could 'say how grateful I am at Your Lordship's recollection of me & especially in connection with so interesting a survival as the Peace Commission of the Cinque Ports, to which I shall be proud to become an addition'.[45]

As he had for some time, Alfred began the new year with a trip abroad. For 1899 the destination was the Swiss Alps. Near Interlaken, at Grindelwald, he took a chalet for a month and spent January at winter pursuits such as tobagganing, skating and sleigh riding. Several celeb-rities were at the resort at the same time, including the cricketer C.R. Studd. From their picturesque lodgings, the Harmsworths could view the progress of a group of young men climbing the famous Eiger. February brought a return to the routine of Carmelite House, where, as in past absences, the businesses had flourished while their chief was away.

Soon after his return, Alfred's first motor car was delivered – a six-horsepower petrol-fuelled Panhard-Levassor, which had been ordered in Paris. Before this, English speed limits and inferior roads had mainly confined his automotive exploits to the Continent. On 30 March he had his 'first ride in England on my automobile'. Delighting in his new possession, Alfred gave demonstrations to those brave enough to join

him on the high-seated yellow machine. Passengers included his
mother, Harold and his brother's children. The little yellow car was
among the first seen on the rural roads of England. Punctures were a
constant problem. Because of flat tyres and other mechanical troubles,
the journey from London to Elmwood often took more than twelve
hours. Despite these annoyances, Alfred insisted on driving whenever
possible, including many visits to his mother and to golf outings.
Pressing on in the open car, even in bad weather, his enthusiasm for his
new hobby remained undiminished. On 24 April the diary records that
a return to town from Elmwood in pouring rain was 'very enjoyable,
though we were all wet through'. Late in April he drove to Epsom to see
Rosebery, whom he took for a ride. The Earl's only complaint was that
the machine would not go faster. Their conversations – described only
as 'most interesting' – continued.

Harmsworth was an early supporter and member of the Automobile
Club of Great Britain, which would become the Royal Automobile
Club. He became friendly with many influential promoters of the new
machine, including Harry Rolls, who visited him to talk about the
subject. Rolls and John Montagu MP (later Lord Montagu of Beaulieu),
another of Alfred's motoring acquaintances, were Britain's representatives in the 201-mile race from Paris to Ostend, the major automobile
event of the year. Alfred afterwards borrowed Rolls's racing machine,
which he proudly showed to his mother. The *Daily Mail* chronicled
Montagu's problems when his petrol-driven Daimler was refused
admittance to Palace Yard, in the Houses of Parliament, because of
fears it would 'set the building on fire'. After a protest to the Speaker,
the machine was admitted.[46]

On 18 June, at one of the many Paris auto shows of this period,
Alfred tested a steam-driven model and bought an electric vehicle. The
six-horsepower Serpollet was delivered in London four days later.
Visiting the London Motor Car Show on 3 July inspired him to take a
100-mile motor trip three days later. In these early years of motoring the
owner of a car normally hired a driver/engineer, and in August 1899
Alfred engaged 'a man called Lancaster', who would stay with him for
several years, until replaced by Pine, who would remain until the end. At
the same time, Alfred again took up his conversations with his neighbour, Rosebery, which must have included the menacing situation in
South Africa, where a renewed imperial confrontation soon completely
dwarfed the Fashoda crisis which had seemed so important the previous year.

4

Boers and Khaki, 1899–1900

IN THE TRANSVAAL, the dreams of Cecil Rhodes for a British Empire stretching from the Cape to Cairo and of Joseph Chamberlain for a united and British-dominated South Africa ran counter to the competing vision of the Boer population for complete independence. One additional British figure, Sir Alfred Milner, also played a leading role in precipitating the unfortunate events of the following three years.[1] High Commissioner at the Cape Colony since 1897, Milner was perhaps even more passionate than Chamberlain and Rhodes in the belief that Britain should rule a united South Africa, and he was ready to commit the country, willing or not, to a course of direct action to gain this objective. While he publicly condemned the Jameson Raid, Milner set out to find another way to overcome the Boer problem.

Milner's aspirations were unintentionally aided by the inflexible nature of Paul Kruger, under whose leadership the Transvaal renounced the uncertain 'suzerainty' granted Britain over its affairs after the brief First South African War of 1880–1. The Transvaal also continued its refusal to grant a five-year franchise demanded by the swarms of 'Uitlanders', the vast majority British immigrants, who had been drawn to the country's goldfields since 1886 and outnumbered the Boer inhabitants. In 1899, 40,000 of these Outlanders signed a petition of grievances which was presented to the Queen and her government by Milner, who, in a dispatch to the Colonial Office, compared their servile position to that of the enslaved helots of ancient Greece. The gold and diamonds that attracted the unwanted British also provided the Boers with the wherewithal to arm themselves with the latest Krupp artillery and Mauser rifles. These descendants of the Dutch would not be swept away as easily as dervishes or Zulu tribesman. Yet, to complete the dreams of Rhodes, Chamberlain and Milner, they had to be squared. It was this dilemma that would lead, in late 1899, to the opening shots of the Boer War.

Unfortunately for Britain's cause, its army was ill prepared. The cautious Lord Lansdowne, Secretary of State for War since the formation of the government in 1895, was hardly the vigorous leader needed in wartime. The British Commander-in-Chief, Lord Wolseley, led an army one-tenth the size of the powers across the Channel and had become an embittered old man in the face of budgetary constraints forced on him by a nation which put the Navy first. On the ground in South Africa 10,000 British troops faced five times that number of Boers, yet Lansdowne rejected Milner's pleas to double their number and to replace their commander, Lieutenant General Sir William Butler.

Cecil Rhodes spent much of 1899 in England rallying support for determined action in South Africa. He visited the Prince of Wales at Sandringham, and was widely fêted in London and at the great country houses. On 12 April Alfred and Harold dined with a group that included Rhodes, the millionaire grocer Sir Thomas Lipton and Schomberg McDonnell. At the beginning of May, Rhodes warned a great City meeting about the 'Boer Pretensions' and the Boers' claim that British suzerainty, agreed to in the settlement after the British humiliation at Majuba, was now abolished.[2] Newspaper articles also revealed the blunt discussions between Kruger and Chamberlain about the situation in the Transvaal. One day after Alfred again met Rhodes, the 6 May *Daily Mail* called it 'England's Duty' to 'Take the Uitlander's Case in Hand'. Two days later, the proprietor took Kennedy Jones for an audience 'to make him known to Mr. Rhodes'.[3] On the 12th, he gave the great man a tour of Carmelite House.

While Rhodes rallied support for intervention in South Africa, Lord Rosebery, who had been silent for some time, also entered the imperial fray in a speech to the City Liberal Club, calling for the Party to cast aside its policy of Home Rule for Ireland and to embrace a 'new Imperial spirit'.[4] In 'The Larger Imperialism', the *Daily Mail* mooted Rosebery's future as a 'Liberal Imperialist'. However, demonstrating its impatience with his vacillation, the newspaper quoted a long list of things that Rosebery had abandoned, taken from the current attacks by his Liberal adversary, Sir William Harcourt. 'Lord Rosebery's Flirtation' painted him as 'a coy lover with no ardour for office', who 'leaves the maiden to propose to him but at each proposal he raises his terms'.[5] On 15 May, at the same time as his newspapers were chiding his companion, Alfred recorded that he and Rosebery walked for an hour.

The next month, prospects for a successful outcome in the continuing negotiations with the Boers at Bloemfontein, capital of the Orange Free State, appeared poor. The 7 June *Daily Mail* dismissed the latest conference as 'A Fiasco' which had broken up without adequate Boer concessions. The situation was, consequently, 'worse instead of better'. The outlook appeared so serious that, the next night, Alfred stayed in his office until 1.30 a.m. because of the 'Transvaal matter'.[6] Over the following days the newspaper repeated Milner's comparison of the outlanders to the Spartan helots of antiquity, called for 'Equal Treatment of All White People', and warned that the Boers were 'Putting Their Trust in Little Englanders'.[7] To reveal the truth, the *Daily Mail* of 10 June demanded the publication of Milner's dispatches and warned of the grave peril of the unarmed English men and women being ruled by armed Boers. A portentous illustration depicted Boer cannon overlooking Johannesburg, their barrels trained on the defenceless houses below. The paper proclaimed the 'Ominous Signs' of 'Free State Boers Arming and Driving' in support of their brothers in the Transvaal.[8] On the 23rd, its owner called at the Colonial Office in search of official news. While the crisis mounted, Alfred took an important step into the British Establishment. Appointed to the Commission of the Peace for the Cinque Ports as a resident of the Isle of Thanet, on 13 June 1899 his diary records that he went 'to the Law Court to take oath of allegiance as a J.P.'.

The next month, the newly appointed Justice of the Peace drove his automobile to Oldham in an attempt to aid young Winston Churchill in his first election bid. The trip was marred by several punctures en route. The result of the vote was equally unsatisfactory. Churchill finished third in a field of four – the same unhappy position Alfred Harmsworth had held four years before at Portsmouth. The loser at Oldham sent his regrets that 'neither of our enterprises were successful . . . But I don't expect my career or your car will be seriously damaged'.[9] Churchill was not the only Conservative candidate aided by Alfred and his newspapers. On 18 July Balfour sent a note of thanks for the 'admirable service' to the Party carried out by the *Daily Mail* at the St Pancras election, where the Conservatives carried the day.[10] Despite this communication, Alfred believed the Party neither properly used the press nor realized how important a tool it could become. He asked Balfour to speak to Richard Middleton, who remained principal party agent, on the subject. Salisbury's second in command replied that he would 'certainly speak to Middleton on the subject of the Press – the importance of which I recognize – and at the same time my own incompetence to advise on it'.[11]

That summer the Harmsworths added two other country residences. Because Elmwood was taken up with Alfred's business interests and was not a suitable place for the scale of social entertainments which Mary envisioned, a large Georgian house, Calcot Park, near Reading, was taken furnished for 'a year's trial'.[12] For the amusement of his bird-shooting friends another house, Thorington Hall, Darsham, Suffolk, was also engaged. The fact that Alfred did not particularly like shooting, plus the constant chills he suffered there, made the latter a short-lived arrangement. Calcot Park, on the other hand, was near the home of Reggie Nicholson, whom Alfred visited often. Calcot also became the base for a growing fleet of cars, and in the same month that the house was taken Alfred had his first recorded motor accident – one of the earliest in England. Surprised by a horse which bolted across their path, the chauffeur overturned the vehicle, trapping its owner underneath. Though his arms were temporarily paralysed, Alfred made a swift and complete recovery. Despite this close call with serious injury, the coach houses at Calcot were filled by automobiles of every type and description, from Gardner-Serpollet steam models to electric vehicles.

Meanwhile, in South Africa, the crisis continued to build. On 9 August the *Daily Mail* described the 'Dangerous Game' being played by the Boers in rejecting Chamberlain's 'Pacifist Overtures'. The next day's edition gave another 'Final Warning', and noted that reinforcements were being sent to the Cape. A 'trustworthy source' predicted that the first clash of the conflict would be at Kimberley, the headquarters of the Rhodes mining interests. Calling him 'The Wrong Man', the *Daily Mail* questioned whether, given the 'proclivities' of the Boers, General Redvers Buller was strong enough to be military commander in South Africa.[13] In September the 'Grave Situation' continued. On the 4th, the editorial, 'Why It May Be War', blamed Kruger for the dangerous situation, because he had surrounded himself with 'German financiers and advisors' with little understanding of the British. The next day's editorial, 'Strong Measures', recounted Salisbury's return to London for a Cabinet meeting at which a probable ultimatum from Kruger would be considered. The newspaper applauded the 'Firmness in the Cause of Peace' shown by the Cabinet's decision to impose on Kruger a time limit in which to recognise British suzerainty. In the opinion of the *Daily Mail*, this would 'very soon dispel any gathering clouds of war', which its owner meanwhile discussed with Lord Selborne, Chamberlain's deputy at the Colonial Office, and George Wyndham, Under-Secretary to Lord Lansdowne at the War Office.[14] A week later the *Daily Mail* repeated Balfour's vow that Great Britain would not give way and declared, 'The Transvaal has made this war; if in this hour it still defies Great Britain, upon the heads of Mr. Kruger and his corrupt cabal be the innocent blood.'[15]

As the conflict appeared more inevitable each day, Alfred made arrangements for additional newspaper coverage. On 18 September he sent Winston Churchill an offer to become a South African correspondent. Churchill used this invitation to extract a more lucrative contract from his friend Oliver Borthwick at the *Morning Post*.[16] Consequently, the Churchill reporting for the *Daily Mail* would be not Winston, but his aunt, Lady Sarah Wilson, a daughter of the seventh Duke of Marlborough, and the first woman war correspondent of the Boer War. The many other correspondents, British and American, whom the *Daily Mail* would send out to cover the crisis included, to name only a few, G.W. Steevens, Charles Hands, Julian Ralph and Edgar Wallace.

In October the nation, and the proprietor of the *Daily Mail*, awaited the Boer attack. The heightened level of crisis again caused Alfred to spend several late nights at Carmelite House, while his newspapers decried such pro-Boer activities at home as Sir William Harcourt's letter to *The Times* which accused Chamberlain of provoking a war.[17] Despite its proprietor's misgivings concerning his abilities, the *Daily Mail* now praised Buller as a capable general and applauded his strategy. Parroting War Office opinion, the paper declared that the 'Boers had shown no capacity for offensive warfare', and added that Britain's troops were entrenched and ready for any attacks. While Boer recruiting and mobilization were estimated to be failures, the newspaper reported more and more British reinforcements arriving daily from India. 'In a word,' it went on, 'President Kruger's game is up, and General Buller now has his troops in his hand.'[18] On the 10th, Kruger's ultimatum was delivered to the British government. The document declared the Boer Republics independent and demanded that the British not only withdraw their troops from the border, but also remove the recently arrived reinforcements from the Cape. The Boer action, Salisbury reportedly commented, had at least alleviated the necessity for the government to justify the war to the British people.

The next day Alfred recorded in his diary, 'Transvaal war nominally began today.' That morning's *Daily Mail* asked, 'Who Will Rule South Africa?' and reported the Boer declaration of war. The newspaper prophesied that, though things might not go well at first, eventually the Anglo-Saxon would defeat the Dutch. Over the next ten days, with no hard news, the paper repeated the many war rumours. These included that the Boers were advancing into British territory to press Mafeking, whose garrison was commanded by Colonel Robert Baden-Powell, and Kimberley, where Cecil Rhodes had chosen to take refuge. The siege of Mafeking and the construction of the myth of Baden-Powell's heroism would prove a popular and continuing story in the following months. During this lull in news, the paper took the opportunity to promote its coverage of the conflict. Drawings of the 'Daily Mail War Express' appeared daily. By means of this special train, it was pledged, the Midlands and the North would receive the latest 'War News By Breakfast Time'.[19]

The *Daily Mail* received the first news of battle, at Glencoe, on 20 October. The next morning's paper proclaimed a 'Brilliant British Victory', but reported heavy losses on both sides. T.P. O'Connor called on Alfred at Carmelite House the same day. Over the next months O'Connor contributed a series on the atmosphere in Parliament. While the *Daily Mail* boasted of 'Victory After Victory' for the British, it also admitted the army was 'Groping in the Fog' and that the Boers had proved a more stubborn and numerous adversary than had been forecast.[20] Amid swirling rumours and alarming stories of 'Boer Treachery', the paper attempted to reassure the public that the situation was not as ominous as some reports held. On the last day of October it reported the 'satisfactory' position at Ladysmith, another British outpost under Boer siege. The paper announced that Buller had arrived in Capetown, and, to buoy public courage, it published Kipling's new poem, 'The Absent-Minded Beggar'. Set to music, the work became one of the popular anthems of the war. Kipling's verse also became the foundation stone for a wartime appeal fund which raised £100,000 in three months and £250,000 by the war's end.[21]

The news which arrived in London over the next two months became progressively more alarming and depressing. The 1 November *Daily Mail* recounted 'Severe Reverses to the British Troops' and the capture of two British regiments, 'Caught in a Trap'. For this disaster, it was reported, 'General White Takes Blame on Himself.' Some papers described the defeat as the 'worst blow in one hundred years'. The *Daily Mail* did not share this extreme view, but admitted that 'we have received a blow the political effects of which are at least as serious to our prestige in South Africa as the actual loss of men'. However, the paper added, 'many histories that start in gloom end in sunshine and providing that General Buller has, in his 50,000 men, arranged a sufficient force . . . there can be only one conclusion to the war!'

Fortunately for the readers of the *Daily Mail*, Lady Sarah Wilson, who had been trapped at Mafeking, was able to send out dispatches. Lady Sarah was the same age as Alfred Harmsworth, and her husband, Lieutenant-Colonel Gordon Chesney Wilson, was aide-de-camp to the besieged city's commander, Baden-Powell. Her first article appeared on 3 November. 'Our Life in Mafeking' told of the British preparations for the siege. An introduction explained that Lady Wilson was 'Recounting Events on the Frontier From the Woman's Point of View'. Three days later G.W. Steevens reported 'The Story of the War From Capetown to Pretoria'. As the British fell back across the board, the paper began to assign blame for the military failures. Why, it asked, after eighteen years' stockpiling of weapons by the Boers, had General Butler taken 'no measures to defend our colonies from the enemy'.[22] Because of his 'lack of preparation', the indictment continued, the British were outnumbered three to one, yet Butler remained in home command. Two days later the newspaper noted that the Commander-in-Chief of the British army, Lord Wolseley, had admitted what the *Daily Mail* had been saying all along: that the Boers were 'more powerful and numerous than we anticipated'.

These reverses forced Salisbury to speak out. On 9 November the Prime Minister vowed that measures would be taken to ensure that the mistakes which had been made in South Africa would not be repeated. Dissatisfied with this promise, the *Daily Mail* called the speech 'vague' and later tagged it 'An Enigma'. The same edition began a series, 'Through Yankee Glasses', by Julian Ralph, which proposed to show 'The War as an American Cousin Sees It'.[23] Late in the month more positive news arrived. The 25 November *Daily Mail* recounted 'The Battle of Belmont' and praised Lord Methuen's victory on the road to Ladysmith. The paper also derided the domestic efforts of the 'Little Englanders' who called for a pro-Boer peace settlement.

At the end of the month Alfred sent a warning to Balfour that statements of Salisbury and others in the government that Britain sought no goldfields or territory in the post-war settlement might cause future problems. Balfour replied from Downing Street that he was much obliged for the communication and that:

> I think certain utterances of my colleagues on the future of South Africa have been misunderstood, and certainly the Government as a whole regarded any determination with arrangements to . . . come after the war as at present premature.
>
> It seems to me, however, absolutely clear that we must never again allow a condition of things to grow up which permits communities within our South African sphere to become armed centres of attack, threatening the very existence of our Empire – and so I shall [state] tomorrow in quite clear language when I speak at Dewsbury.[24]

The *Daily Mail* appraised Balfour's Dewsbury address as 'A Splendid But Inconclusive Speech' which had not clarified the terms of settlement.[25] In a speech a day after Balfour's, Joseph Chamberlain asserted that the 'Boers have given us a clean slate on which we may write what we please'.[26] This was much more to the liking of the proprietor of the *Daily Mail*, which praised the Colonial Secretary's 'Plain Speaking' as 'A Great Speech by Mr. Chamberlain'.

Despite promising reports in its first week, which led the *Daily Mail* to assert that the Boers had 'shot their great bolt', December 1899 proved the darkest month for British arms in a century. On 15 December news arrived that Buller had suffered defeat in his first attempt to cross the river Tugela. The next morning's edition chronicled the 'Serious Reverse'. The paper criticized the 'Government's Inexplicable Delay' in raising and dispatching additional reinforcements, and reported that it received thousands of letters every day which demanded to know who was responsible: the Cabinet, the War Office or the Transport Department? To meet the crisis, it called for a 'A Thorough Awakening' of the nation. Buller's defeat was estimated to be 'sad and unfortunate', but not 'unreconcilable'. The answer to the reverses would be that 50,000 more men would go out to the field. Since Buller had his hands full in Natal, the paper announced the heartening news that Lord Roberts of Kandahar would go out to take command of the war, with Lord Kitchener of Khartoum as his chief of staff.

The targets of the *Daily Mail*'s quest for answers and accountability were all in London. The 'parsimony' of Sir Michael Hicks-Beach, the Chancellor of the Exchequer, underpinned this disaster and, said the paper, had Kitchener been in command earlier he would have 'got that money or resigned'.[27] Blame for defeat was also placed on antiquated British artillery and rifles, which were no match for superior Boer armaments. For this, the journal asked, 'Is Lord Wolseley Responsible?'[28] On 23 December the *Daily Mail* editorial, 'A Black Christmas – and Why', accused the Ordnance Department of supplying Britain's forces with inferior weapons and wondered aloud if even Kitchener and Roberts could prevail under such handicaps in a contest of artillery firing from miles away and of cleverly concealed entrenchments. 'Pluck and dash', said the paper, were not enough in this 'war of field glasses and spades' rather than 'bayonets and swords'. Further, in the opinion of the *Daily Mail*, unless there was a speedy awakening, the 'apathy' of Lords Lansdowne and Wolseley was 'endangering the existence of the Government'. The days after Christmas saw no cessation of the newspaper criticism. The 28 December *Daily Mail* placed the blame for the situation squarely on the 'skinflint' policy of Hicks-Beach and the 'blundering' of either Lansdowne or Wolseley, which combined to send out an army with little cavalry that had 'no chance whatever' against the large bodies of mounted soldiers they faced in the field. The results of this were listed as including at least 750 officers and men killed, 3,500 wounded, 2,000 to 3,000 taken prisoner, 14,000 besieged in Ladysmith, Kimberley and Mafeking, as well as 45,000 troops held in check under Buller, Methuen, Gattacre and French. The newspaper indictment concluded that either Lansdowne or Wolseley should go, and that Hicks-Beach should 'make way for a financier able to manage the huge money affairs of the war'.

The *Daily Mail* was blunt in its criticisms, but other newspapers' leaders on the government and the military leadership had been even more brutal and personal – particularly against the generals. As a consequence, the press came under considerable attack from many quarters, private and official. The 29 December *Daily Mail* editorial, 'Press or Suppress', noted that, in its criticisms, the paper had followed a course similar to that of *The Times*, by aiming its barbs at the politicians. It agreed that generals should not be maligned in the manner adopted by the *Daily Telegraph* and the *Pall Mall Gazette*, but added that the public could tell the difference between 'gallant soldiers' and those at home 'who are even now, sending obsolete guns to the Cape'.[29]

Interest in the South African conflict stimulated newspaper sales to new heights. The *Daily Mail*'s circulation rose above 1 million, then the world's largest. Advertising revenues paralleled the increased circulations; however, the owner limited the types and numbers of advertisements accepted. He preferred selling the classified section, and believed that people bought papers for news and did not wish to be overwhelmed by vulgar product offerings. Alfred told Wareham Smith, who was put in charge of the area in 1900, that he should not 'go out after your advertisers. Wait for them to come to you.'[30]

S.J. Pryor, who had been next in line for the editor's chair, was sent out to South Africa to organize the coverage of the Harmsworth press. His absence allowed Thomas Marlowe to stake a claim to the position which he would not relinquish on Pryor's return. One colourful, if somewhat implausible, version of events has the two men duelling for the single editor's chair, with Marlowe's greater self-control in withstanding the call of nature finally winning the day.

Despite heartening news of British success under the cavalry general John French, as 1899 gave way to 1900 the *Daily Mail* continued its campaign against the politicians. The 2 January editorial, 'War Office Excuses', rejoiced in the recently announced victories, but added that it 'must mention the campaign of excuses' offered by the government. It also denied the 'suggestions' that the *Daily Mail* was trying to turn criticism away from Joseph Chamberlain and the Colonial Office with its attacks. In a continuing campaign, 'The Public and the War', the journal called for readers to send letters to their MPs to ensure that a watchful eye was kept on the government, which it dubbed 'The Oldest Government on Record'.[31] In addition to disparaging their decrepitude, the paper also pointed out the lack of business and organizational experience among Britain's leaders. These factors, according to the *Daily Mail*, had led to 'The Gun Scandal'. Britain's artillery, the newspaper revealed, was inferior to 'long discarded foreign patterns'.[32] By 12 January, the *Daily Mail* wondered aloud, 'Can the Government be Saved?' In its opinion, given the revolt of the Tory MPs in the face of Balfour's 'bland reassurances', reconstruction was the 'Only Chance'.

At the same time as it indicted Balfour's leadership, the newspaper announced the 'War's New Stage', marked by the arrival at the Cape of Lords Roberts and Kitchener.[33] A long article illuminated the difficult task before them and called for more men to support their efforts. A week later Alfred received the news that G.W. Steevens had died of enteric fever at Ladysmith. To extend personal condolences to Steevens's widow, he drove his swiftest motor car to her home, Merton Abbey, near Wimbledon. The art critic C. Lewis Hind remembered that Alfred arrived in a 'very emotional condition . . . sobbing and saying that he could never forgive himself for sending George to Ladysmith and that the blow had destroyed his power to think and to work'.[34] The American war correspondent Richard Harding Davis, who had accompanied Alfred to Merton, was sent to the war front in Steevens's place.

In an attempt to rally the nation, Lord Rosebery spoke out at Chatham on the 'Blessings of War'.[35] The *Daily Mail* applauded Rosebery for pointing out that the conflict had united the Empire and was helping to dissolve the old, worn-out, party lines. He prophesied that 'out of our present strife and conflict shall emerge an Empire stronger, more fully prepared, amply equipped against the worst our foes can do against us'. The failures of the war had forced a re-examination which he hoped would inspire the nation to 'ruthlessly dig away all that is decayed and doubtful, and place things on a rational and sound foundation'.[36] Alfred met Rosebery on the last day of January. His diary records that the two 'had a long chat . . . until midnight on his position in the country during the present crisis'.[37]

The *Daily Mail*, tired of the parliamentary 'chatterings', asked 'Have We A Man?' Which would give the country a lead: the 'Chamberlain Spur or the Rosebery Lash'? The paper praised the Colonial Secretary's remarks in the Commons which showed that

> among the jumble of indecision, senility and evasion that forms our Cabinet there is one man of mind and determination in whom the Empire can have trust. Remove the fossils, let Mr. Wyndham and other able young men join him in the Cabinet, and we shall have a Government we can believe in, which will be able to face the next election without fear of annihilation.

In reply to criticism of the newspaper attacks on the politicians, the journal responded that it was its 'painful duty' to bring faults to the fore, and that, even in face of the victories being reported, it was the responsibility of the press to call for investigations.[38]

While the press attacks on the politicians for their makeshift and inadequate measures went on, the newspapers also chronicled the advances of the British forces at the war front. Lord Roberts led an eastern campaign on the river Modder, while General Buller had modest success in the western sector, having recrossed the river Tugela after earlier being forced to withdraw. The 17 February *Daily Mail* trumpeted 'Success At Last' in the relief of Kimberley by Roberts. Two weeks later it was able to report the relief of Ladysmith by Buller.

The improving military situation, and the criticism he had received, made mid-February a propitious time for Alfred to take his doctor's advice and go abroad for a rest. This allowed him to combine a Continental vacation with his love affair with the automobile. A new twelve-horsepower Panhard had been delivered the previous month, and he drove it to his office for the first time on 2 February. Before going to France, Alfred's driving adventures included riding a new 'motor tricycle' to Hampstead to see his mother. On 14 February he left from Paris for Cap Martin on the Riviera, accompanied by his 'engineer', Lancaster. Though plagued by the usual tyre problems, he found the trip most enjoyable, and for the following month he relaxed in the South of France. Unfortunately, for part of this time Alfred was disabled by a severe cold, which was accompanied by a 'curious numbness' in his chin. On 14 March, somewhat improved, he departed for home via Paris, where he stopped at the offices of the newspaper *Le Figaro*. Back in London, the famous nerve specialist David Ferrier recommended rest and treatments of 'electricity'.

On the war front, March saw success after success for the British army in South Africa. Nevertheless, on the 10th, the *Daily Mail* worried aloud that there would be a 'Peace With Dishonour' which would grant the Boers the independence they demanded as a 'Sine Qua Non'.[39] Four days later the newspaper was pleased to report that Salisbury had refused Kruger's terms. On 15 March the press announced the capture by Roberts of Bloemfontein, and two days later the surrender of the Orange Free State.

Though the battlefield outlook had improved, the war in South Africa had increased Britain's international isolation. One friendly voice, curiously enough, was found in the author of the Kruger Telegram, Kaiser Wilhelm. Despite the hostility of the majority of his subjects towards Britain, made worse by events in South Africa, the Kaiser visited England in 1900 and was hailed by the *Daily Mail* as 'A Friend in Need' after a visit to Windsor. After this, Wilhelm bombarded the royal family with letters and memoranda giving battlefield advice for Lord Roberts. Britain's strategic difficulties in the Boer War only added weight to the Kaiser's conviction that Germany must build an effective battle fleet before she could challenge for world leadership, and the anti-British feeling elicited by the South African conflict helped to pass Admiral Tirpitz's 1900 Navy Law.

France briefly took the place of the German foe as an invasion scare swept Britain. With the Navy and Army engaged in South Africa, the nation was declared to be at the mercy of a Gallic 'bolt from the blue'.[40] In April 1900 Leo Maxse's *National Review* assured the country that the

French could land 50,000 men in England. In the *Daily Mail* this became 80,000, accompanied by 400 pieces of artillery. These revelations elicited loud calls for a new Home Guard and a reorganization of the Territorial Force to meet the danger. After investigation, the government declared the invasion threat to be negligible. Such scares, nevertheless, would be repeated during the following years. Alfred spent April in London reacquainting himself with developments in South Africa. He had gained membership of the Beefsteak Club, where he dined with T.P. O'Connor, who continued his *Daily Mail* articles on parliamentary developments. He also met the American George Harvey, the proprietor of the *North American Review* and *Harper's Magazine*. On the 19th he called on Cecil Rhodes, who, freed from Kimberley, had travelled to London.[41]

While the war raged on, the *Daily Mail* and its owner continued their support of the automobile. The paper worked in alliance with Claude Johnson, secretary of the British Automobile Club, to promote a 'Thousand Mile Trial' through the United Kingdom. On 23 April sixty-five automobiles, including Alfred Harmsworth's new Daimler, started out from Hyde Park Corner to demonstrate the 'revolutionary capabilities' of the vehicle of the future with a tour to Edinburgh and back through the Midlands, putting on public exhibitions along the way. The procession made its first scheduled stop at Calcot Park, where Alfred provided a sumptuous breakfast which included salmon and pâté de foie gras, accompanied by 'bounteous beakers of champagne'.[42] The host was furious when a photographer ventured on to the roof of his stable to take a shot of the affair, but, when asked what he would have done in the man's place, Alfred remarked that he would have 'dragged the ladder up after me'. The Trial proved a milestone for British automobiling. When twenty-three entrants returned successfully, the motor car had to be taken seriously as a long-distance mode of transport. It was no longer a novelty, and its potential was clear, even to those who had remained sceptical since the ramshackle 1896 Emancipation Run.[43]

As its proprietor pursued his motoring hobby, on the war front the *Daily Mail* continued its series from the last of the besieged towns, Mafeking. Another dispatch by Lady Sarah Wilson, 'The Two B-Ps', described Baden-Powell as a quiet, composed and courageous leader who, when not repulsing Boer raids, buoyed up the morale of the besieged British by acting in amateur theatricals.[44] Other articles in the following days carried on this theme of quiet heroism. The 1 May edition asked 'Will Mafeking Be Relieved?' and recounted the mounting public anxiety for the garrison, which, it was believed, could hold out for only three more weeks at most. 'Whether Mafeking falls or is relieved,' the journal gushed, 'the defence of the town will be the most brilliant episode in the war. Nothing could surpass the gallantry, insight and judgment that have been displayed by the defenders. Their surrender could only be the result of the system which has caused so many failures in South Africa.' Though the overall military situation was improving, the muddles and inefficiency revealed by the struggle with the relatively tiny Boer enemy fuelled national worries for the future of Britain and the Empire. Against such anxieties, the 4 May 1900 fourth-anniversary *Daily Mail* declared itself 'the embodiment and the mouthpiece of the Imperial idea' and proclaimed that 'Our Empire has not yet exhausted itself' and that 'a greater destiny awaits us'.

Over the following three weeks, as the national anxiety for Mafeking's garrison mounted, the newspaper carried daily reports of the dwindling food supplies, the gallant defenders' efforts against continued Boer assaults, and the progress of the British relief columns. The 14 May issue proclaimed 'One Week's Food' left. Two days later the journal reported the 'Fight At Mafeking', but during the following days the situation remained a 'Mafeking Mystery' with the country 'Still in Suspense'.[45] At last, after 216 days of 'Siege, Starvation and Bombardment', Mafeking was relieved. The 19 May *Daily Mail* reported the 'Roar of Jubilation' in London the night before, when the news was announced by the lord mayor to a 'shouting multitude'. The police became 'atoms in a mighty sea' in front of the newspaper offices. 'No pen can describe', the journal went on, 'the wildness, the enthusiasm, the glee of that Fleet Street gathering.' Crowds also appeared in the West End, at the War Office and at the house of Baden-Powell's mother, where, a week before, a multitude had congregated because of a false rumour of relief. Late into the night the numbers of revellers grew larger and larger, louder and louder. 'Where the people all came from', said the paper, 'will ever be a mystery.'

The national jubilation, the likes of which had not been seen since the victory at Trafalgar, spilled out of London into the countryside. In the previous days, with the relief of Mafeking imminent, Alfred had been back at his motoring pursuits, using his Daimler to give a driving lesson to Lord Onslow. He had motored to Guildford, Surrey, to visit John St Loe Strachey, the editor and proprietor of the *Spectator*, and was staying at Strachey's house on 18 May when the news of the relief of Mafeking arrived. The next day Alfred drove from Guildford to Calcot and noted in his diary 'the Mafeking jubilations forming a remarkable sight on the road'.

Despite the fact that the last of the besieged towns had been relieved and the Free State had surrendered, Kruger vowed to fight on. The 23 May *Daily Mail* announced that the leader of the Transvaal would 'Defend Johannesburg to the Utmost'. However, a week later the newspaper was able to report that Pretoria and Johannesburg had surrendered and to announce the 'Flight of Mr. Kruger'.[46] Despite all these promising developments, in June the paper warned that the fight was 'Not Over Yet'. Some predicted the British would face a guerrilla war comparable to that which Napoleon had seen in Spain from 1808 to 1813. Because of the sparse Boer population, the *Daily Mail* discounted this possibility, though it did expect continued skirmishing and 'a good deal of trouble'.[47] An interview with the Boer leader Marthinus Steyn, by the *Daily Mail* correspondent Douglas Story, gave evidence that the fighting would go on. However, with the major battles over, the 7 June edition called for the reorganization of South Africa, and dubbed Sir Alfred Milner the man best suited to the task.

In the summer of 1900 the newspaper headlines of the entire world were diverted for a time from South Africa to another, more exotic, locale – China, where the Boxer Rebellion swept the country and forced the foreign contingents to take refuge in their embassy compounds in Peking. The *Daily Mail* was one of the few papers which had given an accurate assessment of the origins and strength of the Boxer movement to expel all outsiders and which had not derided the actions of the Dowager Empress as she played off the European powers one against the other.[48] Once the siege of the foreign embassies began, news of actual events was fragmentary at best. On 19 June the paper reported the 'Battle in China' and the 'Legations Said to Be Captured'. Two weeks later it recounted the 'Grave News From Pekin' that the German minister had been murdered.[49]

Acting on information received from its Shanghai representative, on 13 July the *Daily Mail* broke the story that all the legations had fallen a week earlier and that only two foreigners had escaped. The paper proclaimed 'All Men, Women, and Children Put To The Sword' in the 'Pekin Massacre' and listed the English victims.[50] In reality, however, the British minister, Sir Claude Macdonald, and the others in Peking whose obituaries appeared had not been slaughtered, though their position had been precarious for a time. A memorial service arranged for the victims at St Paul's Cathedral on 23 July was cancelled when doubts began to surface about the veracity of the account from China. The next morning the *Daily Mail* reversed itself in headlines which announced 'Legations Safe!'

However, the paper hedged its bets for the next week as the real situation remained unclear, questioning the 'Many Contradictory Reports From China' and asking 'Are They Living?'[51] On the last day of July, in 'Sir Claude Macdonald Speaks At Last', the paper positively asserted that the British in Peking were secure. The next day the *Daily Mail* was 'Lifting The Veil' and explaining 'How The Legations Held Out'. An international force was sent to relieve the mission, and on 20 August the newspaper reported categorically that British reinforcements were 'In Pekin At Last' and that all was well. The *Daily Mail* was widely attacked over the earlier false report, but in fact had held back the story until it was confirmed by its correspondent. Luckily for the reputation of the newspaper and its proprietor, the major blunder was soon lost among the reports of the continuing conflict in South Africa.

Perhaps the most lasting legacy of the siege in Peking came from the Kaiser, who before long had reason to regret his words to German troops leaving for China: 'Just as the Huns . . . created for themselves a name which men still respect, you should give the name of German such cause to be remembered in China for a thousand years, that no Chinaman . . . will dare to look a German in the face . . . Open the road for culture once and for all.'[52] This utterance provided rich propaganda fodder before and during the Great War.

That summer, mirroring its owner's interests, the *Daily Mail* kept newsworthy motor-car developments before the public, featuring, for example, a drawing of the 'fastest automobile in the world', which could reach sixty miles per hour. The car was owned by the millionaire W.K. Vanderbilt, who, the newspaper noted, already had been fined for 'furious driving'.[53] The paper's proprietor attended the Paris International Exhibition with John Montagu and tested a variety of vehicles on display, including a sixteen-horsepower Mors & St. Germaine and a Peugeot. This world exhibition included, besides automobiles, other technological marvels. Alfred recorded that he saw 'a man go up in a motor-propelled balloon which went against the wind'.[54] Only two months before, the *Daily Mail* had reported the 'Airship's Triumph', a thirty-five-mile flight in Germany by Count Zeppelin's dirigible, calling it an 'Epoch making Event'.[55]

Since their arrangements at Calcot Park and Thorington Hall had not proved completely satisfactory, the Harmsworths sought another country house which would combine the attractions of these in one estate. In June they visited Sutton Place, a historic Tudor mansion near Guildford, which, Alfred noted, they 'liked immensely'. Besides the impressive house, the surrounding farm and shooting rights were included with the property. For a time it was feared that Sutton Place would be lost to another party with a previous claim, but in the end the couple assumed the £1,700 yearly lease, which they kept until 1917.[56] With one of England's showplaces at her disposal, Mary had a home adequate for any social occasion and could attempt to launch the Harmsworths into the highest echelon of British society. The next month their social calendar included the Queen's Garden Party at Buckingham Palace. However, the Harmsworths had little experience in keeping up a large, and old, country house. Necessary renovations and legal complications proved more extensive, and expensive, than they had imagined. While repair work dragged on for months, the couple were forced to use Sutton Park Cottage. The proprietor of the *Daily Mail* kept up his association with Rosebery. In June he visited the Durdans, the Earl's residence near Epsom, and took his friend for a motor-car drive, which, Alfred recorded, Rosebery 'enjoyed very much'.[57]

Though he had ruled out a parliamentary career for himself, Alfred aided and encouraged his siblings as much as possible. Hildebrand, Cecil and Leicester all ran in 1900 under Rosebery's 'Liberal Imperialist' banner, which challenged the traditional party orthodoxy and generally supported the government's policy in South Africa. The Liberals split into three groups over a 25 July Colonial Office vote in the Commons: the Liberal Imperialists, including Asquith, Sir Edward Grey and R.B. Haldane, supported the government; an anti-war faction, including the fiery Welsh pro-Boer David Lloyd George, voted against the government; and a moderate bloc, led by Sir Henry Campbell-Bannerman, abstained.[58] This disarray prompted the *Daily Mail* to begin a series of articles which questioned the future of the party of Gladstone. With an election on the horizon, the newspaper asked where the Liberals stood. Would they support the Empire or those who criticized Britain's actions in the Boer War? During the following two months, before the general election scheduled for early October, the *Daily Mail* beat the drum ceaselessly for the Liberal Imperialist wing as the Party's only hope. On 1 September Leicester was adopted as a candidate for Caithness. Hildebrand followed suit at Gravesend, and Cecil at Droitwich. Hildebrand and Cecil established a magazine along their political lines, the *New Liberal Review*. Alfred took Cecil to speak with Rosebery at Berkeley Square. Cecil recorded that the Earl 'greeted us very kindly and engaged us in conversation on every subject under the sun'.[59] In mid-September the *Daily Mail*, following Rosebery's lead, declared 'Why Liberalism Won't Do'.[60] The old-fashioned 'Little Englander' position, said the paper, by sympathizing with the enemy in the South African crisis, had failed to interpret the sentiment of the nation for 'England and Empire'. According to the journal, for the Liberal Party to survive, its only hope was to regain the trust of the country by support-ing the band of thirty or so Liberal Imperialists, led by Rosebery, Asquith and Grey.[61] The 'issue' for the coming election, set by Joseph Chamberlain, would be the merits of the war and a settlement which would ensure no future threat to the Empire.

While this political skirmishing went on in England, battle-front news from South Africa, though less spectacular than the impressive victories of May and June, continued to garner newspaper headlines. Victory was widely viewed as just over the horizon, despite the fact that the Boer forces, such as those of General Louis Botha, had a discon-certing way of vanishing, to reappear later in guerrilla raids. These minor irritations aside, it appeared that Lord Roberts would soon return home in triumph. The 4 September *Daily Mail* applauded his proclamation that the Transvaal would again be part of the Empire and noted Kruger's flight to Delgoa Bay. Backed by Roberts's assurance that only scattered marauding bands remained, on 21 September the *Daily Mail* proclaimed the 'Boer Army's End'. The war, almost everyone agreed, was practically over.

These salutary developments elevated the election prospects of the government, which had appeared dismal during the previous year. Arthur Balfour promised action to reform the Army if the country's electorate would only 'complete by its votes the work which Lord Roberts' soldiers have begun'.[62] Joseph Chamberlain called on the Boers to accept the situation and become loyal citizens of the Empire. The *Daily Mail* praised Chamberlain's speech of 21 September for making such 'mincemeat' of the Little Englander's position that no 'decent' Englishman could vote for them. Covering the other camp, the journal revealed 'Sir William Harcourt's Radical Diplomacy' which would cheat the country of a proper settlement, and Campbell-Bannerman's opposition to any expansion of British territory.[63]

In addition to his brothers, among the candidates Alfred supported in the 1900 general election was Winston Churchill, who had returned from his stint as a correspondent in South Africa. His daring escape from the Boers had, in some quarters at least, made him a war hero, and he again sought a seat at Oldham. A *Daily Mail* article, 'Lord Randolph's Son and His Traducers', praised the 'young and impetuous' Churchill, who, in the paper's opinion, would capture Oldham for the imperial cause. Churchill's Conservative campaign went even further than the *Daily Mail* in proclaiming the opponents of the government the enemies of Britain and her Empire. One of his posters at Oldham declared, 'Be it known that every vote given to the radicals means 2 pats on the back for Kruger and 2 smacks in the face for our country.'[64]

At the polling for the October 1900 'Khaki Election', the government maintained its majority. Many Liberal Imperialist candidates also won seats; however, two of the three Harmsworth hopefuls were not so fortunate. Hildebrand got a 'bad licking', losing by 768 votes to a Conservative, the novelist Gilbert Parker. Cecil also was defeated, by 268 votes. Only a tiny margin kept it from being a clean sweep against the Harmsworth contingent: Leicester won by 28 votes, in a four-cornered contest at Caithness. The *Daily Mail* announced on 2 October that the other favourite of its proprietor, Winston Churchill, had triumphed at Oldham. The next day the journal declared 'An Imperialist Majority Assured'. Since most of the Liberals who had gained seats in the early voting backed the Empire, the paper proclaimed that it was therefore 'clear that the country would have none of the Little Englanders'.[65] However, over the following days, what had looked to be a Conservative stampede slowed. News of balancing Liberal victories began to turn the momentum, and the Conservative net gain fell to zero. In the later contests, Joseph Chamberlain's declaration that the Liberals were 'traitors' had hurt the government results and united the Opposition, which managed not to lose any more ground than in 1895 – a triumph of sorts, given the conditions.

Even so, the result was a government victory, however mixed. The *Daily Mail* announced the 'Majority 132' that the government continued to enjoy.[66] The newspaper called on Salisbury to reconstruct his Cabinet and to replace men like Lansdowne with younger, more vital, politicians such as St John Brodrick, George Wyndham and Lord Selborne. The Prime Minister did make a few changes. Worn down by his dual burden, Salisbury gave up the Foreign Office to Lansdowne, who vacated the War Office for St John Brodrick. Selborne replaced Goschen as First Lord of the Admiralty. George Wyndham left his duties as Under-Secretary at the War Office to become Chief Secretary for Ireland.

Brodrick had inherited the most troublesome post. Milner immediately warned him that the conflict in South Africa was far from over and that a bitter period of guerrilla warfare was about to open.

While the election was continuing, negotiations concerning *The Times* had been renewed. R.D. Blumenfeld, on the staff of the *Daily Mail*, later recorded that in October he had been Alfred Harmsworth's agent with the Walter family, the majority owners. According to Blumenfeld, Alfred announced:

> There is nothing I would like better in all the world than to obtain control of *The Times*. I do not think they are getting on too well over there. If I went to them they would at once refuse me. Will you make them an offer instead? I've got a million pounds in Consols, and I authorise you to pay up to that sum. It will be a great coup if you can get it.[67]

Blumenfeld, who had done previous business with the Walter brothers, approached Godfrey Walter. After consultation with Arthur, Godfrey's half-brother and the senior partner, the offer was declined. Blumenfeld recollected that Alfred reacted calmly, saying only, 'Never mind. We'll get it sooner or later.' When rumours of a pending sale reached America, Arthur Walter denied them publicly.

The end of the election period saw Alfred bedridden with an illness. While he recuperated, Rosebery looked in, and, when he had recovered, the two men dined together several times in December, before Alfred left England once again for the United States.

5

A New Century, 1900–1903

———————◆———————

IN THE LAST month of 1900, Alfred once again embarked for America, leaving London on 19 December with Mary and Reggie Nicholson. The travellers shared the train from Euston station (and the sea voyage) with Joseph Pulitzer, proprietor of the New York *World*. After yet another rough passage, on the RMS *Teutonic*, they docked at New York on 27 December. Alfred wrote to his mother from the ship that the digitalis he had brought along had seen Mary through and that he wished they had gone instead to 'delightful Cannes'. 'Never again', he continued, would he 'venture on the wild Atlantic at Christmas time.'[1] During this visit the owner of the *Daily Mail* met several important American newspaper figures, including Pulitzer's great rival William Randolph Hearst and his editorial writer Arthur Brisbane.[2] Following a stop at the *Daily Mail*'s New York office, its proprietor toured Pulitzer's premises and joined him at the opera.

It was the proprietor of the *World* who most helped to bring Alfred Harmsworth to the attention of America. Promising 'no interference', for 1 January 1901, the first day of the twentieth century, Pulitzer challenged his British colleague to produce an edition of the *World* representing the future of newspapers. Accepting the dare, Alfred worked several days on the original creation, spending all of 31 December at the *World* offices, where the Harmsworths toasted in the new year. Advertised as 'New in size, new in form, new in style, new in appearance, pictures and methods, but FULL OF NEWS', the tabloid-style issue soon sold out. The 'ears' of the paper declared it the 'Busy Man's

Paper', which contained 'All The News In Sixty Seconds'. A front-page article by its creator claimed that by this system of 'condensed or tabloid journalism' the outline of the day's news could be gathered in a minute and thereby hundreds of working hours could be saved each year. The lead news story told of the vocal celebration of the new century in New York, which was described as a 'roar like Niagara gone mad' at the stroke of twelve. A personal appeal in Alfred Harmsworth's hand asked for the country's 'impartial verdict' on this example of the twentieth-century newspaper.

The novelty received mostly negative reviews throughout the United States. The articles often were accompanied by line portraits of Alfred and Mary which he found less than flattering. The *New York Times* commented in its 'Topics of the Times' column that

> Doubtless every regular reader of our esteemed contemporary The World was much struck with the aspect of that amiable journal on the first day of the new century. If the reader happened to be of a cynical turn of mind, the new face of an old friend may have recalled to him the cheerful cynicism of old Bomba, when his son and successor changed the uniform of the Neapolitan army from Austrian white to the British red: 'As you will, mio caro. Dress them in white, dress them in red; they will always run away.'[3]

The publicity storm raised comparisons of Harmsworth with America's own press magnates, Pulitzer and Hearst. The latter described his British counterpart as having 'a face that presents a mixture of Napoleon, Edison and the left-hand cherub leaning over the frame of Raphael's "Sistine Madonna"'. 'He is busy trying to buy the London *Times*,' Hearst went on, because 'He wants to own a great paper, the greatest paper.' The American wished his colleague well in his endeavours, hoping he would gain *The Times*, so that 'when he gets it, may he show us the real Harmsworth, editing a real newspaper'.[4]

Alfred wrote to his mother that he sought to escape the uproar and warned her to disregard anything she might read in the many invented articles concerning him. However, he added that 'it might please you to know that distinguished people from all parts of the United States have come here to meet me' and that her son was to have 'a private audience with the President'.

The owner of the *Daily Mail* speculated on the future of newspapers in the January 1901 edition of the *North American Review*. The ideal paper of the future, he believed, would be a journal along the lines of the New

York *Sun*, which Alfred considered perhaps the 'best arranged of all American newspapers', controlled by a man with the abilities of a Delane, whom he considered the greatest political editor of *The Times*, backed by an organization as 'perfect as that of the Standard Oil Company' and issued each morning across the continent. It seemed obvious that the power of such a paper 'might become such as we have not seen in the history of the Press'. These 'simultaneous' newspapers would dominate the thought of the country not through editorials, but through a general style and tone. Though he admitted that in the wrong hands such power might be a national disaster, Harmsworth discounted the possibility, pointing to the non-party, national attitude taken by *The Times* in London. In its new form, he believed the press would be even freer than at present. To those that would say that this might be practically government by newspaper, he countered that 'so long as that is only another name for Government by the People, no one need be alarmed at the outlook'. Public sentiment had often forced the hands of the politicians and monopolists, and would also tame a corrupt press. He declared himself a 'firm believer in the sound sense and practical power of the people'.[5]

In addition to his practical and theoretical forays into the American newspaper world, the owner of the *Daily Mail* also rubbed shoulders with business leaders and began several lasting and valuable friendships. He spent a day with Thomas Alva Edison, who realized the value of newspaper publicity, at his West Orange, New Jersey, invention factory. On Wall Street, Alfred visited the House of Morgan and the Stock Exchange. He lunched with the publishing partners Doubleday and Page. The latter, Walter Hines Page, would become a lifelong friend and be appointed American ambassador to Britain before the Great War. The visitors attended a reading by Mark Twain, who, Alfred noted, was in 'great form'.[6] Diversions for Mary included a shopping excursion to Tiffany's. The crowning social achievement of the trip was an invitation to the 1901 Whitney Ball, at which the English couple joined the Astors, Vanderbilts, Jays and Harrimans – the cream of New York and American society.

Alfred's trip in 1901 included another fishing excursion. On 15 January the travellers left the metropolis by train for Florida, arriving in St Augustine the next day. Before leaving for fishing grounds further south, he tested a new Locomobile. Within a few days of his arrival, news reached Florida of Queen Victoria's grave illness. Alfred wired a requested article on the subject to the New York *World*. On 22 January the news of Victoria's death arrived. In London the black-bordered *Daily Mail* – which noted that the German Kaiser had been at Osborne with his grandmother at the end – said of the Queen:

> She has gone from us full of years and honours; by a strange coincidence she had just outlived the longest-lived of previous Sovereigns. And though it is true that the length of a life is not the measure of its greatness, in her case, with an exquisite appropriateness, the two qualities coincide. She will be mourned by all with the deepest and most passionate sorrow – the sincerest tribute which a nation can pay to its benefactress and friend.[7]

More than the death of the Queen, and the passing of an era that it marked, marred Alfred's visit to Florida. Chilly blasts from the North made most of February too cold to fish, and when the boats did go out few large trophies were to be found. Alfred's leg was giving him pain, and he had it X-rayed. By early March, to the influenza he had brought with him from New York had been added a 'malarial fever'. He was advised to seek complete rest, and spent the second week of the month in St Augustine bedridden and very depressed. By the 18th he was well enough to travel and the party left for New York, from where, after ten days of further medical care, they departed for England. Black depression continued during the voyage home, on the *Oceanic.*

Back in England in April 1901, Alfred remained gloomy and beset by health problems. Prostate and back pain joined the depression. Rashes and a sore throat also caused discomfort. However, he had recovered at Elmwood sufficiently by 1 May so that, with George Sutton's help, he could return to work. He wrote to St Loe Strachey that he was 'amazed at the progress' in the USA since his 1894 visit and that he did not think that the 'colossal nature of these huge business combinations is at all understood here, & that their movements are directed entirely against our commerce, the only prize they think worth capturing. I met most of the men concerned. They are to a man able New Englanders, most quite young. Morgan [the financier J.P. Morgan] is, of course, only the figurehead.'[8] Another letter to Strachey commented on American efficiency, asserting that, using the same machines, they made 50 per cent more than the British.[9]

Alfred's experience had made him fear there would be trouble between the two countries over the proposals to build an isthmian canal across Nicaragua. The USA had become dissatisfied with the terms of the 1850 Clayton-Bulwer Treaty, which gave Britain equal rights in any such undertaking. Later in 1901, by the terms of the Hay-Pauncefote Treaty, Britain renounced her canal rights in return for a promise that the United States would make the completed waterway available equally to the ships of all nations. This cleared the way for the Americans, led by Theodore Roosevelt, to build a canal – in Panama, not Nicaragua. Others also noted the potential danger to the pre-eminent position of the British Empire posed by the growing power of the United States. The always gloomy Salisbury told Lord Selborne, 'It is very sad; but I am afraid America is bound to forge ahead and nothing can restore the equality between us. If we had interfered in the Confederate War . . . it was then possible for us to reduce the power of the U.S. to manageable proportions. But two such chances are not given to a nation in the course of its career.'[10] Alfred's own pessimism was lightened, and his health restored, by a trip to Paris. The 20 May diary records, 'A lovely day and felt so well. Drove in Bois. Life worth living.' Though he had passed through this episode, the debilitating malarial symptoms – physical and mental – would recur for the rest of his life.

While in France in May and June 1901, Alfred mixed business with pleasure. In Paris, he lunched with Lord Esher, a confidant of Edward VII. He also spoke with Sir George Newnes about the possibility of buying some or all of his businesses. Newnes had made a number of unwise publishing decisions and had overextended himself. However, after further discussion, the owner of *Tit-Bits* would not accept the terms offered. It must have been an interesting experience for Alfred, who could still recall his first meeting with Newnes in Farringdon Street, hoping to sell an article or two. While in France the motoring experiments continued. A drive in a steam-powered runabout, he recorded, 'went badly'.[11] In the Champagne district, at Reims he visited the Pommery caves and on 27 June watched a motor-car race at Épernay.

At the same time, the conflict in South Africa had moved into a new, and more brutal, stage of guerrilla warfare, with atrocities committed on both sides. In an attempt to control the countryside, the British had, in many areas, concentrated the Boer population into overcrowded detention camps, where conditions rapidly deteriorated. At a 14 June speech at the National Reform Union, Sir Henry Campbell-Bannerman rallied the pro-Boer forces when he denounced the 'methods of barbarism' used by the British in reaction to Boer tactics. The speech was in particular an indictment of the harsh conditions in the detention centres, which had led to many deaths among women and children. This deplorable situation had been brought to light by the reformer Emily Hobhouse, who, with government co-operation, had inspected the camps.

Back in London the next month, Alfred discussed the latest turn of events in South Africa with Rosebery and Rhodes. He took his neighbour, and Arthur Pearson, for late-night automobile rides; Rosebery hoped the excursions would cure his insomnia. Sutton Place was finally getting into shape, although Mary was ill when they visited it in July. On 24 August the Harmsworths at last were able to move into the main house. Alfred sent his mother 'the first letter I write in our new home'.[12]

During this period, the owner of the *Daily Mail* also was forced to deal with problems between his press and the politicians. Since February, when the *Daily Mail* had revealed parts of St John Brodrick's army reform plan before it was submitted to the Commons the next month, the War Office had quarrelled with the journal over leaks of official information. The paper was accused of bribing underpaid clerks. Brodrick's scheme came under attack for weakening the defence of the Empire in favour of European concerns and for its extravagant cost, which, said its opponents, would be better spent on the Navy. The *Daily Mail* concurred and printed the views of the leading critics, including Winston Churchill. In July questions were raised in the House of Commons concerning *Daily Mail* revelations of alleged Boer atrocities at Vlakfontein, based on information allegedly lifted from telegrams between Roberts and Kitchener. After a meeting with Brodrick, on 16 July Alfred recorded in his diary that the 'Government threatened to withdraw official news from the *Daily Mail*'.

The Secretary for War took up the matter, reluctantly, in the Commons on 29 July. Challenged to respond to newspaper stories, Broderick denied any action had been taken against the *Daily Mail* for the Vlakfontein revelations, which had proved true. However, he went on that 'on two occasions in the present year this journal has published statements on impending events based on secret official documents, and it is immaterial in my opinion whether they were obtained by direct purchase or through the means of a correspondent'. In each case, said Brodrick, the information had been refused by another journal on 'patriotic grounds'. He continued that one clerk had already been dismissed for improper use of confidential documents and that he could not 'justify leaving men of moderate income to the temptations which may be offered by a prominent journal'; he asked for the House's assistance 'in my effort to put down these occurrences, which are a disgrace to the public service and a danger to the country'.[13]

In the next day's debate, the attention of the War Secretary was drawn to that morning's *Daily Mail*, which had issued 'A Challenge to Mr. Brodrick'. The article criticized the government for hushing up the Vlakfontein matter and for 'fitting out the preposterous Committee of the Dames to inquire into the state of the women and children in South Africa'. The paper stated its strong objections to Brodrick's accusations of the previous day, and added that it would have 'no hesitation in proceeding against Mr. Brodrick for libel if he ventures to suggest outside the privileged circle of the House of Commons that this newspaper has stolen official documents, and its editor is quite willing to undergo an investigation under the Official Secrets Act'. The Liberal MP Swift MacNeill charged that the newspaper and its owners were guilty of 'a breach of the privileges of this House' and that the article constituted 'a deliberate charge of personal falsehood against a public man in his capacity, not alone as a Minister of the Crown, but also as a Member of the House of Commons'.

After Swift MacNeill's breach-of-privilege motion had been seconded, Broderick rose to present his, less heated, interpretation of the *Daily Mail* article. He told the Commons that he did not believe the journal had said that he had made a deliberately untruthful statement to the House. For the record, and as requested by the owner of the *Daily Mail*, Brodrick read the contents of a letter he had received from Alfred Harmsworth on the matter. Responding particularly to Brodrick's 'temptations offered by a prominent journal' phrase in the previous night's debate, the letter answered:

> This I take to mean, in plain English, that you impute to those who are responsible for the conduct of the *Daily Mail* that they have, either by direct or indirect means, and by the use of corrupt inducements, obtained information from persons in official employ for publication . . . I need scarcely point out to you that this is a very grave charge, and one that I take the earliest opportunity of repudiating. I most emphatically assert that it is without foundation of any kind and anything that has appeared in the *Daily Mail* has been received in the ordinary course of newspaper routine. You have asked me to divulge the name of the *Daily Mail*'s informant to which I can only reply that it is the well-understood practice of journalism not to give up the names of contributors.

After reading the letter into the record, Brodrick told the House that he had met the proprietor of the *Daily Mail* and had asked that secret material be withheld from publication, and that the way in which it was obtained was immaterial.

In the same debate, the Conservative leader in the Commons, Arthur Balfour, manoeuvring to avoid a spectacle in the chamber if the owner of the *Daily Mail* was called before the bar of the House, counselled forbearance for attacks in newspapers. In his opinion, there was nothing to be gained by entering into such contests, and he asked that the House 'pass to the public business of the day'. This view was challenged by the Liberal leader, Campbell-Bannerman, who asserted that Brodrick's reading of Harmsworth's letter had already brought him before the bar and that it was not possible simply 'to pass over so grave a matter'. In the face of this, Balfour withdrew his objection and it was resolved that 'the passages from the *Daily Mail* of this day complained of constitute a breach of the privileges of this House'. The motion proposed was 'That the editor and publisher of the *Daily Mail* do attend at the Bar of this House on Thursday next, at Three of the clock.'[14] When the chamber divided, the matter fell out, as might have been expected, along party lines. The motion to call Alfred Harmsworth before the bar of the House was defeated by a vote of 222 to 128. One Conservative who voted with the Opposition, despite his friendship with the proprietor of the *Daily Mail*, was Winston Churchill.

This vote did not end the matter. Balfour acted as an intermediary to settle the dispute. The Conservative leader told Brodrick that he was 'very anxious' that peace should be made and that it was 'desirable in the public interest that the whole matter should be put on a sound basis'.[15] On 8 August the owner of the *Daily Mail* saw Balfour in Downing Street and later at the House of Commons. Eight days later Alfred visited Brodrick at the War Office. At the end of the month Brodrick's aide Lord Stanley, who also had attacked the *Daily Mail* over the Vlakfontein affair, toured Carmelite House. Balfour sent Alfred a note that he hoped the interviews with Brodrick and Stanley had been 'productive of good result' and offered further help if necessary.[16] Peace was made for a time and the newspaper attacks ceased, in part because of the death of Brodrick's wife.

The Harmsworth press's criticism of the government was attributed in some quarters to its chief's lack of recognition in the honours lists. Gerald Balfour passed along to his brother Arthur a letter he had received from J.C. Lawrence, president of the Institute of Journalists. Lawrence complained that the Salisbury government had not supported its press friends as had its Liberal predecessors, who had bestowed eight honours against two by the Conservatives. One of the cases cited was the failure, three years before, to reward Alfred

Harmsworth after he had started the *Daily Mail*. Noting that Harmsworth was not a member of his organization, Lawrence asserted that 'we attribute the soured state of his mind & his recently ill concealed hostility to the Government, also the recently declared "Roseberyism" of his brothers, mainly to this neglect of the Unionist Press and its supporters'.[17] Prompted by the new King, the government would before too long remedy this situation.

In September 1901 Alfred was back on the Continent. He spent several weeks in France, where he fell ill. While recuperating, he sent a note to Lord Esher, friend and confidant of the King, expressing concern about newspaper rumours of a royal illness. The stories, said the owner of the *Daily Mail*, were 'worrying the West End tradespeople a great deal', and talk was spreading that there would not be a coronation. His own impression was that the King 'was never better', and he asked Esher if it would be wise for him to 'contradict these rumours emphatically'. The two men met for lunch a week later to discuss the matter. Esher described his companion as 'a clever, vain man – not very intelligent about anything except organization and money-making, but full of aspirations for power. The man rather interests me, as all self-made men do.'[18] Two months later Alfred was back in London, and on 23 November he recorded that he went for another 'long walk with Rosebery'.

The former Prime Minister had become increasingly upset with the government for its failure to pursue negotiations with the Boers. Rosebery was also unhappy with the Liberal Party. A sizeable number of imperial-minded Liberals were also restive and ready to follow if only he would lead, but he declared he would not return to active politics. Nevertheless, when it was announced that Rosebery would address a meeting at Chesterfield on 15 December, the attention of the nation was trained on the event. At Epsom the day before the meeting, Alfred had a long talk with his neighbour. Rosebery's speech attacked both the inept policies of the Salisbury government in South Africa and the outmoded Liberal agenda. The Earl called for a magnanimous settlement with the Boers, to whom the English were bound, he said, 'for better or worse, in a permanent, inevitable and fateful marriage'.[19] The Liberal Party, he went on, must rid itself of the Irish Nationalists, 'clean the slate', and reformulate its policies. 'My watchword,' Rosebery went on, 'if I were in office at this moment, would be summed up in the single word Efficiency. If we have not learned in this war that we have greatly lagged behind in efficiency, we have learned nothing.'[20]

This speech, temporarily at least, heartened Rosebery's followers and caused a sensation. The peace arranged the next year would be along the lines called for at Chesterfield; however, no transformation would take place in the Liberal Party, in part because Rosebery continued to refuse to lead, although he did accept the presidency of the imperialist Liberal League. Herbert Asquith and Sir Edward Grey became vice-presidents. They found themselves at odds with the Liberal leader, Campbell-Bannerman.[21] The *Daily Mail* praised Rosebery's speech for putting forward the methods of efficiency, both in politics and elsewhere in the nation, for which it had been calling for some time and that it would continue to support. Its proprietor spent New Year's Eve 1901 at Sutton Place.

Only a few weeks after Rosebery's address, Alfred Harmsworth's other imperial champion, Joseph Chamberlain, also roused the nation and increased his popularity to perhaps its highest point. In the first week of 1902, Alfred cut short a visit to France to hear Chamberlain speak at West Birmingham. The Kaiser's solicitous attitude at the time of Victoria's death had roused the hopes of the Colonial Secretary that some sort of agreement could be reached with Germany, but by late 1901 he had changed his mind about the wisdom of that course. At Edinburgh in October Chamberlain had defended the British treatment of the Boers against foreign criticism, declaring that the actions never approached the barbarity and cruelty of the German record in the Franco-Prussian War and elsewhere. This indelicate statement raised the ire of both the British diplomatic community and Germany's Chancellor, von Bülow. At a 6 January speech attended by the owner of the *Daily Mail*, Chamberlain proclaimed that he regretted that the Germans had taken offence at his remarks but that he would not apologize. He went on that it was 'the duty of the British people to count upon themselves alone, as their ancestors did. I say alone, yes, in a splendid isolation, surrounded and supported by our kinsfolk.'[22] The *Daily Mail* reaffirmed its support of Chamberlain and said of von Bülow's statements of reproach in the Reichstag that 'We are not prepared to accept foreign rebukes, administered with even less tact and discretion, to our public men, or to sit in sack-cloth and ashes at a foreign censor's behest.'[23] Despite Chamberlain's assertion that Britain should remain aloof, the same month, spurred on by the Foreign Secretary, Lansdowne, the signing of an Anglo-Japanese agreement began the cautious process by which the country emerged from its diplomatic solitude.

At the end of January, Alfred returned to France and spent much of the next few weeks in his Serpollet 'steam travelling carriage' on a motor tour to the Riviera and back to Paris. Along the way, one fiery mechanical breakdown had the peasantry – unaccustomed to such clouds of infernal steam – praying for deliverance from the 'devil's work'.[24] February was a time of leisure. The diary for the week of the 13th notes only that 'our daily life consists of motoring, lunching, walking, dining, plenty of sleep, sun and fresh air and a good time together'. During this trip Alfred followed the dirigible exploits of Alberto Santos-Dumont, a young Brazilian aviator living in France, whom he met at Monte Carlo. On 3 March the owner of the *Daily Mail* recorded that he 'went about with Santos-Dumont a good deal' talking of airships.[25]

This period of relaxation was disturbed in late March by the 'sad news' of the death of Cecil Rhodes, who had suffered from heart problems for some time. The *Daily Mail* lamented:

> The British Empire is the poorer to-day by the loss of a man who, whatever the verdict passed upon his career, will always have a place among the greatest of England's sons. With the death of Mr. Rhodes, the heir and successor of Clive . . . has gone from us. Nor is the tragedy of his early end lessened by the fact that he dies, like Pitt, before the cause for which he has fought and worked has finally triumphed . . .
>
> Hesitancy and make-believe, two salient characteristics of modern British statesmanship, did not figure in his disposition . . . He was the dreamer of great dreams, and, wonderful to relate, he realised them in this world of fact . . . He towers above his contemporaries as a colossus, and the virulence with which he has been hated abroad is the measure of his service to England. Fighting with men who used no gloves, he, too, bared his fists . . . With a feeling of profound sorrow will the nation lay upon the bier of this its servant its last tribute of regret to one who added to the Empire a territory as large as Europe, and who leaves as his posterity only the fame of his services and his devotion.[26]

In May Alfred became involved once more in negotiations to buy an interest in *The Times*. On this occasion he was approached by Walter Sibley, one of the minority shareholders, who was unhappy with the management of the paper and with its earnings. The owner of the *Daily Mail* wrote to Arthur Walter that 'You treated me so frankly a few years ago that I should like to have a few minutes' private conversation with you concerning a Dr. Sibley, who has been bothering me a great deal lately, but with whom I have declined to hold any communication.'[27] At this second meeting Alfred apparently offered to go beyond buying Sibley's small interest, and told Walter he was ready to purchase a controlling share. However, as before, the discussions did not lead to an investment. In reply to fresh rumours that control had been taken by Harmsworth, an angry Walter told a correspondent that the whisperings were 'absurd and utterly baseless in point of fact'.

After more than two and a half years, the Boer War finally came to an official end when the Treaty of Vereeniging was signed late on 31 May 1902. The *Daily Mail* recovered some of the prestige lost over the Peking error by being the first to publish the news. However, there was no renewal of the Mafeking celebrations for the newspaper to record. The subdued reaction reflected the fatigue of the nation, which was simply relieved that the long, bloody and costly conflict was finally at an end. The peace was generous to the Boers. They were allowed to keep their weapons and received £3 million with which to rebuild their war-torn country. The nation was equally beneficent to its own heroes. For their efforts on the battle front, Lord Roberts received an earldom, the Garter and £100,000, while Lord Kitchener was rewarded with £50,000, promotion to full general and a viscountcy. Alfred Milner, who had been made a peer in May 1901, was also advanced, becoming Viscount Milner of St James's and Capetown. Unlike the military leaders, however, Milner remained in South Africa as High Commissioner, to direct the difficult reconstruction. With the war officially ended, a Royal Commission under Lord Elgin, a former Viceroy of India, was appointed to investigate the preparations for and conduct of the South African conflict. Its report, which was not published until the following summer, revealed serious problems in War Office administration and organization. A month after the release of the Elgin Commission's findings, Brodrick was moved to the India Office.[28]

Edward VII was scheduled to be crowned in June, but the ceremony had to be postponed. Amid rumours that the King was dying, Alfred was called to Buckingham Palace to receive the latest information. The illness had been exaggerated, but the flare-up of royal appendicitis delayed the coronation until August. While the sovereign recuperated, the owner of the *Daily Mail* took a Continental motor trip, from Paris to Strasbourg and from there by train to Stuttgart. His driving companion was a member of the Automobile Club, Campbell Muir, whom he described as 'a nice young Scotsman'. The uncomfortably hot trip included, he recorded, 'his first sight of Germany'.[29] After Alfred's return to England on the 12th, he again walked with Rosebery. The topics of conversation must have included the resignation of Salisbury, who had hoped to see in the new King as Prime Minister, but who in July, ill and tired of his burden, left office. Arthur Balfour, who had waited patiently for his chance to govern, took his place.

Balfour was among the politicians with whom Alfred had had the most contact in the previous few years. Though languid and aloof in manner, the new Prime Minister was much more approachable than Salisbury, his uncle, and, though he feigned uninterest in the question, Balfour was appreciative of the power of the press. He was also a recent addition to the motor-car fraternity and, like the owner of the *Daily Mail*, used his vehicle to commute from the country to London. The new premier replied to Alfred's note of congratulations on both accounts: 'Your very kind letter has given me much pleasure. Of the two possessions you mention, I really think the first would be scarcely tolerable without the second, or, I ought perhaps to say, without the agreeable anticipations the second suggests. So far I have tried the premiership, but not the motor.'[30] Some believed that Joseph Chamberlain should have succeeded Salisbury, but, realizing his unpopularity with a good portion of the Party, Joe approved of the prize falling to Balfour. Though he once again might have had the Exchequer, where Hicks-Beach was finally replaced by C.T. Ritchie, he was satisfied to remain Colonial Secretary – a better position from which to continue the effort towards imperial unification.

Chamberlain had suggested to the colonial premiers earlier in the year that they take advantage of the coronation to attend the first Imperial Conference since 1897. Alfred Harmsworth entertained several of the distinguished visitors at Sutton Place on 17 June. He took Richard Seddon, the representative from New Zealand, to Clandon in one of his automobiles. Seddon, who had visions of an island empire in the Pacific for his nation, had been the most forthcoming in responding to Chamberlain's request for topics of discussion for the Conference, and had sent the Colonial Secretary a list of seven subjects, including an Imperial Reserve Force to be raised by each colony for emergency use overseas. The aid the Empire had given towards the final victory in the Boer War had raised the hopes of British imperialists that some sort of arrangement could be reached with the self-governing colonies. However, there was little colonial sentiment in favour of imperial federation, even in Australia, where heightened war patriotism had dampened separatist sentiment.

The Conference opened at the end of June and, because the Colonial Secretary was injured in a cab accident, continued until August. Borrowing a phrase from Matthew Arnold, in his opening address Chamberlain told the premiers that 'the weary Titan staggers under the too vast orb of its fate'. Britain, he went on, had 'borne the burden for many years. We think it is time that our children should assist us to support it.'[31] Despite Chamberlain's eloquence, the 1902 sessions, like those of 1897, had little tangible result. His calls for a unifying political institution, economic co-operation and mutual imperial defence arrangements all fell flat. The delegates sidestepped his idea of a permanent council, and agreed only to meet again within four years. Laurier refused a peerage, and his rhetoric was much cooler than in 1897. Before leaving Canada, he told his parliament that he had offered no suggestions for the conference agenda and did not see any need for political reorganization of the Empire. Turning to defence matters, he warned that there was 'a school abroad . . . which wants to bring Canada into the vortex of militarism which is now the curse and blight of Europe. I am not prepared to endorse any such policy.'[32] As a French-Canadian, Laurier had little interest in the talk of an Anglo-Saxon 'race' union, and considered commercial considerations the only topics worth discussing.[33] Though the Colonial Secretary considered Laurier a 'cad', if any understanding was to be reached, Chamberlain came to believe, it would have to follow Canada's commercial lead.[34]

The *Daily Mail* reflected the widespread disappointment that the hopes for a tariffless customs union along the lines of Germany's Zollverein had not been furthered, commenting that 'the dazzling vision remains a vision still'. The paper placed the blame for the disappointing progress since the 1887 Conference on the 'timidity of democratic politicians, who always lag somewhat behind public opinion and wait to be pushed forward'. Another reason for the 'want of progress' sprang from 'the extremely sanguine and confident nature of the British peoples, who believe there is plenty of time to let the union of the Empire grow as a by process of nature. But the wisdom of man can accelerate the processes of nature, and in this life of competition between nations time is everything.'[35] The owners of the Harmsworth papers, involved in their own competition for paper supplies, worried that another international conflict would threaten Scandinavian sources. Harold Harmsworth travelled to North America in search of more secure paper within the British Empire that would also afford more control over prices, which had risen 50 per cent during the Boer

War. Two months' scouting uncovered a promising site for a paper mill at Grand Falls, in the forests of Newfoundland. While the Harmsworths looked to their interests, Joseph Chamberlain, having failed with the colonial premiers, decided to pursue a commercial course to imperial unity. To do this he hoped to take advantage of the system of temporary tariffs put in place by the previous Chancellor of the Exchequer, Hicks-Beach, to pay off the Boer War debt. Balfour was careful to make it clear that this was not a first step towards imperial preference; nevertheless, Chamberlain hoped that a special remission of the tariff for Canadian grain, which Laurier desired, would be a first step in this direction. Before Chamberlain departed in November 1902 for a five-month trip to South Africa, the Colonial Secretary believed that he had gained Cabinet acceptance for this course, over the objections of C.T. Ritchie. As the Colonial Secretary would learn, the supporters of Free Trade in the Cabinet – the new Chancellor among them – took a different view.

From another corner of the Empire, India, Alfred received correspondence from George Curzon. As Viceroy to the jewel in the imperial crown, in the past four years Curzon had struggled to reform the governance of his huge domain, which included 300 million inhabitants, many of whom lived in states ruled by native princes. Making courtesy calls and maintaining good relations with the Indian princes was an important duty of each viceroy. Curzon wrote to Alfred from the 'Viceroy's Camp, India' that 'you would have laughed had you seen me two days ago, in a State carriage and 4, making a triumphal entry into a native city. It ran away with me in the main street, turned clean over, and I landed heavily on the head of the Maharajah in a ditch. Are tours worth the making? Who can doubt it after such an experience?'[36] The *Daily Mail* supported Curzon's course in India, which, in its first years, was relatively successful.

The delayed coronation of Edward VII took place on 9 August. The proprietor of the *Daily Mail* busied himself preparing the 'Coronation number', published two days later. The ceremony and its attendant events rivalled the 1897 Jubilee in magnificence; however, in comparison, the spirit of the affair could hardly help but be subdued by the harsh realities brought to light in the intervening years by the Boer War and the threatening growth in power of rivals such as the United States and Germany. A review of the fleet at Spithead was the final event of the celebration. *The Daily Mail* took the opportunity to sound a warning call for naval building and modernization in response to German activity:

To the casual eye this great fleet, as it lies peacefully at anchor in the historic harbour, makes the bravest of shows. But true wisdom demands that we must look beneath the surface and consider how far it is fit for the purpose for which it was designed. What cannot but strike the observer is that it is much weaker than the fleet assembled in 1897 for the late Queen's Jubilee. No doubt our squadrons abroad are stronger than they were at that date . . . but there is also the fact that in the meantime a powerful navy has grown up in the North Sea which has to be considered in the balance of power.[37]

After the excitement of the coronation, Alfred relaxed with another motoring tour, taking his Mercedes to Mentmore for a 6 September lunch with Rosebery before a week-long tour of Scotland, during which he again saw the Earl, with Winston Churchill, at Dalmeny. The Kaiser was scheduled to visit Rosebery's residence outside Edinburgh two months later. Alfred travelled to Dalmeny on 19 November, the day before Wilhelm arrived. There is no evidence that the Kaiser met the proprietor of one of the newspapers which most loudly sounded the alarm against the German threat; however, after the Great War, Wilhelm listed the founding of the *Daily Mail* as one of the significant European events before the war in his own *Comparative History 1878–1914*.[38]

Alfred drove back to London the day after the Kaiser's visit. From there he departed for a three-week stay at the Ritz in Paris. Fresh from his close encounter with the German foe, he had a 'long interview' with M. Delcassé, the French Foreign Minister, and with various French journalists, to sound the alarm and to do his bit to advance Anglo-French co-operation. In an interview printed soon after in *Le Matin*, the owner of the *Daily Mail* bluntly stated, 'Yes, we detest the Germans, we detest them cordially and they make themselves detested by all of Europe. I will not permit the least thing that might injure France to appear in my paper, but I should not like for anything to appear in it that might be agreeable to Germany.'[39]

In the final month of 1902 the British government took significant action to reform its defence capabilities on land and sea. The new Prime Minister, who was more intimately concerned with military matters than had been his uncle, established the Committee of Imperial Defence (CID), which proved very influential in matters of policy and strategy. This advisory group's original purpose was to promote greater rationality and co-ordination between the War Office and the Admiralty and to foster communication between the civilian department heads and their expert advisers. At the same time, Selborne, the First Lord of the Admiralty, assigned Admiral Sir John Fisher, former chief of the Mediterranean Fleet and presently Second Sea Lord, to carry out the 'Selborne Scheme', aimed at the reform and modernization of naval training and education. The able and dynamic Fisher played a central role in British naval affairs during the following years.[40]

On the automotive front, Alfred edited *Motors and Motor Car Driving,* a volume in the *Badminton Library of Sports and Pastimes.* The contributors made up a *Who's Who* of early car enthusiasts, including, from France, the Marquis de Chasseloup-Laubat. Among the authors from Britain were the Hon. John Scott-Montagu MP, Sir David Salomons, Bart., R.J. McRedy, editor of *Motor News,* and the Hon. C.S. Rolls. The subjects chosen ranged widely, from the state of the British roadways to 'The Choice of a Motor', the editor's single chapter. This advised caution in choosing a car from the hundreds available. The author revealed that at present his own collection included four French, two American, two English, and other motors that were 'practically English'. Three of these were petrol-driven, three steam-powered and two electric. In 1902, he advised, a good petrol engine was 'infinitely the best for all-round work', and of these he recommended the Daimler or its type as the 'wisest purchase'. However, for limited travel, within a twenty-mile radius, he had found that electric vehicles were 'not to be excelled'. His own two – 'quite the most perfect lambs' – were a Columbia Phaeton and a brougham by the City and Suburban Electric Carriage Company.[41] The volume, and its editor, were subjected to some criticism. The *Tatler* revealed that in the previous year Alfred Harmsworth had spent £500 on tyres alone. The paper went on to attack *Motors and Motor Car Driving* for its refusal to register the fact that there were people in England with less than £10,000 a year.[42] In subsequent editions of the book, the editor responded that his collection of cars was 'of the smallest'.

In early February 1903 Alfred and Mary left Paris for a new destination, Russia. They travelled by train, waking in Berlin on the 5th and arriving at St Petersburg the next day. Alfred found much of the sightseeing across the 'thawing, slushy' landscape depressing, but was uplifted by the 'magnificent' Hermitage.[43] On the 8th the Harmsworths attended a 'very wonderful' ballet, at which the Tsar was present, but hidden in the imperial box. Over the next few days, Alfred attended to newspaper matters, for instance meeting the editor of the *Novoë Vrenya.* The couple arrived in Moscow on 11 February, with Mary suffering from flu. The next five days were taken up by sightseeing and numerous courtesy calls. Alfred met the British commercial agent and was also briefed by Tolson, the *Daily Mail* correspondent.

From Moscow, Alfred wrote to Strachey that he had 'not seen an English newspaper since I left home so I do not know whether our national march backward is proceeding more or less rapidly than usual'.[44] He also complained that recent events – particularly the Boer War – had not given the Russians a good impression of England, and that the British needed more trade agents to take advantage of the potentially huge Russian markets. On the 16th, 'after a very pleasant visit', the Harmsworths left Moscow for Warsaw, where they spent a day. Their next stop, Berlin, did not much impress Alfred; however, he did appraise the Unter Den Linden as very fine 'in the evening glow'. In the German capital, the owner of the *Daily Mail* also talked with his representative. Back in London on the 22nd, Alfred continued a correspondence with Brodrick at the War Office concerning attempts to stop official leaks to the newspapers.

Two weeks later, he returned to the Continent to test the latest model Serpollet on the open road. In the French countryside on 9 March, he was 'arrested for going too fast'. The diary continues that 'After much trouble and by dint of going to the palace we were able to take the car home, but had to leave 2000 francs with the Commissaire of Police.' Alfred was in Paris for the start of the ill-fated Paris-Madrid Race, in which ten contestants were killed.

Edward VII was also in France at this time. His royal visit helped both to smooth the somewhat strained relations between Britain and France and to set the stage for the Entente Cordiale of the following year. In the first days of May the *Daily Mail* congratulated the King on his Continental success and expressed the hope that the bad feelings of the Boer War years were now in the past. As the animosities of the South African War began to fade, however, another, even more divisive, issue came to the fore in Britain: the campaign for Tariff Reform.

6

A Tariff Tornado, 1903–1905

JOSEPH CHAMBERLAIN RETURNED from his South African tour with a renewed fervour for imperial federation, and envisioned preferential tariffs as the starting point from which to realize this goal. Unfortunately, in his absence, C.T. Ritchie had dropped from his Budget the corn duty Chamberlain had hoped to use as a first step towards preference for Canada, the linchpin state of any imperial scheme, which had in 1898 and 1900 extended its own preference to British goods. So began an impassioned political battle in Britain between the champions of the deeply ingrained Free Trade tradition and those, led by Chamberlain, who sought to steer a new course, to Tariff Reform.

At a speech at Birmingham on 15 May 1903, the Colonial Secretary, despite the Budget setback, announced his plan to link the Empire with preferential tariffs and called for a national discussion to be opened. The *Daily Mail* described his position as 'A New Policy for a New Situation'. Arthur Balfour declared preference an 'open question' to be debated by the government. By this step the Prime Minister hoped to keep his Cabinet intact, and particularly to hold the politically important Duke of Devonshire in place as Lord President. In the end, however, Balfour's strategy of delay and compromise failed to stop the Unionist Party from splintering into three factions: Tariff Reform supporters of Chamberlain, Unionist Free Traders, including Devonshire and Ritchie, and moderates, led by Balfour. At the same time, Chamberlain's campaign was a godsend to the factious Liberal Party, which rallied round the Free Trade banner.

The day after the 15 May manifesto, the *Daily Mail* commented that Chamberlain

> spoke as a statesman and a patriot . . . He pleaded with his countrymen to sink all minor differences, and work for the consolidation of the Empire, since on what they do in the next few years depends whether we stand together as 'one great free nation' or fall into separate States, each selfishly seeking its own individual interest . . . to his mind the question of Imperial unity is pressing and urgent; it admits of no postponement and no delays.

Turning to Balfour's position, the *Daily Mail* called his statement that he had sympathy for the fiscal scheme, but saw problems, a 'politician's answer'. The paper went on that, while Chamberlain was

> pleading for strenuous and immediate effort, Mr. Balfour can only see the difficulties in the way of Imperial unity, and is postponing all action . . . Mr. Chamberlain's outlook is that of the statesman; Mr. Balfour's that of the politician who waits always for a clear lead from someone else or for the breath of public opinion, instead of taking his place as general at the head of his followers, and playing the general's part in the struggle which is about to begin.[1]

The 'general's part' called for would have required decisive action by Balfour – a course which ill suited the Prime Minister's nature. In his first public declaration on the subject, on 28 May, Balfour agreed with Chamberlain's call for a discussion and, further, asked for a reassessment of Britain's traditional policy.[2]

Like the country, Britain's newspapers were also divided. A portion of the Unionist press supported or was open to Chamberlain's plan. The Liberal journals, with deeply held Free Trade traditions, were united in their abhorrence of preference. The two sides assailed each other with harsh charges. Those opposed to Tariff Reform argued that it was Free Trade that had made the Empire great and that preference would mean the end of Britain's tradition of 'cheap food'. The supporters of Tariff Reform branded their opponents 'Little Englanders' whose adherence to outmoded ideas would inevitably lead to the disintegration of the Empire. The *Daily Mail* and its proprietor attempted to steer a middle way. The paper solicited views from both sides in the debate, and published them in a special section, 'Mr. Chamberlain's Departure, An Open Discussion'. Among those opposed to preference was John St Loe Strachey, editor of the Unionist *Spectator*. In a letter published as part of the *Daily Mail* debate, Strachey took exception to the 'monstrous notion' that those against Chamberlain's plan were 'Little Englanders' who 'had no love for the Empire'. His regard for the Empire, Strachey explained, was what turned him against the scheme, because he felt it would 'ruin the Empire . . . the child of freedom and free trade' which must remain free 'to continue great and to grow greater'. He ended his letter by noting that the *Daily Mail* had long been an upholder of Free Trade, and congratulated the paper 'for its fairness and good sense in inviting opinion from all sides of this momentous issue'.[3]

Besides letters pro and con, the *Daily Mail* also published the declarations of the various politicians on the issue. On 19 May Rosebery gave a speech which, the paper reported, gave 'general support' to Chamberlain's plan. Rosebery sent his neighbour a note of thanks from Windsor Castle for the copy of *Motors and Motor Car Driving* Alfred had sent him. 'I should have thanked you long ago,' said the Earl, 'had I not hoped to see you.' He continued that it was not very easy to make use of the material at the present 'in this tariff tornado'.[4] At Doncaster, Herbert Asquith, the Liberal leader who would be the most constant thorn in Chamberlain's side, stated his 'strong criticism' of the plan.[5] During the following years, Asquith followed the Tariff Reform leaders across the country and carried out an extremely canny campaign of rebuttal, endlessly repeating the argument that food would be dearer under Chamberlain's scheme. On 23 May the *Daily Mail* announced it was closing the correspondence on the fiscal question. Sounding much like the politicians it derided, the paper declared that more details were wanted – on, for example, the link between the tariff revenues and old-age pensions – before a final judgement could be made. On this issue the Harmsworth evening paper more closely reflected the view of its proprietor. The *Evening News* railed against 'Stomach Taxes' (a phrase attributed to its owner), and used this slogan repeatedly in the following weeks. The paper defined its hostility to 'Stomach Taxes' as 'not against food taxes per se, but against a food tax which would raise the cost of living'.[6]

Differences over Tariff Reform finally led to a breach between Strachey and Harmsworth; however, in the summer of 1903 they were allies against food taxes. On 16 July Alfred told his friend:

I see this morning that the *Standard* has completely altered its point of view as to the food part of the tax & that the *Times* is wobbling also . . . Chamberlain can only gain by the divided state of the opposition to him, & he is the only man with a definite plan. I can assure that his organisation has already assumed remarkable proportions. There are over one hundred paid lecturers out already among the humbler folk & 'literature' is being distributed by the ton.[7]

Strachey recommended that the anti-food-tax forces should release a pamphlet, *The Great Bread Riot*. Alfred believed it should be held in reserve, responding that it would be 'a pity to use up such a good piece of ammunition' at this 'early juncture of the fight'. He continued that as far as he could make out 'we are being worsted at every turn in the fight so far, except in the matter of the Press, which, with a few exceptions, will turn round as they see how the contest goes'.[8] A month later, he wrote to Strachey that 'we are making special arrangements for dealing with the great controversy when the time comes, but frankly I believe despite Mr. Chamberlain's reiteration, he will drop the Food tax policy'.[9]

At the end of August the *Daily Mail* published the findings of 2,000 interviews conducted with the public on Chamberlain and the Tariff Reform issue. Twenty per cent of the sample had never heard of the matter, and a majority of those who had were hostile to the idea. Alfred planned a fiscal debate at Sutton Place for 16 September, and Winston Churchill, who sided with the Unionist Free Traders in this controversy, agreed to attend. Both men thought the government was on shaky ground and that, if an election was held, it would be overwhelmed in a defeat of landslide proportions. Churchill congratulated Alfred on the paper's 'fine service' in its criticism of food taxes, but warned that there were many difficulties ahead. He believed the time was ripe for a 'great central Government neither Protectionist nor Pro-Boer, which will deal with the shocking administrative inefficiency which prevails'.[10] Rosebery, Churchill confided, would be the natural leader for such a venture, and if the Earl let the 'opportunity pass, it may never return'. Churchill suggested that Alfred 'have a talk with him'.[11] After at first appearing to support Chamberlain, Rosebery had reversed his stance and declared his opposition to preference. He had come to believe that, rather than make it stronger, the scheme would weaken imperial unity. When the two men spoke at the end of August, Rosebery told his neighbour that he was waiting for the decision of the Cabinet and for Balfour to declare himself before deciding his course for the autumn.

On 1 September 1903 Alfred decided that the time had come for Rosebery, in alliance with the Harmsworth papers, to step forward at last and to lead the forces of 'efficiency' against Chamberlain and Balfour. In this course he was motivated by his frustration at the inaction and muddle shown by those in power, the anti-Tariff Reform feeling his newspaper poll had uncovered, and prodding from Churchill and others for a 'central' government. In an attempt to inspire the Earl to action, he sent Rosebery a list of the major speeches already arranged by the Opposition and a plan in response 'calculated to attract attention equal to that of Mr Gladstone's Midlothian campaign' which Rosebery had orchestrated years before. Alfred exhorted the Earl to follow up his memorable 'National Efficiency' speech at Chesterfield with a series of ten addresses before 15 December to 'frustrate the endeavours of Mr. Chamberlain & Mr Balfour to draw the fiscal red herring across the path of the War disclosures and general ministerial maladministration and to counteract the effect not only of the Tariff speeches of the Protectionists, but also of the endeavours of Sir Henry Campbell Bannerman and others'. In the opinion of the owner of the *Daily Mail*, it would be 'impossible to risk our organisation on anything less' than the programme outlined, and he asked Rosebery to consent to the arrangements suggested – 'which will allow us the chance, by no means a sure one under any circumstances, of carrying our press campaign to a successful issue by giving us the support we ask. Otherwise, with the greatest reluctance in the world, it will be absolutely impossible for us to carry on a contest against such overwhelming odds.' It had been his intention to come to Mentmore to urge this plan on Rosebery in person, but he now thought it best to stay in London to organize the movement, so that 'not a moment will be lost'. He closed by asking Rosebery for an assurance of 'support from you equal to the very urgent need of the occasion'.[12]

The Liberal journalist J.A. Spender was with Rosebery, escaping the unseasonable heat in a tent on the lawn of Mentmore, when the letter arrived. Spender recorded that the Earl laughed aloud when he read the message.[13] It must have been nervous laughter. Rosebery apparently had no idea that his many discussions with his neighbour in Berkeley Square had led Alfred to believe he could speak so bluntly and issue such a summons. He replied that he was surprised by his friend's 'ultimatum' and that it appeared

that you are carrying on a press campaign against overwhelming odds, and that unless I at once fix the dates for at least ten speeches to be delivered by me – two apparently at once and eight in the ensuing two months – it will be impossible for you to carry on the contest ... I do not gather the cause on behalf of which this desperate contest is being waged nor why it depends on me. Is it the cause of Liberal Imperialism? Surely that is healthy enough. Is it the cause of Free Trade? Surely that is not so desperate.

Rosebery went on, 'I doubt if such a letter as this was ever addressed to a public man in this country. In any case it demands reflection and possibly consultation before a definite reply is sent. This hasty note is only an expression of candid perplexity.'[14]

After further thought, Rosebery wrote to Alfred that he had given his letter

> the best consideration that I can, and this only deepens my first impression. I am not ambitious, as you know, and, even if I were, I could not sacrifice my liberty of action, or, I must add, my self-respect. I propose, as I told you on Monday, to await the decision of the Cabinet and the pronouncement of Balfour before I definitely resolve on my course for this autumn. This seems to me the commonsense method in view of the uncertainty of the present position.[15]

He continued:

> Nor do I know, in any case, how far or how long we should agree on policy. You have never consulted me as to the policy of your papers; I do not know what it is, and therefore cannot tell how far we could go together.

The Earl realized the value of the Harmsworth press, but did not propose to be treated as a 'lecturer or a singer on tour'. He was

> sure you have made your proposal – strange and unprecedented as it is – in the friendliest spirit. But I am equally sure that it is impossible that I should hand over the planning of my future course to any one whatever. I think you must realise what would be felt if it was understood that I had assigned this charge to a great newspaper proprietor. It would be said, not unnaturally, that I was being 'run' by him.[16]

His attempt to move Rosebery to action dashed, Alfred considered his own course. Churchill sent a note on the 11th urging him to see Henry Hobhouse MP to talk about a press bureau for the Free Food League, locked in battle with the Tariff Reform League, which had been created by the journalists Leo Maxse and L.S. Amery to carry on the fight for Chamberlain's cause. Churchill said that he was going to Dalmeny to see Rosebery and would attend the Sutton Place fiscal conference, which had been rescheduled for 26 September. He ended with his belief that Chamberlain was 'beaten but he will sell his political life dearly'.[17] Alfred replied that he would see Hobhouse. He went on:

> When I wrote to you I had great hope of hearing that Lord R was about to start on an active political campaign. If he does not do so a Radical

Government is, in my judgment, certain. And when I say Radical, I mean a Government into which Grey and Asquith would be forced.

Lord R does not realise how much his lack of activity injures him in the country, & especially in the provinces.

I almost despair of politics at the present time. Unless I can see some party to which to attach myself, I shall give up politics & go in for buying and organising more newspapers.

... I am not so hopeful of anything resulting from our conference as I was when I wrote to you & before R's state of inanition at that critical time. However, discussion will do no harm.[18]

This letter correctly, if somewhat prematurely, prophesied the entry of Grey and Asquith into the next Liberal government, despite a compact among the Liberal Imperialists to stay out. However, though the owner of the *Daily Mail* did return to 'buying and organising more newspapers', he did not 'give up politics'.

While Rosebery stayed on the political sidelines, Balfour endeavoured to regain the initiative from Chamberlain by proposing a compromise position in which Britain would retaliate against any nation which imposed a protective tariff. Proclaiming 'Light At Last', the 16 September *Daily Mail* praised the Prime Minister for the 'notable courage' of his declaration.[19] Churchill expressed his sorrow to the newspaper's proprietor 'that you have plumped so decidedly for Mr. Balfour's pamphlet. It is only an embroidered curtain to conceal the preparation of the Chamberlain battering rams.'[20] Unable to agree with Balfour's compromise and tired of the restraints caused by his position in the Cabinet, Chamberlain decided to resign so that he might be free to take his arguments directly to the country. However, not wishing to be accused of splitting a second party (a little too late, it seems), he met Balfour and agreed not to attack the government. At the same time, Balfour manoeuvred to keep the Duke of Devonshire in place while ridding himself of several other troublesome Free Traders. On 17 September 1903 Alfred received news of Chamberlain's resignation, which was soon accompanied by those of Ritchie and the Unionist Free Traders Lord Balfour of Burleigh and Lord George Hamilton, Secretaries for Scotland and India respectively.

The audacity of Chamberlain's action appealed strongly to Harmsworth, who decided that, if the plan could be modified to escape the unpopular 'stomach taxes', he would cast his lot with the Tariff Reformers. The next morning's *Daily Mail* hailed Chamberlain as the 'strong man of the Government' who could not accept Balfour's compromise. The paper went on that 'food taxes we have opposed from the beginning, we still oppose, and we shall continue to oppose' but declared, 'it would be an ungrateful and ungracious act indeed if we allowed a man who has borne the burden and heat of Imperial Government for eight strenuous years to leave his post without the expression of our sincere admiration and heartfelt regret that the country must now lose his invaluable services'. Turning to Balfour's reorganization of the government in light of the resignations, it recommended that he follow the report of the Elgin Commission, which had looked into War Office blunders during the Boer War, and rid himself of those it held culpable – meaning particularly Brodrick.

In the reconstruction, Hugh Oakley Arnold-Foster became Secretary of State for War in place of Brodrick, who was shifted to the India Office. Arnold-Foster had a reputation as an expert in both naval and army matters, and since 1900 he had served as Parliamentary Under-Secretary of the Admiralty. To aid the new Secretary for War, Balfour called together a War Office Reconstruction Committee to carry out reforms along lines suggested by Lord Esher, who had been a member of the Elgin Commission.[21] Elsewhere, when Lord Milner refused to serve, Alfred Lyttelton replaced Chamberlain at the Colonial Office. Balfour declared a truce over discussions of fiscal matters in the Cabinet, where the reconstruction only perpetuated the Free Trade/Tariff Reform split. Austen Chamberlain was given the Exchequer, but two Free Traders, Lord Derby and the new Lord Salisbury, who succeeded his father in 1903, also joined the government. The Prime Minister clarified his 'retaliation' stance at Sheffield on 1 October. This gave Devonshire, who had stayed on temporarily, an excuse to leave the Cabinet.

The *Daily Mail* began a series, 'The Fiscal ABC – A Complete Guide to the Great Controversy', which argued for Tariff Reform. Its author, H.W. Wilson, the chief leader writer for the newspaper, was a follower of Chamberlain who had been offered the same position at the more openly supportive *Daily Express*. He reported to Chamberlain that, after he had tendered his resignation, his proprietor had agreed 'that I should be allowed, writing over my own name in the Mail, to fight your cause day by day when the propaganda begins . . . We are to have a kind of newspaper debate.' Alfred had told Wilson that he would 'oppose tooth and nail food taxes', but the writer passed on to Chamberlain that the owner of the *Daily Mail* was 'by no means unfriendly to you; indeed I noted a distinct note of admiration for your conduct which has been missing hitherto'. Much will depend, said Wilson, on 'which way the cat jumps in the next few weeks. If, for example, there came strong demands for preference from the Colonies, that would influence him. He is organising a most formidable propaganda against food taxes . . . but at least I shall be able to meet it in the columns of the Mail.' According to Wilson, his proprietor desired to get rid of Balfour; also to get rid, 'for the moment', of food taxation, because

> he does not believe it will be accepted, and then he thinks that you, having gone to the country and fought for preference, will return to power on the protection basis, and will carry protection. Preference, he says, can only be attained after protection has been accepted by the country – Then he will be with you . . . with him it is protection first, as in the line of least resistance; then when tariff change has once come, he holds the rest will be easy.[22]

Ten days later, after Chamberlain had agreed with this strategy to maintain a friendly voice at the *Daily Mail*, Wilson told him that 'the moment has arrived . . . to make the smallest concession to Harmsworth, so as to save his appearance of consistency, you could put him in your pocket . . . if you were willing to see him, I believe your strong personality might bring him over. In previous attempts to get hold of him, I never got so far as this time.'[23] There is no record of a written reply to this, but a few days later Wilson met Chamberlain and his son Austen. The proprietor of the *Daily Mail* had told the writer that he would support Chamberlain if he did not put up the cost of living, and now Wilson informed Alfred that Chamberlain 'would meet your views, which I have told him were inspired by regard for the poor. He cannot abandon preference; he is bound to it.'[24]

On other matters of political strategy, Wilson reported to Alfred that Chamberlain agreed with him that 'an immediate election with the other side in power would be best'. If Balfour won, it was thought he could do so only 'by a small majority and that would be useless'. Austen had told Wilson that the Tariff Reform forces 'would ride for a fall next year', when the Chamberlains foresaw a possible majority of a hundred or more. Wilson went on that Chamberlain's first speech, at Glasgow, would be developed at Liverpool and other places, adding that 'as soon as his first two or three speeches are over he would like to see you, if you feel that you want to work with him'. The long report on Chamberlain ended by recounting the 'curious' thing he had said: 'Just as Harmsworth knows what the public wants to read, so I know what the elector wants; it is an instinct in both of us.' Heartened by Wilson's revelations, Alfred wrote to Chamberlain that he was 'hoping that your policy will provide for the extinction of the food taxes because then I shall be able to support you as warmly as I did during the Boer War'.[25]

Chamberlain opened his national campaign at Glasgow on 6 October, calling for preference for colonial goods as a first step towards imperial consolidation. In return the colonies were, theoretically, to give preference to British manufactures. The day after the speech, the proprietor of the *Daily Mail* responded in a rare signed editorial. Comparing Chamberlain to Gladstone and Bismarck, the piece commented that

> Whatever the final judgment that may be passed by friends or opponents upon his bold proposals, the sympathy and regard of his countrymen of every shade of party will be with the patriotism, energy and zeal that at the age of sixty-seven have led him to surrender office and to throw himself into a cause which he believes to be vital to the welfare of England and the Empire . . .
>
> For what Mr. Chamberlain is now attempting is a vast programme constructive and destructive, a social and commercial revolution. It involves the uprooting of our beliefs and old principles; and it must be accompanied by some pain to individuals and friction to industry while the national life is being adapted to the changed condition of modern existence.

In the opinion of the owner of *Daily Mail*, the present fiscal structure was 'impossible'. The prevailing situation – in which foreign goods attracted no tariffs, whereas Russia imposed a 123 per cent tax, the United States 73 per cent, France 34 per cent and Germany 25 per cent on British goods – was 'never contemplated by Mr. Cobden'. He went on that the

> injury to British industry that is the result of this system is dangerous alike to the welfare of the individual and of the nation. To the worker it means diminished employment, to the nation it means crippled finances and resources, for trade is the sinew of national existence . . . By protection alone we can obtain some means of replying to foreign powers . . . by protection alone we can give security to capital and labour.

Turning to the method by which the scheme of protection was to be put into force, in the 'humble opinion' of the owner of the *Daily Mail*, Chamberlain had committed an error when he proposed to impose a tax on food and manufactures simultaneously. The editorial suggested that the tax on manufactures should precede that on food, 'so as to permit our British manufactures to expand and afford increased employment before food stuffs are taxed'. There was a great danger that 'if the two different parts of the scheme are to be applied at the same moment the worker will reject both, because he sees and knows only the present loss and is doubtful of the future gain'. The writer was aware that if Chamberlain abandoned food taxes Canada would probably withdraw her 'generous preference since she would gain little under any tariff which did not tax food'. However, if Chamberlain, as he announced, could apply part of the proceeds towards the extinction of the present food taxes, and if he could persuade Canada to wait while Britain taxed manufactures, then the difficulties could be minimized. The question was, 'Can he do this?' So that the Empire would not be injured by partisanship, the editorial called for a committee of British businessmen to look into the matter in an inquiry removed from the 'sphere of party politics'.

After Chamberlain had spoken out again at Newcastle two weeks later, the *Daily Mail* hailed the address as a 'brilliant triumph'. It went on that 'dealing with food taxes Mr. Chamberlain proved that he had advanced further in the direction the "Daily Mail" has demonstrated to be necessary . . . he has set out to accomplish the work which Cavour fulfilled for Italy and Bismarck for Germany'.[26]

While the fiscal debate was carried on, the publishing businesses continued to grow. From the middle of October, Alfred worked with Kennedy Jones and others to settle the 'make-up' of the *Daily Mirror*. This latest experiment was a penny morning paper, written by women and aimed at the female audience. Mary Howarth, who had been the director of the successful *Daily Mail* women's page, was appointed editor. The first issue came off the presses late on 1 November. Alfred recorded that 'after the usual pangs of childbirth produced the first copy at 9.50 P.M. It looks a promising child, but time will show whether we are on a winner or not.'[27] The owner declared in the first editorial that the *Daily Mirror* was 'new, because it represents in journalism a development that is entirely new and modern in the world; it is unlike any other newspaper because it attempts what no other newspaper has ever attempted. It is no mere bulletin of fashion, but a reflection of women's interests, women's thoughts, women's work. The sane and healthy occupation of domestic life.'[28] First-day sales of 265,217 for this 'reflection of women's interests' appeared promising. The usual telegrams of congratulations flooded Carmelite House.

All the applause proved premature as, despite an enormous advertising campaign, sales of the *Daily Mirror* soon plummeted. Within a month circulation was below 25,000 and losses were £3,000 a week. The paper became the greatest publishing blunder of Alfred's career and lost £100,000 before its fortunes were righted. The original idea – that a large female readership could be lured to a penny paper away from sixpenny productions like the *Queen* and *Ladies' Field* – proved absolutely wrong. Harold suggested discontinuing the journal, but Alfred refused to surrender. Instead, to improve circulation, the paper's layout and its exclusively female focus were changed. In addition to a new conception, a more experienced – and male – hand was brought in as editor. (Howarth returned to the *Daily Mail.*) Henry Hamilton Fyfe, formerly G.E. Buckle's secretary at *The Times* and lately editor of the *Morning Advertiser*, took over on 23 November. Over a weekend, Fyfe replaced the feminine furnishings in the editor's office and was delegated the unpleasant task of dismissing much of the female staff. Despite the three months' severance pay given, it was a tearful and painful undertaking on all sides. Fyfe described the task as 'a horrid experience – something like drowning kittens'.[29] The new editor of the *Daily Mirror* spent a weekend at Sutton Place discussing the paper with its proprietor. In consultation with Kennedy Jones, who aided Fyfe in the rehabilitation effort, the decision was made to transform the *Daily Mirror* into the first picture paper.

Another November visitor to the Harmsworth country house was John Evelyn Wrench, a recent interview subject of the *Daily Mail.* Though only twenty, Wrench had already made a fortune in the picture-postcard craze which had swept Britain. During this visit Alfred tested the mettle of his youthful visitor with a drive in his Mercedes, which Wrench described as a 'big snorting monster that stood outside the front hall'. By this time Pine, a lame ex-soldier, had replaced Lancaster as the Harmsworth chauffeur and mechanic. The three, protected by 'French motoring coats with the fur outside, caps and goggles', set out with Alfred at the wheel. Wrench recalled their Sunday morning excursion:

> The car was an open two-seater with a splash board on which Pine wedged himself, though how he managed to cling on I shall never understand ... the empty seat next to the driver was appointed to me: the monster's snorting drowned all human voices. Great leather straps, looking like belts, kept his armour in place. The Chief was a fine driver. In an hour and a half we flew over the surface of half southern England. I clung to my seat. The wind roared past us. I felt as if my eyebrows were being blown off as the air rushed through the chinks of my goggles. I parted my lips for a second, and such was the force of the wind, that I had difficulty in closing them.

We flew through Guildford . . . there was little traffic on the roads . . . up the Hog's Back at sixty miles an hour, on to Godalming, Farnborough, and I didn't know where else. We never stopped, we never talked. How I prayed for villages and sharp turns when we had to slow down! At 11:30 I stumbled out of the car at the front door of Sutton Place with knees and legs aching from the tension of pressing against the floor, with a face tingling from the wind, and with a great sense of relief.[30]

Wrench apparently passed this driving test and soon after, when his postcard enterprise crumbled, joined the staff at Carmelite House as the proprietor's 'confidential secretary'. Before too long, he came to enjoy the rides with his chief.

As he had in the previous year, in 1903 Alfred contributed an essay to a book. *Journalism as a Profession*, edited by Arthur Lawrence, was part of the *A Start in Life* series. In 'The Making of a Newspaper', Alfred asked young men to consider the newspaper profession, which, he declared, had just begun. The essay asserted that, though they previously may have been run by illiterates, modern papers had elevated the position of the journalist, whose prospects were booming. It was widely considered that in France and the United States newspaper men had succeeded further than anywhere else; however, the author listed Lord Milner and Lord Salisbury in England as great men who had worked in journalism. The essay continued that 'No less an authority than the British Ambassador in Paris has told us how greatly the journalist has supplanted the diplomatist, and few politicians would care to attempt to govern without the assistance of the newspapers.'[31] The owner of the *Daily Mail* concluded with a word of caution concerning relations between the press and politicians. He confided that 'some years ago, before I had learned the wiles of politicians and his natural desire that the newspaper should grind his ax, I went among them'. On one occasion he was berated by a Cabinet minister for printing something mentioned at a private dinner. He had had no part in this, but it convinced him that politicians and newsmen were best apart. To maintain their independence, he asserted that proprietors should avoid a wide circle of acquaintances among politicians. This was necessary because it was 'part of the business of a newspaper to get news and print it', whereas it was 'part of the business of a politician to prevent certain news being printed'.[32]

Though he warned against politicians, Alfred closely followed Chamberlain's campaign, which continued at Birmingham on 4 November. He listened to the address through the 'Electrophone' at the *Daily Mail* office. He felt the speech a 'wonderful success' and noted that he 'heard the great man distinctly – distance 113 miles'. The new technology allowed the *Evening News* to bring out a verbatim report within half of an hour of the speech's finish. The *Daily Mail* called the occasion a 'Great Triumph' which brought together all classes of Britons behind Chamberlain in his 'new Pilgrim's Progress'. The address, the paper declared, was 'in essence an appeal to the people of England to ... Treat your friends better than those who would strip you of your trade – this was the gist of his policy.'[33]

Support of Chamberlain brought the proprietor of the *Daily Mail* into alliance with the Tariff Reform League. Arthur Pearson, chairman of the League, wrote to him that the 'weakest point in our armour seems to lie in the fact that definite statements made by Mr. Chamberlain's principal opponents are reported in the Press generally, while owing to the fact that Mr. Chamberlain is practically the only speaker on our side to whose speeches considerable space is given, replies to these statements do not reach the public'.[34] To remedy this, Pearson enclosed a series of retorts used by Tariff Reform speakers in answer to criticisms. In December Alfred met Chamberlain at his London home, 40 Princes Gardens, South Kensington. A few days later he saw Chamberlain's chief organizer, Powell-Williams. The 15 December diary records that two by-elections, at Dulwich and Lewisham, had both been 'fiscal' victories.

These Unionist successes turned a tide of defeats in the preceding years and have been seen as a last opportunity for Balfour to dissolve Parliament with a chance for electoral victory, or for only a narrow loss after which the Party could come together in opposition to the Irish policy to which a Liberal government would be bound.[35] Chamberlain urged this course; however, the Prime Minister continued his policy of delay, intent on ensuring an agreement with France and the completion of a new gun for the Army, both of which he believed the Liberals would destroy. Instead it would be his party and leadership that suffered. On the last day of 1903 the *Daily Mail* asserted that in 'politics and in the whole realm of national affairs, it has been Mr. Chamberlain's year ... Mr. Balfour has lost power and prestige.'

Alfred Harmsworth's support of fiscal reform had been noticed at the highest levels. At this juncture King Edward was sympathetic to Chamberlain and an avid reader of newspapers, including the Harmsworth press, the influence of which he appreciated. The King wrote to his Prime Minister from Sandringham on Christmas Day that the name of Mr. Alfred Harmsworth has been mentioned to me for an Honour. It seems that Lord Salisbury offered him once a Knighthood, which he declined; but I understand he is most anxious for a Baronetcy. He is a great power in the Press & strongly supports the Government as well as Mr. Chamberlain's policy. Should you wish to recommend his name to me, I will certainly give my consent. He is married, but has no children.[36]

Balfour, less rigid than Salisbury had been concerning honours, would before too long follow the recommendation of his sovereign.

After two months of preparation, the first edition of the reborn *Daily Mirror* was published on 25 January 1904. Three days later its proprietor recorded that the newspaper had become the 'first one half illustrated daily' and, to mark the change, the journal was briefly renamed the *Daily Illustrated Mirror*. The price of the new tabloid-styled 'Paper for Men and Women' was dropped to a halfpenny. The journal now devoted itself to pictorial representations of hard news. Another jibe attributed to Salisbury – that 'Mr. Harmsworth had invented a paper for those who could read but could not think, and another for those who could see but could not read' – had finally been realized.[37] More than Fyfe or Kennedy Jones, the person given most credit for turning around the fortunes of the *Daily Mirror* was Arkas Sapt, who brought his expertise in printing illustrations and photographs to the problem. Armed with a new Hoe rotary press, which could print 24,000 pictures of acceptable quality in an hour, Sapt revamped the journal. The proprietor frankly admitted his errors in the 27 February article 'How I Dropped £100,000 on the *Mirror*'.[38]

The *Daily Mirror* benefited from the 'rupture' of Japanese–Russian relations which Alfred noted in his February diary. Coverage of the Russo-Japanese War which began in April gave its correspondents a golden opportunity to perfect their technique on the battle front. Though Britain took no active part, since the signing of the 1902 agreement Japan had been an ally and the British press lauded Japanese successes against the common Russian enemy, which threatened the Empire in India and the Middle East. Among the first photographs in the *Daily Mirror*, at the time of the siege of Port Arthur, were shots of a Japanese admiral and his crew. Two months after war broke out in the Far East, the Entente Cordiale was signed by Britain and France, marking another step away from isolation. The understanding dealt with colonial matters, and Lansdowne, the Foreign Secretary, assured his German counterparts that it was not aimed at their country; however, the *Daily Mail*, and other British papers including *The Times*, welcomed the agreement as a counterbalance to the power across the North Sea.

The month after the understanding with France was signed, Winston Churchill crossed the aisle and joined the Liberals. This parting of the ways over Tariff Reform had been brewing for some time. A deciding incident came at the end of March. When Churchill rose to speak in the Commons after Lloyd George, Balfour, tired of the unceasing criticism of the Member for Oldham, left the chamber and was soon followed by all but a few Free Trade Unionists. The *Daily Mail* reported the 'Chilling Rebuke' as the 'Unionists Refuse to Hear Mr. Churchill' and the 'Strange Scene in the Commons'.[39] On 22 April the unrepentant MP gave a speech in the House attacking government policy towards trade-union legislation – a speech which even the usually sympathetic *Daily Mail* said demonstrated 'Radicalism of the reddest type'.[40] However, the end of this speech betrayed the strain under which Churchill laboured, when he lost his train of thought and could not continue. Alfred Harmsworth was among those who attempted to reassure the shaken parliamentarian that the incident was only a temporary aberration. Nevertheless, the division between the two men over the fiscal question remained.[41] At the end of May, Churchill took a place on the Liberal benches next to Lloyd George, in the same seat his father, Lord Randolph, had occupied when in Opposition.[42]

Elsewhere, on the newspaper front, blocked from acquiring *The Times*, Alfred manoeuvred to add a weighty paper to his battalions. Consequently, he combined with John Montagu MP in an attempt to purchase the Conservative *Standard*, at one time a strong competitor of *The Times*. Though it was still considered influential, particularly among businessmen, the paper's circulation had fallen badly. According to Montagu, he had approached his friend on behalf of the Conservative Party to stand for Parliament at Weybridge in the next election. After Alfred turned down this proposition, their lunch conversation at the Savoy turned to the *Standard*. When Montagu shared his ambitions to buy the paper, he was informed that his friend knew all about the plan. He had had the information from Alfred Watson, editor of the *Badminton Library* series. The owner of the *Daily Mail* suggested that the two join forces; should the purchase be consummated, his position would remain secret while Montagu would run the paper as editor-in-chief. The only proviso added was that the hidden partner would have a veto on the policy of the paper in time of government crisis. In early May a formal agreement was drawn up and Montagu was promised £5,000 a year.[43]

At the same time as Alfred made a run at the *Standard*, he noted casually in his diary that he had had a 'conversation with the King'. Soon after this, Alfred and Mary also attended a reception at the Prime Minister's residence in Downing Street. On 22 June, the owner of the *Daily Mail* recorded that he had 'received official announcement from Mr. Balfour that Baronetcy had been conferred by the King. Wired news to wife at Sutton. Received congratulations from wife, Pearson & others who curiously enough knew in advance.' Mary Harmsworth replied: 'My Darling "Sir Alfred", – I must be the first to tell you how glad and happy I am to know that you have gained recognition for the hard work of years. No one, dear, deserves it more than you – but the happiest thought of all to me is that we began life together and have been together through all the years of work which have earned you distinction and fortune so young.'[44] On 23 June his name was among those published in the King's Birthday Honours List issued in the evening.

An amazing 'avalanche of congratulations' arrived over the next few days. These included a note from Churchill that it was 'appropriate & indeed inevitable that honours should follow in the wake of influence'. The newly minted Liberal could not resist adding, 'But what an awful licking you will get at the election!'[45] The *Daily Telegraph* commented that 'to few men has it been to win so much success in so limited a time'. The *Daily Chronicle* added that 'Mr. Harmsworth's is the name of the most general interest in a list that is more remarkable for quantity than quality.' In this vein, the *Daily News* made a sniffing comparison of the merits of Alfred Harmsworth to a figure like the composer Edward Elgar, a new knight. A friend sent a clipping from the *Pelican*, a London social and theatrical weekly, which gushed that, 'after having been conspicuously passed over for several years, Sir Alfred Harmsworth has arrived at his baronetcy . . . for fitting out the Jackson–Harmsworth Polar Expedition, for his princely charity, for all he did during the Boer War, Sir Alfred well earned his title'. Though he could have had a knighthood for some time before, the paper went on, he previously declined, and now remained the same 'kind hearted man he was before he got fame and fortune'.

Fresh from his achievement, Sir Alfred lunched with Joseph Chamberlain in Princes Gardens. Heartened by comments from Canada and Australia that made some sort of preference agreement seem very possible, Chamberlain revealed his latest plan: to ask Balfour to call a colonial conference. The Prime Minister could enter the meeting uncommitted, but Chamberlain was optimistic that a mutually satisfactory plan could be worked out. The journalist Leo Amery, who was also at the meeting, recorded that 'J.C. unfolded plan of getting A.J.B. into line by device of declaring for Colonial Conference which A.J.B. was to announce at Southampton.'[46] Unfortunately for Chamberlain's scheme, Balfour's reticence and added political complications kept any conference from being held for some time.

In the summer of 1904 the quest for the *Standard* became more heated. In July, Montagu met for the first time Harold Harmsworth to discuss the matter. The financial guide of the Harmsworth enterprises was anxious to move ahead with the purchase and to state a price to Castle & Co., the agents handling the sale for the owners of the paper, the Johnstone family. Alfred balked at immediate action and counselled delay for a few months. However, to meet a deadline imposed by Castle & Co., a bid was tendered which was deemed 'totally inadequate'. The Harmsworths were not interested in raising the offer and, with no other contenders on the horizon, decided to play a waiting game.[47]

That month Alfred saw Lord Curzon, who had returned to England from India for a visit. The Viceroy was made Warden of the Cinque Ports as a reward for his efforts. The sinecure included the use of Walmer Castle. Curzon was also given the freedom of the City at Guildhall. Sir Alfred attended the ceremony and heard Curzon's rousing defence of the Empire – a speech many called the best he ever delivered.[48] On 24 July Chamberlain and his wife visited Sutton Place. Alfred recorded that he 'drove Joe in motor'.

The *Standard* affair came to a conclusion later in 1904. Montagu visited Sutton Place to discuss the stalled negotiations. Since the summer another prospective buyer, Arthur Pearson, had entered the picture. Castle & Co. informed Montagu that Pearson had met the £300,000 asking price and offered an opportunity to counter.[49] The Harmsworths were unwilling to spend anything approaching that amount, which well exceeded their estimation of the paper's value. Unable financially to act alone, Montagu was forced to stand aside as Pearson gained the *Standard*. This proved to be a costly victory. Despite much hard work, the circulation of the paper could never be satisfactorily revived.[50] Before many years had passed, Alfred Harmsworth would turn the tables on Pearson and acquire *The Times*, a much more valuable asset, for only marginally more than the price paid for the vastly less prestigious *Standard*.

In October the Russo-Japanese War intruded into the North Sea, when the nervous Russian fleet mistook British trawlers for Japanese torpedo vessels in the 'Dogger Bank Incident'. Sir Alfred recorded in his diary of the 24th that he had received the news of the 'Baltic Fleet Outrage'. The *Daily Mail* accused the Russians of being 'Drunk as Usual', and congratulated them on the 'First Act of Heroism' of the Baltic Fleet. This international diversion allowed Balfour to ignore the continuing party division over Tariff Reform when he addressed the National Union Conference at Southampton. Sir Alfred attended the speech, in which Balfour explained the agreement reached with Russia over the incident. The 2 November *Daily Mail* proclaimed its dissatisfaction with the Prime Minister's recommendation that the dispute be submitted to the Hague Tribunal for arbitration. The paper soon reported that it was Germany that had advised the Russians about the danger of Japanese torpedo attacks in the North Sea and thus precipitated the whole calamity. Despite official denials, the *Daily Mail* warned that England must remain 'always on the watch for some cleverly devised piece of mischief' from Germany.

The same month that the 'outrage' in the North Sea took place, Admiral Sir John Fisher, one of the most colourful figures in British naval history, gained control at the Admiralty as First Sea Lord. Like the owner of the *Daily Mail*, the sixty-three-year-old Admiral owed nothing to money and influence and everything to his own prodigious energy and talents. He had also maintained a similar boyish enthusiasm and vitality. Fisher believed the German threat was real and that it was only a matter of time before the fleet across the North Sea would test his own. It became his quest to ensure that Britain would be ready when the moment arrived.[51] For the next five years Fisher fought tooth and nail to uphold the traditional 'two-power standard' by which the British had attempted to maintain a fleet twice as large as the combined naval forces of its two most likely foes. In this struggle he found an ally in the Harmsworth press.

Fisher's sweeping reforms ranged from new crew systems and scrapping obsolete ships to the introduction of all-big-gun battleships and cruisers – the 'Dreadnought' revolution. The keel-plate of the original *Dreadnought* was laid a year after Fisher came to power, and the ship was completed in December 1906. As might be expected in a tradition-oriented service, many of the changes were bitterly contested, particularly in crew arrangements and training and the decommissioning of numerous smaller craft which, in Fisher's view at least, were no longer viable. Perhaps the most valid criticism was that scrapping Britain's numerical advantage to construct an all-big-gun navy gave her potential adversaries, particularly Germany, an even start. This, Fisher admitted, was true; however, if Britain did not move first in this direction she would soon be pursuing, rather than leading, the other powers that had the technological capabilities to begin such construction themselves. The agreements with Japan and France and the fact that the United States was no longer considered a possible enemy in Admiralty calculations also brought shifts in the deployment of the British fleets. From 1902 Germany had become the number-one antagonist against whom plans were laid, and consequently the North Sea gained in importance while the Mediterranean diminished.

While the Dogger Bank affair played itself out, November 1904 also saw the publication of yet another Harmsworth newspaper, this one intended to strengthen the 'bonds of empire'. Dubbed the *Overseas Daily Mail*, the new venture was edited by John Evelyn Wrench. Designed to provide news from London, the fourteen-page penny weekly included court and social events and was particularly focused on Canada, which its proprietor believed got too much of her news from the United States. The journal was also designed to provide an imperial perspective for readers in India and Australia, where the papers were, in Sir Alfred's judgement, overly occupied with local developments. Publicity began in the other Harmsworth papers on the 9th, and the first edition came off the presses on 25 November. In a foreword to the first editorial, the owner explained that he had founded the *Overseas Daily Mail* 'because during my several visits to the Dominion of Canada, to many of His Majesty's colonies, and to India, to the United States, and other foreign countries in which the lonely Englishman is found, I have realised that there is a real need for a newspaper that shall come as a Message each week from the Heart of the Empire'.

The new venture was denounced by many as a purely commercial attempt by the Harmsworth press to profit from imperial sentiment. These cries were added to the numerous other barbs directed at Sir Alfred by political and commercial enemies. For example, his former ally Churchill sent a note to the owner of the *Daily Mail* from Dalmeny that he thought friends should not 'bicker politically' and that remarks he had made about 'mammoth newspaper trusts' had been aimed not at him, but at Arthur Pearson, proprietor of the *Daily Express* and the *Standard* and chairman of the Tariff Reform League.[52] Sir Alfred replied that 'A great many people thought your speech referred to me on account of the constant endeavour of my numerous enemies to suggest that my political conscience is even more elastic than it really is. Arthur Pearson has no brothers owning newspapers of divergent views, so they did not apply the speech to him.'[53] Despite their differences, in December 1904, with London under a record fog, Sir Alfred dined with Churchill and the Duchess of Marlborough at Willis's, a favourite destination in this period. Alfred stayed at Elmwood to see in the new year.

When Pearson resigned as chairman of the Tariff Reform League, Chamberlain hoped to replace the loss by attracting the proprietor of the *Daily Mail*. After the attempt failed, the Tariff Reform leader sent a note that he wished 'very much we could have had the advantage of your assistance . . . but I do not wonder at your refusal'.[54] On 7 April Sir Alfred lunched with Mr and Mrs Chamberlain to talk in person about electoral prospects.

That month the operations of the *Daily Mail*, the *Evening News* and the recently acquired *Weekly Dispatch* were incorporated as Associated Newspapers Limited, with a capital of £1,600,000, the shares of which swiftly sold out.[55] Sir Alfred's net income for the year ending 31 March 1905 was £115,000. Apart from the family businesses, he had other stock worth £300,000. But, despite the growing wealth and the baronetcy, Alfred Harmsworth remained dissatisfied with the limited influence that his huge circulations afforded. Attempting to find a solution to this problem would be a major pursuit in the following years.

7

The Youngest Peer Created,
1905–1907

WITH HIS FORTIETH birthday approaching, Sir Alfred Harmsworth had acquired considerable wealth and huge circulations with his popular papers, but still had no journal of opinion taken seriously by the British ruling classes. Having failed to gain the *Standard* and with the purchase of *The Times* blocked, other 'old journalism' properties were considered. As a consequence, the Sunday *Observer* was added to the Harmsworth list. The 3 May 1905 diary simply records 'Purchased "Observer".' Despite a relatively tiny circulation, which varied from 2,000 to 4,000 copies, the journal was London's oldest Sunday paper and one of the most influential, read by many of the same people as the *Standard* and *The Times*. The *Observer* was bought for only £4,000, but it had been losing between £12,000 and £15,000 a year. His income assured from other sources, Sir Alfred was able to accept the losses and the heavy expenditures needed to turn around the paper's fortunes.

Hoping to install a strong figure to guide the political course of the journal, the new proprietor offered the editorship (and a one-third interest) to the highly respected Conservative journalist J.L. Garvin, a staunch champion of imperial consolidation and Tariff Reform, then at the *Outlook*. Garvin turned down the offer, preferring to remain where he was for the time being, but this incident opened a correspondence between the two in which Garvin began to advise Sir Alfred on various political and imperial issues and on the larger question of how influence might be gained by the Harmsworth press. The owner's second choice to lead the *Observer* was L.S. Amery, who was tempted by the offer of twice his salary at *The Times* and one-tenth of the property. However, on the advice of G.E. Buckle, who hoped the younger man would succeed him as editor, Amery decided to remain at *The Times*. Finally, the editorship, without any ownership shares, fell to the journalist Austin Harrison, who did a capable job in his three years with the paper. Since the *Observer* was aimed at a new audience, a more cautious strategy was undertaken to rebuild circulation. Although a team from Carmelite House did descend on the offices at 125 Strand to ensure that economies would be made where possible, the other Harmsworth papers did not boom the *Observer* in their pages as they had all others. The new acquisition brought its owner a considerable amount of ridicule. He later wrote to Garvin that after buying the paper he was regarded as 'a D. F. for doing so'.[1] Such abuse only made him more determined to succeed.

The *Observer* was not the only addition to the newspaper list in May 1905. Sir Alfred had for years complained of the lack of a reliable English-language morning paper in Paris. Spurred on by the increased Anglo-French amity following the Entente Cordiale, it was decided to print a Paris edition of the *Daily Mail*. The contents were phoned from London every morning for distribution well ahead of the arrival of the London papers. Ralph Lane, the manager of the failing Paris *Daily Messenger*, had tried to interest the proprietor of the *Daily Mail* in his journal. Instead, Sir Alfred hired Lane to run the *Continental Daily Mail*. Thus began ten years of close association between two men who were diametrically opposed in their view of the Teutonic threat. While working at the Paris newspaper, Lane, using his middle names Norman Angell, published one of the most influential anti-war books of his time, *Europe's Optical Illusion* (later retitled *The Great Illusion*). Despite their philosophical differences, the two men got along well. Andrew Caird headed the London end of the operation, dealing with many delicate problems, including government relations. The French had made a condition of publication that the newspaper would not include domestic politics. The proprietor told the staff, 'We are guests of the French people. It is not polite to discuss our hosts' internal affairs.'[2] He travelled to the Continent on 8 May to 'look after' the new paper and noted the next day, 'experimental copies very great success'.[3] The first edition for the public was dated 22 May 1905.

Back in England, Sir Alfred corresponded with Chamberlain over the interrelated imperial-preference and election strategies. The latter continued in his attempts to convince Balfour to call an imperial conference before he left office, despite the Prime Minister's pledge at Edinburgh the previous October that he would not introduce preference until after a second general election. On 24 May Chamberlain wrote to Harmsworth that recent events had made a 'great difference in the position and I am now sanguine as to the result of my conference with the Prime Minister'. It seemed likely, he went on, that 'we shall now both work to keep the Government in office over next year when the Conference will be held. If . . . the Conference arrives at a satisfactory result we shall go to the country for it. In this way we get rid of the difficulty of a double election which was from the first one of the most serious obstacles in the way of my agreement.'[4] Whatever Balfour might have led him to believe, Chamberlain's hopes were dashed when opponents in the Commons, claiming that holding a conference before the end of the present government would be a breach of the Edinburgh pledge, put down a censure motion. A meeting of Balfour and Chamberlain in Downing Street on 26 May brought no solution. That month, in response to renewed hysteria on the subject, Balfour also gave the Commons the findings of an investigation into the possibility of invasion, this time carried out by the Committee of Imperial Defence. The report threw cold water on those who cried for increased military spending to ward off an inevitable 'bolt from the blue'.

For his summer 1905 vacation Alfred sampled the fishing in the waters off Norway. He left London on 25 July and returned on 7 August. During this time, he became involved in the power struggle for military control in India between the Viceroy, Lord Curzon, and the military Commander-in-Chief, Lord Kitchener. Curzon had at first believed Kitchener the right man to implement needed army reforms on the subcontinent; however, the Commander soon began intriguing, in India and Britain, to undercut Curzon and all civilian authority over military matters. Under the constitutional system in place, military affairs were divided between two men. One held executive power, the Commander-in-Chief, and one controlled administrative matters, the Military Member. The latter was nominated by the Viceroy and sat on the ruling council which made final decisions on all matters, army and civilian. It was Kitchener's aim to abolish this 'interference' and to combine supply, finance, politics and army control in himself. To do this he set out first to abolish the power of the Military Member, and then to block Curzon's choice, General Sir Edmund Barrow.

Kitchener used his reputation and a network of friends and spies to rally support at home in the press and in the government. The aim was to bring St John Brodrick, now Secretary of State for India, to Kitchener's side in the dispute. It was an uneven battle, as Curzon's aloof manner handicapped him greatly with journalists and his personal honour made him a poor intriguer. Though he disdained journalists and newspapers, Kitchener knew how to use the press to his advantage, and his allies leaked material to sympathetic journals. When the government published controversial Indian documents which supported Kitchener, Curzon remarked that this 'habit was less in accord with their traditions than with those of the Daily Mail'.[5] The paper did back Kitchener in general, but was far from his most vociferous supporter.

By threatening to resign – a ploy he used often – Kitchener was able to get Brodrick to propose a new scheme in which the Military Member was not abolished, but reduced to an advisory capacity and given a new title, Military Supply Member. Curzon, who had also threatened resignation, found the scheme acceptable and assumed that he would be able to designate the appointee. General Barrow's name was duly sent to London for approval. Despite the fact that Kitchener told Barrow that he thought they could work together, he secretly pushed forward the more pliable and aged General Sir C.H. Scott and told Brodrick that Curzon had named Barrow only because he did not believe in the new scheme and wanted to sabotage it. Consequently, the Secretary of State for India notified Curzon that Barrow was unsatisfactory and that he would soon inform him of the Cabinet's choice.

At this point the owner of the *Daily Mail* offered Curzon an opportunity to state his case in print. He replied:

I am very much obliged for your kind telegram. I could not of course while still Viceroy take advantage of your offer.

I greatly regret that the 'Daily Mail' has been against me in this struggle. Firstly, because I think you have been wrong . . . Secondly, because I regard it as a very serious thing from the constitutional point of view that the Viceroy and the United Government of India should be over-ruled in deference to the opinions or threats of one man, supremely ignorant of India, and . . . thirdly, because you have assisted to destroy a most successful form of military administration and to substitute for it a piece of patch work in which not a person in India believes, and which is destined to a brief and inglorious existence, if not to worse disaster.

. . . It is not likely that I should have resigned or jeopardised my whole career unless there were more in the matter than you suppose. As soon as public opinion in England understands the facts, it will come around –

indeed it appears to me to be doing so rapidly already. I should like to think that you will assist the process of enlightenment.

I have spoken with frankness. And for this no apology is needed.[6]

Despite Curzon's plea, the *Daily Mail* did not come to his side in the controversy. It did, however, congratulate him for his work as Viceroy after his resubmitted resignation of 12 August was accepted. To save embarrassment, the government attributed the action to differences over Curzon's proposal to partition Bengal, not the Barrow affair.

Curzon sent his thanks to the proprietor of the *Daily Mail* for the newspaper's 'tribute', despite the fact that the journal had not come around to his view 'on the merits'. His letter attempted to straighten out some of the mis-statements he found in the leader of 21 August, which reflected the many documents which had been made public by Brodrick on the matter. It was not true, said Curzon, that the Secretary of State 'discovered' he had already offered the post to Barrow. It was not true that Barrow had no administrative experience, as Brodrick said: he had eight years in the military and knew, if anything, 'too much about it'. Curzon continued:

> I will let you into the truth on one more aspect. Kitchener ended by denying that he ever accepted Barrow. That is not true. He accepted him absolutely, frankly and without demur to me, to Barrow himself, and to others. If you have any doubt ask Barrow. I could tell you a good many more things that would make you lift your eyebrows.

In a postscript the Viceroy added, 'One thing I should like you to know. The Army in India are almost unanimously on my side – not on that of Kitchener.'[7]

Curzon might have also said that newspaper and public opinion in India were on his side; nevertheless Kitchener prevailed. Moreover, as Curzon had warned, Kitchener's army reforms proved half-hearted and inadequate. On this failure has been laid the responsibility for later disasters in Mesopotamia. Lord Minto would take Curzon's place as Viceroy, and, though Kitchener dreamed of succeeding him, less pliable politicians would soon be installed in London. Putting the Indian controversy behind him, Sir Alfred travelled to Zurich, spending two weeks touring Switzerland and Germany. On 9 September he boarded the Orient Express in Munich for Paris.

Back at home, the collection of cars continued to increase. After being forced for many years to purchase his automobiles abroad, Sir

Alfred was pleased to commission a Rolls-Royce, the company motto of which was 'All British Motor Cars'. In September, Claude Johnson, one of the managers of Rolls-Royce, sent the plans for the new acquisition. Sir Alfred's interest in motorized vehicles extended to public transport as well. He warned the London Traffic Commission, gathering evidence for a report to be published in 1906, that 'the motor-bus is coming'.[8] The *Daily Mail* also proposed a needed extension of the London tramway system. Other public-service campaigns included a call for a clanging bell on fire engines.

In October 1905 growing tension between Germany and Britain intruded into the *Daily Mail* headlines. Six months earlier the paper had detailed the 'Antics of an Emperor' when the Kaiser visited Tangier and ignited a crisis with France when he criticized French ambitions to dominate Morocco, declared he was visiting an independent state, and demanded equal treatment for German commerce. The volatile situation in Morocco had been defused only when the French government refused to support the confrontational policy of Foreign Minister Delcassé, which led to his resignation. Germany's action was, in part, calculated to divide the partners in the Entente Cordiale; however, Wilhelm's advisers miscalculated badly, as the gambit had the opposite effect – Britain strongly supported French claims in Morocco. On 9 October the *Daily Mail* editorial, 'Germany and the Entente Cordiale', repeated arguments from *Le Matin* that 'the trouble between England and Germany has been largely due to the fact that German statesmen say one thing and do another'. For example, 'they say they are friends, but press their naval armaments. Now they attack their neighbour for being England's friend.' To restore the balance of power in Europe and to ensure the 'disappearance of all inducements to schemes of political adventure on the part of German statesmanship', the *Daily Mail* called for England also to become friends with Russia. To settle the Moroccan crisis, an international conference was scheduled for January 1906 at Algeciras in Spain. Up to the outbreak of the Great War, Germany never understood that bluster and threats only frightened potential foes into closer adherence and, step by step, brought war nearer.

On the domestic front, after years of delaying the inevitable, Balfour resigned at last on 4 December, in the hope that the Liberals, divided over Ireland and the Empire, would not be able to form a strong government. The *Daily Mail* praised Balfour's record in office, pointing to advances in diplomacy with Japan and France. In South Africa, he was credited with getting back what Great Britain had 'lost at Majuba

Hill'.[9] At home the achievements listed included the Irish Land Act, the Workmen's Compensation Act, the Education Act and the reconstruction of the Navy. The only fault noted was the failure to address the Army question. The newspaper trumpeted Lord Roberts's Newcastle 'Appeal to England' to look to the Army and his call for a nation trained to resist invasion. To replace Balfour, the King called on Sir Henry Campbell-Bannerman, who successfully put together a Liberal regime.

As the fortunes of 'C.-B.' rose, Lord Rosebery's Liberal League collapsed. Despite a vow not to do so, several prominent members joined the Cabinet, including Herbert Asquith, Sir Edward Grey and R.B. Haldane, at the Exchequer, the Foreign Office and the War Office, respectively. Campbell-Bannerman, who proved much more able as Prime Minister than he had been as party leader, refused to be manoeuvred into the House of Lords as the Liberal Imperialists had plotted. One other appointment of note saw David Lloyd George join the government as President of the Board of Trade. The *Daily Mail* favourably appraised some of the new Liberal ministers, but had reservations. It gave its approval to Grey at the Foreign Office, Lord Elgin at the Colonial Office and Haldane at the War Office. The last was seen as a 'man of front rank in intelligence and grasping a subject'. Although he had in the past been something of a 'blue-water' extremist, the paper believed that he 'may succeed if he obtains the freedom of action a reforming War Minister requires'.[10] Unfortunately, the paper saw the 'seeds of dissension and disintegration' in the Home Rule aspirations of 'Mr. Redmond and the Irish Party'. The new government, according to the *Daily Mail*, had 'now before it the twofold duty of defeating any surrender to separatism in Ireland, and making real the union of the Empire'.[11]

When Balfour presented his Resignation Honours List to the King, the sovereign once again suggested that Alfred Harmsworth's name be appended. Balfour explained to the King that he had not included the owner of the *Daily Mail* because he had so recently been made a baronet, but that he recognized that Sir Alfred was a gentleman to whom the Party owed much, and who occupied a great position in the country and that he would 'be happy to add' his name to the final list.[12] Balfour had left the business of honours largely to the party Chief Whip, Alexander Acland-Hood, who was greatly disturbed by the King's interference. He told J.B. Sandars, Balfour's secretary, that

obviously the king means Harmsworth to have a Peerage. If he doesn't get it now he will get it when CB makes his Peers on taking office – we should then lose all his money and influence – I very much dislike the business, but as we can't stop it in the future why make so handsome a present to the other side! Of course some of our men will be furious and I can't blame them. We have to weigh that . . . against . . . giving an enormous card to the other side – I think in this case we might allow our virtue to be raped.[13]

This was not a very politically astute estimate, as 'CB' would have been more likely to drink hemlock than to have recommended an honour for one of his chief press antagonists. Further, receiving the prize from such a quarter would also have been difficult for the owner of the *Daily Mail*.

Sir Alfred's 8 December diary noted simply, 'heard today the King had conferred a peerage upon me'. Telegrams and letters of congratulations again poured into Carmelite House. The proprietor had been at Reggie Nicholson's when the one which perhaps meant the most to him arrived, from his mother: 'I am feeling very proud today fond love.' Even the usually languid and impassive Balfour reportedly clasped his arm around Alfred's shoulder while telling him that he was 'the youngest peer who has been created' and that he was 'very proud'.[14] He apparently did not tell the new baron that it was the King's intercession that had made the feat possible.

Outrage in some quarters over the peerage was predictable. Many questioned what Alfred Harmsworth had done to merit elevation equal to men such as Sir Algernon Borthwick (Lord Glenesk) of the *Morning Post* and Sir Edward Lawson (Lord Burnham) of the *Daily Telegraph*. A 16 December article in the *Saturday Review* entitled 'The Adulteration of the Peerage' exemplified the outcry, warning that a 'House of Lords composed of plutocrats will not survive the test of modernity'. The piece went on about Harmsworth that

Beginning the world with nothing he has made a very large fortune by the production of certain newspapers. No man makes a pile without the possession of certain qualities, which are obviously rare, but which do not in our opinion necessarily entitle their possessors to a seat in the House of Lords . . . We say advisedly that he has done more than any man of his generation to pervert and enfeeble the mind of the multitude . . . Nor has he even done this mischief for the sake of a political party, for he has been true to no party, and has made himself at different times the mouthpiece of Lord Rosebery, Mr. Chamberlain, and Mr. Balfour . . . We fail to discover in his record any performance of those higher duties to the State or those wider services to humanity, which alone entitle a citizen to become a peer.[15]

The owner of the *Daily Mail* had remarked that 'when I want a peerage I will pay for it like an honest man', and charges that the honour had been bought circulated widely.[16] The King's intercession led to rumours that £100,000 had passed to both Edward and his mistress, Mrs Keppell. Liberal papers reported the large sums that had passed into the coffers of the Opposition. The *Saturday Review* declared that

> the 'fountain of honour' has become . . . a spring of dishonour . . . Two Sterns and a Harmsworth are a severe strain upon the patience and respect of the British nation. Is it true or false that the peerages of Michelham and Northcliffe were sold for so much cash down? And did the cash go into the war-chest of the Conservative party? . . . that these peerages were conferred for a sincere belief in the public merits of the recipients or from any other mercenary considerations is plainly incredible.[17]

However, payment beyond £50,000 recently put into the *Manchester Courier* (and Alfred's other publishing efforts on behalf of the Party since 1894) was probably unnecessary. Although Balfour did not initiate the peerage, currying continued support for the coming election and beyond would have been considered as important as the efforts during the previous decade.

Despite the fact that he had impressed the King sufficiently for him to suggest elevation to the peerage, Alfred Harmsworth would never be accepted by the majority of the Edwardian elite, particularly the landed aristocracy. The attitude he faced has been eloquently summed up by the historian Alfred Gollin:

> a chief source of the hostility that confronted him lay in the fact that he was so different from the other members of the ruling class of his time. They resented his power, his influence, his ability, and most of all, his refusal to conform to their standards . . . the established classes were hostile to Lord Northcliffe because he came from a different background, because he had clawed his way to the top, because he was required, as an outsider, to have recourse to different methods when he sought to clutch at authority and grasp for power. The ordinary rulers of Britain were ruthless enough but a man of Northcliffe's type had to be harder, tougher, more openly brutal, or else he would perish. He had no traditional base to stand upon. The essence of his success lay in the fact that he had always avoided the ordinary course, he had beaten his way to a prominent position by novel means, and was not prepared to abandon them.[18]

Harmsworth also faced the hostility, across the North Sea, of Wilhelm II, who rarely saw eye to eye with his Uncle 'Bertie'. During a Christmas visit to Germany, the South African 'gold-bug' Alfred Beit reported that the Kaiser turned their conversation to the attacks of the British press, which he felt poisoned Anglo-German relations. Beit assured the Kaiser that he would do all he could to improve matters. In response, Wilhelm instructed him to go 'for our chief opponents there, Moberly Bell and Harmsworth, whom His Majesty is making a Lord'.[19]

Untouched by or unaware of all the criticism, Alfred turned to the question of a title for his letters patent. Young Wrench was his aide in consulting the College of Arms. The choice finally leaned towards a title named after the geographical features near Elmwood, such as Kingsgate, but a letter from Lord Avebury, who resided there, asked Alfred not to take the name. Avebury instead suggested St Peter's, another site nearby. Elmwood itself was abandoned because, Alfred said, it was 'the wood they use for coffins'. After Broadstairs was almost chosen, the final designation became Northcliffe, after a feature of the sea coast near Elmwood. In Napoleonic fashion, bees were incorporated in the coat of arms, and the new baron would be able to scrawl the initial 'N' at the end of messages in the imperial manner. The motto 'Beni Qui Sedulo' was translated by one wag as 'Blessed is the busy-body.'[20]

While a title was being chosen, the election campaign began. The Liberals, already united against Tariff Reform, had also made a secret agreement with Ramsay MacDonald, the secretary of the Labour Representation Committee (LRC), an alliance of trade unions and socialists which aimed to elect Labour MPs. This covenant ensured that the two parties would not cancel each other out in a number of constituencies. The outlook for the Unionists, who remained divided over fiscal policy, looked gloomy at best. Echoing the continued reservations of its proprietor about Chamberlain's plan, the *Daily Mail* supported Balfour's hybrid version of protection. The Conservative leader declared himself against a 'general tariff', stating that it would be 'alien' to Britain and that he would not lead a 'party of protection'. The newspaper revealed that, though Balfour was against a general tariff, he did wish to 'strengthen the hand of the British Government in negotiations with foreign states as in the conditions under which British goods are to be appraised in their markets'.[21]

On 21 December, at the Albert Hall, Campbell-Bannerman announced the Liberal programme, in which vague pledges to support

Home Rule and cut defence expenditures were combined with campaigns against food taxes, the unpopular Education Act of 1902 and the policy of 'Chinese Slavery' in South Africa. Free Trade was declared the key issue. The next morning's *Daily Mail* proclaimed that the Liberal Party would 'attack capital, assail private enterprise, undo the Union, reverse the Education Act, cripple the one industry of South Africa, reduce the navy and weaken the army'. The jeremiad continued that the Liberal policies would mean Home Rule for Ireland, revive the Kitchener controversy, tax ground values at home, and stop the importation of Chinese labour to South Africa. This final injustice, the paper asserted, would mean the 'Doom of All Further Expansion' in the colony.[22] On the 27th, the *Daily Mail* revealed its prediction for the election: a 120-vote Liberal–Labour majority.

Attempting to deflect the campaign away from 'food taxes' and 'Chinese Slavery', the New Year's Day 1906 *Daily Mail* declared that Ireland was the clearest campaign issue. 'C-B's Reward' for Home Rule would be the votes of the Irish in Great Britain. The following morning the newspaper revealed the 'Truth About Chinese Labour and Preference' as stated by Balfour and Chamberlain. At Leamington, the Conservative leader dubbed as 'fables' both the stories that Chinese labour kept out British workers and the tales of bad conditions in the mines. In fact the coolies were well paid, worked for five years only, and then were sent home. This policy, argued Balfour, had helped many industries recover from the Boer War. To label the practices 'slavery' was a 'foolish and atrocious falsehood'. In the following weeks the *Daily Mail* called for Campbell-Bannerman to stop the Chinese Slavery 'Hoax'. On the fiscal front the *Daily Mail* repeated Chamberlain's argument that his plan represented reform, not protection, and noted the 'Flow of Vituperation' over the issue.[23] When Chamberlain was 'howled down' at Derby, the *Daily Mail* lectured the 'Free Traders' on 'Free Speech'.[24] However, it approved of some Liberal proclamations, including Haldane's call for efficiency, as well as 'more men and more money if necessary' for the Army.

The *Daily Mail* also closely detailed the many appearances of one of the Liberal candidates, Winston Churchill. The newspaper dubbed him the 'star' of the campaign as he set styles in hats and gave demonstrations of 'Jiu Jitsu'. During the campaign, Churchill often found himself under physical attack by women outraged by his declarations of opposition to female suffrage. Many other candidates were likewise buffeted. To separate these activists from less violent suffragists, the 10 January

Daily Mail has been credited with first applying the diminutive appellation 'Suffragette' to these strident women.[25] Rather than rise to this intended insult, the group, led by the formidable Emmeline Pankhurst, defiantly accepted the label. Northcliffe shared Churchill's views on the question; consequently, his publications attempted to deny the suffragettes the publicity they sought and ignored or downplayed their activities.

Three days before polling began for the general election, Northcliffe returned to London from Monte Carlo, where he had celebrated the New Year. The editors of the *Daily Mail* and its *Overseas* edition, Thomas Marlowe and John Evelyn Wrench, devised a scheme for flashing the results all over London. *Daily Mail* magic lanterns projected the results on the Embankment and in Trafalgar Square. Signal rockets of differing colours were fired off to enlighten more distant watchers. Wrench manned the phones at Carmelite House, relaying the results to Northcliffe at his home.

Balfour was defeated at Manchester on the first day, 13 January – a harbinger of dire things to come for the Conservatives, who were routed in the voting. The final numbers for the new House of Commons showed 401 Liberals, 83 Irish Nationalists and 29 Labour MPs. In the last category, more than half owed their seats to the pre-election agreement with the Liberals. The Opposition was made up of 132 Conservatives and 25 Liberal Unionists.[26] The *Daily Mail* put down the 'terrifying Liberal Hurricane' to multiple causes: the natural swing of the political pendulum after years of Conservative rule; the Chinese-labour question; the political unpopularity both of the Education Act and of the heavy taxation that was a legacy of the Boer War. Finally, the defeat was also laid at the feet of the fiscal question and the unfair cries of 'food taxes' aimed at the Conservative Party. Nevertheless, the paper did not consider the results the victory for Free Trade that many Liberal journals proclaimed. It called for the defeated Party to unite and to regain power through 'fiscal reform, not socialism'.[27] The next day's edition recognized the 'Rise of Labour' in the victory, but predicted that the electoral alliance of socialists and Liberals could not last.

In the aftermath of the election debacle, Balfour, who returned to Parliament when a seat was vacated for him in late February, commented in a letter to Northcliffe that he was

quite confident that there are much deeper causes at work than those with which, for the last 20 years, we have been familiar. I regard the enormous increase in the Labour vote (an increase which cannot be measured merely by the number returned of Labour members strictly so-called) as a reflection in this country – faint I hope – of what is going on on the Continent; and, if so, 1906 will be remarkable for something much more important than the fall of a Government which has been ten years in office![28]

Following Balfour's lead, the *Daily Mail* editorial of 18 January called the result the 'Revolution of 1906', which was more sweeping than that of 1832. The Labour representatives, in the opinion of the journal, knew what they wanted, and the newspaper 'frankly prefers them to old Members who came to Parliament to enrich themselves'. But, in an article by the Labour MP Philip Snowden, 'The People's Party', which made it obvious that Labour would tax heavily the fortunes of the very rich, the journal printed a warning to the 'landed and commercial interest' of what lay before it if more were elected.[29] The next day Wrench saw his chief at lunch and the two discussed 'the absolute change which is coming over English politics'.[30]

Northcliffe also discussed the Unionist future with Chamberlain, who complained of Balfour's intransigence. A serious split in the Unionist ranks was averted by the so-called Valentine Compact, a Valentine's Day exchange of letters by Chamberlain and Balfour, stating their positions. This was widely greeted as a victory for Chamberlain; in reality Balfour and his supporters remained in control of the Party while the onus of 'proving' the necessity of a general tariff and corn tax remained with the supporters of Chamberlain.[31] These received a much more serious blow five months later when Chamberlain suffered a stroke that left him an invalid sequestered at his country home, Highbury. The burden of carrying on the fight and transmitting the messages of his father to the faithful fell to Austen Chamberlain.

Though the Unionist Party had been defeated, for the first time the owner of the *Daily Mail* had a personal reason to look forward to the new Parliament. On 14 February he recorded in his diary, 'I took my seat today in the House of Lords, where I was introduced by Lord Glenesk and Lord Montagu of Beaulieu.'[32] Four days later, Baron Northcliffe of the Isle of Thanet in the County of Kent was back at Westminster for the King's Speech and the opening of Parliament. However, further appearances would be extremely rare. He realized full well his shortcomings in debate, and the many enemies that surrounded him in the House of Lords. He also soon witnessed a close lesson of what could befall even an eloquent statesman in the new political atmosphere. After Lord Milner's maiden speech later that month on the government's South African policy, the former Proconsul found himself pilloried mercilessly for permitting the flogging of Chinese workers during his tenure in South Africa. In the end Milner was censured by the Liberal-dominated Commons, while resolutions of support for his policies were passed in the House of Lords, where the Conservatives maintained control. This episode marked a hardening of inter-party hostility, even beyond the Tariff Reform versus Free Trade bitterness of the three previous years, which would continue until the Great War. Rather than hazard the parliamentary minefield, Northcliffe continued to use his papers to speak out on issues which might have been addressed in the Lords, such as military preparedness and the German threat.

With the election over, other news intruded. The Algeciras Conference on Morocco opened in January with the British represented by Sir Arthur Nicolson. While the Conference met, the *Daily Mail* revealed troop movements and treated the Entente with France as an alliance, much to the displeasure of the new British government. Edgar Wallace, sent to Algeciras by the paper, cabled colourful, pro-French accounts of the proceedings. After three months an accord was reached which seemed to settle the matter, but in fact left France with the upper hand. This result soured Germany on conferences and fed her fears of 'encirclement', which would grow until August 1914. Soon after the Conference, secret meetings began between the British and French to discuss military co-operation against the common foe.

The Liberal rise to power, many believed, made more vital than ever the need for constant pressure on the government to ensure sufficient military preparations were made to protect the Empire. Balfour had stayed in office through many trials in the preceding years in part to ensure that several military programmes were completed. He had declared on 15 January, when defeat was clear, that 'the great Unionist Party should still control, whether in power or whether in opposition, the destinies of this great Empire'.[33] Outside politics, in the previous year Field Marshal Lord Roberts had assumed the presidency of the National Service League, which agitated for compulsory army training and service. Northcliffe and his publications supported the efforts of the League in its unsuccessful campaign to build a British counter to the German 'nation in arms'. The Field Marshal and the press lord joined forces in one of the most notable episodes of the press campaign against Germany.

After four months of scouting locales by the author, in March 1906 the *Daily Mail* published the first instalment of *The Invasion of 1910*, in which the novelist William Le Queux updated his *Answers* campaign of twelve years before in a new serial detailing a German invasion of Britain. Le Queux had met Roberts to ensure that the fictional strategy would be sound, but military considerations were tempered by Northcliffe's concern for sales. Consequently, the routes of the rampaging Uhlan hordes were often determined as much by possible circulation gains as by worth as military objectives.[34] A massive advertising campaign boomed the series. One eyewitness described a 'long file of veterans in spiked helmets and Prussian-blue uniforms parading moodily down Oxford Street . . . They carried sandwich boards to inform all whom it might concern that the great William Le Queux . . . was about to add to his laurels by reporting day by day in the columns of England's most wide-awake newspaper the progress of her great Invasion.'[35] As well as supporting Roberts and the National Service League, Northcliffe also offered aid to other conservative pressure groups, including the Navy League. On the naval front, Wrench recorded in his diary on 10 February that the 'finest battleship in the world was launched today by the King'.[36] After this launching of the *Dreadnought*, nothing would be the same in the armaments race with Germany.

Northcliffe escaped from newspaper and international pressures during a lengthy April stay in France, where he exchanged his ninety-horsepower model for a 'new 35 Mercedes'. Back at Sutton Place he discussed the state of British automobile development with John Montagu and another enthusiast, H.F. Locke King. Northcliffe complained that one reason why Britain's vehicles fared so poorly in international competition was that they had no legal place to be tested at high speeds. Locke King soon drew up plans for a three-mile private circuit at Brooklands, his estate at Weybridge, Surrey. Northcliffe was a charter member of the Brooklands Automobile Racing Club, which opened the next year.[37] On 2 May Northcliffe's knee, which had been troubling him for some time, was operated on. After two weeks in bed he was finally back at his office on 31 May.

Rehabilitation continued in June as Northcliffe sailed again for America, leaving on the 27th on the *Kaiser Wilhelm Der Grosse*. He arrived in New York a week later, nursing a cold. On 6 July he dined with Arthur Brisbane of the New York *Journal* and Sir Joseph Ward, the Prime Minister of New Zealand. In the following days he visited

Newport and Boston, before heading north to Canada, stopping at Montreal and Quebec on his way to Newfoundland. Harold and one of their employees, Mayson Beeton, had scouted a 3,100 square mile tract of seemingly limitless spruce and water power on the Grand Falls of the River of Exploits. This largest of the Harmsworth enterprises – including a town site, railroad, steamship facility and paper mills – was incorporated as the Anglo-Newfoundland Development Company. Following the American example of vertical integration, before many years had passed the family would control almost all aspects of their business, from the tree to the news-stand. Northcliffe spent a week at the site, where he recorded the 'mosquitoes dreadful'.[38] He sent his 'Mummy dear' a note describing the 'vast prosperity of Canada; no poor, homes for millions unborn'.[39]

While at Grand Falls, Northcliffe received the news that his brother St John had been involved in a serious motor-car accident. Northcliffe cut short the visit and returned to London to give what aid he could to his brother's recovery. St John – called 'Bonchie' by the family – had left the publishing businesses to build his own company around the Perrier spring in France. Cecil later wrote that 'the thought of it, the management and control of it, and its advertising were all his'.[40] Even the shape of the bottles and their labels were St John's design. The auto accident, which fractured his spine, left him confined to a wheelchair for life, despite the ministrations of the best medical experts money could buy.

Having done all he could for his brother, Northcliffe travelled to Paris, where his fascination with technology led him to witness the first successful aeroplane flight in Europe. This was carried out by Alberto Santos-Dumont, whose career as a balloonist Alfred had followed with interest in the previous years. On 23 October 1906, at Bagatelle in the Bois de Boulogne, Santos-Dumont managed a flight of fifty metres in a fragile kite-like craft. The fact that the Wright brothers had pioneered aeroplane flight in December 1903 was unknown to the astonished onlookers, most of whom believed they had witnessed a revolutionary milestone. The 25 October *Daily Mail* carried a brief article on the 'Triumph' two days before in France. From this point Northcliffe became a tireless backer of the development of a British aeroplane force, and air power soon joined army and navy preparedness as *Daily Mail* campaign themes. Earlier that year, after the first woman had crossed the English Channel in a balloon, the owner of the *Daily Mail* appointed Harry Harper as the world's first 'Air Correspondent'. The Santos-Dumont flight changed Harper's career for ever. He was dispatched to France to interview the intrepid flyer, and the paper embarked on a campaign to 'make the nation air minded'.

Santos-Dumont flew again on 12 November, this time for 722 feet. A short notice in the *Daily Mail* drew a rebuke to the editor from the proprietor that the news was not that 'Santos-Dumont flies 722 feet', but that 'England is no longer an island. There will be no more sleeping safely behind the wooden walls of old England with the Channel our safety moat. It means the aerial chariots of a foe descending on British soil if war comes.'[41] Santos-Dumont told Harper that within a year he would be able to fly 100 miles, and *Le Matin* offered a £10,000 prize for the winner of a London-to-Paris race in 1908. To foster British development of a competitive machine, the proprietor of the *Daily Mail* matched this with £10,000 for the first 'aeronaut' to fly from London to Manchester. Santos-Dumont sent Northcliffe a note of congratulations on the offer, which, he said, 'will give enormous impetus to the construction of aeroplanes'. Others were less generous. Competitors ridiculed the *Daily Mail* prize as just another publicity stunt. The *Star* offered £10 million 'to the flying machine of any description whatsoever that flies ten miles from London and back to the point of departure . . . One offer is as safe as the other.'[42] It would be only four years before the Manchester-to-London flight became a reality.

In November Northcliffe also attended to more down-to-earth business, travelling to Grimsby to open the new paper mill which was to supply the *Daily Mirror*. At the end of the month furious preparations were in the final stages for a *Daily Mail* Braille edition. Wrench, who was in charge of the project, recorded that he left the office for only ten minutes all day to 'eat a dozen oysters and a glass of champagne to revive me'. He had two 'specially skilled readers' peruse the advance copies. As a relief from the hard work, on the afternoon of 30 November Northcliffe had the Zanzigs, a pair of 'thought-readers', come in from the Alhambra to give what Wrench described as a 'marvellous demonstration in the chief's room'.[43] The edition for the blind was published, at a loss, until the outbreak of the Great War.

Five days before Christmas Northcliffe 'called in to see Berkeley Square for the last time as I have sold the home'.[44] To replace it, a nine years' lease was taken on 22 St James's Place overlooking Green Park. As in Berkeley Square, the new house was a smaller residence surrounded by great mansions of the aristocracy. He was in Monte Carlo for New Year's Eve.

For medical and legal reasons Northcliffe spent a good part of 1907 out of England. He complained of 'burning eyes', and was told by one specialist that an operation would be needed. Continued exhaustion from overwork led the doctors to recommend rest abroad. The legal problems sprang from a newspaper campaign launched against the Lever Brothers' 'Soap Trust'. The *Daily Mail* and its associated papers carried out an American-styled 'muckraking' crusade against the proposed combination of Lever Brothers and several other soap companies, which, the Northcliffe press warned, would destroy competition, increase prices for all, and corner raw-materials markets – all this at the same time as the Harmsworth publications had an ever-increasing share of total circulations and were ensuring their own supply of paper in Newfoundland, where a new town and mill were rising out of the primeval forest. The Lever brothers, William and James, had founded a model industrial city of their own, Port Sunlight, to manufacture their products.

Fewer soap firms also meant reduced advertising revenues, and some have seen this as a major motivating factor behind the newspaper campaign. A £6,000 contract with the *Daily Mail* was among those suspended in a planned £200,000 industry-wide promotional retrenchment.[45] However, Northcliffe was more concerned with keeping up circulations than with advertising. He also admired the trust-busting Theodore Roosevelt and was a friend of S.S. McClure, owner of *McClure's Magazine*, a leading American muckraking journal. The proprietor of the *Daily Mail* commented at the time, 'We already have the tobacco trust operating here. Where is it going to end?'[46] Whatever his motivations – mercenary or enlightened – he soon discovered that the libel laws of the United States allowed its press a latitude not found in Britain.

With no huge oil or money or steel or railway conglomerates to attack, the *Daily Mail*, *Evening News* and *Daily Mirror* had to settle for soap, charging that the Lever proposals were 'Squeezing the Public' and a 'Cruel Blow to the Poor'. The newspapers questioned the contents of soap products, and worried for the workers who would lose their jobs. After Lever Brothers reduced their soap tablets from sixteen ounces to fifteen, the headlines questioned 'How Fifteen Ounces Make a Pound?' and proclaimed 'Trust Soap Already Dearer'. William Lever (later Lord Leverhulme) was caricatured as the grasping owner of 'Port Moonshine', the Soap Trust shop shown adorned with the slogan 'We Don't Care About You. We Want More of Your Money.' The campaign forced the company to return to threepenny one-pound tablets. While

Lever Brothers shares fell drastically in value and sales plummeted by 60 per cent, the *Daily Mail* crowed that 'Public Opinion Smashed the Soap Trust'.[47]

Convinced that he had done nothing wrong and that the attack of the Northcliffe press had been motivated by the loss of advertising revenue and not concern for the public, William Lever decided to strike back. To regain the real losses to his enterprises, and their reputation, Lever, and many of the smaller soap firms, brought legal action. To ascertain whether he had a case, Lever consulted the noted lawyer F.E. Smith (later Lord Birkenhead). Asked to give an answer in one day, Smith fortified himself for a long night of study with a bottle of champagne and two dozen oysters. He replied the next morning that 'There is no answer to this action for libel and the damages must be enormous.'[48] In fact they would be the largest up to that time. Before the dispute went to court, Northcliffe offered a public apology and an agreement to cease the attacks, but matters had gone too far for Lever, who commented that the 'cheek' of the *Daily Mail* and its proprietor was 'simply colossal'.[49] Intervention by Sir Thomas Lipton, a mutual friend of the antagonists, also failed to bring the two together.

Lever's case was argued at Liverpool before Mr Justice A.T. Lawrence by one of the most successful trial advocates of the time, Sir Edward Carson, who had been Solicitor-General in the Balfour government. The defence of the *Daily Mail* and its proprietor was handled by another noted legal mind of the period, Rufus Isaacs (later Lord Reading). Isaacs was a skilled advocate, but no match for Carson, who put his own client in the witness box in July 1907 and called for Isaacs to 'play cricket with us' and do the same.[50] Isaacs had no such intention, and Northcliffe, to escape being compelled to give damning testimony, went abroad. He cabled George Sutton from Paris that he had urged Kennedy Jones 'to stop soap scare that I cannot carry increasing burden of work; unless free from all complications. Told him none of us can be cross-examined on motives of soap cases and that if I am examined should be obliged to tell truth.'[51]

The futility of his position was so apparent after the first day of testimony that Isaacs recommended that his client settle. This was agreed to, and Lever accepted £50,000 in recompense. Unfortunately, this did not end things. Other suits followed which brought the final total to £151,000 in cash and advertising.[52] Northcliffe absorbed much of the loss himself. Trying to put the best possible face on a rather inglorious episode, the *Daily Mail* commented that the 'somewhat embittered controversy' had been undertaken in a 'no doubt mistaken sense of public duty'.[53] For a time it appeared that Thomas Marlowe might be sacked over this affair, but in the end the editor of the *Daily Mail* survived and, in future, was more cautious in following the commands of his chief, on whom he later placed responsibility for the whole campaign.

In the same month that the judgment at Liverpool went against Northcliffe, in another court a decision was rendered that would, in the end, allow him to fulfil a long-held desire – the acquisition of *The Times*.

8

The Times *is Harmsworth's,*
1907–1908

THROUGH A COMBINATION of failed leadership, mismanagement, disagreements among the shareholders, and general decrepitude *The Times* had declined precipitously from its mid-nineteenth-century pinnacle as 'The Thunderer'. For many years the business property had been in two parts. The printing division, which contained the machinery and the freehold at Printing House Square, remained solely in the hands of the founding Walter family, headed by Arthur Walter and his half-brother Godfrey. The brothers also owned the largest block of shares in the other portion, the newspaper. The remaining shares had been subdivided over the years into many pieces. The smaller partners were angered by the exorbitant printing profits they believed were being reaped by the Walters, while their own newspaper dividends suffered.

Another source of dissension at the newspaper sprang from a subsidiary operation which since 1896 had published volumes such as *The Times Atlas*. The modest revenues generated by this activity increased dramatically when the Walters were persuaded to allow two Americans, Horace Everett Hooper and William Montgomery Jackson, to offer a discounted set of the moribund ninth edition of the *Encyclopædia Britannica* to the subscribers of the paper. First-year sales of the encyclopedia in 1898 multiplied the profits of the book-publishing group by more than ten, to £11,830. Such success led other volumes to be added to the list, all sold by 'The *Times* System of Easy Payments'.[1] In the view of many of the minority partners (and many readers), this 'alien' activity was hardly fitting and proper for the dignity of the venerable newspaper. Very few realized that the books, and the advertising reaped from them, kept the journal afloat.[2]

In July 1907 the Chancery Court consented to a minority shareholder's petition in the case *Sibley* v. *Walter* and ordered the dissolution of *The Times* partnership and sale of the newspaper, under the supervision of Mr Justice Warrington. This decision brought to an end the guerrilla war that had been carried on with the controlling Walters since 1885, over the insistence of the family that living shareholders should not dispose of their holdings to outsiders.[3] Among these disgruntled individuals were those with whom Northcliffe had discussed buying into *The Times* more than once over the previous decade. A new struggle now began to resolve the future course of the paper.

By the end of 1907 several groups, according to the rumour mill, were near to completing a deal for control of *The Times*. Arthur Pearson, proprietor of the *Daily Express* and the *Standard*, believed that he had gained the prize after a provisional agreement was reached with the Walters. By one account, Northcliffe learned of this development only because he found himself seated next to Sir Alexander Henderson, one of Pearson's backers, at a dinner party which he had tried his best to dodge. However he gained the knowledge, he was greatly disturbed that he might lose the possession he had so long coveted. To do so to his greatest rival – the same man who had bested him over the *Standard* three years before – would be a double blow. He asked one of his legal advisers, Sir George Lewis, to 'find out what you can',[4] then left for France, leaving the matter in the hands of Lewis and George Sutton. Something of a palace coup – engineered principally by Charles Frederick Moberly Bell, the sixty-one-year-old manager, who had held that post since 1890 – ensured that *The Times* would fall into Northcliffe's hands.

In their negotiations with Pearson, the Walters had not taken into consideration two key employees, both conservative guardians of the paper's traditions: Moberly Bell and George Earle Buckle, the editor since 1884. The staff of *The Times* gained their first warning of the proposed purchase in a piece planted in the 5 January 1908 *Observer* by Northcliffe. Buckle promptly wrote to Arthur Walter that it was a 'shock to me, as the principal servant of the Paper . . . that you should . . . bring in an outsider into the heart of the office . . . without consulting me'.[5] Bell told Walter that he could not 'help feeling deeply hurt at the want of confidence you have shown in one who has tried to serve you faithfully and who regarded you as a friend'.[6] The *Observer* notice, ordered exactly for this purpose, forced *The Times* to make its own announcement two days later that, subject to the approval of the court, the 'business management will be reorganised by Mr. C. Arthur Pearson, the proposed managing director'. This amounted to a public dismissal of Bell and Buckle, neither of whom Pearson was likely to keep in place. When asked by F. Harcourt Kitchin, the assistant manager of the paper, what he was going to do about 'this Pearson business', Bell replied that he meant to 'Smash it.'[7]

Northcliffe sent Pearson a note of congratulations, with a suggestion that he be interviewed by the *Daily Mail*. Pearson demurred, stating that he did not wish to 'rub things in' or seem to 'push myself at all' in the still uncompleted negotiations with the Walter family.[8] Nevertheless, the 8 January *Daily Mail* printed a profile of Pearson, including Joseph Chamberlain's description of him as 'the greatest hustler I have ever known'. The paper went on that Pearson's success sprang from 'the habit he contracted as a young man of never wasting time and always working with extraordinary speed'. From the Ritz in Paris, Northcliffe had contributed to this piece via a series of secret telegrams to Kennedy Jones and Sutton sent in the name of Northcliffe's Austrian valet, Joseph Brunnbauer. Another article in the *Observer*, four days later, spoke of the 'sensational' things Pearson had done in publishing. These disclosures, and others printed at the time, had the intended effect of disturbing those who worried about the reputation and future course of *The Times* – including, most particularly, Arthur Walter and Moberly Bell. Walter began to reconsider his commitment, while Bell actively sought another buyer. Meanwhile, the Pearson forces, believing themselves victorious, held a celebratory dinner at the Savoy, complete with an ice sculpture of *The Times*'s premises at Printing House Square.

At the same hotel, Kennedy Jones arranged a meeting with Horace Hooper, as a result of which Hooper recommended Northcliffe to Bell as a possible financial saviour. Bell was at first opposed to this proposition, seeing little difference between the two leaders of the popular press. Soon, however, with a preliminary hearing before the court looming at the end of January, Bell agreed at least to meet Northcliffe to discover if an agreement might be possible which would rescue the staff and the character of the newspaper. A cable from Kennedy Jones appealed to Northcliffe to save *The Times* for the Empire, but this exhortation was hardly needed. The press lord had made no secret of his desire to own the most prestigious British journal, and, if it was within his ability to do so, he meant to gain control of the newspaper and to thwart Pearson in the bargain.

The first step was to ensure that an ironclad arrangement had not already been reached. From his previous experience, Northcliffe was well aware of the 'very litigious' nature of some of those intimately involved with *The Times*. Before allowing himself to be 'carried away by zeal', he instructed Kennedy Jones to find out the facts.[9] Once he ascertained that the Pearson plan was not, in his chief's words, 'riveted and finished', during the next ten days Kennedy Jones negotiated a draft agreement with Bell. The latter revelled in the great game of intrigue that ensued, at one point speaking to his wife on the telephone in Arabic to shield a planned meeting with Northcliffe. On 18 January he had a notice printed in *The Times* which qualified the first announcement: 'We desire to call attention to the fact that such statement referred only to certain negotiations as being in progress; and further to state, as the fact is, that no sale of *The Times* has yet been effected, nor has any decision been arrived at as to the mode or terms of any such sale'.

To be acceptable to the court, bids for control of the paper had to come from the existing partners. Consequently, Bell persuaded General John Barton Sterling, the largest shareholder outside the Walter brothers, to withdraw his support from the Pearson scheme and to join him. Others besides Sterling made their discontent known to the Walters. Another large shareholder, Sir Edward Tennant, also removed himself from the proposed arrangement. Buckle revealed to Arthur Walter that Balfour, Lansdowne, Curzon, the Chamberlains, Edward Grey and John Morley were 'all agreed in deploring and strongly deprecating the introduction of Pearson'.[10] Meanwhile, secret negotiations, complete with code names for the participants, were carried on to draw up the details of the Bell-Sterling offer to be made with the backing of 'X' – Northcliffe. Rumours swirled of imminent American financial intervention, and the names of a long list of English notables were whispered as alternatives to Pearson. The backing of the Wiener Bank Verein for a rival group led to reports that the Kaiser was involved.

Northcliffe stationed himself on the Continent, in suites at the Hôtel Christol in Boulogne and the Ritz in Paris. He hoped that his remaining out of England would dampen speculation about his involvement and therefore both keep the price as low as possible and prevent a negative reaction similar to that which had greeted the announcement of Pearson's name. Bell – 'Canton' in the coded messages – informed Arthur Walter that he had located a more suitable buyer for the paper than Pearson, but added that he could not disclose a name at present. The harassed owner accepted this peculiar situation on the manager's assurance that he was working in the best interests of *The Times* and because he had also become uneasy about the Pearson arrangement. It is also likely that he knew very well the name that was not mentioned.

Northcliffe crossed to London, and at the Sackville Street offices of his private accountant, T.E. Mackenzie, first talked in person to Bell about the terms on 4 February. The interview was brief, with both men bluntly putting their cards on the table. Northcliffe stated his intention to buy *The Times*, with or without aid. Bell later recalled that, when he asked Northcliffe what he intended to do with the paper, the reply was

> I want to make it worth 3d. I think the printing is bad and the make up abominable. Your law reports and Parliamentary reports are good, but they ought to be fuller. Your City news can be greatly improved. Your foreign correspondents are excellent, but you do not give enough space to foreign news – in fact I want to improve every department of the paper, but as to the policy of the paper, I do not want to interfere at all – that is a matter for the Editor.[11]

With regard to the staff, Northcliffe told Bell, 'I do not know any of them, but I do not want to get rid of anyone who does his work well – I want as little change as possible – the same Editor, the same Foreign Editor, the same Manager, the same Solicitor, and so far as possible the same staff.' Pleased by the forthrightness of these statements and with most of his fears for the staff and the policy of the paper satisfied, Bell agreed to work with Northcliffe to save *The Times*.

On 9 February Bell signed a brief statement which specified that, if Northcliffe gained control, he himself would be appointed managing director for five years. He attempted to impose a list of conditions, but when Northcliffe, through Sutton, threatened to withdraw, Bell agreed to carry out his 'absolute instructions'. This was undertaken in return for an understanding that the 'present policy of the paper in Home & Foreign affairs' should be continued under Buckle and Valentine Chirol, the head of the Foreign Department.[12] Chirol was an important asset of the paper and perhaps the best-known foreign editor in Europe. He was personally acquainted with the important leaders, and had organized *The Times* cable news service, the most extensive in the world. The Bell–Sterling contract, which called for a buyout of the partners for £320,000 in cash, was signed on 11 February. Northcliffe placed that amount in Bell's private account so that he could complete the transaction, which began with a £32,000 deposit. Northcliffe later told Kitchin that he had taken this unusual course, against the advice of his attorneys, because he 'wanted to please old Bell and to show that I, at any rate, believed in him. He had made all sorts of conditions for *The Times* and for the staff, yet had made no condition for himself. It was the least that I could do.'[13]

The next month Bell took the draft of the final sales contract to Northcliffe at Versailles. Because Arthur Walter was reported to be giving assurances that the press lord was not involved in the negotiations, on 8 March Northcliffe instructed Bell to inform Walter, in confidence, of his identity. When Bell did so, it was his impression that the proprietor already knew the name of 'X'. Walter told Bell that bringing in anyone at all was an 'infernal nuisance', but from the little he had seen of Northcliffe he thought him 'all right'.[14] At this point Buckle and Chirol also learned the identity of 'X'. After a heated discussion, the two were persuaded by Bell that Northcliffe would be a lesser evil than Pearson, though to Buckle he was still a 'bitter pill to swallow'.[15] To escape Pearson, Chirol told Bell, 'I should take it [the money] from the Devil himself!' He went on to say that what Bell told him of Northcliffe 'reminds me of what St. Loe Strachey said of him to me: "I hate his methods but there is something very big about him. He seems to be cast in much the same metal as Cecil Rhodes, whose methods were often equally repugnant, but whom everyone admits to have been a very big man."'[16]

Pearson's bid was financed by a hypothetical stock offering and was passed over by the Chancery Court in favour of the Bell-Sterling cash offer. On 16 March, Bell cabled Northcliffe that the purchase had 'Gone through as we wanted.'[17] One week later, when no appeals were filed, the judgement of the court became final. That day Bell told his assistant, 'the easy part is finished, now we've got to keep Him in order'.[18] *The Times*, without disclosing 'His' identity, announced on 17 March that, under the reorganization, 'There will be no change whatever in the political or editorial direction of the paper, which will be conducted by the same Staff on the independent lines pursued uninterruptedly for so many years.' In part because publishing any of the court proceedings was declared to be subject to contempt charges, only the *Daily Chronicle* printed Northcliffe's name, and its account was not believed.

Northcliffe realized a long-held publishing desire when he acquired control of *The Times*. Though its circulation had dwindled, the paper remained the most prestigious British journal and was still viewed by foreign powers as a voice of official government opinion. By adding *The*

Times to his newspaper regiments, Northcliffe gained control of a key organ of the British Establishment – much to the fury of his Liberal critics, once they ascertained that his was the hand behind the purchase. The journal was left a large degree of independence, in part because of the reverence the new chief proprietor held for it as a British institution, but probably more because its conservative views were compatible with his own. Northcliffe promised no editorial interference, with one proviso. He told Kitchin that he would 'leave the Editor unrestricted control, unless he should – which is quite incredible – fail to warn the British people of the coming German peril. I insist upon that duty being discharged.'[19] It was also convenient to leave to Bell the unpleasant and rancorous negotiations with the Walters which completed the bargain by joining the printing works to the newspaper. In August an agreement was reached which transferred 150,000 second preference shares to the Walters and brought the entire business of *The Times* under one ownership.

Many feared that Northcliffe would destroy the paper that he had coveted for years. Instead, reorganization began to bring *The Times* up to date. John Bland was put in charge of replacing the antique machinery, and £60,000 was invested in new Goss presses and the latest Monotype composing equipment. Dispatched to inspect the books, E. Layton Bennett, Northcliffe's long-time company accountant, reported that 'Our friends' ideas of bookkeeping are of an exceedingly vague character.' In reply, the new proprietor advised 'tact in your inquiries, as no one likes the intrusion of newcomers. You would not yourself if you had been in business for 120 years. We want the Printing House Square people to get to like us.'[20] Bell had told Northcliffe that he thought *The Times* was suffering from a lack of abuse. To this the press lord responded, 'Do not worry about lack of abuse . . . When I . . . reveal my identity as controller . . . you will get all the abuse you want.'[21]

Arthur Walter remained in place as chairman of *The Times* Publishing Company created by the purchase. The board of directors included Walter, Moberly Bell, Buckle, Chirol and W.F. Moneypenny, who had been assistant editor, but in 1908 was employed writing a life of Disraeli for the paper, which Buckle would later complete. Northcliffe, who had a 51 per cent interest at first, did not officially join the board for four years. After the purchase was final, the new owner told General Sterling ('Caesar' in the coded messages) that he was gratified to be able to help Bell in keeping *The Times* in the 'hands of English people'. He went on that he was very pleased that the first congratulations he received came from a grandson of 'The Thunderer'.[22] During the negotiations, Bell had used the rumoured German bid to keep Northcliffe on course. The latter told Kitchin that he had 'saved *The Times* from the German Emperor'. He had also saved it from the Liberals, who, led by Campbell-Bannerman, had kept an eye on the proceedings. However, the Prime Minister was too ill to put together a proposed Free Trade syndicate to purchase and manage the paper.

In the first week of April 1908, after a series of heart attacks and months of illness, Campbell-Bannerman resigned his duties and the King called on Herbert Asquith to form a government. The new Prime Minister was fifty-five years of age and at the top of his game. Though he came from the middle class, he had put himself through Balliol and was well connected within Britain's ruling elite. Such was Asquith's renown in Commons debates that Campbell-Bannerman dubbed him 'The Sledgehammer' for his lawyer's ability to pile argument upon argument and overwhelm his opponents.[23] The King requested that Asquith make as few Cabinet changes as possible; nevertheless, his handful of appointees made a great impact in the following years. Two were particularly important: David Lloyd George took the Prime Minister's place at the Exchequer, and Winston Churchill followed Lloyd George to the Board of Trade. In the next few years these partners in the 'New Liberalism' bedevilled the Opposition at every turn with their radical reform proposals. Elsewhere, Lord Tweedmouth, who had been involved in an embarrassing correspondence with the Kaiser over Britain's naval building plans while Northcliffe was negotiating *The Times* sale, was promoted out of the way and replaced at the Admiralty by Reginald McKenna.[24]

Partly because Asquith and Balfour were friends, the Prime Minister invited the Leader of the Opposition to attend the meetings of the Committee of Imperial Defence. The CID arrangement worked because Balfour and Asquith, the former Liberal Imperialist, were in rough agreement over the need to defend the Empire. They were less in tune on other matters, such as Asquith's scheme for old-age pensions in the 1908 Budget, which, since he had prepared it, the Prime Minister introduced himself. The plan for tiny payments at age seventy was to be financed through general taxation. Old-age pensions had detractors across party lines. A hard core of laissez-faire Liberals disagreed with the very idea. Rosebery emerged to declare the 'scheme so prodigal of expenditure' that it would strike 'a blow at the Empire which might be almost mortal'.[25] The Unionists, not prepared to oppose such an electorally popular issue, preferred an insurance arrangement to pay for the measure, rather than increased taxation.

Balfour's party might have defeated the Pension Bill in the House of Lords, but instead declared the measure a financial one (with which the Upper House by tradition did not interfere) and passed it. Since 1906 the Conservative majority in the Lords, led by the Marquess of Lansdowne, had defeated some significant Liberal legislation, such as a Plural Voting Bill and a Licensing Bill; however, fearing the consequences at the polls, Lansdowne allowed several important measures aimed at ameliorating the conditions of workers and unions to pass, the most notable being the Trade Disputes Act of 1906. Campbell-Bannerman had desired to curtail aristocratic interference with the wishes of the elected Commons. His plan was to institute a suspensory veto that would allow the Upper House only to delay Bills by defeating them twice: after a third time through the Commons they would become law. However, C.-B.'s illness and subsequent death, on 22 April 1908, intervened. Reform of the Lords was left to his successors.

Meanwhile, for Northcliffe, the triumph of gaining *The Times* was balanced by problems elsewhere. The *Manchester Courier* continued to lose money, and its proprietor sought local financial backers for the Conservative organ. He wrote to Balfour that the paper had 'arrived at one of its quinquennial crisis [*sic*] . . . A local magnate . . . might, I think, be induced to come forward.' Otherwise, he went on, the paper 'must disappear because for some reasons impossible to fatham [*sic*], the Conservatives will not support it'.[26] The *Courier* also embroiled Northcliffe in a controversy with Winston Churchill, who had been defeated in a rather bitter contest for re-election at North-West Manchester, required when he entered the Cabinet. Consequently, a seat was found for the President of the Board of Trade at Dundee, after its occupant was promoted to the Lords.

Incensed at election slurs in the Northcliffe newspapers, the MP for Dundee made his displeasure widely known. This friction caused some embarrassment to Lady Northcliffe, who moved in the same social circle. The *Manchester Courier*, in particular, was the target of a libel suit by Churchill after it repeated old charges that he had broken his parole while a Boer prisoner. Northcliffe wrote to him that he

was amazed to hear . . . that you considered our criticisms a personal matter. There was a well understood agreement between us that we should use our stage thunder in the furtherance of our mutual interests. You have criticised

me very hotly in and out of Parliament and I have never felt the least put out
about it, as you must have seen by our recent meeting at Lord Lansdowne's.
As we have got to live together more or less in public life & in more ways than
you know, for, I hope, a great many years, I propose we take a walk in St.
James's Park some morning this week and thrash this matter out.[27]

He disclaimed any knowledge of the hostile articles, which had been
printed while he was out of the country. He also told Churchill that
reports of personal remarks disparaging the younger man were false,
and asked him in future not to 'attach importance to rumour or listen to
the words of busybodies'.[28] The MP replied to this that the misunderstanding had been 'completely removed from my mind'. A few months
later, after Churchill's engagement to Miss Clementine Hozier was
announced, Northcliffe sent his congratulations – adding that 'you kept
your secret well or my young men were not in their usual anticipatory
vein, which must be enquired into on my return to town'.[29] He and his
wife sent a wedding present, and Churchill requested that *The Times* –
which he called Northcliffe's 'old paper' – report him 'verbatim at
Dundee, at Manchester, and at Newcastle, and I will see that they get
good copy'.[30]

While he mollified Churchill, Northcliffe also corresponded with
R.B. Haldane at the War Office. Though brilliant, Haldane was an outsider, whose philosophical education at Edinburgh and in Germany
made him seem, to his Oxford- and Cambridge-educated brethren,
somehow foreign. He had made his reputation as a lawyer before the
Court of Appeals and the House of Lords, and had wanted to be made
Lord Chancellor in Campbell-Bannerman's government. Haldane was
not a favourite of the Prime Minister, who dubbed him 'Schopenhauer'.
Instead of gaining the Woolsack, he was assigned the War Office, where
more than one career had foundered. 'We shall see how Schopenhauer
gets on in the Kailyard,' commented the Liberal leader.[31] Surprising his
detractors, the Secretary for War performed admirably for Campbell-
Bannerman and then for Asquith. His regime instituted reforms which
cut expenses, reorganized the regular Army, and laid the foundations
for the British Expeditionary Force that would cross to France in 1914.
Haldane had less success and found more resistance from traditionalists
in his attempts to reform Britain's reserve force, the Territorial Army, so
that it might handle home defence and allow the regulars to be concentrated abroad. Northcliffe relayed to the War Secretary his worries
about the espionage carried out by visiting German officers. This

unofficial practice, carried out by eager young officers of all nations while on leave abroad, had been common for some years. Haldane replied that he had 'not the least doubt that an enormous amount of information is collected by foreign officers here, especially Germans, but they do it when they are on leave and not under any commission'. Since this was the same sort of thing that British officers did, he continued, 'like yourself, I have not got any notion of how to stop it'.[32]

Northcliffe was among those suspicious of Haldane's 'foreign' sympathies. While the Cabinet was being restructured, he complained to Lloyd George about the public perception that the government, and particularly Haldane, were pro-German. Lloyd George replied that he was surprised to hear that the War Ministry was considered suspect. He stated that the only pro-German Liberal he knew was Rosebery, about whom he wondered if he was 'a Liberal at all'. Concerning Haldane, Lloyd George admitted that he had intellectual ties with Germany, but otherwise found nothing on which to base any suspicion that 'we are inclined to a pro-German policy at the expense of the entente with France'.[33] This is the first recorded correspondence between Northcliffe and the canny Welshman, who, more than most politicians, realized full well the value of the press and would loom large in the future history of Britain and Northcliffe.

For the first few months after the sale the new chief proprietor did not show himself in the offices of *The Times*, meeting the senior staff at his house in St James's Place and over country weekends. Besides the London employees of *The Times*, another visitor at Sutton Place in this period was Geoffrey Robinson (later Dawson), editor of the Johannesburg *Star* and a member of Lord Milner's 'kindergarten' of talented young men of Empire trained in South Africa. While in England in June 1908, Robinson, who had also acted as *The Times*'s South African correspondent for the past two years, met Buckle and Bell and spent a weekend with Northcliffe. Robinson recorded in his diary that the other visitors to Sutton Place included the French Foreign Minister Théophile Delcassé, J.L. Garvin, who had joined the *Observer* as editor earlier in the year, Austen Chamberlain, Arthur Lee MP, a Conservative spokesman on defence matters in the Commons, and William Tyrrell, Grey's secretary at the Foreign Office. Northcliffe was greatly impressed by Robinson and his view of the Empire, which was very close to his own. The two walked together and, along with Garvin, discussed a wide range of imperial and national topics.[34] John Evelyn Wrench had also been at Sutton Place, and, after lunch with Robinson,

Northcliffe commented to Wrench that he had just met the future editor of *The Times*.

At Printing House Square, Kennedy Jones became the voice of the proprietor and, moderating his usual gruff manner, he made friends and gained influence. Northcliffe, at first, was full of praise for the newspaper and its staff. His communications exhorted Bell and Buckle to get on with their good efforts, to discontinue Bell's 'squinching' and to spend money freely. In one such 'love letter', as the staff called them, he told Buckle that the paper had

> been so uniformly good for many days past I should like to take this opportunity of thanking you and your staff for its alertness, accuracy . . . and maintenance of tone. So far I do not think we have made any mistakes and I have very little doubt that if the present level can be maintained the depreciation which has been continuous since 1868 will be counteracted and eventually the journal will prosper and gain its old place in the respect of the country.[35]

The editor replied that

> I do not think any paper could have a more willing staff or one more devoted to its success. In the last few years circumstances have naturally weighed our spirits down, but the new arrangement and your vigorous personality have infused hopefulness and buoyancy in us all . . . You have to bring it abreast of modern conditions . . . we must not however go too fast. There must be no doubt that the paper is still *The Times* in essentials, but improved in every respect, brought thoroughly up to date, and made as nearly the ideal newspaper as possible. It is because I know these are your views that I now look forward without misgiving to the future.[36]

To recuperate from the months of negotiations, and the pressures of business in general, Lady Northcliffe persuaded her husband to take a Spanish vacation. Wrench accompanied them as a personal secretary. Also with them on the visit to the Seville Fair were Garvin and his wife, as well as Owen Seaman, the editor of *Punch*. Northcliffe enjoyed the change of scenery, but thought much about his new acquisition and how to elevate its circulation, which had fallen to 38,000. He and Wrench were also able to speak of the younger man's latest idea, an Overseas Club, meant to strengthen the bonds of Empire. The owner promised the full support of the *Overseas Daily Mail*.

After Northcliffe returned to England, Lord Esher visited St James's Place in July on the King's behalf and during their interview the press lord admitted his role in the reorganization of *The Times*. In a letter to

Esher meant for the eyes of the sovereign, Northcliffe reiterated the conversation:

> My position is merely that of one who wishes to see this country represented to the world by an absolutely independent newspaper, always, I trust, in my lifetime, worthy of its high traditions; the organ of neither parties, sects, nor financiers; its columns open to every shade of politics; a newspaper not run as a profit-making machine at all.
>
> The Times is, in fact, in my life what a Yacht or a racing stable is to others – it is merely my hobby.
>
> I propose, if I am spared, to leave in my Will an endowment and a suggestion for its direction by such a Committee as that of the British Museum to preserve it, perhaps, for some generations.[37]

Esher recalled his visit to St James's Place in his diary. He noted that the press lord lived 'simply, his house is furnished with taste, without display, or ostentation of his enormous wealth'. He went on that Northcliffe's

> talk was mainly of *The Times*, and the method, half skill and half luck, of its purchase. Since this talk, he has written to me a curious letter, a confession of his idea in buying control of the paper, and his intentions in regard to it should he die. Both are creditable to him. His mind is that of the organiser and speculator, not of the politician. He evidently loves power, but his education is defective, and he has no idea to what uses power can be put, except by deputy . . . I have no doubt that he will convert *The Times* from a bankrupt to a fine property.[38]

The next month Northcliffe had a similar correspondence with John St Loe Strachey, regarding setting up *The Times* as a 'national institution' in his will.[39] At the same time he confided to Buckle that he had no wish for anyone to know of his association with the newspaper, but that he had revealed the information to a few people, including Arthur Balfour, 'at his obvious desire when I spent an hour with him the other night'.[40]

Sir John Fisher, who almost certainly had already learned the identity of the new owner of *The Times*, wrote to Northcliffe that he should buy the paper and make Garvin editor. 'That would be Napoleonic in its conception', said Fisher, using a favourite phrase, 'and Cromwellian in its thoroughness.'[41] The First Sea Lord reported that Pearson had come to see him when he thought he had *The Times*, 'but he was neither Napoleon nor Cromwell, but only a babbler!' Garvin was not destined to lead *The Times*, but, since the beginning of the year, when he had taken the editor's chair at the *Observer*, he had faithfully defended Fisher's course against all detractors, in and out of the Navy. Fisher supplied secret Admiralty information concerning German naval preparations to Garvin and his chief. He told Northcliffe that 'it would be simple madness of the Germans to make war on England – however, Lord Salisbury once said to me when Prime Minister "One can never tell what great gust of popular passion may not sweep a nation into doing in the shape of some act of madness."'[42]

An anonymous article, by Garvin in the July *Quarterly Review*, entitled 'The German Peril', helped to set off such a public sensation. The piece was designed to stir the country to action and to aid Fisher's naval building plans. It warned of German hostility and, particularly, the danger of invasion because of the nation's weak defences, about which the enemy was well informed. 'Nothing can be much more certain than that, if we are locked in a life and death struggle with Germany, she will attempt invasion. Her naval officers have sounded and sketched our harbours and studied every detail of our coasts. Her military officers have carried out staff-rides in this country . . . the nakedness of our land is spied out.' Further, Garvin revealed that there were 'in this country 50,000 Germans waiters' awaiting their orders at railway stations and near forts, ready to carry out unspoken mayhem.[43]

Within days of the *Quarterly Review* revelations, Count Zeppelin completed a record-breaking journey to Switzerland in the latest incarnation of his dirigible. The timing could not have been better for Garvin's purposes. The *Observer* of 5 July noted the 'epoch-making voyage' of the German airship. For the first time, said Garvin, 'a flying machine has risen in one nation and sailed over the territory of another. As the airship has already crossed mountains, lakes, and international boundaries, we cannot doubt that it will yet cross seas and oceans, kingdoms, and continents, and revolutionise the political relations of the world.' The *Daily Mail* commented that

there is this certain fact with which England must reckon, that Zeppelin No. IV has carried out the most remarkable voyage ever attempted . . . For half a day she hovered above a foreign territory and was controlled with consummate ease. This feat has proved that she is in advance of the types possessed by all other nations. The French 'dirigibles' have accomplished nothing so wonderful, and the British Nulli Secundus makes a very poor show beside her.[44]

The Times also joined the chorus, advising that 'Wake Up England' must be the watchword of the nation.[45]

F.W. Wile, the American-born *Daily Mail* correspondent in Berlin, exposed the enemy plans in a 11 July interview with Rudolf Martin, a German privy counsellor and air expert. Martin asserted that within a few years Germany would be able to construct a Zeppelin fleet capable of delivering 350,000 troops across the Channel to Dover in one night. A separate article by a British expert, Major Baden Fletcher Smyth Baden-Powell, the brother of the hero of Mafeking, seconded the gravity of the situation and called for the government to spend £100,000 on aeronautical research. The sensation caused by the assertions of Wile and Baden-Powell drowned out the more sober words, elsewhere in the paper, which advised that the threat lay well in the future and called on the Admiralty and War Office to take appropriate action.

Britain lagged behind the world not only in dirigibles but also in aeroplanes. At the start of 1908, Europe witnessed its first circular aeroplane flight, by the Frenchman Henri Farman. This was hailed, like the accomplishment of Santos-Dumont at the end of 1906, as an epoch-making event. Once again the French spectators had no idea that the Wright brothers had long before reached this milestone. The Wrights were fanatical about secrecy, fearing they would lose the enormous profits they dreamed of reaping from their aeroplane, the capabilities of which far outstripped any competition. R.B. Haldane believed that the aeroplane was years away from being of military benefit and, though interesting, insignificant in comparison with the potential of the Zeppelin. Therefore, rather than purchase the Wright machines, the War Office constructed its own. This project was carried out in secret at Farnborough. On 23 July 1908 the *Daily Mail* printed the government's assertion that there was nothing to fear from aircraft 'for a long time to come'. When it was possible to fly across the Channel, the statement went on, then 'the War Office may be prepared to regard recent experiments seriously'.

This official arrogance was demolished the next month, when Wilbur Wright brought a machine to France and put on an exhibition that stunned all of Europe. One leader of French aviation, Léon Delagrange, declared, 'We are beaten! We just don't exist!' Northcliffe's previous suspicions concerning the Wrights' achievements dissolved. The 10 August *Daily Mail* proclaimed that 'The scoffer and the sceptic are confounded. Mr. Wilbur Wright last evening made the most marvellous aeroplane flight ever witnessed on this side of the Atlantic . . . A bird could not have shown a more complete mastery.'[46] The owner of the paper asked Wright to come to England in order to make an attempt at the £10,000 prize offered by the newspaper for a London-to-Manchester flight. Wright was tempted, but turned down the invitation at the insistence of his brother. An even larger offer from Northcliffe, for a flight across the English Channel and a public exhibition of the successful craft, was also declined. Meanwhile, after several false starts, a British aeroplane, built by another American aeronaut, Samuel Franklin Cody, neared completion. The craft, strongly influenced by the early ideas of the Wrights, made its first powered flight, and the first in Britain, on 16 October 1908, almost five years after the first flight at Kitty Hawk.[47] In the next year, when the capabilities of Cody's machine proved rather limited, Northcliffe condemned Haldane for Britain's failure.

The destruction of Zeppelin's airship in an August storm did not relieve the tense international climate. Arthur Mee, editor of the Harmsworth *Children's Encylopædia*, suggested that his chief publish a plea to Germany to halt further construction. Northcliffe responded that this could not be done, because 'advances to Germany' were 'entirely mistrusted'. His letter to Mee went on that when 'the Zeppelin airship was burnt the other day Germans at once subscribed over £100,000 . . . I wish you would spend one of your holidays in Germany and try to realise the situation. Every nation has its characteristics. Our people have "sang froid"; the French, jealousy; the Spaniard, pride; the Americans, boastfulness; the Germans, envy and suspicion.'[48] Northcliffe also suggested that Mee look at the German newspapers for proof. When Mee called on Northcliffe to print what the German journals were saying, his chief replied:

> You ask me to do the thing that I think most dangerous. I have for a long time refrained from printing these extracts from German papers. I understand the present Cabinet is well aware of the real state of affairs and are most watchful . . . The best thing to do, as Mr. Spender said [in the *Westminster Gazette*, of which he was editor], is say nothing and be prepared . . . I agree with you that nearly all wars begin by suspicions, and suspicions can best be allayed, in my judgment by saying nothing.[49]

One member of the Cabinet, Lloyd George, had been in Germany on an industrial tour and had witnessed first-hand the fanatical patriotism aroused by the Zeppelin crash and the so-called 'miracle of Echterdingen' by which funds poured in with which to replace the lost craft. He returned to England disturbed by what he had seen, and by the unfriendliness displayed in many quarters.

The hatred of Britain found among the patriotic masses appeared also at the highest levels in Germany. The Kaiser was well known for his intemperate statements and actions – the Tweedmouth correspondence earlier in the year being but one example. Northcliffe obtained a copy of an incendiary interview by Dr William Bayard Hale, an American journalist who was also a clergyman, to whom Wilhelm had spoken in confidence and hence even more directly than normal. The three-hour conversation was so outspoken that Hale felt it would be dangerous to repeat it. As their talk progressed, he reported, Wilhelm paced the room, full of energy, and 'his eyes snapped when he spoke of England his bitterness was so intense'. The Kaiser claimed that Great Britain looked on Germany as her enemy because she was the dominant force on the Continent and it had always been England's way to attack the strongest power. Wilhelm appeared very bitter against his Uncle 'Bertie', and accused him of trying to set the other powers against Germany. He went on that England had been degenerating since the Boer War, which was a war against God, and for that she would be punished like all nations who have done wrong to a weaker power that was in the right. Germany was ready for war at any moment, and, in the view of the Kaiser, the sooner it came the better. He was aching for a fight, not for the sake of war, but to get something unpleasant and inevitable over with as soon as possible.

With regard to the British Empire, Hale reported that the Kaiser seemed well informed and had said that within nine months India would be overrun by one of the bloodiest rebellions in history. Wilhelm blamed this on the Japanese, who had their goods in every bazaar and their agents sowing sedition and treachery in every quarter. Hale gathered that the Kaiser's ambition was to take Egypt from Great Britain and later the Holy Land from Turkey, emulating the Crusaders. As to France and Russia, Wilhelm said they were not worth talking about from a military or naval point of view. He was friendly towards the United States because of the 'march of progress' and the degeneration of Great Britain, and saw the two future dominant forces as the USA and Germany.

Northcliffe sent a copy of the interview to Sir Edward Grey at the Foreign Office. He assured Grey that the interview would not appear in his papers, but that it showed 'there is a danger of something happening before long'. He went on that the threat to the Empire was 'not a dream', as he had been to India himself and had seen the unrest. Army officers had told him that the people at home would not understand the situation until it was too late. 'As you know,' he informed Grey, 'I have at least the news instinct and I did not get through the country "comme un grand seigneur".'[50] Northcliffe had also been in contact with Lord Kitchener in Calcutta. The Commander-in-Chief of the Army in India reported that there might be trouble and that he was prepared to act 'at a moment's notice'. Later in the year William Tyrrell sent a note from the Foreign Office, on behalf of himself and Grey, thanking Northcliffe for withholding the inflammatory piece.[51]

Hale's revelations were suppressed; however, friends of the Kaiser in Britain gathered some of his statements concerning both countries into an 'interview' meant to ameliorate Anglo-German relations and subsequently published in the *Daily Telegraph* of 27 October. The comparatively tame article, which the Kaiser approved, unfortunately had quite the opposite effect to that intended and set off protests in both England and Germany. Wilhelm declared his love for Britain, but revealed that his people did not share his sentiments – hardly a reassuring message in the charged atmosphere of late 1908. He also revealed the advice he had offered during the Boer War and appeared to take credit for directing Lord Roberts towards a winning strategy, which affronted many in Britain. The Kaiser found himself even more heavily criticized at home and, for a time, constrained his public declarations.[52]

In the autumn of 1908 the doctors once again recommended a vacation from business. On 3 October, Northcliffe, his wife and his mother sailed on the *Lusitania* for America. In New York, he and the inventor Marconi were given a dinner by the *New York Times*. Northcliffe also planned to bring back some wildlife to Britain, including American robins and grey squirrels. Regarding this he spoke to Professor Hornaday, of the New York Zoological Society, who helped to arrange for several pairs of both species to be sent to Sutton Place.

From New York, the party travelled to Washington. While sightseeing in the area, Northcliffe's mother refused to visit Mt Vernon, George Washington's home and the final resting place of the first president, because, said Geraldine, she 'would not pay tribute to a rebel'.[53] However, she was persuaded to meet the present occupant of the White House, and the three travellers lunched with Theodore Roosevelt. How the energetic President and the press lord first met is unclear. Northcliffe had had an interview with President McKinley while Roosevelt was vice-president, and the politician made many trips to

Britain when they might have been introduced. The President's 1886 second wedding had taken place in England. The best man was Cecil Spring-Rice, a British diplomat, later ambassador to the United States, and an implacable foe of Northcliffe. However they became acquainted, Roosevelt and Northcliffe each respected the other's accomplishments and shared a vigorous outlook which prized action in the face of life's challenges. Roosevelt was near the end of his second term and only a few months from the start of an extended African and European vacation as a private citizen. During this tour he accepted Northcliffe's hospitality at Sutton Place.

From Washington the travellers next headed north to Canada. At Toronto they visited the sickbed of Wrench, who had fallen ill with typhoid fever while on a tour for the *Overseas Daily Mail*. Northcliffe was fêted at the Canadian Club and met Lord Milner, one of the few British notables to speak in Canada. He was disturbed that no important figure besides Milner had toured Canada, and that no major English financial house had a branch there. On his return he broached these shortcomings with many politicians and businessmen, including Churchill and Balfour. At Ottawa, Northcliffe stayed with the Governor-General, Earl Grey. The two men discussed defence matters, including the training of future officers in the new Canadian Army Cadet Corps, which the Governor-General called 'the most important thing' that had happened during his term. They also agreed on the need for increased immigration from England, to balance the 'flow of people of alien blood from over the border'.[54] Concerning Canadian politics, the Governor-General told Northcliffe that Laurier was angry at attacks made in *The Times* during the general election. Grey had assured the premier that they had also upset the chief proprietor. He also passed along the name of Laurier's suggestion for a local correspondent, John Willison.[55] Willison was already under consideration, and he became *The Times's* representative in Canada.

Grey advised Northcliffe that he did not think commercial treaties of preference should be proposed by Britain as, in his opinion, the Canadian people were hostile to the idea. He believed that the country distrusted visitors such as Milner who came from England as 'physicians' with cures for their problems. Leaving Canada's hand 'entirely free', said Grey, would lead to 'a nearer approximation of Free Trade' between Canada and the United Kingdom. He thought *The Times* and the *Observer* both made a mistake in asserting that imperial sentiment was weakening in Canada, in spite of his efforts, and that Milner had succeeded in 'stiffening opinion'. Grey also believed that Milner had done some good by putting the 'ideals' of Empire before the people.[56] The Governor-General commented to Milner on Northcliffe's visit that the press lord's impact was 'volcanic, a light on the mountain tops'. 'This man', he went on, 'is a Napoleon, full of ideas and energy . . . genuinely possessed by the religion of Empire.'[57]

Back in Britain as 1908 drew to a close, Northcliffe received more disquieting news concerning Germany. In late December, George Saunders, *The Times*'s correspondent in Berlin, sent his chief a telegram which revealed the views of Professor Hans Delbrück, one of Wilhelm's advisers. Saunders – whom a few years before the Kaiser had called a 'first-class swine' – reported that, in Delbrück's opinion, 'England regards the German Empire today as its real opponent and rival and there is a party in the island which considers it necessary to provoke a passage of arms with Germany.' From the *Daily Mail*, H.W. Wilson shared confidential naval intelligence that the 'range tables of the new Krupp guns' had 'staggered the Admiralty'.[58] Wile reported from Berlin that he had had a half-hour interview with Admiral von Tirpitz. The Admiral, said Wile, 'was unmistakably interested in the *Daily Mail* attitude towards German naval development and let me know that he didn't like it. The interview was, in my mind, mainly significant in its proof of the value the highest quarters in Germany put upon the power and influence of the *Daily Mail*.'[59] In the next year the paper would test this 'power and influence' when the Northcliffe press answered the call of Lords Milner, Roberts and others to champion the cause of national defence, on the land, at sea and in the air.

9

Aeroplanes, Dreadnoughts and Budgets, 1909

NORTHCLIFFE WAS ILL for some time following his return from America. He believed that he had contracted food poisoning on the *Lusitania* coming home. Wrench recorded in his diary that the 'chief has not got over his ptomaine poisoning properly and is worrying about his health'.[1] To cheer him up, on New Year's Day 1909 Leo Maxse sent the press lord a copy of Kipling's 'Jungle Stories'. In addition to wishing him a speedy recovery, Maxse's letter also touched on the troubles in the Balkans. 'Our people have hardly realised the gravity of this . . . crisis, which drags on without approaching a settlement,' the editor of the *National Review* warned.[2]

The previous October, Austria-Hungary had taken advantage of the Ottoman Empire's internal problems to annex Bosnia and Hercegovina. Russia had her own aspirations in the Balkans and felt betrayed by the Dual Monarchy, which moved before the Russians had secured their own concessions from the Ottomans. In Maxse's estimation, the world had misjudged the Austrian Foreign Minister, Count Lexa von Aehranthal, who 'realised he could safely proceed with his aggressive policy . . . because force is on his side . . . Russia is in no condition to face a great war, and France is paralysed by her neighbourhood to Germany.' Maxse was correct in his analysis. German support of Austria-Hungary kept Russia from taking aggressive action. However, by absorbing the two troublesome provinces into her polyglot empire, the Dual Monarchy only exacerbated the Southern Slav problem, with disastrous results for the future.

The chief proprietor of *The Times* planned a February trip to Pau in France, both for a rest and to witness a flying demonstration by the Wright brothers. The doctors had diagnosed 'pancreatic trouble', and those around Northcliffe – particularly his wife – had been subjected to an increased irritability in early 1909. Lady Northcliffe and Wrench became close in this period, and had many frank conversations. The younger man apparently became quite smitten with Mary, recording that 'her life is not as happy as I should like to see – but she is wonderful'.[3] In Wrench's opinion, his employer was 'not an easy husband'. Northcliffe told Sutton that his problems were linked to his old malaria, that he felt feeble and cross and was 'lacking interest in the sex, always a bad sign with your devoted chief'.

Northcliffe, his wife and Wrench arrived at Pau in the second week of February, along with Arthur Balfour, who accepted an invitation to join the expedition. Balfour had a keen interest in defence matters, and Northcliffe hoped to recruit him to the support of aeroplanes against Haldane at the War Office. Within a few days of their arrival in France, Lady Northcliffe was able to report to Sutton that her husband was 'much better'. Wilbur and Orville Wright joined the group for lunch. Wilbur told them that flying was 'no more difficult than walking' and predicted that scouting duties would be the aeroplane's role in wartime.[4]

The next day, during the lengthy pre-flight preparations, Northcliffe and Balfour were among those who helped pull the Wright airship into position for launching. With the snow-covered Pyrenees as a backdrop, the group observed the American aviators' twenty-two-minute flight. The usually languid and unflappable former Prime Minister was amazed. The 12 February *Daily Mail* recorded that Balfour said of the demonstration, 'It is the most wonderful sight. It is something worth coming to see. I wish I could be flying with him.' Balfour agreed to inform Haldane of the capabilities of the Wright craft.

Although this exhibition attracted a crowd of international notables, both private and military, the British government sent no official observer. Upset by this failure, Northcliffe informed Haldane that German and French military representatives had been present. He went on that he was

constantly being chaffed by these foreign gentlemen with regard to the British army aeroplane, which they have nicknamed 'the steamroller' ... one of your young men might be sent down here to find out why it is that this aeroplane gets off the ground, and can fly for ten minutes, or ten hours, if it chooses, and your Aldershot aeroplane, which is a very bad copy of the bad French aeroplanes, is unable to leave the ground.[5]

Northcliffe expressed similar sentiments to others. A letter to the staff of *The Times* described Britain's national position in aviation as 'truly pathetic'.[6]

The *Daily Mail* reflected the renewed enthusiasm of its owner for the Wright brothers in a March campaign aimed at forcing the War Office to purchase their machines. The paper praised the Wright aeroplane and criticized government tardiness. Wilbur was soon to visit Britain, and this, said the journal, would give the War Office 'an opportunity of judging the efficiency of his aeroplane'. The *Daily Mail* was also careful to note the first flights of the 'Imperial Airship I', the first Zeppelin built with German-government funding, with flights, it was reported, being carried out by a 'purely military crew'. Other reports, from F.W. Wile in Berlin, speculated on how many troops the new craft could carry, and whether they were armed with new 'aerial torpedoes'.[7]

At the same time as the *Daily Mail* campaigned for a British fleet, at the *Observer* J.L. Garvin led a renewed agitation for naval building. The anxieties of the previous year over Germany's fleet were re-ignited by reports that her naval expansion was proceeding at a much more rapid pace than had been believed possible. Britain remained divided over the peril and the appropriate response. This split made its way even into the Liberal government. The First Lord of the Admiralty, Reginald McKenna, was a strong advocate of Sir John Fisher's schemes, which Lloyd George and Churchill thought needlessly extravagant. Lloyd George's opposition prompted a comment to the staff of *The Times* from Northcliffe that 'the emptiness of the Chancellor's head will soon become painfully apparent to the country'.[8] In February 1909 Sir Edward Grey threw his support behind McKenna, who, along with the entire Admiralty Board, threatened to resign if the six Dreadnoughts called for in the Naval Estimates were not approved. Asquith, as usual, came up with a compromise to save the day, in the Cabinet at least – four ships at once, with plans made for four more if warranted. The Prime Minister's scheme soothed the Liberal division, but was attacked as inadequate in the Unionist press, led by Garvin and the *Observer*, which soon called for the full complement of ships, under the slogan 'We Want Eight and We Won't Wait.'[9] Northcliffe agreed with the course taken by Garvin and had the *Daily Mail* follow the same line on the Navy, even though the proprietor had some concern that Garvin was too much under the influence of Fisher.[10]

In the Commons, the Opposition sounded the alarm over accelerated German shipbuilding and attacked the government after the 1909–10 Naval Estimates were made public on 12 March. The *Daily Mail* quoted Balfour's declaration concerning the 'Great Naval Crisis' that he had been 'forced most reluctantly to the conclusion that now for the very first time in modern history, we are face to face with a naval situation so new, so dangerous, that it is difficult for us to realise all it imports'.[11] A letter to Earl Grey from Northcliffe commented on the naval threat, and the political scene in general. In the press lord's opinion, Asquith was

not nearly strong enough for his job. Hence the continual revolts of Churchill and Lloyd George. I asked Winston the other morning what was wrong with the Cabinet. He was perfectly frank and said they had not got a master. The chief feature of Parliament at the moment is the dominance of Balfour. I was at the naval debate and have never seen a more cowed collection of Liberals on the front bench.[12]

Backed by his proprietor and supplied with secret information from Fisher, Garvin unleashed an unrestrained attack in the *Observer* of 21 March, which called for 'the Eight, the whole Eight and nothing but the Eight'. If Asquith should refuse, asked Garvin, 'Will there remain no means of enforcing the national will?' The editor answered his own question. 'Yes, there will remain one last resource . . . with a full sense of gravity of the words we use we say that the Peers must reject the Budget and force a dissolution.'

The *Observer* had taken the lead among the Unionist papers in the naval agitation, and it was also recognized to be the Party's premier voice in the struggle over fiscal reform that soon overshadowed the Navy question and dominated the remainder of the year. Tangled up in the fiscal battle was the problem of the sabotage carried on by the House of Lords against the legislative programme of the government. Angered by the defeat of a Licensing Bill late in the previous year, Asquith had announced to his party in December that in 1909 he meant to take the offensive on two issues in particular: the Budget and reform of the Upper House. 'I invite the Liberal party', said Asquith at the National Liberal Club, 'to treat the veto of the House of Lords as the dominating issue in politics . . . because in the long run it overshadows and absorbs every other.' The next Budget, he went on, would 'stand at the very centre of our work' and 'may be found to be . . . a partial solvent of what, under existing Constitutional conditions, would otherwise be insoluble problems'.[13]

In part because the increased naval building added £3 million, Lloyd George's 1909 Budget came in with a deficit of £16 million. Most of this amount, the Chancellor became determined, would come from the wealthy, through taxes on income, urban and mineral land values, and other items, including liquor duties. On Budget Day, 29 April, he laid out his plan for social reform, and how he proposed to pay for it. The conclusion of his four-and-a-half-hour speech was nothing short of a call to arms:

> This is a war Budget. It is for raising money to wage implacable warfare against poverty and squalidness. I cannot help hoping and believing that before this generation has passed away we shall have advanced a great step towards that good time when poverty, and the wretchedness and human degradation which always follow in its camp, will be as remote to the people of this country as the wolves which once infested its forests.[14]

The wolves which would howl the loudest were in the House of Lords.

Austen Chamberlain's immediate response for the Opposition was rather mild; he actually admitted sympathy for some of what the Chancellor proposed. Balfour was more critical. On 3 May he defended personal wealth and attacked the land and liquor taxes. Calling the proposed rise in taxation 'almost dangerously steep', he condemned Lloyd George for betraying his 'fiscal ancestors' and for the 'blind and ignorant' attack on property in the land taxes.[15] The radical nature of the 1909 Budget also brought Joseph Chamberlain back to England from a rest in the South of France. Though still an invalid, he used his reputation and his 'smothered words', as Garvin put it, to urge the forces of Tariff Reform to reject the Budget in the House of Lords.[16]

While the Budget controversy was going on, Northcliffe travelled to Germany. This trip had two objectives. The London physicians recommended that his eyes be examined by a German specialist, and he also wanted to assess at first hand the militarism across the North Sea, which, a growing number of people argued, must lead to war. Before he left England, Northcliffe corresponded with John Galsworthy, who had written a series on Germany for the *Daily Mail*. Northcliffe told Galsworthy that he did not want war and 'as to the war question, it is one of the most difficult in the world at the moment. Nobody wants it in this country'. He continued:

I feel my own responsibility in this matter very greatly, and having German relations and knowing intimately the feeling in both countries, I wish to make the readers of my newspapers as well acquainted as it is possible to be with the exact state of affairs. Two of my greatest difficulties are, firstly, English ignorance of Germany, and secondly, German's [*sic*] somewhat natural indignation at our suggestion that they should alter their navy to suit us.[17]

In Frankfurt, Northcliffe consulted a noted oculist, Dr Solm, concerning his eyesight, which he feared he would lose as had Joseph Pulitzer. In the doctor's judgement there was no disease, but, to keep the proper use of his eyes, Solm advised his patient to take care that he took holidays often and that he had treatment twice a year. Otherwise, warned the doctor, Northcliffe would have to retire from active participation in his businesses within three or four years.[18] Northcliffe told Kennedy Jones, 'I must try and organise my life and business accordingly, as I have no desire to be a second Pulitzer.'[19] However, the diagnosis, at least temporarily, calmed Northcliffe's worst fears. He sent Sutton a note that Solm 'considers my eyes *greatly* improved'.[20]

Middle age was showing itself in other areas besides eyesight. Northcliffe's teeth had been giving serious problems for some time, and he had been fitted with a denture. The same letter to Sutton went on that 'a careless chambermaid here threw away my teeth and I must go to Paris *Saturday* to get more. An infernal nuisance. No teeth and a painful eye treatment – not much of a holiday.' On the advice of the oculist to rest his eyes, he began to wear tortoiseshell-rimmed dark glasses, indoors and out. He also gave up reading himself to sleep, delegating the duty to his secretaries. Though his favourite author was probably Dickens, a wide range of other material, historical and literary, from Flaubert to Kipling, was included in these nocturnal recitations.

While addressing his medical problems, Northcliffe also investigated the reality behind the naval tension and the forecasts of war. He informed Earl Grey that he was 'trying to make it my business to find out about Germany. The problem is an immensely difficult one. I do not believe the Germans seriously contemplate invasion at all, but what they do intend is threat, backed up by the power to execute that threat.'[21] Northcliffe witnessed that power wherever he travelled. He told Buckle that in the 350-mile journey to Berlin he had seen a 'country all dotted with factories, and model factories at that – not the patched-up make-shifts so often seen at home'.[22] To H.W. Wilson, at the *Daily Mail*, he noted that after four motoring trips through Germany he was 'amazed at the industrial strides made in practically every town we came to. Everyone [*sic*] of these new factory chimneys is a gun pointed at England.'[23]

The threatening prosperity and the anti-English feeling that Northcliffe found in Germany convinced him that only a Unionist government could be trusted to undertake the necessary countermeasures at home. Garvin reported that Balfour and Lansdowne were both against forcing an election by defeating the Budget in the Lords, unless some great popular movement for that course became evident. Northcliffe replied that he was sorry to hear it, as he was 'inclined to think it would have been a very wise move. The country is at present sick of the Government and rightly so.'[24] Its owner ensured that the *Daily Mail* followed the anti-Budget lead of the *Observer* over the next months. This course brought down on him the wrath of the Liberal press. The 3 May *Daily News* commented on the wealthy men opposed to the Budget that

> It is they who own the newspapers, and when we remember that 'The Times', the 'Daily Mail', and the 'Observer', not to mention a host of minor organs in London and the provinces, are all controlled by one man, it is easy to realise how vast a political power capital exerts by this means alone . . . The confused efforts of the 'Daily Mail' are . . . splendidly eclipsed by the emotional person who pens the leading article of the 'Observer'.

In May, Northcliffe also corresponded with his employees concerning the latest scare in England over German Zeppelins, for which the *Daily Mail* air campaign, which had begun two months earlier and continued in May with unconfirmed reports of airships over Peterborough, must receive some blame. He commented to the editor of *The Times* that 'these ridiculous balloon and other scares make English people look very foolish in Germany just now'.[25] To remedy this, he sent a signed article, published in the 21 May *Daily Mail*, which pointed out the harm that the phantom-airship stories were doing to Britain's reputation on the Continent, pointing out that the immediate danger, if any, lay in Germany's navy, not its dirigibles. The article ended with a warning that 'the Germans, who have so long been accustomed to regard Great Britain as a model of national deportment, poise, and cool-headed men, are beginning to believe that England is becoming the home of mere nervous degenerates.' Leo Maxse told Northcliffe that 'People . . . required shutting up as you have done. The real thing is so serious that it is maddening to have people going off at tangent.'[26] Nevertheless, at the end of May, Count Zeppelin established a new endurance record for his aircraft, which attracted widespread attention, and the *Daily Mail* continued to publicize aeroplane developments and called for the government to establish a British aeroplane fleet and a Military Air Service for the defence of the nation.

Nothing the newspaper printed, however – including a notice that France was buying 100 Wright aircraft – deflected the Secretary for War from his deliberate and cautious approach to the issue. The previous year, Haldane had had an Aerial Navigation Sub-Committee of the Committee of Imperial Defence consider the dangers, advantages and costs involved in developing a British air force. On the recommendation of this group, which was dominated by military men hostile to innovation, Britain's fledgling aeroplane programme was abandoned. Haldane believed a more scientific, methodical approach was needed to solve the complex problems of flight, which had obviously eluded the tinkerers at Farnborough. He informed Northcliffe on 3 May that 'we have at last elaborated our plans for the foundation of a system of Aerial Navigation for the Army and Navy and constructed . . . a real scientific Department of State for the study of aerial navigation. Lord Rayleigh is to preside . . . The Prime Minister will tomorrow . . . announce the new institution.'[27] Northcliffe was not impressed with this development. He replied to Haldane from Germany that except for Rayleigh, who had won the Nobel Prize for physics a few years previously, the composition of the committee had no practical air experience and was 'lamentable'. Instead, he suggested a 'practical sub-committee should be formed to study the Wright and Voisin planes and make a copy of a zeppelin'. To do the latter, he added, 'much could be ascertained by any intelligent observer who came to Germany for a few months and stationed himself fairly closely to one of the numerous balloon sheds'. He hoped to bring some 'useful' dirigible information himself when he returned in June.[28]

With regard to Haldane's army reforms, the same letter informed the War Secretary that Northcliffe had found that much more was 'known here about your Territorials than in England and apart from the artillery, which is laughed at, the rifle, which is poor, and the short time of service, they are more seriously regarded than in some quarters at home'. On his return, he expressed a wish to talk to Haldane about newspaper publicity for the Territorial scheme. On the related topic of press censorship in wartime, Northcliffe told the War Secretary that he 'had something in mind like a practical military demonstration, with a practical test of press censorship. The handling of the press during war is, in my humble opinion, almost as important as the handling of troops. One knows how Moltke, Von Roon and Bismarck watched and used the Press, and in those days the newspaper machine was in its infancy.' The training of press censors, he went on, 'might be commenced this year. The present system of appointing an ordinary officer, however intelligent, to superintend the work of an army of keen and able men sent out at great expense by newspapers, will not do . . . During the last [Boer] war I had twenty-two and they can tell curious tales of the censorship.'

Haldane replied to Northcliffe's long list of criticisms point by point. He accepted the suggestion to use the forthcoming Territorial manoeuvres to test the censorship. On the aerial front, the War Secretary defended the 'practicability' of the new committee, stating that England was, unfortunately, behind in general scientific knowledge. In his opinion, undue alarm was uncalled for, as 'the naval and military experts have demonstrated to the Defence Committee that dirigibles and still more aeroplanes are a very long way off indeed being the slightest practical use in war'.[29]

Rallying the support of the Empire for the mother country in time of war was one of the objectives of the Imperial Press Conference, which convened in London on 5 June 1909. Since the beginning of the year, Northcliffe (as the hon. treasurer and a member of the Executive Committee) had been involved in planning the event. This meeting of editors and proprietors from the self-governing colonies had been proposed and organized by the journalist and publicist Harry Brittain, who acted as conference secretary and had enlisted Lord Burnham, proprietor of the *Daily Telegraph*, to preside over the affair. Strengthening imperial unity and defence, as well as imperial communications, were the key objectives of the gathering, which opened with an inspirational dinner address from Lord Rosebery at the Shepherd's Bush Exhibition Hall.

The speech, which was equal parts flattery and admonition, welcomed home the sixty colonial representatives to the heart of the British Empire. Rosebery told the journalists that he believed theirs was a meeting of 'vast importance' because, unlike the transient politicians he was used to speaking to, good newspapers 'should be eternal'. The power of a great paper to guide and embody public opinion was, said Rosebery, 'immeasurably greater than that of any statesman could be'. During their visit, the Earl went on, the representatives would see 'an ancient and stately civilization . . . embodied in our old abbeys and cathedrals . . . in the ancient colleges of Oxford and Cambridge . . . you will see the little villages clustered about the heaven-directed spires . . . and you will see the ancient mother of all Parliaments'. Besides these symbols of antiquity and tradition, the journalists would also see the 'teeming communities which represent the manufactures, the industry, the alertness of commercial life in Britain. And last of all, surrounding all and guarding it, you will see a . . . prodigious, but always inadequate armada. All of these, gentleman, are yours as much as ours. Your possessions, your pride, your home.'[30]

Moving on to the goals of the Conference, Rosebery declared that imperial defence was the most vital topic on the agenda. He warned that never before in the history of the world was there 'so threatening and overpowering a preparation for war'. Without mentioning Germany by name, he continued, 'They cannot, indeed, arm any more men upon land, so they have to seek new armaments upon the sea, piling up this enormous preparation as if for some approaching Armageddon.' He urged the audience that, while they were in the country, they should 'compare carefully the armaments of Europe with our preparations to meet them, and give your impressions to the Empire in return'. It would be their duty to 'take back to your young dominions across the seas this message and this impression: that some personal duty for national defence rests on every man and citizen of the Empire'.

Rosebery ended as he began, welcoming the delegates to 'the home of your language, your liberties and your race . . . the source of your parliaments, your free institutions and of this immeasurable Empire'. Wrench, who with Northcliffe was among the 600 British press members present, recalled that 'Rosebery made the best speech I ever heard . . . What an orator he is. If only there were something behind such eloquence.' Nevertheless, Wrench believed that the conference was 'going to be the turning point in the history of the Imperial relationship'.[31]

During the following days the delegates and members of the British press attended sessions on the interrelated topics of imperial communications, defence and foreign policy. The first business meeting, which Northcliffe and Moberly Bell attended, was held at the Foreign Office and chaired by Lord Crewe, the Colonial Secretary. The subject was cable news services and press intercommunication. Sydney Buxton, the Postmaster-General, led the discussion. Out of this a Cable Committee was appointed to look into the matter and to report back on methods of facilitating cheaper communications. This group later met Asquith,

Buxton and Colonel J.E.B. Seely, the Under-Secretary at the Colonial Office, to discuss the high cost of cablegrams. These efforts resulted in a rate reduction. On the first afternoon, a reception in Westminster Hall was given by those members from the Commons and the Lords with journalistic or writing experience. Those in attendance included Lords Curzon, Cromer and Milner, as well as Winston Churchill, Sir Charles Dilke and T.P. O'Connor. The second day's session was led by Sir Edward Grey, the Foreign Secretary, and Reginald McKenna, the First Lord of the Admiralty. Grey echoed Rosebery's remarks, telling the delegates that the extensive expenditure on armaments 'cannot be overrated'. McKenna stressed the need to keep Britain's Navy strong enough to 'keep open the highroad of the seas'.[32]

The imperial delegates were fêted in London and the countryside. They were presented to the King, and attended a reception at Marlborough House hosted by the Prince of Wales. On 6 June Northcliffe and Wrench motored to Sutton Place to make preparations for a lunch visit of the colonial editors two days later. Northcliffe told Wrench that he agreed with him that there was 'a waking up in England in many directions'. A special train took the journalists – including Geoffrey Robinson, who commented on the 'glorious weather' – from Waterloo to Worplesdon. The rest of the trip to Sutton Place was made in a fleet of Standard automobiles. The company of journalists and notables listened attentively to Northcliffe's descriptions of what he had just seen in Germany. Garvin wrote that the editors were noticeably impressed 'and some depressed' by the disclosures.[33]

In addition to lectures by the politicians, the delegates also were given demonstrations by the armed forces – including an impressive sham battle by the Army at Aldershot. However, from a propaganda point of view, the high point of the Imperial Press Conference was the 12 June naval review at Spithead, organized by Admiral Fisher. Wrench joined Kennedy Jones, Thomas Marlowe, Reggie Nicholson and Geoffrey Robinson on the Admiralty tug *Volcano* for a trip down eighteen miles of warships. He recorded that it was a 'wonderful sight and made me realise what British seapower is'. The fleet included seven Dreadnought-class ships – 'so far the only ones afloat,' he noted.[34] Tea was laid out for the imperial editors on the original *Dreadnought*, from which the company watched destroyers practise firing torpedoes at submarines. Not to be outdone by the Army, Fisher also arranged for the delegates to witness a mock hostile landing on Whale Island, the property of the Naval Gunnery School.

During the conference, Northcliffe revealed to Harry Brittain that some 'rascal' had spread the rumour that he, Northcliffe, was about to start an Australian newspaper. Alluding to his continuing eye trouble, he told Brittain:

> You are aware that I am much more likely to extend my business in the direction of a blind man's dog, a stick, and a tin cup, and shall undoubtedly have to relinquish a great deal of my work. Apart from that I am hardly likely to act as one of the hosts of our friends from over seas, and give them a stab in the back by starting Papers against them.[35]

One young Australian journalist present at the conference, Keith Murdoch, was in London looking for work, unsuccessfully as it turned out. Although he would not meet Northcliffe until the dire events of the Great War threw them together, Murdoch was well aware of the press lord. He wrote to his father that Northcliffe was

> a prominent figure. He never speaks, but his management can be detected in all the arrangements . . . He is tall, fair, with a large head and a very kindly face. He does not give an impression of great strength (although certainly strength is there) but rather a clear-sighted, deep general capability. He seems to have great knowledge and to be simple and direct in his purposes. That, I think, is the secret of his success . . . he knows what he wants and goes straight for it. I expected to find him a bounding, unscrupulous showy man of the world, but he seems to be simple and kind (he wears steel-framed spectacles), and I must say I like his appearance.[36]

The delegates spent the last week of their two-week visit touring England and Scotland, from Oxford to Edinburgh. They returned to London for a final session, chaired by Lord Esher, on 26 June, when the role of the colonies in imperial defence was considered. Northcliffe attended the farewell reception at the Waldorf that evening.

When Fisher sent congratulations on the success of the Conference, Northcliffe called it 'one of the most important gatherings that has ever taken place in England', while downplaying his own role.[37] Those who attended it undoubtedly returned home with a heightened awareness of their ties to the mother country and of the needs of imperial defence. Many of these men remained in positions of influence when hostilities erupted in 1914 and the Empire rallied to Britain's aid. However, the greatest concrete achievement of the meeting in 1909 involved the facilitation of cable communications across the far-flung Empire.

Much work, nevertheless, remained to be done. Northcliffe

suggested to Brittain that to 'tackle this Press cable-rate business thoroughly', it would be a good idea to start a 'permanent Imperial Press Council' with a paid secretary. Otherwise, he continued, he was 'afraid that your splendid work may be wasted when the conference evaporates'. In his estimation there was 'at least several years work in the cable-rate business'.[38] Should Brittain accept the job of secretary to such a council, Northcliffe affirmed his willingness to contribute towards the salary. In July Brittain sent Northcliffe the articles of association of the Empire Press Union. The new organization was designed to improve the cable distribution of news throughout the Empire and to provide a permanent organization for representatives of newspapers published in the British Empire.[39] Northcliffe agreed to become its hon. treasurer.

In the summer of 1909 aerial concerns again were brought to the fore when the first aeroplane crossed the English Channel from Calais to Dover and captured the prize which the *Daily Mail* had offered in the previous October. In June, several aviators – all French – were in Calais making preparations, with *Daily Mail* correspondents in place to cover the take-off and landing. The feat was finally accomplished by Louis Blériot, who bested his competitors on 25 July 1909. Northcliffe presented the pilot with the £1,000 cheque the following day at a ceremony at the Savoy. The *Daily Mail* commented that the deed

> stuns the imagination by its far-reaching possibilities and marks the dawn of a new age for man . . . Thus have the sceptics been put to scorn. When, less than a year ago, we offered our prize there were many who declared it ridiculous to imagine that man would ever fly across the Channel . . .
>
> Now, however, we have to reckon with the fact that a small and inexpensive machine, which can readily be multiplied by the hundred, has bridged the Channel . . . British insularity has vanished . . . Men who can navigate the air know nothing of frontiers and can laugh at the 'blue streak' . . .
>
> The British people have hitherto dwelt secure in their islands . . . But locomotion is now being transferred to an element where Dreadnoughts are useless and sea power no shield against attack . . . Such a dramatic moment in human history occurred yesterday.[40]

Elsewhere, on the political front, the struggle over the Finance Bill continued. Rosebery issued a statement that the measure was 'not a Budget, but a revolution; a social and political revolution of the first magnitude', which, he feared, would be passed 'over the heads of the people'. The Unionists welcomed this criticism from within the Liberal camp and argued that the Commons had run amok and that some sort of popular referendum was needed before the country embarked on such a radical departure. Lansdowne, the Conservative leader in the Lords, asserted his willingness to protect the country from rash action.[41] In a speech to his constituents in the City of London on 27 July, Balfour endorsed Tariff Reform and challenged the government to hold an election to test which financial plan the voters supported.

Lloyd George replied to the Unionists three days later from the Edinburgh Castle meeting house in Limehouse, where he gave perhaps the most famous and effective speech of his career. He began his address by excoriating the rich for their reluctance to pay for the Dreadnoughts they demanded: 'We wanted money to pay for the building; so we sent the hat around . . . amongst workmen . . . they all dropped in their coppers. We went round Belgravia, and there has been such a howl ever since that it has well-nigh deafened us.' Turning to the Budget's social programme, he went on that it was 'rather a shame that a rich country like ours . . . should allow those who have toiled all their days to end in penury and possibly starvation . . . There are many in the country blessed by Providence with great wealth, and if there are amongst them men who grudge out of their riches a fair contribution towards the less fortunate . . . they are very shabby rich men.'[42]

The Chancellor then turned to a defence of his proposed land and mineral taxes, using as vivid examples the miserly activities of a number of dukes. The first example, Northumberland, had demanded £900 an acre for a plot needed for a school which, said Lloyd George, would 'train the children which in due course would become the men labouring on his property'. His contribution to the rates on this land was on the basis of thirty shillings an acre. 'All we can say is this,' the Chancellor went on, 'if it is worth £900, let him pay taxes on £900.' After giving several of Northumberland's brethren similarly harsh treatment, he ended the defence of his Budget with a challenge to the House of Lords: 'I do not believe in their threats. They have threatened . . . like this before, but . . . have seen it is not in their interests to carry out their futile menaces.'

The Limehouse address caused a sensation and helped to turn the political tide, which had been running against the Budget.[43] It rallied the Liberals, confounded the Unionists, and elicited a complaint from the King to Asquith that no previous Chancellor had spoken so violently while in office.

The audacity of the speech impressed Northcliffe, whose continued enthusiasm for automobiles had brought him into contact with Lloyd George the month before, over government import and export regulations. In June, after apologizing for bothering him during the Budget crisis, Northcliffe had complained to the Chancellor (whom he had yet to meet in person) that foreign cars were being held up needlessly by Customs when they entered England.[44] Apparently eager to find a way to mend fences with one of his most influential newspaper opponents, Lloyd George responded that he would call a meeting of Customs officials over the matter and invited Northcliffe to visit the Treasury to discuss the issue.[45] Though Northcliffe replied that he was 'sorry I cannot accept the very kind invitation you make because I am one of those people who believe that journalists should be read and not seen', four days after the Limehouse speech, on 3 August, he visited the Peers' Gallery of the Commons.[46]

This rare occurrence caught the attention of Cecil Harmsworth and of Henry Dalziel MP, a newspaper proprietor who supported Lloyd George in his *Reynold's Illustrated News*. When told that Northcliffe had never met the Welshman, Dalziel arranged for a conference in the Chancellor's private room behind the Speaker's chair. Cecil Harmsworth described the occasion:

> There were cordial greetings. N. and I stayed with Ll. G. for upwards of an hour. The whole of this time Ll. G. devoted all his powers to capturing N. It was a dazzling performance. Private Secretaries and Ministers looked in at the door, to be wafted away by a wave of Ll. G's hand. The spell was not to be broken by anybody or for any purpose.[47]

Finding Northcliffe unbending on the Budget, Lloyd George changed his subject to the Development of the Roads Bill, over which they had previously corresponded. He took the bold step of giving the owner of the *Daily Mail* a draft of his proposal for developing national routes before it had been presented to the Commons, telling him to make any use of it he wished, including publication. Cecil recorded that his brother was 'delighted in Ll. G's splendid imprudence'.[48] Lloyd George reported to his own brother that Northcliffe had told him that 'the Budget has completely destroyed the Tariff Reform propaganda in the country. He said they had all miscalculated the popularity of the Land Clauses. He wants to trim.'[49]

This first meeting of these two figures, poles apart politically, was widely noted. Lloyd George came under criticism from the Liberal Party for the liaison, and during the next decade he faced harsh reproof for continuing a relationship with the press lord. The Liberal *Daily News* suggested that the first meeting had prompted a moderation in Northcliffe's view of the Budget, as reflected in the 4 August Political Notes section of *The Times*, which commented that it sensed a change comparable 'to the turn of the tide upon an estuary when the moored boats swing slowly around'. The *Daily News* statement, Northcliffe told the staff of *The Times*, was an 'entire concoction'. However, the *Daily Mail* of 5 August admitted that the agitation against the Budget appeared to have fallen flat and that the Liberal cause had been rejuvenated by Lloyd George's Limehouse declaration. Despite the fact that the paper never supported the Finance Bill and that the *Daily Mail* leader of 6 August was 'How to Fight the Budget', the feeling at the time, abetted by the Liberal papers, was that the Northcliffe press had turned its back on the Unionist cause.[50]

That day an alarmed Garvin sent his chief, whom he feared had gone over to the enemy in the Budget battle, a seventeen-page letter. The editor's exhausting campaign for eight Dreadnoughts had recently come to what appeared to be a successful conclusion. Because Italy and Austria had launched similar programmes, McKenna announced in the Commons on 26 July that the government would go ahead with the four contingent Dreadnoughts. A little more than a week after this victory, Garvin entreated Northcliffe

> not to encourage by indirect means in your papers thoughts of a surrender on the Budget which would ruin the Empire. In my admiration for your genius, and seeing you growing as I thought every day, I boasted that you were a Napoleon who would never come to his Moscow. But now I am not so sure, and I am more alarmed for you than for the Empire and the party. Oh, believe me, half England will not sit down to be despoiled without fighting; and if your papers won't fight their battle they will turn to the papers that will.[51]

In response to this emotional plea, the owner of the *Observer* told Garvin that he was worried about his editor's health and the strain he was under.

In Northcliffe's view, the Conservative Party was handicapped both by a lack of speakers outside Parliament and by the absence of a clearly defined social programme to offer the electorate. He discussed the need for Unionist proposals with the *Daily Mail* writer Henry Hamilton Fyfe, who was in full agreement. Fyfe sent his chief a series of articles on the subject, written earlier in the year, which the proprietor now had published in the *Daily Mail*.[52] The Party was also hampered, Northcliffe told Buckle, 'by the egregious Budget Protest League'. This organization had been started in June by the Unionist MP Walter Long to fight alongside the Tariff Reform League against Lloyd George's creation. Unfortunately for the Unionist cause, the Liberal Budget League, also organized in June, was much more successful in rousing the country and, in addition, the Unionists had no speakers to match the eloquence and fire of Lloyd George and Churchill. Instead they had newspapers, which proved inadequate for the task.

With Joseph Chamberlain sidelined by a stroke, the *Daily Mail* supported his son, Austen. Northcliffe asked the *Daily Mail* writer Frank Dilnot to do a personal sketch for publication. He told Dilnot that Austen, despite being overshadowed by his father, had 'certainly "come on" enormously this Session, but does not get credit for the great ability he has displayed. I was particularly struck by the comments made about him by the Imperial Press Conference men.'[53] Northcliffe attempted to encourage Austen to action outside the Commons. He suggested 'a strong constructive fighting speech' from 'some prominent platform', promising 'very careful arrangements for its reporting in all my newspapers'. Further, if the speech could 'hint at some possibility of social reform', Northcliffe believed 'it would do a good deal to stem the tide of reaction, which, despite the views of those who do not take the trouble to find out, is spreading – and rapidly'.[54] In a long letter, Chamberlain responded that he had 'gone some way to meet your wishes' and that, at his father's invitation, Balfour had agreed to address a great Unionist demonstration at Birmingham after a visit by Asquith.[55]

Northcliffe responded that he was pleased at the planned visit of Balfour to Birmingham, but advised that 'we have to carry on a discussion for perhaps six weeks before that'. This would require more speeches outside the Commons. The splendid debates, the press lord complained, were not properly covered in the papers, while the Liberals were making strong speeches every day. 'Whatever you may have been told to the contrary,' he confided, 'we are strongly handicapped, and in many quarters there is a good deal of ridiculous optimism. The Budget Protest League is, in my humble opinion, no match for the Budget League, and while they allege that their speakers are allowed to talk tariff reform, that was not true up to last week.'[56] He also deplored the fact that the elder Chamberlain's illness had kept him out of the fray.

The cautious policy of *The Times* concerning Tariff Reform and the

Budget, added to the continuing losses at the paper, had worn thin the patience of the chief proprietor. To keep a closer watch, Northcliffe replaced Bell's assistant, Kitchin, with Reggie Nicholson.[57] Bell told Buckle that Northcliffe had threatened to transfer his shares to someone who would run the newspaper 'from the purely commercial point of view'. This prompted the editor to seek a reaffirmation of the proprietor's pledge to stay the course for five years, or, if he relinquished control, to place the paper with a group of trustees who would run it 'in allowance with its traditions'. Buckle warned Northcliffe that both his reputation and that of *The Times* would 'be damaged by any premature change'. He admitted that the newspaper was conservative in journalistic matters, but asserted that this was a part of its tradition. The letter ended with a plea not to 'rustle' the newspaper too much or 'change its character and destroy its influence. Hitherto you have always seemed to recognise this. I ask you again to return to that sound opinion.'[58] Northcliffe replied that his statements had only been attempts to 'get Bell to move', and that he found the manager of *The Times* a difficult person with whom to deal. He went on that he had fought a year-long 'battle of accounts' to get the newspaper on the 'same clear system' used by his other concerns.[59] It had taken that long to learn the true financial state of the paper and of *The Times* Book Club, which Northcliffe considered the firm's greatest liability.

In August 1909 Northcliffe attended the first great international flying meeting, held on the plain of Bétheny, north of Reims. Unlike earlier in the year at Pau, the British government was represented; however, there was only one English aviator, George Cockburn, among the thirty-eight entrants in the competition. On the 25th, *The Times* remarked that in 'centuries hence the students of social, industrial, and probably also military history will look back to these windy days of August as to the turbulent birthday of a new era . . . Now, for the first time, the flying men have emerged . . . and definitely grouped themselves as the pioneers of a new epoch in the eyes of attentive humanity.' Besides several British military representatives, Lloyd George also attended. The Chancellor commented to a *Daily Mail* representative that 'It was one of the most marvellous sights I ever set eyes on . . . A feeling one could not resist was this: How hopelessly behind we are in these great and historic experiments. I really felt, as a "Britisher", rather ashamed that we were so completely out of it.'[60] Cockburn complained to Northcliffe that there were not enough places in England for pilots to learn to fly, and the press lord passed along this information to

Haldane. The War Secretary, as before, denied the seriousness of the problem, while assuring Northcliffe that everything possible was being done to assist aviators.

However, by the time Haldane's reply arrived, Northcliffe and a travelling party which included his wife, Moberly Bell and Wrench had already departed on the *Empress of Britain* for North America. They planned a train tour of Canada and the United States, before returning to Newfoundland for the opening ceremonies of the Grand Falls development. The group left Montreal on 3 September on a two-week trip across the continent to Vancouver in the private rail car *Independence*. Their progress through the scenic country was slowed by numerous stops and one wash-out of the tracks. Along the way Wrench collected local newspapers for his chief. From Vancouver, the group then proceeded south along the Pacific coast by rail into the United States, through Seattle and Portland, arriving at San Franciso on 21 September. The *San Francisco Chronicle* asked Northcliffe and Bell for their views on the tension between England and Germany. The newspaper reported that both men called a war as 'inevitable as was the clash between Germany and France in 1870 and the struggle between Russia and Japan in 1904'. Bell was quoted as saying 'the situation was like that of two trains rushing towards each other on a single track'.[61]

The US leg of the journey included stops at the Grand Canyon, Santa Fe and Kansas City. From the last, Northcliffe sent Kennedy Jones a report on their progress:

> We are on a nine days' journey from San Francisco to Grand Falls, and except the intense heat in Arizona, do not mind it in the least. This morning we have been passing through the state of Kansas and it looks much like Norfolk. The Canadian North-west is the place and I greatly fear a rush of Americans there. The Western Canadian papers give absolutely no English news at all except about the English suffragettes, so, of the Budget I know very little. I don't know when I shall be back, but I am determined when at Grand Falls to learn the whole business of that place.[62]

Moberly Bell had been included in the group at Northcliffe's insistence, in part to remove him from Printing House Square, if only temporarily. The manager of *The Times* was exhausted by the five weeks with his chief, partly because Northcliffe constantly harried him over a variety of newspaper topics, including the lukewarm support he felt the paper gave to the Tariff Reform cause against Lloyd George's Budget. Wrench was troubled by the treatment of 'Old Bell', and recorded some 'unpleasant scenes'.

While the others went on to Grand Falls, Wrench and Bell left the party and returned to England. Northcliffe warned Kennedy Jones that

> Shortly after this reaches you, old Bell will arrive home. He is under the impression that we are trying to deprive him of his rights and privileges at Printing House Square. He has been . . . not a more difficult travelling companion than I expected, but quite difficult enough . . . I am convinced that the only way to deal with him is to jump on him at once. When he sees you are in earnest he becomes duly obedient. The truth of the matter is that the old man is older than his years . . . I think also he is inclined to be an intriguer. He is elated at the least sign of prosperity of *The Times* and doesn't believe there is any need for watchfulness. What he really thinks is, if we leave *The Times* alone, all will be well and 'Belled'.[63]

Northcliffe should have known full well that Bell was an 'intriguer', as it was his sabotage of Pearson that had delivered *The Times* into the press lord's hands.

At Grand Falls a two-day festival marked the official opening of the development after three years of preparation. The Governor-General of Canada, the premier of Newfoundland and their retinues attended the ceremonies which set the machinery at the mills in motion. An arch of electric lights, which spelled out 'Welcome to the Chief', greeted Northcliffe, who had a house built for himself and Lady Northcliffe on the site – meant to be a 'little bit of England' in the wilderness.[64] English investors supported the huge venture, which controlled 3,100 square miles of timber, despite the many critics who said the project was doomed for a variety of reasons, including the climate and the remote location. American interests also attempted to stir up controversy, calling the project another example of a British appropriation of resources that rightly belonged to Canada.

After the opening, on 20 October, Northcliffe sent Kennedy Jones a note that the ceremonies had been a great success and 'did us a great deal of good in this very suspicious island, and the American attacks, although they shook the place . . . for a time, have on the whole done us some good'. He went on that 'they have at any rate quite dispelled the theory that we had stolen the nation's birthright'. In his estimation the enterprise was a good investment and, if properly protected, the potential of the forests was 'limitless'. The plant he described as 'perfection', and the delays 'not anything in so gigantic an undertaking . . . the same kind of toothing troubles we have gone through in our other enterprises'.[65]

With the celebration in Newfoundland completed, Northcliffe turned his mind to England and *The Times*. Another letter to Kennedy Jones complained:

> It is rather difficult to drag ourselves away from this monstrous enterprise to the smoky squalor of Printing House Square, but the thought that occurs to me every day about the 'Times' is 'Is it good enough?' I suppose it is better than before we had it, but it is certainly not so good as it was immediately after we bought it, in our first burst of enthusiasm. It lacks initiative in policy and in news. Its attitude on the Budget has been a joke throughout Canada ... it is very careless – Grand Rapids for Grand Falls – Good God! It wants energising.[66]

On 30 November, only a few days before Northcliffe arrived back in London, the House of Lords rejected the Budget. A week before, the *Daily Mail* had hailed 'Lord Lansdowne's Challenge', which invited his colleagues to refer the Budget to the people. In this action, said the newspaper, the House of Lords would be not 'attacking the privileges of the Commons . . . only discharging its moral obligation'. According to Lansdowne, it was the responsibility of the Lords to 'see that principles so new and revolutionary as those comprised in the Finance Bill shall not become the law of the land until the country has had an opportunity of expressing its opinion thereon'.[67] The day after the rejection, the *Daily Mail* declared that the Lords had 'acted both bravely and wisely' in voting 350 to 75 against the Finance Bill, which represented an 'audacious attempt to force socialism on the country without consulting the people'. Amid the furore over the unprecedented action of the Lords, the next morning's issue also noted the retirement of Sir John Fisher, who was to be elevated to the House of Lords as Baron Fisher and replaced at the Admiralty by Sir Arthur Wilson.

Northcliffe granted a Sutton Place interview to the *New York Times*. He declared his delight with the long tour of the USA and Canada, 'where he saw great prosperity only equalled by that of Germany'. He told the American correspondent that he had returned for the national Budget debate, a fight for a British tariff versus the 'present obsolete Free Trade System'.[68] In his estimation, the Liberals were being forced to a vote by the efforts of J.L. Garvin, whose *Observer* had 'driven them into a corner', and the coming election, said Northcliffe, would be a 'smashing blow for the Liberal party'. The *Observer* called for a 'New Government For the New Year', and the Unionist Party expected a good result. Unfortunately, it would not be quite good enough.

10

The Peers, the People and the Press,
1909–1911

I~N EARLY DECEMBER~ 1909, Northcliffe suffered an attack of nervous exhaustion which forced him to consult his physicians. On doctors' orders, he once again travelled to Paris for a rest cure. His wife soon reported to Sutton that he was much improved, although plagued by many people who wished to see him, including J.P. Morgan. At the same time, campaigning began for the January 1910 general election, the first in four years. The Unionist Party again offered Tariff Reform as the cure for the nation's persistent unemployment problems, while branding the Liberals as socialist radicals who were criminally lax in matters of national defence. In the editorial 'Why Germany Wants the Free Traders to Win', the *Daily Mail* declared that a victory for the Liberals would be a victory for Germany. The journal applauded 'Mr. Balfour's Strong Lead' in making Tariff Reform the 'first plank' in the Unionist platform. It also approved of Balfour's attacks on Liberal neglect of the Navy, and condemned the electoral deals being made with Labour as a 'Liberal Surrender to Socialism'.[1]

In a speech at the National Liberal Club on 3 December, Lloyd George commented on the Budget crisis that all the 'weightiest papers on the Conservative side', including *The Times*, had been against him. The *Daily Mail*, he went on, had hesitated, and 'only came in at the last moment' when it placed 'at the disposal of the wreckers that passion for accuracy of statement which has been so dear to it'. The 'rabidest of the lot', he said, had been the *Observer*, edited by Garvin, the maddest of the 'Mad Mullahs'.[2] The next morning's *Daily Mail* commented that the attack had not disturbed the paper's 'peace of mind', and went on that 'we have no doubt that Mr J.L. Garvin . . . whom the Chancellor also assailed in a very unusual manner, is capable of taking care of himself'. The attack did, however, temporarily prompt Garvin to cease writing anonymous pieces for the *Daily Mail*, so that he could deny the charge that he was behind the paper's campaign.

Asquith formally opened the Liberal campaign with an address to 10,000 supporters at the Albert Hall. This speech – made under a banner which asked 'Shall the People be Ruled by the Peers?' – rallied the anti-Unionist forces and made plain that the Liberals meant to centre on the House of Lords and its rejection of the Budget. The Prime Minister declared, 'We shall not assume office, and we shall not hold office, unless we can secure the safeguards which experience shows us to be necessary for the legislative utility and honour of the party of progress.'[3] What these safeguards might be – whether statutory or a pledge from the King to create enough peers to carry the Liberal programme – was left unstated. Besides the social-reform benefits of the Budget for the working class, Asquith also promised education reform to the Nonconformists, another Licensing Bill to the anti-drink forces, franchise reforms for the radicals, disestablishment to the Welsh, land and rent reform to the Scots, and, last but far from least, Home Rule to the Irish. The next day *The Times* called the speech an 'orgy of promises made to all the fanatical and disruptive forces in political life'. Despite the many other promises, the constitutional issue was crucial for the Liberal campaign. The Unionists, on the other hand, wished to bring their fiscal alternative to the Budget to the fore.

Illness forced Balfour to issue his 10 December election address in the newspapers. This less than stirring document concentrated on a defence of the Lords and lacked Asquith's fire. The address disappointed those in the Party who wanted a strong pro-Tariff Reform stance. Because *The Times* had difficulty obtaining an advance copy of Balfour's statement from Conservative Central Office, Northcliffe had his staff discuss press co-ordination for the election effort with Balfour's secretary, J.S. Sandars. However, in the end, efficient co-operation was frustrated by Central Office fears that Northcliffe was attempting to take over. Garvin and Sandars nevertheless schemed to keep the proprietor of *The Times* 'well disposed' to the Party. Sandars reported to Balfour that they also planned to save Northcliffe 'from the embraces of Winston who flatters him and toadies him in a sickening way, and then laughs behind his back'.[4]

Despite his ill health, Northcliffe became more involved in this election than in any since his own run for Parliament fifteen years before. Lancashire, because the Unionists had been so overwhelmed there in the 1906 debacle, became the cockpit of the January 1910 contest. This assault on the bastion of Free Trade ensured that the fiscal question would be well aired. Garvin told Sandars that his chief had been unwell, but that 'from his pillow he is driving things splendidly, taking in hand himself the Lancashire campaign; and the *Daily Mail* as a political organ was never half so good as now'. The arrangements included special *Daily Mail* election editions for Lancashire, East Anglia and North-East England, in addition to a temporary newspaper at Newcastle. These measures were meant to supplement the efforts of Lancashire's Unionist magnate, Lord Derby, who, Northcliffe told Sandars, had been 'very badly out manoeuvred by the enemy'. Balfour's secretary praised the *Daily Mail* to its owner for its admirable service to the Party. 'It is the most potent auxiliary,' Sandars went on. 'Everyone reads it: it is a brief for all our speakers. Its arguments, its facts, its criticisms supply the best and most modern ammunition.'[5]

A December 1909 *Daily Mail* series by Robert Blatchford, a former Army sergeant and proprietor of the socialist *Clarion*, was aimed at underscoring the Liberal government's blindness to the German threat, at sea and elsewhere. In the first instalment, Blatchford explained that he was writing 'these articles because I believe that Germany is deliberately preparing to destroy the British Empire; and because I know that we are not able or ready to defend ourselves against a sudden and formidable attack'. He went on that he had taken this course 'against my own interests and against the feeling of most of my political and many of my private friends'. He spoke out in the *Daily Mail* 'in the hope of arousing the public from the fatal apathy and complacent optimism which blind them to the greatest peril the nation has ever been called upon to face'.[6] As evidence for his assertions, in the following weeks he chronicled the growth of Germany's navy, her militarism, her will for world power through 'Blood and Iron', and her record of attacking without warning whenever she believed conditions favourable for victory. Britain, said Blatchford, was to be Germany's next target, but the British people refused to believe it. Britons, he said, 'take little interest in foreign affairs and less in military matters'. They 'do not want to bother, they do not want to pay, they do not want to fight, and they regard as cranks or nuisances all who try to warn them of their danger'. He also claimed that the British government was afraid to tell its people the truth.

Blatchford prophesied that the greatest danger – more menacing than invasion – lay in France and the Channel ports, which, in the hands of Germany, would be a 'pistol pointed at the heart of England'.[7] The problem of British defence, he went on, was the problem of the defence of France. To accomplish this the country must build a first-class army of at least 500,000 men, and he recommended that Lord Kitchener be put in command. 'Soldiering or Slavery' were the alternatives. The 'blue-water' navalists were wrong and Lord Roberts was right. To keep their Empire, their liberty and their trade, Blatchford proclaimed that the British would have to submit both to conscription and to the taxation needed to pay for the cost of peace. If £300 million could be found to pay for the Boer War, he believed the money could now be found to pay for more ships and more soldiers.

The *Daily Mail* series was belittled as 'Ravings' by the Liberal *Daily News*. Other Liberal journals joined in against the *Daily Mail* and what was described as a Tory election trick. The *Manchester Guardian* accused the newspaper of 'deliberately raking the fires of hell for votes'. Blatchford responded, 'What has the danger to the Empire have to do with votes? I wrote these articles for men and women, not for votes.'[8] The *Daily Mail* expressed its pleasure that nothing that had appeared in its pages 'in recent years has attracted more attention, has aroused more discussion, or has been followed by our readers with closer interest'. By the end of January, 1,600,000 copies of the series in pamphlet form had been sold, with another 250,000 given away.[9]

In mid-December, Balfour sent Northcliffe his regrets that their respective illnesses had kept them from meeting to discuss affairs.[10] The Conservative leader told Northcliffe that the 'Notes on the Navy' he had sent to him seemed 'admirably done', and continued that 'the difficulty I feel in dealing with the Navy on the platform is that it is so hard to make the public understand the danger of the position without saying things about Germany which hardly seem discreet in the mouth of an ex-Prime Minister'.[11] Nevertheless, Balfour used the naval issue and a strong appeal for Tariff Reform to bring the Unionists back into the long contest. On the naval front, Balfour championed the two-to-one standard in a 4 January 'solemn warning' to the nation. According to Balfour, the country's supremacy at sea was threatened and the Navy generally was in 'the weakest position in memory'. He told his audience at Hanley that the statesmen of the lesser European powers were agreed that a struggle between Britain and Germany was inevitable and that 'we are predestined to succumb'.[12]

In the view of the *Daily Mail* the country had to choose between two very clear-cut policies in the coming election. The Unionist policy offered a sufficient navy, Tariff Reform and small landownership with State-aided purchase. The radical policy entailed an insufficient navy, single-chamber government, Home Rule for Ireland, increased taxation (with a 'new inquisition' over collection), appropriation of profits, the export of British capital, Church disestablishment, and a fresh licensing Bill. The newspaper asked, 'Can there be the slightest hesitation as to which the nation should choose?'

The entry of Balfour into the naval arena gave the agitation an added weight which the *Daily Mail* sought to exploit. The 'First Issue', declared the journal of 7 January, was the choice between 'A Weak Navy Or Command of the Sea'. Balfour's recovery and return to the fight also helped to energize the Unionist fiscal cause. At Aberdeen he labelled the Liberal policy as contrary to the 'experience of civilised mankind'. A major speech at York a few days before the polling began pledged import duties 'over a wide fiscal field' and matched the Liberal vow to maintain 'Cheap Food'. The *Daily Mail* proclaimed his 'Clear Promise' that there would be 'No Dearer Bread and Tea' and, in fact, a 'Probable Reduction of Present Food Taxes'.[13]

On the first morning of the voting, which began on 15 January and lasted until 10 February, the *Daily Mail* called the election the most momentous since 1832. *The Times* and *Daily Mail* both predicted – correctly as it turned out – that neither party would be able to secure a majority and that the Irish Nationalists would be presented with a pivotal role. Early returns heartened the Tariff Reform supporters. The 19 January *Daily Mail* called the previous day's results, 'A Great Day', with two ministers defeated and fifteen Tariff Reform victories. Two days later the newspaper reported 'Sweeping Victories' and 'The Death of Free Trade'. The Unionists' early electoral gains did not last, however. Wins in the South of England were balanced by Liberal strength in the North. Lancashire, despite Northcliffe's best efforts, held firm. Though the Party could take satisfaction in an overall net gain of 105 seats, it was not enough. The final tally showed 275 Liberal, 273 Unionist, 82 Irish Nationalist and 40 Labour MPs. Although the Liberals had lost their absolute majority, the promise for Home Rule to the Irish contingent, led by John Redmond MP, allowed them to continue in office with Irish support. The *Daily Mail* dubbed Redmond the 'Dollar Dictator' because of the money he raised in America for the Irish cause.

Even before the final numbers were tallied, Garvin fired what can be seen as the opening volley of the next election in the 23 January *Observer*, declaring that the Liberals' 'absolute majority is smashed, pulverised, annihilated . . . Mr. Asquith and his Government must exist in subjection to Mr. Redmond . . . or they cannot exist at all.' He asked two questions: 'Is the Second Chamber to be destroyed by the Irish vote?' and 'Are free imports to be forced upon the neck of British Labour by the money that has been raised in the Protectionist United States?' The *Daily Mail* declared the election, for the great parties, a 'dead heat' in which a majority in the United Kingdom, including Ireland, had 'pronounced against the Budget'.[14] Referring to the possibility that enough Liberal peers would have to be created to pass the Finance Bill and to reform the House of Lords, the journal suggested that 274 radicals in the Commons be elevated to the Lords so that there could be 274 by-elections and more Tariff Reform members. The country, said the *Daily Mail*, did not want to be dominated by a single chamber or a single man – meaning Redmond. However, the lack of a Liberal majority lessened the immediate pressure on the King to create peers without another election, and for several months the Asquith government pursued a 'wait and see' policy of drift.

With the general election behind the country, Northcliffe turned his attention to *The Times*. Garvin, among others, had complained of its lacklustre performance in the contest. Expenses and the 'obstinate incapacity and ignorance' of Bell also exasperated the chief proprietor. He warned Buckle that 'drastic reform' was needed, and complained that it was 'a thousand pities' that the efforts of such men as Jones and Nicholson should be nullified by the optimism that brought *The Times* 'on the rocks'. The staff, he felt, should be made acquainted with the real facts. He went on that it was 'lamentable to have to say that every communication we send has to be put in the hands of those, who, I think, most ungratefully, resent our efforts to save the paper. In any case I trust you will preserve this letter so that I may be relieved in future from blame.'[15] Buckle responded that improvements made at the newspaper were being ignored and that he did not know 'to whom you refer as nullifying the efforts' of Jones and Nicholson. He was endeavouring to help them. 'Nor do I understand', he added, 'what you mean by saying it is lamentable that every communication you send has to be put into the hands of those who ungratefully resent your efforts to save the Paper . . . Probably you are referring to Bell; if you mean more please tell me.'[16] He apologized for any 'misunderstanding between us' and promised he would not allow his confidence in his owner to be shaken. He hoped that by the next Christmas the paper would be in a position to 'meet its obligations.'[17]

The staff of *The Times* received a reprieve from the attention of the chief proprietor in February 1910, when Northcliffe's physician, Dr Bertrand Dawson, confined him to a nursing home for a complete rest. The illnesses that had plagued him since his return from America – variously described as neurasthenia, inflammation of the pancreas and indigestion due to overwork – had refused to abate. Garvin wrote to Sandars that he had 'helped to manoeuvre' Northcliffe 'into a real rest where they even take away his pencils; and if he is well and cheerful and assured of more enjoyment of life, he will do priceless things for us'.[18] Garvin had recommended to Northcliffe that he should 'take a little more pause, a real pause – not setting up your mental dynamo in Paris and calling it a holiday – in order to increase the enjoyment and extend the efficiency of your indispensable existence . . . How much your complete restoration of health will mean to us all and the Empire.'[19] It was not long, however, before the 'pause' became insufferable to the patient. In a letter from 'The Asylum', Manchester Street, London, Northcliffe complained to Sutton on 5 February that he was 'not very well' and that the facility was 'like a prison'.[20] His doctor, he reported, was being very strict and had cut his reading down to the *Daily Mail* and the *Observer* and also insisted on no work until June.

While Northcliffe was confined, the chairman of *The Times*, Arthur Walter, died. His place at Printing House Square was taken by his son, John Walter, who had been at the newspaper for twelve years as an assistant to Bell and, more recently, correspondent in Portugal and Spain. The chief proprietor sent a sympathy card from the convalescent home pledging his support to the new chairman 'in your endeavour to maintain the Paper in the high station your greatly respected father desired it to hold in the worlds of Government and of Letters'. The letter continued that 'I do firmly believe that when we are rid of some of our inevitable initial troubles a bright era will dawn at Printing House Square.'[21]

In April, Northcliffe transferred his recuperation to the Continent, where the doctors insisted he maintain 'absolute rest and no mental effort'. His entourage included his wife, Garvin and an old friend, the writer Charles Whibley. The group made their way via Paris to Valescure, Saint-Raphaël. Rumours had spread in England and France that Northcliffe had suffered a complete nervous collapse. Lady

Northcliffe reported to Sutton that her husband was making 'a little progress every day, but is still very easily fatigued – nervous – and a long way off work yet'. Even Garvin and Whibley were only allowed to see the patient for fifteen minutes a day. Northcliffe managed to smuggle out a request to Sutton for copies of all the London papers. Before long, he wrote to Hamilton Fyfe that he was 'weary of the roses and the nightingales of Valescure and longed for Fleet Street'. He told his 'Darling Mums' that he was 'sticking to my cure closely. It is a slow business. I am so weak.'

In late April two contestants, one British and one French, vied for the £10,000 prize the *Daily Mail* had announced four years before for the first person to complete an aeroplane flight from London to Manchester. The breakdown of Claude Grahame-White's Farman craft, the *White Eagle*, two-thirds of the way to Manchester, opened the door for the French contestant, Louis Paulhan, who completed the 186-mile test on 28 April in another Farman biplane. Although Grahame-White had failed, Northcliffe arranged for him to receive a 100-guinea cup in recognition of the pluck he had showed by making the first night flight in Europe while trying to overtake Paulhan. The contest between a Briton and a Frenchman caused a national sensation and greatly aided the efforts of Northcliffe to make the nation 'air-minded'. The publicity surrounding Paulhan's victory and a series in *The Times* by the military correspondent, Colonel Repington, helped to spur the government into reassessing and then reopening its aeroplane programme.[22]

The day after Paulhan landed in Manchester, the 1909 Budget became law at last. The Liberals had awakened sufficiently from their slumber to prepare a Parliament Bill which called for the reform of the Lords along much the same lines as Campbell-Bannerman's 1907 proposal. The Bill limited the veto power of the Upper House to only a two-session delay and withdrew completely the Lords' interdiction on financial Bills. In addition, the maximum life of the Commons was reduced from seven to five years. The reform battle was postponed, however, by the sudden death of the King, upon whom the constitutional crisis had lain very heavily, on 6 May 1910. Northcliffe, whose own convalescence continued, confided to his mother that his physician, Dawson, had been the 'youngest and ablest by our dear king's bedside'.[23]

The country went into a period of mourning which rivalled that for Queen Victoria; 250,000 people filed past the catafalque at Westminster Hall to pay their last respects. Sir Schomberg McDonnell, secretary to

His Majesty's Office of Works, recorded that the mourners were led by 'three women of the seamstress class: very poorly dressed and very reverent'. In contrast, McDonnell noted that the 'Prime Minister was there with Miss Asquith leaning against one of the lamp standards and watching the people pass. I thought his attitude and general demeanour rather offensive. I fear he had dined well and he seemed to regard the occasion as a mere show.'[24] The false story spread that, when Asquith called to view Edward's body, Queen Alexandra told him, 'Look at your handiwork!' The Queen allowed the *Daily Mirror* to publish a photograph of her husband lying in state. Huge crowds lined the funeral route on 20 May. Eight kings, one emperor and a former President followed the gun carriage upon which the coffin rested, behind which trailed Edward's faithful fox terrier, Caesar. Kaiser Wilhelm, George V and the Duke of Connaught made up the first human row. The Kaiser commented that 'he had done many things in his life, but he had never before been obliged to yield precedence to a dog'.[25]

The American representative, Theodore Roosevelt, arrived in England just after the monarch's passing. Following a lengthy hunting expedition in Africa, in the spring of 1910 Roosevelt had travelled to Europe, where he was treated as if he were still president. Among other activities, he met the King and Queen of Italy and reviewed the Kaiser's troops. Against the advice of the US ambassador, the former President stayed at Chequers, the house of Arthur Lee MP, who had been with Roosevelt at the Battle of San Juan Hill during the Spanish-American War, where the reputation of the 'Roughrider' had been made. Lee reported to Northcliffe on 24 May that Roosevelt would be with him until he sailed for home on 10 June. He commented, apropos the energy of the American, that 'we are having a fairly strenuous time as you can imagine'. Roosevelt's throat was troubling him, but Lee told Northcliffe that he still planned to 'fire a shot' at Guildhall on the 31st, 'which will give immense satisfaction to people like you and me who care, above all things, for the maintenance of our "goodly heritage" throughout the Empire'.[26] Lee expressed the hope that Northcliffe was recovering from his own illness, and extended an invitation to visit Chequers, the restoration of which, he said, had been aimed at the standard of Sutton Place.

By late May Northcliffe's condition had improved. Cecil Harmsworth commented after seeing his brother at Boulogne on the 26th that he was apparently a good deal better after his rest at Saint-Raphaël. Unfortunately, continuing weakness kept him from

Roosevelt's Guildhall address. The American sent a note that he regretted his 'absence and its cause. I had looked forward to seeing you.'[27] It appeared that the two would not meet before Roosevelt's return to the USA; however, in early June the former President managed to fit a visit to Sutton Place into his schedule. On the day he landed in New York, Roosevelt thanked Northcliffe for a 'mighty nice telegram', and especially his contention that the trip had been 'the most difficult speaking tour on record'. Roosevelt was 'inclined to believe you are right'. The letter went on that 'One of the pleasantest features of the tour was our stop at your house, and seeing Lady Northcliffe and you. I look forward to seeing both of you in America.'[28] Wrench noted in his 10 June diary that the 'Chief looked bronzed and not so fat, but restless, and his health is unquestionably getting on his nerves.' Northcliffe's improving mood was given a temporary setback by the news of the death of his old vanquished rival Sir George Newnes, at his house at Lynton on 9 June. The proprietor dictated a respectful *Daily Mail* obituary for the man who had helped to start his career in Fleet Street.

Arthur and Ruth Lee visited Sutton Place several times that summer, in the company of Garvin and St Loe Strachey, among others. Lee's diary recalls that there was 'much high talk, fine music, and always a sense of being at the heart of things'. Of Lady Northcliffe, he noted that she was a 'very remarkable woman, not strictly beautiful in the classic sense and yet lovely to look at. She knew how to make the best of her every point, was always perfectly dressed, and everything in her house and garden was as finished and exquisite as her own person.' Lee went on that 'she had few illusions about Northcliffe, who, while lavishly generous about money and gifts and almost courtly in his outward devotion, took little pains to dispel the impression that he esteemed his mother above all other women. So much so that in all crises he turned like a little boy to his mother's knee.'[29]

In times of political crisis, Northcliffe continued to seek the advice of the editor of the *Observer*. The death of Edward VII and the inexperience of George V inspired Garvin to suggest a political conference in an attempt to solve the constitutional and other problems. 'If King Edward on his deathbed', he wrote in the 8 May *Observer*, 'could have sent a last message to his people, he would have asked us to lay party passion aside, to sign a truce of God over his grave, to seek ... some fair means of making a common effort for our common country ... Let conference take place before conflict is irrevocably joined on terms of war to the knife.'[30] Garvin's call for a 'truce of God' was supported in

The Times by the Unionist political writer F.S. Oliver, under the name 'Pacificus', and within the Liberal Party by the Chief Whip, Alexander Murray, Master of Elibank.[31]

Garvin helped convene the inter-party Constitutional Conference, which came together not without difficulty, as some Unionists held Asquith responsible for the King's premature death. The first of more than twenty meetings during the following months took place on 17 June in Asquith's room at the Commons. The Liberal participants included the Prime Minister, Lord Crewe, Asquith's close adviser, Lloyd George and Augustine Birrell, the Irish Secretary. On the Unionist side, Balfour, Lansdowne, Lord Cawdor and Austen Chamberlain joined the sessions. The Conference began with a discussion of reform for the House of Lords, and at first went well. The Unionist side was willing to surrender to many of the Liberal demands, but insisted that the Upper House retain enough power to block Irish Home Rule without an election or referendum on the question. This point would prove the undoing of all subsequent efforts at conciliation and coalition.

That summer Northcliffe accepted the invitation of Sir John Knill, the lord mayor of London, to join the King Edward VII Memorial Committee. His activity on the Committee, however, was limited by a trip to Newfoundland. He wrote to Knill that he would be leaving on 20 August and returning the first week in October.[32] This trip to the Grand Falls development, a year after the opening, was meant to be a vacation in the fresh air of Canada. However, tempered by his illness and the intervening events, the optimism of 1909 was replaced by a foreboding over possible labour problems and other projected difficulties. On this trip, Northcliffe met Dr Seymour Price, who had travelled from London to Newfoundland to report on health conditions at the development. Northcliffe was so impressed with Price that he added him to his staff as a medical consultant. Price discovered valve damage to his new employer's heart.

Strengthening the imperial bond with Canada was one of Northcliffe's keenest desires and a central aim of the 'Overseas Club', founded by Wrench, who continued to be editor of the *Overseas Daily Mail*, as well as manager of the periodical list, brought together as the Amalgamated Press. The creation of the non-party imperial organization was announced in the *Overseas Daily Mail* on 27 August 1910, and news of the club became a weekly feature. Northcliffe pledged his full support to the venture, the headquarters of which were at Carmelite House. The Members' Creed proudly declared, 'Believing the British

Empire to stand for justice, freedom, order and good government, we pledge ourselves, as citizens of the greatest Empire in the world, to maintain the heritage handed down to us by our fathers.' The objects of the Club were:

> To help one another.
> To urge on every able-bodied man the necessity of being able to bear arms.
> To draw together in the bond of comradeship the peoples now living under the folds of the British flag.
> To insist on the vital necessity to the Empire of British Supremacy on the sea.[33]

There was no fee for membership, but a shilling bought the Club's lapel badge, a red 'S' within a white 'O'. Gold badges were available for a more sizeable contribution.

Wrench proposed that Northcliffe become the president of the Overseas Club, which by September 1910 already had 267 branches across the Empire. He told his chief, who accepted the presidency, that he saw 'no reason why we should not become the greatest force for keeping the Empire together. A membership of 1,100,000 like the Germany Navy League should not be beyond our organisation.'[34] By 19 November, reported Wrench, the Overseas Club had 6,075 members and 1,107 branches in formation in North and South America, Europe, Asia, the West Indies, Australasia and Africa, from Chicago to Johannesburg. From Paris, Northcliffe cautioned Wrench to be careful before going further with what he agreed might become a huge organization. He advised the study of the mistakes of similar efforts, and warned that the branches must be kept out of the hands of bad men and swindlers. The letter continued, 'In a short time, I propose to give a fourth page two-column article to the subject in the "Daily Mail". Where the matter is of most importance is in Canada, of course, and Australia. I should like soon to have my own gold badge, so as to be able to wear it where it can be seen.'[35] At the same time, the Northcliffe press campaigned against the Declaration of London, which was perceived as a threat to the Empire. This agreement codified the rules of naval engagement and blockade in case of war. As the leading sea power, Britain had the most at stake in the negotiations. The *Daily Mail* condemned the agreement as 'Sea Law Made in Germany' which would lead to a 'Paralysis of Seapower'.[36]

Back on the political front, after three months of meetings the Constitutional Conference appeared stalemated and doomed to failure.

In October Garvin persuaded his chief to support a plan promoted by Lloyd George for a larger settlement entailing a new programme of 'federalism' for the Empire and Ireland and a coalition government. The *Daily Mail* backed both the 'Home Rule All Around' plan and the *Observer* for a discussion of the idea. In *The Times*, 'Pacificus' also pushed forward the federal solution. Unfortunately, Garvin was unable to sway Chamberlain and Balfour, who rejected the coalition idea on 1 November.[37] Balfour's main consideration throughout had been maintaining the unity of his party, to which he refused to be another Peel.

The unsuccessful end of the Constitutional Conference meant another general election, this time fought primarily over the House of Lords and Irish Home Rule. Northcliffe told Balfour's cousin Lord Robert Cecil that he had done his 'very best to prevent the breaking up of the Conference'. He felt that 'almost any concession' would have been better than an election.[38] Before the dissolution of Parliament on 28 November, Asquith obtained a secret pledge from a doubtful George V to create sufficient Liberal peers to carry reform of the Lords if the Party won the contest. This commitment was gained only after the King was misled by one of his secretaries into believing that, if asked, Balfour would refuse to form a government. The Unionist campaign opened at Nottingham on 17 November. The next morning's *Daily Mail* hailed Balfour's speech, which made a 'Non-Party Appeal for the Navy', laid out a 'Clear Plan for the Lords' and declared yet another 'Solemn Pledge of Cheap Food'. Austen Chamberlain attempted to uphold his father's policy on food. He and Andrew Bonar Law MP, a 'coming man' in the Unionist Party, met Northcliffe in a futile effort to convince him that no new assurances on food taxes were needed.[39]

By mid-November Northcliffe's health had improved enough for his wife to write to Sutton that the 'Chief looks to me better than he has done for ten years – younger, firmer – better altogether. He eats well and sleeps perfectly. But he is rather nervous about himself and more inclined to run from London.'[40] Northcliffe's renewed vitality was reflected in a flurry of election messages from Paris to his employees. He instructed Walter Fish, news editor at the *Daily Mail*, to follow up and repeat the paper's 'National Service Appeal' and, if necessary, to see Lord Roberts on the subject; he dismissed that morning's paragraph on the matter as 'useless'. Andrew Caird was told to 'develop Bonar Law's challenge to Lancashire Free Traders'. Kennedy Jones was advised that the papers should continuously press the unpopularity of the 'Dollar

Dictator's Christmas Election' and 'dear tea' as well. The cable continued, 'Is not tea one of the chief household items? . . . Should we not continuously publish simple list of food prices under Free Trade?'[41]

Two days later another cable to Kennedy Jones proposed 'fresh words of warning by Blatchford in form of letters to editor think this essential to preserve consistency and prove neither Blatchford or ourselves scaremongers'. Consequently, three further *Daily Mail* reminders from the editor of the *Clarion* again raised 'The Greatest Issue of All' – the German menace. 'The danger to-day', said Blatchford, 'is greater than it was a year ago; our readiness to avert or meet it is relatively smaller.' Reginald McKenna responded to the series in a speech at North Monmouthshire, saying that, in order to divert attention from the House of Lords, a 'well-known socialist writer has been pressed into the service of a Tory newspaper in order to make your blood creep with horrible imaginings as to the designs of a great friendly foreign power'. Nonetheless, he declared that he was sure that the articles would 'have no influence on a single vote'. Blatchford replied in the *Daily Mail*, 'Votes! Votes! What has the danger of the Empire to do with votes?'[42]

During the campaign, many Unionists came to believe that the Party's cause could be saved only by a pledge from Balfour that Tariff Reform would not be enacted before it was put before the people in a referendum. Lord Robert Cecil was among those who foresaw electoral disaster without such a pledge. The Unionists, he told Northcliffe, 'appear to me to be rushing on to their destruction, which may involve the downfall of the Constitution. I have made every appeal that I can think of to the Leaders of the Party to take the necessary action to avert the catastrophe.' He went on:

> There is only one power that can now save us, and that is the Press . . . Our only hope lies with the moderate men . . . If they can be induced to believe that the Constitution really is in danger they may put aside all their political opinions and vote against the Government. But before doing that they must be satisfied that their votes are not sought merely for party advantage.[43]

Northcliffe replied from Paris to this appeal:

> So strongly do I feel with you, that I went over to England last week, called upon Mr. Sandars, and spent one hour with him . . . devoted nearly three hours . . . to an interview with Mr. Balfour, Mr. Austen Chamberlain, and Mr. Bonar Law, urging the very points you name. Chamberlain says he would have to resign Politics, if the step you and I suggest were contemplated.

Bonar Law agreed that the mixing up of Preference with Tariff Reform had been an original mistake. Mr. Balfour, I am sure, agreed with us, but it was made very plain that the Party would smash on the eve of the most dangerous Election in our history, if the plan you and I suggest were adopted.

I, therefore, out of loyalty to Mr. Balfour, promised to use my many newspapers in the general interest, though I hate this present situation. You know that I am a very keen Tariff Reformer, but that is not the discussion at the moment. The brutal fact is, of course, that we are all under the influence of the invalid at Highbury [Joseph Chamberlain], who is never allowed to hear the truth. I do not, however, take so pessimist a view as to the result of the Election as you do . . .[44]

While Northcliffe waited for Balfour to give the Party a lead, Garvin began the call for a referendum pledge in the 27 November *Observer.* Other Unionist figures soon followed suit, and the *Daily Mail* commented positively on Garvin's declaration. Asquith even joined the cry and challenged his opponents to submit food taxes to a direct vote. Balfour, meanwhile, considered his position and consulted with Bonar Law and Austen Chamberlain. He explained to Chamberlain that, after weighing the pros and cons, he had decided to declare for a referendum. He also pointed out that the idea had been taken up by the *Daily Mail*, from which, he said, 'so many of our candidates get their speeches'.[45] At the Albert Hall on 29 November, Balfour proclaimed that a referendum should be held on Tariff Reform. The 1 December *Daily Mail* praised the 'Effect of Mr. Balfour's Declaration' in creating consternation among the radicals. More articles followed in the next days supporting the referendum pledge.

The polling began on 3 December. The first figures, said the *Daily Mail* two days later, constituted a 'Good Beginning'. One of the early Conservative victors, in a whirlwind ten-day campaign, was the Canadian financier Max Aitken, a political novice, who took a seat at Ashton-under-Lyne. The *Daily Mail* remarked that Aitken 'Stands for a new type in Parliament' and that it was 'not without significance that one of the most striking victories of the campaign has been won by a new-comer from over-seas, who looks on our problems and opportunities with the fresh and broad vision of the illimitable West'.[46] The election of Aitken – who later, as Lord Beaverbrook, would become a press power himself – was one of the few Unionist bright spots in December 1910. It very soon became apparent that polling would not alter the balance of political power. The *Daily Mail* dubbed the futile exercise the 'No Change' election, and blamed the waste and expense on Redmond and Asquith. The only ones pleased, said the newspaper, were the radicals.[47]

The final numbers again reflected failure for the Unionists, who tied with the Liberals at 272 seats. The Irish held the balance, with 84 MPs, to maintain Asquith in office. *The Times*, the *Observer* and their proprietor put the blame for the defeat on the party organization. Many Unionists also became convinced that the result was somehow unfair and that drastic measures to resist the government were justified.[48] In the aftermath, Northcliffe remained dissatisfied with the use politicians made of his press weapon. He told Lord Curzon that, for a general election, the modern newspaper had 'entirely superseded the Meeting'. The latest contest had left the party needing to 'turn over 235,000 votes' and he believed this could be 'as largely done by able speeches on Tariff Reform as by indefatigable local canvassing'.[49] With the election results disheartening, Northcliffe turned to pleasures elsewhere. He had taken delivery of a new Rolls-Royce and wrote to Claude Johnson that he was very happy with his test drive.[50]

With his own health problems in mind, Northcliffe recommended a rest to Balfour, who, he said, despite the disappointing result, had 'given the party a magnificent lead'. His letter went on that 'not before in my lifetime has our country been so greatly in need of leadership for I notice from a careful study of the German Press – of what it is printing and what it is not printing – that our friends across the North Sea are in no wise slackening their preparations, while we are amusing ourselves with an unnecessary General Election'.[51] Balfour thanked him for his note and added, '*Apropos* of what you say about the Germans, I shall trust that the Government will give us good Naval Estimates. It all turns, I suppose, on whether they are more afraid of the Germans or of their own tail – an unhappy position for the rulers of a great country!'[52]

Though Northcliffe complimented his leadership, two failures at the polls in 1910 and the referendum pledge cost Balfour party support. In Tariff Reform and other quarters the perceived weakness at the top began to be seen as the reason for the two narrow losses. Leo Maxse, who declared that 'Balfour Must Go' in the *National Review*, complained to Northcliffe of the 'hopelessness' of the Unionist leader and sent a plan for a party reorganization. In his opinion, a continuation of the status quo would mean the 'permanent impotence of our Party . . . Balfour's charm is not only the curse of the Unionist Party, but it is going to be the ruin of our country because enfeebled Unionism means the continuous ascendancy of the demagogues'.[53]

Away from politics, in early 1911 Northcliffe began preparations to replace Buckle with Geoffrey Robinson, whose opinions – particularly concerning the Empire – the proprietor of *The Times* found closer to his own. On 5 January, Robinson visited Sutton Place for a long weekend of discussions. Two days later he recorded in his diary that Northcliffe 'frankly offered me a position on The Times'. Though rather nervous at the prospect, Robinson found the opportunity 'much too attractive to refuse'.[54] He talked more with his chief over the next days, and drove back to London with him, ten days later returning to Sutton Place with Lord Milner for further talks. During the next weeks Robinson met Bell, Buckle, Nicholson and the chief proprietor in more 'planning' sessions. He officially joined the staff at Printing House Square on 14 February, as Buckle's assistant.

At the same time, Northcliffe also continued to be gravely concerned with Canada, which was not responding to a British scheme for preference on wheat, meant to counteract a plan for reciprocity between Canada and the United States. Since September 1910 the *Daily Mail* had warned its readers of the damage such an agreement would do to the bonds of Empire. When the details became known, on 28 January 1911, the paper commented that the US-Canadian understanding represented an unrepairable 'breach in the wall' which put an end to the hope of commercial union between Great Britain and Canada. Two days later the editorial 'Exit Imperial Preference' laid to rest Joseph Chamberlain's fiscal plan, and in the following days further articles dismissed 'the gospel of Highbury' from imperial politics. These events forced Garvin to choose between his loyalties to Northcliffe and to Chamberlain. Northcliffe hoped that the editor of the *Observer* would follow his lead, but Garvin soon made his position clear in a letter which declared that he had 'never dreamed of dropping Imperial Preference' and that he believed the policy was 'not dead but is going before long to play a far bigger political role than ever – far bigger, stronger, wider'.[55] The *Daily Mail* of 4 February responded for its chief in the editorial 'The End of the Food Tax'.

Northcliffe viewed the new MP Max Aitken as a man with invaluable practical experience on the subject of Canada, and invited him to Elmwood on 2 February to 'talk about politics'.[56] Aitken, who was a close ally and adviser to Bonar Law, did not think that preference would attract his country's wheat to the English market, as opposed to the American. He told Northcliffe that he would go along with the majority on the proposed agreement, but thought 'preference on food stuffs was of no further advantage to Canada, and an enormous disadvantage to the party in England'.[57] At a Unionist Party meeting, Aitken recommended abandoning food taxes, but the suggestion got only lukewarm support. As an alternative, he sent Northcliffe a preference plan for Canadian colonial bonds and stocks, a subject with which the financier was intimately familiar. Aitken arranged for Northcliffe and Bonar Law to meet at his London flat. Aitken afterwards reported that Bonar Law privately 'favours our views' but was 'apprehensive for serious opposition'.[58]

The most serious opposition to any revision in fiscal policy continued to come from the Chamberlains and from Garvin at the *Observer*. Northcliffe invited Garvin to visit him at Elmwood for a talk, telling him that he could not 'possibly be associated with a policy that I believe by its hopeless ignoring of new facts would certainly help to lose Canada'. Despite this veiled threat, the editor responded that it was impossible for him to leave London until the following week, and that a meeting would only be a 'miserable & futile ordeal for us both'.[59] This meant that the 5 February *Observer* continued to defy its proprietor's view. That day Garvin pointed out that the US-Canadian agreement had not yet been ratified, but that, if it was, this development should be looked upon as an opportunity for Britain to negotiate lower trade barriers and expand into the lucrative US market. The article also dismissed the talk that the *Daily Mail* had raised of 'other means' of lowering tariffs besides food, declaring that Chamberlain had considered all other avenues before pursuing his course.

After reading Garvin's rebuttal, Northcliffe complained to Aitken, whom he had hoped to use to convince the editor of the error of his ways, that 'Chamberlain yesterday and Garvin today show you that our party is in the clouds and many will be grateful if it is brought to solid earth'.[60] The next day he dissociated himself from the *Observer* by resigning from the board of directors and met Aitken and Bonar Law to plan a combined strategy against food taxes. The Liberal press was not slow to take advantage of the Unionist rift. The 6 February *Daily News* gloated over the 'spectacle' of the *Daily Mail* 'winding up a week's campaign in favour of Unionists dropping their food taxes, and yesterday being savagely trounced' by the *Observer* 'for such treason'. This, the paper went on, was 'not the least remarkable of the series of dissolving views which for years now have taken the place with Unionist politicians of . . . an intelligible policy'.

Despite an attempt by Aitken to smooth over their differences,

Northcliffe gave Garvin three weeks to find another proprietor for the *Observer*, putting George Sutton in charge of the matter. Sutton was instructed either to negotiate a sale or to purchase Garvin's shares. There was no effort made to force the editor to resign. Northcliffe informed Aitken that so far as he was concerned the *Observer* was nothing; however, it was 'everything to Garvin'. He went on, 'Under no circumstances will I continue . . . with Garvin. I am extremely fond of him, but I think that he acted with great unwisdom in declining to take a mere two hour railway journey to discuss this matter, before plunging himself into his present very difficult situation.'[61] Two months later the *Observer* was sold to the millionaire MP Waldorf Astor for £45,000. With Garvin out of Northcliffe's constellation of advisers, the press lord turned to others for advice on domestic and foreign-policy questions, including Geoffrey Robinson and a new voice, Henry Wickham Steed, the Vienna correspondent of *The Times*.

In March 1911 Northcliffe continued to be actively hostile to British ratification of the Declaration of London. When *The Times* did not follow this line, he made his displeasure known to Buckle through Reggie Nicholson. Buckle wrote to the chief proprietor that he had heard that he was unhappy about the newspaper's support of ratification. He explained to Northcliffe that, since it was negotiated in 1909, he had never heard any verdict on the treaty from him. At the present point, said Buckle, it would be extremely damaging to the reputation of the newspaper to change course. He also called the incident a 'test' of the independence of *The Times*.[62] Northcliffe replied that he thought Nicholson had made it plain that he would not 'devote one farthing of my fortune to supporting that which I know would be an injury to my country, and this, therefore, is to acknowledge, with much regret, the receipt of your letter and this is my final communication on the subject'.[63] The employees of *The Times* became more and more concerned that Northcliffe would completely forget his pledge of non-interference and bring the newspaper into line with his other publications as a de luxe edition of the *Daily Mail*.

Moberly Bell, the foremost guardian of the newspaper against such action, was in poor health. His wife told Northcliffe that her husband's doctors had told him to slow down. Northcliffe replied that he wished Bell 'could be induced to do what I did – cut himself off from work and worry until the doctor approves . . . If the present Times experiment is not a success, further great steps must be taken which will impose more work on Bell, and everybody else.'[64] On 5 April, three days after his sixty-fourth birthday, Bell, writing on the Copyright Bill before Parliament, died at his desk at Printing House Square. Northcliffe's letter of condolence from Paris to Mrs Bell included the opinion of many: that this was the end that her husband would have chosen. The chief proprietor also regretted that he had not insisted that Bell take a vacation to Egypt. Northcliffe had had his differences with the manager; nonetheless, he later commented that he had 'no doubt that there was one moment in the history of *The Times* when he saved its life'.[65]

The next years before the Great War would see more change at Printing House Square and elsewhere. From the Unionist Party to labour, women and the Irish question, the period was among the most tumultuous in British history. The first battle, however, would be fought over the House of Lords.

I I

Prelude to War, 1911–1914

D ESPITE NORTHCLIFFE'S ATTEMPTS to keep the German peril fresh in the public mind, the attention of the nation and the newspapers in the years before the Great War was, in the main, trained closer to home: on the continual crises among unruly peers, striking workers and marching suffragettes, or on the turmoil, both in Ireland and in Parliament, over Home Rule. Northcliffe did not wish to see bloodshed in his place of birth, but was against a forced settlement and leaned toward the cause of Ulster and its champion, Sir Edward Carson, who, though from the South, was chairman of the Ulster Unionist Council. Northcliffe was sympathetic to working men and to women; however, he decried violent methods and strikes, and flatly opposed the extremes of the suffragettes. In the House of Lords battle, the owner of the *Daily Mail* supported the party leadership against the 'Diehard' faction which vowed to fight reform until the end.

Away from these national crises, in 1911 golf helped Northcliffe finally to overcome his long bout of ill health. 'Steal one working day a week for this game,' he recommended to Garvin. 'Nothing ever did me so much good.' His enthusiasm led him to construct a first-class nine-hole course at Sutton Place, which opened in May 1911. The new course drew a long list of political visitors, including Balfour, Bonar Law and Austen Chamberlain. Some, such as Balfour, enjoyed the game; others did not. Northcliffe's secretary Russell Wakefield recorded that Chamberlain told his host that he could not 'conceive how you can have fallen prey to that lamentable pastime. Its nomenclature alone revolts me – those "bunkers", "bogeys" and "slymies".' '"Slymies?"' replied Northcliffe. 'You're thinking of the popular name for politicians.'[1] Guests from outside the world of politics included Frederick Selous, a renowned big-game hunter, who had accompanied Roosevelt on his African safari, the feminist Lady Betty Balfour and the flyer Claude Grahame-White. A landing strip on the property allowed visitors to arrive by aeroplane.

Northcliffe attended a 12 May demonstration at Hendon by Grahame-White during which the aviator scored a direct hit on the outline of a battleship from 2,000 feet with a 100lb sandbag. Also present in the distinguished crowd that day were Asquith, Haldane, Balfour and Reginald McKenna, the First Lord of the Admiralty. The last two accepted Grahame-White's invitation to fly with him. Northcliffe's first flight, a short excursion with the Frenchman Paulhan in his Farman aeroplane, terrified Geraldine Harmsworth. She made her son sign a declaration, dated 31 May 1911, that he would 'not go out in any aeroplane or flying machine whatever without the written consent of my mother'.[2] Despite the exhibition at Hendon, Haldane continued in his cautious view of aviation.

In the summer of 1911 the *Daily Mail* and its proprietor continued the battle against the Declaration of London. The writer George Curnock led the fight. Northcliffe apologized to an ally in the controversy, Lord Desborough, for venturing 'to write to Mr. Balfour at your house – a thing I would not have done had I not been so anxious about the Declaration of London. Mr. Curnock was in better spirits about it last (Friday) night. If you can succeed it will be the greatest triumph of our times.'[3] Northcliffe's letter to Balfour called the Declaration matter 'more vital than any other measures now being discussed'.[4] In the Commons, the Conservative leader declared himself against the Declaration and helped to defeat its passage. He had assured Northcliffe that he meant 'to do his best over the Declaration of London, – if I am alive after the coronation ceremonies!'[5]

On 22 June, hundreds of thousands of spectators watched George V's coronation procession make its way from Buckingham Palace to Westminster Abbey, the route lined by 50,000 troops under the command of Lord Kitchener. To the *Daily Mail* the new King was a 'symbol and link of an Empire which embraces millions of the human race and the upholder of a common law which is a guarantee of the rights and liberties of every subject of the Empire, irrespective of race and creed and language'. 'In his sacred person', the paper went on, 'are embodied the centuries of history and romance which in the next few days will find their expression in a manner which neither Babylon in its splendour nor Rome in its pride could have presented.'[6] The coronation also spawned the final pre-war Imperial Conference, with the same results as its predecessors. For a final time Laurier was present to undercut any hope for closer union or the creation of a standing organization with real influence. Yet another Review of the Fleet at Spithead, with seven columns of ships stretching five miles, capped that summer's celebration.

John Evelyn Wrench used the Conference to convene a first general meeting of the Overseas Club. Northcliffe, L.S. Amery and Sir Harry Brittain joined Wrench on the platform before 300 members representing 62 different club branches from throughout the Empire. The premier of Alberta and the Lieutenant-Governor of Ontario were also present.[7] Wrench proposed to undertake a tour of Canada on behalf of the club. He wrote to Northcliffe that the moment was 'ripe for an active imperial campaign in the Dominion'.[8] Northcliffe agreed with the plan, but asked Wrench to combine some business with the Overseas Club agenda. Northcliffe never developed Wrench's almost religious zeal for the organization. His interest, though strong, remained tempered by business concerns. The owner of the *Overseas Daily Mail* was dissatisfied with the circulation figures, which hovered around 40,000, and complained that the paper, and Wrench, devoted too much time to the Overseas Club.[9]

Later that summer the confrontation between the Conservative House of Lords and the Liberal House of Commons came to a climax. Faced with a vote in the Lords on the Parliament Bill, the Unionists divided into 'ditchers', opposed to giving in to government threats to create Liberal peers, and 'hedgers' who planned to abstain or to support the measure if necessary to avert the swamping of the Upper House. Northcliffe and his newspapers supported the latter course, while Garvin aligned himself with the Diehard faction. Buckle told his chief that he hoped 'we shall defeat Garvin and his wild peers'.[10] The press lord managed to obtain a copy of the list of proposed peers which Asquith had deputed Alexander Murray, Master of Elibank and Liberal Chief Whip, to draw up. Northcliffe commented to Lord Curzon, who backed using Unionist votes to pass the Parliament Bill if necessary, that

I gather that there is now no doubt about the new Peers. The real list is *not* a bad list. I fear that the thing is out of control, and short of a pretext of saving the Royal dignity, I cannot see how the revolution can be averted. The public is not in the least interested. I have never seen fewer 'Letters to the Editor' on any great topic, and that remark applies equally to the 'Times' and the 'Daily Mail' – its London and Paris editions. The interest is confined to the politicians on both sides.[11]

Two days later, on 20 July, Asquith informed Balfour and Lansdowne by letter that, if the Lords continued their recalcitrance, he had received an assurance from the King that enough peers would be created to pass the Parliament Bill. The next day, rather than allow Conservative power in the Upper House to be lost, the Unionist leaders decided to allow the Parliament Bill to pass. Lansdowne, as leader in the Lords, sent a printed letter on the crisis, dated 24 July 1911, to his supporters, including Northcliffe:

The announcement made by the Prime Minister leaves no room for doubt that His Majesty's Government are now empowered to force the passage of the Parliament Bill through the House of Lords by means of a practically unlimited creation of Peers.

We shall therefore have to decide whether, by desisting from further opposition, we shall render it possible for His Majesty's Government to carry the Bill in the House of Lords as at present constituted, or whether, by insisting on amendments, we shall bring about a creation of Peers in numbers which may overwhelm the present House, and paralyse its action in the future without in any way retarding the passage of the Parliament Bill.

I have come to the conclusion that the former alternative is preferable in the interests of the House, the Unionist Party and the country.

Nor can I bring myself to believe that our supporters will not realize that we are no longer free agents, and that the course which I have indicated involves no responsibility for the Bill and no complicity for those who are promoting it.

It is of the utmost importance that I should be made aware of the views of those Peers who usually act with us and I should therefore be grateful if your Lordship would, with the least possible delay, let me know whether you are prepared to support me in the course which I feel it my duty to recommend.[12]

In reply, Northcliffe pledged his personal and newspaper aid to Lansdowne and contacted the Earl of Orford in the cause. He told Lansdowne that Orford was in Norway, but that a cable 'would get his adhesion. I have wired him urging him to give it.'[13] Northcliffe wrote to the Earl that he was sweltering in London amidst the veto crisis and envied Orford his 'pleasant surroundings, but I absolutely cannot get away as I am used. I have become a slave to the machine. I took the liberty to-day of telegraphing you with reference to the attempted revolt against Lord Lansdowne among a few stupid Peers.'[14]

Northcliffe was pessimistic about the outcome of the battle in Parliament. He reported to Lord Roberts that he had come to London to see him, but had got caught up 'in the vortex of the most extraordinary situation'. His letter went on that

> personally I am sorry that they are about to create these peers and turn the House of Lords into a Radical body. I do not think the House of Lords is particularly popular with anybody and there certainly are lots of people in the lower middle class who would like to see it smashed – quite forgetting it is the only barrier they have against the growth of socialist taxation. I fear it means good bye to National Service.[15]

However, Northcliffe's fears did not come to pass, and a mass creation of peers was averted, when on 10 August the Upper House passed the Parliament Bill, with the help of thirty-seven Unionist votes. Buckle wrote to his chief, 'I think we may congratulate ourselves. It was a narrow margin, but it was on the right side.'[16] Northcliffe replied, 'I can truly say that I have never been so pleased with the "Times" as during the Parliament Bill discussion. You laboured against very heavy odds.' He went on, 'Unfortunately our leaders do not understand newspapers and pay very much more attention to those of their enemies than to those of their friends.'[17]

The German menace also re-emerged in the eventful summer of 1911. That July, the Kaiser ordered a gunboat, the *Panther*, to Agadir in Morocco. This action was a warning to the French, whose troops had occupied Fez in what Germany viewed as a breach of the Algeciras agreement, and also was calculated to advance German claims for compensation in Central Africa. The incident also constituted a challenge to the Entente Cordiale. This was answered from the Mansion House by Lloyd George, who unleashed a sharp warning to Germany which turned up the international temperature and drew the support of the *Daily Mail*. F.W. Wile reported to Northcliffe that he had interviewed Count Bernstorff, the German ambassador in Washington, who stated that he had dined with the Kaiser and that the consensus of feeling at the table had been that Lloyd George's speech was 'as provocative an affront to German honour as was the telegram of Napoleon III, which had precipitated the Franco-German War'. The sentiment was expressed that Germany should have gone to war over the insult. The consequent humiliation, said Bernstorff, 'would leave its sting for many a year'. The ambassador also told Wile that Germany would 'not consent to permanent acknowledgment of British naval supremacy'. Bernstorff compared Anglo-German relations to two bulldogs 'perpetually barking at each other', who would continue to bark 'until one flew at the other's throat'.[18] Despite the warning from Wile, Northcliffe did not believe the present situation would lead to war, and the *Daily Mail* and *The Times* kept moderate tones in their articles. Nevertheless, the cavalry general Sir John French reported that the Kaiser had complained to him that the only way that France and Germany would come to blows would be at the encouragement of Britain and her press. He named the *Daily Mail* and *The Times* as 'the most hostile' and 'doing the most harm'.[19]

One effect of the Agadir crisis was the transformation of Winston Churchill from dove to hawk. Northcliffe advised Churchill in September that many of his colleagues 'look supremely foolish in view of the present no doubt to be smoothed over situation. Few of them apparently ever go to Germany or France.' If they did, said Northcliffe, they would learn that Germany was short of capital and that her army was handicapped both by red tape and by out-of-date traditions. In his opinion, Germany was bluffing. France in 1911, on the other hand, was not the same weakling of 1870 or 1875. His letter went on:

> Your Cabinet seems neither to get nor to send for information. If they had a good service of information they would know that the Germans are as much afraid of the French Army of today as they are of our ships, they will try but not succeed in separating these forces. My newspapers have never been provocative about Germany. Germany resents my printing the facts about her forces and intentions.[20]

Within a few weeks of this letter Churchill became the First Lord of the Admiralty and turned all his considerable energy to preparing for the German threat against which Northcliffe had been warning for two decades.

Elsewhere on the political front, Balfour finally tired of the criticism aimed at him and decided to lay down his burden in November 1911. The leadership of the Unionist Party passed into the hands of Andrew Bonar Law, who emerged as a compromise choice when support for the two favourites, Walter Long and Austen Chamberlain, became deadlocked.[21] An MP only since 1900, Bonar Law had never held a Cabinet

1. Alfred Harmsworth, aged two, with his mother, Geraldine Harmsworth

e young journalist: Alfred
nsworth in 1885

3. Mary Harmsworth, née Milner

4. Cartoon from the *Portsmouth Mail*, 1895

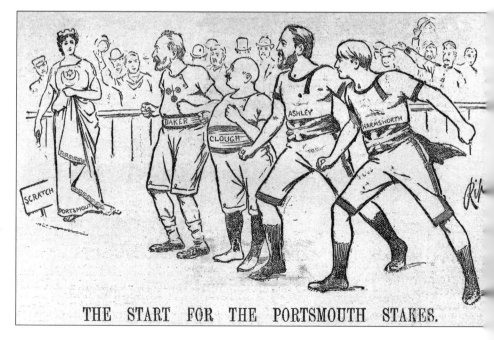

5. The coming man: Alfred Harmsworth in 1896

6. Elmwood

7. Thomas Marlowe, editor of the *Daily Mail*

8. Harold Harmsworth, later Lord Rothermere

. Cecil Harmsworth, later Lord
Harmsworth

10. Leicester Harmsworth

11. A growing collection of automobiles, about 1903

12. Puncture repair

13. Sutton Place

14. Sir Alfred and Lady
Harmsworth at Sutton Place,
1905

15. Northcliffe with Arthur Balfour and the Wright aeroplane at Pau, 1909

16. Northcliffe with Blériot
in London after the first
cross–Channel flight, 1909

17. William Kennedy Jones,
Northcliffe and George Sutton

. Northcliffe and Geoffrey
obinson (later Dawson) at Sutton
ace, during the Imperial Press
onference, June 1909

19. John Walter and
Northcliffe

20. Northcliffe and Winston Churchill

21. At the height of his power: Northcliffe, 1916

22. 'The Passing of the Failures', from the *Daily Mail*, 9 December 1916

23. Curzon and Northcliffe, outside the Air
Board, 1916

ir Cecil Spring Rice and
hcliffe in Washington, 1917

29. Henry Wickham Steed and Northcliffe in Washington, 1921

30. Northcliffe golfing during his world tour, 1921

post. Of Ulster descent, he had been born in Canada and raised in Glasgow. He came to Parliament from a successful business career. Bonar Law's background and direct style appealed to the many Unionists tired of philosophy and drift and ready for more active leadership. When she heard Bonar Law speak for the first time, Lady Dawkins commented that she found his Glasgow accent a little disconcerting at first, 'rather as if I were being addressed by my highly educated carpenter'. However, she was soon inspired 'with such confidence as he went on that I forgot that, and of course one has to recognise that a new era in political life has dawned . . . the old aristocratic school is practically swept out of it, it is the dawn of a new regime'.[22] In the new Parliament, Bonar Law reportedly told Asquith that he was 'afraid I shall have to show myself very vicious . . . this session, I hope you will understand.'[23] Northcliffe wrote to Sutton that he was 'very pleased that our prospective leader' was a Canadian, and hoped that it would have a great effect in the Dominion. He went on that on the 'two occasions I saw Bonar Law I liked him immensely; and I do not suppose I will have any difficulty in giving him my full support, though I am not, as you know, a strict Party man'.[24] Lloyd George declared that 'the fools have stumbled on the right man by accident'.

At the same time, the Agadir crisis was settled by an agreement in which Germany recognized France's position in Morocco in return for concessions in the Congo. Nonetheless, on 8 November, at Guildhall, Churchill proclaimed that Britain would continue to match Germany's naval expenditure. Northcliffe responded to a query from the First Lord that he had no German news, but advised that Churchill would 'find that a firm attitude towards Germany will meet with the usual result in dealing with this greatly misunderstood, hysterical people . . . One of my German relations said "We are a nation of land crabs. If you advance, we retreat; if you retreat, we advance."' His letter went on, 'I judge public men on their public form, and I believe that your inquiring, industrious mind is alive to our national danger. My newspapers have no connexion with any Party in regard to Germany, the fleet and Canada, three subjects which . . . seem most vital to our national well-being.'[25] Northcliffe and his employees called often at the Admiralty. The owner of *The Times* introduced Geoffrey Robinson as 'a dear young man', but insisted that 'behind that quiet manner lies one of the ablest brains in England'.[26]

While the Agadir crisis had occupied centre stage, Italy had taken the opportunity to assert an imperial claim in Tripoli against the Ottoman

Empire. The Unionist press at first condemned the action, but soon tempered its criticism rather than drive Italy further into the arms of Austria-Hungary and Germany, her partners in the Triple Alliance. Henry Wickham Steed, the long-time Vienna correspondent of *The Times*, was also familiar with conditions in Italy. He wrote to his chief that he was 'glad that the Paper is now standing firm on the Tripoli question. There was at first a tendency to wobble.' He went on that the Countess de Castellane had confided to him that the French general staff expected war the next spring. Steed told Northcliffe that he 'should be surprised if war were to come in the next six months, but I should not care to predict the maintenance of peace for more than a year'. He felt that the 'precarious position of German industry and the determination of the German Junker class to force on, if possible, some foreign complication to prevent the destruction of Junker privileges by internal reform are, to my mind, the main elements of the situation. In different ways both of them make for war.' In Steed's opinion, England must get her Army and reserves in order, as well as armaments and ammunition 'sufficient for all possible emergencies'.[27] Northcliffe agreed that the British should refrain from harshness with Italy over the Tripoli affair, so as not to strengthen her alliance with Germany. He also advised Steed to tell the Countess not to worry too much about the Entente, because he was 'a firm adherent and am always working, privately and publicly, for it'.[28] Within a few months, Valentine Chirol resigned his duties as foreign editor of *The Times* and, after some delay, was succeeded by Steed, whose European expertise became increasingly important to Northcliffe. Chirol's departure marked another step in the changing of the old guard at Printing House Square.

The first months of 1912 brought the women's suffrage question to the fore once again. Northcliffe told Curzon that his papers were 'going to do anything they can for the anti-Suffrage party, but I am one of those people who believe that the whole suffrage movement is a bluff'. He went on that he had 'strong reasons . . . for believing that there are very few people anywhere who are sincerely anxious about the securing of the suffrage for women. If it were not for the support of one or two wealthy women of my acquaintance we should hear very little of the matter.'[29] Lord Cromer invited him to a 28 February Albert Hall protest against votes for women. The Lord Chancellor, Lord Loreburn, and the Colonial Secretary, Lewis Harcourt, were scheduled to make addresses and, Cromer added, it was possible the Prime Minister might also speak.

For the Conservatives, Curzon would take the podium.[30] Northcliffe replied:

My view of the position of newspaper owners is that they should be read and not seen. The less they appear in person the better for the influence of their newspapers. That is why I never appear on public platforms.

As to the woman's suffrage business, I am one of those people who believe the whole thing to be a bubble, blown by a few wealthy women who employ their less prosperous sisters to do the work.

I judge public interest in the matter by the correspondence received. We never get any letters apart from those from the stage army of suffragettes. Newspapers devoted to the interests of women in this country, many of which have vast circulations receive, as I happen to know, practically no letters.[31]

At *The Times*, Northcliffe had been grooming Geoffrey Robinson for more than a year and had made him a director in April. That summer the chief proprietor decided that the moment had come for a change in editorship. Buckle, who often threatened to leave the paper, asked his chief in July if, as John Walter had told him, Northcliffe wanted his resignation. He requested confirmation, as he could not take action on a 'mere message'. Northcliffe replied that he greatly regretted the tone of Buckle's letter and had sent no 'message' about his retirement. He went on that 'Mr. Walter has told me that you had repeatedly suggested that you were contemplating resignation. You have said so to me. I am in entire accord with him and consider it his duty as Chairman . . . to prepare for the change . . . by the exercise of ordinary foresight.'[32] To this reproach, Buckle sent an apology and prepared to take his leave. Robinson recalled that when he talked to the editor on the 29th Buckle seemed 'sore' about his treatment, 'though entirely well disposed to my succession'.[33] The editor of *The Times* tendered his secret resignation to the board on 31 July in what Robinson described as a 'long and admirable letter'. When the news was published in the *Pall Mall Gazette*, Northcliffe was forced to issue a statement on the matter. On the same day, 8 August, he sent congratulations to the new editor. He told Robinson 'I hope and believe we shall work well together. I do not think that either of us are unreasonable people, and I know that we have many Imperial ideas in common.'[34]

The imperial ideas the two shared included a common view of the danger of Home Rule. The change at *The Times* took place soon after Bonar Law, in response to the pending Home Rule Bill including

Ulster, declared at Blenheim on 29 July that he could 'imagine no length of resistance to which Ulster will go, in which I shall not be ready to support them, and in which they will not be supported by the overwhelming majority of the British people'.[35] After *The Times* had warned against the use of physical force, Northcliffe informed Robinson on 12 August that he liked the leader that morning as he had 'not cared for the violent Ulster language of Bonar Law, Carson and others'.[36] He agreed with his relatives in Ulster, who had told him that many people did not approve of such declarations and thought them dangerous. However, at Belfast at the end of the following month, Sir Edward Carson was the first to sign the Ulster Covenant, a pledge to use all means necessary 'to defeat the present conspiracy to set up a Home Rule Parliament in Ireland'.[37] Nearly half a million Irishmen added their signatures.

At the same time, Wrench reached Canada, which he hoped would be only the first stop on a tour of the Empire for the Overseas Club. The editor of the *Overseas Daily Mail* more and more longed to give up his business duties to be free to devote himself exclusively to the Club. Wrench warned his chief that western Canada would be absorbed by the United States unless some organization like the Overseas Club was very diligent. He received a cable in Alberta from his employer saying that Northcliffe was 'surprised at lack of recognition of myself as inventor and founder' of the club.[38] Wrench replied that at every public meeting he gave credit to the success of the movement in Canada to three men: first, to Cecil Rhodes, for the 'inception of the Overseas Club idea'; second, to Northcliffe, 'for placing the Overseas Mail at the disposal of the movement'; and, third, to Lord Grey, president of the Canadian section of the Overseas Club, 'who did a great deal to interest Canadians in the aims of the society & who roped in most of our prominent members here'.[39] Wrench asked Northcliffe to question Willison, *The Times*'s correspondent in Canada, for an unbiased view of whether justice was done to him, and offered to resign if he was not satisfied.

This apparently mollified Northcliffe, who allowed Wrench to continue around the Empire on behalf of the Overseas Club and the Amalgamated Press. Wrench sent a letter of appreciation for the opportunity, and told Northcliffe that he would send 'papers from time to time & I will take good care that all the members realise all that you have done for the Overseas Club. I am looking forward to my wanderings more that I can say.' He added that he wanted 'to make it as great a success as possible from *your* standpoint just to show you what I feel about you'.[40] Wrench's first report – from Wellington, New Zealand – revealed that during a town-hall meeting the night before, attended by Lord Islington, the Governor-General, the mention of Northcliffe's name by Wrench drew a round of applause, although the papers did not pick this up. He neglected to tell his chief that he was continually forced to defend the Club against charges that it was simply a publicity scheme for the Northcliffe press. The letter went on that New Zealand was a 'great country. I only wish there were two or three million more of them in other parts of the Empire that I could mention.'[41]

Northcliffe also continued to urge British statesmen to visit Canada, in August 1912 asking Winston Churchill to undertake a speaking tour.[42] At this time, Churchill found himself a particular target of physical attack by the militant suffragettes. He wrote to Northcliffe that the walking stick the press lord had given him should come in handy in fending off such advances. The First Lord of the Admiralty also asked when Northcliffe could be available to go down in a submarine.[43] A few months later Churchill again proposed to take Northcliffe on an undersea voyage, as a reward for the fine way he felt *The Times* and the *Daily Mail* had treated the Admiralty – adding to his invitation, 'Return to surface guaranteed.' Northcliffe replied that he would be happy to take such a trip, but suggested that Churchill not go along, so that, if there was a mishap, they would not both be lost. 'If anything goes wrong with the submarine with both of us in it,' he added wryly, 'I am sure it will be a cause of much satisfaction to many.'[44]

In October 1912 war broke out in the Balkans when Serbia and her allies, including Bulgaria, began a campaign to drive the Turks out of Europe. Before the first shots were fired, the writer Alfred Stead, son of W.T., cabled Northcliffe from Paris:

> Only one possibility remains prevent war within few days which may involve Europe and only you can do anything. If England declares herself ready aid and co-operate with Turkey execution reforms as great Mohameddan power Servia Bulgaria will gladly accept since can assure you they more anxious find possibility avoiding war than precipitating hostilities. Time perilously short but strong lead this sense in Time and Mail tomorrow may save situation yet and success means everything future British Empire.[45]

However, British newspaper calls for reason proved inadequate. Rapid Serbian successes in what Austria-Hungary considered her rightful domain soon brought fears, in Northcliffe and others, that the conflict would spread into a Europe-wide war in which Russia would support

Serbia against Austria-Hungary and Germany and, consequently, trigger the Entente with Russia's ally France. Northcliffe told Pomeroy Burton, business manager at *The Times*, that 'Any person who follows current politics closely must be a plus six fool among fools if he does not realise every day that we are moving to and fro round the crater of a volcano.'[46] The owner instructed the editor of the *Daily Mail* that Henry Hamilton Fyfe should be recalled from America, where he was covering the three-way political battle between Roosevelt, his hand-picked successor William Howard Taft, and Woodrow Wilson. In 'view of the fact that the Presidential Election will be snowed under by the War,' said Northcliffe, 'We want men here, and we want to save money.'[47]

In October and November the possibility of a European conflagration seemed very real. When Serbian troops reached the Adriatic, Austria-Hungary was unwilling to stand idly by while her enemy gained a port. The Dual Monarchy demanded the creation of an Albanian state to block this occurrence. The *Times* of 26 November 1912 asked, 'Is there no means of evading war?' It continued:

> In England men will learn with amazement and incredulity that war is pos-
> sible over the question of a Serbian port, or even over the larger issues which
> are said to lie behind it. Yet that is whither the nations are blindly drifting.
> Who, then, makes war? The answer is to be found in the Chancelleries of
> Europe, among the men who too long played with human lives as pawns in a
> game of chess, who have become so enmeshed in formulas and the jargon of
> diplomacy that they have ceased to be conscious of the poignant realities with
> which they trifle.

However, in December cooler heads prevailed and Russia, Germany and Austria-Hungary came to a peaceful solution. In future, however, the prestige of the various parties in the Balkans crisis of 1912, particularly Serbia's champion Russia, would not allow another such humiliation.

The near miss in 1912 stimulated the efforts of a considerable peace faction in Britain. Sir Frank Lascelles, British president of the Anglo-German Understanding Conference Committee, asked Northcliffe to promote benevolence between the two nations by reading a paper at a London meeting on how newspapers could help defuse the tense international situation.[48] In the same vein, Northcliffe's nephew and godson Vyvyan Harmsworth, Harold's eldest son, sent a letter from Christ Church, Oxford, which included a circular on the Anglo-German

Debating Society, meant to further goodwill between the countries. He invited his godfather to Oxford for a dinner in support of the Society. It appears that neither of these invitations was successful; however, several months later, after the immediate crisis had passed, Northcliffe suggested to Vyvyan that he take a tour of Germany and recommended Hanover as the best part, saying the Hanoverians were no more like the Berliners 'than the East End rough' was like the Scotsman. His letter continued:

> I think the German Empire is in a very tight corner, and I do not wonder at its anxieties – the Russian colossus on the East, a much-weakened Austria, Italy a very doubtful ally, France like a hungry tiger with its claws very much sharpened of late, and one or two small English vessels in the North Sea. I am rejoiced to see you take so fair and intelligent a view . . . I do believe some great change is going to take place slowly.[49]

Northcliffe also lent his aid to another, more warlike, nephew, Lucas King. The young man's mother, Northcliffe's older sister Geraldine, was anxious to ensure that her son joined a good regiment after Sandhurst. She suggested the King's Royal Rifles (under the King) or the Rifle Brigade (under the Duke of Connaught). Northcliffe replied to his sister that he had contacted the people she had requested and that Lord Roberts had written as well and wanted Lucas to go and see him.[50] The owner of *The Times* remained a strong supporter of the Field Marshal's National Service League, and instructed his editor to aid the efforts of Roberts and to remain vigilant about the European military build-up. Robinson replied that he quite agreed 'that the new arming of Europe is definitely serious and very difficult to handle without inflaming popular excitement and passion' and promised he would not 'let the subject go'. He feared the greatest danger at the moment was that the rearmament of France might 'degenerate into an aggressive jingoism which will alienate this country' and saw this as an 'obstacle to Lord Roberts' campaign', which was 'otherwise going admirably'.[51]

Northcliffe also kept up his contacts in the USA. William Bayard Hale, whose interview with the Kaiser the press lord had suppressed in 1908, enquired about a newspaper position in Washington. In his letter, Hale confided that Walter Hines Page would be announced as American ambassador the next day.[52] Northcliffe responded that his arrangements in Washington were set, so he could not use Hale. He went on that he knew 'Page a little, as you may be aware, and my newspapers and my homes will do everything in their power to see that he is made happy. I have not the honour of the President's acquaintance, but he might perhaps permit me to say, through you, that the dignified appointment of Mr Page has given great pleasure in diplomatic and other circles in England.'[53] Once Page had assumed his post, Northcliffe wrote directly to him that if he himself had not been away from London he would have congratulated him personally and that he had sent a letter to Woodrow Wilson, the new American President, saying that the appointment was 'ideal'. Page replied that 'it was your prompt and encouraging cablegram that stiffened me up for this job from the very beginning and now you are kind enough to continue that process by taking the trouble to write about me to the President. I hope to see you soon and see you often.'[54]

In 1913 the Unionists accused several members of the government of shady dealings concerning a contract awarded to the British Marconi Company to build a series of transmitting stations to link the Empire. Reports surfaced that Lloyd George, Rufus Isaacs (in 1913 the Attorney-General) and others had traded in the shares of the American Marconi Company. The fact that Isaacs's brother, Godfrey, was managing director of the Marconi Company, lent credence to the charges. The American company was not, at least directly, involved in the contract, and, after Churchill had convinced him there was nothing illegal in their stock transactions, Northcliffe supported the two men against charges in the Unionist press of official impropriety. The Attorney-General (who would soon be elevated to Lord Chief Justice as Lord Reading) sent a note of appreciation for the 'generous treatment' of him over the affair. Lloyd George also thanked the press lord for 'the chivalrous manner in which you have treated the Advocate-General [*sic*] and myself over the case . . . I feel grateful for a great kindness done to me for I know the power you wield.'[55] Northcliffe replied:

> I adopted my line about this Marconi business because five minutes lucid explanation showed me that it was the fairest one . . . I am not personally hostile to you . . . You gave me some shrewd blows and I replied to them . . . A weekend glance at the French and German newspapers, convinces me that this country has more urgent business before it than personal or party issues.[56]

In September, Northcliffe made another journey to the United States and Canada, where the manager and designing hand behind the Grand Falls development, Mayson Beeton, was threatening to retire. Northcliffe reported to Sutton that 'We had a very strenuous time at

Grand Falls, but I know we did good and I know [the development] is a good thing . . . but Muzzy [Beeton] spoils everything. He is the Old Man of the Sea, much as I like him as a friend.' He wrote to his mother, 'Very busy investigating, inspecting, handshaking, speechmaking, travelling . . . you, Darling Mum, are always in my heart. The town is electrically decorated for us. There is a huge letter N with coronet, 35 feet on top of a tower. It looks brilliant and can be seen twenty miles away in the forest.'[57]

He returned to England to find that the writer Keble Howard had published a fictional work, *Lord London*, the plot of which closely paralleled the rise of the Harmsworth family to prominence. Howard, who had worked briefly for the *Daily Mail*, sent the book to Marlowe and his chief for approval. He wrote to Northcliffe that if he disapproved he would call in the copies on sale, adding that it was written 'as a wholehearted admirer and an eager partizan – perhaps a little too eager'.[58] Northcliffe took exception to the author's presentation of the fictional father of the family as a violin-playing recluse shut away in an attic. Howard agreed to expunge the objectionable passages, as well as a reference in the preface that he knew the press lord.[59] Northcliffe told the publisher William Heinemann that 'As a public man I have to put up with publicity. But I will not have my father insulted.'[60] To soothe the family, he celebrated Christmas 1913 with his mother at her home, Poynters Hall, in Totteridge. Two days later he drove to Beaconsfield to make a presentation to Lord Burnham, proprietor of the *Daily Telegraph*, on the occasion of his eightieth birthday. The 1914 New Year Honour's List included a peerage for Sir Harold Harmsworth, who was introduced in the House of Lords as Baron Rothermere of Hemsted, in Kent.

In the first month of the new year Northcliffe renewed his criticism of *The Times*. He complained to Howard Corbett, the newly appointed assistant manager, that six years' experience of Printing House Square had taught him that 'nothing happens' there. Much was 'discussed', but 'nothing happens'. On the 24th he wrote to Robinson that 'Yesterday's inquiry into the finances of *The Times* was a revelation and does not reflect credit on the establishment. The salaries paid are eighty-four thousand pound per annum . . . and the mouse that issues is, this morning, certainly a ridiculous one.'[61] Robinson noted in his January diary, 'fearful worry and chaos in the office. N. raging about and giving contradictory orders'. The tribulations of Robinson and the staff were eased only when Northcliffe left for Paris at the end of the month, to see another eye specialist. His visit to Burnham, who had become blind, had triggered a renewed concern for the care of his own vision.

Despite all efforts to invigorate sales of *The Times*, the paper's average circulation stayed at 46,000. The price, which had already been dropped from threepence to two, was further reduced to one penny on 16 March 1914. The first one-penny edition sold 281,000 copies, and daily sales settled at an average of 145,000, ensuring the continued success of the paper. Increased circulations brought a change in Northcliffe's tone. Robinson sent his chief a note thanking him for his praise of *The Times*. His letter went on:

> I hear it well spoken of everywhere and increasingly so. The article on syndi-calism this morning has attracted much attention. I think of going to Belfast at Easter for a couple of days. We must have someone in any case to garnish the report of Bonar Law, & I want to see the serried ranks of Ulster Puritans with the light of battle in their eyes![62]

Shortly before this, Sir Edward Carson had been fêted at the Ritz in London by Lord Milner, Lord Roberts and others who had signed a British declaration in support of the Ulster Covenant. In April, Milner reported to Carson that signatures for this British Covenant were coming in at 30,000 a day.

Civil war in Ulster and political revolt in sympathy at home appeared to be very real possibilities over the impending enactment of Home Rule, which had been blocked for as long as possible by the Lords and would become law in the autumn. In response to the Curragh incident, in which serving British Army officers declared they would choose res-ignation rather than obey orders to coerce Ireland, Cecil Harmsworth MP recorded in his 28 March diary, 'Greater excitement in the House this week than have ever known.' In an otherwise gloomy chamber, Harmsworth found Winston Churchill 'singing blithely to himself in the lavatory behind the Speaker's chair'. Churchill explained to his col-league that it was his 'habit to confront difficult situations with an outward serenity of aspect'.[63] The First Lord also openly called for the use of the fleet, or whatever other means necessary, to force Home Rule on all of Ireland and in particular Ulster.

Though opposed to violence, Northcliffe supported the Unionist side in demanding the permanent exclusion of Ulster from Home Rule, while the Liberals in the end would agree only to a temporary exclusion of six years to allow the Opposition a chance to change the law. On 1 April he replied to Churchill, who had suggested a lunch to discuss affairs, that he would like to see him but that these were not 'lunching times'. The letter went on that he had

> stood by you and [Lloyd] George on many occasions, and have incurred plenteous abuse because of it, but as one who does happen to know the Irish people pretty well – I was born in Ireland and have a home there . . . I can only regard recent outrageous threatenings as aberration due to too much work . . . Any attempt to overcome the Ulster Protestants will mean Civil War. A tragic aspect of the situation is that the South of Ireland does not particularly want Home Rule. I went into the matter minutely on my last visit, and was surprised at the apathy existing. Your position seems completely out of touch with the real views of the English as well as the Irish peoples.[64]

Churchill replied that their pleasant personal relations had always proceeded on the basis of independent political and newspaper action, and that their lunch could wait for 'better times'.[65]

In the following months the *Daily Mail* headlines, editorials and articles concentrated on the Irish question, but also found space for the occasional sensational photograph either of suffragettes being dragged off to prison or of street scenes of worker unrest. For example, the 18 May leading article, titled 'Provoking Ulster', was followed a few days later by coverage of the 'Scene in the House' over Ireland, which shared the page with pictures of Mrs Emmeline Pankhurst and other women being arrested at Buckingham Palace.[66] The battle over Lloyd George's latest Budget took centre stage in the 23 June leading article, 'Mr Lloyd George's Surrender'.

Five days later, on Sunday 28 June 1914, the Austrian Archduke Franz Ferdinand was murdered by a Slav nationalist at Sarajevo in Bosnia. The next morning's *Daily Mail* recounted the events in Sarajevo, and sympathetically traced other Habsburg family tragedies in an article by the foreign correspondent Valentine Williams.[67] Though newsworthy, the event was not seen to involve the direct interests of England. The *Daily Mail* did send one of its leading writers, George Ward Price, to Austria to cover the funeral of the Archduke, and his account was published on 3 July.[68] Otherwise, events on the Continent seemed almost normal. The automobile correspondent, John Prioleau, continued a series of articles on his driving tour of Germany. The 1 July *Daily Mail* editorial, 'Drifting to Disaster', referred to the Irish question, not the Balkans.

Northcliffe's attention was riveted on Ulster, to which he made a personal visit. While inspecting the quality of the press coverage of the emergency, he met Irish leaders. He wrote to his mother that he had 'seen enough drilling of these auspicious and determined Scotch and English Irish to know they cannot be put down'.[69] Amid mounting tensions, the 7 July *Daily Mail* supported 'No Surrender' in Ulster. Three days later the newspaper traced Sir Edward Carson's trip to Belfast and his defiant speech the night before. Twelve *Daily Mail* representatives spread out from Belfast to cover the story 'Ireland Under Arms: The War Preparations'. One of the correspondents, J.M.N. Jeffries, later wrote that 'several of us had gone from the Reporters' Room over the wrong channel'.[70]

Meanwhile, the Prime Minister attempted to find a peaceful solution for Ireland, where two to three hundred thousand armed men on the opposing Nationalist and Ulster sides daily drilled in the glare of newspaper publicity. Asquith's 'wait and see', compromising style maddened his opponents, including Northcliffe, who wanted decisive action.[71] In turn, the Prime Minister was not an admirer of newspapers – even those of sympathetic persuasion.[72] Unquestionably, he reserved a special antipathy for Northcliffe, whose press had condemned the Liberals throughout their eight years of power. On 10 July the Premier wrote to his confidante Venetia Stanley that

> Northcliffe, who has been spending a week in Ulster, and has been well fed up by the Orangemen with every species of lurid lie, has returned in a panic. The Master [Lord Murray of Elibank] . . . is anxious that I should see him. I hate & distrust the fellow & all his works . . . so I merely said that if he chose to ask me directly to see him, & he had anything really new to communicate, I would not refuse. I know of few men in this world who are responsible for more mischief, and deserve a longer punishment in the next.[73]

However contemptuous Asquith was of Northcliffe, he did meet him about the Irish situation. Another letter to Miss Stanley, on 13 July, revealed this clandestine conference at Lord Murray's London flat, reporting that Northcliffe had 'been "doing" Ulster, & is much struck with the Convenanters, whom he regards . . . as a very formidable tho' most unattractive crew. I talked over the question . . . with him, & tried to impress upon him the importance of making *The Times* a responsible newspaper.'[74] Rothermere reported to Murray that the interview with Asquith had made a 'profound impression' on his brother; nevertheless, the *Times* leader of 14 July remained critical of government efforts. This was not pleasing to Murray, who voiced his rancour to the Prime Minister. Two days later, however, the *Daily Mail* editorial, 'Time to

Make Peace', reflected a change in course brought on by Asquith's plea and Northcliffe's own reading of the situation. Still, much to the premier's annoyance, *The Times* and the *Daily Mail* of 20 July revealed Asquith's secret plan to bring the King into the Irish settlement. He wrote to Venetia Stanley that 'it is annoying on every ground, & puts the whole Liberal press in the worst of tempers: they are as jealous as cats & naturally resent the notion that *The Times* has been preferred to them'.[75]

While Britain watched Ireland, events in Austria-Hungary and Germany proceeded relentlessly towards war. The assassination of Franz Ferdinand had given the Dual Monarchy the excuse it had long awaited to take action against the South Slav problem. Spurred on by Germany, Austria prepared to move. A note was drafted to hand to the Serbians 'framed in terms which no self-respecting state could accept'.[76] Almost lost among the reports of the King's efforts to find a peaceful settlement for Ireland, a small article, 'Austria Angry', in the 22 July *Daily Mail* revealed the firm note to Serbia demanding the right to follow up the investigations of the assassination on Serbian soil. Two days later, while the King's exertions towards an Irish settlement failed, the crisis in Europe for the first time merited extensive space in the *Daily Mail*. The paper's report on the 'Austrian Note' told of the demands to Serbia of 'no more plots' and a reply by the following day concerning the other Austrian conditions, including the suppression of societies in Bosnia which had preached revolt. In the writer's opinion, Serbia was not likely to comply, even in the face of seven Austrian army corps marshalled on the frontier. The paper predicted that Russia would support Serbia, and pointed out that President Raymond Poincaré and Prime Minister René Viviani of France happened to be in St Petersburg at present for consultations.

Britain's 'drift to commitment' in the days leading up to the declaration of hostilities with Germany has been well documented.[77] In the last days of July, Asquith and Sir Edward Grey skilfully manoeuvred the wavering Liberal Party towards support for action against Germany if necessary, predominantly because it was in Britain's best interest to do so. The war coincidentally saved the Liberal Party from what appeared to be a gloomy electoral future by dwarfing the many problems of 1914 in comparison. The *Daily Mail* reflected the dwindling chances for peace. On 27 July an editorial-page article by Valentine Williams, 'The Crisis in Europe', outlined the questions involved and the alliances, and included a map of Europe clearly illustrating the projected military consequences. In Williams's words, 'the appalling conflagration which would then inevitably result could not leave Great Britain indifferent'. That day's political news page asserted there was still time for peace in Europe since Austria had not yet declared war, but also recounted the panics on European stock exchanges, the return of the Kaiser from his Norwegian trip, and the 'war excitement' in Berlin. Ireland was relegated to a distant second place. The 28 July editorial, 'Sir Edward Grey's Effort for Peace', supported a conference of Great Britain, France, Germany and Italy to offer mediation to Austria-Hungary, Russia and Serbia, and warned of the grave consequences of failure. It ended with a hope that reports of an Austrian attack were false. Once this attack was confirmed the next day, the newspaper condemned Austria's decision for war, but nonetheless prayed that the spread of hostilities could be avoided, for 'if not Europe is face to face with the greatest catastrophe in human history'.

On the last day of July 1914 the *Daily Mail* proclaimed that the British people were united behind the King and the government and that the Opposition leaders Bonar Law and Carson had announced that they would support the nation. However, in a first discordant note even before the entrance of Britain into the conflict, the paper also made it clear that, in its opinion, it was the government's previous neglect of defence that had brought England to this perilous position. Calling the threat in Europe one 'not seen since the time of Napoleon', it commented that there were:

signs in every direction that the conflagration that Austria has so precipitantly and wantonly kindled is about to spread . . . The Austrian onslaught . . . will, it is to be feared, draw Russia into the field . . . in its turn [this] will be followed by German action. Germany's entrance will compel France . . . When France is in peril, and fighting for her very existence, Great Britain cannot stand by and see her friend stricken down . . . The hope is now only of the faintest that the war can be localised, because it is developing into a deliberate assault upon the Triple Entente. We must stand by our friends, if for no other and heroic reason, because without their aid we cannot be safe. The failure to organise and arm the British nation so as to meet the new conditions of Europe has left us dependent on Foreign allies. We have forfeited our old independent position, and as the direct consequence we may be drawn into a quarrel with which we have no immediate concern. But at least we can be true to our duty today if we have neglected it in the past.

With the diplomats 'almost exhausted' amid 'vast preparations for war', the paper's tone was no longer hopeful. Now the *Daily Mail* justified why Great Britain should be involved in maintaining the European balance of power. Most portentously, a *'Daily Mail* Eyewitness' reported the 'Shelling of Belgrade' in the first of countless news stories from the war fronts that would follow in the next four years.

I 2

Awakening the Nation, 1914–1915

IN THE FIRST days of August 1914 Northcliffe believed that the country lay literally at the mercy of the enemy. His entreaties for a stronger air defence had fallen largely on deaf ears, and things seemed little better on the ground. The British, he felt, could not spare any divisions for France's defence; the country's meagre ground forces were needed at home to repel a likely German invasion. Further, he doubted how well prepared the Army was for any campaign after eight years of Liberal government. He received information from his sources close to the French President, Poincaré, that there would be a German invasion of Belgium, but he feared that an air attack on Britain would be Germany's first stroke of the war and a prelude to invasion.[1]

His own press forces were redeployed from Ireland to the Continent by the London editors. Each man carried £200 in gold to cover initial expenses. Valentine Williams arranged for a corps of couriers to ferry news back and forth. The leading writers – Henry Hamilton Fyfe and George Ward Price – hurried to Paris for transport to the Franco-German frontier, where the brunt of the action was expected. To support them, a supplemental body of young correspondents rode out from Paris by bicycle and car to observe the French army. The Belgian post was assigned to J.M.N. Jeffries, the youngest of the group. The *Daily Mail* news editor, W.G. Fish, informed Jeffries that 'Belgium should prove an excellent news centre.' Thomas Marlowe, who perhaps knew more about Belgian conditions than he let on to Jeffries, calmly instructed him to make sure of the facts in his stories. Marlowe's parting words were hardly reassuring, 'remember . . . a deceased correspondent is of no use to his newspaper.'[2]

Northcliffe himself remained in London, either at his offices or telephoning them continually. At a 1 August conference at Printing House Square, he revealed that he had information that the government was going to 'rat' on Britain's Entente partners. The question was, how should his newspapers respond? Should they openly attack the government in this hour of national distress? Steed, *The Times*'s foreign editor, believed the paper had to speak out to preserve its dignity as a 'national institution'. On the other hand, the editor of the *Daily Mail* feared 'the country would never forgive us' for an attack on the government.[3]

Events on the Continent ensured that Northcliffe would not have to run the risk of public censure. British participation in the war appeared inevitable after the Russian mobilization of 30 July triggered the timetables of the German Schlieffen Plan. According to this decade-old master strategy, France had to be knocked out quickly to avoid a war on two fronts. The bald aggression of Germany's thrust into Belgium to carry out the Plan's first objective, and the Belgian King's 3 August plea for help, healed the remaining division in the British Cabinet and swayed public opinion away from the position of neutrality that was widely called for at the time. These developments cleared the way for the Foreign Secretary, Sir Edward Grey, head of the pro-intervention faction, to deliver an ultimatum which called for Germany to withdraw from Belgian soil by 11 p.m. on 4 August or face war with Britain. The *Daily Mail* proclaimed 'GREAT WAR BEGUN BY GERMANY – FRANCE ATTACKED WITHOUT A DECLARATION.' The editorial declared that

> [the] shadow of an immense catastrophe broods over Europe today. All hope
> of peace has disappeared with a crash . . . Europe might have been spared all
> this turmoil and anguish if Great Britain had only been armed and organised
> for war as the needs of our age demand. The precaution has not been taken,
> but in this solemn hour we shall utter no reproaches on that account. Our
> duty is to go forward into the valley of the shadow of death with courage and
> faith – with courage to suffer, with faith in God and our country.[4]

When Grey's warning was ignored by the Germans, Britain joined the combatants in the most horrifying war the world had yet seen.

Northcliffe agreed with the majority that believed the British navy would win the war and that the few divisions of the British Expeditionary Force (BEF) would be insignificant among the grand armies of France and Germany. The threat of German invasion was his paramount concern. On 5 August, at the Admiralty, he protested to Winston Churchill, the First Lord, against any plan to dispatch the BEF.[5] During a Carmelite House conference the same night, the proprietor declared, 'not a single soldier shall leave this country. We have a superb Fleet, which shall give all the assistance in its power, but I will not support the sending out of this country of a single British soldier. What about invasion? What about our own country? Put that in the leader . . . Say so in the paper tomorrow.'[6] In one of the rare cases in which he stood up to his chief successfully, Marlowe had Northcliffe's *Daily Mail* editorial along these lines replaced. Once the final decision was made to send the BEF to the Continent, Northcliffe put his misgivings aside. Winning the war became his mission.[7]

To lead the nation into battle, on 5 August Lord Kitchener was appointed Secretary of State for War – a decision viewed in some quarters as a triumph for the Northcliffe press. One biographer credited 'the persistence of Lord Northcliffe and the insistence of the public' with ensuring the choice.[8] No other military figure so commanded the respect of the nation as Kitchener, who had been lionized by the press for successfully fighting the country's little wars for decades and now was looked to for salvation in this larger emergency. The *Daily Mail* and *The Times* both lauded him, while vigorously attacking a rumoured plan to bring back Haldane. The 5 August *Daily Mail* noted that for the past two days Haldane (who had stepped down as Secretary for War in 1912 to become Lord Chancellor) had been presiding over the War Office and asked what he was doing there and whether he was delaying war preparations. Whatever Asquith privately might have wished to do, political and public opinion forced him to the 'hazardous experiment' of bringing a soldier into the Cabinet to sit at his right hand and direct the war.[9]

Despite Sir Edward Grey's often-repeated declaration that 'the lamps are going out all over Europe; we shall not see them lit again in our lifetime', the consensus in Britain held that the war would be brief.[10] It was widely believed that the intertwined national economies of 1914 could not stand more than a few months of conflict. Military experts predicted that the war would involve battles of movement, fought by professional armies which would be home by Christmas. The British Navy would make the crucial difference by defeating the enemy fleet and blockading Germany. Kitchener disagreed with all these assumptions and looked down upon the regular Army because he thought it too small for the part he believed it would have to play. He shared Northcliffe's fear of invasion, and both men also disagreed with the great majority that forecast a brief war.[11]

The Liberal government Kitchener joined was committed by its pre-1914 planning to a 'business as usual' course in which the Navy and economic support to the nation's allies, rather than a Continental-sized army, would be Britain's contributions. Sacrificing any more to the war effort, it was felt, would be disastrous. All this changed in the following months as Kitchener's plans for a 'nation in arms' held sway. Parliament was asked to increase the size of the Army by 500,000 men, and this was granted on 7 August. The same day, the Secretary for War issued his first appeal for 100,000 volunteers and Britain was soon papered over with his image, a pointing finger emphasizing the message 'Your Country Needs You!' The response overwhelmed the nation's recruitment centres. Meanwhile, the BEF, under the command of Field Marshal Sir John French, embarked for the Continent and concentrated near Amiens.[12]

After the outbreak of hostilities, conditions on the Continent were understandably chaotic. Although the French Ministry of War announced that correspondents were not to be allowed at the front, many reporters nevertheless used the general disorder to mask trips out to the fighting. Northcliffe tried to ensure both that his press coverage in France would not break down and that his papers would provide the best reports from the field. He saw Paris as the obvious news centre, and insisted that his office there be properly manned at all times. He instructed *Daily Mail* correspondent G.W. Price not to leave the French capital, because 'from all we hear, the correspondents are going to be kept in cages like wild animals, and Paris provides a far better opportunity for you and the paper than the front'.[13] This message represents one of his first remarks about government efforts to control war news.

After 5 August, Kitchener became the most important factor concerning the censorship. The War Secretary, who felt his reputation had been sullied in the aftermath of Omdurman and in the Boer War, had only contempt for the press. To make matters worse, confidences he shared with Repington, the military correspondent of *The Times*, appeared in print on 15 August. In response to angry charges of favouritism to the Northcliffe press, Kitchener proclaimed a total ban on correspondents with the BEF.[14] To guide the press and control war news, a Press Bureau was organized under Kitchener's choice, F.E. Smith.[15] Anxious to stay on good terms with the most powerful press lord, two days after he assumed his duties Smith sent a message to Northcliffe that 'we are bound to make mistakes at the start. Give me the advantage throughout of any advice which your experience suggests.'[16]

The Bureau served mainly as a lightning rod for criticism, for the real power stayed at the Admiralty and the War Office. Smith soon commented that 'Kitchener cannot understand that he is working in a democratic country. He rather thinks he is in Egypt where the press is represented by a dozen mangy newspaper correspondents whom he can throw in the Nile if they object to the way they are treated.' Whether for reasons of patriotism or for fear of government action, the British press was, in the main, self-censoring during the course of the war. Nevertheless, there were powerful written and unwritten strictures in place. Though the system was called 'voluntary', in addition to being subject to the statutory powers of the 1911 Official Secrets Act, the press was covered by several of the regulations of the first Defence of the Realm Act (DORA), passed by Parliament in August 1914.[17] Northcliffe was certainly well aware of possible penalties and, as we shall see, his publications faced government action more than once during the war.

While the British and French forbade correspondents, the Germans gave the press access to their initial victorious march across Belgium and France. To the owner of the *Daily Mail*, the enemy appeared to be controlling the world's press, as well as winning it over to their side.[18] In addition to international opinion, there was in Northcliffe's view the more important question of home morale to consider. The *Daily Mail* challenged the government to 'have the great courage to tell the British people the truth'.[19] Noting French press revelations from the battlefield in August, the newspaper questioned whether

> public enthusiasm for our army is not being chilled by the insufficiency of news concerning the British troops at the front. The newspapers do not wish to publish . . . anything that might be injurious to the military interests of the nation . . . while all will agree that a careful censorship is necessary for success, it might seem that the reticence in Great Britain has been carried to an unnecessary extreme.[20]

While censorship was being put in place in England, the BEF had secretly disembarked in France between 9 and 14 August. The 18 August *Daily Mail* congratulated the Army on the successful transportation of the BEF to France 'without a casualty'. Three days later Sir John French and the 90,000-man British contingent were advancing on the enemy. Though small by Continental standards, the BEF was well trained and its morale was high. The secrecy and misinformation concerning its transport had been effective; the Germans had no idea the British were even in France on the 23rd at the beginning of the Battle of Mons. However, because of the retreat of the French army, the BEF was soon engaged in a hazardous tactical withdrawal to escape being outflanked by the Germans.

Although disturbing rumours made their way to Britain, little was printed at first about the peril faced by the BEF. The Allied news blackout had left British newspapers to take a hopeful tone, in an attempt to bolster the morale of the nation. The *Daily Mail* filled its pages with general articles about the probable course of events, illustrated with maps carefully labelled as only estimates of the positions of the opposing forces. Then, on 30 August, *The Times* (in a special Sunday edition) and the *Weekly Dispatch* published the first reports of the British retreat from Mons.[21] *The Times* reported that

[since] Sunday morning last the German advance has been one of almost incredible rapidity . . . The Germans, fulfilling one of the best of all precepts in war, never gave the retreating army one single moment's rest. The pursuit was immediate, relentless, unresting. Aeroplanes, Zeppelins, armoured motors, were loosed like an arrow from the bow . . . Regiments were grievously injured, and the broken army fought its way desperately with many stands, forced backwards and ever backwards by the sheer unconquerable mass of numbers . . . Our losses are very great. I have seen the broken bits of many regiments . . . The German commanders in the north advance their men as if they had an inexhaustible supply.

These detailed and graphic 'Amiens dispatches', written by Arthur Moore for *The Times* and by Hamilton Fyfe for the *Weekly Dispatch*, shattered weeks of press optimism.[22] On Monday 31 August the *Daily Mail* continued the story of the BEF's 'heroic retreat', and in the following days it assumed the defence of its Sunday associate from the widespread attacks that the articles stimulated. Not only were the reports passed by F.E. Smith at the Press Bureau; in fact, he made significant changes and additions, to the stunned surprise of the editors, who fully expected the accounts would be suppressed. On 1 September *The Times* and the *Daily Mail* printed Smith's addition: 'England should realise, and realise at once, that she must send reinforcements, and still send them. Is an army of exhaustless valour to be borne down by the sheer weight of numbers, while young Englishmen at home play golf and cricket? We want men and we want them now.'

The Amiens dispatches created a storm of criticism directed at Northcliffe. Asquith rebuked *The Times* in the Commons, while elsewhere the reports were called exaggerated, defeatist and a malicious attack on the Army. Smith, who was forced to resign, was furious and vowed vengeance on the editors of *The Times*, who, he felt, had betrayed him. He called Northcliffe a 'dirty dog' who could not be trusted.[23] Smith was replaced at the Press Bureau by Sir Stanley (later Lord) Buckmaster, the Solicitor-General.[24] To reassure the public, Asquith had Churchill compose an official press communiqué (published anonymously on 5 September) on the retreat. The First Lord of the Admiralty wrote to Northcliffe:

> I think you ought to realize the [damage] that has been done by Sunday's publication in the 'Times'. I do not think you can possibly shelter yourself behind the Press Bureau, although their mistake was obvious. I never saw such panic-stricken stuff written by any war correspondent before; and this served up on the authority of the 'Times' can be made, and has been made, a weapon against us in every doubtful state.[25]

To this the press lord replied:

> This is not a time for Englishmen to quarrel, so I will not say all that I might about the publication of the Amiens message in The Times. Nor will I discuss the facts and tone of the message, beyond saying that it came from one of the most experienced correspondents in the service of the paper. I understand that not a single member of the staff on duty last Saturday night expected to see it passed by the Press Bureau. *But when it was not merely passed, but carefully edited, and accompanied by a definite appeal to publish it,* there was no other possible conclusion except that this was the Government's definite wish.[26]

The Amiens-dispatches affair put Northcliffe firmly in opposition to the government and its censorship policy, whatever his pre-war sympathies might have been. He wrote to Lord Murray of Elibank that, 'Some things are far more than flesh and blood can stand. So far as I am concerned, I propose to keep aloof from members of this Government until the war is over.'[27] Though he pretended to be unruffled by the affair, he told one of his writers, R. MacNair Wilson, that the attacks which labelled him an enemy of the Army 'hurt me more than anything else in my life'. The criticism was all the more painful, said Northcliffe, because 'it was true what we said about the retreat from Mons. If only we had turned that glorious truth to our advantage.'[28] This incident also confirmed Churchill's extreme view of naval censorship. No warship in action was able to find room for a correspondent; naval information had to be gleaned from the occasional official communiqués the Admiralty saw fit to issue. Though the dispatches confirmed Kitchener's worst suspicions about the press, the War Office was also moved to take action. It had become apparent that some news must be allowed; however, instead of authorizing press correspondents, the War Office announced that its reports would be supplied by an official 'Eyewitness', Major Ernest Swinton.[29]

In early September the advance of the German army to the outskirts of Paris became the most important story. The 3 September *Daily Mail* showcased a map of the fighting near the city. Jeffries and Fyfe reported the German advance to within twenty-nine miles of the capital. The Northcliffe newspapers and the French government prepared to move to Bordeaux, and the *Continental Daily Mail* was being published there by Monday 7 September. Soon after this, the early battlefield misfortunes of the Allies were reversed when their armies successfully counter-attacked at the Battle of the Marne. This stroke halted the German advance, saved Paris, and spelled the end of any remaining German illusions of swift victory in the West. By 15 September the *Daily Mail* staff had returned to their Paris office. The Marne victory also convinced Northcliffe that Germany would be defeated provided Britain could be persuaded to exert her full strength.[30] To this end, he spent the remainder of the war attempting to awaken the public to the magnitude of the challenge at hand.

Northcliffe made his first of many trips to the front in early October. By this time the *Daily Mail* was supplying 10,000 free copies of each edition for the troops. Major Swinton, the official 'Eyewitness', had responsibility for the dispersal of the papers, and met Northcliffe in Paris. Swinton was soon charmed by the owner of the *Daily Mail*. Northcliffe asked Swinton to pass along a request to visit Army Headquarters to Sir John French, and put the considerable intelligence resources of the newspapers at his disposal.[31] Though Northcliffe apparently did not personally meet the British commander on this first trip, he visited the Belgian and French armies and was able to make some contact with British troops. He thoroughly enjoyed the adventure. His companion, Hamilton Fyfe, recorded that during the trip their car, driving at night without lights, had several near misses with disaster and that the two men experienced a shell bombardment at Pervyse. After watching an air raid, Northcliffe commented, 'We shall have those fellows dropping bombs on London before long.'[32] At this time he also sent Sir John French a scheme for airborne propaganda against the Germans, but nothing came of it. When he then presented the notion to General Sir Henry Wilson, the Director of Military Operations replied that propaganda was only a minor matter: the thing to do was 'to kill Germans'.[33]

In October and November, *Daily Mail* maps followed the so-called 'race to the sea' in which the opposing armies tried to outflank each other. The triumph of modern defence over attack was demonstrated in the defeat of the German attempt to break through at the First Battle of Ypres. The stalemated front soon extended from the Swiss border to the Channel, beginning years of trench warfare.

Winston Churchill's actions at the Admiralty came under increasing press attack. The nation expected great things of the Navy, and had been disappointed by the escape of the German battle-cruiser *Goeben* to Turkey, the sinking of three British cruisers in one day, and losses at Antwerp by the Royal Naval Division. The failed defence of Antwerp personally involved Churchill.[34] Asking 'Who is Responsible?', the *Daily Mail* rebuked the First Lord for interfering 'in fields which do not properly concern him' and called for his colleagues to see that he did no more 'mischief'. In a harbinger of future developments, the piece ended with a warning that though 'this last incident was not vital . . . some future commitment might be'.[35]

In response to widespread public and press demands (led by Northcliffe), at the end of October Lord Fisher was recalled from retirement to right the Admiralty's course. The chief proprietor of *The Times* took Geoffrey Robinson and the writer Lovat Fraser to visit the First Sea Lord so that they could see 'what manner of man it is in whom our destiny lies'. He assured Fisher that he was 'at one with' him and wanted to ensure that his papers would be as well.[36] Northcliffe cabled Arthur Brisbane, at the *New York Evening Journal*, that the one big change in the first few months of the war had come with the return of Fisher, adding that he did not think naval arrangements could be in better hands than those of the First Sea Lord, who was 'a most daring and original man – the youngest thing of seventy-four in the world, I should think'.[37] Nevertheless, Admiralty censorship continued unabated under the new regime.

To circumvent the Press Bureau, the Northcliffe newspapers often quoted American and other journals. For example, the 4 December 1914 *Daily Mail* carried excerpts from the *Saturday Evening Post* of 'the only interview Lord Kitchener has given since the outbreak of war', by the American journalist Irvin Cobb. The article revealed Kitchener's prediction that the war effort would need at least three more years and that Germany would be defeated, because 'there is no other possible contingency'. This policy infuriated Buckmaster, at the Press Bureau, who claimed he had proof that Northcliffe had US papers attack the British censorship so that his newspapers could print their comments. Buckmaster complained that he was not supported by the Cabinet in his calls for sterner measures and that Churchill and Kitchener were afraid to use DORA to court-martial the press lord. In Cabinet discussions Lloyd George often defended the press and Northcliffe. Sir George Riddell, a confidant of Lloyd George and proprietor of the *News of the World*, noted that 'L.G. not very keen about attacking the Harmsworth crowd' and felt that there was 'no doubt some sort of understanding between him and Northcliffe'.[38]

The Northcliffe press joined the rest of the British newspapers in howls of righteous indignation over German 'atrocities' in Belgium and France. On 12 and 17 August the *Daily Mail* carried accounts of 'German Brutality' including the murder of five civilians, corroborated by sworn statements. A 21 August article by Fyfe chronicled the 'sins against civilization' and the 'barbarity' of the Germans. A week later, in a story based on accounts by wounded British troops, Fyfe continued to list atrocities such as Germans cutting off the hands of Red Cross workers and using women and children as shields in battle.[39] At the end of August the Belgian Legation in London began releasing official reports of German 'excesses'. The 26 August *Daily Mail* declared that

[the] measured, detailed, and we fear unanswerable indictment of Germany's conduct of the war issued yesterday by the Belgian minister is a catalogue of horrors that will indelibly brand the German name in the eyes of all mankind ... this is no ordinary arraignment ... concerned not with hearsay evidence, but with incidents that in each case have been carefully investigated ... After making every deduction for national bias and the possibility of error, there remains a record of sheer brutality that will neither be forgiven or forgotten.

In September the *Daily Mail* reported the 'Horror of Louvain' and continued with subsequent revelations of German outrages at Malines, Reims and elsewhere. The 18 September issue carried a full page of atrocity photographs, including, according to the caption, a Belgian civilian holding up the charred remains of his daughter's foot. An investigative committee convened under the former British ambassador to the United States, Lord Bryce, published a condemnation of German brutalities, including reports of the impaling of babies and amputations of women's breasts. Besides the domestic audience, these broadsides also were aimed at world, and most importantly American, opinion.[40]

Almost immediately after the outbreak of war the *Daily Mail* had begun to warn of enemy publicity in the United States.[41] While his newspapers publicly proclaimed the failure of the German 'campaigns of falsehoods', privately Northcliffe believed otherwise. He wrote about the matter in September to the *Times* correspondent in Washington, Arthur Willert, who reported that educated opinion was on the side of Britain and passed on many positive comments from Americans. However, he sent his chief a letter – identified only as from a British sympathizer in California – which confirmed the press lord's worst suspicions of German propaganda gains.[42] At the same time, fearing the use German propagandists would make of any negative comments, Northcliffe gave instructions that 'no criticism of the US was to appear in my newspapers until the American Fleet bombarded Liverpool'.[43] To foster US understanding of Britain's position, Northcliffe gave personal interviews which played on the notoriety he had gained in many trips across the Atlantic. In the 30 December 1914 New York *Sun* he asserted that, although it might take years, Germany would be defeated if the Allies marshalled all their resources, including manpower. He wrote to Arthur Brisbane that the British were preparing for 'a three years' war' with many ups and downs and admitted that the British had lost heavily. The same letter revealed his concern that 'we may not be preparing sufficiently for invasion. I am inclined myself to think that we are not – perhaps because I should be one of the first people to be hanged if the Germans got here'.[44]

In addition to the effects of German propaganda in the United States, Northcliffe was also concerned with American reaction to the effects of the British blockade on US trade. At the beginning of the war it was assumed that the British fleet would soon defeat the enemy and barricade the German coast. When the German navy stayed at anchor and refused to engage, the British erected a barrier to intercept contraband and waited for the foe to emerge. Northcliffe agreed that Germany must be blockaded, but not at the cost of completely alienating US official and public opinion, which he felt the Foreign Office slighted.[45] Willert reinforced this belief with a report that the main difficulty in relations between the two countries was that 'Washington is ignored to a most surprising extent'.[46] In an attempt to remedy this shortcoming, Northcliffe forwarded press clippings from the United States to Sir Edward Grey which illustrated both American hostility to the blockade and the success of German propaganda efforts.[47]

The Zeppelin raids and naval bombardments on civilian targets which began in the last month of 1914 brought directly home to the English population for the first time the bitter reality of twentieth-century warfare. Two months before, the newspaper had appealed for better air-defence preparations 'instantly' against the 50 to 100 airships being prepared in Germany for an assault. Now the *Daily Mail* howled over the 'inhuman and malignant action' of the German shelling of Scarborough and other coastal towns, which killed many women and children.[48] But, despite their sensational coverage in the press, Northcliffe remained confident that the attacks would not cause the terror and panic which the Germans hoped. At year's end the *Daily Mail* pledged in 1915 'never to sheathe the sword' until the whole of France was cleared of the enemy and Belgium was regained. The fundamental job ahead, continued the paper, was to destroy Prussian militarism, even though this 'can only be carried out by the invasion of Germany'.[49]

In the first week of January 1915 Northcliffe left for a second visit to the front. As before, his journey added fuel to his frustration with the lethargic attitude of the Asquith ministry. The government, he feared, was bungling relations with France and also with the most important neutral – the United States. He told the correspondent Samuel Storey soon after leaving the fighting line that he feared 'we are muddling and dallying'. The government, he went on, that 'did not see the war coming, apparently does not see that America is coming, and that the trouble with the French is developing rapidly'. American friends had written to him that they would

> not have their commerce directed by us. Our French friends say that England does not understand that we are fighting Germany on French territory or that one-eighth of the richest part of France is held by the Germans . . . starving to death two millions of French people behind the German lines . . . You know, of course, that Germany has approached France twice about a separate peace.

The letter ended with the warning that his press was 'dealing very gently with the Government now, because the public, who know nothing about the war, will not tolerate criticism of our public men; but, believe me, we shall not be patient much longer'.[50]

Germany's announcement of its February submarine blockade of Britain was labelled a 'bluff' by the *Daily Mail*, which called for a 'real blockade' in response.[51] Northcliffe, whose press operations had already been hampered by the loss of many men to the armed forces, for the first time felt his paper supply threatened and planned for the worst. In a letter of complaint to Geoffrey Robinson at *The Times* about the downward trend in circulation and measures that might have to be taken, he added that 'our difficulties are going to be increased because it is said that owing to the blockade the price of paper is about to rise, and we must issue small papers I fear'.[52] The British responded to Germany's submarine campaign by tightening their own surface blockade. Three months later the German campaign came to a climax with the sinking of the *Lusitania* off the Irish coast and the resulting loss of 128 American lives. The 8 May *Daily Mail* labelled the action 'Premeditated Murder'. Two days later the paper printed photographs of dead women and children lined up at the 'charnel house' at Queenstown (now Cóbh), County Cork. Some expected the Americans now to join the war, in the spirit of Wilson's stated rule of 'strict accountability', but his 'Too Proud to Fight' speech soon disabused them of the idea. After the disaster, Willert wrote to Northcliffe from New York that 'the row with Germany by no means precludes a further unpleasant controversy over our blockade. As things stand today only actual war can prevent that'.[53]

On the home front, Northcliffe fully realized how unpopular he was making himself in some quarters by his constant newspaper criticisms and reminders of the long and difficult task ahead for the country. By March 1915, however, increased numbers of politicians from both parties also questioned the methods of the Asquith government and the Kitchener mystique. Conservatives, particularly Walter Long and the Unionist Business Committee, muzzled by the continuing 'party truce' and unhappy with the progress of the war, were increasingly impatient. Some Liberals were also restive. At Bangor, Lloyd George began a series of public pronouncements. The 1 March *Daily Mail* printed his remark that

we are conducting a war as if there was no war. I have never been doubtful about the result of the war. Nor have I been doubtful, I am sorry to say, about the length of the war and its seriousness . . . we need men, but we need arms more than men and every day that produces delay is full of peril to this country.

Northcliffe joined forces with Lloyd George over the issue that would dominate the next few months – the shortage of shells.

No one on either side had foreseen the unprecedented scale of Western Front artillery bombardments, but by October 1914 the need for an increased supply of munitions had become apparent. A Shells Committee, including Lloyd George, was created to examine and propose solutions to the problem. This civilian invasion of the army sphere was resented and blocked by Kitchener and the War Office; however, the Committee was able to manage some improvements. Lloyd George complained that the War Secretary treated his colleagues with 'the usual mixture of military contempt and apprehension'.[54]

Because he had to take into consideration the Empire and Britain's allies, Kitchener was one of the few British military figures amenable to diversions of men and material away from the Western Front. Russian pleas for assistance in early 1915 made him open to a naval plan proposed by Churchill to breach the Dardanelles and to open a warm-water supply route to the eastern ally. The First Lord of the Admiralty insisted that few troops would be required.[55] Unfortunately, the naval bombardment failed and, rather than face a humiliating withdrawal, Kitchener was forced to divert troops and supplies from the Western Front to the Dardanelles. This further infuriated Sir John French, who continued to plead for more resources.

Since the first months of the war the British commander had complained about munition shortages, which often forced miserly rationing of shells. The lack of ammunition – particularly high-explosive shells – came to a head after the Battle of Neuve Chapelle (10–13 March) had once again demonstrated the futility of using shrapnel against heavily entrenched German positions. Kitchener's frugal habits led him to call French's use of shells during the Battle of Neuve Chapelle 'recklessly extravagant'.[56] Faced with War Office intransigence, French appealed for help outside of army channels, including politicians and the press. Even before Neuve Chapelle, Northcliffe was in contact with French about munitions and their production, including the problem of motivating worker support for the war. A 3 March letter expressed the hope that French would 'shortly receive the munitions' for his 'great enterprise'.[57] The Field Marshal and the press lord both considered 'lamentable' the division of British forces created by the Dardanelles expedition, and Northcliffe assured French that his newspapers would not 'cease to urge the sending of men to your army'.[58] French replied that he 'rejoiced to hear the view which you take in regard to the division of our forces. I entirely agree . . . and I earnestly hope you will do your utmost in your powerful control of the Press to insist upon concentration of all available forces in this theatre.'[59]

Reports of the Neuve Chapelle failure got out in letters to the papers, from Members of Parliament and from the accounts of wounded soldiers in England. Northcliffe visited the hospital established by his wife at Sutton Place. Kitchener broke the government silence and admitted his worries over munitions in the House of Lords on 15 March 1915, yet he told Asquith two weeks later he would resign if another Shells Committee were appointed.[60] The failure of the naval bombardment to breach the Dardanelles on 18 March added to the criticism of the government. In a 29 March *Daily Mail* interview, Sir John French stated that 'the protraction of the war depends entirely on the supply of men and munitions'. The military setbacks strengthened rumours that the Conservatives, their press allies and others were scheming to discredit the Prime Minister and force a coalition. Churchill and Lloyd George were accused of working from within to undermine the government. Lloyd George, in particular, was brought under suspicion because he had been lauded recently in the Northcliffe press. The Home Secretary, Reginald McKenna, passed along the whisperings to the Prime Minister.[61] Asquith told Venetia Stanley on 29 March:

> There is, in the Tory press a dead set being made against me personally. Witness the articles in *The Times* & the *Morning Post*. As you know, I am fairly indifferent to press criticism. I honestly don't care one damn about that. McKenna came to see me . . . with a tragic history of intrigue. The idea is that Northcliffe (for some unknown reason) has been engineering a campaign to supplant me by Ll. G! McK is . . . quite certain that Ll. G. & perhaps Winston are 'in it'. Which I don't believe. However, he (McK) . . . has a certain amount of evidence as to Ll. G. to go upon.[62]

Asquith appears to have been correct in his belief that Lloyd George remained loyal in this period. No evidence to support McKenna's charges has surfaced.

In April 1915 Northcliffe made his third visit to the front. While on the Continent he saw Field Marshal French and also met General Joffre, the French army commander. The press lord wrote to his mother that he had had a 'long talk with Sir John French' and a 'pleasant dinner at which was the prince of Wales'.[63] At British GHQ, Northcliffe composed a rare handwritten note to his old friend Alexander Kenealy, former editor of the *Weekly Dispatch*.

All here most confident that by prolonged massed artillery fire on a tremendous scale they can break the German line & the next few weeks will be momentous in history I feel sure. General French [i]s calm, able & certain, & by necessity a terrific worker. I sat with him till late last night. We need shells. Today I go to stay with Joffre whose headquarters are at Chantilly a long motor ride from here right along the war front, at many places.[64]

Kitchener used Joffre's objection to correspondents as a rationale for excluding them from the British Army. To dispel this argument, Northcliffe met Joffre. His efforts were rewarded when Joffre agreed to a suggestion that a Reuters correspondent should report news from the French army.[65] At the same time, Sir George Riddell and other press figures at home urged Kitchener to allow correspondents with the British forces. In May the War Secretary finally allowed press representatives at British GHQ in France, where, although their movements were limited, they remained for the rest of the war. Valentine Williams credited Northcliffe's visit to Joffre and his own 19 April Neuve Chapelle story with forcing Kitchener to remove his ban.[66]

The conference with Joffre increased Northcliffe's dissatisfaction with Britain's prosecution of the war. The owner of *The Times* felt recent articles in that paper had whitewashed government blunders. He wrote to Lovat Fraser, on the staff of *The Times*, that

[anyone] who has studied this war knows that our army in France is unable to move . . . It cannot move for three reasons: Firstly, because many of the shells that should have been sent to it have been dispatched to the Dardanelles; Secondly, because the 29th Division, which was promised to the French, has been sent to the Dardanelles; and, Thirdly, because the Government has not availed itself of the small contractors who have offered to supply shells.

He went on that he had 'reason to believe, privately, that General French is on his way over to England to make urgent representations . . . to the Cabinet'. The same letter particularly condemned the government over the shortage of shells:

The whole question of the supply of munitions of war is one on which the Cabinet cannot be arraigned too sharply . . .
When recently, I saw those splendid boys of ours toiling along the roads to the front, weary, but keen and bright-eyed . . . I could not help feeling very, very bitter at the thought that many of them were on the way to certain mutilation and death by reason of the abominable neglect of the people here.
. . . 'The Times' . . . has a tremendous duty and responsibility – more

especially as I feel my duty greater because I have now made three visits to this war, have talked with hundreds of people – both English and French – concerned with it, and know that, while we are talking about the alleged drunken habits of the working man (in which I do not believe), the guns at the front are starved for want of the only means of putting an end to this frightful slaughter of the best which any nation has to give.[67]

The Drink Question mentioned above became another national issue of debate at this time. Lloyd George blamed alcohol for many of the country's production and labour problems, and considered nationalization of the liquor industry.[68] Northcliffe disagreed with him on this issue, and had his newspapers say so. Lloyd George unsuccessfully attempted to enlist Northcliffe's aid for his anti-drink programme. 'I am anxious to have a talk with you on the government proposals about Drink,' he wrote, 'we have overwhelming evidence of the grave mischief in the munitions and transport areas caused by excessive drinking and we must take strong action otherwise the war will go on forever . . . your influence is essential.'[69] Despite this flattery, Northcliffe was not persuaded and remained hostile to further proposals.

At the same time, the Northcliffe newspapers called for the publication of Sir John French's Neuve Chapelle dispatches to coincide with the week's recruiting drive, charging that 'the constant suppression of news with regard to the operations in Flanders and the mysterious Dardanelles Expedition is, indeed, a matter which requires the attention of Parliament'.[70] A chart (reproduced from *Le Matin*) showed the relative miles of trench line occupied by each army – with France holding 543½, the British 31¼ and the Belgians 17½. Two days later French was quoted as stating that

In war as it is today between civilised nations, armed to the teeth with the present deadly rifle and machine gun, heavy casualties are absolutely unavoidable . . . loss and waste of life can, however, be shortened and lessened if the attacks are supported by the most efficient and powerful force of artillery available; but an almost limitless supply of ammunition is necessary and a most liberal discretionary power as to its use must be given to the artillery commanders.[71]

Based on information from French, Kitchener assured Asquith that the supply of shells was adequate. Eager to demonstrate the wickedness of Northcliffe, the Prime Minister declared at Newcastle on 20 April 1915 that

I saw a statement the other day that the operations . . . of our army . . . were being crippled, or at any rate, hampered, by our failure to provide the necessary ammunition. I say there is not a word of truth in that statement, which is the more mischievous, because, if it were believed, it is calculated to dishearten our troops, to discourage our Allies, and to stimulate the hopes and activities of our enemies.[72]

This speech drew immediate and widespread press criticism. *The Times* and the *Daily Mail* asked how Asquith's remarks could be reconciled with statements by Lloyd George and Kitchener on the shortage of shells. Asquith wrote again to Venetia Stanley:

I am so glad that you liked my speech; if you think it good, I don't care a two-penny damn what anyone else thinks about it – let alone Northcliffe & his obscene crew. I don't think we shall hear much more now on this particular line of attack, as after a very curious rapprochement between K & Ll. G . . . the latter was allowed – for the first time – to give a number of most convincing figures to the House yesterday.[73]

Rather than smoothing the waters, Lloyd George's revelations in the House of Commons caused Northcliffe further concern. On 1 May he warned French that he would soon be held responsible for the military failures:

On April 21st, Mr. Lloyd George, in the House of Commons said that there were 36 divisions at the front . . . People are asking . . . If Sir John French has three quarters of a million men, why is he only occupying thirty miles of line? . . . Early this week Lord Kitchener expressly forbade the newspapers analysing Mr. Lloyd George's statement, and you are therefore believed to have this vast army at your disposal . . .

In the absence of some strong statement from you the Government have your friends at their mercy, because they are able to get their newspapers to say that any agitation for less secrecy is unpatriotic and playing the enemy's game.

As a further result of secrecy, Mr. Asquith is able to assure the nation that your operations have never been hampered for want of ammunition . . .

A short and very vigorous statement from you to a private correspondent (the usual way of making things public in England) would, I believe, render the Government's position impossible, and enable you to secure the publication of that which would tell the people here the truth and thus bring public pressure on the Government to stop men and munitions pouring away to the Dardanelles, as they are at present.[74]

Soon after the Battle of Festubert began on 9 May, Kitchener notified French that 20,000 rounds (20 per cent of his reserve) were to be earmarked for the Dardanelles. A few days later, frustrated by failure on the battlefield, French decided to act. He shared the War Office correspondence over the shells with Repington, and sent his personal secretary, Colonel Brinsley Fitzgerald, and his ADC, Captain Frederick Guest, to London to show the same material to Lloyd George, Bonar Law and Arthur Balfour.[75] Repington's account, published in *The Times* of 14 May, of the failed attack on the Aubers Ridge, five days before, charged that 'the want of an unlimited supply of high explosives was a fatal bar to our success'. The 'Shells Scandal' which followed was the end product of months of newspaper demands for more shells and a reorganization of the country's munitions production. The article has also been viewed as the final straw which prompted Lloyd George to inform Asquith that he could not go on in the government.[76] The same day Northcliffe was notified that his nephew Lucas King had been killed in action. On 15 May Lord Fisher, unable to contain his bitter disagreement with Churchill over the Dardanelles, tendered his resignation from the Admiralty. Northcliffe met Lloyd George two days later to discuss the growing crisis. During the next week a coalition government was formed.

When it became apparent that Kitchener would remain in charge of the War Office in the reformed government, Northcliffe felt he had to take drastic action. 'I don't care what they do to me, the circulation of the *Daily Mail* may go down to two and the *Times* to one – I don't care,' he told H.W. Wilson. 'The thing has to be done! Better to lose circulation than to lose the war.'[77] Driven by his fear for the nation and his personal grief, Northcliffe composed the 21 May *Daily Mail* editorial, 'Tragedy of the Shells – Lord Kitchener's Grave Error', which called for the Army and Navy to be 'placed in the best available hands'. At the Admiralty, it advised that Fisher should remain 'untrammelled'. For Lord Kitchener and the War Office, the piece was nothing short of an open indictment:

In the dark days when Lord Haldane . . . showed signs of renewed tinkering with the Army, the *Daily Mail* suggested that Lord Kitchener should take charge of raising the new troops . . . that part of the work was done as well as anyone could do it . . . the soldiers are there. How many, nobody knows . . . *What we do know is that Lord Kitchener has starved the army in France of high explosive shells* . . .

It has never been pretended that Lord Kitchener is a soldier in the sense that Sir John French is a soldier. Lord Kitchener is a gatherer of men – and a very fine gatherer too. But his record in the South African war as a fighting general . . . was not brilliant . . .

The admitted fact is that Lord Kitchener *ordered the wrong kind of shells* – the same kind of shell which he used against the Boers in 1900. He persisted in sending shrapnel – a useless weapon in trench warfare. He was warned repeatedly that the kind of shell required was a violently explosive bomb which would dynamite its way through the German trenches and entanglements and enable our brave men to advance safely. The kind of shell our poor soldiers have has caused the death of thousands of them. Incidentally it has brought about a Cabinet crisis and the formation of what we hope is going to be a National Government.[78]

This editorial had exactly the opposite effect to that which Northcliffe wished. An affronted nation condemned the press lord and all his works and rose in fervent defence of Kitchener. *Daily Mail* circulation and advertising plummeted, and copies of the papers were burned in the street and at the Stock Exchange, which sent messages of confidence to Asquith and Kitchener, and gave three cheers for Kitchener and three groans for Northcliffe. A placard inscribed 'The Allies of the Huns' was hung outside the City office of the *Daily Mail*.[79] London clubs banned the *Daily Mail*, *The Times*, the *Evening News* and the *Weekly Dispatch* from their premises. The leaders of the Army also rallied to the defence of the War Secretary. General Haig informed Kitchener how 'thoroughly disgusted we all are here at the attacks which the Harmsworth reptile press have made on Lord Kitchener'.[80] General Hamilton informed Kitchener that 'the infamous attack upon you of the Harmsworth Press . . . is bitterly resented throughout the forces . . . They say a nation gets the Press it deserves, but surely the British Empire has never done anything bad enough to earn itself a Harmsworth!'[81] The day after the *Daily Mail* salvo, A.G. Gardiner, the editor of the *Daily News*, returned fire. 'Northcliffe and Kitchener, The Meaning of the Vendetta' blamed the press lord, not Churchill, Fisher or Kitchener, for the crisis. To Gardiner, the biggest problem the country now faced was not who would form the new government, but what it would do with Northcliffe. The *Daily News* continued the story of the 'growing chorus of protests' in the following week. On 28 May it reported 'resolutions from all quarters', including protests from Bristol and Liverpool. Three days later the paper disclosed the hostile responses of several weekly reviews: the *Spectator* called Northcliffe's methods 'outrageous'; the *Nation* accused him of instilling the 'poison of uncertainty in our national mind', and a *New Witness* article, 'The Harmsworth Plot', alleged that Northcliffe had clamoured for the appointment of Kitchener only so that he could then tear him down to show his power, but that Lord Kitchener 'refused to conduct the War Office under orders from Carmelite Street'.

In the face of this deluge of criticism, the owner of the *Daily Mail* remained defiant. Wrench later recalled walking with him on 'the very day when the *Daily Mail* was burnt in the City of London and advertisers were cancelling their contracts by thousands . . . Never did Northcliffe appear to me of more heroic mould. Northcliffe knew his facts were right, he was intensely patriotic and nothing could deflect him from his purpose of telling the people the truth.'[82] As a countermeasure, the *Daily Mail* began a 'Truth Will Out' campaign. The 24 May editorial described the people angry at the newspapers as 'the dupes of official secrecy and unthinking optimism'. However, the paper was certain that 'the truth cannot be hidden for long and it will be found that those who are now so active in criticising the *Daily Mail* will . . . turn their criticism in the right direction'. In its own defence, the paper quoted other journals, including J.L. Garvin's comment in the *Observer* that 'we must hold it to be true that the failure and the casualties . . . on Sunday week were largely due to want of sufficient ammunition of the right kind . . . we need far more high explosive . . . in vast and almost unimaginable quantities'.[83]

To straighten out the muddled shells situation, Lloyd George accepted the new post of Minister for Munitions in the coalition government. The 26 May *Daily Mail* declared that 'the appointment of Mr. Lloyd George to this new office meets a great many of the criticisms of the *Daily Mail* and we think it will satisfy the country'. In a note to him, Northcliffe described Lloyd George's place in the government as the 'heaviest responsibility that has fallen on any Briton for 100 years'.[84] Beyond this selection, however, Northcliffe had little cause for celebration at the membership of the new administration. Contrary to his wishes, Asquith remained Prime Minister and the Liberals predominant. Kitchener stayed at the War Office, while Fisher's resignation was accepted. Although Churchill left the Admiralty (where Balfour was installed), he remained in the Cabinet at the Duchy of Lancaster. Bonar Law, somewhat surprisingly, accepted the Colonial Office. In one other positive step from Northcliffe's point of view, Haldane was replaced as

Lord Chancellor (by Buckmaster) and left the government. The Northcliffe press had attacked both Churchill and Haldane, but had been especially brutal to the latter, whose ties to Germany were unceasingly trumpeted. The *Daily Mail* found most useful Haldane's reported remark about his college days in Germany, which he had called his 'spiritual home'.[85]

In response to charges in the House of Commons by John Dillon, an Irish Nationalist MP, that the actions of the *Daily Mail* had led to the downfall of the government, the paper responded on 9 June that 'what caused the formation of the new Government was the revelation that our men were hampered by the lack of an unlimited supply of high explosive shells . . . not any articles in the *Daily Mail*'. Nevertheless, the newspaper campaign Northcliffe carried out against Asquith and various members of his government from the beginning of the war to May 1915 must be given some credit for shaping the new situation. It has been suggested by several historians that the press campaign over the shells cleared the way for Lloyd George and the new Ministry of Munitions.[86] If there was a 'conspiracy' to unseat Asquith, the historian Bentley Gilbert has written, it was Northcliffe who began it, not Lloyd George.[87] Although not the most important factor, continuing press revelations in the months leading up to May 1915 fostered a climate of unrest which made a government change possible and, when added to the continuing military setbacks, inevitable.

Perhaps the most important factor in the fall of the Liberal government was the failure of the Allies to have any significant success in the war. The string of 1915 disasters on the Western Front and in the Dardanelles resulted in unrest among the Conservatives which was finally voiced by their leader, Bonar Law. With Bonar Law and Lloyd George both convinced of the need for change, Asquith was forced to act. Winston Churchill later wrote that, with the Liberal Party and Parliament unable to counteract the 'tireless detraction' of the press, 'there remained . . . as the reply to remorseless depreciation, only victory in the field. Victory would have carried all before it, but victory was unprocurable.'[88] Unfortunately, victories would continue to be rare as the war moved into its second year.

13

Stalemate, 1915–1916

ON 15 JULY 1915 Northcliffe celebrated his fiftieth birthday. The Associated Newspaper employees gave their chief a luncheon at the Ritz.[1] In a speech afterwards he told the assembly that he intended 'to continue his policy of criticizing the Government till such a time as we apply ourselves as scientifically as Germany to carrying on the war'. He added that 'If only all this munition problem had been tackled six months ago, things would have been in a very different state.'[2] Northcliffe's spirits were high. Only two months after copies of the *Daily Mail* and *The Times* had been publicly burned, circulation had more than recovered as the truth of the shells accusations became apparent to the nation both from debates in Parliament and from further newspaper revelations.

Northcliffe found his influence revived along with his papers. He was widely credited with bringing down the old government. Although they might profess otherwise, anxious officials curried his favour. General Sir Ian Hamilton, who became the target of the *Daily Mail* and *The Times* over the disastrous Gallipoli campaign, recalled a visit to an 'administrator' who was 'admonishing me as to the unsuitability of a public servant having a journalistic acquaintance when, suddenly, the door opened; the parlour maid entered and said, "Lord Northcliffe is on the phone."'[3] Winston Churchill later wrote of his enhanced stature:

> The furious onslaughts of the Northcliffe Press had been accompanied by the collapse of the Administration. To the minds of the public the two events

presented themselves broadly as cause and effect. Henceforward Lord Northcliffe felt himself to be possessed of formidable power. Armed with the solemn prestige of *The Times* in one hand and the ubiquity of the *Daily Mail* in the other, he aspired to exercise a commanding influence upon events. The inherent instability and obvious infirmity of the first Coalition Government offered favourable conditions for the advancement of these claims. The recurring crises on the subject of conscription presented numerous occasions for their assertion.[4]

The *Daily Mail*, which now declared itself '*THE PAPER THAT REVEALED THE SHELL TRAGEDY*', began to call for conscription during the spring press agitation over shells. Northcliffe believed conscription to be the fairest course and the one that would prove Britain's resolve to her allies and forestall France and Russia from making a separate peace with Germany. Lloyd George shared this view, and both men believed there must be a more vigorous effort to mobilize the nation's resources. To that end Northcliffe fed information to the Minister, whom he saw as a dynamic alternative to Asquith.[5]

Besides Lloyd George, several other government insiders also communicated with Northcliffe. Prominent among them was the Attorney-General, Sir Edward Carson, who, in Northcliffe's estimation, was second only to Lloyd George in ability.[6] Carson was one of the very few non-soldiers to whom Northcliffe deferred on war matters, and he could also intimidate the press lord – a rare talent. The two men corresponded and met over various war issues, including conscription and the Dardanelles. In response to Northcliffe's letter lauding his entry into the government, Carson replied, 'It was kind of you to write me . . . The work will be very heavy and anxious. Like yourself I have always had misgivings about the Dardanelles, but being a mere outsider I could not estimate the Pros & Cons. It will be a very anxious consideration for us all.'[7] In August, after the Suvla Bay landing of more men for the Dardanelles operation had brought matters to a crisis, Carson joined the government's Dardanelles Committee, which oversaw war policy. About Gallipoli, Northcliffe asked Carson, 'Is it not wise to discuss this disastrous expedition in my newspapers . . . the Germans are intimately informed of our impending catastrophe. *Can nothing be done to minimise it?*'[8]

At the same time, certain that the coalition government would have to be pressured into implementing compulsory service, Northcliffe launched a major push for conscription. The 16 August *Daily Mail* published a 'Manifesto' in support of national service, including a

pro-conscription form to be filled out and mailed to the government.
The same issue also criticized the 'unfairness' of the National Register
announced the previous day – requiring all citizens aged fifteen to sixty-
five to report their names, occupations and any war-work skills –
because it lacked any regulatory power over 'slackers'. In the following
weeks *Daily Mail* articles and editorials hammered away at the subject.
The 28 August editorial, 'Hush! Don't Mention Compulsion', attacked
Liberal press calls to wait for a government lead on the question. Soon
after the formation of the coalition, Asquith had written to the King
that future press transgressions were to be put in the hands of the
Public Prosecutor, who had full power 'to suppress by executive action
offending newspapers without previous prosecution'.[9] As Attorney-
General, Carson pondered action against both *The Times* and the *Daily
Mail*. The *Daily Mail*'s offence was found in the 7 September article
'Recruiting by Blackmail', which decried 'sneaking and haphazard compulsion under the guise of "moral pressure"'. The *Times*'s fault came
three days later in the article 'The Government and the Pink Forms',
which protested at the 'fresh campaign of private pressure'. When the
evidence was found too weak to take to court, F.E. Smith, who had
been consulted in the matter, wrote to Carson that he wished the
government had had a case.[10]

During the conscription campaign, revelations concerning the
Dardanelles operation came to the attention of the Cabinet. Charges of
official mismanagement and neglect were made in a damning report by
the Australian journalist Keith Murdoch. General Sir Ian Hamilton, the
commander at Gallipoli, had allowed Murdoch to visit the Anzac
(Australian and New Zealand Army Corps) zone in an inspection of
postal arrangements for the Australian government.[11] The journalist had
been shocked by the squalor, sickness and depression he saw during a
brief visit to the Australian beachhead. His dire report pointed out the
extremely tenuous position of his countrymen, and indicted Hamilton
and the British for ignorance and incapacity in their treatment of the
Anzac forces. Murdoch's United Cable Service office was located in
Printing House Square. When he told his harrowing story to Geoffrey
Robinson, the editor of *The Times* had Murdoch repeat his account for
Carson.[12] A copy of the report was also given to Northcliffe, who discussed it with Lloyd George. Northcliffe wrote to Murdoch that he would

> not be able to rest until the true story of this lamentable adventure was so
> well known as to force immediate steps to be taken to remedy the state of

affairs. The matter has haunted me ever since I learned about it . . . Merely the minor part of your statement, to the effect that the men are being sent out with summer clothing is enough to indict the state of muddle which is existing.[13]

Lloyd George, who preferred an operation in Salonica to the Dardanelles, passed the document on to Asquith. The Prime Minister, without allowing Hamilton to defend himself against its accusations, had it printed and circulated to the members of the Dardanelles Committee.[14] It was before them when the decision was made to send either Kitchener or Sir Douglas Haig (commander of BEF First Corps) for a direct inspection of the situation.

The evacuation of the Dardanelles, Northcliffe and others believed, would be the wisest course. Northcliffe asked Carson's support for this policy:

It requires no imagination to realise that the Dardanelles tragedy, which the Australians and New Zealanders are determined to reveal to the world, will for all time be a theme of universal discussion. I am now assured that the men can be got away with the loss of only 2,500. The public know nothing about the expedition, and are still hopeful and confident . . . that victory [is] near at hand.[15]

The blundering in the Dardanelles, added to Britain's lack of support for Serbia, led Carson to resign from the government. Before the official announcement of his departure, *The Times* rose to his defence on 18 October, declaring that 'No resignation is tolerable at this stage except in a man who has foreseen a long series of blunders into which the want of a policy had led us, and has striven to warn his colleagues and has failed. That, we must assume, is the case of Sir Edward Carson.' When the official announcement was made the next day, *The Times* called his resignation 'a political event of the first magnitude – none the less because for the moment it seems likely to stand alone.'

In late October, General Sir Charles Monro was sent to take the Dardanelles command from Hamilton. Monro agreed with Northcliffe's view that the operation should be ended. He recommended withdrawal to Kitchener, and forecast the cost as as high as 40,000 casualties. The War Secretary had been the eventual choice to assess the situation in the Dardanelles, leaving in November, and his inspection tour took him out of the country for some time. While he was absent the government undercut his powers by appointing Sir

William Robertson as Chief of the Imperial General Staff (CIGS). Robertson became the government's chief military adviser and overlord of the army command in France, where Sir John French, Northcliffe's former ally in the shells agitation, felt his position slipping away. For French, the Battle of Loos in September and October proved the final failure. Haig took command of the British forces on the Western Front in December 1915.

When Kitchener returned from his inspection of the Dardanelles, the government decided on evacuation. This was carried out with an almost miraculous lack of casualties. The *Daily Mail* characterized the withdrawal as a government admission that the operation had been a 'stupendous blunder'.[16] The 21 December editorial charged that 'too late is written in letters of fire upon the record of the Government. We were "too late" in aiding Belgium, we have been "too late" to save Serbia,' and 'we sent our expeditionary force to the Dardanelles "too late"'.

The final months of 1915 also marked the death throes of British voluntarism. By October 1915 recruiting was almost exhausted. Over 3 million men, including the patriotic and adventurous cream of British manhood, had answered Kitchener's call. Asquith, however, continued to delay conscription. A War Policy Committee under Lord Crewe was appointed to consider the question. In a supplementary report, its Labour Party member, Arthur Henderson, called for a final voluntary effort to demonstrate to the working classes that all alternative methods had been tried. Asquith and Kitchener managed to convince Lord Derby to lead the final voluntary push. Derby was a great landed aristocrat, a remnant of a previous era, dubbed the 'King' of Lancashire. In the first year of the war his record in recruiting stood second only to Kitchener's. On 5 October 1915 he was put in charge of what would prove to be the last government effort to raise the men needed by the Army before resorting to compulsion. Under the 'Derby Scheme', all men between the ages of eighteen and forty-one whose names appeared on the recent National Register would be asked either to enlist or to 'attest' their willingness to serve with the armed forces when called.[17]

Since the spring of 1915 Northcliffe had been in touch with Derby on manpower questions. Though Northcliffe wanted conscription, Derby's pledge to seek out the remaining unmarried men prompted him to offer his assistance to this final voluntary effort which both probably believed would ultimately fail. Their goal was to supply badly needed men for the Army, by whatever method possible, and they realized that the campaign brought conscription closer, no matter how the campaign itself turned out. The 18 October *Daily Mail* profiled Derby and congratulated him for his 'Single Men First' declaration. Northcliffe wrote to him, 'I am going to help your scheme as much as I can – and I think I can help it.'[18] Derby gladly accepted his support.

While Northcliffe and his papers supported the Derby Scheme, the government prepared evidence against Northcliffe to lay before the Cabinet. The head of the Foreign Office Press Bureau, increasingly frustrated by the many uses the enemy made of the attacks on the government by Northcliffe's newspapers, complained to J.C.C. Davidson, Bonar Law's assistant at the Treasury, that 'practically the whole of his time was taken up in counteracting the influence and effect of *The Times* in allied and neutral countries'.[19] In co-operation with the Home Secretary, Sir John Simon, the Foreign Office Press Bureau prepared a secret report for the Cabinet, *The Northcliffe Press and Foreign Opinion*, which detailed the use of the Northcliffe papers in anti-British propaganda in Germany and neutral countries like the USA. This document, apparently laid before the Cabinet in November, listed extracts from German papers quoting *The Times* on topics from blockade failures and recruiting, to the Dardanelles campaign and Lord Kitchener.[20] Despite the desires of some officials, notably Simon, the Cabinet refused to ban or prosecute Northcliffe's newspapers. Measures were taken against others, however. On 6 November the *Globe*, an ultra-Conservative evening paper, falsely reported that Kitchener had resigned from the Cabinet because of conflicts with his colleagues. It was suppressed by the government under DORA regulations against publishing 'false statements tending to depress His Majesty's subjects and give comfort to the enemy'.[21] In a Guildhall speech at the Lord Mayor's Banquet soon after, Asquith denied that the suppression raised the question of the freedom of the press, because, he said, the *Globe* had spread a 'malignant lie . . . after it was contradicted on the highest authority'. He then went on to compliment the patriotic self-restraint of the press during the war, 'with two notorious exceptions' – an unspoken reference to *The Times* and the *Daily Mail.*[22]

Meanwhile, the Derby campaign reached its finale and the *Daily Mail* kept up the cry. The 5 December edition noted that, despite the fact that 'Lord Derby has done all that man can do', the single men had not yet come forward in the numbers needed; however, it said, voluntarism might yet be saved by their swift action. On the final morning, the *Daily Mail* exhorted single men to 'JOIN FIRST THING TODAY.'[23] A pictorial feature displayed the 'Closing Scenes in the Great Recruiting Campaign'. At its conclusion, except as a delaying strategy for the Asquith government, Derby's 'Great Campaign' proved a failure. Despite the best efforts of many people, including Northcliffe, it ultimately produced only 340,000 men – well short of the goal of 500,000. The disappointing results made it evident that voluntarism could no longer fill the manpower needs of the nation. Also, for the government to keep its pledge to the married, compulsion would have to be aimed first at single men.[24]

In the ensuing weeks of political turmoil over this issue, Northcliffe stayed in close touch with Lloyd George, to the decided discomfort of many of those around the Minister for Munitions. C.P. Scott, editor of the *Manchester Guardian*, recorded that on Sunday 12 December he met Northcliffe and his wife before lunch at Walton Heath, Lloyd George's residence. Scott agreed with Garvin of the *Observer*, who felt the Minister had 'suffered from his recent intimate association with Lord Northcliffe'.[25] A Cabinet crisis, which included a resignation threat from Lloyd George if compulsion was not brought in, came to a climax in the last few days of December. Kitchener agreed at last that unmarried men should be conscripted, and a Bill to that effect was passed in January 1916. Asquith once again proved his political skill by holding together the coalition – with the sole resignation of Simon.[26] The *Daily Mail* declared 'The End of the Voluntary System. And Sir John Simon.'[27]

Convinced that the Germans would soon bombard England with their more powerful fighting aircraft, in the first half of 1916 Northcliffe had his newspapers call for an increased and co-ordinated air defence. Eighteen months into the conflict, British air power remained divided between the War Office and the Admiralty, with resulting confusion and jealousy as to the responsibilities of each.[28] The *Daily Mail*, now '*THE PAPER THAT DEVELOPED AIRMANSHIP*', stepped up its air campaign and asked, 'Who is Responsible?'[29] The 10 February edition blamed the division of the air service between the Army and Navy for allowing the air raids on London. In the face of this harsh newspaper criticism, Bonar Law arranged for Northcliffe to discuss the question with General Sir David Henderson, who was in charge of the Royal Air Corps, the Army branch of the air service. The meeting between the three men did not leave Northcliffe much impressed with Henderson, whom the Conservative leader defended. The *Daily Mail* described Henderson as 'chiefly known for his 1914 statement that "for airships to drop bombs on London would be quite opposed to the ethics of war"'.[30]

In a *British Weekly* article, 'Work For Lord Northcliffe', Sir William Robertson Nicoll called for the government to use the press lord's expertise by appointing him Air Minister.[31] This, Nicoll argued, would serve the dual purpose of disarming the government's chief critic and showing what he could do. In response to this suggestion, Lloyd George told Sir George Riddell, 'Northcliffe would not be a success. He has no experience of acting with equals. He would be especially handicapped in a Cabinet of twenty-two . . . he is best where he is.'[32] The *Daily Mail* called for an air minister 'instantly', and replied to Nicoll's suggestion of Northcliffe 'that there are men better able than he is to undertake the task; and, furthermore, that he could not conscientiously take part in a Government that is fighting a defensive rather than an offensive war'.[33]

In late February Lord Derby was put in charge of a Cabinet committee to co-ordinate the Royal Air Corps and the Royal Naval Air Service.[34] He soon asked for Northcliffe's aid in his new task. Northcliffe responded, 'Unless you privately get at the truth from the actual flying men and not from the people on top you will unknowingly incur a responsibility of unspeakable dimensions. Some of the horrible facts are getting known. I suggest you see Lord Peel and Sir Charles Nicholson, the Liberal member for Doncaster. They know a little.' He went on that the 'Farnborough establishment should be at once put in the hands of a person like Sir William Lever, Lord Devonport, Sir Richard Burbidge, of Harrods, or Guy Galthrop, of the North Western Railway. The whole air service is chaos.'[35] Derby took some of this advice, conferring with 'actual' airmen, as well as Peel and Nicholson. From them, he told Northcliffe, he 'learned a good deal'.[36] But after only a month on the job, tired of presiding over endless squabbles between inflexible Army and Navy officers and frustrated because he had no power to force action, Derby resigned. His letter of resignation advocated a combined air service to Asquith.

Though the Prime Minister thought its creation would only increase problems, in May he approved the appointment of an Air Board. The new enterprise was headed by Lord Curzon, who had had little useful work to do since joining the Cabinet as Lord Privy Seal. His appointment was greeted by the 13 May *Daily Mail* editorial, 'The Wrong Man. What Does Lord Curzon Know About Aircraft?' Nonetheless, the Air Board proved useful, though Curzon's abrasive manner added to the complaints of his colleagues.[37] Northcliffe's depth of feeling on the air issue brought him to make an extremely rare appearance in the House of Lords. On 23 May 1916 he rose to speak during a debate on the air service.[38] As always, he called for more speed in the matter and hoped that 'this somewhat shadowy Board must develop into an Air Ministry'. He urged Curzon to encourage inventors by setting up a separate Board of Inventions, and manufacturers by giving financial assistance. His final recommendation was that the government increase provision for the training of flying men.

Northcliffe made his sixth visit to the front in late February, this time at the invitation of the French government. Steed, who accompanied him, was impressed by Northcliffe's physical stamina and his 'cheerfulness and patience under discomfort'.[39] This trip coincided with the beginning of months of massive assaults by the Germans on the fortresses surrounding the French city of Verdun. When the military authorities stopped the pair's progress towards Verdun, Northcliffe appealed directly to Prime Minister Aristide Briand and they were soon allowed to continue. Their automobile's overheating radiator had repeatedly to be filled with snow from the roadside, and they were forced to share a crust of bread for dinner at Bar-le-Duc amid a multitude of refugees. They completed their journey to General Pétain's headquarters in a French army lorry. Northcliffe sent home dispatches, published internationally, on the great battle which praised Pétain and the French army.[40] Both sides suffered immense casualties, but after early German successes, the French rallied behind Pétain and held the line. The horrors he witnessed at Verdun deeply affected Northcliffe. He returned to England in so agitated a state that his family and friends were concerned for his health.[41]

When conscription for single men was put into force in the first months of 1916, it soon became apparent that the numbers supplied would be insufficient. The CIGS, Sir William Robertson, called for the government to act on the manpower question. Asquith followed his usual pattern of delay in face of insistence from Robertson, Lloyd George and others that conscription must be widened to include married men. The *Daily Mail* described the government's inaction as 'Fiddling While Rome Burns'.[42] The 11 April 'Message From the Chief' to the *Daily Mail* staff predicted that the latest 'vigorous' *Daily Mail* appeal for compulsion 'will, I am sure, have great effect on our wobbly rulers'. H.G. Wells, who represented the living voice of the science which Northcliffe wished to see applied to the manpower question and the war in general, was among those who praised the press lord's efforts. He congratulated him for 'playing a supremely useful part in goading on our remarkable Government . . . The war has brought you into open and active conflict with the system as it is.'[43] In reply, Northcliffe explained the method of his attacks on the government over conscription and other questions, and professed his lack of personal ambition:

> I find the only way to get anything done is to attack the coalition incident by incident, muddle by muddle. If the armies already raised were scientifically used there would be no need of compulsion at this juncture, quite apart from the million and a half men in khaki in England. Havre, Boulogne, Rouen, Calais, Abbeville and environs are alive with soldiers doing civilian and women's work. It makes one['s] blood boil to know that while France has called up boys and men of fifty, our Army Pay Department is packed with young men doing the clerical work of girls . . . I have no ambition in this matter, and am not likely to give up the strength of my presses for the powerlessness of a portfolio.[44]

The *Daily Mail* campaign for conscription continued into late April and linked the problem to Britain's unwieldy Cabinet system. In 'The 23 Scandal. How Much Longer?' the paper called for a concentration of power in as few hands as possible, noting 'there is no instance in history of a war being successfully conducted by a large committee' such as the present twenty-three-man Cabinet.[45] More important than the press in extending conscription were Lloyd George's threatened resignation and pressure from Bonar Law. In this latest political crisis Asquith once again gave way and survived in office. Compulsion was extended to all able-bodied men between eighteen and forty-one in May 1916. The 3 May *Daily Mail* hailed 'Compulsion At Last'.

That year, 1916, also saw a reawakening of the Irish problem, which had been overshadowed by the war. The executions carried out by the British in the aftermath of the bloody April 'Easter Rising' centred in Dublin only created martyrs and radicalized Irish opinion in favour of Sinn Fein, which had not been involved in the insurgency. The rash British action also brought cries of indignation from the American government and public, and further complicated relations with the most powerful neutral. Lloyd George was enlisted to tackle this latest Irish crisis. The *Daily Mail* loudly applauded the choice, calling him the 'handyman of the Coalition'.[46] In Northcliffe's view, Ireland's problems could not be solved until economic conditions in the country were improved. He returned to this theme again and again for the remainder of the war, and during this period he often met Lloyd George. On 27 May Riddell recorded in his diary that 'L.G. never tells me about his meetings with Northcliffe, but I am sure they are in daily contact.'[47] Cecil Harmsworth called this time 'a period of something like friendship between them – they were collaborating for a settlement of the Irish problem'.[48] Unfortunately, at this time, as so often before, the question proved insoluble.

The problem of what to do with Lord Kitchener was finally settled by a German mine. Sent on a mission to Russia in June, his cruiser, the *Hampshire*, sank with almost all hands. On hearing the news, Northcliffe reportedly proclaimed, 'Providence is on the side of the British Empire after all.'[49] He saw the event as a golden opportunity to replace Asquith. When Lloyd George, who had long been dissatisfied with Asquith and considered resignation, was offered the War Office, Northcliffe advised against acceptance on the grounds that it would 'give the Government a new lease on life and that it will be impossible to turn them out'.[50] However, Lloyd George was unable to resist the new post, even with the reduced powers that Kitchener had lost to Sir William Robertson, which the Welshman tried, unsuccessfully, to regain. The *Daily Mail* announcement of 7 July was much more subdued than that which had greeted the Irish appointment six weeks before. Though disappointed, Northcliffe did not burn his bridges. Maurice Hankey, secretary of the War Committee, recorded in his diary that Northcliffe and Churchill were among the first to call on Lloyd George at the War Office.[51]

Sir William Robertson and Sir Douglas Haig made a powerful military combination with which the new Secretary for War had to contend. The CIGS had close relations with Repington, to whom he fed information backing his western strategy and the idea that politicians should not meddle in Army affairs. The Commander-in-Chief, on the other hand, resisted newspaper aid. Since his experience in the Sudan with Kitchener, Haig had felt only disdain and revulsion for the press. He likened Sir John French's 1915 alliance with the newspapers and Northcliffe to 'carrying on with a whore'.[52] Robertson attempted to change his attitude, writing to him in June, 'I am sure things would be much better if we got the press on our side . . . My idea is that we ought to send out, on your invitation, 4 or 5 of the big newspaper Proprietors e.g. Northcliffe, Burnham etc for a few days to some part of our front.'[53] Haig replied that the present was not an opportune time for a visit of the proprietors, as secret preparations were under way for a new offensive. This operation on the river Somme would prove the most bloody battle of the war for the British, after which nothing would be the same.

The Battle of the Somme began disastrously on 1 July 1916, when the unprecedented artillery barrage that preceded it failed to clear away the German defences. The British suffered more than 50,000 casualties on that single day – with only meagre gains to show for their sacrifice. As the toll mounted during the following weeks and months, Sir Douglas stubbornly continued the bloody frontal assaults. The Somme marked a new direction in Haig's relations with the press, which, he realized, could be useful in explaining that the campaign was not a failure, despite the dreadful human wastage. Three weeks into the battle, at the Commander-in-Chief's invitation, Northcliffe arrived at Saint-Omer, the British headquarters. This tour marked his first substantial discussions with Haig. Sir Douglas took twenty minutes from his pressing schedule for a talk alone with him before they shared lunch with General Lancelot Kiggell, Haig's Chief of Staff, and General John Charteris, his Head of Intelligence. The Commander-in-Chief recorded in his diary that he 'was favourably impressed' with the proprietor's 'desire to do his best to help win the war. He was most anxious not to make a mistake in anything he advocated in his newspapers, and for this he was desirous of seeing what was taking place. I am therefore letting him see everything and talk to anyone he pleases.'[54] Northcliffe described Haig in his journal as 'a quiet, determined, level-headed, easy mannered, blue-eyed Scottish gentleman with a Scottish accent, neither optimist or pessimist, the kind of man who sets puzzles for Prussians.'[55] The men attended church services together two days later, and the chief proprietor of *The Times* requested that Haig report anything in the paper not to his liking.[56]

Enthralled both by Haig and by the improved conditions he saw on his visit, Northcliffe pledged his complete support. He recorded in his journal that Haig 'showed me his plans. Each time I see him I am convinced of his qualities. We talked of the wobble of politicians.'[57] The politicians soon received Northcliffe's appraisal. He sent Lloyd George a glowing report which described a demoralized enemy and renewed British confidence. He found 'no comparison whatever with the state of affairs in August 1916 and the state of affairs at any other time at which I have been to the war', and strongly urged the Secretary for War 'to spend at least two weeks with the army . . . You will find yourself in the midst of an organisation which . . . is as well nigh perfect as it can be.'[58] Lord Derby, by this time Under-Secretary at the War Office, received a similar letter of praise.[59] Lloyd George did not agree with Northcliffe's adoring assessment of Sir Douglas Haig and the Army. He viewed the Somme as a larger repetition of the Neuve Chapelle and Loos failures.

Appalled at the British casualties, his aim was to reduce the carnage in France and Flanders – if necessary by diverting troops elsewhere or holding them in Britain. This difference of opinion developed into a serious rift between the two men.

Northcliffe and Steed again visited the British Army on 9 September and were shown the preparations for a second great offensive planned to begin within days. On Haig's recommendation that he view something called a 'tank', the press lord visited General Sir Julian Byng at Canadian headquarters. Expecting storage devices, Northcliffe and Steed were understandably surprised (and at first inclined to laugh) at the 'rumbling caterpillar leviathans'.[60] Steed described his chief's personal experience with one of the vehicles:

> Northcliffe tried to enter one of them by the manhole on the top; but as his girth was some inches larger than the hole, he stuck midway and had to be hauled down to the inside by the feet while I sat on his shoulders above. Getting him out again was an even harder matter, though presently he emerged minus some buttons.[61]

After some initial success in the 15 September offensive, the tanks either suffered mechanical failures or bogged down, but showed the promise of this innovation. The 16 September *Daily Mail* hailed the 'Great Successes on the Somme' and noted the new methods and weapons being used, particularly 'a new type of heavy armoured car' and the 'tactical use of aeroplanes and their remarkable feats of machine-gunning'.

In the following months, Northcliffe kept in close touch with Haig through the latter's personal secretary, Sir Philip Sassoon. 'I must write to you how much we all liked the Times leader of the 18th,' Sassoon announced the next day. 'It must have made people realise for the first time the true significance of our victory of the 15th – the C in C was quite delighted with it.'[62] When Lloyd George visited the front in September he failed to take Northcliffe's advice to spend time with the British rank and file and make himself known as something other than a politician. Though he stayed two weeks, most of his time was spent in Paris or with senior officers far from the front.[63] Sassoon complained to his press ally that the War Secretary was rude to the French, would not follow any of the plans made for him, and, in general, 'did not make a favourable impression either in the British or French army'. 'If *this* is the man some people would like to see P.M.,' Sasoon continued, 'I prefer old Squiff any day with all his faults!'[64]

Though Northcliffe and Lloyd George differed on strategic questions, they nevertheless stayed in contact. Both men worried about the effect in Britain and abroad of what they considered defeatist talk of a negotiated peace with Germany. The Americans continued to offer mediation through President Wilson's personal envoy, Colonel Edward M. House. In late September, Northcliffe urged the War Secretary to give a statement to Roy Howard of the American United Press, who had stopped in London on his way to Germany. Lloyd George took his advice, and their conversation – published internationally – became famous as the 'Knock-Out Blow' interview.[65] In it the War Secretary made it plain that the Allies intended to fight to the finish and would not agree to a compromise peace. The 29 September *Daily Mail* printed the interview and congratulated the Welshman for his 'straight from the shoulder language that Americans appreciate'. The bold and unauthorized statement by Lloyd George bolstered home and Allied morale and sent a clear signal to the Americans and the Germans. It gained him, however, only a brief reprieve from Northcliffe's ire.

In October the intrigues against the Army came to a climax. Against the advice of Robertson, Lloyd George called for increased numbers of troops for Arabia and the Balkans, particularly for the support of Romania, which had joined the Allies in August and whose position was dire.[66] In the first few days of the month Northcliffe met Derby to discuss the problem. At this time he told Sassoon, 'You are dealing with people, some of whom are very thick-skinned, others very unscrupulous, but all afraid of newspapers. It was urgently necessary that they should be told . . . "Hands off the army".'[67] On 4 October he had Repington assure Robertson that he would support him. The following day's *Daily Mail* editorial, 'Comb Out or 45. The Chief of Staff Speaks Out', supported Robertson's call for 'more men *now*', with conscription being extended to forty-five-year-olds.

On 10 October the strategic differences between the Secretary for War and his military advisers developed into an open breach. Completely out of patience, an angry Lloyd George called for an Allied conference to save Britain's 'prestige' and 'honour' and to keep Romania from becoming another disaster like the fall of Serbia. Robertson notified Lloyd George in writing that if his views were ignored he 'could not be responsible for conducting this very difficult war under these conditions'.[68] Northcliffe offered his help, and urged Robertson to take his case to the Prime Minister. The Chief of Staff replied, 'The Boche gives me no trouble compared with what I meet in London. So any help you can give me will be of Imperial value.'[69]

After Northcliffe heard from Repington that Robertson could not sleep because of Lloyd George's latest 'interference', he made a personal visit to the War Office. A letter to Sassoon described his confrontation with Lloyd George's secretary, J.T. Davies, in which the press lord told Davies that he could no longer support the War Secretary and that

> if further interference took place with Sir William Robertson I was going to the House of Lords to lay matters before the world, and hammer them daily in my newspapers. This may seem a brusque and drastic thing to do, but I think I know the combination I am dealing with better than you folks who are so engrossed in your splendid and absorbing task . . .
>
> I have heard nothing since, because I am in the country, but Geoffrey Robinson tells me that General Robertson says that matters are better. I also heard that Winston has been going about libelling me in extra vigorous style, which is a good sign.
>
> . . . I am a believer in the War Secretary of State to a very great extent, but he is always being egged on by Churchill . . . and other little but venomous people.[70]

Lloyd George used Northcliffe's outburst as an opportunity for a counterstroke against Robertson over the issue of official leaks to the press. In a strongly worded reply to Robertson's ultimatum, Lloyd George stated that he refused, as War Secretary, to play the part of a 'mere dummy'. His rebuttal made particular reference to Northcliffe's confrontation with Davies.[71] Though the War Committee did agree to limit communications with the press, Lloyd George found himself fighting a losing battle over strategy. He was forced to bide his time in his conflict with the generals and their press allies.

The Northcliffe newspapers backed up their proprietor's pledge to Robertson. Coining the alliterative slogan '*Ministerial meddling means military muddling*', the 13 October *Daily Mail* reminded the country of the Antwerp and Gallipoli blunders and declared that the government should limit itself to supplying men. That day's 'Message From The Chief' declared:

> If we continue to grind into the public mind the horrible fact that political interference means an increase in the death roll of our army, Sir Douglas Haig and Sir William Robertson will not be worried as they are at present. This was a scandalous attempt to weaken the Army in France at the moment of

Victory – an attempt to send our soldiers on mad, wild expeditions to distant places.

The campaign against government interference hit home. Lloyd George told Riddell that Northcliffe was 'taking up a strong line against him and is endeavouring to make friends with Asquith', who planned to 'leave him severely alone'. He also said that Northcliffe's vanity was 'colossal, that he wants to be a Dictator', but that he did not intend to be 'dictated to'.[72] Northcliffe and Lloyd George bitterly disagreed, and tempers flared on both sides; however, the two men needed each other. Northcliffe knew that the Welshman represented the best, perhaps the only, realistic alternative to Asquith. For him, this fact overrode their other differences, including war strategy. Lloyd George in turn realized the power over public and private opinion that Northcliffe wielded. He was not a man to let disagreements override political practicalities.

At the end of the Battle of the Somme in November 1916, the British had precious little to show in exchange for their 400,000 casualties. The war again struck home for Northcliffe when another nephew, Vere, Rothermere's second son, was killed in the fighting that month.[73] Haig, despite mounting criticism over his seeming disregard of British lives, survived as Commander-in-Chief. Northcliffe's support helped ensure that he stayed in place. The battle did have other results. The Somme and Verdun campaigns had taken a physical toll on the German army and affected its morale. If they did not before, the Germans now realized that the British, with their conscript army, were a serious military power. In addition, at home, the Somme brought more open criticism of the Asquith government. On 8 November the Nigeria debate in the Commons revealed the serious division in the Conservative ranks and threatened the position of Bonar Law.[74] In the middle of the month Lloyd George began (through Sir Max Aitken) negotiations to meet the Conservative leader. The men finally came together, with Sir Edward Carson, on 20 November to formulate a plan for a small War Council which would be presented to Asquith. Carson, like Northcliffe, wanted Asquith removed. At this point Bonar Law and Lloyd George were less willing to act so drastically.

Largely because of his feud with Lloyd George over strategy, during November Northcliffe was shut out of the inner circle of political intrigue, but at the end of the month Geoffrey Robinson worked to involve him. Robinson visited Arthur Lee, in 1916 one of Lloyd George's parliamentary secretaries, with the aim of patching up the

differences between their chiefs. The efforts of Robinson and Lee succeeded; however, Lee complained at the time to his wife, Ruth, of the
danger of being caught between Lloyd George and Northcliffe: 'It is all
very well this going about like a Dove of Peace, with an olive branch in
one's beak, but one is apt to get taken for a bloody pigeon and get shot
at by both sides.'[75]

In the first days of December, Robinson's chief regularly visited the
War Office while, at the same time, Lloyd George attempted to per-
suade Asquith to agree to a small War Committee. The *Times* of 2
December 1916 called the political crisis 'The Turning-point of the
War' and demanded a small Cabinet which would rid the country of
'worn and weary' men such as Grey, Crewe, Lansdowne and Balfour.
Another meeting between the War Secretary and Northcliffe resulted in
Evening News placards which proclaimed 'Lloyd George Packing Up!'
On Sunday 3 December Lloyd George and Asquith met and, in the War
Secretary's view at least, came to a suitable agreement about a small War
Council. Unlike Northcliffe, Lloyd George did not wish Asquith to
resign. That day's *Weekly Dispatch* revealed 'Mr. Lloyd George's Proposal
For a Small War Council', the interviews and meetings of the day
before, and the positions of Asquith, Balfour and Bonar Law. Cecil
Harmsworth recorded in his diary that 'Alfred has been actively at work
with Ll. G. with a view to bringing a change.'[76]

Other newspapers may have been better informed in the first week
of December, but none carried the weight of *The Times*, whose editorial
of the 4th, 'Towards Reconstruction', contained delicate information
which seemed to point to Lloyd George as the source. This editorial
was widely believed to have been Northcliffe's work, but was actually
written by Geoffrey Robinson with information from Carson.[77]
Regardless, Northcliffe must have seen and approved it in advance. *The
Times*'s disclosure – written with what has been called a 'calculated
offensiveness' – discussed the continuing negotiations and revealed the
Prime Minister's capitulation, in the face of 'Mr. Lloyd George's stand',
to create a small War Council.[78] Infuriated, the Prime Minister wrote to
Lloyd George that

> Such productions as the first leading article in today's 'Times', showing the
> infinite possibilities for misunderstanding and misrepresentation of such an
> arrangement as we discussed yesterday, make me at least doubtful of its fea-
> sibility. Unless the impression is at once corrected that I am being relegated
> to the position of an irresponsible spectator of the War, I cannot go on.[79]

Lloyd George responded that he had not seen the *Times* article, but hoped Asquith would

> not attach undue importance to these effusions. I have had these misrepresentations to put up with for months Northcliffe frankly wants a smash. Derby and I do not. Northcliffe would like to make this or any other arrangement under your premiership impossible. Derby and I attach great importance to your retaining your present position – effectively. I cannot restrain, nor I fear influence Northcliffe.[80]

After consulting Reginald McKenna and others hostile to Lloyd George, the Prime Minister decided to test his strength by attempting to reconstruct the government, rather than give in to the War Secretary's demands. Before Asquith called on the King, Edwin Montagu, the Minister of Munitions, found him very angry about the 'Northcliffe article'. Montagu had seen the press lord at the War Office the day before the *Times* assault, assumed he had obtained the information from Lloyd George, and almost certainly shared this assumption with the Prime Minister.[81] He urged Asquith 'not to be put off by the Northcliffe article; he had never paid any attention to newspapers, why should he give up now because of Northcliffe?' Asquith replied that it was because the article 'showed quite clearly the spirit in which the arrangement was going to be worked by its authors'.[82]

Despite the advice of Lloyd George and Montagu, Asquith continued in a stubborn attempt at reconstruction which was destined to fail. He resigned on 5 December, and the King turned first to Andrew Bonar Law, as the Leader of the Opposition, to form a government. When this proved impossible, Lloyd George, who had overcome his own reluctance in the face of Asquith's affronted change of heart, began negotiations with the disparate political groupings whose support was needed to form an administration. *The Times* described the situation as being 'in the melting pot'.[83] During a visit to the War Office, Robinson was asked by Lloyd George to tell Northcliffe 'that it did not help him when the Daily Mail and the Evening News assumed too intimate a knowledge of his actions and intentions. Also that too much vituperation of individuals was not so useful as insistence that the whole system of Government was unsound and could not win the war'.[84] Cecil Harmsworth recorded on 6 December that 'the London Liberal daily papers are full of denunciations of Northcliffe, whom they regard as the arch-wrecker of the Asquith Govt. There is truth in this of course, but not all the truth.'[85]

A.G. Gardiner's *Daily News* and other Liberal journals had trumpeted warnings of Northcliffe's evil influence from the beginning of the Cabinet crisis. The 2 December edition foresaw doom for 'any Government which lives by the sanction of a press dictator'. On the 5th it stated that the enemy was 'looking for a rupture not less cheerfully than Lord Northcliffe is working for one, and if that gentleman were the ally of the enemy he could not be doing more priceless service to them than he is doing at this moment'. A 7 December *Daily Chronicle* article, 'The Press Vendetta, Tyranny and Torture', claimed that Asquith had been too lenient in allowing the yellow press to attack him and his allies, and now the 'new Ministry, however constituted, will have to deal with the Press menace as well as the submarine menace; otherwise Ministries will be subject to tyranny and torture by daily attacks impugning their patriotism and earnestness to win the war'.

While this war of headlines was carried out, the political negotiations continued. In order to form a government, it was necessary for Lloyd George to give assurances concerning his relationship with Northcliffe. He promised the Conservatives that Northcliffe (and Churchill) would not be included. One of Lloyd George's pledges to a Labour Party delegation was that he and his government would not give large newspapers preferential treatment and that he would treat 'Lord Northcliffe in exactly the same way as he would treat a labourer'.[86] In Northcliffe's view, the Foreign Office and its blockade policy were in need of new leadership. He was disturbed to hear that Arthur Balfour might be removed from the Admiralty – only to be made Foreign Secretary. The *Daily Mail* and the *Evening News* called for the exclusion of Balfour and his cousin Lord Robert Cecil from the new government. Their campaign failed. Lloyd George needed Balfour to cement Conservative support, and the latter accepted the Foreign Office. Lord Robert remained in place as Under-Secretary and Blockade Minister. Northcliffe, however, was not completely without influence. He was instrumental in ensuring that the businessman Sir Albert Stanley was appointed to the Board of Trade. Northcliffe also aided Lord Devonport in attaining the new position of Food Controller. The historian Alfred Gollin has viewed Milner's inclusion in the War Cabinet as, in part, a friendly gesture to the press lord.[87] On 7 December Lloyd George became Prime Minister, and the next day he moved to 10 Downing Street. The new five-member War Cabinet was made up of the Prime Minister, Lords Milner and Curzon, Bonar Law and a Labour Party representative, Arthur Henderson.

Despite Northcliffe's repeated protestations that he did not choose to become a minister (including a 7 December *New York Times* interview in which he defended his own course and stated that he would not join the Cabinet), his considerable vanity must have been wounded when Lloyd George did not at least offer him a place in the government which he believed he had helped to make possible. He was also undoubtedly informed of the promises concerning him that Lloyd George had made to the Conservatives and to Labour. In Lord Beaverbrook's account of events, when Lloyd George offered conciliation the owner of the *Daily Mail* declined a proposed meeting, telling Beaverbrook that 'Lord Northcliffe sees no advantage in any interview between him and the Prime Minister at the present moment.'[88] Damaged pride best explains his refusal. The *Times* of 8 December stated that Northcliffe preferred 'to sit in Printing House Square and Carmelite House'. However, two days later Sir Maurice Hankey reported that during a visit to Lloyd George's home to discuss the formation of the Cabinet Secretariat (which would play an important future role) he overheard the new Prime Minister in 'a long talk on the telephone with Lord Northcliffe, whom he seems to funk'.[89]

The 9 December *Daily Mail* proclaimed the new government 'A Ministry of Action At Last' and revelled in 'The Passing of the Failures'. A page of photographs showed the outgoing ministers with accompanying captions across their chests, including Asquith ('Wait and See'), Grey ('Belgium, Serbia, Bulgaria, Greece, Rumania') and McKenna ('German Banks Still "Winding Up"'). Though Sir John Simon had left office over conscription in early 1916, he was also displayed, with a 'No Compulsion, Down with Daily Mail' slogan. Haldane ('My Spiritual Home is Germany') and Churchill ('Antwerp & Gallipoli') were also presented. Northcliffe had ordered this feature, and congratulated the newspaper's picture department (with which he was often at loggerheads) on the results.[90] The same day's *Daily News* countered that the country must choose between newspaper 'Placards or Parliament'. Gardiner commented, however, that there was

> one advantage which Mr. Lloyd George's Government will have over its predecessor. It will be subject to a friendly organised and responsible criticism which will aim at sustaining it and not destroying it. The fall of the late Government and most of its failures were due to the absence of such a criticism. It became the target . . . of a ruthless and uncritical press campaign which appealed directly to the passions of the mob against the authority of Parliament.

For once Gardiner was partly correct. Northcliffe was ready to aid at least the new men in the government. He instructed his employees at Printing House Square, 'We must do our best to get the new ministers known, and thus strengthen their position in the country.'[91] How long he would continue his support became the question.

From the evidence, it appears that Northcliffe and his newspapers should be given more credit than they have generally received for the demise of the Asquith government in December 1916. Whether or not Northcliffe wrote the *Times* article of 4 December which triggered Asquith's reneging on his agreement with Lloyd George, the belief of his involvement proved decisive. Asquith's anger over the supposed collusion with Northcliffe, combined with Reginald McKenna's advice, provoked the Prime Minister to fight the humiliating terms which Lloyd George presented. In the longer view, however, more important than the *Times* piece was the eighteen-month campaign the Northcliffe press had carried out against the government, practically acting as the Opposition since the spring 1915 shells agitation. Unlike the many voices that deserted Asquith only at the end, the Northcliffe press condemnations in early December were only marginally more strident than they had been since early in the war. The cumulative effect of Northcliffe's personal and newspaper campaign against the government helped to wear down Asquith's resistance and left him a bitter man who, in a speech to a Liberal Party meeting at the Reform Club on 8 December, openly admitted that the *Times* article of 4 December was a precipitating factor in his subsequent course. Asquith's refusal either to compromise with Northcliffe (as Lloyd George did) or to have the government muzzle his attacks finally cost him dear. The failed Somme campaign and the unrest among the Conservatives forced the politicians to act at last, as had similar forces in May 1915 when the coalition government was formed. The most remarkable attribute of the Asquith coalition may be not that it fell in December 1916, but that it lasted as long as it did.

On 10 December the *Weekly Dispatch* published Northcliffe's United Press article 'Fashioning the New England', printed worldwide.[92] In this piece, the press lord reviewed the progress of the war and roundly praised Lloyd George for his courage, even though he admitted that the two had often been on opposite sides of vital issues. The article described the new Prime Minister as a 'human dynamo' whose 'every erg of energy is focused on the immediate task at hand. He combines the persuasiveness of the Irishman with the concentration of the American and the thoroughness of the Englishman.' For this occasion,

Northcliffe broke his own rule about newspaper prophecy. To those who asserted that the new government and Lloyd George would not last, he declared, 'I believe that he will be at the head of the Government that wins the war: that brings a settlement of the Irish question and maintains that essential factor goodwill between the people of the English speaking nations of the British Empire and the people of the United States.'

Across the Atlantic, the newly re-elected Wilson administration watched the December political upheaval in Britain with dismay. The 1916 presidential election had been won with a pledge to keep America out of the war. Sentiment coincided most closely with the Liberalism of Asquith and Sir Edward Grey, not Lloyd George, who was considered a reactionary.[93] Colonel House, Wilson's close adviser and his agent for peace negotiations, had written to the President that he was watching British developments closely and predicted that if the 'Lloyd-George–Northcliffe–Carson combination succeed in overthrowing the Government and getting control' England then would be under 'a military dictatorship' and there 'will be no chance for peace until they run their course'.[94] Nevertheless, Wilson continued his attempts to broker a negotiated peace. In response to a tentative German peace move, the American Secretary of State, Robert Lansing, sent identical notes to Britain and Germany asking them to state their war aims.

Northcliffe found the prospect of a negotiated peace unthinkable, but, not wishing to offend Wilson, he tempered the response of his newspapers. The US ambassador in London, Walter Hines Page, wrote to Lansing that the British were angry because the note seemed to place the Allies and the central powers 'on the same moral level'. He went on that Northcliffe had assured him that his papers would continue to say 'as little as possible', but that 'the people are mad as hell'.[95] Northcliffe advised Lloyd George that the 'delay in the British reply to Wilson is all to the advantage of Germany'.[96] In 1917, the Prime Minister ensured that Northcliffe would have an opportunity personally to affect Anglo-American relations and the course of the war.

14

Pegasus in Harness, 1917

Outside the stalemated military fronts, the most immediate problems of 1917 for Britain were food and finance. The country was
near bankruptcy, and the depredations of the German U-boats reduced
the national larder to a six weeks' supply at one point. The 9 January
Daily Mail described the 'Food Crisis' as yet another legacy of the 'wait
and see' Asquith government. Northcliffe urged Lord Devonport, the
Food Controller, to implement strict rationing. According to private
information he had from Germany, Northcliffe reported to Devonport,
the submarine campaign would increase greatly as soon as the enemy
could get their latest submarines, being built all over Germany, into the
water. He was concerned that Sir Edward Carson was not keeping
Devonport up to date on the submarine sinkings, which, he warned,
'have so much to do with your work'.[1] However, the increased enemy
submarine activity had one positive effect from the British point of
view. Germany's declaration that from 1 February 1917 all vessels
bound for Britain would be subject to unrestricted attack all but guaranteed the entrance of the United States into the conflict.

With America on the verge of joining the Allied cause, propaganda in
the USA came to the fore in early 1917. Since August 1914 the British
and the Germans had been locked in a propaganda duel over American
opinion. British efforts had concentrated on counteracting German
publicity, with the aim of ensuring America's continued sympathy for
the Allies.[2] Charles Masterman had been appointed director of the War
Propaganda Bureau at Wellington House in London. The Bureau aimed

its literate, low-key and covert efforts at the American elite, mainly on the east coast. Sir Gilbert Parker, a well-known author of the time, headed the effort directed at the United States. Northcliffe believed that the Bureau preached to the converted and that the mass public had been dangerously overlooked. He also had an understandable prejudice towards newspaper and magazine propaganda that Masterman and Parker did not share. If the United States joined the war, a different sort of appeal would be needed that would ensure the British received their fair share of American aid and would help to mobilize the new partner for the struggle. The subject consumed Northcliffe, who reported to Lloyd George the 'disconcerting reading' that the last American mail had brought. He warned that steps must be taken 'to hearten the pro-Allies in the United States, or we shall have a food embargo, which is what the Germans are working at. What we are winning by projectiles we look like losing by lack of propaganda.' He continued that the Prime Minister's recent interview in *Everybody's Magazine* by Isaac Marcosson, one of America's leading journalists, was 'the best thing that has happened for us. It is read in every village in the United States and was immensely advertised.'[3]

Frustrated with what he perceived as government bungling, Northcliffe dispatched Pomeroy Burton, the manager of Associated Newspapers among other duties, on a fact-finding trip to the USA in late 1916. Burton reported back at the end of January 1917. Calling the whole English 'so-called propaganda scheme' wrong, Burton enclosed a memo which laid out his plan for a 'War Intelligence Department, Or, Special War News Service'. By utilizing the direct and improved facilities he proposed, American journalists would be able to get the facts for themselves, and, for the first time, 'be able to tell the people of America the truth, and the whole truth, about the war'.[4] Northcliffe shared Burton's report with Lloyd George and Lord Milner, who attempted to recruit the press lord's services for a propaganda department designed to co-ordinate the many conflicting government efforts. Unlike Asquith, Lloyd George believed that properly handled publicity could be very valuable, particularly in the USA. Once he became Prime Minister, for the first time serious attempts were made to strengthen and co-ordinate the British propaganda effort.[5]

The writer John Buchan, who had been serving in France on General Charteris's Intelligence Staff, was chosen to head the new department, but only after the job had been offered to several notables, very likely including Northcliffe. Buchan was made director of a new Department of Information, headquartered in the Foreign Office, on 9 February. Northcliffe appeared to be pleased with the choice, notifying Charteris that the new appointment was 'good news' and that Buchan 'understands the Army point of view, and will, I trust, get rid of our appalling cumbersome Press Bureau'.[6] Buchan was inclined to make greater use of newspapers and film than his predecessor, Masterman, and it was a priority of his department to keep American opinion informed. He therefore took up Northcliffe's suggestion to supply British papers to those American journals that did not already get them.[7] In addition to more news for the United States, under Buchan's direction the British also increased the scale of their propaganda effort. A British Information Bureau was set up in New York, and numbers of American newspapermen were invited to visit Britain and the front. The newly enlarged staff distributed a much larger quantity of less high-minded material than previously employed.

At the same time that British propaganda was being rearranged, Lloyd George continued his struggle with the Army. With Lord Derby at the War Office, military strategy remained securely in the hands of Sir Douglas Haig and Sir William Robertson. Northcliffe arrived on New Year's Day at GHQ, where he again met Haig, who repeated his argument that all possible men and material should be concentrated in France. In full accord, the press lord promptly travelled to Paris, where he tackled Lloyd George and Lord Milner over the matter and threatened, once again, to turn his papers against the government. Haig recorded in his diary that he spoke to Northcliffe again on 5 January about the danger of Lloyd George's interference and that although Northcliffe had 'much confidence in Milner and thinks he holds sound views on strategy . . . N. is determined to keep Lloyd George on right lines or force him to resign the Premiership'.[8] In mid-January Northcliffe and Repington rejoiced at news from Robertson that, at the Rome Allied Conference, General Cadorna and the Italians refused to send any men to Salonica in the face of strong French pressure. This, at least temporarily, halted efforts to reinforce the Balkans.

Britain's allies were also feeling the strain of two and a half years of war. The amounts of munitions and other supplies sent to the Eastern Front never satisfied Russian demands, and the British feared that the defeat or withdrawal of their giant partner would free all the might of Germany to be hurled against the West. Milner headed a mission, with Sir Henry Wilson as military representative, which travelled to Petrograd in January to appraise the deteriorating military and political situation. Russia refused to co-ordinate major military support for a proposed offensive in the West planned for 1917 under the leadership of the French commander, Robert Nivelle. Milner did not foresee the March revolution, which followed his visit by two weeks. The abdication of the Tsar and the rise of a provisional government, which the British immediately recognized, brought new concerns. Some optimists hoped the revolution might bring a renewed vigour to Russia, as had happened in 1790s France, but by the end of March such dreams of an improved war effort were dashed by the reality that military and industrial conditions had grown worse, not better.[9] Robertson and Haig – never sanguine concerning the planned Nivelle offensive – felt that without Russian support such an action would be dangerous. Further, Robertson warned, in the event that Russia left the war, the Allies would lose their numerical superiority and all forces would have to be concentrated in France to face Germany.[10] Whatever the doubts of his generals, Lloyd George wanted a victory before the British public wearied completely of the war. The charming and optimistic Nivelle persuaded the Prime Minister and his French counterparts that he had found a way to break through the German lines. An Anglo-French offensive was authorized for no later than 1 April.[11]

Northcliffe's varied activities in support of the British war effort resulted in direct enemy retaliation. Elmwood, on the coast of Kent near Broadstairs, came under a German destroyer barrage on 25 February 1917. The next day's 'Message From the Chief' reported that 'the paper was nearly deprived of its chief Proprietor last night – a source of mingled feelings among the staff'. The account went on that

[At] 11.30 my house was lit up by 20 star shells from the sea, so that the place was illuminated as if by lightning. Shrapnel burst all over the place, some of it hitting the Library in which these notes are prepared every day, and killing a poor woman and baby within 50 yards of my home and badly wounding two others ... The Authorities have no doubt that my house was aimed at and the shooting was by no means bad. I understand that the destroyer was three miles out.[12]

In addition to shells, German propaganda also took aim at the press lord. He corresponded with Sir Reginald Brade at the War Office about leaflets from Switzerland that solicited subscriptions for a German *Anti-Northcliffe Daily Mail*.

Undaunted by the attacks of the enemy, Northcliffe continued to campaign against British waste in material and manpower. A particular target was the newly created National Service Department and its head, Neville Chamberlain, another of Joseph Chamberlain's sons. For example, Northcliffe criticized the Department's leaflet propaganda as 'grossly wasteful' and 'involving the use of much labour'.[13] He complained directly to Frederick Higginbottom, at the offending department, that offers for free advertising from periodicals, including his own Amalgamated Press, had been turned down. Higginbottom replied that he had remedied the situation and had met Northcliffe's people, as well as representatives of other periodicals.[14] Northcliffe lodged numerous complaints about Chamberlain with the Prime Minister through J.T. Davies, and also through Sir George Riddell.

An April article in Rothermere's *Sunday Pictorial* called for Northcliffe to take over National Service. Lord Cowdray, who had recently been named president of the Air Board, assumed that Northcliffe would indeed soon replace Chamberlain, and sent him a message that he hoped the new post would not require all his time and that he could still lend a hand in air matters.[15] Northcliffe replied that he 'had nothing to do with the little leading article . . . I do not believe the matter can be put right without compulsory powers, limited only by the authority of the War Cabinet. The delay is making the matter more and more contentious, as I can see by reading reports of meetings of workers throughout the country.'[16] Unable to come to an understanding with Lloyd George about his duties at the National Service Department, or to quell the criticism of the Northcliffe press, Chamberlain left his post in August. He returned to Birmingham nursing a bitter hatred of both men.[17]

Cowdray asked Northcliffe to act as chairman of a committee designed to look into and report on commercial aviation matters, telling him that his involvement would 'ensure that it did its work effectively & comprehensively. Commercial aviation would be sure of development & years of possible delay would be avoided.' Replying that he was glad Cowdray had not forgotten about commercial aviation, Northcliffe told him that he would 'be glad to do anything you ask me to do – especially if I may choose some of the members of the Committee myself'.[18] In late March he assumed the chairmanship of the new Civil Aerial Transport Committee – his first official post of the war. Sir Arthur Pearson sent a note of delight at hearing of Northcliffe's appointment, expressing the hope that this 'first official position which you have cared to accept will . . . only be a prelude to others of even greater importance. I wish they would get you to settle the Irish question.'[19]

In March 1917 Northcliffe took a public stand on Ireland. The visit of the Dominion prime ministers, he believed, offered an exceptional opportunity. He wrote to Geoffrey Robinson at *The Times*, 'This is the golden moment for a Settlement. From a conversation with Sir Robert Borden [Canadian Prime Minister] at Brighton last Friday night I inferred [that] the Dominion Prime Ministers over here have little to do beyond inspecting their own troops. It is a question not of weeks but of days to get this Irish Question settled.'[20] At a St Patrick's Day speech to the pro-Nationalist Irish Club in London, he revealed his proposals to 'remake' the troubled isle.

He told his audience that he chose to address his remarks to a club composed of those with whose political views he was not in accord because he believed it a 'waste of time to talk to those with whom one agrees' and because he 'was born in Ireland' and 'should have some of your national pugnacity'.[21] In his opinion, Ireland was at an urgent moment in her history. All the other Allied countries were gaining a substantial war bonus in the form of industrial legislation, better economic conditions and other benefits. He asserted that only industrialization, and the better jobs it would bring, would make a lasting settlement possible. Turning to the question of Irish self-government, Northcliffe called 'unanswerable' the argument that British government of Ireland had been badly managed. Though the British system was, in his opinion, the very best in the world, in Ireland it had not been as adaptable as in other parts of the Empire and 'strangely neglectful' in sharing industrial development during the war. His plan would begin with a personal investigation into Irish affairs, outside the passion and discussion of 'bygone' wrongs that plagued Parliament. The inquiry need not take place in Belfast or Dublin; he could suggest half a dozen quiet Irish towns where calm deliberations could be made and witnesses speedily be drawn from all parts of Ireland. He ended his talk with an entreaty to his Northern friends to consult their countrymen and to point out to the British government that, for Ireland to play her proper role in the war, 'fresh development' and 'Irish happiness' were needed. Looking to the future, he pointed out that, in order to appeal to the world after the war, Ireland needed to take her proper place in the war effort now.

Northcliffe took personal charge of his newspapers' coverage of his declaration. The journalist Michael MacDonagh was assigned to cover the event for *The Times*, and his report also appeared in the *Daily Mail*. Northcliffe wrote to Geoffrey Robinson at *The Times* that

Last night I talked with a great many Irish people – mostly, of course, of the Sinn Fein variety. Quite a number of them had come over specially for the meeting. They seemed to be more hostile to the Irish Members than to Carson. What took place privately was more interesting than the formal speech making. I had rather a job to get them to drink the King's toast, but, with a few exceptions the whole room rose.[22]

He instructed Thomas Marlowe at the *Daily Mail*:

I am sorry to burden the Paper with the speech that I made on Saturday night but it is part of a plan that I have to try and get some sort of an Irish Settlement. I want you, therefore, to give the space to it on the Turn-Page, the report being as given by *The Times* representative, whose version I shall correct myself.[23]

This attempt by Northcliffe to shape an Irish settlement sank below the waves, as did all such wartime endeavours. It received little attention in Britain, but it was noticed and applauded in the USA, from where Pomeroy Burton cabled his chief that the statement had made a strong impression.

On 6 April 1917, mainly in response to German submarine sinkings of her merchantmen, the United States officially entered the war. Even so, the Americans were careful to designate themselves as 'Associates', not Allies. The *Daily Mail* praised Wilson's 2 April war address as 'the most tremendous monument of the war' and compared it to 'Lincoln's great speeches for its gravity and pathos'.[24]

Two days before the official US war declaration, Northcliffe forwarded to Lloyd George a telegram he had received from Pomeroy Burton in the USA with a request from Howard Coffin, of the American Council of National Defense, asking for British aid in America's mobilization effort. Northcliffe told the Prime Minister that 'If speedily acted upon it will give the American government an idea of our national promptitude and also bring us all sorts of help quickly.'[25] Lloyd George replied the same day that 'we are sending over immediately a very strong mission to America to deal with all the subjects referred to in Mr. Pomeroy Burton's cable; but in addition to those topics we are anxious to get the American co-operation in the matter of American shipping and food supplies'.[26] The mission Lloyd George mentioned was headed by Arthur Balfour. Northcliffe sent the Foreign Secretary a congratulatory note on 5 April, and six days later he advised him that 'America is a land of pitfalls for English people. Twenty-one visits have convinced me that it needs a great deal of knowing.'[27] About this time, Northcliffe later told his wife, he refused an offer from Lloyd George to go to the United States as ambassador in place of Sir Cecil Spring-Rice.[28]

Although Britain was heartened by the entry of the United States into the war, the country still faced critical problems, most prominently the worsening food situation. In face of mounting losses to submarines, the Food Controller initiated stricter rules – to the applause of the *Daily Mail*, which called for bread rationing. The newspaper described the situation as 'very grave' and called for the submarines to 'be dealt with as they have not yet been dealt with by the Navy'. It also called for food consumption to be cut down 'within the strictest limits'.[29]

Three days after the United States joined the war, the Anglo-French assault under Nivelle was launched, despite the criticism of Haig and Pétain and the fact that the Germans had withdrawn to a more defensible line. The 11 April *Daily Mail* editorial, 'The Battle of Arras, Haig's Great Results', poured praise on the Field Marshal for his 'consummate generalship' in the new Allied offensive. However, Nivelle's strategy was soon countered by the enemy, and the push collapsed – as did the fragile morale of the French army.

Though Northcliffe had been reluctant to do so before, the unrelenting losses to the submarines and the resulting food crisis finally moved him to unleash his newspapers on the Admiralty. The 2 May *Daily Mail* editorial, 'Behind the Scenes at the Admiralty, Too Much Civilian Control', complained that the Admiralty was 'not a Board of Strategy, but mainly a Board of Supply'. The paper also became increasingly strident in a series on the related food problem. The 9 May editorial, 'IF', repeated the call for compulsory measures and warned of Lord Devonport's 'grave responsibility' if his voluntary rationing system failed. The next day's editorial, 'Hardships Yet Unknown', quoted the recent statements of several ministers, including Lloyd George and Curzon, on the peril, commenting that 'wait and see had obvious dangers as a food policy'.

As his newspapers opened fire on the Admiralty, Northcliffe distributed information from the USA to members of the government. Arthur Willert, the *Times* correspondent in Washington, cabled that Congress was procrastinating and that the executive was not yet organized or giving the necessary leadership.[30] Willert's chief passed this information along to the Prime Minister. Northcliffe also received a cable from Garet Garrett, managing editor of the *New York Tribune*, which warned that the possibility of Germany winning the war had not 'penetrated' the 'American intelligence'. To wake up the people, Garrett wished to 'cast the truth upon them' and asked Northcliffe to 'tell us in your own forcible language' what the situation really was and 'how long England can stand destruction of tonnage at this rate'.[31] In response to this, Northcliffe notified Balfour in the United States, 'American newspapers cabling me asking whether the submarine menace really serious. They state that United States cannot be impressed unless it knows the facts. Could you urge Foreign Office to allow me to give the facts which I know?'[32] He then proceeded to write a series of articles for the *New York Tribune* on the lessons that America should learn from Britain's experience.

At this time, Lloyd George considered who would succeed Balfour in America. The Foreign Secretary recommended Sir Edward Grey. Rather than send another diplomat, the Prime Minister and the War Cabinet were inclined to appoint a businessman to organize the British supply and financial arrangements. Lord Robert Cecil notified Balfour in America, through Balfour's secretary, Eric Drummond, that the 'Prime Minister wants to send a businessman. I believe, though he has not said so to me, that he is thinking of sending Northcliffe. I could not make myself responsible for such an appointment & if he presses it I shall tell him so & beg that he will wait for your return so you can approve it.'[33] Balfour was horrified at the idea. He replied to Cecil that to 'send a commercial man or Northcliffe might in my opinion have an unfortunate effect on the present and future relations of the two countries and I earnestly trust that no such decision will be taken until I have the opportunity of explaining situation here, which perhaps Cabinet hardly appreciate'.[34]

Unaware of the discussions concerning him, at the end of May Northcliffe wrote to Repington that he was kept busy with his Civil Aerial Transport Committee duties.[35] At the same time, the *Daily Mail* prophesied a future 'Invasion By Air' of massed German bombers, quite unlike the latest 'mere baby-killing expedition'.[36] However dire his newspapers made the situation seem, Northcliffe reported in a more encouraging letter to Lady Ripon that the American Commander-in-Chief, General John J. Pershing, would 'be in London next week, though this is not generally known. The first United States army will consist of 40,000 men – not much, but it is a beginning. They will join the French forces.' He went on:

As for the Government, I think it is in a stronger position now than it has been for some time. Lloyd George's vitality is astonishing. As you know, he and Lord Milner constitute the Government, the rest of the cabinet being more or less ciphers as regards the war . . . The submarines have not been doing well just lately – from the German point of view – that is, up to last Saturday. I have not seen the figures since.[37]

On 29 May the Civil Aerial Transport Committee published a visionary *Private and Confidential* Memorandum (signed by Northcliffe as chairman) which called for further study of such post-war questions as the role of the government, air-mail services, aerial law and meteorological investigations.[38] The next day, the press lord agreed to head the British War Mission to the United States.

This appointment (and its acceptance) was not so surprising as it might appear at first sight. Rumours had been circulating since the beginning of the year that Northcliffe might be asked to go on some sort of American mission, and in April an offer had apparently been made by the Prime Minister. Both men realized the extreme urgency of organizing the United States for war, and both agreed that British publicity there must be strengthened. The prospect of getting Northcliffe to tackle this must have appealed to Lloyd George on several counts. First, Northcliffe had the expertise needed to organize both the business and the publicity sides of the mission. In addition, the Prime Minister was well aware of Northcliffe's varied experience of the United States, his reputation there, and his belief in the USA's absolute importance. A final, and perhaps decisive, factor was that Northcliffe's loose-cannon activities had been a constant irritation to Lloyd George, and the mission would remove him for an extended period.[39]

Many reasons, besides the considerable persuasive powers of the Prime Minister, can be listed for Northcliffe's accepting the job. As Lloyd George must have known when he made the offer, the task combined two of Northcliffe's wartime passions: America and propaganda. Also, in May the mission no longer included onerous diplomatic duties and by the end of that month the submarine peril appeared to be abating. Further, Northcliffe had already taken a step towards breaking his vows not to join in the government by taking on his duties with the Civil Aerial Transport Committee. Perhaps the most important factor was that he was at last ready to assume a more substantial role in the war. Too old to serve in the military, for almost three frustrating years he had been limited to criticism from the sidelines, however influential, while younger family members died of their wounds. He felt each loss deeply. Whatever his previous doubts and fears, once he accepted the job the decision seemed to have a calming affect, as though some inner tension had been released. Maurice Hankey, secretary of the War Cabinet, noted in his 31 May diary that Northcliffe 'was very quiet and restrained, and much pleasanter than I found him before'.[40]

The announcement of the appointment was met with astonishment and anger in most British circles. The friends of Balfour were particularly incensed when *The Times* called Northcliffe the 'Successor to Mr. Balfour'. The Prime Minister defended the choice to C.P. Scott, whose allegiance it had shaken, on the grounds that 'Dr. [Walter Hines] Page when consulted had welcomed the idea' and that 'it was essential to get rid of him. He had become so "jumpy" as to be really a public danger and it was necessary to "harness" him in order to find occupation for his superfluous energies. I had to do this . . . "if I was to avoid a public quarrel with him".'[41] A cartoon which appeared at this time in *London Opinion* showed Carson and Lloyd George celebrating Northcliffe's absence; it bore the caption 'If Asquith had conceived such a splendid idea, he would have been Prime Minister still!'[42] But, however convenient and restful it was for Lloyd George to have Northcliffe out of the country, the Prime Minister must also have believed that the man who was his chief press critic and ally could also perform his duties suitably. Organizing the effort in America was too vital to Britain for Lloyd George to have acted lightly.

The Prime Minister had stressed the urgency of his mission to Northcliffe and had told him, falsely, that Balfour had requested he leave immediately. Consequently, after accepting the position on Wednesday evening and being hurriedly briefed in the next two days, he left on the morning of Saturday 2 June, on the USMS *St Paul*, with only a valet.[43] His ship and Balfour's crossed in the passage. With Northcliffe in America before Balfour could confront the Prime Minister about the appointment, Lloyd George thus presented the Foreign Office and the United States with a fait accompli that both were forced to accept.

The terms of reference which listed Northcliffe's duties were broad enough to leave him some flexibility of action.[44] The primary task – the control of British operations – included the recruiting of British citizens, and the manufacture, purchase and transport over land and sea of all supplies. The instructions gave him full authority to reorganize the independent and often conflicting Treasury, Admiralty, War Office, Ministry of Munitions, Ministry of Shipping and Ministry of Food missions already in place, in order to 'prevent overlapping and secure better results'. He was granted direct access, as needed, to the Prime Minister or the heads of these departments, with the power to resolve their conflicting claims. The issue of publicity was not addressed in the mission terms; however, they did include the establishment and maintenance of the 'friendliest possible relations, not only with the United States authorities, but also with the representatives of our Allies'. One additional instruction of note stated that Northcliffe was to 'keep the British Ambassador at Washington generally informed of the main lines of his action', and was to 'profit by the Ambassador's advice and assistance, whenever these may be required'. Unfortunately, this would prove difficult.

Northcliffe was well aware that, by sending him to America, the Prime Minister hoped to muzzle his newspapers' criticism and their support of the Army. Steed later commented that 'one of the reasons which induced Mr. Lloyd George to ask Northcliffe . . . was a wish to utilize his knowledge of America . . . while removing his influence from the military wrangle at home. If so, Mr. Lloyd George was mistaken. Before Northcliffe started he left general instructions to the editors . . . to "back the soldiers".'[45] The *Daily Mail* kept Field Marshal Haig's name before the public. The 9 June editorial celebrated 'Haig's Triumph, The Victory at Messines'. That month the *Daily Mail* also kept up its attacks on the government's food policy and called for punishment for the 'Mesopotamia Culprits' after the publication of the Mesopotamia Report on Britain's Middle East failures. Other instructions to Northcliffe's newspapers included a 7 June 'Message from the Chief' which announced his departure and instructed the *Daily Mail* and its associated papers not to publish 'one line of criticism of the United States . . . only those who know the Fenian, pro-German and anti-English pressmen in America can realize the minute efforts they make for anti-British attack'.[46] To further prevent any 'distorted account' being published in American newspapers, Northcliffe sent Lloyd George's secretary a press release with his own version of the mission objectives.[47]

When the statement appeared in the 7 June *New York Times*, Colonel House wrote to Wilson that he was sorry Northcliffe was coming. He had believed Balfour had 'headed him off', and now feared his visit would 'stir up the anti-British feeling here that at present is lying dormant'.[48] Some Americans, however, were cheered by the news. Two days before Northcliffe arrived, Roy Howard, of the United Press, cabled:

We are delighted to have you with us. We are a bit fed up on British and French compliments and are sorely in need of word for someone who knows . . . enough to frankly tell Americans what a rotten demonstration we are making of our much talked about speed and enterprise. We have been so completely lulled into a state of asinine self-satisfaction that nothing short of a kick in the hip-pocket will establish our sense of proportion. Hoping you are bringing the kick with you.[49]

The *St Paul* docked at New York on 11 June.

After first considering whether 'to let him run amuck', Colonel House and Sir William Wiseman, the British Military Intelligence officer who kept an eye on Northcliffe during the mission, conspired to surround him with people who would 'keep him straight'.[50] These included Arthur Willert, who joined the mission staff. House sent his immediate greetings and asked Northcliffe to call on him if he could be of assistance. Northcliffe sent thanks the same day for this offer, to which he replied, 'I shall not hesitate to avail myself.'[51] House informed Wilson that he had asked Wiseman to advise Northcliffe not to talk through the press and not to 'attempt to force his opinions upon our people'.[52] Nevertheless, Northcliffe immediately launched a personal public-relations campaign, hosting almost daily luncheon parties in his suite at the Gotham Hotel. Willert wrote that 'nothing would ever convince him that publicity was not part of his duty'.[53]

The new head of the British War Mission was a magnet for the American press. Following a brief session with journalists at his hotel suite, a 12 June 1917 article in the New York *Sun* described Northcliffe as

> maker and unmaker of ministries; furious critic of slovenliness and incapacity and certainly regarded at home as the most powerful figure in British public life outside a responsible Ministry . . . in this country to take up his duties as Head of the British War Mission . . . a post assigned to him because a man of extraordinary energy and executive capacity, as well as tact and accurate understanding of the American people was needed to coordinate the activities of the various British war commissions.

A *Brooklyn Daily Eagle* interview soon after noted how Northcliffe was 'bringing the realities of war and Germanism home to us . . . here was one who had seen what the Germans had done – who had heard the stories from the lips of those who had suffered'. George Harvey, a friend of Northcliffe and editor of the *North American Review*, dubbed him the 'Man of the War' and the 'electric engine of the armies of democracy'.[54]

However, as always, Northcliffe had his critics, in the press and elsewhere. In the 16 June *Daily News*, A.G. Gardiner reacted to a *New York Tribune* article which credited the press lord with the fall of Asquith by proclaiming it 'only amusing as an illustration of the game which the Newspaper Potentate plays with the public of two worlds'. On the same day, the *New Republic*, an American weekly review sympathetic to Gardiner, asserted that Northcliffe had been sent to the United States because 'he exercised an enormous influence on British opinion' and the British government 'rejoiced at the opportunity of installing him in a public office situated in a foreign country'. By the standards of diplomats like Lord Hardinge of Penshurst, the Permanent Under-Secretary at the Foreign Office, the socializing and the amount of publicity Northcliffe generated were disreputable. Hardinge later described Northcliffe as 'a business hustler' who 'hoped to effect some big *coup* for his own glorification'.[55]

Since his mission had no diplomatic status, Northcliffe needed the co-operation of the British ambassador in Washington on matters of protocol. Unfortunately, the hostility of Sir Cecil Spring-Rice represented a real impediment. While en route, Northcliffe had already notified the Prime Minister that he was disturbed by reports of Spring-Rice's interference and that, although he would attempt to 'work with him in every way', if he found him to be 'a man of small parts inclined to make mischief' he would return.[56] On his arrival in New York, in stark contrast to Balfour's reception, no one from the British Embassy greeted him – to Northcliffe's fury. Determined to get on with his job, he put his anger aside and travelled to Washington. At this time he confided in his mother, to whom he wrote almost daily, that his four days in America seemed like four weeks. The letter went on, 'It is barely more than a fortnight since I resolved that it was my duty to make this great sacrifice & I have had to adjust and readjust my view of the tremendous task I have in hand . . . The American Govt is very nice to me. *They are a mighty people these Americans & will end the war.*'[57]

On 15 June, with Spring-Rice, Northcliffe called on several members of Wilson's Cabinet. Josephus Daniels, the Secretary of the Navy, recorded that during their interview Northcliffe criticized the British for withholding information on submarine activity and called the censorship 'stupid' because the knowledge withheld would 'stimulate both patriotism and sacrifice'.[58] Daniels was also a member of the American

279

government's Committee on Public Information (CPI), which had been organized in April under the reforming journalist George Creel. The CPI's main task was to persuade the American public, which had supported neutrality, to a view of the war consonant with Wilson's moral vision of a crusade to 'Make the World Safe for Democracy'. Though Northcliffe thought this idealism naive at best, for a time the CPI shared his view of the harm caused by repressive censorship and also espoused the idea that publicity should be honest and seek to educate, rather than mislead, the citizenry.

Northcliffe and Spring-Rice also visited Counselor Frank Polk at the State Department. Polk reported to House that his two British visitors 'were polite to one another, but it is easy to see that they are not close friends'.[59] That evening they had a tense encounter at the British Embassy before a formal dinner, in which the diplomat raised the personal attacks he believed *The Times* had made upon him. Only the arrival of the French ambassador prevented Northcliffe from storming out. His first mission report to Lloyd George recounted this confrontation with Spring-Rice, describing him as 'an odd person . . . either overwrought by the strain of the war', or 'not quite right in the head'.[60]

The first meeting between the new chairman of the British Mission and Woodrow Wilson took place on 16 June 1917. In a letter to his wife, Northcliffe described the President as

> [a] determined looking gentleman with whom one would not care to be in antagonism, he is about as tall as I am, more slightly built, very quiet in his manner, compresses more meaning into a few words than any other American I have met . . . bears his worries remarkably well, is quite humorous and amusing and, incidentally, the most powerful individual in the world.[61]

Three days after the meeting, House wrote to the President that 'you charmed Northcliffe in your few minutes talk with him . . . I have heard from many directions of his enthusiastic praise of you. You seem to have been a revelation to him. I am glad you treated him so kindly for he has shown a desire to work in harmony with everyone.'[62] Willert reported to Geoffrey Robinson at *The Times* that Northcliffe 'has started well. He has made a good impression. He was expected . . . to do all sorts of indiscreet things. He has instead lain low and . . . his conversation with officials has been tactful and to the point. The President, who had expected a political ogre . . . has expressed himself to be agreeably surprised.'[63]

A cable to the Prime Minister from Northcliffe described his reception by the President as 'cordiality itself'. The message also recounted, however, that Wilson and several of his advisers complained of a lack of submarine news. Before they could expect their own people to make sacrifices, they argued, it was necessary to demonstrate the severity of the conditions under which Britain suffered. Numbers of Americans thought the British exaggerated the submarine peril, the report continued, or still believed they had been tricked into the war. Others objected to 'joining a bankrupt concern'. Northcliffe added that the American-Irish were more powerful than he had thought and that he was meeting a number of their leaders. He concluded by assuring Lloyd George that he would do all in his power to work with Spring-Rice and that 'no effort at conciliation on my part will be lacking, even if my personal dignity suffers'.[64]

In part because of the friction between himself and the ambassador, Northcliffe established his own office at 681 Fifth Avenue in New York, away from the diplomatic scene in Washington, where Charles Gordon, a Canadian financial expert and mission vice-chairman, eventually took command. As the centre of American finance, journalism, commerce and railways, New York also made a more practical site from which to discharge mission business efficiently. The office was staffed largely with *Daily Mail* employees, in order 'to secure reliability and prevent the leakage of confidential information'.[65] The major official challenges Northcliffe faced involved finance, organization and supply. Publicity in the United States, which he considered of equal value to these other areas, he tackled on his own. The area in which he was least experienced and prepared – international finance – soon surpassed all other concerns. On 28 June Balfour cabled House that the British were 'on the verge of a financial disaster which would be worse than defeat in the field. If we cannot keep up exchange neither we nor our allies can pay our dollar debts. We should be driven off the gold basis and purchases for the U.S.A. would immediately cease and Allies' credit would be shattered.'[66]

Northcliffe was sent a similar message. After conferring with House as to the wisest course of action, he travelled to Washington and on 30 June 1917 met Wilson again, this time to discuss Britain's desperate financial situation. The President directed him to the Secretary of the Treasury, William Gibbs McAdoo.[67] Stunned by the immense sums requested – $200 million a month – the Americans asked for facts and figures to back up the British government's dire predictions of financial collapse and to ensure that the supplies requested were absolutely necessary. Northcliffe informed House and McAdoo that, by the middle of 1917, Britain had spent £3.71 billion on the war and had loaned almost £1 billion to its allies. He estimated that the British had already disbursed perhaps $5 billion in the United States.[68] McAdoo complained to House that he was 'somewhat confused by the number of people who are undertaking to speak for Great Britain'. He added that the British needed a 'big man over here' to deal with the financial crisis. He could not yet judge 'how practical' Northcliffe was on matters of finance, but he struck McAdoo as 'a man of great energy and purpose'.[69]

Northcliffe realized his limitations in the realm of international finance, but he was, at the time, the biggest man the British had on the scene. He knew that the Allies needed to co-ordinate their monetary requests, and he worked closely with André Tardieu, his French counterpart. The good relations he established with McAdoo and Tardieu proved invaluable. The three men managed to arrange $185 million in American credits which temporarily averted the disastrous possibility of a suspension of the loans. Tardieu later wrote that without 'means of payments in dollars . . . the Allies would have been beaten before the end of 1917. America's entry in the war saved them. Before the American soldier, the American dollar turned the tide.'[70] While he helped to solve the immediate crisis, Northcliffe realized that assistance was needed for the further loan arrangements that still remained to be made with the United States. The Americans also called for separate full-time British financial liaison. In discussion with House, it was decided that Lord Reading would be the best choice to take over the financial end of the Mission's duties. Reading, the Lord Chief Justice, had previously negotiated a 1915 Allied loan agreement with the United States. Northcliffe underlined the seriousness of the need in repeated cables to his government.

In addition to Treasury negotiations, under Northcliffe's control the War Mission included Admiralty, Purchasing, Munitions, Food, Shipping and War Office groups. These were further subdivided into separate departments, twenty-eight in all.[71] The procurement of munitions was put under the control of Charles Gordon in Washington. After Gordon's appointment the British also began to handle their own purchase arrangements, which had previously been negotiated by J.P. Morgan & Company. One notable addition to Northcliffe's team in the United States was Colonel Campbell Stuart, a Canadian officer who had been assigned to the British Embassy in Washington. Stuart assisted

Northcliffe for the remainder of the war, and afterwards helped to manage the British publishing businesses. In total the Mission employed 10,000 people in the United States and Canada and spent $10 million a day. These colossal expenditures resulted in Northcliffe being called the 'World's Champion Spender' in American newspapers.[72]

Food supplies for Britain, which had been cut to the bone by the submarine campaign, for a time had priority even over munitions. Northcliffe notified the Prime Minister that he was seeing members of the American Cabinet personally, but that the 'slow passage of the food bill and lack of power of requisition, with other difficulties, make for delay'.[73] Special arrangements finally were made to ensure both supply and railroad transportation to ports. Northcliffe met Herbert Hoover, head of the American Food Administration, over the matter. He was impressed by the wide powers given Hoover, who, he told the Prime Minister, was a sincere friend of the Allies, but was discontented with British policy.[74] Hoover complained that high food prices in the United States were successfully used by German propagandists, because the war was not yet understood in America.

By September the British food situation had improved somewhat, partly because losses to submarines had been brought to manageable levels by the convoy system. This innovation, which grouped merchantmen for their voyages under the protection of destroyers and other anti-submarine craft, had first been experimented with in April. Northcliffe continued, however, to think that the shipping losses, though reduced, remained at excessive levels and that the Prime Minister foolishly downplayed the U-boat threat.

Northcliffe's genuine efforts to do his best had overcome House's earlier apprehensions. The Colonel cabled Wiseman (in England to consult with the government) that the press lord was 'doing good work and is getting along well with everyone'.[75] In fact, House began to feel duplicitous because he deliberately withheld information and had so much contact with the British government behind Northcliffe's back.[76] He also was careful in what he disclosed, because he knew that Northcliffe's confidants included members of the political opposition, such as Theodore Roosevelt. Northcliffe saw the former President several times during his visit, but realized that, although immensely popular in the country, he was an enemy of the Wilson administration.

In London, Wiseman discussed Spring-Rice's interference with the government. He informed House that the 'tendency' was to support

Northcliffe and that, in fact, there were calls for him to be made ambassador.[77] After discussing the matter with House, Northcliffe cabled Wiseman that Spring-Rice should be given a long leave of absence, not dismissed, because 'people would say that Northcliff [*sic*] had done it'.[78]

Meanwhile, the mission chairman attempted to stop a US plan under which ships being built for the British would be confiscated for the USA's own needs. Northcliffe cabled his government that 'in regard to the imminent confiscation of ships . . . whatever is done should be done quickly' and suggested that an urgent protest should be lodged with the President.[79] On 25 August he pleaded with House that the seizure would 'create a very bad impression in Europe . . . Is there not some possible compromise? . . . My instructions are to point out that my Government will keenly feel the blow, which will be a very serious one for England, if these ships are taken over by your Government.'[80] Despite his best efforts, however, most of the ships were ultimately seized. Though he failed in this instance, Northcliffe otherwise performed well under difficult circumstances. Regardless of the reasons for his controversial appointment, he turned out to be a capable choice.

After many weeks of delay because of political wrangling in Britain, in September Lord Reading arrived as chief financial negotiator. Anxious that no 'jar from England should mar his very difficult work', Northcliffe was put in the ironic position of pleading with the government to muzzle British press hostility to Reading. Soon after his arrival, House wrote to Lloyd George that the 'coming of the Lord Chief Justice has already resulted in good. Lord Northcliffe is helping to make his visit a success.'[81] Northcliffe informed Steed at *The Times* in London that the Americans had become the 'complete masters of the situation' as regards the Allies. He continued that 'if loan stops, war stops'.[82]

With the financial negotiations in Reading's expert hands, Northcliffe was freed to concentrate on publicity. A letter to his family complained that the 'ignorance about the war is absolutely colossal and lack of knowledge of our tremendous effort and mighty sacrifice deplorable. If there is ever any hanging from lampposts, those who are responsible for our form of censorship should be the first to be strung up.'[83]

To spread his message, Northcliffe used whatever methods made themselves available. American journalists competed with each other to publish his views on the war, and he also wrote or authorized numerous additional pieces. To counteract what he considered his government's dangerously optimistic proclamations about the losses to submarines, he gave Roy Howard a series of interviews which, while complimenting the 'American Spirit', and efforts in the air service, warned of the lack of shipbuilding because of the hiding of the truth concerning German submarine activity. Some of his writing caused official consternation, on both sides of the Atlantic, and at least one piece was edited by the censorship.

The most controversial Northcliffe article appeared in the October 1917 edition of the American journal *Current Opinion*. This directly challenged President Wilson's idealistic explanation for American participation in the war. Though Northcliffe had great admiration for Wilson, he did not believe appeals to idealism would be as effective as appeals to self-interest. Consequently, he asserted that

> [the] motive which brought the United States in was not sympathy for any other nation, was not desire for gain, was not an abstract fondness for democratic as opposed to autocratic government: it was self-interest, self-preservation, self-respect. The American People are not fighting to make the world safe for democracy, but to make the world safe for themselves.[84]

House recorded in his diary that Northcliffe could get in 'serious trouble should the President chance to see' the *Current Opinion* piece.[85] Wilson was well aware that Northcliffe was constantly promoting Britain's interests, with an eye on war aims and the peace settlement.[86] However, in this instance, the President either did not notice or, more likely, chose to avoid the controversy and did not directly answer the challenge to his view of the war.

In addition to his written appeals, Northcliffe also carried out a speaking campaign. He was uncomfortable before an audience, his voice was rather weak, and he spoke from notes. However, with practice he improved, and he gained confidence from the enthusiasm of the crowds he faced. The early talks in America emphasized several themes: the enormity of Britain's contribution (masked by the censorship); that the war would be a long one; and the immediate need for the United States to mobilize all her resources to help the Allies overcome the Prussian menace. Northcliffe's first opportunity to voice his opinions before a large crowd came on 21 July 1917, during British Recruiting Week, to a rally of 14,000 at Madison Square Garden in New York. Although his speaking voice was not powerful enough to reach the whole arena, he received an enthusiastic reception. The next day's *New York Times* reported that another of the speakers, Alexander Humphries, 'voiced the enthusiasm of the audience by exclaiming – I wish to God we had in this country a Lord Northcliffe. We need one perhaps more than Great Britain did'. Northcliffe's recruiting activities also led him to make a speech at AT&T headquarters which was 'radiated' over the entire early radio system. He told his mother that he had had the 'amazing experience of talking to ten American towns, distant from New York between 500 and 3,000 miles. I was also the first man to have a telephone receiver at each ear and to hear on the right the waves of the Atlantic and on the left the waves of the Pacific.'[87] After the success at Madison Square Garden, Northcliffe spoke in almost every city he visited.

Perhaps Northcliffe's most notable United States propaganda success came in his late-October tour of the American Midwest, an area with a large German-American population which the British considered to be a hotbed of pro-German sympathy.[88] During the tour, which began in Detroit, he gave 'advice to everyone from big industry down to housewives'.[89] One of his first tasks was to appease an angry Henry Ford. The American industrialist felt insulted by British handling of an offer to supply, at cost, 6,000 of his new and inexpensive agricultural tractors for the Food Production Ministry.[90] As a result, Ford refused to allow any Englishmen into his factories. Northcliffe told Winston Churchill, who had become Minister for Munitions in July, that Ford had twice put him off, but that he would gladly go to Detroit and 'eat humble pie'.[91] Thomas Edison, an acquaintance of both men, finally arranged a mid-October meeting at which the misunderstanding was laid to rest. Northcliffe toured Ford's plant, and even took a turn behind the wheel of one of the tractors in a ploughing demonstration.

The first Midwest speech was made to a capacity crowd at the Cleveland Armory on 22 October. Northcliffe was introduced by Myron Herrick, a former governor of Ohio and ambassador to France, as 'England's most powerful man', whose 'fearless courage had saved the situation for the Allies'.[92] Northcliffe's address rallied support for the second Liberty Loan and called for more ships, while warning of the continued strength of Germany. As an eyewitness to the war, he also condemned the 'malicious' rumours that the British were holding back troops and that there would be an early peace.[93] While in Cleveland, Northcliffe also gave an interview aimed at a female audience to Kate Carter of *The Press*. He appealed to American homemakers to conserve food, using sugar as an example of a habit which only 'brings on all sorts of trouble', like diabetes, so that doing without it is actually a 'benefit not a sacrifice'. Carter described Northcliffe for her readers as having 'none of the manner or appearance of the movie, stage or best-seller Englishman. There's no monocle, no drawl. His manner of speech is crisp and jerky, clear, forceful. The words and phrases he uses are American.'[94]

Northcliffe's next destination was Chicago. He spoke at the University Club to a thousand leading citizens, to whom he repeated the points he had made in Cleveland. In response to German attempts to frighten the American public with threats to sink troop ships, he reassured his audience that the convoy system now in place was effective and pointed out that almost no Canadian troops had been lost in the crossing. Surrounded constantly by burly bodyguards, behind whom he could hardly see, Northcliffe toured the Chicago naval installation and met Josephus Daniels. On 24 October he was guest of honour at a Chamber of Commerce meeting. After a wheatless and liquorless dinner, his address again underlined the vital need for ships. The *Chicago Herald* declared that

> Lord Northcliffe knows. For over two years in England he led the fight against the murderous inertia of red tape and the suicidal policy of 'wait and see' . . . He has seen with his own eyes the red reckoning of the war . . . Probably no other man in this country today knows so well the necessities of his nation . . . necessities to be supplied by America or not at all. We can accept his statements . . . as facts and his conclusions as sound.[95]

The next day, Northcliffe arrived in Kansas City, where he spoke to a luncheon meeting of leading newspapermen from Kansas, Missouri, Iowa, Nebraska, Oklahoma and Arkansas. The press lord told his fellows that they had misled their readers by emphasizing news that Germany was weakening and by slighting discouraging reports. Dubbing him 'The British Kingmaker', the 26 October *Kansas City Star* called his criticism 'just' and agreed that it was dangerous to create the impression that Germany was weak. The same day's *Kansas City Times* editorial, 'Lord Northcliffe's Warning', praised the frank language he used to convince those who doubted the seriousness of the war. The paper added that

> Lord Northcliffe has unmasked for us the true face of war and has bidden us to accustom ourselves to look upon it. It is something perhaps no American could have done, and for that reason it should make all the more sober the reflections with which the warning is received, for it comes to us paid for with a price by disillusioned England while we are yet unscathed.

At his next destination, St Louis, in front of yet another capacity crowd at a Chamber of Commerce luncheon, Northcliffe praised the enthusiasm he had found on his tour. His address emphasized the concentrated efforts of businessmen needed to win the war, as well as the sacrifices of all Americans – men and women. In a newspaper interview, he saluted the American effort in providing men and training facilities for them, as well as the progress made in aviation. However, he again warned of the shipping shortage and the problems of supplying a huge army in France, and predicted a long war which would require mandatory food conservation.[96] In Dayton, Ohio, the final stop of the tour, Northcliffe presented Orville Wright with the Albert Medal in recognition of his accomplishments in aviation.

Though he believed much more remained to be done, the vast potential he saw in the Midwest heartened the press lord. Josephus Daniels wrote in his diary that Northcliffe returned to the east coast 'happy over the splendid spirit of the patriotic West'.[97] In a 1 November *Daily Mail* article, the 'Middle West's War Spirit', Hamilton Fyfe recounted the warm welcome given Northcliffe and the enthusiasm he had witnessed.[98]

By the autumn of 1917, the strain of his duties and the unaccustomed American heat had combined to tax Northcliffe's energy and stamina. With the Mission on its feet and running smoothly, he proposed to return to Britain in November for a short visit, and suggested that his brother, Lord Rothermere, act as a temporary replacement.[99] Even though some of his activities had caused concern in official British circles, before his departure Northcliffe received a message of thanks from Lloyd George for

> the invaluable work you have done in the United States as head of the British War Mission. It was an appointment requiring exceptional tact and vigour and the War Cabinet desire to express to you their complete satisfaction . . . They would also like to congratulate you on the great energy and effect with which you have striven to explain what Great Britain has been doing and the needs of the Allies to the American public, and the successes of your efforts to combat attempts of the enemy to sow dissension between the people of the U.S. and Great Britain.[100]

A week after the Midwest tour ended, Northcliffe sailed for England, leaving New York on 3 November and arriving in London nine days later. He would not cross the Atlantic again until after the war. Lord Reading eventually succeeded him as head of the War Mission in

February 1918. He also took the British ambassador's post, eliminating the squabbling that had marred Northcliffe's tenure. Arthur Willert wrote of the different contributions of the two men that Reading 'could not have contributed to the awakening of America as Northcliffe did, Northcliffe could not have assisted the American government to take advantage of the awakening as Reading did, and no professional diplomat could have performed either task'.[101]

Northcliffe returned to Britain at the peak of his wartime popularity and influence, his work in America widely acclaimed. To the amazement of many, he had shown that he could fulfil duties of the highest responsibility and importance, and he would continue to serve the country, as he best saw fit, in the year of war remaining.

15

An Unruly Member, 1917–1918

NORTHCLIFFE RETURNED FROM the United States with grave misgivings about the British political situation. During the preceding months he had received disturbing reports of unrest, gloom and weakness at home. The 'virile' American atmosphere left him impatient with his government, including the Prime Minister, who, during the press lord's absence, had enjoyed a partial respite from his newspapers. Without its owner's stewardship, compared to the previous years, the *Daily Mail* campaigns lacked vigour. However, the Northcliffe journals continued to support the generals, even though Northcliffe himself was increasingly disillusioned with the western strategy of attrition.

The deadlock between the Prime Minister and his contumacious generals continued, partly because press support made it politically impossible to replace them. With his leadership secure, Haig had gained approval for yet another offensive, which began on 31 July 1917 in Flanders. The British Army soon found itself mired in nightmarish mud created by a combination of rain and shelling. The Commander-in-Chief, however, pressed his generals to keep up the attacks, while being less than honest about casualties and results. Based on Army information, the newspapers printed stories of British success. In November, as the battle slogged towards its end, once again little progress had been made while the British Army had suffered grievous casualties.

Allied setbacks made it possible for Lloyd George to enjoy one victory over the generals. At Rapallo on 6–7 November, in the aftermath of the Italian military debacle at Caporetto, the Allied leaders agreed to set up a Supreme War Council at Versailles to superintend the general conduct of the war. The Prime Minister appointed Sir Henry Wilson, who had been his unofficial adviser for some time, as the British military representative to the Council. Theoretically, unity of action had been established and a step had been taken to curb the power of Robertson and Haig. On his way home, the Prime Minister made a speech in Paris to publicize the Rapallo agreement. The address underlined the grave errors of the past, to demonstrate the need for co-ordination of Allied efforts. In addition to his Army problems, Lloyd George returned to London to find turmoil over manpower and over the creation of a unified Air Ministry. The *Daily Mail* compared the need for an 'adequate and effective air service' to the shells emergency of 1915.[1]

This was the charged atmosphere which greeted Northcliffe on 12 November when he reached London. That day Repington, the military correspondent of *The Times*, asked to see him as soon as possible about the 'Allied staff created at Paris contrary to the desires of our leading soldiers at home and abroad, and contrary to the public interest'.[2] Northcliffe, however, agreed with Lloyd George that co-ordination was needed. The 14 November *Daily Mail* declared its support for 'unified control and the establishment of a permanent military council', although it disagreed with Lloyd George's assertion at Paris that the German line was 'an impenetrable barrier' and his criticism of the 'appalling casualties' of the Somme.

Northcliffe's greatest worry at this time was that relations with the United States would be mismanaged. A few days before he left New York, he had told Josephus Daniels that he was going to London for the Allied meetings (which would include Colonel House), but that he 'feared there would be no commanding figure, with initiative'.[3] House arrived in London a few days before Northcliffe, and the two worked closely to keep the Prime Minister on the proper course. On 14 November Northcliffe briefed Lloyd George on the Americans' prepar-ations, particularly their air services. He telephoned House that the Prime Minister wished him to join the Cabinet, but that he declined to join 'so spineless a body' and to be put in a position where he could not criticize. 'It is common knowledge', recorded House, 'that N treats LG as if he, the PM, was subordinate and speculation is rife as to when the worm will turn.'[4]

After the Prime Minister had told House that he did not believe he would go to the Paris Inter-Allied Conference, the Colonel and Sir

William Wiseman decided to 'read the riot act to LG'.[5] At House's suggestion, Wiseman phoned Northcliffe and said that, if Lloyd George did
not go, the Colonel would advise the French government to call the
Conference off. This, Wiseman went on, would have a 'disastrous effect
throughout the Allied countries and would exhilarate Germany'.
Northcliffe agreed and, with Wiseman, had lunch with the Prime
Minister to discuss the situation. At this 15 November luncheon the
men also spoke of the planned Air Ministry and who would head it.
Since Northcliffe had called for such a unified organization for years, the
position must have been very appealing. Whether Lloyd George actually
offered the job or not, Northcliffe apparently left the Prime Minister
with the impression that he would take the post. House met Lloyd
George that evening and agreed to delay the Paris Conference by one
week. The Colonel recorded that he now had 'Reading and N, LG's
closest friends, working to force the PM to coordinate the work we have
in hand. N delights in this. He is as eager as a hound on a trail. Today he
refused another offer from George to become a member of the Cabinet.
He wished N to become Minister of the Air services.'[6]

It was in this environment of intrigue between Northcliffe and
House to pressure Lloyd George into more active co-operation that on
16 November, four days after his return, *The Times* published a letter
(dated the day before) from its chief proprietor to the Prime Minister.
This public declaration, which Lloyd George claimed he had not previously seen, took the government to task for continuing to make the
same mistakes concerning the censorship, the control of sedition and
other necessary compulsory war measures that the more 'vital'
Americans and Canadians had already enacted and which the
Northcliffe press had been supporting for years. The letter condemned
the government's obstruction and delay, such as earlier had delayed the
start of Reading's mission, and the 'absurd secrecy' which masked the
continuing British efforts in America. Northcliffe also blamed the
British failure to counteract German propaganda as being partly
responsible for Allied 'tragedies' in Russia and Italy. Instead of being
punished, the letter charged, those responsible for the many blunders
had been retained and even promoted. The most embarrassing disclosure for the Prime Minister was Northcliffe's public refusal of the Air
Ministry. Despite Lloyd George's 'repeated invitation', the press lord
declared that he 'could do better work' if he maintained his 'independence' and was not 'gagged by a loyalty that I do not feel towards the
whole of your administration'.[7]

The Prime Minister played golf with Sir George Riddell the day after the letter was published and told him that Northcliffe could not be relied upon, that he had 'no sense of loyalty and there is something of the cad about him'.[8] Lloyd George also believed the press lord was 'angling for the Premiership'. However, a week later he informed Riddell that Northcliffe had apologized for improperly mentioning the air post in his newspapers.[9] In any case, the premier was too thick-skinned to allow his personal feelings to intrude in political calculations, and Northcliffe remained too powerful a force for a politician in his precarious position to alienate.

Before attending the Paris Inter-Allied Conference, on 24 November 1917 Northcliffe was rewarded for his American efforts by being elevated a step in the peerage, from baron to viscount. Wiseman reported to House that the King had talked of Northcliffe in a 'denunciatory way. However, he was compelled to make N a Viscount the next day. He must have done it with a wry face.'[10] Reading explained to Wiseman that, despite Northcliffe's recent attack, Lloyd George had not the Liberal, the Labour nor the Conservative members behind him, but he did have a majority of the newspapers (if Northcliffe's were counted). With an election impossible for the time being, it was therefore necessary to 'placate' Northcliffe in every way possible, including the appointment of Rothermere as Air Minister, which was announced in the 27 November *Daily Mail*.[11] House was disappointed in the results of the Paris talks. He returned to the United States disheartened by the 'utter lack of virile unity of purpose and control' he found in Europe.[12] Before departing, he sent Northcliffe a note of thanks for the assistance and co-operation he had given, 'with characteristic energy and generosity the value of which it would be hard to estimate'.[13]

While the Paris Conference was in session, Lord Lansdowne had a letter published in the 29 November *Daily Telegraph* which called for negotiations with Germany for a reasonable compromise peace. The Conservative elder statesman had originally submitted this to *The Times*, but the editor, Geoffrey Dawson (who had changed his name from Robinson as a condition of an inheritance), refused to print it, fearing it would damage the effectiveness of the first meeting of the Supreme War Council scheduled within days. This decision angered Northcliffe, who was in Paris at the time but was nevertheless accused of violating traditional policy by keeping the letter out of *The Times*.[14] The press lord told Lloyd George in Paris that he would have published the letter side by side with a 'stinging leader'.[15] The 30 November *Daily Mail* declared, 'If

Lord Lansdowne raises the white flag he is alone in his surrender.' *The Times* commented that 'the letter reflects no responsible phase of British opinion . . . in all the Allied countries it will be read with universal regret and reprobation'.

After the adjournment of the Inter-Allied Conference, Northcliffe visited the front. At British General Headquarters, Charteris, Haig's Head of Intelligence, recorded that the Army's press ally 'was very strong in his condemnation of the Government, much impressed with American methods as opposed to ours, and bubbling over with the importance of his own mission and full of himself. Unfortunately, D.H. was too pre-occupied to respond and Northcliffe was rather wounded in his self-esteem.'[16] Haig had good reason for his preoccupation. Battlefield developments in France, after appearing promising, had recently foundered. In the first few days following the 20 November push at Cambrai, the British Army had made impressive gains. The 22 November *Daily Mail* called the assault a 'Splendid Success', and a full-page headline proclaimed, 'HAIG THROUGH THE HINDENBURG LINE.' Unfortunately, the momentum of the British spearhead of 400 tanks was soon reversed when reserves were not brought up fast enough either to exploit the breakthrough or to halt the German counterattack. By the time Northcliffe visited GHQ the gain was lost, although Haig apparently did not share this information. A national celebration of ringing church bells prompted by over-enthusiastic reports of victory soon turned into anger and disillusionment at the suppression of news of the following reversals.

Cambrai proved the final straw which broke Northcliffe's previously solid support of the generals. By mid-December, at the same time as he pressed the authorities about manpower, he complained to Haig's sec-retary, Sir Philip Sassoon, that 'in some quarters it is asked, what is the use of sending out men to be "Cambrai-sed"'.[17] The Northcliffe news-papers began a campaign aimed at Robertson and his western strategy. The *Times* of 12 December featured the article 'A Case for Inquiry', which called for the punishment of those culpable for Cambrai. The next day the *Daily Mail* followed suit. Meanwhile, Northcliffe defended Haig, who he felt was being misled by his incompetent staff. The press lord warned Sir Douglas, through Sassoon, about the intense popular resentment which was spreading to Parliament.[18]

As Northcliffe returned to the familiar role of crusading newspaper owner, the chances of his returning to the United States dwindled. 'The only possible solution of the leadership of the Mission,' he informed

Reading in late December, was that 'it should be incorporated with your work. When you come back to England I will take charge of it . . . I congratulate myself that the organization is well constructed.'[19] He had been asked to organize the London end of the War Mission, and wrote to Andrew Caird (with the Mission in America) that he was 'glad to stay for other reasons. This Government is always on thin ice, half of it just as wobbly as it has always been . . . I watch these people vigilantly day and night.'[20] A final decision was made in January that, when Reading returned, Northcliffe would stay in London.

That month the continuing attacks of the Northcliffe press on Robertson caused the military correspondent of *The Times* to tender his resignation. Repington did not share his chief's disillusion with the generals, and he felt Northcliffe had 'tied himself to L.G's chariot wheels'.[21] *The Times*, charged Repington's resignation letter to its manager, had assumed a 'subservient and apologetic attitude' towards the War Cabinet in 'neglect of the vital interests of the Army'.[22] Strachey commiserated with Repington:

> It is obvious . . . that you could not have gone on after the Northcliffe Press opened its guns upon Robertson and Haig. I don't pretend to understand the whole depths of the intrigue, but I feel pretty well convinced that Northcliffe and his entourage are out for the Premiership. The fact that he performs the 'nolo episcopari' stunt only convinces me the more that he desires to be Prime Minister . . . Of course a great many people will say that it is absurd and that I am fighting a shadow, but from many indications I have had, I deem this not to be the case . . . I hope you will agree with me that though we won't have Northcliffe, we must get rid of L. G., or at any rate get rid of him from the seat of supreme power.[23]

Repington replied that he 'most heartily' agreed with Strachey 'in your views about Lloyd George and Northcliffe. I think they are a curse to the country. I have no doubt myself, though I have no direct evidence, that they are directing this odious campaign against the high command and I can't think why the Army Council does not take up Northcliffe, Marlowe and Fraser and have them shot.'[24] Repington soon found more sympathetic employment with the *Morning Post*, and became the most outspoken adversary of his former chief's attacks on army strategy.

Though accused of attacking the Commander-in-Chief, Northcliffe attempted to shield Haig's reputation in his newspapers. For example, Lovat Fraser noted in a précis of his article 'Things Hidden', which called for the truth about Cambrai, that he had 'completely eliminated points which tell against Haig'.[25] Published in the 21 January *Daily Mail*, this attack on Robertson described western strategy as 'the strategy of the stone age' and called the theory of attrition 'ridiculous'. Articles in the following week asked further questions about Cambrai and, for the first time, accused the general staff of blaming the politicians or a lack of men for their own failures. The *Daily Mail* campaign, its owner gleefully noted, was 'getting plenty of free advertising' in the other newspapers, which reminded him of the 'good old days of the shells'.[26] Lloyd George, who wished to replace both Haig and Robertson, was incensed at Northcliffe's attack, because he feared it would only rally support for them. General Smuts, in France testing the waters for a change, noted renewed support for Haig. In Parliament, the Unionist War Committee passed a resolution which called on the government to condemn the Northcliffe press. The Prime Minister urged Northcliffe to suspend his campaign and told Lord Stamfordham, the King's private secretary, on 22 January that he 'could have taken him out and shot him'.[27] Lloyd George was also considering shifting Milner to the War Office in place of Lord Derby, who was staunch in his defence of Robertson. He told Amery that Northcliffe's clamour had made it 'impossible to sack Robertson or Derby for some time to come'.[28]

At the same time, another resignation – by Carson in January 1918 – presented an opportunity to reorganize propaganda, which had been under Carson's nominal control. Lord Beaverbrook (formerly Sir Max Aitken), to whom Lloyd George now entrusted the task, approached Northcliffe with the latest government plan. Despite Lloyd George's anger over the anti-Robertson campaign, Beaverbrook had pointed out to the Prime Minister that 'a friendly arrangement' with the owner of the *Daily Mail* was vital to his administration, since he had no party and depended upon the support of the press.[29] The premier needed little persuasion. He had come to believe that propaganda was the troublesome press lord's true talent. Harnessing his energies would also have the added benefit of keeping him too busy to meddle elsewhere. In the discussions with Beaverbrook, Northcliffe again refused to consider Cabinet office, in order to stay independent and to continue his criticism. He did, however, agree to take over foreign propaganda if Beaverbrook took office as Chancellor of the Duchy of Lancaster, with overall control of the British effort. He also gave Beaverbrook assurances of his loyalty to the Prime Minister. It was agreed that Northcliffe would report directly to Lloyd George and would assume the job at his request.[30]

However, for the next ten days the Prime Minister delayed in appointing Beaverbrook to the Duchy (mainly because of royal objections). The resultant climate of rumour, which reminded him of what had happened when he went to America, prompted Northcliffe to withdraw in a letter to Beaverbrook, who sent Lloyd George his own resignation the same day. This action spurred the Prime Minister to go ahead with the appointment despite the King's disapproval. After further negotiations, Northcliffe was brought back into the fold. He accepted a more limited job as head of Propaganda in Enemy Countries on 13 February, while Beaverbrook became head of the renamed Ministry of Information. Rumours soon spread that the press lord was moving into rooms adjoining 10 Downing Street.[31] The day after he accepted Enemy Propaganda, Northcliffe wrote to the Prime Minister that a 'bold stroke' was needed to settle the army question.

Lloyd George had finally had all he could take of Robertson's intransigence and, after he had given the King a choice between himself and the CIGS, replaced him with Sir Henry Wilson. When Lord Derby, out of loyalty to Robertson, threatened to resign as War Secretary, Haig advised him to stay in office. The Field Marshal recorded in his diary that Derby accepted his advice, adding that, 'If he left, Lord Northcliffe would probably succeed him. This would be fatal to the Army and the Empire.'[32] The *Daily Mail* of 18 February, calling itself '*THE SOLDIER'S FRIEND*', supported the choice of 'Ugly Wilson' to replace Robertson, and announced Northcliffe's new duties. The 'riddance of Robertson ought to do good,' Northcliffe reported to Lord Rosebery, 'as also the changes on Haig's Staff'.[33] Notable among the changes was the reassignment of Charteris, who wrote that after this time Haig 'was unwilling even to meet with Lord Northcliffe'.[34] The Commander-in-Chief, like his predecessors in Northcliffe's esteem, found he could not control his troublesome newspaper ally.

The fall of Robertson, added to the inclusion of Northcliffe and Beaverbrook in the government, caused considerable unrest in Parliament. During the 19 February debate on the Army Estimates, Lloyd George successfully defended his administration over the replacement of Robertson, whose views, he said, had unfortunately proved 'incompatible' with British and Allied war policy.[35] Austen Chamberlain, who had been forced to resign as Secretary for India over the July 1917 Mesopotamia Report, used the occasion to call the press attacks on Army and Navy officers both 'deplorable' and 'cowardly'. He urged the Prime Minister to 'cut away the root of evil' by severing his connections with Northcliffe, Rothermere and Beaverbrook. This attack expressed the long-pent-up feelings of many in the Commons. Chamberlain was widely congratulated for his remarks, and he followed up with letters to Lords Curzon and Milner, urging them to 'take action inside the Government'.[36] Lloyd George made no answer to Chamberlain's February remarks about the press lords until 11 March, when he responded in the House of Commons. He defended his choices by pointing out that every Allied government had the press represented, and that Beaverbrook, Rothermere and Northcliffe were highly qualified for the posts they had been given. The owner of the *Daily Mail*, the Prime Minister declared, 'in addition to being a great news organizer', had made a 'special study during the War of conditions in enemy countries' and was therefore invited to take charge of that department. 'No man better qualified for that difficult task could', in Lloyd George's opinion, 'be found in the Empire.'[37]

As the parliamentary storms of February and March passed, the Enemy Propaganda operation settled down to its work. It became known simply as Crewe House, after moving into Lord Crewe's Curzon Street mansion. As Northcliffe's adviser on foreign affairs, Steed convinced his chief that the new department should concentrate its initial efforts against Austria-Hungary, the enemy's weak link. The two men formed an effective combination. While Steed formulated the details and travelled into the field to implement them, Northcliffe fought on the home front against Foreign Office and War Cabinet objections. The press lord's wartime propaganda activities (most often directed at America) had already brought him into conflict with the Foreign Office, and from February 1918 he intruded his 'amateur' efforts into Europe, becoming even more of a threat to traditionalists. Steed's plan for Austria-Hungary required the British government to state plainly that British war aims supported the liberation of the peoples of the Dual Monarchy and its break-up.

War aims had been a bone of contention for some time. In recent months, the Lansdowne letter had also called for Britain to state her aims, which made Lloyd George hostile to the idea. However, when it was revealed that negotiations going on at Brest-Litovsk between the Bolsheviks (who had overthrown the provisional Russian government in November 1917) and the Germans included such topics as self-determination and open diplomacy, the Prime Minister felt it necessary to speak out in response. Because the continuing removal of men for military service was causing considerable friction among British workers,

Lloyd George hoped a public declaration of unselfish principles would help calm the waters and counter Bolshevik appeals to Allied workers to join a worldwide revolt. His speech was also designed both to reassure Britain's allies that they would continue to be supported and to appeal directly to the peoples of the Central powers with the argument that it was their governments that stood in the way of peace. Before a trade-union conference on 5 January 1918, a few days before President Wilson made public his Fourteen Points as a basis for peace negotiations, Lloyd George called for the restoration of Belgium, reparations for her recovery, the re-establishment of the 'sanctity of treaties', a territorial settlement based on the ideal of self-determination, and the creation of 'some international organization' to limit armaments and diminish the probability of war. The speech also called for an independent Poland, but stated that 'the break-up of Austria-Hungary was no part of our war aims'. At the same time the Prime Minister declared, 'we feel that, unless genuine self-government on true democratic principles is granted to those Austro-Hungarian nationalities who have long desired it, it is impossible to hope for the removal of those causes of unrest in that part of Europe which have so long threatened its general peace'.[38] In the *Times* of 7 January, Steed called Lloyd George's proclamation 'the most important State document issued since the declaration of war'.

Balfour, the ever-cautious British Foreign Secretary, did not believe that explicit war aims were in Britain's best interests. He had consistently advised delay in the matter, hoping a separate peace could be arranged with Austria without revealing Britain's diplomatic hand. Already personally hostile to Northcliffe, he was less than receptive to his 24 February letter which asked the government to declare its policy toward the 'various nationalities composing the Dual Monarchy'.[39] The most effective propaganda weapon, Northcliffe asserted, would be for the Allied governments and President Wilson to insist upon 'democratic freedom' for the races of Austria-Hungary on the principle of 'government by consent of the governed'. However, the ultimate aim of Allied policy should be, not to form a number of small states, but to create a non-German Confederation of Central European and Danubian States. The territorial promises made to Italy at the London Convention of April 1915 constituted a stumbling-block; however, recent civilian unrest and military reversals had made the Italian government more amenable to compromise. On all sides, Northcliffe asserted, the time seemed ripe for a speedy implementation of his suggestions.

Prompt action was made more urgent by intelligence that a strong offensive against Italy would be launched within the next two months. To weaken this thrust, or to turn it into a defeat, Northcliffe argued that Allied propaganda must begin at once.[40] He wished his department's efforts to be based on Allied and British policy. For this reason, he urged the War Cabinet not to delay its own decision on a propaganda campaign, and to obtain a verdict from France, Italy and the United States as quickly as possible.

After deliberation, oral consent was given for Northcliffe's department to encourage the anti-German and pro-Ally elements in the Dual Monarchy, up to the point of promising independence. Though dissatisfied with this response, the press lord decided to carry on. For the campaign, Steed had Northcliffe obtain the services of Dr R.W. Seton-Watson, who Steed called 'the best official expert on Austria-Hungary'.[41] Steed and Seton-Watson became co-directors of the Austro-Hungarian section of Crewe House. After some problems with the Foreign Office, the pair travelled to Italy, the base of propaganda against Austria-Hungary, where the Pact of Rome between Italy and Yugoslavia, which modified the territorial promises made to Italy, was adopted on 7 March 1918.

As his propaganda plans made some progress, Northcliffe was less than happy with the *Daily Mail*'s war coverage in France. Henry Hamilton Fyfe, who had been returned to the field to address this problem, wrote that he was sorry his chief did not like the latest articles, but explained, 'My view is that people at home, & the men out here, want to read about the little, every-day incidents of Army life & are sick of reading War with a W unless there is something really big on, which there probably will be very soon now.'[42] Fyfe was certainly correct that something 'really big' was about to happen. On 21 March 1918 the German army, reinforced by divisions freed from the Russian front, began a massive assault meant to end the war in France. British casualties in the first few days of this attempt to split the British and French armies were reported to be 150,000. The *Daily Mail* called it the 'Greatest Battle of All', which would decide whether the British would be 'Free Men or Slaves'.[43] On 24 March Northcliffe wrote to the *Daily Mail*'s New York correspondent, W.F. Bullock, that 'we are at the beginning of the great battle which may decide the future history of the world for some centuries. I do wish that our American friends were quicker. Those I know here use very violent language towards their own Government. Every man available will be wanted.'[44]

Meanwhile, in an attempt to blunt the Austrian offensive expected on 10 April, millions of leaflets and other appeals were distributed across the Italian front by aeroplane, rocket, special rifle grenade and contact patrols. Northcliffe gained permission from the War Cabinet, preoccupied by matters in France, for the propaganda literature to proclaim the independence of the 'subject races'.[45] Gramophone records in the no man's land between the trenches played Czech, Slovak and Southern Slav songs to stir the national aspirations and pride of those serving the Austrians. The desertions and disaffection stimulated by this non-violent barrage were substantial factors in delaying the planned Austrian offensive. Subsequent military intelligence credited the campaign with forcing the Austrians to replace some front-line regiments with more trustworthy troops.[46]

While some success was achieved in Italy, the military crisis in France brought calls for Northcliffe to withdraw his support of the government before a premature peace was made. With the storm 'steadily rising,' Leo Maxse asked him to

> reconsider your present disposition to back up Lloyd George and Co. as from all accounts they are at least as capable as Squiff and Co. . . . of going off around the corner, thoroughly rattled as the P.M. frequently is, and making a suicidal peace with the Boche . . . There would appear to be hardly one stout heart in the War Cabinet, all of whose members I am told were gibbering at the recent crisis.[47]

'I often hear remarks like those in your letter,' Northcliffe replied, 'but I never hear the names of any persons with whom to replace the present Government.'[48] Maxse wrote again a few days later 'as a friend' who was deeply concerned that Northcliffe was so 'intimately identified with the Lloyd George Government, backing it up . . . and treating the War Cabinet as a sort of God Almighty, whereas it contains . . . four or five of the biggest b—— f——s in the country'. Maxse had feared this would happen from the time Northcliffe went to America, which, he said, 'was Lloyd George's only object in offering it to you'.[49] In response, Northcliffe repeated his request for the names of those he should support, and Maxse could offer only Robertson. Northcliffe retorted that when Maxse found a 'dictator who is not afraid of the politicians, I shall support him'.[50]

Beaverbrook later commented that, in this crisis, Northcliffe held himself in reserve for duty as an emergency premier should the British be driven from the Continent and the Lloyd George government fall.[51]

However, there is no evidence to support this contention, and it seems unlikely. Those who believed that the owner of the *Daily Mail* aimed for the premiership misjudged him. While the thought of leading the country to victory over the German foe must have appealed to his considerable vanity, Northcliffe prized the freedom to criticize more than government rank. He wanted action, not power. He told a publishing colleague, 'I have no desire to be Prime Minister. I have twice refused Cabinet rank because I believe that I can be more useful in my present position as an independent critic. A good many of our radical friends want me in the Government in order to shut me up.'[52]

The German advance cast a pall over the nation and its leaders. The House of Commons was in 'utmost gloom', Cecil Harmsworth recorded in his diary. There was 'not merely anxiety', but 'stupefication and bewilderment at the hurried and confused retreat of our glorious army – just as if they were so many Italians or Rumanians'.[53] As had happened throughout the war, military reversals brought changes in the government. To invigorate the War Office, in mid-April Lloyd George removed Derby and installed Lord Milner as War Secretary. Rumours spread that Austen Chamberlain was to take Milner's former place in the War Cabinet. In response, the *Daily Mail* warned against the appointment of an 'ineffective mediocrity' whose career had come to an end in the Mesopotamia failure.[54] After the choice was made official, the *Daily Mail* editorial 'How to Lose' attacked the government for playing politics in this time of crisis with 'party manoeuvres to placate tariff reformers'.[55] On the other hand, the *Yorkshire Post* marked Chamberlain's selection as 'a personal triumph for him over the Harmsworth influence; but more important still, it indicates that Mr. Lloyd George has determined openly to ignore it'.[56]

The 'vote catching bargain with Mr. Chamberlain' and the exclusion of Milner from the War Cabinet combined to rouse Northcliffe to tender his resignation. Recuperating at Elmwood from influenza and bronchitis, he suggested to Beaverbrook that Sir Campbell Stuart, in London since November 1917 and already doing most of the work as vice-chairman, become head of the London headquarters of the British War Mission. At Beaverbrook's insistence, Northcliffe agreed on 19 April to stay another month, only because 'certain matters are pending which render it unwise for any sudden change to take place'.[57] He told Beaverbrook, 'I want to get away from any connection whatever with this alleged War Cabinet, in order that I may say what I think of it . . . Will you please let the Prime Minister know of my decision at once, as I propose making a public statement on the matter, but do not wish to embarrass him unnecessarily.'[58]

After Lloyd George sent a note (along with the promised evidence of the value of Northcliffe's work) that, if the German offensive could be stopped as the British military chiefs hoped, Austria might 'fall to pieces', once again Northcliffe relented.[59] Under the circumstances, he agreed to stay until a replacement could be found, but notified the Prime Minister of one important condition:

> Though no binding assurances have been given, or engagement entered into, a very precise impression has been conveyed, under my responsibility, that this country, at least, favours a policy of Liberation of the Hapsburg subject races with a view to their constitution, in the event of an allied victory, into a non-German polity, or Danubian Confederation.
>
> I, therefore, regard myself as entitled to be informed and consulted before any steps are taken, direct or indirect, public or secret, that might involve a departure from this line of policy.
>
> It is not only a question of consistency in our methods, it is also a question of keeping faith with the representatives of the Hapsburg subject races who are being encouraged to fight on the side of the Allies for the liberation of their own peoples and for the Allied cause in general.[60]

Northcliffe's personal effort was limited by a series of illnesses, including bronchitis, influenza and laryngitis, that plagued him in this period and led him to put Sir Campbell Stuart in day-to-day charge of Crewe House until he could recover. Stuart acted as chair of the Propaganda Committee meetings until October, and handled organizational and administrative duties while others, such as Steed, saw to the propaganda details.

H.G. Wells was persuaded to direct the campaign against Germany. Wells believed that some sort of world government was necessary, and had promoted the idea of a League of Nations. When the two men met at Crewe House to discuss propaganda, Wells reported that Northcliffe told him, 'You want a world revolution . . . Isn't our sitting here social revolution enough for you?'[61] Wells's plan for German propaganda called for four simultaneous approaches: one underlined German responsibility for the war, another emphasized the probability of defeat, a third pointed out the waste and loss involved in continuing the war, and the fourth proposed a 'League of Free Nations' as a nobler replacement for the German dream of world domination. Wells dubbed the last appeal the 'Great Propaganda'.[62] This plan for world organization –

meant to change Germany by luring the population away from dreams of 'Berlin–Baghdad' and 'Mitteleuropa' – became the cornerstone of the campaign.

Crewe House strategy for Germany was refined in a special 31 May meeting of the Committee for Enemy Propaganda. A Wells memorandum called for a 'clear and full statement' of the war aims of the Allies – including an international congress or 'League of Nations' – to be used as 'the standard of their activities'. He blamed the present disaster on the German ruling classes, and called for all British propaganda to draw 'the sharpest distinction' between Germany and 'its present Junker Government'.[63] The Crewe House scheme for Germany was submitted to Balfour in a 10 June 1918 letter from Northcliffe which called for the Allies to 'put in the forefront' their ultimate objectives and the use they would make of victory.[64]

While propaganda against the enemy was planned in London, on the battle front the German army once again came within forty miles of Paris. The 10 June *Daily Mail* editorial, 'The Battle for Paris: Mr. Clemenceau's Heroic Lead', recounted the struggle, while the newspaper planned for evacuation. George Curnock reported to his chief that arrangements had been made to transfer the *Daily Mail* office to Nantes if need be; however, he added that it was 'not believed here that Paris will fall; but it is anticipated the Boche will endeavour to get near enough the next time to bring the city under a naval gun bombardment and treat it like Rheims and Amiens. In such an event there would be a great exodus. Already 1,600,000 have gone.'[65] But, as in 1914, the Allies stiffened before Paris and began to drive back the enemy the next month.

In Northcliffe's estimation, to accept anything less than total victory would be an unpardonable sin. June revelations of peace initiatives at Russia's expense, led by Milner, reached him via Steed and Clifford Sharp, the *Times* correspondent in Stockholm. This episode destroyed Northcliffe's former staunch faith in Milner and he began to speak of Milner's German connections – the War Secretary had been born in Germany, where his father lectured at Tübingen University – as he did those of Haldane. Both Northcliffe and Steed believed that any peace which gave Germany a free hand to exploit the vast resources of Russia would only mean a future, more powerful, attack on the West by a regenerate enemy. The 21 June *Daily Mail* declared that any ministers who made a peace which allowed Germany 'a free hand in the East' would 'deserve to be . . . hanged by their indignant fellow countrymen

. . . who would not suffer the war to end in so shameful a betrayal'. When this blast brought only silence from the government, Northcliffe told Steed that 'We've hit the bull's eye!'[66]

Northcliffe's health improved in July as preparations began for a general election based on the newly enlarged franchise.[67] The widespread industrial unrest during the war had convinced him that the new electorate would not support a government made up of the same old Conservative faces that presently surrounded Lloyd George. He feared that revolution would follow the return of such an old-fashioned and reactionary crew. He also believed that the armed-services vote would be crucial. Since it was expected that the poll would be held before the end of the war, newspaper coverage of the campaign would be critical for the soldiers overseas. He backed a redistribution of land to returning veterans who wanted it, and lectured his employees on the question.

In mid-July, Wells was angered by Campbell Stuart's dismissal of a young Crewe House assistant who, it had been discovered, had come to Britain from Germany at the age of thirteen. As the son of an enemy alien, his employment was contrary to tightened government regulations. Wells complained to Northcliffe that his 'most useful assistant' had been 'swept away . . . by this infernally indiscriminate anti-German wave'. In the same letter, Wells pressed Northcliffe over the foreign-affairs line taken by his newspapers. 'Lord Northcliffe of Crewe House has sent Mr. Balfour a very remarkable document,' said Wells, 'embodying his conception of the Allied War Aims. Will he not now induce Lord Northcliffe of Printing House Square and Carmelite House to insist upon that document becoming the guiding memorandum upon foreign affairs of the Times, the Daily Mail and the Evening News?'[68] Northcliffe answered abruptly: 'Let me say at once that I entirely agree with the policy adopted by my newspapers, which I do not propose to discuss with anyone . . . if you will wait you will find that I will unearth much sinister and alive Prussianism in England.'[69] Wells responded that he was 'sorry that you insist on being two people when God has only made you one. I cannot, for my own part, separate "The Evening News" from Crewe House while you remain one person.'[70]

This was only one incident in a continuing dispute between Northcliffe and Wells over the treatment of Germans in Britain and proposals for the post-war period. The distance between their conciliatory and punitive positions finally led to the resignation of Wells. In response, Northcliffe wrote to him, 'I cannot say how sorry I am that you have deprived Crewe House of your valuable services, and I want to thank you for laying the foundation of the great work that will be carried on ... I hope you will not resign from our Committee. All committees need stimulus and criticism.'[71]

At the same time, the German army's last hopes for military victory collapsed when the Allied forces, unified under the command of Marshal Foch, attacked and caught the enemy off guard. Afterwards, General Ludendorff always called 8 August 1918 the 'Black Day of the German Army'. However, even those closest to battlefield developments predicted that the war would last well into 1919 or longer, with the Germans entrenched on a shorter line in fierce defence of their own soil. Allied planning and strategy were made on that basis, despite continuing rumours of peace. Northcliffe agreed with those who thought that the war would last at least another year. He sent his nephew Esmond Harmsworth, Rothermere's only surviving son, a note which predicted that, though the war would be long, it would 'end with the total dispersal of the German tribes'.[72]

On the propaganda front, Northcliffe called for an Inter-Allied Conference, which began in London at Crewe House on 14 August and focused on Germany. The forty participants shared information and created a permanent London Inter-Allied Propaganda Committee to unite the efforts of the Allied and Associated powers.[73] Northcliffe also proposed to the Prime Minister that one consolidated organization, to be called the British War Mission, should act as an umbrella for all his responsibilities. He wrote that he would 'be glad to accept the Chairmanship of this Mission' to carry on his work, which, in his opinion, was 'daily growing in importance'.[74] Lloyd George approved this change. In the June–August period almost 8 million leaflets of all kinds were distributed over the German lines. Enemy newspapers called for a similar campaign in retaliation.

As their battlefield position deteriorated, the military leaders of Germany also acknowledged the British propaganda campaign. General von Hutier warned his troops against the 'last resort' of the Allies to a programme of 'ruses, trickery and other underhand methods' aimed at inducing 'in the minds of the German people a doubt in their invincibility'. Northcliffe, 'the most thorough-going rascal of the Entente', received special attention as master of this campaign of forgery, for which he had been given 'billions' in funding. A few days after von Hutier's declaration, Hindenburg released a 'Manifesto to the German People' which warned of the Allied war against the 'German spirit'.[75] Surveying the myriad appeals made by the Allies – which he called a 'drum-fire of printed paper' intended to 'kill the soul' – the German Field Marshal warned his people not to allow themselves to be fooled by the propaganda of those who wished to 'annihilate us'. Haig's secretary, Sassoon, congratulated Northcliffe on his work, writing that 'Hindenburg's manifesto was a great tribute to the success of your propaganda'.[76]

By 7 September the Allied military position had become promising enough for the *Daily Mail* to warn of an expected 'armistice dodge' from Germany. Speaking to an audience of foresters in Scotland, Northcliffe called for Prussia to pay 'town for town, village for village, ship for ship, jewel for jewel, picture for picture, dollar for dollar . . . she must pay full compensation for all she has . . . stolen, sacked and burnt'.[77] In late September, Bulgaria signed an armistice and left the war. Crewe House moved swiftly to include this victory in the propaganda campaign. On the basis of a letter in *The Times*, Lovat Fraser feared the Bulgarians would be dealt with too lightly. He wrote to his chief:

> That narrow, grasping peasant nation was not in the least led astray when it joined the Germans. It went in on the make, exactly as the Sikhs would do . . . if we are going to throw all the blame on the Kings and shed tears over the peoples we shall have a rotten peace. If we begin by saying that the Bulgarians are not to blame, but only their King, we shall end by saying the same thing about the Germans.[78]

This mirrored Northcliffe's own concern exactly.

While the Allies were taking control on the battlefield, Lloyd George began the 1918 election campaign with a major address at Manchester on 12 September. Negotiations had also started with the Asquithian Liberals for places in the prospective coalition government. At the end of the month, Rothermere and Lord Murray of Elibank approached the Prime Minister with a proposal for what Sir George Riddell called an 'old gang' coalition to include Asquith as Lord Chancellor. The following day Rothermere visited Lloyd George with Northcliffe in tow. Riddell was unsure how much the owner of the *Daily Mail* knew of the plan and felt Rothermere might be using his brother for a 'bit of domestic humbug . . . to dust the eyes of L. G. and others as to Northcliffe's actual knowledge of and participation in the ramp'.[79] On 2 October Northcliffe visited Lloyd George at Riddell's house, Danny Park. The next day he warned Riddell that the old gang were 'trying to lay hold of the legs of the Prime Minister and drag him down'. They would succeed, Northcliffe believed, unless Lloyd George realised his position and stopped giving so much credence to the 'little people' in the government, such as Walter Long and Austen Chamberlain, who had no real standing in the country. He urged Riddell not to let the Prime Minister be fooled. The coming election, he said, would turn on the soldier's vote and could be won by a Paris *Daily Mail* appeal to the troops. He offered to go to France for this work, but refused to do so 'for the return of the Old Gang'.[80]

Northcliffe was disillusioned because he had been assured (or at least believed he had been assured) by the Prime Minister that a new government of experts would be formed 'immediately the new Register became legal'.[81] Under political pressure, Lloyd George now wavered from this earlier position. Northcliffe therefore wrote to Riddell that he did not propose to use his newspapers and personal influence to 'support a new Government elected at the most critical period of the history of the British nations' unless he knew 'definitely and in writing' and could approve 'the personal constitution of the Government'.[82] When Riddell passed along this demand for the names of his prospective ministers to Lloyd George, the Prime Minister responded that he would 'give no undertaking as to the constitution of the Government and would not dream of doing such a thing'. Riddell recorded that he 'communicated this to N., who said very little'.[83] With Northcliffe's support in serious question, Lloyd George moved to shore up the newspapers on which he could count. A group of his political allies completed the purchase of the *Daily Chronicle* in October.

As the end of the worldwide struggle became only a matter of time, Northcliffe convened (at Steed's suggestion) a new Policy Committee of the British War Mission to consider the transition from war to peace. This new committee was designed to assist in furnishing materials for drawing up and revising the various peace proposals.[84] In response to a German peace note to President Wilson and his reply, the Committee came together in an emergency session, with Northcliffe in the chair, to draft a statement of propaganda policy. A 9 October 1918 meeting approved a draft of a 'Memorandum on Propaganda Peace Policy' to be sent to the Foreign Office and, if approved, to Colonel House.[85] At the same time, the *Daily Mail* labelled the German request for an armistice 'not peace but trickery', and printed a warning to the Allies (attributed to a German in Switzerland): 'They will cheat you yet, those junkers! Having won half the world by bloody murder, they are going to win the other half with tears in their eyes, crying for mercy.'[86]

Northcliffe took Steed and Captain Chalmers Mitchell, who had joined Crewe House from the War Office propaganda branch, to a meeting with Lloyd George to discuss their Propaganda Peace Policy memorandum. The men were disappointed in the Prime Minister's reaction. He told Steed and Mitchell, 'I can't have this . . . Here you are laying down principles and conditions which only the Allied Governments are competent to decide.' Further, he refused to have his hands bound by 'announcing things of this sort'. When asked for his specific objections, Lloyd George replied that he could not 'be bound by principles and programmes such as you lay down. I am a lawyer . . . possession is nine tenths of the law', and said that, when the Peace Conference met, the British would have the Germans 'in our hands'.[87] However, after further discussion, Lloyd George agreed that, if the men could persuade Balfour, the memorandum might be used as terms of propaganda. After changes were made concerning the German colonies, the Foreign Office authorized the revised document to be used 'unofficially'. The resulting 'Propaganda Peace Policy' listed thirteen non-negotiable and three negotiable conditions for peace with Germany.[88]

On 22 October Northcliffe spoke at the Washington Inn, an American officers club in London. He previewed his department's peace policy, and discussed the need for a united programme against the Germans. He also attacked Milner's 17 October interview in the *Evening Standard*, which supported conditional surrender terms for Germany in order to stave off Bolshevism. Northcliffe countered that 'the way to create Bolshevism was to let the Hun off'. He worried not about the threat of revolution in Germany, but about the 'real danger of social upheaval . . . in this country and in other Allied countries, *if an unsatisfactory peace is made*'.[89] The *Evening News* of 28 October included the veiled threat to Milner that 'his German origin is not forgotten and the man in the street declares that he is acting as a Prussian. Lord Milner should take care. If this impression were to spread the results might surprise him.' In the House of Commons, critical note was taken of the statements of both Milner and Northcliffe. The Irish MP John Dillon complained that MPs were being treated 'like a lot of school children' concerning the peace terms, while the press lord was allowed to make public declarations.

The collapse of Austria-Hungary and Turkey in October left Germany alone. Northcliffe's greatest fear was that too lenient a peace would be made with Britain's paramount enemy, and he called for an unconditional surrender in *The Times*. The *Daily Mail* featured 'The Great War of 1938', which would have occurred only because the Allies had not 'seen the thing through' in 1918. With peace talks looming on the horizon, Colonel House arrived in Britain. Northcliffe sent a note that he was glad to find House 'on this side in these critical days', and that he was looking forward very much to seeing him. He gave the Colonel a copy of his Propaganda Peace Policy in order to 'prepare the ground for full co-ordination of propaganda policy between the Associated countries'.[90] On 28 October the document was distributed to all the members of the Inter-Allied Propaganda Committee. As preliminary peace discussions began in Paris, the 30 October *Daily Mail* renewed its 'They will cheat you yet, those Junkers' warning to the 'Softies' in the government.

In France for an Inter-Allied Propaganda Committee meeting, Northcliffe sought an official peacemaking role for himself and his department after the cessation of hostilities. He met Lloyd George, who told him to arrange for a house in Paris. The press lord believed he had been given assurances that the British War Mission would continue and that he had approval to carry out publicity before and during the Peace Conference. He wrote to the Prime Minister for confirmation of his understanding:

> The prospective disappearance of enemy countries properly so called naturally brings into greater prominence this aspect of the activities of the British War Mission.
> They will henceforth be directed increasingly to the dissemination of knowledge of the essential conditions of peace and of the reasons why these conditions are essential.
> It seems therefore indispensable that, pending the convocation of the Peace Conference and during its deliberations, the British War Mission should be definitely entrusted with this work both because it is the logical sequel to the work it has done with considerable success hitherto, and because there is no other organization in existence that possesses in the same degree its special qualifications.
> Therefore, in view of the urgency of the matter, I request that I be given, with the least possible delay, authority as Chairman of the British War Mission to undertake this Peace Terms propaganda in the closest collaboration with the various departments of state until the final peace settlement has been concluded.[91]

The Prime Minister had come to believe that Northcliffe wanted more than the control of publicity: he thought his ambitions included a

seat at the Peace Conference table as a member of the British delegation.[92] When the two men spoke on 3 November, Lloyd George bluntly
stated that he intended Northcliffe's position in Paris to be only
unofficial and advisory. He later recalled that the press lord was 'visibly
astonished and upset at my declining to accede to his request'.[93]

The day after his meeting with Lloyd George, a signed Northcliffe
article, 'From War to Peace', appeared in the *Daily Mail* and *The Times*.
This statement, syndicated internationally, listed and explained, as parts
of a three-stage process, the terms of his department's Peace Policy. The
Daily Mail also included a further denunciation of the War Secretary,
'Lord Milner's Blunder: Encouraging the Enemy and Discouraging Our
Friends'. In the Commons on the same day, John Dillon asked about
the nature of Northcliffe's trip to Paris and if the views revealed in his
'From War to Peace' article were private or official.[94] Bonar Law replied
for the government that Northcliffe had travelled to Paris on private
business, though he might have discussed propaganda, and that the
article expressed only his private position.

Despite Lloyd George's rejection of him during their 3 November
meeting, Northcliffe did not give up hope for a role in Paris. Two days
later, Sir Campbell Stuart saw J.T. Davies in an attempt to smooth over
the differences. However, any peacemaking effort was complicated by
the *Daily Mail* campaign against Milner, which continued with a 6
November editorial, 'Milner's Mischief'. Along with Northcliffe's public
announcement of peace terms – which were soon called 'Northcliffe's
Thirteen Points' – the anti-Milner campaign gave the Prime Minister an
example of the sort of behaviour he could expect if he took the press
lord to Paris in any capacity. The two men had a final meeting at this time
at which Lloyd George, wearied by Northcliffe's conditions for support,
claimed he told him to 'go to Hades'.[95] Sir Auckland Geddes, who saw
both men after this confrontation, later commented that each 'described
the other as impossible and intolerable' and that he did not believe that
Northcliffe had asked for a seat at the Peace Conference, because, if he
had, Lloyd George would have 'blurted it out all over the place and there
would have been a cloud of witnesses'.[96]

The Prime Minister apparently did tell at least one person: Sir
Edward Carson.[97] With Northcliffe's supposed impertinence to Lloyd
George and the newspaper offensive against Lord Milner both fresh in
his mind, Carson rose during the 7 November Commons debate on
funding for the Ministry of Information to unleash perhaps the most
telling attack on Northcliffe of the war:

I am quite alive to the fact that it is almost high treason to say a word against Lord Northcliffe. I know his power and that he does not hesitate to exercise it to try to drive anybody out of any office or a public position if they incur his royal displeasure. But as at my time of life neither office nor its emoluments, nor anything connected with Governments, or indeed public life, makes the slightest difference . . . I venture to incur even the possibility of the odium of this great trust owner who monopolises in his own person so great a part of the Press of this country . . .

Within the last few days there has been an attack made by this noble Lord's papers upon Lord Milner . . . [who] seems to have given an interview to a rival paper . . . [H]aving read it and having read the criticism of some of Lord Northcliffe's papers upon it, I believed that it has been purposefully and intentionally misrepresented and misunderstood . . . [I]t seems to me to be nothing but indecent that the gentleman engaged in foreign propaganda on behalf of His Majesty's Government should make part of his propaganda an attack on the Secretary of State for War in the Government under which he purports to serve . . .

I think it is really time to put an end to this kind of thing. The Government may imagine that they gain power and support, but I do not believe it for a moment. I believe that all the best elements in the country resent this kind of thing . . . At this present moment, when Lord Milner is in France . . . dealing with . . . matters of vital importance to this country . . . come these attacks from an official of the Government . . . to drive him out of his office. For what? In order that Lord Northcliffe may get it or get into the War Cabinet, so that he may be present at the Peace Conference . . . The whole thing is a disgrace to public life in England and a disgrace to journalism.[98]

After this, Milner informed Carson, he had a 'shower of letters from friends simply delighted with the trouncing you gave Northcliffe'. Milner thought it was high time that 'somebody other than myself' spoke out, and added that Northcliffe was 'only a scarecrow, but still the fact remains that most public men are in terror of him'.[99]

On the day when Carson was 'trouncing' Northcliffe in the Commons, the press lord was in Paris attending a luncheon given in appreciation of the efforts of his propaganda colleagues and the staff of the *Continental Daily Mail*. At the gathering, he announced that the signing of the Armistice would mean the end of his government service. He remarked that, 'We have to some extent hastened the end . . . Ours has been a bloodless campaign and a costless one. I wish that we had embarked upon it at an earlier stage of the War.'[100] Though he had not got the unconditional surrender he wanted from Germany, shortening the war and thereby saving lives had been Northcliffe's primary aim, and in that his department had succeeded. Crewe House had helped speed the downfall first of Austria-Hungary and then of Germany. British propaganda did not create the conditions that led to the enemy's final collapse, but it has rightly been credited with exploiting and accelerating the process.[101]

The day after the Armistice was signed, Northcliffe sent his resignation to Lloyd George; it was accepted at once. The Prime Minister replied that he wished 'to assure you how grateful I am for the great services you have rendered to the Allied Cause while holding this important post. I have had many direct evidences of the success of your invaluable work and of the extent to which it has contributed to the dramatic collapse of enemy strength in Austria and Germany.'[102] The next day Northcliffe notified his other great wartime antagonist, Arthur Balfour, that he had resigned and thanked him for the 'courtesy and promptness' with which the Foreign Office had dealt with him and his departments.[103] Balfour replied with the same studied courtesy he had shown throughout:

> Though I rejoice in the cause, I am indeed sorry that our cooperation has come to an end. It is a great pleasure to me to feel that our two Departments have worked so smoothly together; and while I am grateful for what you say about the Foreign Office I know that such harmony can only be the result of mutual goodwill.[104]

However, it was not with goodwill, but with trepidation that Northcliffe looked towards the election of 1918 and the Peace Conference of 1919 that followed.

16

The Road to Ruin, 1918–1919

WHILE OTHERS REJOICED in Britain's victory after more than four bloody and brutal years of total war, Northcliffe found little tranquillity. For him the war had not had the 'Glorious End' proclaimed by the *Daily Mail*.[1] The Armistice fell far short of his demands for a total surrender and the complete destruction of Prussian militarism. Denied an official role at the Peace Conference which would decide Britain's place in the post-war world, he feared Germany would be treated lightly and had little faith that the politicians could make a truly lasting settlement. 'The Huns Must Pay', the *Daily Mail* editorial of 13 November, began a drumbeat that would last well beyond the signing of the Versailles Treaty in June 1919. Northcliffe did not doubt that Lloyd George would win the election set for December 1918, but predicted that revolution would follow the return of a government dominated by what he saw as Tory remnants of the old regime. Additionally, the press lord's health worsened; a visible lump had appeared on his throat. Ordered to rest by his doctors, he wrote to the Earl of Selborne from Elmwood that he was 'doing my part of the election from here'.[2]

The election season opened in earnest after the Armistice was signed. Despite his calculation that, as 'The Man Who Won The War', he would triumph, Lloyd George remained unsure of the outcome until the final results were tabulated. He promised far-reaching social and economic reconstruction to a Liberal Party meeting on 12 November, but, nevertheless, continued his alliance with the Conservatives. To his party, Bonar Law explained his decision to carry on with Lloyd George as the only course to head off Bolshevist radicalism.[3] The Lloyd George–Bonar Law coalition programme was published on 18 November and supplemented thereafter by regular manifestoes which outlined policy. Having led the country to victory, the new coalition would have as its mission the reconstruction of Britain into a 'fit country for heroes'. The Asquithian segment of the Liberal Party was proscribed from the list of approved candidates given the 'Coupon' of approval by Lloyd George and Bonar Law. One element of the wartime government, Labour, decided not to continue in the coalition into peacetime. With the exception of George Barnes and a few others, Labour withdrew, and became the official Opposition.

Unless the needs of the working classes and the soldiers were met, Northcliffe feared a socialist revolution would spread from the Continent. Consequently, he attempted to use his newspapers as a bulwark against Bolshevism. Hamilton Fyfe wrote to his chief about the general feeling that Northcliffe held the power 'to restrain the forces which threaten to drive Labour into adopting revolutionary methods'.[4] Fyfe urged him to give Labour 'a fair show' to keep it on 'constitutional lines'. He was in contact with Arthur Henderson, the Labour leader, and urged Northcliffe to meet him to dispel the notion among party members that he, Northcliffe, was an ogre. Since Labour had no daily newspaper of its own, the *Daily Mail* donated free space to the Party, under a disclaimer that the paper was not responsible for the opinions offered.

The millions of men in the armed forces, Northcliffe believed, would decide the election. In the months after the Armistice, delays in demobilization of the troops became a major problem. The press lord received numerous letters of complaint from the soldiers and their families about the matter, and serious unrest developed in Britain and France. To defuse the situation, he instructed Marlowe to publish an article on demobilization, 'carefully explained by someone who understands it'.[5] He also feared that many soldiers would lose their votes because of the confusion resulting from the constituency changes made in the Representation of the People Act. Northcliffe demanded that the returning soldiers receive a just reward. He explained to his brother Cecil, one of the Coalition candidates, that the men had been 'through horrors unspeakable, unwritable, unbelievable, and they must not be fobbed off with mere promises and speeches. I will see to it that they are not so treated.'[6] The *Daily Mail* labelled the land-for-soldiers issue a 'test question' for the voters and declared that, if money was able to be found to buy land for redistribution in Ireland in the past, surely the country could 'do no less for the soldiers of England, Scotland, and Wales'.

With official channels of propaganda closed after his resignation from the British War Mission, Northcliffe's publications gained a renewed importance as instruments to reflect his opinions. He also had more time to devote to them – particularly *The Times*. Thus began a struggle between the chief proprietor and the editor over election and peace issues which culminated in February 1919 with Dawson's resignation.[7] In July 1918 the newspaper agreed with Northcliffe's view of the election, but by late November it had become more conciliatory towards the government. Northcliffe had allowed *The Times* a semi-independent course during much of the war, but the disastrous result he foresaw moved him to inform Dawson that he did 'not propose to speak any more with two voices'.[8] He warned his editor that 'unless we speak now' Lloyd George would be influenced by men like Sir George Younger, who ran the 'party of wealth', into forming a reactionary government which would not allow the Prime Minister to carry out the reforms needed to prevent revolution. He told Dawson:

> There have been moments in history when *The Times* has rendered great service to the nation. You can render no greater service, in my judgement, than in asking the Prime Minister who are the men that the country is to be asked to vote for. Such a course will strengthen his hands. Surely, it is very simple, if he has the backbone to do it . . . If I have not made myself plain, then I am afraid I am incapable of coherence.[9]

Another issue over which Northcliffe and Dawson quarrelled was reparations, which became a major focus of the election. Despite the Prime Minister's increasingly anti-German statements during the course of the campaign, Northcliffe suspected that, after his victory at the polls, Lloyd George would make too lenient a peace.[10] He complained to Dawson that he had a great responsibility as chief proprietor of *The Times* and that the paper had 'lagged woefully' behind his other journals in pointing out that the Prime Minister was 'evading main issues' and acting in accord with the German financiers in Britain who sought to prevent Germany from having to pay for the war.[11]

In his early election speeches the Prime Minister had pledged that Germany should be forced to pay 'up to the limit of her capacity'. In the heat of the campaign this had been increased to 'the uttermost farthing' and 'until the pips squeak' by various Coalition figures. When it appeared that Lloyd George was wavering on the issue, Northcliffe

cabled him in Leeds. He had heard that the French had named a reparations figure for their own country and told the Prime Minister that 'the
public are expecting you to say definitely amount of cash we shall get
from Germany. They are very dissatisfied with the phrase "limit of her
ability" which . . . may mean anything or nothing.'[12] Lloyd George
responded, 'You are quite wrong about France. No ally has named
figure. Allies in complete agreement as to demand for indemnity. Inter-
Allied Commission will investigate on behalf of all on identical principles. Don't always be making mischief.'[13] However, the Prime Minister's
rhetoric in the following days moved closer to the position of the *Daily
Mail* and its proprietor, including a trial for the Kaiser and the 'fullest
indemnities'. At Bristol Lloyd George called for Germany to pay 'the
whole cost of the war', and the *Daily Mail* crowned it 'his best speech of
the campaign'.[14] Nevertheless, as the election moved into its last
week, the *Daily Mail* warned that the Prime Minister was still avoiding
many of the main issues. The paper cautioned its readers that the time
had come to 'pin the candidates down to a definite pledge' concerning
support for the points it had listed during the preceding weeks: speed-
ing the return of Britain's soldiers, a trial for the Kaiser, 'ample provision' for new houses, collecting a full indemnity from Germany, the
expulsion of enemy aliens, restrictions on German immigration, and
the reform of pensions and allowances.[15] By the end of the campaign,
the aims of the *Daily Mail* and the Coalition had become remarkably
similar. The final Coalition manifesto, published on 11 December, listed
five: punish the Kaiser, make Germany pay, get the soldiers home as
quickly as possible, fair treatment for the returned soldiers and sailors,
and better housing and social conditions.[16]

While electioneering came to an end in Britain, the Peace Conference
took shape in Paris. Arthur Willert alerted Northcliffe from Washington
of the developing problems concerning the Freedom of the Seas issue
(the second of Wilson's Fourteen Points) and of the general bad feeling
towards Britain. Louis Tracy, assigned to the British Bureau of
Information within the British War Mission in New York, seconded
these opinions and complained to Northcliffe about the planned
closing of his office.[17] Northcliffe opposed the rapid dismantling of the
British propaganda establishment that was being carried out at his
British Mission and at the Ministry of Information. He thought closing
the British Bureau in New York would be pure folly, replying to Tracy
that he had 'done his best in the matter, and I think something will be
done'.[18] After negotiation, the Foreign Office, which had resumed

control of propaganda, allowed the Bureau to operate for another six months. The 9 December 'Message From the Chief' suggested to the *Daily Mail* employees that 'Anglo-American relations are in a very delicate condition', and insisted on 'the utmost care being used in what we print both from and about the United States'.

Northcliffe also became involved in the question of whether Woodrow Wilson should take part in the Peace Conference. Some in America doubted whether it was proper for the President to attend, and also whether the Europeans would welcome him. Northcliffe replied to a telegram from E.L. Keen of the United Press that

> it would be unthinkable for us that Lloyd George would not be at the Peace Conference . . . It is apparent from cables that we are now getting that many citizens of the United States . . . object to the President's voyage. I can only say that we cannot comprehend that situation . . . if these conferences are held without President Wilson, the whole European world would think there was something very wrong indeed with these conferences.[19]

Northcliffe cabled Wilson, through the President's secretary, Joseph Tumulty, that it was 'unthinkable that the head of the United States should be absent' and that the 'fervour of his reception will exceed that of any foreign visitor on record'.[20] In December, the chief proprietor of *The Times* told his editor about the extraordinary greeting that Wilson received on his arrival in France. He also recorded the dissatisfaction in the President's entourage over the delay in starting the Conference, and the 'infinite harm' that was being done by the Prime Minister's tardiness in coming over, while the President was anxious to get to work.[21]

While waiting for the talks to begin, Colonel House proposed that Wilson should visit England. Northcliffe sent his strong approval of the idea to Balfour, who agreed with the potential importance of a visit by the President.[22] Northcliffe assured Lord Reading that, although some Americans believed Wilson would receive a chilly reception in Britain, he was sure the President would 'receive a very hearty welcome' and that a visit to England would 'be all to our benefit and . . . remove from the minds of the entourage any misapprehensions'.[23]

Before the President travelled to Britain on 26 December, House secured a Paris interview with Wilson for Northcliffe, printed in *The Times* and the *Daily Mail* on 21 December. The published version spent little time on weighty matters, but did report Wilson's view that the main business of the Conference was to 'create a safeguard against future wars'. Concerning the Freedom of the Seas issue, Wilson reassured Northcliffe that he respected Britain's 'peculiar position as an Island Empire'. Reading congratulated Northcliffe on his journalistic coup, stating that he 'liked its tone' and found it very 'valuable and opportune'.[24] On the other hand, Dawson, in whose absence the interview had been published, called it 'appalling'.

Preparations for the Peace Conference were interrupted by the announcement of the British election results at the end of December. In a decisive victory, 484 Coalition candidates were returned. Labour captured 59 seats, surpassing the Asquithian Liberals, who took only 26. The *Daily Mail*, reporting the 'Thumping Unionist Majority', commented that

> Sir George Younger, Lord Downham (Mr. Hayes Fisher), and Mr. Bonar Law have manoeuvred our gallant little Welsh wizard into a position in which he is almost entirely dependent on the votes of those whom he so vigorously denounced at Limehouse a few years ago. He is now at the mercy of his recent enemies. Will they cajole the Prime Minister, or will he cajole them?[25]

However, the paper discerned at least two bright spots in the result. First, the many seats lost by the Liberal old gang, including Asquith, and, second, the gains made by Labour. Though uneasy over the large number of Coalition reactionaries that had been returned, Northcliffe nevertheless felt there was a slim chance that something could still be salvaged from the situation. He confided in Rothermere that 'the Prime Minister has an immense opportunity, but I doubt he will take it. The country would support him in a clean sweep of the Old Gang people . . . The Foreign Office, Diplomatic and . . . Consular Services could be put right in three months.'[26] The *Daily Mail*, however, soon recounted the 'ugly rumours about' concerning the formation of an 'Old Gang Tory Cabinet . . . a tied Prime Minister, and the crack of the Tory whip'.[27]

The most ominous results of the election came from Ireland, where 73 Sinn Feiners were victorious. They did not take their seats in London, but those who were not in prison gathered instead in Dublin on 21 January 1919 as an Irish parliament, the Dáil Éireann, and declared an independent Irish Republic. The British newspapers were at first inclined to ridicule the event. *The Times* declared that the proceedings resembled a 'stage play at the Mansion House'. The *Daily Mail* commented that 'Whether Sinn Fein will perish either in a shriek of laughter or in a de profundis for the dead in a country where comedy and tragedy walk hand in hand none may prophesy.'[28] Soon, however, the tone of derision dissolved in the face of escalating violence.

Northcliffe had been ordered to rest by his doctors and, with the election behind him, prepared to depart for an extended stay in France. After a stop in Paris, his final destination was to be La Dragonnière, Rothermere's villa at Cap Martin, near Monte Carlo. Before leaving, he instructed the papers to take care in Anglo-American relations, to keep an eye on the demobilization delays, and to watch Ireland. The 7 January 'Message From the Chief' warned that in his place of birth there was 'cause for great anxiety. I am very certain that something will happen soon . . . to bring the Irish question before the world.' He had reason to believe that Viscount French, the Lord Lieutenant, whom the Irish Republican Army had tried to assassinate on 19 December, was preparing to extend martial law. The message went on that French, Northcliffe's former ally in the shells agitation of 1915, 'had the nerve to ask for the loan of one of my staff to act as military censor. If he starts shooting in Ireland, the noise of his machine-guns will travel to a far greater distance than he imagines. Hands should be sent to Ireland at once.'

When the membership of the new government was announced on 10 January, Northcliffe was appalled at most of Lloyd George's choices, even though they included Cecil Harmsworth, who was elevated from the Prime Minister's secretariat to a Foreign Office under-secretaryship. Unfortunately, in Northcliffe's view at least, political considerations had once again overridden all other factors. He complained to Andrew Caird, back at the *Daily Mail* and *The Times*, that the 'original plan was that the Prime Minister should go to the country on his own, forming a Government of 'All the Talents' and Parties . . . Then Sir George Younger stampeded the Prime Minister . . . even worse than what I foretold has happened. A Government that is a scandal has been formed.'[29] Disgusted with a timid article about the new regime, Northcliffe cabled Charles Beattie, night editor of the *Daily Mail*, at Carmelite House, 'No wonder people say they can tell the difference in the Daily Mail when I have left England.'[30]

Prominent among the new ministers who came in for immediate criticism was Winston Churchill, Secretary of State for War and Air. The recombination of the separate Air Ministry, which Northcliffe and his press had fought for tirelessly until its creation in late 1917, brought a sharp reaction. The 11 January *Daily Mail* warned that if 'we are to return to the chaos from which we were delivered in 1917 . . . this union under such a man as Mr. Churchill is asking for trouble, and is a sure cause of future mischief.' However, the press lord and his newspapers co-operated with Churchill over another issue: demobilization. Churchill curried favour by sending Northcliffe the details of his plan and the reasoning behind it. Northcliffe replied from the South of France that he would instruct his editors to give the 'first in first out' scheme all their support, and did so. This measure, seen as much more just than the original demobilization procedure, was successful in calming the troops.

Because he felt his unheeded calls for stronger criticisms had allowed Lloyd George a free hand in the creation of a reactionary Cabinet, Northcliffe's displeasure descended on Dawson at *The Times*. A letter to his editor reported that the French were 'amazed at the new Cabinet' and went on

> I am not given to saying . . . 'I told you so', but I saw the possibilities of the present deplorable Cabinet when I asked you to begin that campaign last summer.
>
> I blame myself greatly for my lack of vigour in regard to 'The Times' when I was ill at Elmwood in November and December. The sending of an emissary to me showed that George knew perfectly well that I was the only force that could stop his really timid nature . . . Never again will I allow myself to be overruled in a matter like that. I am very willing to be led in matters I do not understand, but I do understand character . . .
>
> By the appointment of my brother he has no doubt hopes of deflecting criticism through which I yet trust that I may be able to change the Government and avert a semi-Revolution in England. The giving of office, either to brothers or friends, will not move me to the extent of a single column or comma.[31]

Northcliffe was also out of patience with Dawson for his slackness in criticizing the delays in starting the Peace Conference. He gave an ultimatum:

> If you do not like my attitude, I beg you to do either one of two things – endeavour to see eye to eye with me, or relinquish your position. *The Times* could have accelerated the peace conference . . . Unless the peace conference can be speeded, I can assure you from my knowledge of what is going on among our troops in France that we may have serious trouble. My ownership and control of The Times are a great responsibility, and as long as I have health I will act up to that responsibility to the full. In the last three months I have, against my will and owing largely to the inertia of ill-health, fallen far short in my conception of my duty.[32]

To make matters worse, Northcliffe received reports from Rothermere and others concerning 'indiscreet' comments by Dawson to his circle of friends, most of whom, like Milner, were decidedly hostile to the press lord. The tenure of the editor of *The Times* was nearing its end.

Once the Peace Conference opened, in mid-January, Lloyd George found himself trapped between, on the one hand, the passionate demands of Clemenceau for a peace settlement which would cripple Germany and, on the other, Wilson's Fourteen Points, capped with a League of Nations to ensure the peace. The Prime Minister wished Germany again to become a major trading partner of Britain, but he was constantly reminded of his election pledges to make the enemy pay dearly. After Wilson returned from a visit to the United States in February, the important business of the Conference took place in the private meetings of the Council of Four, which added Vittorio Orlando of Italy to Clemenceau, Lloyd George and Wilson.

Sir Campbell Stuart and Steed became perhaps the two most important members of the Northcliffe newspaper team in Paris. While their owner recuperated in the South of France, Stuart joined the *Daily Mail* staff in Paris and became a liaison to all the Northcliffe newspapers. He kept in touch with such figures as House, who, Stuart informed his chief, had become 'as you foresaw, the real power of the Conference. Things are not going well, as Steed will have written you.'[33] The Colonel was particularly close to Steed, who became Northcliffe's principal source of information and his adviser on the complicated negotiations. Beginning in mid-January, the foreign editor of *The Times* sent his chief regular memoranda on the work of the Conference and also wrote almost daily leaders for the *Continental Daily Mail*. Northcliffe told Steed that, for the time being, the Paris *Daily Mail* was 'the most important newspaper in the world, because the English-speaking delegates would read it with their morning coffee'.[34] Steed had been for some time Northcliffe's counsellor on foreign affairs, which the Peace Conference brought to the forefront. He was also the man the proprietor of *The Times* had in mind to take over its editorship after Dawson, who refused to follow the line Northcliffe demanded and resigned officially in February. Stuart became the agent in the successful negotiations with Steed to assume the position. The new editor of *The Times* was far more philosophically in tune with, and more able to influence, Northcliffe than his predecessor. Steed was also more compliant – in fact fawning – in his relations with the press lord.[35]

During the conference, Steed allied himself with House and the

French when Wilson and his chief adviser split over compromises in the peace terms. Northcliffe sympathized with House, but still did not wish his newspapers to be overly critical of Wilson. Gordon Auchinloss, House's secretary at the Conference, was also in close touch with Steed. Auchinloss met Northcliffe in late March and recorded that they discussed 'the reparations matter, the Russian situation, the German territorial situation and Lloyd George's attitude towards the president's position'.[36] Auchinloss found Northcliffe 'very complimentary to the Colonel and the work that he has done'.[37]

Relocated from the South of France to Paris, in April Northcliffe became more directly involved in the press coverage of the Peace Conference. Other Americans present noted his activities. The journalist Ray Stannard Baker wrote that in mid-April House was 'still working with Clemenceau and Northcliffe and opposes Lloyd George, while the President works with Lloyd George – and finds Clemenceau his hardest opponent'.[38] The press lord remained anxious over reparations and the terms in general, and exhorted his newspapers to keep up the pressure on the Prime Minister. However, the feud with Lloyd George made it difficult for Northcliffe's correspondents to gain inside information. Consequently, the competition often scooped the *Daily Mail*, much to its owner's displeasure. An interview with a 'high authority' (widely believed to be Lloyd George) published in the 28 March *Westminster Gazette* made it appear that the Prime Minister was 'going soft' on reparations. Disturbed by this declaration, Northcliffe directed Marlowe to admonish Lloyd George to carry out his election promises and not to put the cost of war on the backs of the British people.[39] 'They Will Cheat You Yet, Those Junkers' once again became the battle cry of the *Daily Mail*. The newspaper's calls for a statement of the amount of reparations due to Britain infuriated the Prime Minister, who told Riddell that he would not 'state the terms' and complained of the 'disgraceful' attacks of the Northcliffe press, which, he said, called him a pro-German. He considered a libel action in the matter, but Riddell counselled against it. 'I shall certainly say in public what I think about Northcliffe,' continued Lloyd George. 'His action is due to vanity and spleen . . . His advice has not been asked about a single subject. I ran the election without him and I beat him. He is full of disappointment and bitterness.'[40] The Prime Minister had come to the view that the treaty should not state a total figure, but that the matter should be left to a reparations commission to decide.

The Prime Minister's course led an old newspaper associate of

Northcliffe's, Kennedy Jones, now an MP, to contact his former boss for advice and support. Though often dismissed as a 'satellite' of Northcliffe, Jones followed his own path, which reflected the unrest among many in the Commons who had made rather extravagant election pledges on reparations and were concerned at Lloyd George's hedging. After the publication of the *Westminster Gazette* article, Jones sought Northcliffe's opinion and the press lord recommended that the strongest possible protest should be made from Parliament. On 8 April, several hundred Members signed a telegram to Lloyd George asking for reassurances on reparations, and a furious Prime Minister saw Northcliffe behind the affair. The next day Northcliffe wrote to Jones that the Prime Minister was giving in to the pressure of German financial agents, who claimed the country would go Bolshevik if forced to assume a large debt. 'That he is being bluffed is obvious,' he declared.

> His entourage says that the reasons the Peace terms cannot be published is that the British Government would fall at once, as the people would realize they had been had . . . it is a deplorable thing that after all our sufferings and the sacrifices of all the gallant boys that have gone that in the end we should be beaten by financiers.[41]

Though it was widely believed that Northcliffe was hostile to President Wilson, he went on to tell Jones that Wilson should not be blamed, that he had tried to help and had even snubbed an Irish delegation, which would cost him votes. The continuing agitation for Ireland to be granted 'self-determination' in the same fashion as the other small states of Europe had gained considerable success in the United States, where the House of Representatives had passed a resolution of support. In Britain, finalizing a settlement with Germany temporarily overshadowed the violent Irish 'Troubles' which began in 1919.

Northcliffe's nephew Esmond Harmsworth was on Lloyd George's staff at the Peace Conference. His uncle wrote to him that he feared 'your chief is giving away the show. He always seems to be led by the nose by those who were at the bottom of the poll at the last election.'[42] When Northcliffe heard that Esmond's father, Rothermere, was going to see Lloyd George, he told his brother that he would be doing a great service if he gave the Prime Minister the truth about the national 'exasperation' caused by the many conflicting statements on the financial settlement.[43] He also sent a statement of his views meant for the eyes of Lloyd George. After his meeting with the Prime Minister, Rothermere visited Northcliffe at Fontainebleau. The two men played golf, and Rothermere attempted to make peace. His mission was a failure.

Rebuked in this latest attempt at reconciliation and fed up with Northcliffe's interference and criticism, Lloyd George returned from Paris to defend himself in the Commons, determined to 'declare war to the knife' and to follow through with his threats of a public statement.[44] According to Paul Mantoux – the interpreter and the only person taking notes at the Council of Four Sessions – before he left, Lloyd George told the Council that he had to return to London to face his critics on the reparations issue. He promised he would be back within a few days, 'unless the House of Commons refuses me its confidence, in which case it will be with Lord Northcliffe or Horatio Bottomley that you will be resuming these talks'.[45]

On 16 April, speaking on the subject of the Peace Conference, the Prime Minister brutally denounced Northcliffe in the Commons. Turning aside the *Westminster Gazette* article as the cause of the telegram from Parliament, Lloyd George instead blamed Kennedy Jones's instigation of the affair on the cable of a 'reliable source' (undoubtedly Northcliffe) in Paris. Without ever naming his target, the Prime Minister continued:

At the beginning of the conference there were appeals to everybody all around to support President Wilson and his great ideals. Where did these come from? From the same 'reliable source' that is now hysterically attacking all these great ideals . . . Reliable! That is the last adjective I would use. It is here to-day, jumping there to-morrow, and there the next day. I would as soon rely on a grasshopper.

Still I am willing to make some allowance . . . when a man is labouring under a keen sense of disappointment, however unjustified and . . . ridiculous the expectations may have been . . . [w]hen a man deludes himself, and all the people whom he ever permits to go near him into the belief that he is the only man who can win the War, and is waiting for the clamour of the multitude that is going to demand his presence there to direct the destinies of the world, and there is not a whisper, not a sound, it is rather disappointing; it is unnerving; it is upsetting.

Then the War is won without him. There must be something wrong. Of course it must be the Government. Then, at any rate, he is the only man to make peace . . . So he publishes the Peace Terms, and he waits for the 'call'. It does not come . . . Under these conditions I am prepared to make allowances; but let me say this, that when that kind of diseased vanity is carried to the point of sowing dissension between great Allies, whose unity is essential to the peace and happiness of the world . . . then I say that not even that kind of disease is a justification for so black a crime against humanity.[46]

During this denunciation, as he spoke the words 'diseased vanity', Lloyd George tapped his forehead to indicate Northcliffe's infirmity.

The Prime Minister ended his indictment with an apology for taking up the time of the House with the matter, which, he explained, was necessary only because he had been many weeks in France, where it was still believed that *The Times* was a 'serious organ' and it was not known it was 'merely a threepenny edition' of the *Daily Mail.* 'On the continent,' said Lloyd George, 'they really have an idea that it is a semi-official organ of the Government. That shows how long these traditions take to die out . . . This is my only apology for taking notice of that kind of trash, with which some of these papers have been filled during the last few weeks.'

The Prime Minister's performance was widely acclaimed, and Riddell reported that Lloyd George was in 'great spirits' afterward. Lord Robert Cecil remarked to him, 'I expect N. will burst.'[47] Not only had the occasion allowed the Prime Minister to strike at his chief press critic; the theatrics had enabled him to sidestep any detailed discussion of the peace settlement. Bonar Law commented a few weeks later that the attack had been 'very dexterous, but that the speech as a whole was open to serious Parliamentary criticism, had there been anyone to criticise'.[48] Besides the fact that the speech cleverly diverted the discussion away from the real subject, Bonar Law would have pointed out the Prime Minister's previous alliance with Northcliffe, the fact that he had appointed him to two offices, and that 'nothing had occurred warranting LG's change in attitude except the fact that N had the temerity to disagree with him'. Expecting an equally stinging response from *The Times* and its chief proprietor, Lord Esher told a confidant on 18 April that he believed the newspaper would survive the battle, but added melodramatically, 'No one can say what the result of the conflict will be that now opens between L. G. and Northcliffe.'[49]

However, the response of *The Times* under its new editor, Steed, was measured, and Northcliffe chose not to wage a public battle with the Prime Minister. At his chief's suggestion, Steed had travelled from Paris to witness Lloyd George's attack. He recalled that the Commons 'roared with delight' at the performance; however, in his opinion, the address 'showed no critical faculty whatever' and, in 'view of the gravity of the position in Paris', he found the 'spectacle hardly comforting'.[50] He reported back that the Prime Minister's attack was 'really beneath contempt. I thought the best way to treat him was to be dignified . . . and to give him better than he sent. From the number of letters I have received these tactics seem to have been successful.'[51] Northcliffe replied, 'Your handling of our Petty P. M. was perfect', and recommended the same course to his other journals.[52]

A month after the rather one-sided tilt with the Prime Minister, Northcliffe's role as critic of the Peace Conference came to an end when his failing health forced him to see a series of doctors about his throat. In their opinion, it was imperative that he have the adenoma that had developed on his thyroid gland removed as soon as possible. The surgery was successfully completed on 18 June. Ten days later, as he recovered, the Versailles Treaty with Germany was signed in Paris. Before returning home, the Prime Minister of Australia, W.M. Hughes, sent a note that 'I know your impatient spirit chafes, but for the sake of England and the Empire, rest and let Nature do her healing in her own way.'[53]

After weeks in bed recuperating, Northcliffe prepared to leave London for further rest in Scotland. He warned Marlowe at the *Daily Mail* that the 'satellites' of the Prime Minister were 'going about saying that we are anxious to apologise to him for our criticism which led to his "grasshopper" hopping. See to it that none of our people get near his press bureau . . . Downing Street is desperately anxious for our support, they approach me in every kind of way.' His attitude, he said, was not personal. When Lloyd George 'does what I think right I say so; when he does what I think wrong I equally say so'.[54]

With the Versailles settlement resolved, the stage was cleared for the next battleground between the press lord and the Prime Minister – a settlement for Ireland, where the violence intensified daily.

Apparently without his knowledge, 'satellites' of Northcliffe had also been making approaches to the Prime Minister. In July, Sir Campbell Stuart visited Riddell and offered to share *The Times'*s plan for Ireland (as well as the credit for any success) with Lloyd George. After Riddell had conveyed this message to the Prime Minister, he recorded that 'naturally L. G. laughed at this, as "The Times" had been running the question hard for weeks', but Lloyd George did agree to see Stuart when he returned to London. A week later Lloyd George and Riddell talked of Northcliffe. The Prime Minister enquired whether the owner of the *Daily Mail* was better, and Riddell told him that he was recovering slowly. Lloyd George declared that Northcliffe would have to

make up his mind what line he intends to take. If he goes on attacking me I shall have something more to say about him . . . Things that he will not like.

No one likes ridicule. If he and I have a reconciliation, what has happened will make him more careful in the future. He will know that he cannot attack me with impunity. I don't propose to allow matters to rest. I shall let the public know and fully realise that he is my enemy and that he is attacking me and my Government for personal reasons.[55]

Northcliffe had been warned to stay away from business for three to six months and then to limit himself to three days' work a week. Nevertheless, he directed a stream of messages to Steed, who drafted the Irish policy of *The Times*. Northcliffe pronounced himself happy with the paper and, consequently, told Steed the price could be maintained at 3d, to make the journal 'completely independent of advertising'.[56] He advised Steed that Sir Robert Hudson, a friend of the Northcliffes, had suggested he get the views of the colonial premiers on a settlement, and he added that the editor should stay in consultation with Hudson, who was 'on the extreme inside of politics'.[57]

Northcliffe also gave Steed his views on politics and finance. He blamed Britain's precarious financial position on the 'feeble figure-head Treasury', which continued to use mid-Victorian methods to raise money. To remedy this situation, he told Steed, there should be an 'explanatory propaganda to the people conducted by the ablest propagandists we have showing that they must spend nothing abroad, if possible, and send as much goods abroad as possible'. Its chief asserted that *The Times* should have a 'definite financial and political policy', and instructed Steed to 'draw up a group formula about the attitude of my newspapers towards the politicians, so that we each can give exactly the same reply in public affairs'. He planned to leave England for 'three moons', and asked for a copy of the policy before he departed.[58] The newspapers soon embarked on a 'Road to Ruin' anti-waste campaign which promoted British goods and called for government retrenchment and efficiency.

In mid-July Northcliffe suffered an attack of neuritis which, he told Steed, had given him the 'worst four days of his life'. Even morphine and opium had no effect on the pain. While he recovered from this latest reverse, on 24 July *The Times* published a four-column 'basis for a solution' of the Irish problem. The paper declared that, since the government had shown itself reluctant to make a statement on the issue, it offered the outline for peace freely as a starting point for discussion. The plan to replace the unimplemented Home Rule Act of 1914 proposed, as a first stage, the partition of Ireland into two states: one the historic province of Ulster in the north, and the other made up of the remaining three historic southern provinces. Each state would have its own legislature with full power over internal affairs and an executive branch answerable to the legislature. After this was accomplished, the paper suggested the creation of a joint all-Ireland parliament, with powers and responsibilities to be decided upon with 'utmost care'. In this federal system, each state legislature would have a veto in its domain over the application of legislation passed by the all-Irish parliament. A limited number of Irish MPs and peers would continue to sit in the parliament of the United Kingdom, which would retain considerable powers, including such matters as decisions of peace and war, defence, foreign relations and coinage. The responsibilities of the all-Irish parliament would include the collection of taxation, borrowing on the credit of Ireland, fixing and collecting customs and excise duties, land purchase, labour exchanges, national insurance and pensions, the post, telegraph and telephone systems, and education. The office of Lord Lieutenant was to be continued with powers similar to that of a Dominion governor-general, such as a veto on legislation. *The Times* printed its outline for a settlement with the full realization that it would undoubtedly be attacked, but nevertheless offered it in 'an earnest endeavour to point the way towards a just and generous solution of the Irish problem'.[59]

The next day the chief proprietor of *The Times* informed the editor that he had read the plan for Ireland twice and 'it could not have been better'. Northcliffe predicted that the Prime Minister's next step would be to drop the question. He instructed Steed to 'Push it. Report speakers and writers on it. From my knowledge of the Prime Minister he will resort to one of two courses – either say that we stole the scheme from him . . . or he will let the matter drop till we are forgotten and then take it up again.'[60] At the same time, Northcliffe wrote to Joseph Devlin, the Ulster leader, that he had heard through his brother Cecil that Devlin wished to see him, and that he regretted that his illness had prevented their meeting.[61] Devlin replied that he disagreed with the settlement proposed by *The Times*, but called it a 'bold and statesmanlike attempt to solve the problem'.[62] Irish sentiment outside Ulster and in the United States echoed Devlin. For example, the *Gaelic American* labelled the newspaper's plan 'Northcliffe's Fake Home Rule', a 'crazy quilt' of ideas taken from former Home Rule efforts to which the press lord had merely added a few of his own. Consequently, said the journal, the new plan had all the faults of the previous attempts, plus a few new ones.

The primary shortcomings were that it continued to insist on the supremacy of the English imperial parliament and divided Ireland into two parts with separate legislatures. The paper did, however, credit Northcliffe for having 'more courage than the British Government' in daring 'to propose a specific and immediate solution of the Irish Problems'.[63]

In the hope that the Prime Minister would adopt the *Times*'s plan, Sir Campbell Stuart had furnished advance copies to Riddell. He told Lloyd George's confidant that he had been holding back Northcliffe and Steed, who had wanted to publish sooner. Stuart also warned Riddell that *The Times* meant to attack the government for its inaction.[64] Lloyd George responded to further overtures in August, 'Is it war or peace? It must be one thing or another. I could not work with N. on his Irish policy if he were continually attacking me on other subjects.'[65] Stuart could give no assurances, but believed that, if Lloyd George took up the plan, the criticism would end or diminish. The Prime Minister was ready to resume his attacks on Northcliffe when he was recovered, and, in Riddell's view, it suited Lloyd George's purposes that it was known there was a 'blood feud', as it made the attacks of the newspapers seem personal.

In August, partly because of the action of *The Times*, rumours spread that Northcliffe was to be named Lord Lieutenant of Ireland. A letter to Steed from his chief noted the 'many paragraphs' which mooted the appointment. The rumours also stated that Northcliffe had recently bought the 'family mansion' in Ireland where he was born. Actually it was Cecil Harmsworth who recently had bought Irish property; Northcliffe had long owned his birthplace at Chapelizod. 'All these paragraphs,' Northcliffe told Steed, 'come from Downing Street.'[66] The editor replied that the 'Irish business is really biting deep, and if we can avoid tactical blunders I think we may get something done in the early autumn'. He went on that he personally was co-ordinating policy with the *Daily Mail*, and that Stuart was keeping an eye on the *Evening News*. A postscript added that 'in many quarters the P.M.'s remarks about our "unfriendliness" are thought to be an olive branch'.[67] Northcliffe wrote to his brother Cecil of the rumours of the Irish Lieutenancy, 'Does any human being imagine that I would compromise my power and independence by a footman's job like that?'[68] At the same time, in response to the warfare in Ireland, the government 'proclaimed' illegal both Sinn Fein and the Dáil and introduced new military units, the infamous 'Black and Tans' – hardened veterans who would use whatever means were deemed necessary to deal with the unrest.

Largely because of the Irish situation, Northcliffe was anxious about Anglo-American relations. Lord Grey of Fallodon (formerly Sir Edward Grey) agreed temporarily to replace Lord Reading in Washington. Though Northcliffe had been critical of Grey during the war, because of his age and failing eyesight, he was swayed by Colonel House's enthusiastic approval of the choice. Northcliffe wrote to Grey that he was 'grateful for the sacrifices' he was about to make, and went on that, since his first visit to the USA twenty-five years before, he had 'realised that our relations with its people are a paramount question. Labour troubles, economic questions, and the rest of our national worries may solve themselves, but on the other side of the Atlantic is a latent series of hostile elements that nullify the strong friendship and admiration felt for the British Empire in many . . . influential circles.'[69] He also wrote to George Sutton from Scotland that

> the crisis must come about Home Rule. Lord Grey has gone to America under the promise that Ireland will be dealt with before Christmas, then we shall see what we shall see. I have had little to do with the papers since I have been away, except to urge the Road to Ruin Campaign, which I shall continue. I am taking none of the Prime Minister's overtures, nor shall I mix up in any of Beaverbrook's rather clumsy wire pulling.

At the end of September Northcliffe returned south from Nairn by automobile with Lady Northcliffe – stopping at York and Lincoln, he reported, to 'ransack the antique shops'. Back in London, the two took up residence in their seventh town house, at 1 Carlton Gardens.

However far-fetched it might seem, Northcliffe had begun to worry that, if the Irish Question was not resolved, a conflict might break out between Britain and the United States. He told Edward Price Bell, of the Chicago *Daily News*, 'one way to avert war . . . is to give and enforce a reasonable settlement and spend at least ten million pounds in placing the settlement before the peoples of the United States, Canada and Australia'. The British government, he went on, was apathetic, indifferent and ignorant of the situation, and felt there was nothing to fear. Although he had urged the Foreign Office to set up a special section for American affairs, using knowledgable men like Sir William Tyrell and Sir William Wiseman, nothing had been done. He complained that 'having no personal influence with the Government, I am unable to do anything about the Foreign Office'. Even his own brother Cecil, Parliamentary Under-Secretary for Foreign Affairs, knew little. The situation, he believed, was comparable to twenty years before, when he had warned of a coming war with Germany which could not be averted. He wanted to avert this one. Northcliffe was glad Bell was an optimist, but, because of the shared British and American 'capacity for flare up', he believed:

> optimism on my part would be fatal for it would cause me and my news-papers to turn a careless eye towards anti-British manifestations which . . . if known here would cause a violent outbreak of public opinion . . . meanwhile I never cease to study the situation from half past six o'clock when I begin work until ten when I go to bed.[70]

Though Northcliffe complained that he had no influence at the Foreign Office, he continued to correspond with both Tyrell and Grey, to whom he recommended an American oculist. Tyrell told Northcliffe that he wanted to develop a relationship with the United States in which the Americans would seek British advice rather than having it obtruded upon them. In Tyrell's opinion, the United States was the only power that Britain need worry about. Unlike Northcliffe, he thought it a good thing that the British had very ostentatiously shut down their propaganda offices, because the Americans were very sensitive to Irish charges that a huge British operation continued. Tyrell preferred light 'cultural' publicity, and asked for Valentine Williams to help in this area. As an example of this light approach, he felt the recent visit of the Prince of Wales had been a public-relations triumph. He also discussed with Northcliffe the Versailles Treaty (and the League of Nations), which had run aground in the US Senate.[71] Northcliffe disagreed with Tyrell's analysis, telling Lord Robert Cecil that he was 'very unhappy about Anglo-American affairs, and am not at all influenced by the successes of our gallant little Prince of Wales in Canada, New York and Washington'.[72]

As his health gradually improved, Northcliffe took closer notice of his newspapers. Despite a booming circulation of well over 1 million copies, the *Daily Mail* drew his particular ire. He gave instructions that the writers' names were to appear on the contents bills, so that 'the punishment may fit the crime', and warned that he did not want the bills changed unless something extraordinary occurred – like 'Winston assassinating Lloyd George'. The 7 November 'Message From the Chief' attributed the impressive sales of the *Daily Mail* to 'momentum not excellence'. The paper, the owner continued, stood for nothing in particular and needed a policy. To return it to the vigour of its old crusading days, it also needed more distinctive news, as well as an infusion of talent among the staff and leader writers. The proprietor suggested that the paper come out for Free Trade and the enlightenment of labour through education, while taking a stand against government control, subsidies, doles and nationalization.

Spurred to action in part by public outrage at the escalating violence in Ireland, on 22 December 1919 Lloyd George introduced a settlement plan similar to that earlier put forward by *The Times*. This compromise 'Bill for the Better Government of Ireland' proposed separate parliaments for the twenty-six southern and six north-eastern counties, with a joint council to deal with some subjects. Irish representatives would continue to sit in the imperial parliament, and the British government reserved considerable power in financial and foreign affairs. Asked for his estimate of the proposal by Ralph Pulitzer for the New York *World*, Northcliffe responded that he believed that the Prime Minister's plan was 'based on sound principles'. He went on:

A temporary division of Ireland, much as I dislike the idea is probably the shortest path to eventual Union. The Commonwealth of Australia grew from separate colonies. So did the Dominion of Canada and the Union of South Africa. But the Government scheme is far from perfect. If Ireland is to be divided the historic province of Ulster should be a unit. The link of the proposed Irish Council might be made stronger. Why should it not be an Irish Congress or House of Representatives? The right of the Irish people to full fiscal autonomy should definitely be recognised. The scheme is however a beginning and I hope the Government will have the courage to go on.

At the same time, Northcliffe told Lord Reading that he was anxious about Anglo-American affairs and that Sir Edward Carson 'often advises me about my newspapers. I feel inclined to advise him to go to the United States, and make counter-propaganda. If he did so, they would then understand the justice of Dominion Home Rule for Ireland.'[73] Carson's view of the press lord is shown by a bit of 'blasphemy' he sent to Bonar Law a month later, 'The Northcliffe Creed':

So Northcliffe is *The Times*, Northcliffe is the *Daily Mail*, and Northcliffe is the *Evening News*.

And in this trinity neither is before or behind: and there is not top or bottom.

So that in all things as is foresaid: Northcliffe in three papers and three papers in Northcliffe must be worshipped.[74]

In the last days of the year Riddell, who had just learned that he had been recommended for a peerage, spoke to Lloyd George and once again their discussions turned to the owner of the *Daily Mail*. The Prime Minister said that 'he thought of bringing in a Bill which would allow a member of the House of Commons to attend and speak in the Lords in support of any Bill of which he might be in charge, and vice versa'. He went on, 'I shall attend and I shall write to Northcliffe telling him that I shall be there and that if he wants to challenge my actions that is the proper place and not from behind the hedge of a newspaper. I shall publish the letter, and people will know what to think if he fails to accept my challenge.' Riddell added that 'as he said this his eyes flamed as if Northcliffe had been in the room'.[75]

Though the Prime Minister might dream of a showdown with his press adversary in Parliament, he received no such satisfaction. In the new year the *The Times* and the *Daily Mail* continued their criticisms of the government's handling of worker unrest, the Irish problem and the reparations question, and gave Lloyd George fresh reasons to complain.

17

Strikes and Troubles, 1920–1921

AT THE END of January 1920 Cecil Harmsworth, worried about his brother's appearance, recommended that Northcliffe 'get a little sunshine into your blood before the summer comes and Home Rule, Bolshevism, falling exchanges and a tottering Government absorb your energies'.[1] The press lord took his advice. Before departing for the South of France, he instructed Lovat Fraser to keep up the anti-waste campaign aimed at government spending. Northcliffe told Marlowe that he was going away for air and rest, but was pleased to leave 'the business in a much better state than it has been for some years'. He feared, however, that difficult times might be approaching, and instructed the editor of the *Daily Mail* to 'consult closely' with Steed, whose opinion would prevail, 'so that there may be no dissonance in the views of my newspapers – views for which I am publicly held responsible'.[2]

He was certainly held responsible by the Prime Minister, who, according to Riddell, continued to be 'obsessed by Northcliffe and his villainies'. In Riddell's opinion, the Prime Minister's problems lay in his failure to provide the 'fit country for heroes' he had promised in the 1918 election. Riddell told Lloyd George, 'The British people are not fools. They judge by results. You have been ruined by the failure of your housing scheme. If you could wave a magic wand and produce 200,000 houses, Northcliffe's criticisms would not matter.'[3] Sir Campbell Stuart told Riddell that Northcliffe was also obsessed with the quarrel and was determined to topple Lloyd George. Because of this he was supporting the Labour Party. Stuart believed that if the King could be persuaded to offer his chief the Lord Lieutenancy of Ireland, Northcliffe might accept. This, said Stuart, 'would gratify his ambitions and form a bridge for reconciliation'. The following day Riddell told Lloyd George of this conversation and was surprised that the idea was not immediately ridiculed. On the contrary, the Prime Minister seemed seriously to contemplate the notion, although he mentioned he was also considering another attack on the press lord.[4]

Once the stresses of the war were lifted, relations improved between Northcliffe and Haig, whom a grateful nation had rewarded with an earldom and £100,000. When the former Commander-in-Chief visited Broadstairs, Northcliffe offered him 'the first and only honorary membership of the North Foreland Golf Club'. Haig accepted the gift, and wrote to Northcliffe in the South of France that he hoped they could play together soon and that 'he was able to enjoy things notwithstanding the politicians and the Budget'.[5] The Earl became the leader of the British Legion, a national association of war veterans, behind which Northcliffe put his newspapers. At the same time, another military ally and antagonist, Lord Fisher, passed away. Cecil Fisher sent a note of thanks to the chief proprietor of *The Times* for the newspaper's 'truly beautiful and moving account' of his father's funeral. Northcliffe replied that the Admiral had been 'an old and a greatly valued friend of mine; and I shall always think of him with deepest affection'.[6]

Another wartime associate, the Australian journalist Keith Murdoch, sent a note before he left England for a visit home, to

> express something of my gratitude to you for all you have been to me and done for me since I came here, four years ago. I will not say more than you have been the biggest influence and the biggest force over me here; largely on account of the many kindnesses you have shown me, but even more largely from the example I have steadily seen in you and the standard you have set me. I am certainly coming back, but if I never met you again I would retain this influence to the end of my life.[7]

Among the many wartime reminiscences published in 1920 was the *Diary of Sir Ian Hamilton*, which attempted to rehabilitate Hamilton's reputation and in doing so dealt rather harshly with Murdoch's actions in 1915, at one point stating 'Murdoch must be mad.' The journalist requested that Northcliffe answer for him in *The Times* and the *Daily Mail*. Northcliffe replied succinctly, 'Book dead but will expose in Mail.'

By April 1920 the post-war boom that the British economy had enjoyed, outside a few industries like coal, began to evaporate alongside the success of the legerdemain practised by Lloyd George to avert work stoppages. A recovering world market and the inefficiencies found in many ageing British industries only worsened the situation. In the face of mounting inflation, trade-union calls for nationalization were transformed into demands for higher wages that brought widespread industrial action, which included the Northcliffe enterprises. The following period was marked by increasing numbers of strikes, as well as growing unemployment, which would not again fall below 1 million until the next world war. The continued international haggling over reparations further complicated Britain's economic malaise. Germany had been given an initial bill of £1,000 million to be paid while a reparations commission considered the total due, finally assessed in April 1921 at £6,600 million. Though Lloyd George had made bellicose noises on the subject during the 1918 election, he believed that, to remain a viable trading partner for Britain, the former foe should not be treated too harshly. Northcliffe had called for continuing a complete embargo on German goods, but before long the realities of international trade softened his stance too. He told Harold Hardy, proprietor of a London importing firm, that his 'feeling about Germany is that we must take one of two courses – trade with her and press for reparation, or boycott her and abandon any hope of reparation. We cannot have it both ways. I am reluctantly in favour of trading with her.'

In late May, Lords Northcliffe, Riddell and Burnham presided at the ceremony opening the Printers' Sanatorium. Riddell recorded that Northcliffe was friendly as usual, but did 'not look well. He says he suffers from a cough and cannot stand the dampness. He has grown very stout.' Riddell felt very sorry to see him 'so much under the weather in regard to his health. He is very plucky about it, but evidently thinks he is seriously ill.'[8] Continuing health problems led Northcliffe to consult Sir James Mackenzie, a renowned authority on the fatigue and exhaustion that plagued him. He reported to Stuart that Mackenzie had told him 'if I go slow and rest in the afternoon, I shall last a long time'.[9] He felt well enough by mid-June to attend a landmark performance by Dame Nellie Melba. Always interested in new technology, Northcliffe and the *Daily Mail* arranged for Melba to give the first radio concert from the Marconi wireless transmitting station at Chelmsford. He wrote to the diva that her appearance was a 'triumph' and that at the parties afterwards (though he seldom attended such events) there was unanimous applause.[10]

There was more party-going, and party-giving, by the Northcliffes in the summer of 1920 than there had been for some time. Sir Robert Horne and Arthur Lee – created Lord Lee of Fareham at the end of the war – attended a large dinner party at 1 Carlton Gardens in June. Northcliffe told Ruth Lee that Horne, recently appointed President of the Board of Trade, was the 'only politician I ever allow in my house'. As her husband was in the government as head of the Board of Agriculture, she took this as a compliment, recording that Northcliffe replied, 'Yes. Of course he is not a politician, and never has been.'[11] Margot Asquith wrote to Northcliffe the next month that she 'would like to know what you really think of the Government you created – I hear you had a delightful party the other night, but you never asked me!'[12] Mrs Asquith, whom the press lord loathed as cordially as she did him, had recently sold her autobiography and complained to Northcliffe that the publishers had not advanced her what she thought the book was worth. To drum up publicity, she suggested a *Daily Mail* interview.

That summer, labour problems, particularly in the coalfields, commanded the attention of the nation. In June, a demand by the miners for increased wages raised the spectre of a general strike by the Triple Alliance of miners, railwaymen and transport workers. Northcliffe believed no compromises should be made to such 'blackmail', and his papers called for a 'fight to the finish'. The press lord advised Sir Robert Horne that his 'provincial reporters, without exception, say that the miners are convinced that at the last moment the Government will back down. I do not know whether the Government proposes to give in. It has that kind of reputation and it is unfortunate that the colliers should be imbued with this belief.'[13] In reply Horne assured him that the government would not 'give way rather than fight' and that it appeared the miners would have to accept a 'serious rebuff'. He added that he would like to 'express my great admiration of the notable services which your Press has rendered to the stability of public opinion at the present time'.[14]

After two false alarms, the threatened coal strike finally began on 16 October. Attacks on the government response in *The Times* and the *Daily Mail* brought a predictable reaction from the Prime Minister. Riddell recorded:

LG very critical about Northcliffe's actions, which he says make negotiations of this sort very difficult. He said: 'What is Northcliffe at? Is he veering over to the Labour party?' . . . Referring again to Northcliffe, LG said, 'Has he really been ill?' I said, 'Yes, he has had a swelling in his neck which has had to be removed.' LG remarked, 'He has also got a swollen head. It is a pity they did not remove that too!'[15]

The other members of the Triple Alliance voted to strike in support of the miners on 24 October, but a tough government stance – including the passage of an Emergency Powers Act which harkened back to the DORA wartime regulations – kept the railwaymen and transport workers from joining the action. The coal strike was settled, at least for a time, on 28 October. After he had met Northcliffe in the following month, Riddell found the Prime Minister much interested in their discussion; however, both Stuart and Riddell believed a reconciliation between their chiefs was impossible.[16]

From the United States, Northcliffe received word on the presidential election. With Wilson out of the race, the campaign pitted the Democrat James Cox against the Republican Warren G. Harding. Bullock reported that the Hearst press was claiming that an army of well-financed propagandists, led by Northcliffe, was supporting Cox. The headlines read, '10,000 Agents Left Behind By Propaganda Chief of British Empire.'[17] Herbert Fowler, who had designed two golf courses for the press lord in the UK, warned that Cox was making inflammatory remarks about Ireland, including that there should be an Irish seat in the League of Nations. Should Cox win and this policy be implemented, the 'logical conclusion', said Fowler, 'would be a war between Great Britain and the United States'.[18] After Harding had been elected, Northcliffe replied to Fowler that he had urged the British government to spend £10 million to 'deny the more outrageous lies' being spread in the United States. Unfortunately, he said, some of the 'lies' were true.[19]

In an effort to further Anglo-French relations, which he felt were suffering because of the reparations question, Northcliffe gave an interview in Paris to the *Journal des débats*, published on 20 November. To counter the belief that the British government was unsympathetic to France, he suggested that 'a constantly sitting Anglo-French Council would be wiser than these hurried and theatrical San Remo and Spa gatherings'. He also asserted that the newspapers friendly to the Lloyd George government 'do not represent British public opinion'. More important were the millions of Britons who had been in France and knew the sacrifices the country had made. He called for 'uncompromising firmness' from France at the next reparations meeting, asserting that unless France is firm I foresee more trouble. Germany *can* pay and *will* pay. Our Government has promised to search their pockets. Instead of which, so far as England is concerned, it is the pocket of the unfortunate British taxpayer that is being searched . . . Whatever our Government may suggest, we people in England are determined that prosperous Hun financiers and manufacturers, the countless war Boche profiteers should pay.

Turning to British domestic affairs, Northcliffe went on that the country had been occupied with Ireland and the miners' strike. The latter had now been settled, he said, 'without any bitterness on either side, without the loss of a life'. In his opinion, the labour extremists in Britain 'amount to nothing'. About Ireland – 'our other and much more difficult preoccupation' – he found that much that he read in France was half-truth. A solution would be much closer, he asserted, if the government had devoted one or two Cabinet members to the problem full time, in the manner of a Secretary of State in other matters. Instead, 'To-day Ireland, according to the Prime Minister, is in a state of war.' Three hundred had been killed and 500 wounded in the last month, mostly Irish police and Sinn Fein, although innocents had perished as well. Northcliffe felt that a settlement by force would only be 'provocative of bitterness that would extend to all the Irish communities of the United States, Canada and Australia, a bitterness that would last for years'. Unlike some, he did not despair of a settlement, for he claimed that the extremists were not entirely in control and there was a 'vast body of moderate Sinn Feiners who wish for Ireland something like the Government of Canada'. The interview ended with an old theme: that the press lord was a great believer in the future economic development of Ireland and looked a little further than those who merely saw 'endless bloodshed and turmoil'.

Lloyd George viewed Northcliffe's support of France in the reparations arena as dangerous interference. When Derby remarked that he was going to visit Northcliffe in an attempt to raise money to bring French soldiers to Britain as visitors, the Prime Minister reacted violently. Calling the owner of the *Daily Mail* 'a damned scoundrel', he declared that Northcliffe was 'doing his best to make mischief between France and Gt Britain, and has been trying to do so for months past. I don't mind what he says about home politics, but when it comes to stirring up international strife, that is another matter.'[20] In an attempt to weaken *The Times*, Lloyd George fed special political intelligence to the *Daily Telegraph*.

Back in London, Northcliffe confronted worker demands at

Carmelite House. On 25 November he told union leaders that if any action took place 'the directors, immediately, and with the deepest regret, well aware of the suffering that it will entail upon you and your families, will issue legal notice to terminate all contracts throughout the building and will stop the publication of our four newspapers. This is not a threat. I never threaten. It is a fact.'[21] The next month the National Union of Journalists put forward new demands, including increased wages and a system of staff grading which Northcliffe labelled 'degrading'. The scheme, he declared, would bring journalism down to 'jam factory level'. *Daily Mail* articles reiterated that the paper would be shut down if necessary, and called the union plan 'Jam Factory Journalism'. A settlement satisfactory to both sides was reached three months later without a work stoppage.

Newspaper labour relations were also troublesome on the Continent. The printers of several journals, including the *Continental Daily Mail* and the Paris edition of the New York *Herald*, demanded higher wages. Northcliffe told Frank Munsey, the proprietor of the *Herald*, that 'presuming on our generosity your printers and mine' were 'demanding still further money'. Since they were already paid much more than French printers, he vowed that he would shut down his papers rather than be 'further blackmailed'.[22] At the Paris office, he told a delegation of workers that, if they had come to discuss increased wages, there was 'nothing doing . . . I have neither the nerve nor the desire to go back to London and tell our shareholders that men who receive the highest rate of pay in France now want even more money.'[23]

At Printing House Square, late 1920 saw disagreements between the chief proprietor and the chairman, John Walter. The first occurred over the appointment of Sir Campbell Stuart as managing director of *The Times*. Northcliffe championed Stuart as a replacement for Andrew Caird. Walter claimed that the newspaper had a valid agreement with Caird; however, in October 1920 Caird was reassigned and Stuart took his place.

The other divergence of opinion came over Ireland. Accusations that the paper had reversed its long-held policy and swung around to sympathy for Sinn Fein hurt circulation and led to threats on the chief proprietor's life. After a photograph of Northcliffe with a bullet hole through the forehead was delivered to him at *The Times*, he engaged an armed escort. A 30 November article in the paper condemned the policy of reprisals by the Black and Tans, declaring that everywhere in Ireland the cry was heard, 'if only the people of England knew'. The piece asked, 'Why are servants of the Crown charged with pillage and arson and what amounts to lynch law, and even with drunkenness and murder? How can the reign of terror be stopped?' The next day, Walter wrote to Northcliffe:

> Is not the present a favourable opportunity for the paper to reconsider its attitude towards Ireland? I allude not so much to its policy as its tone, which has been creating an impression for some time past that we are more anxious to damage L.G. than to see his Government achieve a settlement with the Irish. I believe this attitude is losing the paper its authority as well as its readers. It does not appear to carry its former weight in Irish affairs, either with the Government or the opposition.[24]

Steed informed Northcliffe that Walter was 'working steadily against you, the paper and me' and reconfirmed his own loyalty. 'No one', he went on, 'shall succeed in making bad blood between us, as many people would like to do.'[25]

Northcliffe was convinced that the paper's policies across the board were correct and should not be altered. *The Times*, he told its employees, was pursuing causes

> temporarily distasteful to the unthinking public. We are for friendship with the United States, and nine out of ten people say 'Damn the Americans. Let them mind their own business.' Then again, we are supposed to be in sympathy with Sinn Fein. We support the League of Nations, which most people are bored by and do not believe in. Our sometimes tactless pinpricking of the Prime Minister has created the impression . . . that we have a personal vendetta against him. Yet I believe that we must maintain our policies. They are right.[26]

However, while Northcliffe's other publishing interests thrived, the circulation figures of *The Times* had fallen to the lowest point in years as costs continued to climb. The proprietor warned Steed to prepare for reductions. Telling Stuart that the only thing that ever moved the staff of *The Times* to efficiency was fear, he announced to the employees on 11 December that

> Not the four thousand square miles of Newfoundland, with my ships and railways, social problems of the increasing population; nor the Paper Mills at Gravesend; nor the Amalgamated Press with seventy publications; nor the *Daily Mail*, whose circulation has increased even in the month of December, cause me even one featherweight of annoyance. Some day there will come a limit to my capacity to stand *The Times* annoyance.

Before leaving on doctor's orders to rest in France, Northcliffe told Steed that he was preparing himself for one final endeavour to 'get *The Times* situation right'. He added that he was considering transferring his 'obligation to other shoulders – the best that I can find in the interests of the paper. I am looking around.' Meanwhile, the paper 'must cut its coat according to its cloth and set out to get features that will overcome its partially necessary unpopularity. It must be a lesser anxiety to me than it is.'[27] The same month, as per their agreement, Walter informed Northcliffe that Sir John Ellerman, who already owned the third largest block of shares after Northcliffe's and Walter's, had approached him about buying more. The chief proprietor had no objections, since it would not affect their agreement as to control. This small sale, amounting to only 10,700 of Walter's 225,700 shares, fed rumours that there was a power struggle going on within *The Times*.

At the same time, Northcliffe began to plan for group action among the leading proprietors should the national plague of strikes hit the newspaper industry, as appeared likely. A 19 December note invited Lords Beaverbrook, Burnham, Riddell and Rothermere, as well as Sir Henry Dalziel, Edward Hulton and William Berry (later Lord Camrose), to 'simple repast and pow wow' at 1 Carlton Gardens. At the meeting four days later, those present discussed the 'eventualities which seem to be upon us'.[28]

Beaverbrook was also in attendance that month at a dinner at Bonar Law's London home, where the conversation turned once again to the possibility of Northcliffe going to Ireland in an official capacity. Also present at this affair was Hamar Greenwood, since April the Chief Secretary for Ireland. Lloyd George was asked who would be made Viceroy after the Government of Ireland Bill, about to become law, came into force. The Prime Minister, with a straight face, replied:

Northcliffe, the most eminent Irishman living. He has all the qualities for the post. He would not do at a time like this, but he would do well in the role of a great pacifier. He is energetic and can make himself very pleasant. Furthermore, he has no history at the back of him which would tend to dim his efforts. He would come fresh to the task.

Lloyd George later told Riddell that Beaverbrook's jaw dropped, as he had expected an attack on Northcliffe. When Bonar Law asked whose leg the Prime Minister was pulling, he replied, 'No one's! I am perfectly serious.'[29] Though, to Riddell, Lloyd George explained away this episode as a joke, two weeks later Derby sent a message to Northcliffe in Paris that 'the authorities' were still hoping to designate him Lord Lieutenant.

In America, Warren Harding's election victory had doomed any slim chance which remained for the Versailles Treaty and the League of Nations to be accepted by the United States. As an alternative, the President-elect suggested in early 1921 that the great powers confer on disarmament and the Far East and Pacific questions. Japanese naval building and territorial ambitions troubled both the USA and Britain, whose alliance with Japan was due for renewal. The New York *Herald* cabled Northcliffe to see how such an idea would be received. He replied, 'Even if League of Nations should be utter failure, which I don't anticipate, and if United States should definitely decide against any participation in any combination of nations for purpose securing peace of world, which I don't discuss, agreement between principal states of world for that purpose might be next best.'

However, the idea of Britain being rendered more vulnerable in a hostile world by reducing her fleet had little appeal to Northcliffe, who came into conflict over naval matters with a wartime associate, Josephus Daniels, the US Secretary of the Navy. When Northcliffe heard that Daniels was promoting the continuation of American shipbuilding against a possible hostile combination, he remarked 'perhaps some Washington correspondent will give my love to Mr. Daniels and ask him to name his combination'. The London office of the Associated Press passed along a response from Daniels, who commented that he was glad to have heard from Northcliffe and feared he had reacted to reports that he was going to recommend three more years of building if the USA was certain to stay out of the League or any other association of nations. The 'only basis to peace', he went on, was 'to have all nations come in as a buttress in the world against evil'. The cable ended with the comment that Northcliffe was 'a good fellow. We are fellow newspapermen [Daniels had been in the newspaper business before he entered government service] only he is rich and I am poor. He has a lot of mighty fine ideas.'

In answer, Northcliffe released a signed statement that gave his views on disarmament, for which he said he had sympathy, but which, because of past experience, he distrusted. However, he thought a proposed naval shipbuilding holiday might have merit, if public opinion could be mobilized behind the idea as the world's press was presently trying to do. He went on that 'the chief thing is to avoid disappointment for that breeds suspicion'. Any discussions would have to take place in an environment of friendly fairness and good faith, with 'all the cards on the table'. He believed this possible between Britain and the USA, which, he explained, was why he had 'asked Mr. Daniels to name any combination to which Great Britain could possibly be a party against the United States'. If Britain's Japanese allies were building warships for use against the United States, said Northcliffe, they were 'lacking in sense of proportion'.[30] Daniels responded to this that he had never said that there was a possible combination against the USA, did not care to enter into a long-distance controversy with Northcliffe, and agreed with Lloyd George's latest statements, that all nations must disarm together. The Secretary of the Navy reiterated his position: that the best solution would be for all nations to enter the League of Nations, including his own.[31]

Besides the war of words with Daniels, Northcliffe also entered into a conflict with Lord Lee of Fareham, his old friend and ally in aviation and other matters and, after February 1921, First Lord of the Admiralty. An article, 'The New Press Gang', in the 18 December 1920 *Outlook*, owned by Lee's sister-in-law, so infuriated the press lord that he gave instructions that none of his people were to communicate with the family. In a letter to Sir Robert Hudson, Northcliffe called Lee a 'parasite [who] attacks me in this journal kept by his wife's money'.[32] He informed Lee that he did not consider the article 'within the bounds of friendly criticism' and, since Lee was a director of the journal, he withdrew an invitation to the Lees to join him at Roquebrune in France.[33] Lee, who had just arranged to turn over his house, Chequers, to the nation and, along with his wife, had planned to spend some time in France with the Northcliffes, replied that he regretted that Northcliffe had sent 'such an insulting message to an old friend'. He claimed he had had no connection with *Outlook* since 1919, when his sister-in-law had turned over its direction to the editor pending its sale. He had therefore not seen and took no responsibility for the article in question, and declared himself amazed at Northcliffe's 'gross discourtesy – not merely to me, but to my wife who has honoured you with her loyal and gentle friendship for nearly fifteen years'.[34] Northcliffe's refusal to accept this explanation led to another letter from Lee stating that he had given the 'true facts', but that his former friend had chosen to repeat a 'contemptible lie' and therefore had brought their acquaintance to an end.[35] These seemingly irrational quarrels with Daniels and Lee – two friends of some years' standing – indicate a marked deterioration in Northcliffe's judgement, and a touchiness also reflected in his relations with Printing House Square.

By this time Northcliffe harboured serious doubts concerning

Steed's capabilities as editor of *The Times*. Steed had been ill, and his chief recommended a golf vacation cure. Steed's companion, Madame Clémence Rose, thanked Northcliffe for his concern and advised him to 'unburden yourself if you can. Your burdens would be too much for two giants.'[36] Northcliffe replied that he was delighted Steed had gone on holiday and recommended another rest at Easter. About his own health, he told Madame Rose that 'the doctor says I have not been better than I am now for a long time, that my blood pressure is good and has almost quite recovered'. He admitted that he worried about *The Times*, but explained that this was because he was one of the few people who understood the real situation. He planned to return soon from the Riviera to give the paper a 'little push'. The worst part, he continued, was that the 'advertisers do not get a response to their announcements. This is bad because they all belong to one or two associations and tell each other.'[37] The general economic depression was reflected in a drop in advertising revenues, and plans were laid to reduce the size of all the papers, and perhaps prices as well. Northcliffe, however, told Sutton not to cut the price of the *Daily Mail*, unless the *Daily Telegraph* cut its price.[38]

To discuss the difficult times facing the nation, Northcliffe called a meeting at the end of January 1921 which included Lords Desborough, Reading and Rothermere, as well as Sir Auckland Geddes, Sir Robert Horne, Keith Murdoch and Lovat Fraser. Afterwards, Northcliffe informed Bullock in the USA that he had had 'two long talks' with Geddes, who had replaced Grey in Washington as ambassador, and was 'very pleased to find that we have in the US a man who can talk and think American'.[39] The two had spoken of the Japanese-controlled Island of Yap (which the Americans considered a key cable-station site), Anglo-American oil concerns, the US fleet and Ireland. Soon after this, Northcliffe said goodbye to Reading, who had given up his duties as Lord Chief Justice to become Viceroy in India. Northcliffe told Bullock that this would be 'a great loss to this Government, which is obviously beginning to crack'. Bullock sent better news from New York. Northcliffe was pleased to hear that Charles Evans Hughes, the US Secretary of State, had privately made reassuring statements regarding Anglo-American relations and, according to Bullock, had authorized a cable to the Prime Minister that harmony was a 'paramount consideration'.[40]

Just as the American situation seemed more promising, the reparations question once more reared its head. The chief proprietor of *The*

Times believed that Germany, already in default for the initial £1,000 million owed, was taking advantage of the general economic downturn to escape restitution. He sent Stuart an article in a series he proposed called 'Germany Shamming Dead: The Facts From Inside'. He hoped that the articles would have two effects: to 'stiffen' the Prime Minister for the reparations conference the next week and to 'awake our workers to the real situation'.[41] He cabled Marlowe from France, 'Suggest strong leading article urging tariff against forthcoming huge dump German goods as indicated in our Shamming Dead revelation. Such tariff only way to prevent general unemployment.'[42]

Problems at the War Office Air Ministry came to Northcliffe's attention in early 1921. By this time the Royal Air Force had dwindled from being the largest in the world at the war's end to three squadrons, while France maintained forty-seven. When Churchill moved to the Colonial Office from the War Office on 14 February, *The Times* commented that he left 'the body of British flying at that last gasp when a military funeral would be all that would be left for it'. Chalmers Mitchell, who had briefly worked for Northcliffe at the Enemy Propaganda operation, sent a memo which charged that the Air Ministry was divided into a 'starved civilian section' under Sir Fredrick Sykes and a military section under Air Marshal Trenchard, where, he alleged, millions were wasted.[43] Mitchell believed Sykes should be encouraged, because civilian aviation could be made self-supporting and it would be more efficient for its craft to be diverted into military purposes, if need be, than vice versa.

Northcliffe also stayed abreast of Irish developments. A letter from Roquebrune to Archibald Kerr, the British agent at Tangier, commented that

> As for our part of the world, Ireland, with its abominable effect on American and Australian opinion, is the thing that really matters . . . Many private nego-tiations with Sinn Fein take place, but all have synchronised with unfortunate incidents which have abruptly stopped *pourparlers* . . . The unfortunate Greenwood is what the Americans call the 'goat' of the piece – no authority, and all the blame.

Northcliffe reported that the Irish Secretary had come

> to see me in London last week and has become an ancient man in the last three or four months. I suggested that hanging six young men at intervals of two hours on the same day was hardly good propaganda in view of our great difficulty with the United States (which was the cause of Auckland Geddes

sudden appearance in London). Greenwood replied that he could only get one executioner, an Englishman who could not come very often, so that the four executions had to be hurried forward in order to suit the hangman's convenience. Thus we are governed.[44]

While Northcliffe rested in France, the British government was considerably altered. Bonar Law used his health as an excuse to retire, and was replaced by Austen Chamberlain as leader of both the Conservative Party and the Commons. Sir Robert Horne succeeded Chamberlain at the Exchequer, while Stanley Baldwin, for several years the Financial Secretary to the Treasury, replaced Horne at the Board of Trade. Steed reported from London that, within half an hour of the announcement of Bonar Law's retirement, Chamberlain had sent an emissary to Printing House Square to ascertain whether *The Times* would support him as Conservative leader. In the editor's opinion, since there seemed to be 'no one else in the running', Chamberlain was entitled to the job and, further, Steed passed on the good news that the whole episode had upset the Prime Minister, who was not 'at all happy with the idea of working closely with Austen'.[45] Northcliffe commented to Kerr that

> We have a small ripple of excitement in the political stream at home. Bonar Law has been threatening to retire for a long time, is said to have found the Russian agreement more than he could swallow. There is a fine piece of film work in the House of Commons as a result – the PM in tears; Asquith heavy with grief. Bonar, who is here, looks extremely well.

In the spring of 1921 the Harding administration named Northcliffe's friend George Harvey as ambassador to the Court of St James. Not surprisingly, *The Times* lauded the selection. Its chief proprietor and others suggested that a parliamentary reception be arranged for the diplomat, in the interests of Anglo-American amity. Northcliffe told George Lambert MP, another who backed the idea, that Harvey was an able man who understood and liked England, and had been appointed despite the fact that he had made enemies in both American parties with his pen. Harvey was a Democrat in a Republican administration of which, Northcliffe feared, 'we shall be asking favours very soon'.[46] Northcliffe shared his good estimation of the new ambassador with Cecil Harmsworth at the Foreign Office. The Under-Secretary assured his brother that he agreed with his assessment, and pledged to work for 'most friendly relations with him'.[47] Harvey, Northcliffe told Riddell, had 'immense influence with the President' and was coming to England for what the press lord believed was 'the most difficult period in Anglo-American relations since the Venezuela Affair'.[48] The following month, Northcliffe and his wife gave a welcoming party for Harvey at 1 Carlton Gardens.

The potential for disaster represented by the many Americans visiting the Irish war zone worried Northcliffe. He wrote to Greenwood from France that the friends of England in the United States were 'very anxious lest any Americans, other than those actually engaged in the rebellion, be killed'. He went on that such an event would play to the 'immense publicity' given to Ireland in the USA. Greenwood replied that he would do all he could to avert such a 'catastrophe', and added that he wanted to see Northcliffe on his return.[49] In April the suggestions that the press lord should go to Ireland as Lord Lieutenant were brought to an end when, in a conciliatory gesture, Lloyd George appointed Lord Edmund Talbot, the first Roman Catholic selected for that post, and made him Viscount Fitzalan. That month Northcliffe and his wife visited Sir John Cowans, who was staying in France nearby and dying of cancer. Cowans, Northcliffe told Stuart, was 'a very old friend, and his condition casts as black a shadow over this beautiful region as does the coal trouble in England'.[50]

On 1 April 1921 Britain's coal miners again went out on strike, when the wages agreement made the previous October and government control of the industry both ended and the owners implemented wage cuts. To link wages to profits, the miners' settlement plan called for the creation of a National Wages Board to draw on revenues from a 'national pool' of coal-mining revenues. Once again the spectre of a general strike moved the government to invoke the Emergency Powers Act. However, a special Defence Force created to meet the potentially revolutionary threat was never called on to respond. The Triple Alliance called off the sympathy strike on 15 April – afterwards called trade unionism's 'Black Friday'. Deserted by their allies, the miners carried on the fight alone. One solution to the stalemate was presented in a letter from Lord Londonderry published in *The Times*. Calling the coal miners' suggestions 'mere palliatives', Londonderry also wrote directly to Northcliffe seeking aid for a plan which suggested an 'amalgamation' or 'trustification' of the industry to make it more efficient and competitive. Londonderry asserted that getting their way during the war had made the miners think the government was 'squeezable', and he believed that Lloyd George would in fact give in rather than face 'industrial warfare'.[51] Northcliffe replied that he was very interested in the subject

349

and was going himself to the coalfields to inspect and 'learn a little of the subject at first hand'. His letter continued, 'I do know something about organisation, and if I consider trustification will produce efficiency I will say so.'[52]

Northcliffe's criticisms of *The Times* and Steed continued. Rumours spread that the paper was to be sold and that Steed was to be replaced – either by B.K. Long, of the paper's Foreign Department, or by Campbell Stuart. After a usually well-informed City friend warned of a 'deep-seated plot' against him, the beleaguered editor broached the subject in a 22 March letter to his chief. 'You will be interested to know', he wrote, 'that I am to be dismissed and you are to be ousted from *The Times* by the end of the year.'[53] Steed was persuaded to take a short vacation, during which no action was taken. Meanwhile, Northcliffe reassured Stuart that, although he believed that newspapers were going to go 'through Hell for the next year or two' and that a great many would disappear, *The Times* would not be among them. 'Those who remain', he predicted, would 'share a prosperity not hitherto known in Newspaperdom'.[54] Despite this, Northcliffe continued to pressure his editor, informing Steed on 24 April that after the last three editions he was ready to part with *The Times* and that he had three suitable buyers lined up. Selling to a reputable purchaser would, he continued, conform 'to the urgent wishes of my medical and other advisers to get rid of a very trying responsibility'.[55] Steed replied that his chief could count on the goodwill and affection of himself and the staff should he carry out his decision, but added, 'I feel sure you would feel sorry to the end of your days that you had vacated the premier position in journalism in which you have done so much for England, and that, while relieving yourself of some financial and political responsibility, you would be acquiring a burden of regret that would weigh you down.'[56]

Several possible reasons have been suggested by those who believe that Northcliffe did seriously consider selling *The Times*. These include the alleged backing of the paper for a 'pooling' settlement to the coal strike despite his objections, his depression over Cowans, and the suggestion of Rothermere that he concentrate on the *Daily Mail*. *The History of The Times* suggests that behind all this was Rothermere: a proprietor who hated disobedient editors, wanted to deflect the criticism of the newspaper away from Lloyd George, whom he supported, and possibly desired to acquire the paper for himself.[57] But Steed was hardly the rebellious figure Geoffrey Dawson had been, and there is little other evidence to support this theory. A more sensible explanation, given

Northcliffe's comments to Stuart shortly before, is that this was simply one more attempt to shake things up at Printing House Square and to give the editor the 'little push' the press lord spoke of to Madame Rose.

At the end of April, Northcliffe returned to England to attend the twenty-fifth anniversary celebration of the *Daily Mail*, at which, it was whispered, he would announce the sale of *The Times*. The gala was held on 1 May at the Olympia Hall, London, where a banquet was laid out for 7,000 employees and guests. Northcliffe was accompanied by his wife and mother, both of whom apparently were upset by the rumours of the sale of *The Times*. Because the proprietor's voice continued to be too weak for public speaking, a recorded address was played on a specially amplified gramophone machine. Northcliffe used the occasion to further Anglo-American relations. Each table was decorated with a flag of the interwoven Union Flag and the Stars and Stripes, one of which he waved when given a spontaneous round of applause by the gathering. Northcliffe also took advantage of the affair to recognize George Isaacs, one of the *Daily Mail* union leaders, in preference to the editorial and managerial staffs. The *Morning Post* commented that 'On Sunday last Lord Northcliffe entertained 7,000 of his employees at Olympia. We understand that he has engaged the Salisbury Plain in order to give a summer picnic to those who *have been* in his employ.'

Whether there had ever been any serious intention to sell *The Times*, or it had all been simply a bluff, Northcliffe made no mention of it during the *Daily Mail* ceremonies.[58] The following month he commented to Herbert Swope, the editor of the New York *World*, that there had 'never been any battle about "The Times". The whole story was concocted by the German papers. I never explain or complain.'[59]

With Northcliffe focused on the labour problems in Britain, his own first taste of strike action came from across the Atlantic, in Newfoundland. Cheap Scandinavian paper had forced price reductions which brought a 20 per cent wage cut at Grand Falls. As the press lord prepared to tour the coalfields, he was notified in a 9 May cable from the Grand Falls Employees' Committee that, because of the wage cuts, the workers were on strike from that day. He responded that he deeply regretted the 'hasty action' that had brought 'the first strike in the history of our many businesses'.[60] The message went on that the Newfoundland mill employees must realize that paper was being sold in London for less than it could be made for at Grand Falls, and that newspapers could not exist with paper at war prices. He reiterated that he had the fullest confidence in Mr Harris, the Grand Falls manager, and strongly urged the Committee to confer with him. The Employees' Committee responded that they were willing to talk and had gone out on strike because they had been given only five days' notice of the cuts. The new wage, they complained, would mean 'extreme poverty' for the workers. Though he communicated with the employees, Northcliffe left the solution of the Newfoundland troubles to Rothermere and the management in London and Canada. His brother assured him that he had 'no reason' to worry about the trouble, which had been fully anticipated. The American mills, said Rothermere, were cutting wages 30 per cent, while Harris had reduced wages by only 20. He believed that in two to three weeks the workers would return on the new terms.[61]

In mid-May Northcliffe embarked on his fact-finding mission to the coalfields. During his tour he consulted a variety of people, from the miners to the owners, for their views on a settlement. He told Sir Henry Keith that he had put Keith's solution – a 'living wage' based on cost-of-living-index figures – before a 'very high quarter'. His letter continued:

> In my opinion the lack of modern facilities, modern underground transport, and the disgraceful houses I have seen in Lanarkshire have a good deal to do with the state of affairs . . . there are faults on both sides . . . about equally distributed. The fact that the matter is in the hands of Sir Robert Horne . . . formerly the agent of the miners, makes all of those I have met very suspicious.[62]

The proprietor instructed his papers to continue their moderate tone on the strike and to report both sides fully. A week in the mining districts convinced Northcliffe that Londonderry's amalgamation idea had merit. He reported to him that he had just made an 800-mile tour from Yorkshire to Lancashire and agreed with him, as did most of the mining executives and mine owners' agents to whom he had talked. Londonderry replied that he wanted to meet to discuss his plan.[63]

Northcliffe sent Steed a summary of his findings, which the editor passed on to Horne. The press lord reported that he did 'not hear of the many mechanical improvements in use in Illinois, Pennsylvania and Westphalia' and that he found 'large numbers of little collieries muddling along as the little railways muddled along until they were amalgamated in the fifties and sixties last century'. He did not find one person who did not agree that the 'break in wages has been too sudden and severe', and he believed that Horne would have to offer the men something like standard pre-war wages plus about 120 per cent. The strikers were 'very resolute', and a system of communal kitchens was developing rapidly which would lengthen the dispute. 'If you drive these people underground with insufficient wages,' Northcliffe warned Horne, 'you will have trouble in the country and get very little coal.'[64]

Horne responded that the 'problem, as you observe, is a wages problem'. However, he went on, 'the result of establishing a wage 120 per cent above prewar earnings' would be that the South Wales and other coalfields would be put out of business. He was sure that Northcliffe was correct that much could be done by improvements in equipment and that amalgamation would increase efficiency, and he hoped that both matters would be taken in hand. Unfortunately, as both meant the expenditure of considerable time, they would 'not effect any solution to the present strike difficulty'. Horne added that he wanted to talk further with Northcliffe about some other ideas, such as the creation of a board to set coal wages for the next twelve months.[65]

While Northcliffe was in the coalfields, Sir William Robertson Nicoll's *British Weekly* once again suggested that the press lord take office to solve some of the nation's pressing problems. Northcliffe wrote to Nicoll that his attention had been called to the 'kind paragraphs about me. I am not worthy of them.' His letter went on:

> You ask: Why should a journalist be confined in his 'box'? I am confined to my box for two considerations – one is a throat which constantly gives trouble if I speak above my normal pitch; the other is the fact that, if I accept office, my newspapers are from that moment silenced. The combination of newspapers [*sic*] work and Government has never yet succeeded.[66]

Nicoll responded to this that he would not 'argue with you, but I know that a very few years will find you at the head of the Empire. It must be so.'[67]

Efforts continued to build a bridge between Northcliffe and the Prime Minister. The writer Gerald Maxwell, who had been on the *Daily Mail* staff, asked for five minutes of Northcliffe's time to 'see if a good undertaking could not be re-established . . . without any sacrifice of independence on either side. I have, of course, already ascertained that this is his desire.'[68] Thanking Maxwell for his trouble, Northcliffe replied that

> Politicians and newspapers and financiers and newspapers are better apart. Some politicians seem to think that newspapers act from personal motives. Mine certainly do not. I have often expressed my great admiration for the part the Prime Minister played in keeping up the public spirit during the war.

When he does what my newspapers conscientiously believe to be right, they will say so. I do not think he has been right about Ireland, a country I know as well as some people, and I do not think he is right about national expenses, and I shall say so. But please disabuse your mind of the idea that I have any ill-feeling about the Prime Minister or any politician.[69]

In Ireland, Ulster accepted the partition mandated by the Government of Ireland Act, which had become law in December 1920, while the South refused to acknowledge the statute and continued its rebellion. George V, who had sent several protests to his ministers over the reprisals of the Black and Tans in the South, had been invited to Belfast in June 1921 to open the new parliament of Northern Ireland. Several figures, including the South African general Jan Smuts, had suggested to the King that this occasion might be an auspicious one to appeal for peace. Steed had also written to this effect to Lord Stamfordham, the King's secretary, warning of the danger of such a trip, but urging that if the sovereign was determined to go he might use his visit to call for a truce. After Lloyd George was brought around to the merits of this idea, his secretary, Sir Edward Grigg (later Lord Altrincham), who had served on the staff of *The Times* in the decade before the war, drafted a statement for the King which was further revised by several people, including Balfour. This address, delivered on 22 June at Belfast, called for all Irishmen to 'stretch out the hand of forbearance and conciliation, to forgive and forget, and to join in making for the land which they love a new era of peace, contentment and good-will'.[70] The strong support of *The Times* and the *Daily Mail* prompted a letter of thanks from the King to Northcliffe for helping to ensure the success of his trip.

The government used the good feeling elicited by the royal declaration to arrange an Irish truce, which began on 11 July, after which negotiations began that would finally lead to an agreement. Ten days before this, the coal strike also came to an end. The starving miners were forced to accept a wage reduction, while a government subsidy kept the mines open. With these two major national storms at least somewhat calmed, Northcliffe prepared to escape from domestic and business affairs and to inspect for himself the Japanese menace in the Pacific during a trip around the Empire and the world.

18

World Whirl, 1921–1922

E ARLY IN JULY 1921 Northcliffe corresponded with Lord Inchcape, chairman of the Peninsular and Oriental (P&O) steamship line, concerning both travel and accommodation for his world tour. He requested a letter from Inchcape to his 'various agents' for use in case he ran into difficulties.[1] The P&O staff responded with detailed travel plans and numerous letters of introduction. In gratitude, Northcliffe told Inchcape that he would begin the account of his expedition in *The Times* with a 'description of my visit to the P&O office because, as I said to my companions when I left that office, this is the real beginning of my journey'.[2]

This pilgrimage was undertaken for several reasons, including health. Sir James Mackenzie recommended six months' rest away from England. Northcliffe also desired to visit those parts of the Empire he had not seen personally. Some of these, he believed, were imperilled by Japan's ambitions, which had overshadowed any real or imagined threat from the United States to Britain and her possessions. Northcliffe told his brother St John that 'There are those who say that a second Great World War is unthinkable and impossible, but Japan is undoubtedly preparing for war.'[3] Concern with the Pacific and Far East questions – both topics, with disarmament, to be discussed at the Washington Conference proposed by the Harding administration – led him to include Japan, China, Korea and Indo-China in the itinerary. The first stop was to be the United States, followed by a rail crossing of Canada before a steamship voyage to Australia and the Orient, with the return to Europe made via India, the Suez Canal and Palestine.

During his absence, Northcliffe arranged for Sutton, Campbell
Stuart and William Graham, one of his solicitors, to have power of
attorney. Because of bad experiences with inaccurate stories from the
United States in 1917, he warned Marlowe not to publish any
announcements of his travels except those from their own correspondents. At a final Carmelite House staff meeting before his departure,
Northcliffe demanded that a sub-editor name the best story in that
morning's *Daily Mail.* The man replied without losing a beat, 'Viscount
Northcliffe is leaving tomorrow on a world tour and will be away several
months.' The unsmiling proprietor broke the shocked silence in the
room with instructions to his secretary to reward the remark with a
£100 bonus.[4] *Punch* divulged that on 'Lord Thanet's World Pilgrimage'
he would 'visit the North and South Poles, ascend Mount Everest and
descend to the centre of the earth'.

Northcliffe left on 16 July, the day after his fifty-sixth birthday, on the
gigantic Cunard liner *Aquitania,* and was one of 600 in first class. He was
accompanied by two secretaries, John Prioleau and Harold Snoad, as
well as his chauffeur, Pine, and valet, Frederick Foulger. The proprietor
dictated an article for the *Daily Mail* which dubbed the *Aquitania* the
'Wonder Ship', a 'country house at sea with just the right number of
people'. He told Sir Robert Hudson that the liner was 'doubtless the
best in the world' and that he had 'no idea what Ocean travelling had
come to'.[5] Hudson had been looking after Lady Northcliffe, whose
illness excused her from the world tour. Worried about her health,
Northcliffe had advised his wife to remain at her house at
Crowborough, but told Hudson that he had 'not given any further
admonitions to my Lady. She will do as she will.'

At the last minute, Northcliffe insisted that Steed join him on at least
the first leg of the journey. The editor already planned to represent *The
Times* at the Washington Conference. He used the trip to familiarize
himself with the United States, which he had never visited. Steed's companion, Madame Rose, lauded the press lord for again going out to be
involved in 'Big Things' and hoped that he would return rejuvenated.
Steed, Northcliffe told her, would be 'invaluable at the Washington
Conference, for there is no one in the world who knows so much as he
does as to what happens at Conferences'.[6] At the same time, Lloyd
George, engaged in London with a conference of imperial prime ministers, was suspicious of the US proposal to meet in November and made
counter-suggestions which the Americans declined. The Prime
Minister told Churchill that the whole US conference conception was

amateurish in the extreme . . . The worst of it is there will be a newspaper campaign to force us into an acceptance of the extreme American position. Northcliffe will be got at as soon as he arrives at Washington. However, the British Empire must not be given away in order to secure a good reception for the Pilgrim of Printing House Square.[7]

Following Steed's instructions, *The Times* had declared that neither Lloyd George nor Curzon, the Foreign Secretary, should represent Britain at Washington. Curzon was rebuked for his 'pompous and pretentious manner', his 'business incapacity' and his 'obsequious docility' to the wishes of the Prime Minister, who was described as 'probably the most distrusted statesman' in Europe. *The Times* went on that the 'great qualification needed from the representatives of the Empire is a character for conspicuous straightforwardness and honour. We have many such men in our public life, but Mr. Lloyd George is not one of them.'[8] This attack and a separate statement by the proprietor that the Prime Minister and the foreign Secretary, like Wilson in 1918, did not represent the public opinion of their country, infuriated both men and drew a Foreign Office boycott of the Northcliffe press. Campbell Stuart told Riddell that the articles had been produced by Steed, who, Stuart believed, would have lost his job over the affair except that Curzon's boycott had rallied the proprietor's support for the editor.[9] Whether this was true or not, from Northcliffe's point of view the fact that Lloyd George and Steed did not get on was in his editor's favour. Northcliffe told Madame Rose that he thought that 'if the Prime Minister gets to know that Steed is in Washington, the Prime Minister will not go there'. He also suggested that whatever the editor sent to London should also be provided to the *New York Times*, so that Steed would have a daily organ on the spot, as he did in Paris in 1919.

While Northcliffe and Steed crossed the Atlantic, Lloyd George responded to the newspaper criticisms. E.L. Keen, of the United Press, sent a wireless message to the press lord asking for comment on an outburst in the Commons by the Prime Minister on 18 July, informing him that Lloyd George had labelled the attack on Curzon, 'peculiarly offensive', and stated that, since people continued to believe that *The Times* represented official opinion, the government had to strike back. The Prime Minister had announced that the 'favours' accorded the newspaper by the traditions of the past had been 'entirely withdrawn'.[10] Northcliffe replied to Keen that it was 'kind and characteristic of the Prime Minister to wait until I am in mid-Atlantic for one of his monthly attacks'. He went on that 'Curzon's boycott of our newspapers in no way affects our news services which are infinitely superior to those of the Foreign Office whose communications to the press as a rule show singular lack of accuracy. Having only seen an abbreviated account of the Prime Minister's attack, I must defer reply till I reach New York.'[11]

The *Aquitania* docked on 23 July, and Northcliffe met reporters in the same suite at the Gotham Hotel which had been his headquarters in 1917. He declined to comment on the Far East before he had seen things for himself, but declared that he had hopes for Ireland. He lauded Harding's call for a conference, professed his support for disarmament, as any 'sane' person would, while noting that England was already cutting its Navy. The US journals, the press lord told Sutton, had been 'very kind to me about the L.G. controversy. If he comes here he will do so in an atmosphere of deep suspicion. His mental acrobatics are talked of by the best writers.'[12] Northcliffe told reporters that he was not greatly disturbed by the Foreign Office boycott of his trip, or all the publicity. His final comment before boarding a train for Washington was, 'Somebody has said that Lord Curzon and the Premier are the best members of my newspaper staff, and it looks as if that is right.'[13]

An already tense situation was worsened when an interview given by Steed in Northcliffe's name was published in the *New York Times* of 24 July. Among other things, it recounted a conversation between the King and the Prime Minister in which Lloyd George had been asked if he was going to shoot all the people in Ireland. The sovereign then demanded that the government come to an agreement as 'I cannot have my people killed in this manner.' An inexperienced assistant at the New York *Daily Mail* office cabled the interview to London, where Stuart prevented its publication in *The Times* and the *Daily Mail*; however, the piece appeared in the Irish edition of the *Daily Mail* and in the *Evening Standard* and the *Daily Express*. In the Commons on 29 July, Lloyd George read a statement by the King which called the comments attributed to him a 'complete fabrication'. The Prime Minister went on that he hoped the announcement would 'sterilize the effects of the criminal malignity which, for personal ends, is endeavouring to stir up mischief between the Allies, and misunderstanding between the British Empire and the United States, and to frustrate the hopes of peace in Ireland'.[14]

Northcliffe first heard of the matter the same day, while attending a luncheon at the Washington Overseas Writers' Club. He immediately cabled the King's secretary, Lord Stamfordham: 'Please convey to His Majesty . . . my denial of ever having ascribed to His Majesty the words or any such words as were stated by the Prime Minister yesterday. I gave no such interview.' Stamfordham replied that he had 'communicated to the King your message . . . His Majesty is glad that it confirms the statement made on his authority by the Prime Minister in the House of Commons yesterday.'[15] The telegram to Stamfordham ended the matter as far as Northcliffe was concerned. He wrote to his mother, 'I daresay you saw a ridiculous fuss in the papers about something I was supposed to say about the king. A complete fabrication. I am afraid I did not fuss at all but went on with my golf and novel reading as usual.'[16]

Although Steed apparently had never made the comments attributed to him, at least for publication, in Britain the incident drew a storm of protest against the editor and his chief. John Walter and Rothermere, among others, called for Steed's head. Northcliffe responded to the furore at home in a telegram to Rothermere copied to Lady Northcliffe, Sutton, Walter and others: 'Steed did not give interview and complained last Monday about it. I did not hear of it until Parliamentary discussion Friday. Am giving no interviews, but cannot prevent correspondents following and writing . . . Am not worrying and my golf excellent.'[17] Lady Northcliffe responded, 'Thank you for your cable my dear . . . all well, everyone sends love.'[18] Northcliffe commented to Sutton that the US newspapers were wondering if Lloyd George would apologize for his having attacked under false pretences. The Prime Minister, however, was not in a forgiving mood. He told Riddell that he thought Northcliffe and Steed had 'done themselves an enormous amount of harm,' and that it was 'a serious thing to have two wild men gyrating round the world making poisonous statements concerning their own country'.[19]

Because of this incident, and the earlier attacks on Curzon and Lloyd George, a dinner and an invitation to stay at the British Embassy at Washington were both cancelled. Northcliffe commented that he did not know the reason for this, but, 'knowing the methods in India of Lord Curzon', he was 'pretty certain that Lord Curzon has adopted these methods here'. The British ambassador, Sir Auckland Geddes, Northcliffe told Sutton, was

> what they call the goat of the piece. He asked me whether he should resign . . . Can any sane person imagine me mentioning the King over here? I have mentioned the Prime Minister twice. Once when he attacked me when I was in Mid-Atlantic, and in a statement I made before leaving England that his position is the same as Wilson's was in 1918 – a perfectly proper statement to make and more than true.[20]

A letter home commented that it was 'a triumph of Nemesis that I should be pursued round the world partly by a monster of my own creating – the Press'.[21]

Though snubbed by the Washington Embassy on the instructions of Curzon, Northcliffe was granted an hour-and-twenty-minute interview with Harding which had been arranged with the help of Geddes. Afterwards, he would not comment about whether disarmament had been discussed, saying, 'I am not to be drawn, I have been in the game too long myself.' He did reveal that 'We had a most enjoyable chat, but we did not discuss international affairs. The President told me about the "Marion Star" and his life as a journalist.'[22] Northcliffe told Stuart that he 'liked Harding immensely. He has grown bigger since I met him in 1917.' He also found Charles Evan Hughes, the Secretary of State, 'more a man of the world than he was – less lawyer'.[23] With the embassy dinner cancelled, a night at the home of the pre-eminent Washington hostess, Mrs McLean, was substituted. Hughes, General Pershing and many senators were present. The banquet at the McLean house, Northcliffe reported, was 'like a cinema show play', with a ragtime band and a 'movie show' after dinner. The evening, and the rest of the visit, gave the press lord some 'hearty laughter in Washington'.

After the visit to the US capital, Northcliffe made his way by rail, via New York, to Toronto, a departure point for Vancouver on the Pacific coast. The Canadian leg of his travels was marked by the usual 'rising of the ghosts' – people the press lord had known long before and forgotten, such as a sub-editor from *Bicycling News* last seen in Coventry in 1886. These phantoms appeared throughout the world. At Vancouver, which Northcliffe considered a 'very fine' city that had grown since his visit in 1909, he spoke to the Canadian Club, fulfilling a promise made years before. He called for 'mental disarmament', and declared that failure at Washington 'would be a catastrophe'. In Europe, he declared, Germany remained 'unrepentant, vengeful and watchful'. However, it was not Germany, but Japan about which he found people concerned. He heard many complaints of the Japanese 'tentacles' in British Columbia and California, and for the final 300 miles approaching the Pacific coast he had noticed Japanese by the hundreds. At Vancouver a long interview, which he had not given, appeared in the local Japanese newspaper.[24]

Northcliffe left Canada on 7 August on the SS *Makura* bound for New Zealand, via Hawaii and Fiji. The ship, much smaller than the *Aquitania*, was filled with boisterous New Zealanders and Australians (including Keith Murdoch), but Northcliffe found his quarters comfortable and decorated them with a 'shrine' of photographs and mementoes from home, including the parting gift his mother had given him, a book of devotional readings from Scripture entitled *Daily Light on the Daily Path*. Mother and son arranged to read passages from it at the same time every day: seven in the morning and seven at night. Sir Robert Hudson sent good news of Lady Northcliffe's health and of the success of the Westminster Abbey appeal fund, to which the owner of the *Daily Mail* had donated generously. Northcliffe replied that he had been 'thinking a great deal' of his wife on the voyage, and that he 'had three of her portraits in my cabin'.[25]

After the oppressive heat of the USA and Canada, the cooler weather at sea was a pleasant change. Northcliffe busied himself reading books on the Japanese question and Australian novels. A message to Sutton from the *Makura* complained that he could not 'avoid this being something like a royal progression when I come to towns and cities. I dodge ... in every way I can ... these official receptions and entertainments by saying I am staying at Lord Inchcape's houses. His shipping company has a private house everywhere. He seems to control the oceans.'[26] He reported to Sutton he had only seen *Answers* and the *Overseas Daily Mail* since he left, and that the Americans were flooding Canada with cheap publications. He feared the same conditions prevailed in Australia. The message went on that, in case any more alleged statements surfaced, he was giving no interviews. A few days later, some good business news intervened and the press lord recorded that he was 'in a better temper than usual, having received welcome cable saying the strike at Grand Falls is over'.[27]

At Honolulu, Northcliffe paid a courtesy call on Governor Farrington, who lived in the old royal palace of the Hawaiian king and queen. At the British Club, he was greeted by the consul and delegates of the Overseas Club, wearing their badges. He was impressed by the two local papers and by the amount of news provided by the US government naval wireless. 'Like the Germans and the Japanese,' he wrote home, 'they regard news as vital. I wish our people did.'[28]

Keith Murdoch joined him for a golf outing. Although he had complained of the press attention, Northcliffe told Sutton 'I play much better with cinematograph machines working' and joked that perhaps he 'had better have a movie operator with him all the times in future'.[29] Besides enjoying golf, Northcliffe witnessed demonstrations of several local sports, including the shooting of flying fish from boats and 'surf riding' on boards. Murdoch, he wrote to W.F. Bullock, had been telling him for years about the beautiful girls at Waikiki Beach. Bullock's chief went on, 'I got him out there and though the fish in the aquarium were wonderful, the girls were repellent. I now remind him that he has always been talking of the girls of Auckland and now we are approaching Auckland.'[30] Though he apparently enjoyed needling Murdoch, Northcliffe told Bullock that he was a 'great travelling companion and a veritable dynamo of energy'. The press lord had become very fond of the Australian, and regarded him almost as a son.

After Hawaii, next came a week's voyage south to Fiji. The heat once again became bothersome, although the constant trade winds and the ceiling fans gave some relief. Forced to live in white clothes, Northcliffe changed suits four times a day. He wrote to his mother that, because of the heat, 'I sleep in the costume you gave me on 15 July 1865.'[31] The noise of the nightly dancing and entertainment often kept him awake, but he refrained from complaint. However, as chairman of the Passenger Committee, Northcliffe received various protests – for example, of the shockingly scanty apparel worn by some of the younger women, including backless gowns, of which he disapproved. For the fancy-dress ball, he wore an antique mandarin robe and wrote home that he was becoming 'quite frivolous'. At Fiji he spoke to another Overseas Club delegation, on the subject of disarmament. He found the group more interested in the monthly ship starting to London.

From the tropical heat of Fiji, the voyagers dipped into the winter cold of New Zealand. At Auckland the acting Prime Minister, Sir Francis Bell, played host. The New Zealand veterans of the trenches in France gave the press lord a rousing demonstration of their gratitude when Bell mentioned the shells agitation of 1915 at a luncheon given by the local newspaper owners. Northcliffe was delighted by the Dominion's natural splendours and especially by his golfing adventures among the volcanic geysers at Rotorua, 170 miles inland. He found the people 'absolutely English', and was surprised at their lack of accent. He investigated and spoke on the question of immigration from Britain to the Empire during his tour. In New Zealand he saw 'room for millions', and discovered that 'young skilled British dairy farmers, industrious, married preferably, but not with large families', could get 'immediate engagements' on a milk-sharing partner basis, but that they 'must learn colonial ways'.[32]

On 3 September the company left Auckland for Sydney on a small steamer, the *Maheno*. The weather continued glorious, and in 13,000 miles, Northcliffe wrote home, they had not seen any sea 'rougher than a smooth day between Dublin and Holyhead'. After only a few weeks he had already had enough sunshine to last a lifetime. His reception by the 'diggers', the returned Australian soldiers, touched him. At lunches for the Institute of Journalists and the Empire Press Union, Northcliffe was lauded for the shells campaign, the *Daily Mail* Gallipoli revelations and, more recently, the criticism of the delegates to the Washington Conference. The proprietor told the gatherings that, as treasurer of the Empire Press Union, he had helped make progress in obtaining cheaper cable rates for Canada and hoped to do the same for Australia. Amazed at the low prices for food and housing, he wrote home that he could not 'bear to contrast our vast slums with the sunshine and plenty here. I was taken to what they call a slum here, but there was no slum about it. Butcher-shops are as plentiful as lamp-posts.'[33]

He travelled by train to Melbourne, where he spoke on immigration and warned of Japan's ambitions. The 'only way you can keep Australia white', he told one interviewer, was by 'carefully selected agricultural immigration'.[34] Unfortunately, Northcliffe found most Australians fearful of and hostile to increased immigration. Since Pine had little else to do, he became his employer's eyes and ears among the working classes, reporting back 'what they say and how they are treated'. The chauffeur, Northcliffe recorded, was 'becoming a most efficient reporter'. There was no effective official propaganda at home, he complained, to spread the message about the empty continent. The press lord visited the offices of the Melbourne *Herald* and the *Weekly Times* and was fêted by the Lord Mayor at the Town Hall. Sir Joseph Cook, the acting Prime Minister, welcomed him as a 'man who sees his duty and does it . . . not only a man of vision, he is a man of action. Shall I call him a great imperial pathfinder? . . . I believe that as a result of Lord Northcliffe's visit to Australia a great fillip will be given to all those things that tend to strengthen and bind and consolidate the Empire.'[35] Besides continuing his unsuccessful quest to find an Australian slum, Northcliffe also called on Dame Nellie Melba at her home, Coombe Cottage, near Coldstream. He described it as 'a cottage as the cottages of the American millionaires at Newport . . . on the scale of the very biggest villa on the Riviera'.[36]

'Those who predicted I should be back in about two months,' Northcliffe wrote to Sutton from Melbourne, 'evidently don't know me. I am learning every day things of great importance, which will become very useful in my journalistic and political future.' The Australians, he was relieved to find, wanted English news and did not like American publications. It was 'extraordinary', he told Sutton, 'to be away in a country where everything is the same as in England, except the weather, and see practically no signs of our publications'.[37] His remedy was for a young man to come out and put some energy into their journalism. There were some other differences, however. Compared to the average Englishman, the people, and the politicians, he met were giants. The dispatches home also commented on the 'awful' pronunciations and accents. 'It is a knock-down blow at first', said the press lord, 'when well dressed handsome young men and beautiful young girls address you with the accent of White Chapel.' He found the speech 'largely based on Cockney, with a dash of Irish'.[38]

Sutton sent business and political news from London. In two by-elections, at Lewisham and Westminster, he reported that Rothermere's Anti-Waste League candidates had done badly, since all the candidates proclaimed themselves anti-waste. The League, he felt, was 'done'. 'Your papers', Sutton added, 'just reported the Elections; gave no advice, as I instructed them, though we did *not* help the Coalition man in disguise . . . In the meantime Government Waste continues. At the present moment the Irish Question may go either way, but the general view is not too optimistic, at the moment, the negotiations have broken down.'[39]

After a brief side trip to Tasmania, Northcliffe left Sydney on 1 October on the *St Albans*, a well-appointed 4,000-ton steam yacht bound for Yokohama. Leaving Australia behind, he reported to Lady Sophie Hall that the St Christopher's medal she had given him had worked so far and that he was on a thirty-eight-day leg of the journey, which would include Borneo, the Philippines and Hong Kong. He was 'in the Tropics – all white clothes and electric fans'. The places he had seen were like the Riviera, but with more flowers and flowering trees. Of the 'little courts' held by the various colonial governors, he commented that 'if they were not so very tiresome, they would be very humorous'. The people were 'astonishing ignorant' of Great Britain – 'almost as much as we are of them' – and he noted that the colonials 'work less, play more, bet more, eat more, and some say drink more than we do'. Northcliffe was struck by the 'plenitude' of food and by tea at 11 a.m. At present, he told Lady Hall, Australia was 'a working man's paradise, and will be until the Japanese get it, which they are almost certain to do, either by peaceful penetration or by war'.[40]

Before leaving Sydney, Northcliffe had issued a statement on the

immigration question which underlined the emptiness and defenceless-
ness of Australia and New Zealand. He declared himself 'amazed at
your indifference to the events and portents in the outside world, and
especially in Asia . . . Within a fortnight's steam . . . you have thousands
of millions of people, all of whom are crowded and restless, and some
ambitious and powerful.' The key, he went on, was population:

> You must increase your slender garrison by the multiplication of your people.
> Only numbers will save you. The world will not tolerate an empty and idle
> Australia . . . You have no option. Tens of millions will come to you whether
> you wish it or not . . . Make your foundations safe, and play about with social
> reforms and State Socialism and all the rest . . . afterwards.[41]

Though he wrote home that his comments on immigration were well
received, Northcliffe found it 'impossible to arouse these people to
realise the imminent danger which threatens them in the Pacific'. The
inhabitants did not realize that Japan's new possessions were within two
and a half days of Australia and that there were quite a lot of Japanese
already in Northern Queensland, allegedly pearl divers. 'They think they
are invincible,' he went on, 'they believe the Australians alone won the
war, and measure the rest of the world by its inferiority at cricket.'[42]
Wrench cabled him 'heartiest congratulations' for his 'fine utterances'
and requested that the first speech he give on his return be made to the
London Overseas Club.[43]

On 21 October the *St Albans* arrived at Manila, where General
Leonard Wood, whom Northcliffe had known since before the Great
War, had been recently installed as US governor. Northcliffe accompanied Wood to the University of the Philippines and addressed the students. He found the Americans in the Philippines the 'most British' he
had ever met, and commented that there was no 'swank' or 'brag' about
them and that they were unanimous in the opinion that the USA and
Britain had to 'get together and keep together'. In a speech to the
Manila Rotary Club, he called for Anglo-American co-operation in the
Far East against 'events which, possibly, we do not like to name'. He
'dreaded to think' what would happen if the Washington Conference
failed and the 'mad race for armaments' continued. After months of
preliminaries, the Conference convened at last on 11 November, with
Arthur Balfour and Lord Lee of Fareham, the First Lord of the
Admiralty, as Britain's chief delegates.

Two months of travel across the Pacific made the press lord aware
of many problems with the foreign arrangements of his journals. He

complained to Marlowe that the *Daily Mail*'s foreign correspondents never heard from Valentine Williams, the head of the Foreign News Department. Northcliffe came to the conclusion that a trip by an expert was needed to repair the muddle. In the remote areas he recommended one man for both *The Times* and the *Daily Mail*. A critique sent to London remarked that

> [the] whole thing shows a mighty poor foreign organisation on the part of both papers. Look at the map and realise that the Fiji Islands are covered from Sydney! Sydney has as much connection with the Fiji Islands as London has with Bulgaria. Also, would you believe that Bullock, of New York, covers Manila. It sounds almost incredible. How the devil can Bullock cover Manila?[44]

Northcliffe found the harbour of the next destination, Hong Kong, one of the loveliest in the world. The city, he said, 'makes one proud to be British'. Not wishing to enter Japan under false colours, at Hong Kong he issued a statement against the renewal of the Anglo-Japanese alliance. Bullock wrote to his chief from New York that the statement had 'created a sensation'. He also shared a story from the 'enemy camp', generated in the continuing fallout of the fraudulent Steed interview, that the Prince of Wales, after reading of the matter, remarked that 'Lord Northcliffe has no daughter, but if he had he would make me marry her I am sure.'[45]

En route to Japan, the party made a brief stop at Canton, where Northcliffe was staggered by the hundreds of boats that greeted the ship. He met a Cantonese leader, who informed him that the Chinese delegation to the Washington Conference was under Japanese influence. After the consul-general agreed with this assessment, the owner of the *Daily Mail* warned Marlowe that according to 'high British authorities' the Chinese delegation in Washington was 'under Japanese domination'.[46] Japan, he wrote home, had 'blackmailed us and blackmailed the Chinese, a fact I have been reminded of in every conversation I have had since leaving Australia'. Nevertheless, he found the British flag everywhere about Canton, and recorded that, even though the Japanese alliance had degraded Britain's 'prestige in the eyes of the East, we are still a very considerable people'.[47]

On 2 November, from the deck of the *St Albans*, Northcliffe caught his first sight of Fujiyama, which he called the 'most beautiful mountain in the world'. Though the approaches to Yokohama were scenic, he found the city itself rather 'mean' looking. After a round of golf, he left on an electric train for Tokyo. The bustling station reminded him of an open-air tube stop in London, such as Earls Court or Finsbury Park. At Tokyo he stayed at the Imperial Court Hotel. He 'got ahead' of the Japanese newspapers by inviting their representatives to a dinner at the Maple Club, complete with geisha dancing. His principal guest was Mr Murayama, the owner of the *Asahi* newspaper, which the press lord considered the *Times* of Japan. Northcliffe's declaration of a week before against the Anglo-Japanese alliance had caused 'quite a stir'; however, since *The Times* for years had supported the alliance, he had expected more outrage at the change of course. He was surprised, as well, by the many voices that agreed with his position, including the *Jiji*, a respected paper. Northcliffe warned Steed, at Washington for the conference sessions, that the Japanese were 'out to pull the leg of the conference, and I rely on you not to let them. They are as like Prussians as they can be – inquisitive, flattering, yea, verily, even goose stepping. Go in and win.'[48]

On his second day in Tokyo, after a visit to the Meiji Shrine, Northcliffe called on a 'little bit of England', the red-brick British Embassy, where he was received cordially by the ambassador, Sir Charles Eliot. The first Japanese house the owner of the *Daily Mail* visited was that of Baron Goto, the mayor of Tokyo. Northcliffe was much interested in the paper screens and lack of furniture. At the picturesque garden of the industrialist Mr Yamamoto, he commented that he 'looked back at the little company that trooped behind us. I thought it was like being in a dreamland – exactly like Japan of the idealists.' He was also initiated into the 'Tea Ceremony', about which he had heard a little. He described Mrs Yamamoto's performance as the most graceful he had ever seen. The journalists of Tokyo returned the press lord's hospitality with a night at the Imperial Theatre. He enjoyed that evening's meal as much as any at the Ritz in Paris.

The next morning Northcliffe departed on an 'excellent modern train' for Kyoto. His few days in the country had made him understand the 'Japanese craze that affects so many English visitors who do not realise the other Japan – the Japan whose brutality is notorious, the Japan who is obviously trying to rule China in order that she may rule the world'.[49] Though he considered the Japanese to be expansionist on the German model, no one in his party had seen anything like German rudeness, pushing or staring. He found the aristocratic Japanese much like the English, and the middle classes he saw in the restaurant car like the 'French and Italians – very exuberant'. On the train, Northcliffe encountered a young Japanese reading *The Mirrors of Downing Street*,

which included a brief, and biting, chapter on the press lord. This criticized his 'reckless variability', dubbed him the 'Spring-Heeled Jack of
Journalism', and suggested that an 'admirable title for his biography
would be "The Fits and Starts of a Discontinuous Soul"'. Though he
was not a 'deliberately bad man', the anonymous author concluded that
'at the seat of judgment' Northcliffe would have to answer for the
degraded 'moral and intellectual condition of the world'.[50] Northcliffe
confided in the youthful reader that it was a 'very wicked book'.

After sightseeing at Kyoto, the travellers embarked for Osaka, the
'Manchester of Japan'. They arrived on the day of a children's flower
festival, and were festooned with blossoms. Asked if he would visit the
Japanese fleet, Northcliffe told the representatives of the Osaka *Asahi*
that 'In a brief visit, I do not want to look at things with ugly meanings,
like battleships.'[51] All across Japan, Northcliffe was struck by the
crowds, by the 'nerve-racking' automobile rides through the narrow
streets, and by incongruities such as the pictures of Charlie Chaplin
outside many theatres. Though he remained suspicious of Japanese
motives, the complex people, he wrote home, were 'poetic, fond of tradition, polite, brave' and, despite their reputation, 'in many ways very
inefficient'. They were, in his estimation, also 'spying, very imitative,
and very quick to learn'.[52] To escape being embroiled in a diplomatic
controversy, Northcliffe avoided meeting Hara, the Prime Minister,
who was, much to Northcliffe's regret, assassinated while the owner of
the *Daily Mail* was in Japan. Northcliffe enjoyed his time in Japan
immensely, and was sorry when the time came to leave for Fusan in
Japanese-occupied Korea on 9 November, en route to Peking.

At the Chinese capital, the press lord was surprised to find the Hotel
de Pekin full of Europeans and as big and comfortable as the London
Ritz. The climate reminded him of Monte Carlo, and he declared Peking
the 'world's most marvellous city . . . unlike anything else in the world'.
It was the only place he had visited where the British and Americans he
met did not want to go home. Northcliffe wrote to Rothermere:

> I touch wood when I say that I have never been so well before. Sir James
> Mackenzie told me that, between fifty and sixty, a man should have a holiday
> of at least six months away from his affairs with different people, different
> food, and different climate. The whole thing here is very interesting. I am
> afraid I shall find things at home very tame after it.[53]

His sightseeing and shopping included an expedition, at his wife's
behest, for celadon porcelain, much of which he considered 'very heavy

and ugly'. A British expert accompanied him to ensure that he bought the genuine article. Northcliffe was offered porcelain gifts, but, not wishing to be indebted to the bestowers, turned them down. The guide, something of a gossip, informed him that when Lord Kitchener had visited he had accepted an especially rare celadon bowl and had insisted that it was the British custom that another should be received as well. On Kitchener's return to England the pair, it was said, soon made their way to a London antique dealer's window.[54] Northcliffe purchased several Ming-period examples, as well as some jade. He had also promised to bring home some souvenir bricks from the Great Wall of China, and six of these were delivered by a railway official who had been informed of his wish. Before leaving Peking, the proprietor cabled Steed instructions for *The Times* to advocate the immediate termination of the Anglo-Japanese alliance and to work for Anglo-American unity.

Northcliffe travelled by private rail car to Tientsin on the way to Shanghai, where the sea voyage would continue. As he passed through Shantung, Japanese troops were everywhere and attempted to 'peep' into his car. 'They have as much right to be in Shantung', he recorded, 'as they have to be at Birmingham.'[55] At Nanking and Shanghai reporters deluged him with requests for interviews. His statements about the Anglo-Japanese alliance, he commented, had 'brought the Chinese very much on my side'. He reported to Sutton from China that he had never felt so well in his life. 'I was flabby before I left home and sometimes a little worried about myself, though I did not tell anyone so. Here I feel full of . . . strength . . . Lord what a lot I did not know! . . . How big the great world is. How old fashioned our little island is becoming.' He feared that the energy of the English was 'flagging', and wondered if 'twelve months sunshine would wake up England?' His travels, Northcliffe wrote to Sutton, also had shown him that high-priced newspapers would not go and he declared that the price of *The Times* would have to be cut. He asked for a computation of loss figures at 1d and 1½d.[56]

Even on the other side of the world, the continuing Irish negotiations intruded. In November, confused by garbled accounts from London and afraid of a government capitulation, Northcliffe instructed Marlowe, 'Absolutely no further concessions Irish. Situation unclear. Give support Birkenhead and Churchill.'[57] After seeing Lord Birkenhead (formerly F.E. Smith), Marlowe replied that

in reference your communication he thought you may be imperfectly informed as to mutual situation. He and Winston are both of opinion

Government proposals completely carry out policy which you and your newspapers have so long advocated. They think further that supreme effort at this moment may secure permanent solution with immense beneficial result to Empire as a whole and our relations with America. The need of moment in their opinion is to persuade Ulster and Bonar Law to be reasonable.[58]

Northcliffe replied that Marlowe should thank Birkenhead for clearing up the matter for him, as he had feared another government surrender.[59]

At the end of November, Northcliffe notified Sir Robert Hudson that he was sending Pine ahead with 'propitiary offerings' for Lady Northcliffe and, if she wished, to drive her to the South of France to meet him. His letter also commented on the Japanese mastery of doctoring news. The Reuters man at Tokyo had confided to him that the 'Germans were babies at propaganda' in comparison. Northcliffe told Hudson that he regarded the Japanese as 'first rate second rate people, plus oriental cunning at diplomacy. They apparently play with our Foreign Office.'[60] He spoke of the same subject in a letter to Murdoch:

> The conclusion I have come to about Japan is that fifty-five per cent are for war and forty-five per cent are for peace . . . They know very much more about Australia than we expected. The road to world peace, we were informed by one pundit, would be to 'open Australia to the Japanese and settle those Australians who don't like it in other British Dominions'.[61]

The next month Northcliffe's Australian protégé felt he had found his 'big chance' to gain control of the Sydney *Evening News* and the Melbourne *Herald*. So that he might take advantage of the golden opportunity, Murdoch asked the press lord for a 'few thousands' in financial assistance. Northcliffe was more than happy to aid the younger man, and cabled him, 'Gladyest [*sic*] invest five thousand as encouragement to others and proof my complete confidence in you. Name and amount should be published together [and] fact you have complete control. One man control essential newspaper business.'[62] Besides delivering the promised financial backing, in the following months Northcliffe took the time to send detailed criticisms of his new papers to Murdoch.

At the same time, Northcliffe's mother became highly agitated at the line taken by *The Times* concerning Ireland. She had been told that it and the other Northcliffe newspapers were calling for Ulster to be compelled to accept a settlement. Consequently, Geraldine Harmsworth sent her oldest son a 'stiff' telegram at Java which read: 'All your papers are supporting coercion of Ulster. Do you approve? Very anxious and concerned. Reply. Mother.' The press lord responded that he was 'very disturbed by your Ulster message most darling one. I hate to think that while I am whirling round the world you should be for a moment unhappy about a matter I am too far off to help.'[63] Afraid that some illness had prompted this outburst, Northcliffe contacted Sutton and Rothermere. 'My peace of mind on the tour', he cabled Sutton, 'has depended entirely on my mother's health. I was very worried by her cable about Ulster, not so much by the cable itself, but the fact that an old lady of 83 should be disturbed and anxious.'[64] Sutton informed his chief, 'Shall succeed in satisfying all your mother's anxieties without changing your policy. She misunderstands. Have not and do not intend support coercion Ulster.' Rothermere cabled, 'Have seen Sutton and Mother's telegram and am quite satisfied that without changing policy of papers her anxieties can be relieved. She is thoroughly well, but in anxious frame of mind. Am seeing her three or four times a week.'[65] On 6 December Sutton cabled his chief that 'Sinn Fein delegates came to agreement with Government early this morning. Proposals will be submitted to Ulster today.'[66] After Stuart had informed him that the settlement had been signed, Northcliffe cabled that he hoped *The Times* would be given the 'fullest credit' it deserved for its efforts in the matter.[67]

With this Irish diversion behind him, Northcliffe was able to turn his mind back to the tour. The next destination was Saigon, reached via Singapore on the SS *Admiral Latouche Tréville*. He found the overloaded ship dirty-looking and untidy. The 600 surly foreign legionnaires in steerage and the shortage of lifeboats for the thousand total passengers made him rather nervous. The best parts, he declared, were the cuisine and the 'good-looking and well-dressed' ladies on board – mainly the daughters and wives of officers going out to Tonkin and Saigon. The press lord found himself, 'entirely in France here', with a 'complete absence of the stiffness and self-consciousness of English passengers and the little class distinctions at meals and elsewhere. Everybody does what he likes; no one minds, but the result is pandemonium.'[68]

Northcliffe's arrival at Saigon was marred by the news of the death of Sir Arthur Pearson. He commented in the 13 December dispatch home that 'I have known him since 1884 – a strange, erratic and in some ways noble character. He is in my mind today of course.' Several other friends and rivals also passed away while Northcliffe was abroad. These included Kennedy Jones, his exact contemporary, whose memoir *Fleet Street and Downing Street* had been published the year before and had claimed considerable credit for the author in the growth of the Harmsworth newspaper empire. A brief note of condolence to the widow from Northcliffe regretted that 'his political work, and my frequent absences abroad had rendered our meetings rare of late, but I always preserved and shall always preserve my regard for a colleague of ability, worth and character'.[69]

From the wide boulevards and shops to the cuisine, Northcliffe found Saigon a 'miniature Paris'. The French colonial government arranged a hectic day-and-night schedule. This included a motor-car excursion to Phnom Penh, the Cambodian capital, and a tour of the ruins at Angkor, where he attended a two-day festival. The immense site reminded Prioleau of the Oxford colleges, on a monster scale. Northcliffe was impressed by the huge faces of Buddha, as large as the Sphinx, and the 'Cloisters nine hundred yards long and bas reliefs in perfect condition.' At Angkor, the party was met by Marshal Joffre and other notables, including the jewel-encrusted King of Cambodia, who presided over the colourful pageant and held the mail boat to Bangkok for his guests. The eighty-three-year-old King arrived with a hundred attendants and wives – including, Northcliffe did not fail to notice, 'an extremely good-looking new addition, aged nineteen'.[70]

Aboard the SS *Donai*, on the way to Siam – 'the kingdom of Lilliput', as the press lord called it – he learned that 'oriental cock roaches are as big as prawns. I jumped high, tired as I was, when I saw one crawling on my bed last night and threatened Frederick with instant "sack" if he didn't get it. He got the beastly thing after a struggle.'[71] Much of the Siamese court had been educated in England; consequently at Bangkok Northcliffe was able to dispense with his 'fluent but erratic' French. On 21 December he dined with the Siamese King at the royal residence, which Northcliffe described as much like Buckingham Palace. Topics of conversation at the magnificent banquet included King Edward, Queen Alexandra and Balmoral. In the local press reports of the affair, Northcliffe was dubbed the 'King of all the editors in the world.' One Bangkok paper was an almost exact replica of the *Daily Mail*. The owner of the original quit Siam with great regret, calling it 'an interesting and unknown country'. However, at Bangkok he exhibited a striking fit of temper. Snoad recorded in his diary that, when he was unable to produce a newspaper his chief demanded, Northcliffe shoved him out of a room and down some stairs into the arms of four purple-clad servants of the King. The next day no sign of the eruption remained and the party left by train for the Federated Malay States.

In the Malay Peninsula the party transferred to a British train for the first time since leaving Australia. Northcliffe complained that the government-provided car was 'unclean and old' and that, compared to Siam's, the railway system was overall a 'disgrace to the British Empire'. At Kuala Lumpur preparations were under way for the visit of the Prince of Wales. The only English papers evident were the *Overseas Daily Mail* and the weekly edition of *The Times*. This observation brightened an otherwise undistinguished leg of the journey. Resting at Penang, which he considered one of the most beautiful seaside places he had ever visited, Northcliffe had time to look through a large stack of Christmas and New Year's cables, including one from President Harding. The new year 1922 had just begun in England when Snoad brought in a cable from Lady Northcliffe and one from a London publisher asking for a book, which Northcliffe remarked he had 'no intention of writing'. He had also started a 'thinning regime', determined to return to Marseilles weighing twelve stone and six pounds.

From Ceylon (Sri Lanka), where Northcliffe was briefed on Indian affairs and made some purchases at a renowned gem market, he advised Steed that his Washington dispatches were being twisted in the Far East to appear pro-Japanese. He went on that he had no doubt that *The Times* 'had been got at for years. By whom and how I don't know' and that he had had some 'unpleasant personal experiences' as a result of the attitude of the newspaper.[72] Steed replied that his chief's 'astounding prescience about the Washington Conference and the uncanny accuracy of your instincts about the United States were borne in upon me more and more the longer I was over there . . . we have, I think, scored very heavily in the United States.' The editor reported that, to combat a Hearst campaign against England and the Conference, his articles had appeared in numerous papers, including the Washington *Post* and *Herald*, the San Francisco *Chronicle*, the Munsey press in New York, and 400 newspapers in the West and Midwest. Steed told Northcliffe that Geddes and Balfour had done 'splendidly', as had the Dominion representatives.[73] Before the Washington Conference adjourned the following month, two agreements would be signed which, at the time, seemed great victories for Balfour and Britain. A Five Power Treaty extricated the British from an expensive and futile naval race with the United States by setting limits on shipbuilding. The troublesome Anglo-Japanese alliance was replaced by a Four Power Treaty to maintain the status quo in the Far East and the Pacific. Balfour returned home in triumph and was awarded with an earldom and the Garter.[74]

While these developments unfolded in Washington, Northcliffe's party began the longest Asian rail segment of the journey, to Delhi. 'The shadow on our trip', the press lord wrote, was the 'Indian news, or the lack of it'. The party was constantly asked about the Prince of Wales, who was also touring the subcontinent. British officials, Northcliffe recorded, 'never realise that silence means rumours, especially among these gossiping Orientals'. Indians were everywhere, he went on, and all used the same argument: that the British must be afraid of Mahatma Gandhi, the leader of the Congress movement for home rule, 'otherwise they would arrest him. Therefore he is more powerful than the British Raj.'[75]

The passage from Ceylon to the coast of India – fittingly on a vessel called the *Curzon* – was the roughest of their travels. Northcliffe had not seen India since 1897, and had grown no fonder of the place in the intervening years. Even travelling in a private car, he found it 'uncomfortable' and 'wearisome'. The crowds made him uneasy, as did the religious division which convulsed the country. He did not know 'Why we should keep the Mohammedans and Hindus from cutting each others throats . . . What do we want India for?' he went on. 'Prestige? Perhaps. Cash? We certainly don't get any from it.' What the British got was the responsibility of 'defending these ungrateful people'. The thousands of able Britons in India, he felt, could do far better elsewhere. The weather was rainy, and he slept most of the time between Madras and Delhi. The chief news was the resignation in Ireland of Éamon de Valera as President of the Republic after the Dáil accepted the Irish settlement. De Valera, Northcliffe recorded, was a 'great personage in India, compared to Gandhi'.

At Delhi, Northcliffe stayed at the Viceregal Lodge with Lord and Lady Reading. Both were very kind to him. He also dined with Lord Rawlinson, the commander-in-chief, whom he had not seen since the Battle of the Somme. He revisited the Pearl Mosque, the Fort, the Red Palace and several of the remains of the Great Mutiny of 1857, such as the Kashmir Gate. After touring the 'vast new Delhi', Northcliffe recorded that it was a 'wonderful pre-war conception' but very unpopular. The natives called it the 'grave of the British Empire', and repeated the superstition that this eighth Delhi would see the passing of British rule. Golfing with Reading, the party was followed by detectives, which reminded him of his experience in the USA in 1917. Northcliffe commented that 'all are anxious here, very, very anxious – almost as anxious as in 1857'.[76]

Northcliffe praised Reading for having the 'faculty of being unperturbed, ready with a laugh that makes others laugh, during this very, very trying time in India'. The native newspapers attacked the Viceroy for his 'repressive' methods, which filled the prisons with those who would, said Northcliffe, be in jail at home for the same actions. He feared that by the time he got to Jerusalem 'there may have been bloodshed in India. Nobody knows.' He felt like a deserter for not staying longer, as Reading requested, to greet the Prince of Wales, but longed for Elmwood and home.[77] Lady Reading sent a note from the Viceregal Lodge to Lady Northcliffe, informing her that her husband had left after 'all too short a stay' and that he had been 'really comfortable here and liked it'. She went on, 'I must tell you how well he looks, quite rejuvenated, so different to when I last saw him in London and he was in excellent spirits.'[78] Lord Reading reported to Edwin Montagu, the Secretary of State for India, that he hoped Northcliffe's visit would 'do good. He is proposing to keep one of his best men here for a time in order that the British public may be better acquainted with the difficulties and perplexities you and I have to encounter.' The Viceroy believed the press lord was 'undoubtedly desirous of helping in the present trying state of affairs and will give greater publicity to Indian news and situation'.[79]

As he promised Reading, when Northcliffe reached Port Said he dispatched Arthur Moore to India to bolster the *Times*'s coverage. The days of the Raj, Northcliffe believed, were numbered. The predicament, he confided in Sutton, was as 'ugly a one as the British Empire has been in. For the first time in history the Moslems and Hindus have got together.'[80] Reading, he went on, was unhappy that his warnings about the 'Moslem situation' were not addressed. Northcliffe complained a few weeks later that *The Times* 'criticised Lord Reading but I believe the fact is that he cannot get replies from London and is interfered with . . . probably in view of desire to attract labour vote at next election. It was obvious to me that there was a difference of opinion between him and our Government.'[81]

From the SS *Naldera* on the Red Sea, on the final leg of his peregrination, Northcliffe wrote to Stuart that our little trip is ending. I think that all of us are better for it. I thought I knew something of the British Empire before I started, but I didn't. John Bull is very much the top dog in the vast world of the Far East. How such a tiny island as ours does it, I do not know, but it docs.[82]

News arrived from Sutton that *The Times* was running a campaign against a possible general election, which it dubbed 'The Unpopular Election'. In Sutton's opinion, Lloyd George would push for a poll before the rift among his Tory supporters got any worse.[83] Northcliffe replied that he had heard nothing of these events except that Lloyd George was uncertain. At Bombay he had received a cable from Churchill, the Colonial Secretary; this 'did not refer to an election, but my suspicions were at once aroused. Your letter confirms that he is going to the Prime Minister, which explains why the cable to me was sent.'

Northcliffe sent Hudson his thoughts on the political situations he had encountered along the way. He commented that 'Politics in India means anxious white men. Politics in China means trade. Politics in Japan means suspicion and propaganda. Politics in Australia means basic wages and how to keep out emigrants.' Everywhere he went, he was asked about Lloyd George. He told Hudson, 'They always talk of my alleged relations with the Prime Minister. I have never had any to speak of, as you know; I don't remember his ever having been to our house. I don't remember ever having been to his.'[84]

At almost the same time, Lloyd George, having failed to shore up his position with a diplomatic breakthrough at a Cannes meeting with France to pursue the peace process, considered what would be needed to make things up with his greatest press enemy. He asked Riddell whether he thought it would be possible to reach a settlement, adding that he had at his disposal a Knighthood of St Patrick which he had meant for Carson, whose present attitude made it impossible to honour him. 'I might give it to Northcliffe,' the Prime Minister went on, 'if one felt that one could rely on him . . . He has defeated none of my policies. I have beaten him all along the line, and there is really no reason why he and I should not be friends.' Riddell replied to this that he believed that what Northcliffe wanted was an earldom, to which Lloyd George responded, 'Well, it might be done.' When Riddell suggested that he make the proposal indirectly, the Prime Minister countered that it might be wiser and safer for Hamar Greenwood, who was known to talk in a 'rather wild way, to raise the point'. The fact that Northcliffe was by this

time en route to Palestine made it difficult to get in touch with him
before an election might be called. Lloyd George decided that the best
course would be to wait until Parliament met and to see the attitude of
the Conservatives. 'If they want me to go on,' he told Riddell, 'I will. If
they don't I shall retire and write my book.'[85]

While the Prime Minister made his political calculations, Northcliffe
arrived at the final stops of the world tour. In Cairo, he met Lord
Allenby, the Egyptian High Commissioner, and stayed at the Official
Residence. Northcliffe described Allenby as a 'tall, large-headed, good-
looking, distinguished gentleman . . . believed to have been one of the
best generals in the war'. Allenby had been summoned to England to
explain his policy: to grant nominal sovereignty to Egypt. In
Northcliffe's opinion, if enough troops were kept in the country it
would not 'matter much as to Indian or Egyptian independence'. The
High Commissioner escorted Northcliffe to his great chamber at the
Residence and revealed that it was where Kitchener had always slept.
Northcliffe commented to his family, 'I am writing this early in the
morning of the last day of January in the bed of that Mammoth Myth.'
Lord Cromer had slept there as well; consequently Northcliffe recorded
the wish that he might 'imbibe some of Cromer's wisdom and
Kitchener's capacity for collecting china'. The local newspapers were
both 'very naughty' and 'most flattering'. 'I suppose', the press lord
recorded, 'there is something to be said for both points of view.'[86] The
Egyptian Gazette's epithet for him, 'Northcliffe the Kingmaker', he
noted, was 'perhaps a teeny weeny bit overdone'. To one of his secretaries at Carmelite House he wrote, 'by the time you get this I shall be in
Palestine. I am told that it is very cold there . . . We must wear sheep-
skins – not the first time my affectionate critics will say this wolf has
gone forth so clad.'[87]

Travelling with Northcliffe to Britain's mandate in the Middle East as
'secretary and correspondent pro tem' was Philip Graves, Cairo correspondent of *The Times*. Graves was a moderate on the Palestine question, which had in many ways been created by the Balfour Declaration
of November 1917, which stated, in part, that the British government
viewed 'with favour the establishment in Palestine of a national home
for the Jewish people, and will use their best endeavours to facilitate the
achievement of this object'.[88] While Northcliffe had been occupied in
the United States as head of the War Mission, *The Times*, with Dawson
and Steed in agreement, had supported the Declaration. The contradictory promises made to the Zionists and Arabs during the war had

fostered unrest and violence in the disputed lands. During his journey, Northcliffe had received telegrams from Arab, Jewish and Christian groups requesting that he hear their respective grievances, and at Gaza he met the first Arab deputation. The Arabs argued, and he agreed to a certain extent, that Britain had, 'without sufficient thought, guaranteed Palestine as a home for the Jews despite the fact that 700,000 Arab moslems live there and own it'. Northcliffe noted that 'Arabs and Christians have now joined up against the Jews. There is hatred and there has been bloodshed.'[89] At Ludd a large and unruly demonstration about the problem was stopped and Northcliffe's motorcade was joined by an armoured escort.

In Jerusalem the owner of *The Times* stayed on the Mount of Olives at Government House, a 'vast Rhine Schloss' originally built by the Kaiser. The High Commissioner, Herbert Samuel, was ill; consequently, Northcliffe was greeted by his assistant, Sir Wyndham Deedes. From Jerusalem the press lord made an excursion to a Jewish colony at Rishon le-Zion, where, he noted, Hebrew was being revived as was Irish in Ireland. He cautioned the settlers, whom he found arrogant and bad-mannered, that not everyone in Britain supported the Zionist cause as rabidly as they seemed to believe and that they needed to be careful not to 'tire out our people' by secretly importing more arms to fight the Arabs. The 'recent importation of undesirable Jews, Bolshevists and others', he told the colonists, 'was the partial cause of the regrettable troubles with the Arabs'.[90]

Northcliffe visited the holy places of all sides, including the Jewish Wailing Wall, the Christian Church of the Holy Sepulchre and the Muslim Mosque of Omar. At the last he met several Muslim leaders. Deputations from every faction attempted to extract an opinion from him on Palestine. 'All lie profusely,' he recorded: 'the Moslems outrageously, the Zionists artistically.' The only declaration he made was that the 'immigration of new Jews, unused to liberty and plenty, should be done with great care'.[91] He also travelled out to Trans-Jordania for a meeting with its nominal ruler, Emir Abdullah, son of the King of Hejaz. At the Emir's camp, the press lord was introduced to a 'swarm of sheikhs'. He returned to Jerusalem, which, he recorded, looked like 'Jerusalem the Golden in the sunlight'. His final pronouncement was 'There will be trouble in Palestine', which, he feared, would be 'another Ireland'.

After a brief visit to Beirut, Northcliffe arrived on 13 February at Port Said, where he boarded the *Egypt*, bound for Marseilles. Passing

Corsica, he recorded, 'Every ship has its odd characters. Among those of the Egypt is a former fat man, now in skeleton class, who beginning life as a reporter at sixteen, is now said to have more papers than he can count and more money than brains. Is finishing whirl round world and ready for another one tomorrow.'[92] Unfortunately, there would be few tomorrows left to the returning voyager.

19

Into the Darkness, 1922

ON 18 FEBRUARY 1922 Northcliffe received a warm official welcome on arrival at Marseilles, where, to the Chamber of Commerce, he delivered in French a speech drafted by Steed. He sent thanks for the words, which were, he said, 'much applauded'.[1] The editor of *The Times* advised his chief that the address was purposely non-controversial, because the British government was 'very shaky' and his words would be 'watched and maliciously exploited'. Lord Grey of Fallodon, in the editor's estimation, had become the leading contender to unseat the Prime Minister, although in the current situation 'anything' might happen. In the aftermath of the Washington Conference, Steed reported that Balfour had become a great man and, consequently, Lloyd George's jealousy of him was 'almost pathological'. The editor went on:

> you probably hardly realise the personal and political importance you have acquired during the last few months. Both as regards the situation at home and the situation in Europe – to say nothing of America – you are now in the position of a statesman wielding far greater power than you have ever possessed and enjoying the peculiar advantage of immunity from overthrow by Parliaments or by elections.[2]

Rigorous dieting had allowed Northcliffe to reach his weight goal – twelve stone and six pounds – and the *Daily Mail* report of his arrival at Marseilles commented that he 'appeared to be in the best of health'. Lady Northcliffe joined him at the Eden Hotel at Cap d'Ail, from where he cabled Rothermere on arrival, 'Energy doubled.' Nevertheless, on the advice of the doctors, rather than return immediately to England after so many months in the tropics, he planned to reacclimatize himself in France. However, it was not likely, for personal and business reasons, that he would stay there long. He was eager to see his mother at Totteridge, and he had returned to Europe full of schemes to reenergize the *Daily Mail* and *The Times*, which in particular he thought had grown old and dull.

Four days after the chief proprietor's arrival at Marseilles, a message to Steed and Campbell Stuart called for a plan to be prepared, in consultation with Sutton and Caird, to revamp *The Times*. He cabled Stuart, 'In view of the appalling gross figures just received am returning immediately. Figures are worse than I predicted two years ago. All those explanations and statistics with which it was attempted to dope me make very pathetic reading today . . . Whole enterprise requires careful scrutiny and more initiative.'[3] At Carmelite House, Sutton was instructed to inform Marlowe of a 'complete revolution Foreign Department immediately I arrive. There is no Foreign Department.'[4] Northcliffe planned to combine the foreign services of *The Times* and the *Daily Mail* outside the major news centres, and to institute yearly inspections. Since he had found the weekly edition of *The Times* to be more popular abroad than the *Overseas Daily Mail*, he instructed Marlowe to place in it a 'line up' of announcements of the other Northcliffe newspapers. He also engaged Sir William Beach Thomas to make an extended voyage to write an 'Imperial Guide to Emigration'.

While abroad, besides the problems he found with his newspapers, Northcliffe had also been appalled at the disarray he encountered at many of the Overseas Club branches along the route. A cable to John Evelyn Wrench, who after the war had left publishing to devote himself full time to the Overseas Club and the English-Speaking Union, questioned if he was aware of the condition of the Club in various parts of the world. 'Is it right,' the press lord asked, that 'we should go on misrepresenting the thing as we do?' He told Wrench he wanted to discuss the matter when he returned, and added, 'frankly, I think I ought to tell the truth'.[5] Wrench defended the Club, responding that he knew of no misrepresentation and was confused by Northcliffe's message. The troublesome Melbourne branch, he replied, had been disowned and the Club remained 'the strongest Empire movement in existence', with a membership of 26,000 – greater by 10,000 than that of the Colonial Institute, with which there was discussion of a possible merger.[6]

Before leaving France, Northcliffe stopped in Paris to deal with fresh union salary demands at the *Continental Daily Mail.* He dealt roughly with this latest 'blackmail' at a late-night meeting at his hotel suite, physically removing a union leader from his room, while denouncing the man as 'a damned ungrateful swine'.[7] Back in England, Northcliffe accompanied his wife to her house at Crowborough, where he was cheered once again to enjoy the simple pleasures of the English countryside – the birds and the early spring flowers. Although Lady Northcliffe was not alarmed by his appearance or manner, the slimming regime led several of those who met her husband at Victoria station to describe him as 'haggard' and 'shrunken' in appearance. His old friend Max Pemberton, seeing him at the London town house, was shocked at the change in eight months. 'The robust figure, the upright bearing, the buoyant manner', Pemberton recorded, 'were gone. I saw a stooping, wizened, shrunken old man and the first glance at him told me that he was doomed.'[8]

Despite this dire prophecy, for a time Northcliffe showed considerable energy – too much for many of his employees. From Carlton Gardens, Northcliffe telephoned George Isaacs, the *Daily Mail* trade-union leader, for an appraisal of the state of labour relations. Isaacs complained of a proposal by the Newspaper Proprietors' Association to cut salaries, which the press lord thought as unjustified as the opposing union calls for wage increases. Differences with the other proprietors prompted the owner of the *Daily Mail* to withdraw from the NPA and to begin writing a pamphlet setting out his opinions on newspaper ownership. The plain-speaking W.J. Evans, managing editor of the *Evening News*, wrote to his chief that he believed the NPA resignation was a mistake and that Northcliffe's personal negotiations with 'that man Isaacs' had 'dulled our reputation'.

The *Evening News* did not escape the scrutiny of its proprietor. A poor appraisal of the paper by Northcliffe, posted at Carmelite House, was torn down by an indignant staff. Evans, who had known his chief for thirty years, sent a frank note to his employer that 'the message you sent to be posted was a profound mistake. Its effect on the staff is disastrous. Good men . . . don't mind criticism and are ready to profit by it, but they resent unnecessary complaint and they won't stand abuse.' The managing editor was well aware of the owner's method of 'keeping young men up to the mark by alternatively praising and blaming them', but, he said, Northcliffe's actions had reduced the employees 'to a state of simply watching your moods and saying whatever they think likely to please you'. Evans professed his 'care for the business and for yourself', but admitted that he did not 'like some aspects of recent happenings because they put you in a bad light with those who don't know you and don't make allowances for one who has so many cares, worries and responsibilities'. Northcliffe replied from Paris that he liked 'frank criticism' and hoped that he was not too 'swell-headed' to be unaware that men in his position were surrounded by 'flatterers and sycophants'. However, he felt Evans had become a trifle 'touchy and inclined to take for himself reproofs in no way intended for him'. Northcliffe added that, on his return, Evans was the 'only important associate' that had not sent a word of greeting. 'I was not hurt,' he went on. 'I ascribed the silence to work and preoccupation with the difficult problems we all face.'[9]

In addition to alterations in the newspaper offices, another result of Northcliffe's voyage was a call for an inquiry into the Palestine question. Dr Chaim Weizmann, in 1920 elected president of the World Zionist Organization, accepted the proposal in a letter published in *The Times* on the day Northcliffe landed at Marseilles. The paper commented, 'We trust that the Zionist leaders will be able to act vigorously and authoritatively in making it clear that Zionism, if it is to succeed, must move step by step, in close and friendly co-operation with the Moslem and Christian natives of Palestine.'[10] The *Daily Mail* was less measured in its pronouncements, declaring in headlines that 'Lord Northcliffe's Remedy' to the 'Palestine Waste, Bolsheviks and Incessant Arms Smuggling' was to 'Stop the Immigration' of Jews.[11] This hostility led Weizmann to seek an interview with the press lord. The Zionist leader commented to an American correspondent that the attacks by the Northcliffe press were reviving the Arab cause, which had been 'dying a natural death'. Fortunately, said Weizmann, the British Government 'has so far not wavered from its position; in fact Northcliffe's attacks would rather strengthen our case . . . but its effects on our financial situation and on the situation in Palestine are of a different nature'. He went on, 'I hope to see Lord Northcliffe within the next few days and a great deal will turn on the results of that interview.'[12]

In early March Weizmann was granted an interview at Carlton Gardens, where he was surprised to find that Northcliffe had set up a debate with Leo Maxse on the Palestine question. Both Weizmann and Maxse were given five minutes to state their positions, while Northcliffe's secretary, H.G. Price, took notes. In Weizmann's account, it was the host that dominated the conversation. When the two disputants had gone, Price asked his chief if he wanted the notes typed out.

'Good Lord no! Forget it,' was the reply.[13] In a series 'Some Truths About Palestine', by Philip Graves, *The Times* concluded that, rather than support a national 'political' home in Palestine, Britain should support 'spiritual' Zionism.[14]

Another legacy of Northcliffe's journey was his involvement in Indian questions. He agreed to Edwin Montagu's request from the India Office that 'if you can spare the time, I should be very glad to learn from you at first hand the views which you have formed as to the Indian situation'.[15] Northcliffe commented in a letter to Stuart that he was 'told in India that Montagu and Reading had not been seeing eye to eye for a long time, but Reading himself said nothing on the subject. I have every confidence in him as Viceroy, if he is let alone. He succeeded a very weak man, Chelmsford, whose policy was to let everything slide.'[16] The press lord did not believe that Reading was exaggerating the Muslim situation as some newspapers claimed. The government, Northcliffe asserted, should have acted on the many warnings. Now they faced a Muslim population 'aroused as they have never been before'. 'What are the members of the Indian Government to do,' he went on, 'when their letters and protests are ignored?' If the policy of 'firmness' was interfered with, Reading had vowed to resign. This, said Northcliffe, would be 'disastrous'.[17] The Viceroy sent his thanks for Northcliffe's help and support in England. It was 'a great encouragement', said Reading, that Northcliffe knew and understood the 'difficulties of the task here'.[18]

Back at Printing House Square, the 2 March editorial conference was called in the larger boardroom rather than Steed's office, in order to announce Northcliffe's new arrangements for *The Times*. At this meeting, which had been expanded to include sub-editors and others, H.G. Price read a statement by the chief proprietor which complained, among other things, that he

> had not returned to a bed of roses as far as P.H.S. is concerned. In spite of the warnings that I and others gave, readers have been deserting the Paper for years and recent editorial gaffes are, I am sure, losing us more.
>
> The unpopular policies I do not mind. I am responsible for them, as for the entire policy. The blunders I do mind, because they hurt the paper and still further alienate its reading circle, now down to 108,000.
>
> I am not going to be quite as gentle in the future as in the past, and if pressure is put upon me by the other Proprietors, as seems likely . . . I shall institute a root and branch enquiry into the administration of the Times, the expenses thereof, and the personnel.

Northcliffe's secretary also announced that the price of *The Times* was to be halved, from 3d to 1½d. This, the message continued, would be 'the greatest leap in the dark in the history of Printing House Square'.[19] When Price was finished, Steed asked, 'Is that all?' Price replied 'That is all' and retired.

This incident soon became public knowledge. Stuart told Riddell that he did not agree with this strategy of humiliation and that he had discussed terms with an outraged Steed for leaving the paper.[20] The editor, however, decided to bide his time, while consulting an attorney, Sir Charles Russell, who advised him to stay in place and, according to Steed, confided that, at a recent lunch, Northcliffe's 'abnormal' condition had convinced him that the proprietor's days were numbered.[21]

The drop in price of *The Times* raised circulation, but did not stop the financial haemorrhage, which amounted to £1,000 a week. Rothermere sent a telegram of 'Best Wishes' for the 'new Times development', while at the same time reminding his brother that there was 'such a thing as bankruptcy'. Northcliffe commented to H.G. Price that his brother was 'moaning about money again'. The chief proprietor complained that the staff of *The Times* 'seemed to be ever more diligently devoted to the past, labouring under the delusion that news like wine improves with keeping'.[22] He planned to return to France, leaving Stuart – whom he warned would be held to 'very strict account' – in charge. Before he left England, he sent Lord Inchcape reports on his world voyage and on the sterling performance of the shipping magnate's operations. He added that 'as the Eastern doctors predicted, the sudden change after so many weeks in the Tropics have disturbed my throat and eyes which are much inflamed. I am therefore, going to the Pyrenees over the March winds.'[23]

From Pau, Northcliffe told John Prioleau that at Cap d'Ail he had caught a chill which had inflamed his eyes, throat and temper. Nonetheless, he went on that he hoped Prioleau had

> felt the benefit of our journey as much as I did. I feel very strong and full of pip, punch and kick. I am writing a little review of our world whizz which I now begin to see in its proper proportion . . . I wound up my family diary by saying 'Prioleau and I went round the world without a single contretemps which says much for Prioleau'.[24]

Though he got along with Prioleau, Northcliffe's relations with others at the newspapers continued to suffer. His captious criticisms of the *Daily Mail* drew a resignation from Marlowe. Stuart, unable to reach a suitable financial arrangement with the editor, interceded and an apology from the owner brought Marlowe's return.

Northcliffe found that the mountain scenery 'quietened his nerves'; however, his golf pro, Sandy Thomson, noted that something was 'on his mind . . . He's worrying.' Northcliffe's touchiness and loss of mental balance would increasingly be reflected elsewhere, but until the end the ardently dutiful son sent calm and reassuring messages to his mother. From Pau he wrote to her that he was 'fighting the good fight, and retain my figure and eat very little and only drink at one meal daily'. The continuation of the strict regimen begun on the voyage may well have speeded his physical and mental deterioration during the next months. His personal physician, Dr Seymour Price, later told Pemberton that 'Instead of half starving himself as he did, he should have taken as much food as possible. Instead of denying himself all drink, he should have drunk consistently.'[25]

From London, Rothermere cabled of the 'considerable anxiety throughout the newspaper trade' because of the printing-trade-union wage demands. Northcliffe instructed his managers not to follow his brother's 'tendency to panic'. When he refused to join the NPA discussions of wage cuts, the compositors of Carmelite House sent 'heartfelt thanks'. A letter to H.G. Price commented that he was not 'likely to join combinations of rich men for grinding down poor men'. Near the end of his time at Pau, Northcliffe sent a letter of warning to Sir Andrew Caird at Printing House Square that he hoped 'once more to make the building vibrate with energy, and to pursue with vigorous communiqués the numberless Diehards – "We'd Better Nots," "We've Never Done It Before", and "It Can't Be Doners"'. A mounting torrent of cables flooded the newspaper offices from Pau. About *The Times*, Northcliffe told Stuart, 'It is now or never.' Despite their differences, Steed had remained in place as editor, but a 'gaffe' in regard to the Far East reminded the chief proprietor of the New York interview affair of the previous year. Northcliffe told Stuart that Steed knew a great deal about Central Europe, but that in discussing other areas with him he felt at times as though he was 'talking to a pinhead'.[26]

In the face of renewed economic woes – the most recent in agriculture – Conservative discontent with the Lloyd George government led to rumours of a Cabinet reorganization or even the resignation of the Prime Minister. In Paris on 14 March Northcliffe discussed the shifting domestic political sands with Lord Derby, the British ambassador. The press lord reported to his mother that Derby 'cannot make up his mind.

Evidently he wants to be Prime Minister, but he is frightened of the criticism of Lloyd George's newspapers, and of Birkenhead and Winston.' Northcliffe informed the ambassador that his newspapers would be hostile to his joining the present government because it would 'temporarily strengthen this wretched gang of people who are making us pay six shillings in the pound Income Tax, causing us trouble in India, Egypt, Palestine and making the French hate us, all the rest of it'.[27] Hudson informed Northcliffe that 'the Fat Man was sorely tempted for 48 hours, but considerations of personal safety finally triumphed'.[28] The friends of the Prime Minister, he went on, had the door slammed in their faces when they tried to arrange a reorganization to prolong the government. Lloyd George commented to Sir Edward Grigg that he failed to see why he should resign and seem to yield 'to the howls of enemies like Northcliffe'.[29]

At the same time, Northcliffe sent Stuart instructions on a number of subjects. He hoped that Steed was leaving at once for the Far East Conference in Paris and that he would work publicly and privately in support of Reading in India. He called for a 'short, sharp leader' on the Genoa economic conference scheduled for April, and *The Times* published two articles which argued against both the Prime Minister's going to Genoa and his proposal to extend official recognition to Russia.[30]

Stuart felt the most important recent development was Lloyd George's desire for a vote of confidence over the Russian policy. 'We must endeavour', said Stuart, 'to see that he does not get that vote.' Without committing Northcliffe, he was trying to get the Conservatives to agree on an alternative to Chamberlain, who was 'putty in Lloyd George's hands'.[31] All attempts to deny Lloyd George the vote of confidence and to find another Conservative leader failed. On the day of the vote, 3 April, the Prime Minister entertained the Commons with his comments on the hostile press:

> judging by the criticism of the 'grotesque conglomerate' who were in opposition, he could only imagine that their new Government would have its principles enunciated and expounded by the *Morning Post*, the *Daily Herald*, the *Westminster Gazette*, the *Daily Mail* and *Comic Cuts*. I do not mention *The Times*, because that is only a tasteless rehash of the *Daily Mail*.[32]

Despite his victory, Lloyd George departed for Genoa needing an international success to restore his weakened position at home.

Steed resisted travelling to the Genoa meeting, which opened on 10 April, because he believed it would only make Europe's 'confusion worse confounded'.[33] Northcliffe by this time had in mind shifting Steed back to foreign affairs and making other arrangements for the managing editor's position. He overruled all objections and from Pau insisted that Steed attend the conference.

On the Genoa agenda was a discussion of reopening relations with Bolshevik Russia, which Northcliffe publicly called 'shaking hands with murder'. While the conference was in session, on 17 April the world was shocked by the news that, at Rapallo, Germany and Russia had signed an agreement of their own which seemed to imperil the European balance of power. *The Times* declared that the Allies had been 'duped', and it appeared the conference might collapse. Winston Churchill agreed with Northcliffe's anti-Russian sentiments. After hearing that the Colonial Secretary had taken a bad fall at Eaton Hall, the press lord sent a telegram wishing him a speedy recovery and remarking that he must be glad not to be at Genoa in the circumstances. Churchill replied, 'Yes, I am very glad not to be at Genoa. You probably know what my views on that subject are, so I need not commit the impropriety of repeating them.'[34]

The government was further infuriated by Steed, who, after speaking privately with the chief French delegate, M. Barthou, suggested in *The Times* that Lloyd George planned to repudiate the Entente with France. The Prime Minister cabled Chamberlain that there was 'not a word of truth in it' and that the French were outraged. He told the press at Genoa that Steed's allegations were 'the ravings of a person who is insane with desire to wreck the conference', and he instructed Sir Edward Grigg to tell the press representatives not to believe any statements about the Genoa conference made in the Northcliffe press and that he would deal with them once again in Parliament. Chamberlain in turn told the Commons that *The Times* statement was a 'wicked and malicious invention'.[35] Chamberlain confided in Riddell that 'Northcliffe has been the best friend L.G. had at the Conference. His action has created public sympathy for L.G. amongst people who are strongly opposed to his policy.'[36]

Northcliffe congratulated Steed for saving the Entente. A letter to Murdoch commented that Lloyd George 'has had an awful fall at Genoa, which may do him good'.[37] However, when Barthou repudiated Steed's revelations, Northcliffe reversed course. He considered asking for the editor's resignation, believing, whether Steed's assertions were true or not, that he had been duped once again. In the end, he had Stuart tell Steed that he still believed 'good will result' from the episode.

It appears in this instance that the editor was guilty only of publishing off-the-record remarks, in much the same manner as he had himself been quoted in the United States. This affair moved Sutton to suggest to Northcliffe that the time had come to replace Steed; otherwise, he wrote, 'you and the old paper will be continually involved in some trouble'.[38]

Once again Lloyd George found a way out of his difficulties, in this instance aided by what were seen to be personal newspaper attacks. In the *Observer* the next month, Garvin welcomed him home from Genoa with praise. His article defended the Prime Minister against 'men like Northcliffe, with their preaching of a three-fold lunacy of hatred and suspicion', who 'will never be happy . . . until they drive Germany, Russia and Japan into one another's arms with ultimate consequences . . . destructive of every sane hope and aim'. It warned particularly of the 'hundred gramophones' of one man who was 'full of personal kinks and political hallucinations'.[39]

While the Genoa conference was in session, Northcliffe came to the end of his patience with the advertising in the *Daily Mail*, which, he declared, was ruling the paper. He told Price that he proposed to train the hall porter of thirty years, Robert Glover, and that 'If the present state of affairs be ever repeated on any one day, I will put him in charge of the Advertising Department.' When this threat did not have the desired result, Glover, who had been apprised of his employer's view of offensive advertising, was installed, very briefly, as 'head critic of advertisements'. Immediately after the meeting with the advertising staff at which Glover was introduced, Price recorded that he saw Northcliffe 'sitting with his head in his hands, his shoulders heaving with laughter, like a schoolboy who has played a successful trick'. Reacting to whispers that 'the Old Man is a bit off his head', a bulletin from the proprietor replied that 'The Old Man, the Mr Alfred of earlier days, may be off his head, but he has stopped the big bludgeoning advertisements getting in the paper.'[40] Northcliffe's last appearance at Carmelite House took place on 4 May at the retirement luncheon for W.J. Evans, who was generously pensioned off after twenty-eight years of service. In his final speech to his employees, Northcliffe spoke wistfully of the past.

At the same time, Northcliffe published the pamphlet *Newspapers and Their Millionaires*, meant to expose the wealthy outsiders he felt were corrupting Fleet Street. The pamphlet criticized, mildly, several of his fellow proprietors, who, 'ignorant of Fleet Street dictate terms to those who have spent their lives trying to understand the complex questions of a newspaper'. It argued against the wage cuts proposed by the NPA, giving as justification the danger that British printers would flee to more lucrative positions in the USA if not properly paid. In revealing something of the other Fleet Street proprietors in his publication, Northcliffe said, he was simply repaying the 'favours' many of them had done him over the years by printing so many stories about himself. The work also contained a little-noticed prophecy that newspapers would soon be challenged by a new technological development, the radio, already sweeping the United States. During his world tour, Northcliffe had stayed in a house with a 'loud-speaking broadcast wireless', which, being a newspaper man, he declared he did not like. The pamphlet had little impact outside the environs of Fleet Street. The *New Statesman* commented that 'Lord Northcliffe is perfectly justified in poking fun at his "millionaire" colleagues' and that conditions had arisen in which 'journalists of all political colours are almost driven to pray for more Northcliffes'. Northcliffe himself told C.H. Lea, who wrote an article critical of the work, that he had not had time to read Lea's effort, but that he knew the printing trade well and that the point of the book was that he would not have his 'affairs dominated by people who do not know the trade'.[41]

At Carmelite House and Printing House Square the proprietor's daily detailed criticisms made life increasingly intolerable for the employees, and stories of his mental imbalance abounded. Steed, perhaps understandably, in particular found him unreasonable and ill-tempered, whereas Sutton, Stuart and Price took longer to admit alarm, still able to place his actions within the boundaries of a prior history of restless, impulsive autocracy. On Easter Sunday Northcliffe's luncheon hostess had been shocked to hear him, on the phone to *The Times*, use an expletive – something completely new to her long experience. A month later, a sudden vendetta against nepotism cost several people their jobs, including a relative of Caird, who was especially irate and talking of legal remedy. The manager, Lints Smith, and others were fed up and near rebellion, a confidant at *The Times* told Riddell.

Northcliffe's last public function was an 18 May speech to the Australia and New Zealand Club in London. During his address, which was well received, he hinted that he would be visiting Germany. The newspapers in his proposed destination soon reacted. The *Neueste Nachrichten* declared that 'nobody had been so hated in Germany since Napoleon'. Another journal reminded its readers that he was 'the one man in the whole world that hates Germany most. We trust that employers, officials and workmen who are in contact with him will not forget it.'[42] The 'Message From the Chief' a week after his speech announced that 'Before this reaches you all I shall be out of England on a very interesting mission of which you will hear nothing and of which you know nothing now although you may think you do.' Sutton was left in charge, once again with power of attorney.

John Walter, who saw Northcliffe on 24 May concerning the possibility of selling his shares in *The Times*, noted no abnormality; however, before Northcliffe left for Germany, the Elmwood staff commented on his 'permanent anger' with them all. To anger was added paranoia when he demanded that fire alarms be installed because 'people were coming down from London to set fire to the house'. His 'tempers' led the head gardener and his housekeeper wife to give notice after eleven years of service. The gardens of Elmwood brought no peace, and even the success of a new periodical, *Popular Wireless*, failed to interest him. A member of the staff told Pine that 'no one seem[ed] to realise how ill' Northcliffe was. The time for excusing his behaviour as simply that of an imperious autocrat was nearing an end.

Germany was an especially quixotic destination. It had not been included in the grand plan Northcliffe had drawn up to survey the parts of the world missed on his recent voyage, such as South and Central America. The trip to the Continent, under the name 'Leonard Brown', marks an unmistakable tip into disease-induced psychosis. Northcliffe's angry mood continued on the cross-Channel steamer and was experienced first-hand by the stewards who drew his wrath. The party included Pine, the golf pro, Thomson, and a valet. Northcliffe showed Pine a Colt revolver – carried, he said, for self-protection.

The first Continental stop was the Hôtel Christol at Boulogne. The press lord's fears were augmented by threatening letters sent to Printing House Square and to his hotel. Sir Alexander Godley, the British Commander-in-Chief on the Rhine, invited Northcliffe to stay with him at Cologne. Godley downplayed the risks, but told Northcliffe that there was 'no doubt that at this moment you are probably the Englishman who is most hated in Germany'.

On his way to Cologne, across countryside still clearly marked by the ravages of war, Northcliffe stopped at several battlefields. He also sharpened his skills with the revolver, using trees as targets. He arrived at Cologne on 31 May in a staff car sent to meet him at the Belgian frontier because he feared his blue Rolls-Royce would be too well known. He was ill during the trip, attributing his symptoms to food poisoning or the heat, and at Cologne he retreated immediately to bed. The next day was spent resting in Godley's garden. The Commander-in-Chief described his guest as 'obviously a very sick man' who was 'extremely egotistical' and 'talked incessantly'.[43] Northcliffe reported to Carmelite House that 'I have had a curious illness. Some people think I have been poisoned. Personally I cannot believe that but I know I have been very bad.' Before returning to Boulogne, he sent the usual reassuring message to Totteridge: 'Am very well and always thinking of my darling Mother.'[44] He also cabled his wife at Évian-les-Bains on Lake Geneva that he had had a 'very interesting and adventurous time among the Bosche'.

On his journey the press lord alternately scolded the London staff for forwarding business correspondence and attacked them for withholding information. At Boulogne he received a cable from Sutton, who had been left in charge of the negotiations to purchase John Walter's shares in *The Times*. Sutton asked what Northcliffe thought was a fair valuation. Northcliffe replied, 'Please, please, please, please, please, please, don't consult me about old one. Will do exactly what you choose. Wish to get as many shares as I can. Have absolute confidence in future, but shall make clean sweep of office when Campbell returns. Am very tired after anxious German visit.'[45] The next day he cabled Sutton that he was not desirous that Steed should leave *The Times*. He went on that as 'special correspondent Europe he is unexcelled. That matter was too rushed.' He declared himself 'extremely fond' of Steed, and continued that he regarded him as 'a naughty boy' who 'loses his head when in difficulty'.[46]

At the same time Northcliffe began to question his own balance. He cabled Sir Robert Hudson – at Évian-les-Bains with Lady Northcliffe – to obtain the opinion of Sir Frederick Treves, 'the most distinguished medical man in the world', as to 'my sanity'. Whether it was 'too little work and too much money' or whether it was 'simply decay of my faculties' he did not know, but, he told Hudson, 'I think I am going mad.' He asked Hudson to 'wire me at once to relieve my suspicions'.[47] A temporary secretary, Douglas Reed, sent from Printing House Square to Boulogne, later commented that he found Northcliffe an extremely sick man on whom the 'shadows were already closing relentlessly in'. The press lord, Reed later wrote, 'felt himself surrounded by treachery'. Northcliffe showed the secretary a black silk bag – the 'colour of death', he commented – that had been left for him as Mr Leonard Brown. 'How do they know that I am here?' he asked Reed.[48] He reported to Price that he liked Reed 'extremely. He has been with me during one of the worst weeks of my life, and has not been gushing, but quiet and sympathetic.' He also told H.G. Price that he had found writing on Germany difficult, but sent two unexceptional articles, published as 'Incognito in Germany' in *The Times* and the *Daily Mail*. Northcliffe complained, before the articles appeared, that, even though he had risked his life to obtain them, they were receiving little advance publicity. The third and fourth articles that followed were so confused that Sutton blocked their publication.

Despite his deteriorating state, Northcliffe's travel schedule continued. He planned to meet his wife at Évian-les-Bains. On the way, he invited Steed to meet him at the Hôtel Plaza-Athénée in Paris. A cable to the editor announced, 'Have purchased entire Walter interest thus sacking two of your chief enemies Lints Smith and Walter . . . Am pleased you are coming.' Sutton had completed the negotiations and signed an agreement to buy Walter's 215,000 shares and end his family's association with *The Times*. A cable to George Brumwell, assistant editor of *The Times*, exulted that 'for the first time I shall have freedom'. In the reorganization, said Northcliffe, 'it is not at all sure that we shall appoint an Editor at all'. If Steed was retained, he went on, 'it will be purely as Travelling Correspondent' who would go 'exactly where we tell him'.[49]

From this point, the flood of messages to the newspapers became increasingly insulting and incoherent. H.G. Price fled the office under a barrage of abusive telegrams. On one Price wrote in the margin, 'Poor Chief'. Even Sutton had to admit that steps might be needed to take Northcliffe in hand. He telegraphed him that he was 'sorry you have been ill . . . afraid you are overworked . . . suggest you drop all detail work and telegrams . . . your health only concern'. Northcliffe protested that he was not overworked and that he was suffering from a 'sort of blood poisoning' which some people told him had been 'deliberately activated in Germany'.[50] He was correct that his blood was poisoned, but it was no German concoction. The pistol he carried could not protect him from the streptococcus in his bloodstream – a herald of the endocarditis that would soon end his life.

At Paris his condition deteriorated swiftly. He arrived so weak that he had to be helped along the train platform. In the lobby of the Plaza-Athénée, the owner of *The Times* by chance encountered Colonel House, who was shocked at his appearance and by the 'crude embrace' with which Northcliffe greeted Mrs House. The episode convinced the Colonel that his friend had little time left. The following day Steed met Northcliffe at the hotel and recorded that he had the same wild

393

'diagonal squint' in his eye that the editor had seen in a friend who had died of GPI – the final stage of syphilis. This was the amateur diagnosis he soon shared with others. Steed spent the night talking to Northcliffe, who, he later reported, was raving, with intervals of alarming over-lucidity, on European politics and other, more personal, subjects. One of his delusions took the form of a conviction that a dressing gown hung on a door was a man trying to shoot him. The press lord threatened the gown with his revolver. Twice Northcliffe left the chamber for the bathroom. Each time Steed tried to extract the bullets. The first time he failed utterly; the second time he nearly succeeded, but had to drop the weapon on his chief's sudden return. Finally, near dawn, Northcliffe fell asleep and the revolver was unloaded.[51]

Northcliffe, Steed and four others left for Évian-les-Bains on 12 June. The ten-hour train journey, Steed later told Sir Arthur Willert, was a nightmare. Between Paris and Bellegarde, where Hudson met them with a car for the fifty-mile drive to Évian-les-Bains, Northcliffe was 'raving mad'. Usually clean-mouthed, he shouted the 'worst obscenities' to his fellow travellers. These included a Miss Rudge, who, according to Steed, was the former chief telephonist of *The Times* and head of Northcliffe's espionage system at the paper.[52] The proprietor asked Steed, 'Did I go a little too far with that girl? Don't you think I am mad? Am I mad?'

Reaching Évian-les-Bains, the situation only grew worse. At the Hôtel Royal, Northcliffe greeted old acquaintances with crude language and insults. According to one account, he called Sir Frederick Treves, who came to examine him, an 'old imbecile'. Abuse was also aimed at Lady Northcliffe, who was driven from his room in tears. Somehow he was able to maintain enough composure to telegraph his mother, 'I am in a delightful place where intend to spend some time . . . announcing my indisposition in newspapers though in reality am perfectly well.'[53] A Lausanne neurologist was brought in to examine the press lord, who agreed to see him only after being told he was an expert on German poisons. Steed told Willert and others that Northcliffe was certified as insane at Évian and probably would have been detained there had not the editor wired Prime Minister Poincaré to call off the local authorities.

Whether or not a certificate was signed remains in question; however, Northcliffe at this point passed into the care of Dr Seymour Price, who arrived with Leicester Harmsworth to take the case out of the hands of the local physicians. Dr Price telegraphed London that he believed Northcliffe would recover, but that at present 'sense of proportion nil'. Steed arranged that the only messages from the press lord which were not intercepted were reassuring telegrams to his mother. Northcliffe was persuaded to return to England only because he was told his mother wished to see him. On 16 June Hudson wrote to Sutton, 'This business is the devil! He is driving everyone around him into a condition which will soon resemble his own state! Everyone is to be dismissed as soon as he gets back to London, so pack your kit!' Hudson went on that the party would reach Carlton Gardens the following morning; then Northcliffe would 'pass under purely medical control. Telephones will be cut off. No letters or telegrams allowed to pass in or out. No newspapers and no letters allowed! Of course, this will raise hell, but the drs. and nurses must face that.'[54] The *Daily Mail* announced that, because of his 'indisposition', the owner had been ordered to abstain from work for the present and publication of his articles on Germany would be 'temporarily suspended'.[55] At *The Times* meanwhile, Lints Smith had a guard put on the door in case the proprietor recovered sufficiently to carry out his threat of descending on Printing House Square and sacking everyone.

Rumours had already reached London that the press lord had gone mad. Caird visited Riddell at Walton Heath with the news that Northcliffe had lost his mind. Riddell believed that his actions, and the recent German articles, reflected tertiary syphilis. After he passed along the gossip on the phone to Lloyd George, he recorded that he could see the Prime Minister's 'eyes glistening at the other end of the wire'. Lloyd George, in Riddell's opinion, had extraordinary luck: all of his enemies seemed to 'go down under the hand of fate'. At golf a few days later the two men speculated as to what would happen to *The Times* if Northcliffe succumbed to his illness. To stop Beaverbrook 'or someone else who would make things difficult' from gaining control, the Prime Minister proposed that friends of his acquire the paper. He told his companion that, if the stories about Northcliffe were true, it was a 'tragic business, and that he felt sorry to see him end in this way'.[56]

Once Northcliffe arrived in London, the respected physician Sir Thomas Horder took supervisory charge of the case. The patient was confined at 1 Carlton Gardens in the care of a team of doctors and a squad of around-the-clock male nurses, one of whom he attacked with a poker. Her nerves badly frayed by the ordeal, Lady Northcliffe retired to a hotel. Horder almost immediately suspected septic endocarditis, which, he recorded, was confirmed by blood tests showing the characteristic streptococcus and no evidence of venereal disease.[57] He explained the lethal implications to the family. By 22 July Northcliffe's condition was so grave that his mother, who had hitherto been kept away, was brought to his bedside. Among his last audible words were 'tell mother she is the only one'.

By late July it was widely known that the press lord was unlikely to recover. The manoeuvring for position and control at his various newspapers had already begun. Rothermere was reported to be casting covetous eyes at *The Times*; however, he told Lloyd George that the property would have to be sold to pay the £2 million in death duties that would become due on Northcliffe's £5 million estate. Rothermere also informed Churchill that no one had ever recovered from his brother's condition. Churchill confided the news to his wife, adding 'Sic transit gloria mundi. I cannot help feeling sorry – altho God knows how cruel he was to me in those evil days of 1916. Our revered leader is no doubt greatly relieved on this score.'[58] Later in the month, Riddell asked the Prime Minister how he would describe the founder of the *Daily Mail*. After some reflection, Lloyd George replied:

> I should describe him as a great journalistic Barnum. He had the knack of divining what the public wanted, say, a white elephant, and of seeking one out and getting it into his menagerie. Having got it he knew how to advertise it . . . Northcliffe did many good things, but the truth is that he had a bad effect on the public mind.[59]

In August, as Northcliffe's condition worsened, daily bulletins were released and a guard was put on the door to keep out the curious and well-wishers alike. Because of the summer heat, on 9 August Horder decided the patient needed fresh air. After an inspection revealed that the roof of 1 Carlton Gardens would not support it, a wooden cabin was constructed atop the neighbouring house, with the permission of the owner, the Duke of Devonshire. Five days later, brothers Vyvyan and Cecil were with Northcliffe when he died shortly after 10 a.m., peaceful at the end. He would have been upset that the *Star*, not the *Evening News*, was the first newspaper out with the story. The owner of *The Times* had left instructions that his death was to be marked by 'a page reviewing my life-work by someone who really knows and a leading article by the best man on the night'. Steed wrote the memorial, which was published along with letters of condolence from the King and Queen and numerous other luminaries.

The funeral was held at Westminster Abbey. Neither Winston Churchill nor Lloyd George attended. The Prime Minister sent in his stead Sir Edward Grigg, who had worked for Northcliffe at *The Times* before the war and held no bitterness towards him. Grigg wrote to J.T. Davies that

> I was also glad to go on my own behalf . . . The circumstances of his death are very tragic the more one thinks them over. I had always hoped he would live to see beyond the advice of the time-servers and sycophants by whom he was surrounded, and would come to do a really great public service by his treatment of 'The Times'.
>
> It is sad that a man with so much of the elements of greatness in him should go down after so many months of madness which must blur the record. Contemporary judgments are seldom sound, but I think that posterity will judge him to have been less indeed than his ardent admirers supposed him to be, but far greater than his many imitators amongst the owners of the modern press.[60]

Northcliffe had left instructions for his burial that he wished 'to be laid as near Mother as possible at North [*sic*] Finchley and I do not wish anything erect from the ground or any words except my name and the year I was born and this year upon the stone'. He was laid to rest next to his grandfather and father, to await his mother, who lived several more years.

To pay the heavy death duties on his estate and to settle the bequests (including three months' salary to all employees) set out in his will, the family was forced to dismantle Northcliffe's press kingdom. Though Rothermere and Lloyd George both desired control of *The Times*, neither man gained the prize, which passed to John Jacob Astor. Rothermere added the *Daily Mail* and the other Associated Newspapers titles to his own list of journals. After litigation, which dragged on for some time, the Amalgamated Press periodical list, including *Answers*, the foundation of the Harmsworth family fortune, was sold to Sir William Berry, later Lord Camrose. Lady Northcliffe settled with the family over her portion of the estate and, within a year of Northcliffe's death, married Sir Robert Hudson.

Northcliffe had commented to Sir William Robertson Nicoll in 1914 that he wondered 'if there will be anyone sorry when I am dead'. His own, rather modest, answer had been 'I think there will. I have given employment to many people and at good wages.' Nicoll was more generous in his summation of his colleague, calling him the 'greatest transforming force that has appeared in British journalism' and, after all deductions, a 'faithful servant of his country'.[61]

Two other judgements printed in the days after his death are appropriate for the end of Northcliffe's story. The *Manchester Guardian* commented that he 'accepted the Empire as Mr. Kipling dreamt it, and worked spasmodically, but hard to increase its strength'.[62] Except that he lacked the poet's romantic regard for India, this is true. Finally, Beaverbrook, who vied with Rothermere to assume the vacant leadership of Fleet Street, remembered Northcliffe as the 'greatest journalist England has ever seen – if we are to judge greatness, as we must in public life, by the influence a man brings to bear on the age in which he lives'. Unlike Delane, perhaps the greatest editor of *The Times*, Northcliffe

not only conducted newspapers both on their editorial and business side with infinitely greater range than the 'Times', but he created them. And in doing so created through his own efforts directly and through those of his imitators indirectly, an entirely new public atmosphere. The classes enfranchised in the later nineteenth century at last found a medium of instruction in public affairs and a method of making their opinions felt – not once every five or six years but continuously, from day to day. Such an achievement ranks Northcliffe finally among the makers of history.[63]

Notes

ABBREVIATIONS

BL – British Library
HA – Harmsworth Archive
HLRO – House of Lords Record Office
NADM – Northcliffe Additional Manuscripts
NLS – National Library of Scotland
PRO – Public Record Office
TA – Archive of *The Times*
WAM – Wrench Additional Manuscripts

PREFACE

1. 7 June 1921, NADM, 62365, BL.
2. Stephen Koss, *The Rise and Fall of the Political Press in Britain, The Nineteenth Century* (Chapel Hill, 2 vols., 1981, 1984), Vol. 1, p. 369.
3. A.B. Cooke and John Vincent, *The Governing Passion: Cabinet, Government and Party Politics in Britain, 1885–86* (New York, 1974), p. 5, quoted in Koss, *Political Press*, p. 265.
4. Kenneth O. Morgan, *Consensus and Disunity: The Lloyd George Coalition Government, 1918–1922* (London, 1979), p. 169.

CHAPTER I: FROM ADONIS TO ANSWERS, 1865–1894

1. Lord Beaverbrook, *Men and Power, 1917–1918* (London, 1956), pp. 90, 358.
2. For the details of the family history, see Reginald Pound and Geoffrey Harmsworth, *Northcliffe* (London, 1959).
3. 'The Remaking of Ireland', *The Times*, 19 March 1917. In addition to the heightened opportunities the metropolis offered, there had been recent anti-English Fenian activity in the vicinity of Dublin which, whether real or imagined, made leaving seem a sensible course. Alfred recorded in his diary that he had been 'Reading law with my sword on my knee'. Pound and Harmsworth, *Northcliffe*, p. 15.
4. A.P. Ryan, *Lord Northcliffe* (London, 1953), p. 29.
5. Tom Clarke, *My Northcliffe Diary* (London, 1931), pp. 18–19.

6. 'An Article Full of Capital Is', *Answers*, 28 May 1892.
7. Pound and Harmsworth, *Northcliffe*, p. 29.
8. Ibid., p. 35.
9. Max Pemberton, *Lord Northcliffe: A Memoir* (London, 1922), p. 1.
10. Pound and Harmsworth, *Northcliffe*, p. 41.
11. Cecil King, *Strictly Personal* (London, 1969), p. 60.
12. Paul Ferris, *The House of Northcliffe* (London, 1972), p. 25.
13. Pemberton, *Lord Northcliffe*, p. 23.
14. Pound and Harmsworth, *Northcliffe*. p. 54.
15. S.J. Taylor, *The Great Outsiders: Northcliffe, Rothermere and the Daily Mail* (London, 1996), p. 12.
16. Alfred respected William Iliffe as well, later commenting that 'when the bicycle was regarded as a toy, he saw that it would be the beginning of a revolution'. Ryan, *Northcliffe*, p. 36.
17. S.J. Taylor, *The Great Outsiders*, p. 13.
18. Pound and Harmsworth, *Northcliffe*, p. 67.
19. T.R. Nevett, *Advertising in Britain* (London, 1982), p. 104.
20. Pound and Harmsworth, *Northcliffe*, p. 91.
21. F.A. Mackenzie, *The Rise and Progress of the Harmsworth Publications* (London, 1897), p. 7. Puzzle clubs were organized throughout the country. Two hundred contestants gathered at the London offices to compete for a £50 national prize awarded to the swiftest solution. Before the craze ran its course, millions of the puzzle boxes were distributed all over the globe.
22. The realignment also grew out of business friction in the offices of Carr & Co. and the increased demand for *Answers*, the management of which was transferred to Answers Company Limited. The 600 shares of the new venture were divided with Beaumont and his wife having 150 shares, Markwick 140, Annie Rowley 10, Carr and his spouse 100, and Alfred and Mary 200. The men all became directors of the new firm.
23. Pound and Harmsworth, *Northcliffe*, p. 109.
24. Ibid., p. 114.
25. The oldest, Geraldine, who had left London in late 1890 to marry Lucas White King, a civil servant in India, was given a belated wedding allotment. To make provision for the younger siblings, not yet able to take an active part in the business, the Harmsworth Trust was drawn up. Funding came from thirty shares in the latest publishing venture, 'The Periodical Publishing Corporation Limited,' begun with £500 of capital in November 1891. The remaining shares were divided between Alfred (300), Harold (150), and Cecil and Leicester (10 each). Payments also began to be made to support Alfred's natural son, Alfred Benjamin Smith. Since the marriage of the mother, Louisa Jane, the boy had been in the care of his maternal grandparents.
26. Mackenzie, *Harmsworth Publications*, p. 11.
27. For example, see 20 October entry, 1891 diary, NADM, 62379, BL.
28. 1892 diary, NADM, 62380, BL.
29. Ibid.
30. *Answers*, 23 July 1892. Many years later, Northcliffe would refer to Gladstone's habit of charging for interviews – including this one, which Northcliffe claimed cost £400.
31. Ibid.
32. Pound and Harmsworth, *Northcliffe*, p. 145.
33. First editions were published on 11 November 1893 for the *Halfpenny Marvel*, 28

November 1894 for the *Union Jack*, and 2 February 1895 for the *Boy's Friend*. The *Union Jack* promoted the Empire with tales of British endeavour on land and sea. In addition to stories on Britain's imperial heroes, the journal explained the origins of each possession. The *Boy's Friend* was devoted to the 'high-class' fiction of the day, with stories by the best boys writers of the time, such as J. Harwood Panting, S. Clarke Hook and C.J. Mansford, author of *Shafts from an Eastern Quiver*. Mackenzie, *Harmsworth Publications*, pp. 11–13.

34. 1894 diary, NADM, 62382, BL.
35. 31 December entry, 1894 diary, NADM, 62382, BL.
36. In 1894 more titles aimed at boys were added in the form of the *Union Jack Library*, the *Pluck Library* and the *Comic Home Journal* (later the *Boy's Home Journal*), all of which sold well. Domestic enterprise was exalted in journals such as *Home Sweet Home*. The Harmsworths also made a start into a new area, religious publishing, with the *Sunday Companion*.
37. For this, see John Maxtone-Graham, *Safe Return Doubtful: The Heroic Age of Polar Exploration* (New York, 1988).
38. Frederick G. Jackson, *A Thousand Days in the Arctic* (London, 1899), p. 5.
39. Pound and Harmsworth, *Northcliffe*, p. 162.
40. The *Mail* (Portsmouth), 12 July 1895.
41. Ibid.

CHAPTER 2: NEWSPAPERS AND POLITICS, 1894–1897
1. Such a move, on a smaller scale, had already been discussed within the organization. Talks with William Iliffe about his paper in Coventry had proved fruitless, and there also had been unconsummated flirtations with two weeklies, the *National Observer* and the *Islington Gazette*. Meetings were held in 1893 to discuss buying an interest in the *Sun*, a halfpenny evening Liberal paper edited by T.P. O'Connor, the offices of which were opposite the *Answers* establishment in Tudor Street. Political differences prevented an agreement with O'Connor, and Alfred also probably wished to find an editor who would be more tractable than the independent-minded 'Tay Pay'.
2. Kennedy Jones, *Fleet Street and Downing Street* (London, 1920), p. 118. Jones calls himself 'news-editor'.
3. Pound and Harmsworth, *Northcliffe* (London, 1959), p. 172. Unhappy with his position, Tracy would leave the paper and sell his shares – an act which would prove rather unwise financially.
4. Raymond Schults, *Crusader in Babylon: W.T. Stead and the Pall Mall Gazette* (Lincoln, Nebraska, 1972), pp. 24–33.
5. 31 December entry, 1894 diary, NADM, 62382, BL.
6. For this question, see Koss, *Political Press*.
7. Richard Shannon, *The Age of Salisbury, 1881–1902: Unionism and Empire* (London, 1996), pp. 321, 430.
8. 21 November 1894, NADM, 62292A, f. 4, BL.
9. Pound and Harmsworth, *Northcliffe*, p. 181.
10. Ibid., p. 151. An 1891 *Answers* article, 'Why the Germans Come to England', had begun the warnings.
11. William Le Queux, *The Great War in England in 1897* (London, 1894), p. 5.
12. Brian Roberts, *Cecil Rhodes: Flawed Colossus* (London, 1987), p. 209. The writer H. Rider Haggard remembered a similar breakfast experience with Rhodes at the Burlington Hotel in London: 'Already before breakfast a number of people, some of them well-known . . . were waiting about in the ante-rooms on the chance of

getting a word with or a favour from the great man . . . in a china bowl on a table I observed a great accumulation of unopened letters . . . it was . . . one of the habits of Rhodes not to trouble to open letters that came by post . . . they only attended to those sent by hand, or to telegrams.' Robert Rotberg, *The Founder: Cecil Rhodes and the Pursuit of Power* (Oxford, 1988), p. 516.

13. 22 January entry, 1895 diary, NADM, 62383, BL.
14. 9 May entry, 1895 diary, NADM, 62383, BL.
15. 10 May 1895, Salisbury Papers, Hatfield.
16. 14 May 1895, Salisbury Papers, Hatfield.
17. Though not written by Le Queux, the storyline bore a striking resemblance to the *Answers* 'Poisoned Bullet' serial of the previous year. For examples of the continuing serial, see the *Mail* (Portsmouth), 18, 19 June and 4, 16 July 1895.
18. The *Mail* (Portsmouth), 3 July 1895. Age sixty-seven, Baker was considered the most vulnerable of the two adversaries, despite his long public service in Portsmouth, including a term as mayor.
19. The *Mail* (Portsmouth), 12 July 1895.
20. Maxtone-Graham, *Safe Return Doubtful*, pp. 159–61.
21. The *Mail* (Portsmouth), 16 July 1895.
22. D.A. Hamer, *Liberal Politics in the Age of Gladstone and Rosebery* (Oxford, 1972), p. 207; Shannon, *Age of Salisbury*, p. 414.
23. *Evening News* (London), 18 July 1895.
24. 16 July entry, 1895 diary, NADM, 62383, BL.
25. The *Mail* (Portsmouth), 17 July, 1895.
26. This declaration was not so outlandish as it might seem. In this period two other proprietors who had given the Conservative Party newspaper aid – Algernon Borthwick of the *Morning Post* and Henry Hucks Gibbs of the *St James's Gazette* – were elevated as Lords Glenesk and Aldenham. Shannon, *Age of Salisbury*, p. 340.
27. Jones, *Fleet Street and Downing Street*, pp. 94–5.
28. *Evening News* (London), 6 January 1896.
29. A.N. Porter, *The Origins of the South African War: Joseph Chamberlain and the Diplomacy of Imperialism, 1895–99* (Manchester, 1980), pp. 55–6.
30. *Evening News* (London), 4 January 1896.
31. E.L. Woodward, *Great Britain and the German Navy* (London, 1964), pp. 23–4.
32. 25 January entry, 1896 diary, NADM 62383, BL.
33. The imperial 'Colossus' was unsure how he stood in England, but later commented that, after his arrival, he 'found all the busmen smiling at me . . . and then I knew it was all right'. Roberts, *Cecil Rhodes*, p. 222.
34. Thomas Pakenham, *The Scramble for Africa: White Man's Conquest of the Dark Continent from 1876 to 1912* (New York, 1991), pp. 502–3.
35. Shannon, *Age of Salisbury*, p. 430.
36. 5 May 1896, Salisbury Papers, Hatfield.
37. 7 May 1896, in Pound and Harmsworth, *Northcliffe*, pp. 202–3.
38. Ibid., p. 200.
39. Piers Brendon, *The Life and Death of the Press Barons* (New York, 1983), p. 114.
40. Consultation with Mr Robin Harcourt Williams, librarian of the Salisbury papers at Hatfield House, has failed to locate a written source for this remark.
41. 19 May entry, 1896 diary, NADM, 62384, BL.
42. David Gilmour, *Curzon* (London, 1994), p. 62.
43. 8 May 1896, in Pound and Harmsworth, *Northcliffe*, p. 208.
44. Hamilton Fyfe, *Northcliffe: An Intimate Biography* (New York, 1930), p. 87. For Steevens's career, see Roger Stearn, 'G.W. Steevens and the Message of Empire,' *Journal of Imperial and Commonwealth History*, **17**, 2 (1989), p. 213.

45. N.d., Salisbury Papers, Hatfield.
46. 21 July 1896, Salisbury Papers, Hatfield.
47. Hamer, *Liberal Politics in the Age of Gladstone and Rosebery*, pp. 237–49, 255.
48. Rosebery diary, 8 October 1896, quoted in The Marquess of Crewe, *Lord Rosebery* (London, 1931), p. 429. The interviewer had a 'most pleasant time'. 8 October entry, 1896 diary, NADM, 62384, BL.
49. 9 October entry, 1896 diary, NADM, 62384, BL.
50. 'For His Country's Good', *Daily Mail*, 9 October 1896.
51. Although an 1878 revision of the law had made the red flag unnecessary, to symbolize the occasion the Earl of Winchelsea attempted to tear one in two before the start. That a penknife had to be produced before the cloth could be divided would be emblematic of the disarray of the Emancipation Run. Anthony Bird, *The Motor Car 1765–1914* (London, 1960), p. 109.
52. Piers Brendon, *The Motoring Century: The Story of the Royal Automobile Club* (London, 1997), p. 28.
53. William Plowden, *The Motor Car and Politics* (London, 1971), p. 34.
54. *Daily Mail*, 8 February 1897.
55. Ibid., 16 February 1897.
56. 'Under the Yellow Flag', the final series article, *Daily Mail*, 25 February 1897.

CHAPTER 3: UPBUILDER OF EMPIRE, 1897–1899

1. *Daily Mail*, 20 February 1897; Roberts, *Cecil Rhodes*, p. 247.
2. *Daily Mail*, 24 February 1897.
3. The findings of the committee, released several months later, cleared Chamberlain and his ministry and declared Rhodes responsible, even though it concluded that Jameson had gone in on his own. No sanctions, against either the chartered company or its founder, were mentioned. An attempt in the House of Commons to demand some punishment for Rhodes was soundly defeated. He commented that 'I notice the Home Committee have made me the sacrificial lamb. I wonder whether the decay of our race will come through unctuous rectitude.' Rotberg, *The Founder*, p. 550.
4. 'What the Committee Says,' *Daily Mail*, 14 July 1897.
5. 28 April 1897, Salisbury Papers, Hatfield.
6. 30 April 1897, Salisbury Papers, Hatfield.
7. *Daily Mail*, 23 June 1897.
8. 22 June entry, 1897 diary, NADM, 62385, BL.
9. 26 June entry, 1897 diary, NADM, 62385, BL. A campaign in the *Daily Mail* helped ensure that the colonial troopers would be able to see the review as well. The original plan had been for them to visit the fleet a few days later, but the Admiralty relented under newspaper pressure. The 22 June issue called the reversal 'A "Daily Mail" Victory'.
10. 21 June entry, 1897 diary, NADM, 62385, BL.
11. John Kendle, *The Colonial and Imperial Conferences 1887–1911* (London, 1967), p. 25.
12. Joseph Schull, *Laurier: The First Canadian* (Toronto, 1965), pp. 356–7.
13. *Daily Mail*, 7 July 1897. To succeed, the article continued, the Conference would need to address five questions brought up by the Canadian: the representation of the colonies in the imperial parliament; preferential trade; Asiatic immigration; the Pacific Cable; and imperial penny postage.
14. Kendle, *Colonial and Imperial Conferences*, p. 30.
15. S.J. Taylor, *The Great Outsiders*, p. 47.
16. Pound and Harmsworth, *Northcliffe*, p. 163.
17. Gilmour, *Curzon*, p. 30.

18. 6 November entry, 1897 diary, NADM, 62385, BL.
19. At the end of 1897 these included warnings of a possible civil war in Spain and of Russian action in China.
20. 6 September 1901, in Malcolm MacColl, *Memoirs and Correspondence*, ed. George Russell (London, 1914), p. 283.
21. 6 January entry, 1898 diary, NADM, 62386, BL.
22. Philip Magnus, *Kitchener: Portrait of an Imperialist* (London, 1959), p. 134.
23. 14 January entry, 1898 diary, NADM, 62386, BL.
24. Anthony Sattin, *Lifting the Veil: British Society in Egypt 1768–1956* (London, 1988), p. 126.
25. 11 February entry, 1898 diary, NADM 62386, BL.
26. 9 February 1898, in Pound and Harmsworth, *Northcliffe*, p. 235.
27. 17 February entry, 1898 diary, NADM, 62386, BL.
28. 6 March 1898, in Pound and Harmsworth, *Northcliffe*, pp. 235–6.
29. *Daily Mail*, 26 April, 1898.
30. Ibid., 25 November 1898.
31. The guests included brothers Harold and Cecil, the Duke of Abercorn, Colonel John Hay, Lord Granby, E.T. Cook, editor of the *Daily News*, J.A. Spender, editor of the *Westminster Gazette*, Sir George Newnes, Evelyn Ashley, H.W. Massingham, editor of the *Daily Chronicle*, and Sir Douglas Straight, editor of the *Pall Mall Gazette*.
32. 27 July entry, 1898 diary, NADM, 62386, BL.
33. Pakenham, *The Scramble for Africa*, pp. 546–7.
34. *Daily Mail*, 5 September 1898.
35. Ibid., 9 September 1898.
36. Ibid., 13 September 1898.
37. Ibid., 15, 16 September 1898.
38. Ibid., 7 October, 1898.
39. Ibid., 13, 18, 20 October 1898.
40. Ibid., 24, 25, 26 October 1898. The ubiquitous Steevens would also produce a book on the Dreyfus Affair from his articles.
41. Ibid., 1 November, 1898. The next day's editorial, 'The Press and War', considered the 'delicate question' of the duties and responsibilities of a newspaper during a conflict, which, said the paper, 'cannot but engage the attention of every earnest and patriotic journalist'. Reviewing the role of the press from the time of Napoleon to the present, the editorial continued that 'the time is a good one for careful consideration by naval and military authorities and journalists of the problems involved in the modern extension of newspaper enterprise' and that 'until some hard and fast regulations' were provided by the authorities it was not easy for even 'the most conscientious journalist to know what to print and what to omit'. The piece ended with the hope that the government would confer with the leaders of the press 'as to the best means to be adopted to prevent the publication of news likely to be injurious to the national welfare'.
42. Quoted in William Langer, *The Diplomacy of Imperialism 1890–1902* (New York, 1965), p. 85.
43. 18 October 1898, in Pound and Harmsworth, *Northcliffe*, pp. 233–4.
44. Lowther to McDonnell, 8 November 1898, Salisbury Papers, 3M/AA1, Hatfield.
45. 25 November 1898, Salisbury Papers, 3M/AA1, Hatfield.
46. Paul Tritton, *John Montagu of Beaulieu 1866–1929: Motoring Pioneer and Prophet* (London, 1985), p. 53.

CHAPTER 4: BOERS AND KHAKI, 1899–1900

1. Milner's imperial reputation was made with his 1892 book *England in Egypt*, a spirited defence of Britain's course which inspired others including Winston Churchill, who later recalled that at the time the book's words 'rang like a trumpet-call which rallies the soldiers after the parapets are stormed, and summons them to complete the victory'. A.M. Gollin, *Proconsul in Politics: A Study of Lord Milner in Opposition and in Power* (London, 1964), p. 26.
2. *Daily Mail*, 3 May 1899.
3. 8 May entry, 1899 diary, NADM, 62387, BL.
4. Robert Rhodes James, *Rosebery* (London, 1963), pp. 407–8.
5. *Daily Mail*, 9 May 1899.
6. 8 June entry, 1899 diary, NADM, 62387, BL.
7. *Daily Mail*, 8, 9 June 1899.
8. Ibid., 21 June 1899.
9. 7 July 1899, NADM, 62156, BL, in Pound and Harmsworth, *Northcliffe*, pp. 255–6.
10. Balfour to Harmsworth, 18 July 1899, NADM, 62153, BL.
11. Balfour to Harmsworth, 25 July 1899, NADM, 62153, BL.
12. Pound and Harmsworth, *Northcliffe*, p. 255.
13. *Daily Mail*, 8 July 1899. On 16 August the paper reported that the War Office had decided that Buller would be replaced by Sir F. Forestier Walker. This proved incorrect, as Buller was in fact sent out as commander of the British forces.
14. 22 September entry, 1899 diary, NADM, 62387, BL.
15. *Daily Mail*, 29 September 1899.
16. Randolph Churchill, *Winston S. Churchill, Vol. 1: Youth, 1874–1900* (Boston, 1966), p. 437.
17. *Daily Mail*, 5 October 1899.
18. Ibid., 10 October 1899.
19. Ibid., 18 October 1899.
20. Ibid., 23, 24 October 1899.
21. Among other good works, the Absent-Minded Beggar Fund paid for the construction of the Treloar Cripples Hospital, completed in 1903.
22. *Daily Mail*, 6 November 1899.
23. Ibid., 10 November 1899.
24. 27 November 1899, NADM, 62153, BL.
25. *Daily Mail*, 29 November 1899.
26. Ibid., 30 November 1899.
27. Ibid., 18 December 1899.
28. Ibid., 20 December 1899.
29. Northcliffe said little about government policy during the war concerning newspapers, but did comment some years later to Lord Roberts that the management of the press had been 'scandalous' and that the censors had allowed dangerous messages to pass, but withheld interesting but quite valueless messages. Worst of all he charged that the censors interpolated the names of friends in action, in order to bring public notice to them. 19 June 1909, NADM, 62155, BL.
30. Nevett, *Advertising in Britain*, p. 82.
31. *Daily Mail*, 4 January 1900.
32. Ibid., 10 January 1900.
33. Ibid., 11 January 1900.
34. Pound and Harmsworth, *Northcliffe*, p. 253.
35. *Daily Mail*, 24 January 1900.
36. The *Daily Mail* of 30 January echoed Rosebery, calling it the 'Duty of Parliament' to

see to it that England's military organization was thoroughly overhauled and the country put in the position to meet 'the worst the world can bring against us'.

37. 31 January entry, 1900 diary, NADM, 62388, BL.
38. *Daily Mail*, 5, 6, 9 February 1900.
39. Ibid., 10 March 1900.
40. A.J.A. Morris, *The Scaremongers: The Advocacy of War and Rearmament 1896–1914*, (London, 1984), p. 101.
41. 19 April entry, 1900 diary, NADM, 62388, BL.
42. Brendon, *The Motoring Century*, pp. 62–4.
43. Bird, *The Motor Car 1765–1914*, p. 123.
44. *Daily Mail*, 20 April 1900.
45. Ibid., 17, 18 May 1900.
46. Ibid., 31 May 1900.
47. Ibid., 2 June 1900.
48. For an analysis of the press coverage of the events in China, see Jane Elliot, 'Who Seeks the Truth Should Be of No Country: British and American Journalists Report the Boxer Rebellion, June 1900', *American Journalism*, **13** (1996), pp. 255–85.
49. *Daily Mail*, 2 July 1900.
50. Ibid., 13, 16, 17 July 1900.
51. Ibid., 30 July 1900.
52. Quoted in Morris, *The Scaremongers*, p. 35.
53. *Daily Mail*, 4 August 1900.
54. 19 September entry, 1900 diary, NADM, 62388, BL.
55. *Daily Mail*, 3 July 1900.
56. Pound and Harmsworth, *Northcliffe*, p. 261.
57. 7 June entry, 1900 diary, NADM, 62388, BL.
58. John Grigg, *The Young Lloyd George* (London, 1973), p. 267.
59. Tom Clarke, *Northcliffe in History* (London, 1950), p. 186.
60. *Daily Mail*, 17 September 1900.
61. Ibid., 18, 20 September 1900. For this movement, see H.C.G. Matthew, *The Liberal Imperialists* (Oxford, 1973).
62. *Daily Mail*, 21 September 1900.
63. Ibid., 22 September 1900.
64. Thomas Pakenham, *The Boer War* (London, 1979), p. 492.
65. *Daily Mail*, 3 October 1900.
66. Ibid., 17 October 1900. The actual majority over the combined Liberals and Irish Nationalists was 134.
67. Ralph D. Blumenfeld, *R. D. B.'s Diary* (London, 1930), pp. 95–6.

CHAPTER 5: A NEW CENTURY, 1900–1903

1. Pound and Harmsworth, *Northcliffe*, pp. 265–6.
2. 29 December entry, 1900 diary, NADM, 62388, BL.
3. *New York Times*, 3 January 1901.
4. Pound and Harmsworth, *Northcliffe*, p. 268.
5. 'The Simultaneous Newspapers of the Twentieth Century', *North American Review*, vol. 172, DXXX.
6. 9 January entry, 1901 diary, NADM, 62389, BL.
7. *Daily Mail*, 23 January 1901.
8. 3 May 1901, Strachey Papers, S/11/4/2, HLRO.
9. 18 May 1901, Strachey Papers, S/11/4, HLRO.
10. 13 March 1902, Selborne Papers, Box 5, Bodleian Library.

11. 22 June entry, 1901 diary, NADM, 62389, BL.
12. Pound and Harmsworth, *Northcliffe*, p. 271.
13. *Parliamentary Debates*, Commons, 4th Series, XCVII, col. 380.
14. Ibid., cols. 592–3.
15. Quoted in Morris, *The Scaremongers*, p. 95.
16. 19 August 1901, NADM, 62153, BL. Brodrick later claimed that during this interview the owner of the *Daily Mail* asked him for a letter absolving him of guilt if he ever ran for future office and was charged with knowingly buying secrets. Morris, *The Scaremongers*, p. 95.
17. 2 December 1901, Arthur Balfour correspondence, Salisbury Papers, Hatfield.
18. Viscount Esher, *Journals and Letters of Reginald, Viscount Esher*, ed. Maurice Brett (Vols. 1 and 2) and Oliver, Viscount Esher (Vols. 3 and 4) (London, 4 vols., 1934–8), Vol. 1, pp. 309–11.
19. Rhodes James, *Rosebery*, p. 430–3. This speech contained one of Rosebery's most quoted phrases, in which he attacked the backwardness to be found in those Liberals, who 'sit still with the fly-blown phylacteries of obsolete policies bound round their foreheads, who do not remember that while they have been mumbling their incantations to themselves, the world has been marching and revolving . . . I hope, therefore, that when you have to write on your clean slate, you will write on it a policy adapted to 1901 or 1902, and not . . . 1892 or 1885.' Campbell-Bannerman commented about the speech to Herbert Gladstone, 'All that he said about the clean slate and efficiency was an affront to Liberalism and was pure clap-trap. Efficiency as a watchword! Who is against it? . . . What is a "fly-blown phylactery"? Fly-blow is the result of a fly laying the egg from which maggots come in meat; no fly out of Bedlam would chose a phylactery . . . for such a purpose.'
20. E.T. Raymond, *The Life of Rosebery* (New York, 1923), pp. 194–5. For this topic, see G.R. Seale, *The Quest for National Efficiency: A Study in British Politics and Political Thought, 1899–1914* (Berkeley, 1971).
21. For this see, Matthew, *The Liberal Imperialists*.
22. Peter T. Marsh, *Joseph Chamberlain: Entrepreneur in Politics* (London, 1994), p. 516–17.
23. *Daily Mail*, 9 January 1902.
24. Pound and Harmsworth, *Northcliffe*, p. 272.
25. 1902 diary, NADM, 62390, BL.
26. *Daily Mail*, 27 March 1902.
27. 30 May 1902, in *The History of The Times*, (London, 4 vols., 1935–52), Vol. 3, p. 439.
28. Rhodri Williams, *Defending the Empire: The Conservative Party and British Defence Policy 1899–1915* (London, 1991), pp. 15–16.
29. 11 July entry, 1902 diary, NADM, 62390, BL.
30. 17 July 1902, NADM, 62513, BL.
31. Marsh, *Joseph Chamberlain*, p. 532.
32. Schull, *Laurier*, p. 407.
33. Kendle, *Colonial and Imperial Conferences*, p. 41.
34. Dr Jim, leader of the Jameson Raid, commented of Laurier that 'the damn dancin' master' had 'bitched the whole show', Schull, *Laurier*, p. 410.
35. *Daily Mail*, 12 August 1902.
36. Pound and Harmsworth, *Northcliffe*, p. 274.
37. *Daily Mail*, 16 August 1902.
38. Wilhelm II, *Comparative History 1878–1914* (London, 1922), p. 49.
39. Quoted in Oron James Hale, *Germany and the Diplomatic Revolution: A Study in Diplomacy and the Press 1904–1906* (London, 1931), p. 17.
40. Williams, *Defending the Empire*, pp. 22, 35.

41. Alfred C. Harmsworth, *Motors and Motor Car Driving* (London, 1902), p. 41.
42. 21 May 1902, quoted in Jamie Camplin, *The Rise of the Plutocrats* (London, 1978), p. 234.
43. 7 February entry, 1903 diary, NADM, 62391, BL.
44. 15 February 1905, Strachey Papers, S/11/4/7, HLRO.

CHAPTER 6: A TARIFF TORNADO, 1903–1905

1. *Daily Mail*, 16 May 1903.
2. Alan Sykes, *Tariff Reform in British Politics 1903–1914* (Oxford, 1979), p. 38.
3. *Daily Mail*, 20 May 1903.
4. 19 June 1903, NADM, 62154, BL.
5. *Daily Mail*, 22 May 1903.
6. Quoted in A.M. Gollin, 'Lord Northcliffe's Change of Course', *Journalism Quarterly*, **39** (1962), p. 48.
7. Strachey Papers, S/11/4/9, HLRO.
8. 17 July 1903, Strachey Papers, S/11/4, HLRO.
9. 20 August 1903, Strachey Papers, S/11/4, HLRO.
10. 1 September 1903, NADM, 62156, BL.
11. 26 August 1903, NADM, 62156, BL. Rosebery's aide in the Liberal League, Robert Perks MP, made the same recommendation. Churchill was also in contact with the Duke of Devonshire. Another Unionist Free Trader, Lord Hugh Cecil, cautioned Churchill about telling Alfred Harmsworth too much about their schemes, writing him, 'As to Harmsworth I shd not advise taking him too far into confidence. He is not a very trustworthy man . . . nothing could be more deplorable than to give the impression that the Duke of Devonshire was being run by you & me & the *Daily Mail*!!!' Randolph S. Churchill, *Winston S. Churchill*, Vol. 2 Companion, Pt 1 (London, 1969), p. 222.
12. 1 September 1903, NADM, 62154, BL.
13. J.A. Spender, *Life, Journalism and Politics* (London, 2 vols., 1927), Vol. 2, pp. 171–2, quoted in Gollin, 'Northcliffe's Change of Course', pp. 48–9.
14. 2 September 1903, NADM, 62154, BL.
15. 5 September 1903, NADM, 62154, BL.
16. Rosebery's lieutenant Robert Perks told the proprietor of the *Daily Mail* that 'He [Rosebery] is conscious, as everyone must be, of the powerful influence legitimately exerted by your various journals but as the former leader (& in my own judgment the future leader also) of a great political party it would be impossible . . . to enter into a compact with a vast journalistic combination which might seriously fetter him, as well possibly as his political associates, in the inception and practical application of his policy. Lord Rosebery spoke, as he always does, most kindly of you: but I may say to you *very privately* that he said he had not seen in the Daily Mail much evidence of the support which you led him to think he would receive if he "came out" as he has done.' 3 September 1903, NADM, 62154, BL.
17. 11 September 1903, NADM, 52156. BL.
18. 14 September 1903, in R.S. Churchill, *Churchill*, Vol. 2 Companion, Pt 1, p. 224.
19. Balfour's policy, which called for the British government to have the 'fiscal freedom to make commercial treaties without regard to any specific economic doctrine', was later published as the pamphlet *Notes on Insular Free Trade*. Sykes, *Tariff Reform in British Politics*, p. 45.
20. 18 September 1903, NADM, 52156, BL.
21. Besides Esher, the other two members of the new group were Sir George Clarke, first secretary of the Committee of Imperial Defence, and Admiral Sir John Fisher.

One mission of the Esher Committee was to reform the War Office along Admiralty lines. Williams, *Defending the Empire*, p. 38.
22. Wilson to Chamberlain, 19 September 1903, quoted in Julian Amery, *Joseph Chamberlain and the Tariff Reform Campaign* (London, 1969), p. 296.
23. 28 September 1903, in ibid., p. 297.
24. 1 October 1903, NADM, 62201, BL. Alfred told Leo Maxse that, since so much of his family's fortune came from the poor, it would be 'criminal of me' to support preferential tariffs 'unless a very large portion of the money received from the taxation of foreign manufactured articles is allocated to the practical extinction of food taxes'. Quoted in James D. Startt, 'Northcliffe the Imperialist: The Lesser Known Years, 1902–1914', *The Historian*, **51**, 1 (November 1988), p. 28.
25. Quoted in J. Amery, *Joseph Chamberlain and the Tariff Reform Campaign*, p. 298.
26. *Daily Mail*, 21 October 1903.
27. 1903 diary, NADM, 62391, BL.
28. *Daily Mirror*, 2 November 1903, in Robert Allen and John Frost, *Daily Mirror* (Cambridge, 1981), p. 5.
29. Pound and Harmsworth, *Northcliffe*, p. 278.
30. John Evelyn Wrench, *Uphill: The First Stage in a Strenuous Life* (London, 1934), pp. 139–41.
31. 'The Making of a Newspaper', in Arthur Lawrence, ed., *Journalism as a Profession* (London, 1903), p. 172.
32. Ibid., pp. 184–5.
33. *Daily Mail*, 5 November 1903.
34. 25 November 1903, NADM, 62172, BL.
35. John Ramsden, *The Age of Balfour and Baldwin 1902–1940* (London, 1978), p. 13.
36. Quoted in Alfred Gollin, *Balfour's Burden: Arthur Balfour and Imperial Preference* (London, 1965), p. 205.
37. Quoted in J.L. Hammond, *C.P. Scott of the Manchester Guardian* (London, 1934), p. 95.
38. Elsewhere, an agreement was signed with Sir George Newnes to purchase the faltering Sunday *Weekly Dispatch*, which, because the paper's circulation had dwindled to 5,000 copies, Newnes was willing to sell for £25,000. Alexander Kenealy, who had been at the *Daily Express*, accepted a three-year arrangement to manage the journal. A new ownership company, the Pictorial Newspaper Company Limited, was created in 1904. Its shares were held by the Daily Mail Publishing Company (27,393), Alfred (10,000), Kennedy Jones, (2,500), Harold (1,000) and Leicester (750).
39. *Daily Mail*, 30 March 1904.
40. Randolph S. Churchill, *Winston S. Churchill, Vol. 2: Young Statesman, 1901–1914* (London, 1967), p. 77.
41. The same night the owner of the *Daily Mail* attended the inaugural dinner of the Compatriots Club, organized by Leo Amery to ensure that the Tariff Reform movement kept its imperial nature and did not fall into the hands of the manufacturers and whose membership before long included Lord Milner.
42. R.S. Churchill, *Churchill: Young Statesman*, p. 79. Henry Lucy – 'Toby, MP' of *Punch* – commented at the time that 'Winston Churchill may be safely counted upon to make himself quite as disagreeable on the Liberal side as he did on the Unionist. But he will be handicapped by the aversion that always pertains to a man who, in whatsoever honourable circumstances, has turned his coat. In running for the prize of office he will, moreover, be brought in competition with many able men of his own age who, having been loyal to Liberalism throughout, will resent being set aside in favour of a late-comer to the vineyard.'

43. Tritton, *John Montagu*, pp. 105–8.
44. Pound and Harmsworth, *Northcliffe*, p. 282.
45. 27 June 1904, NADM, 62156, BL.
46. J. Amery, *Joseph Chamberlain and the Tariff Reform Campaign*, p. 609.
47. Tritton, *John Montagu*, pp. 109–10.
48. Gilmour, *Curzon*, p. 285.
49. Tritton, *John Montagu*, pp. 110–11.
50. Sidney Dark, *The Life of Sir Arthur Pearson* (London, 1920), p. 125.
51. Arthur J. Marder, *Fear God and Dread Nought: The Correspondence of Admiral of the Fleet Lord Fisher of Kilverstone, Vol 2: Years of Power 1904–1914* (London, 1956), p. 20. Famous for his aggressiveness, in late 1904 the new First Sea Lord suggested to the King that the British should launch a pre-emptive strike on the growing German fleet before it grew any stronger. To this the sovereign is supposed to have replied, 'My God, Fisher, you must be mad!'
52. 16 November 1904, Strachey papers, S/11/4/15, HLRO.
53. R.S. Churchill, *Churchill*, Vol. 2 Companion, Pt 1, pp. 373–4.
54. 21 March 1905, quoted in Gollin, 'Lord Northcliffe's Change of Course', p. 51.
55. Pound and Harmsworth, *Northcliffe*, p. 290.

CHAPTER 7: THE YOUNGEST PEER CREATED, 1905–1907

1. Alfred M. Gollin, *The Observer and J.L. Garvin, 1908–1914: A Study in Great Editorship* (London, 1960), p. 7.
2. Pound and Harmsworth, *Northcliffe*, p. 291.
3. 9 May entry, 1905 diary, NADM, 62393, BL.
4. J. Amery, *Joseph Chamberlain and the Tariff Reform Campaign*, pp. 702–3.
5. Peter King, *The Viceroy's Fall: How Kitchener Destroyed Curzon* (London, 1986), p. 170.
6. 3 August 1905, NADM, 62153, BL.
7. 14 September 1905, NADM, 62153, BL.
8. Pound and Harmsworth, *Northcliffe*, p. 287.
9. *Daily Mail*, 5 December 1905.
10. Ibid., 11 December 1905.
11. Ibid., 8 December 1905.
12. N.d., quoted in Gollin, *Balfour's Burden*, p. 241. As evidence that Harmsworth may have known about the honour well in advance, Gollin also cites a letter to Strachey in June 1904 in which Alfred jokes that he is 'starting to learn Yiddish with a view to speech making in the Lords'.
13. 5 December 1905, quoted in G.R. Searle, *Corruption in British Politics 1895–1930* (Oxford, 1987), p. 93. Despite his statement at the time, Acland-Hood would later claim that he turned down a 'very large cheque' offered by Harmsworth after he received the peerage. 8 May 1919 entry, in John Ramsden, *Real Old Tory Politics: The Political Diaries of Robert Sanders, Lord Bayford* (London, 1984), p. 125.
14. Pound and Harmsworth, *Northcliffe*, p. 295.
15. Quoted in Gollin, 'Lord Northcliffe's Change of Course', p. 52.
16. Pound and Harmsworth, *Northcliffe*, p. 295.
17. 20 July 1907, quoted in John Wilson, *CB: A Life of Sir Henry Campbell-Bannerman* (London, 1973) pp. 80–1.
18. Gollin, *Proconsul in Politics*, p. 575.
19. Quoted in Morris, *The Scaremongers*, p. 70.
20. Pound and Harmsworth, *Northcliffe*, p. 295. The journalist R.D. Blumenfeld spoke to Northcliffe years later about the episode. He was surprised when told that 'Lord Harmsworth' had been the first choice. This was not, as Blumenfeld believed, to

advertise the publications, but, confided the press lord, out of 'pardonable family pride'. According to Blumenfeld, Northcliffe explained that the 'authorities who distill red blood into blue . . . would not let me use the name Harmsworth for the reason you mention – advertising – so I had to fall back on the usual territorial descriptive title'. Ralph D. Blumenfeld, *R. D. B.'s Procession* (New York, 1935), p. 183. Brother Cecil, not so personally identified with the publishing business, would later be allowed to take the title 'Lord Harmsworth'.

21. *Daily Mail*, 19, 20 December 1905.
22. Ibid., 23 December 1905.
23. Ibid.
24. Ibid., 5 January 1906.
25. Jill Liddington and Jill Norris, *One Hand Tied Behind Us: The Rise of the Women's Suffrage Movement* (London, 1978), p. 62.
26. Colin Cross, *The Liberals in Power, 1905–1914* (Westport, 1963), p. 23.
27. *Daily Mail*, 15 January 1906.
28. 17 January 1906, in Pound and Harmsworth, *Northcliffe*, p. 296.
29. *Daily Mail*, 23 January 1906.
30. 19 January entry, 1906 diary, WAM, 59562, BL.
31. For this compromise, see Marsh, *Joseph Chamberlain*, pp. 633–7.
32. 1906 diary, NADM, 62394, BL.
33. Cross, *Liberals in Power*, p. 23.
34. I.F. Clarke, *Voices Prophesying War 1763–1984* (London, 1964), p. 144.
35. Ibid., p. 145. When published in book form Le Queux's work sold a million copies and was translated into twenty-seven languages. In the English edition, a foreword by Lord Roberts called for preparedness to prevent such a catastrophe from occurring in reality.
36. 1906 diary, WAM, 59562, BL.
37. Tritton, *John Montagu*, pp. 147–8.
38. 16 July entry, 1906 diary, NADM, 62394, BL.
39. Pound and Harmsworth, *Northcliffe*, p. 298.
40. Ibid., p. 290.
41. Graham Wallace, *Flying Witness: Harry Harper and the Golden Age of Aviation* (London, 1958), p. 52; Alfred Gollin, *No Longer an Island: Britain and the Wright Brothers 1902–1909* (London, 1984), p. 193.
42. Wallace, *Flying Witness*, p. 53.
43. 30 November entry, 1906 diary, WAM, 59562, BL.
44. 1906 diary, NADM, 62394, BL.
45. Charles Wilson, *The History of Unilever* (London, 1954), p. 79.
46. H. Montgomery Hyde, *Lord Reading* (London, 1967), p. 74.
47. Pound and Harmsworth, *Northcliffe*, p. 303.
48. C. Wilson, *History of Unilever*, p. 84.
49. Ibid., p. 85.
50. Edward Marjoribanks (Vol. 1) and Ian Colvin (Vols. 2 and 3), *The Life of Lord Carson* (London, 3 vols., 1932), Vol. 1, p. 407.
51. Pound and Harmsworth, *Northcliffe*, pp. 302–3.
52. C. Wilson, *History of Unilever*, p. 85; Pound and Harmsworth, *Northcliffe*, p. 304.
53. Montgomery Hyde, *Lord Reading*, p. 74.

CHAPTER 8: *THE TIMES* IS HARMSWORTH'S, 1907–1908

1. *History of The Times*, Vol. 3, p. 444.
2. In 1904 sales of the *Encyclopædia Britannica* were suspended pending the tenth

edition. To increase the declining revenues which resulted, the next year an outlet of The *Times* Book Club was opened in New Bond Street, for the first time giving the enterprise direct marketing contact with its customers, the subscribers of *The Times*. This step led to a further complication, a 'Book War' with the commercial publishers, incensed at the paper's blatant intrusion into their trade at lower prices than they offered.

3. Oliver Woods and James Bishop, *The Story of The Times* (London, 1985), p. 194.
4. Pound and Harmsworth, *Northcliffe*, p. 309. The account of *The History of The Times* has Northcliffe learning of the Pearson bid first from Lewis, through George Sutton. This version of the episode also has Northcliffe acting much too calmly in the face of this intrusion by Pearson. Though Northcliffe may have feigned indifference as a negotiating ploy, he desperately wanted *The Times*, no matter how many other publishing properties he owned. Others could be disposed of, and were, subsequently.
5. 6 January 1908, in Pound and Harmsworth, *Northcliffe*, p. 309.
6. *History of The Times*, Vol. 3, p. 517.
7. F. Harcourt Kitchin, *Moberly Bell and His Times* (London, 1925), p. 213.
8. 7 January 1908, in Pound and Harmsworth, *Northcliffe*, p. 310.
9. 7 January 1908, in *History of The Times*, Vol. 3, p. 539.
10. *History of The Times*, Vol. 3, p. 526.
11. Bell to Chirol, 26 January 1910, Buckle Papers, PPG/1, TA.
12. *History of the Times*, Vol. 3, p. 549.
13. Kitchin, *Moberly Bell*, pp. 234–5.
14. *History of The Times*, Vol. 3, p. 557.
15. James D. Startt, 'G. E. Buckle, Lord Northcliffe and the Conservative Revolution at *The Times*, 1908–1912', *Journal of Newspaper and Periodical History*, 7 (1991), p. 15.
16. Pound and Harmsworth, *Northcliffe*, p. 321.
17. *History of the Times*, Vol. 3, p. 570.
18. Kitchin, *Moberly Bell*, p. 251.
19. Ibid., p. 238.
20. Pound and Harmsworth, *Northcliffe*, p. 330.
21. Lord Northcliffe, *Newspapers and Their Millionaires* (London, 1922), p. 20.
22. 19 April 1908, NADM, 62296, BL.
23. Cross, *Liberals in Power*, p. 37.
24. This affair had been revealed by the military correspondent of *The Times*, Charles à Court Repington. Northcliffe told Leo Maxse that his silence and his newspaper's muted response to the 'disgraceful Tweedmouth matter' sprang from his fear that the enemy might have beaten his price for *The Times* if his identity had been known.
25. Cross, *Liberals in Power*, p. 68.
26. 29 July 1908, NADM, 62153, BL.
27. 11 May 1908, in Martin Gilbert, *Winston S. Churchill*, Vol. 3, Companion, Pt 2 (London, 1972), pp. 791–2.
28. 13 May 1908, in Pound and Harmsworth, *Northcliffe*, p. 324.
29. 15 August 1908, in Gilbert, *Churchill*, Vol. 3, Companion, Pt 2, p. 805.
30. 30 August 1908, in Pound and Harmsworth, *Northcliffe*, p. 334.
31. Cross, *Liberals in Power*, p. 91.
32. 17 July 1908, NADM, 62155, BL.
33. 9 April 1908, NADM, 62157, BL.
34. 11–30 June entries, 1908 diary, Dawson Mss., Bodleian Library.
35. 22 June 1908, Buckle Papers, PPG/1, TA.
36. 23 June 1908, NADM, 62243, BL. Buckle's sacrifices to keep the reputation of *The*

Times 'unsullied' had included turning down a baronetcy offered by Balfour in December 1905, at the same time as Northcliffe gained his peerage. The editor sent the correspondence concerning the proposed honour to his new chief, who returned it with a note that he was 'gratified to think that I am associated with one whose ideals for the future of the Times are so lofty and glad to feel that I may have been the means of preserving traditions which led you to decline that which the majority of our countrymen consider high reward'. 3 July 1908, NADM, 62243, BL.
37. 9 July 1908, NADM, 62298B, BL.
38. Esher, *Journals and Letters*, Vol. 2, p. 327.
39. Strachey Papers, S/11/4/19, HLRO.
40. 14 August 1908, Buckle Papers, PPG/1, TA.
41. 23 July 1908, NADM, 62159, BL.
42. 29 August 1908, NADM, 62159, BL.
43. Quoted in Gollin, *No Longer an Island*, p. 333.
44. *Daily Mail*, 11 July 1908.
45. Repington had been carrying out his own invasion-scare gambit for several years in *The Times*, but on behalf of a larger army. For this see W. Michael Ryan, 'The Invasion Controversy of 1906–1908: Lieutenant-Colonel Charles à Court Repington and British Perceptions of the German Menace', *Military Affairs*, February 1980.
46. Gollin, *No Longer an Island*, pp. 363–4.
47. Ibid., p. 303.
48. 22 August 1908, NADM, 62183, BL.
49. 28 August 1908, NADM, 62183, BL.
50. 26 August 1908, NADM, 62299, BL. This was returned, along with a note of thanks, by Hubert Montgomery, Grey's aide at the Foreign Office. The US administration also sent Grey a summary of the interview, part of which was printed in the 22 November New York *World*. Raymond Esthus, *Theodore Roosevelt and the International Rivalries* (Waltham, Mass., 1970), pp. 126–30.
51. 23 December 1908, NADM, 62300, BL.
52. Lamar Cecil, *Wilhelm II* (Chapel Hill, 2 vols., 1989–96), Vol. 2, p. 137.
53. Wrench, *Uphill*, p. 141.
54. Pound and Harmsworth, *Northcliffe*, p. 336.
55. 7 December 1908, NADM, 62155, BL.
56. 19 January 1909, NADM, 62155, BL.
57. Quoted in Morris, *The Scaremongers*, p. 207.
58. Pound and Harmsworth, *Northcliffe*, p. 337.
59. Ibid., p. 332.

CHAPTER 9: AEROPLANES, DREADNOUGHTS AND BUDGETS, 1909
1. 2 January entry, 1909 diary, WAM, 59569, BL.
2. NADM, 62175, BL.
3. 3 January entry, 1909 diary, WAM, 59569, BL.
4. 14 February entry, 1909 diary, WAM, 59569, BL.
5. 19 February 1909, in Pound and Harmsworth, *Northcliffe*, p. 353.
6. Ibid., p. 354.
7. *Daily Mail*, 10, 11, 18, 19, 22 March 1909, quoted in Gollin, *No Longer an Island*, pp. 443–4.
8. Quoted in Morris, *The Scaremongers*, p. 203. The irony of this situation was that the First Lord who inherited and used the Dreadnoughts needed in 1914 was one of the men who had fought against them, Churchill.

9. This slogan has been credited variously to George Wyndham and Arthur Lee, later Lord Lee of Fareham.

10. Garvin commented in the *Observer* on the four provisional Dreadnoughts that 'As a lady's letter puts its meaning in a postscript, the most significant feature of Mr. McKenna's proposals is contained in a footnote.' Northcliffe was impressed by Garvin's articles and pleased to see the *Observer* evident at Calais on his return to England from a rest in Paris. He wrote to the editor, 'I was very glad to see your naval article. I find it has been much *observed.*' 17 March 1909, quoted in Gollin, *The Observer and J.L. Garvin*, p. 76.

11. *Daily Mail,* 17 March 1909.

12. N.d., NADM, 62155, BL.

13. Cross, *Liberals in Power,* p. 82; John Grigg, *Lloyd George: The People's Champion* (London, 1978), pp. 173–4.

14. Grigg, *Lloyd George: The People's Champion*, p. 192.

15. Ibid., p. 195.

16. On 3 May *The Times* reported the comments of Lord Ridley, the chairman of the Tariff Reform League, that the Upper House had a 'perfect right' to throw out the measure, as well as a 'perfect constitutional right to amend the Budget, and that circumstances might arise in which it would be desirable to assert that right'. The peers, said Ridley, had in the past gone along with the other chamber on financial affairs 'because the Government had hitherto been conducted by sane men, but there was now a House of Commons controlled by a pack of madmen, and they had to take different measures'.

17. 28 April 1909, NADM, 62303, BL.

18. Solm to Northcliffe, 12 May 1909, NADM, 62304, BL.

19. 22 May 1909, NADM, 62196, BL.

20. N.d., NADM, 62184A, BL.

21. 12 May 1909, NADM, 62155, BL.

22. 18 May 1909, NADM, 62243, BL.

23. 19 May 1909, NADM, 62201, BL.

24. 7 May 1909, quoted in Gollin, *The Observer and J.L. Garvin*, p. 100.

25. 20 May 1909, NADM, 62243, BL.

26. 26 May 1909, NADM, 62175, BL.

27. 4 May 1909, NADM, 62155, BL.

28. 9 May 1909, NADM, 62155, BL.

29. 18 May 1909, NADM, 62155, BL.

30. Rosebery's address is reproduced in Thomas Hardman, *A Parliament of the Press: The First Imperial Press Conference* (London, 1909), pp. 10–14. According to one account, Rosebery tried to escape this chore and 'had almost to be brought up to London by force'. Pound and Harmsworth, *Northcliffe*, p. 369.

31. 5 June entry, 1909 diary, WAM, 59569, BL.

32. Hardman, *Parliament of the Press*, p. 48.

33. Pound and Harmsworth, *Northcliffe*, p.369.

34. 12 June entry, 1909 diary, WAM, 59569, BL.

35. 11 June 1909, NADM, 62166, BL.

36. Quoted in Desmond Zwar, *In Search of Keith Murdoch* (Melbourne, 1980), p. 55.

37. Pound and Harmsworth, *Northcliffe*, p. 369.

38. 12 June 1909, NADM, 62166, BL.

39. 19 July 1909, NADM, 62166, BL.

40. *Daily Mail,* 26 July 1909, quoted in Alfred Gollin, *The Impact of Air Power on the British People and Their Government, 1909–1914* (Stanford, 1989), pp. 71–2.

41. At the National Union of Conservative Associations annual dinner on 16 July, Lansdowne commented that he did not think that the Upper House was 'at all likely to proclaim that it has no responsibility at all for the Bill, and that because it is mixed up in the financial affairs of the nation we are obliged to swallow it whole and without hesitation'. Grigg, *Lloyd George: The People's Champion*, pp. 198–201.
42. Ibid., pp. 203–8.
43. Bruce K. Murray, *The People's Budget 1909–10: Lloyd George and Liberal Politics* (Oxford, 1980), p. 175.
44. 19 June 1909, NADM, 62157, BL.
45. 22 June 1909, NADM, 62157, BL.
46. Quoted in Grigg, *Lloyd George: The People's Champion*, p. 214, n. 4.
47. 3 August 1909 entry, Cecil Harmsworth diary, Lord Harmsworth Papers; Pound and Harmsworth, *Northcliffe*, p. 376–7.
48. Ibid.
49. Grigg, *Lloyd George: The People's Champion*, p. 214.
50. For this see Gollin, *The Observer and J.L. Garvin*, pp. 106–7. Gollin (pp. 119–20) calls this a 'mischievous alteration of course'.
51. Pound and Harmsworth, *Northcliffe*, p. 377.
52. Fyfe to Northcliffe, 9 August 1909, Northcliffe to Fyfe, 11 August 1909, NADM, 62206, BL.
53. 8 August 1909, NADM, 62307, BL.
54. 8 August 1909, NADM, 62307, BL.
55. 11 August 1909, NADM, 62307, BL.
56. 12 August 1909, NADM, 62307, BL.
57. For Kitchin's account of the 'infinite tact and patience' with which the process was carried out, see his *Moberly Bell*, pp. 290–1.
58. 9 August 1909, in Pound and Harmsworth, *Northcliffe*, pp. 378–9.
59. 11 August 1909, NADM, 62243, BL.
60. Quoted in Gollin, *The Impact of Air Power*, pp. 90–1.
61. Quoted in Pound and Harmsworth, *Northcliffe*, p. 383.
62. 27 September 1909, NADM, 62196, BL.
63. Pound and Harmsworth, *Northcliffe*, p. 383.
64. The design, however, came from the USA. Mark Twain had sent the drawings of his house, which Northcliffe greatly admired, to be used in Newfoundland. Louise Owen, *The Real Lord Northcliffe* (London, 1922), p. 19.
65. NADM, 62196, BL.
66. 1 November 1909, NADM, 62196, BL.
67. *Daily Mail*, 23 November 1909.
68. Undated interview copy, NADM, 62308, BL.

CHAPTER 10: THE PEERS, THE PEOPLE AND THE PRESS, 1909–1911
1. *Daily Mail*, 2, 8 December 1909.
2. Quoted in Koss, *Political Press*, Vol. 2, p. 133.
3. Quoted in Neal Blewett, *The Peers, the Parties and the People: The British General Elections of 1910* (London, 1972), p. 92.
4. Quoted in Morris, *The Scaremongers*, p. 210.
5. Koss, *Political Press*, Vol. 2, p. 128; Sandars to Northcliffe, 13 December 1909, quoted in Koss, *Political Press*, Vol. 2, p. 130.
6. *Daily Mail*, 13 December 1909.
7. Ibid., 18 December 1909.
8. Pound and Harmsworth, *Northcliffe*, p. 389.

9. Blewett, *The Peers, the Parties and the People*, p. 127. This pamphlet would be reissued in August 1914.
10. 16 December 1909, NADM, 62153, BL.
11. 3 January 1910, NADM, 62153, BL.
12. *Daily Mail*, 5 January 1910; *The Times*, 5 January 1910.
13. *Daily Mail*, 13, 14 January 1910.
14. Ibid., 29, 31 January 1910.
15. 9 December 1909, Buckle Papers, PPG/1, TA.
16. 15 December 1909, in Pound and Harmsworth, *Northcliffe*, p. 387.
17. Pound and Harmsworth, *Northcliffe*, p. 388.
18. Quoted in Koss, *Political Press*, Vol. 2, pp. 132–3.
19. Quoted in Gollin, *The Observer and J.L. Garvin*, p. 134.
20. Pound and Harmsworth, *Northcliffe*, p. 391.
21. 24 February 1910, in Pound and Harmsworth, *Northcliffe*, p. 392.
22. Gollin, *The Impact of Air Power*, pp. 140–51.
23. Pound and Harmsworth, *Northcliffe*, pp. 392–3.
24. Kenneth Rose, *King George V* (London, 1984), p. 76.
25. Ibid., pp. 76–7.
26. 24 May 1910, NADM, 62310, BL. Lee was an ally of Northcliffe in the calls for aeroplane and Dreadnought construction.
27. 31 May 1910, NADM, 62310, BL.
28. 18 June 1910, NADM, 62310, BL.
29. Quoted in Viscount Lee of Fareham, *'A Good Innings': The Private Papers of Viscount Lee of Fareham*, ed. Alan Clark (London, 1974), pp. 109–10.
30. Garvin later told Northcliffe that 'When the King died the conference idea came to me in a flash with absolute conviction as the new policy for a wholly new situation.' 13 June 1910, quoted in Gollin, *The Observer and J.L. Garvin*, p. 185.
31. Grigg, *Lloyd George: The People's Champion*, pp. 259–60. In March, Murray had suggested some sort of conference to the future George V.
32. 8 August 1910, NADM, 62311, BL.
33. *Overseas Daily Mail*, 27 August 1910.
34. 29 September 1910, NADM, 62222, BL.
35. 21 November 1910, NADM, 62222, BL.
36. *Daily Mail*, 8 November 1910.
37. John Ramsden, *The Age of Balfour and Baldwin 1902–1940* (London, 1978), p. 35.
38. 22 November 1910, NADM, 62311, BL. Northcliffe also supported the Free Trader Lord Robert, and his brother, Lord Hugh Cecil, against the attempts of a group of stalwarts called the 'Compatriots' to force the Cecils out of the Unionist Party.
39. Gollin, *The Observer and J.L. Garvin*, p. 247. For the future Prime Minister, see R.J.Q. Adams, *Bonar Law* (London, 1999).
40. 16 November 1910, in Pound and Harmsworth, *Northcliffe*, p. 399.
41. Northcliffe to Fish, 20 November 1910, NADM, 62201, BL; Northcliffe to Caird, 20 November 1910, NADM, 62188, BL; Northcliffe to Kennedy Jones, 20 November 1910, 62196, BL.
42. Twells Brex, *'Scaremongerings' From the Daily Mail* (London, 1914), pp. 85–93.
43. 18 November 1910, NADM, 62311, BL.
44. 22 November 1910, NADM, 62311, BL.
45. Quoted in Gollin, *The Observer and J.L. Garvin*, pp. 264–5.
46. *Daily Mail*, 8 December 1910.
47. Ibid., 9, 10, 21 December 1910.

48. Ramsden, *Age of Balfour and Baldwin*, p. 37; Cross, *Liberals in Power*, p. 123.
49. 18 December 1910, NADM, 62153, BL.
50. 20 December 1910, NADM, 62279A, BL.
51. 13 December 1910, NADM, 62153, BL.
52. 17 December 1910, NADM, 62153, BL.
53. 30 January 1911, NADM, 62175, BL.
54. 7 January entry, Dawson diary, in John Evelyn Wrench, *Geoffrey Dawson and Our Times* (London, 1955), p. 78.
55. 1 February 1911, quoted in Gollin, *The Observer and J.L. Garvin*, p. 288.
56. 2 February 1911, Beaverbrook Papers, C261, HLRO.
57. 22 February 1911, Beaverbrook Papers, C261, HLRO.
58. Aitken to Northcliffe, 4 February 1911, Beaverbrook Papers, C261, HLRO.
59. Quoted in Gollin, *The Observer and J.L. Garvin*, p. 289.
60. 5 February 1911, Beaverbrook Papers, C261, HLRO.
61. 21 February 1911, Beaverbrook Papers, C261, HLRO.
62. 1 March 1911, NADM, 62243, BL.
63. 3 March 1911, NADM, 62243, BL.
64. Pound and Harmsworth, *Northcliffe*, p. 409.
65. Northcliffe, *Newspapers and Their Millionaires*, p. 20.

CHAPTER 11: PRELUDE TO WAR, 1911–1914

1. Pound and Harmsworth, *Northcliffe*, p. 405–6.
2. Ibid., p. 420.
3. 17 June 1911, NADM, 62315, BL.
4. 17 June 1911, NADM, 62153, BL.
5. 20 June 1911, NADM, 62153, BL.
6. *Daily Mail*, 19 June 1911.
7. Wrench, *Uphill*, p. 250.
8. 30 June 1911, NADM, 62222, BL.
9. 17, 20 July 1911, NADM, 62222, BL.
10. 23 July 1911, NADM, 62243, BL. For the 'wild peers', see Gregory Phillips, *The Diehards: Aristocratic Society and Politics in Edwardian England* (London, 1979).
11. 18 July 1911, NADM, 62153, BL.
12. Lansdowne to Northcliffe, 24 July 1911, NADM, 62316, BL.
13. 28 July 1911, NADM, 62316, BL.
14. 28 July 1911, NADM, 62316, BL.
15. 3 August 1911, NADM, 62155, BL.
16. 12 August 1911, NADM, 62243, BL.
17. 12 August 1911, NADM, 62243, BL.
18. Pound and Harmsworth, *Northcliffe*, p. 423.
19. Quoted in Morris, *The Scaremongers*, p. 296.
20. 18 September 1911, NADM, 62156, BL.
21. For this episode, see Adams, *Bonar Law*.
22. Ramsden, *Age of Balfour and Baldwin*, p. 91.
23. Cross, *Liberals in Power*, p. 137.
24. 11 November 1911, Beaverbrook Papers, C261, HLRO.
25. 11 November 1911, NADM, 62156, BL.
26. Northcliffe to Churchill, 24 November 1911, NADM, 62156, BL.
27. 11 November 1911, NADM, 62246A, BL.
28. 16 November 1911, NADM, 62246A, BL.
29. 16 February 1912, NADM, 62153, BL.

30. 31 January 1912, NADM, 62318, BL.
31. N.d., NADM, 62318, BL.
32. Buckle to Northcliffe, 8 July 1912, Northcliffe to Buckle, 10 July 1912, NADM, 62243, BL.
33. 29 July 1912 entry, Dawson diary, Dawson Mss., Bodleian Library.
34. 8 August 1912, Dawson Mss., Box 62, Bodleian Library.
35. Adams, *Bonar Law*, p. 109; Marjoribanks and Colvin, *Lord Carson*, Vol. 2, p. 129.
36. 13 August 1912, NADM, 62244, BL.
37. Colvin, *Lord Carson*, Vol. 2, p. 149.
38. N.d., NADM, 62222, BL.
39. 25 June 1912, NADM, 62222, BL; also in Pound and Harmsworth, *Northcliffe*, p. 432.
40. N.d., 12 October 1913, NADM, 62222, BL.
41. 26 November 1913, NADM, 62222, BL.
42. 12 August 1912, NADM, 62156, BL.
43. 15 October 1912, NADM, 62156, BL.
44. 11 April 1913, NADM, 62156, BL.
45. 13 October 1912, NADM, 62320, BL. The forms 'Serbia' and 'Servia' were both used in this period.
46. N.d., in Pound and Harmsworth, *Northcliffe*, p. 435.
47. 16 October 1912, NADM, 62198, BL.
48. N.d., NADM, 62322, BL.
49. Harmsworth to Northcliffe, n.d., Northcliffe to Harmsworth, 19 April 1913, NADM, 62323, BL.
50. Mrs White King (Katherine Harmsworth) to Northcliffe, 7 November, Northcliffe to Mrs White King, 11 November 1912, NADM, 62320, BL.
51. 2 March 1913, in Pound and Harmsworth, *Northcliffe*, p. 440.
52. 30 March 1913, NADM, 62322, BL. Hale told Northcliffe that he could have had the ambassador's job, but his income was not large enough. Hale had written a biography of Woodrow Wilson and also *The New Freedom*, which outlined the President's brand of progressive politics. His letter continued that 'Mr. Wilson is anxious to be understood in England and he needs to be led to understand England better. There is a chance just now to do some telling work in such a position as *Times* or *Daily Mail* correspondent here.'
53. 19 April 1913, NADM, 62323, BL.
54. Northcliffe to Page, 27 May, Page to Northcliffe, 29 May 1913, NADM, 62323, BL.
55. Isaacs to Northcliffe, n.d., NADM, 62156, BL; Lloyd George to Northcliffe, 21 March 1913, Lloyd George Papers, C/6/8/2, HLRO.
56. 24 March 1913, Lloyd George Papers, C/6/8/1a, HLRO. Brother Harold had also written in support of Isaacs particularly. Pound and Harmsworth, *Northcliffe*, p. 441.
57. Northcliffe to Sutton, 21 September, Northcliffe to Geraldine Harmsworth, 19 September 1913, in Pound and Harmsworth, *Northcliffe*, pp. 446–7.
58. 8 November 1913, NADM, 62324, BL.
59. Howard to Northcliffe, 11 November 1913, NADM, 62324, BL.
60. Pound and Harmsworth, *Northcliffe*, p. 450.
61. Ibid., p. 448.
62. 25 March 1914, NADM, 62244, BL.
63. Pound and Harmsworth, *Northcliffe*, p. 454.
64. 1 April 1914, NADM, 62156, BL.
65. 1 April 1914, NADM, 62156, BL.
66. *Daily Mail*, 22 May 1914.

67. 'The Hapsburg Tragedy', *Daily Mail*, 29 June 1914.
68. J.M.N. Jeffries, *Front Everywhere* (London, 1935), p. 63.
69. 3 July 1914, in Pound and Harmsworth, *Northcliffe*, p. 456.
70. Jeffries, *Front Everywhere*, p. 64.
71. L.S. Amery wrote anonymously of Asquith that 'for twenty years he had held a season ticket on the line of least resistance and has gone wherever the train of events has taken him, lucidly justifying his position at whatever point he has happened to find himself ... And if Civil War breaks out ... next month, or the month after, he will still be found letting things take their course, and justifying himself with dignity, conciseness and lucidity.' 'The Home Rule Crisis', *Quarterly Review*, 440 (July 1914), p. 276.
72. Two years before he had remarked that 'the Liberal press was written by boobies for boobies'. Koss, *Political Press*, Vol. 2, p. 191.
73. H.H. Asquith, *Letters to Venetia Stanley*, ed. Michael and Eleanor Brock (Oxford, 1982), pp. 99–100. Asquith's biographer Roy Jenkins considers these letters to Miss Stanley to be the most truly representative record of Asquith's innermost thoughts.
74. Ibid., pp. 100–1.
75. Ibid., pp. 104, 107.
76. L.C.F. Turner, *Origins of the First World War* (New York, 1970), p. 88.
77. Cameron Hazlehurst, *Politicians at War July 1914 to May 1915: A Prologue to the triumph of Lloyd George* (London, 1971), p. 14.

CHAPTER 12: AWAKENING THE NATION, 1914–1915
1. For a more detailed examination of Northcliffe's activities in the Great War than is possible here, see J. Lee Thompson, *Politicians, the Press and Propaganda: Lord Northcliffe and the Great War* (London, 1999).
2. Valentine Williams, *World of Action* (Boston, 1938), p. 137; Pound and Harmsworth, *Northcliffe*, p. 461; Jeffries, *Front Everywhere*, pp. 66–7.
3. H.W. Steed, *Through Thirty Years, 1892–1922* (London, 2 vols., 1924), Vol. 2, pp. 10–11; Pound and Harmsworth, *Northcliffe*, p. 463.
4. *Daily Mail*, 3 August 1914.
5. Lord Beaverbrook, *Politicians and the War 1914–1916* (London, 1960), pp. 36–7. Beaverbrook reported that Churchill 'stood out strongly for the despatch ... all the more strongly perhaps because of Northcliffe's intervention'.
6. T. Clarke, *My Northcliffe Diary*, p. 53.
7. Steed commented that Northcliffe developed a 'war mind' which 'divided men into two classes – those who felt that there could be no way out except through victory, and those who bewailed the loss of peace, or sought compromises, or failed to bend all their energies to the hitting of the enemy, constantly and hard by arms and by policy'. *Through Thirty Years*, Vol. 2, p. 34.
8. Sir George Arthur, *Lord Kitchener* (New York, 3 vols., 1920), Vol. 3, p. 3.
9. Earl of Oxford and Asquith, *Memories and Reflections, 1852–1927* (Boston, 2 vols., 1928) Vol. 2, p. 30. Roy Jenkins, *Asquith* (London, 1964), p. 342.
10. Viscount Grey of Fallodon, *Twenty-Five Years* (New York, 2 vols., 1925), Vol. 2, p. 20.
11. Philip Magnus, *Kitchener: Portrait of an Imperialist* (New York, 1959), pp. 278–9; Steed recorded in *Through Thirty Years*, Vol. 2, p. 33, that Northcliffe told him on 6 August 1914 'this is going to be a long, long war'. Magnus states that Kitchener foresaw a war of three or four years. *Kitchener*, p. 282.
12. David French, *British Economic and Strategic Planning, 1905–1915* (London, 1982), pp. 51–70, 124–35; Magnus, *Kitchener*, pp. 288, 279–81.

13. 18 August 1914, NADM, 62210B, BL.
14. George Cassar, *Kitchener: Architect of Victory* (London, 1977), pp. 350–1; J.M. McEwen, '"Brass Hats" and the British Press During the First World War', *Journal of Contemporary History*, **18** (April 1983), pp. 45–6.
15. Lord Riddell, *Lord Riddell's War Diary 1914–1918* (London, 1933), p. 9. The Press Bureau, staffed mainly with over-aged military men brought out of retirement, opened in a decrepit Admiralty building in Charing Cross on 10 August.
16. 12 August 1914, Northcliffe Papers, HA.
17. Regulation 18 forbade the collection and publication of information useful to the enemy. Regulation 27 forbade the spread of false reports which would cause disaffection among the armed forces to prejudice Britain's relations with its allies. Regulation 51 gave powers to the military both to search and to seize machinery at any place suspected of breaching these regulations. Infringements were punishable by court martial, with possible life sentences.
18. Those allowed with the German army included neutral journalists, many of them Americans. The German general staff even had the temerity to offer their communiqués to *The Times*, which immediately turned them down. Soon, however, *The Times* and *Daily Mail* did report 'official' German news, as being better than no news.
19. Robert Blatchford, 'Do You Understand?', *Daily Mail*, 25 August 1914.
20. *Daily Mail*, 27 August 1914.
21. During the war, *Daily Mail* correspondents placed important weekend news in the *Weekly Dispatch*.
22. Since the British Army would not officially allow correspondents, the two men had been forced to glean their stories from reports given them by retreating soldiers they came upon on the road to Amiens. Hamilton Fyfe, *My Seven Selves* (London, 1935), pp. 177–80. Fyfe's first reports based on the accounts of the wounded from Mons appeared in the Friday 28 August 1914 *Daily Mail*. The original Amiens dispatch, with F.E. Smith's changes, is at the Archive of *The Times*. See Amiens Dispatch File, World War I Box.
23. Entry beginning 25 August 1914, Riddell diary. Add. Mss., 62974, BL. In Riddell's opinion, Smith had no doubt been 'endeavouring to curry favour' with Northcliffe, so he had 'only himself to blame'.
24. Buckmaster was replaced in May 1915 by the colonial administrator Sir Frank Swettenham, who shared duties with the Liberal editor Sir Edward Cook. Cook served to the end of the war.
25. 5 September 1914, NADM, 62156, BL.
26. 7 September 1914, NADM, 62156, BL.
27. 1 December 1914, NADM, 62158, BL.
28. R. MacNair Wilson, *Lord Northcliffe: A Study* (Philadelphia, 1927), p. 206.
29. Swinton went to France on 14 September 1914 and continued his reports until the middle of July 1915. His name was not announced, but soon became common knowledge. He was recommended to Kitchener by Churchill, and was later better known as one of the fathers of the tank. For his account of the assignment, see Major General Sir Ernest Swinton, *Eyewitness: Being Personal Reminiscences of Certain Phases of the Great War, Including the Genesis of the Tank* (1933; reprint, New York, 1972).
30. R. MacN. Wilson, *Lord Northcliffe*, p. 205; John Evelyn Wrench, *Struggle, 1914–1920* (London, 1935), p. 117.
31. Swinton, *Eyewitness*, pp. 38–9. In Swinton's view, though Northcliffe's patriotism was obvious, to favour one newspaper proprietor over another with a personal visit was not wise.

32. Fyfe, *Northcliffe*, p. 179.
33. Northcliffe to General Charteris, 6 August 1916, NADM, 62159, BL.
34. He led a volunteer force across the Channel which suffered heavy casualties. Further, the foray was blamed (because it gave false hope) for delaying and therefore making more costly the retreat of the Belgian army.
35. *Daily Mail*, 14 October 1914.
36. 24 November 1914, Fisher Papers, Churchill College Archive, Cambridge.
37. 22 December 1914, NADM, 62180, BL.
38. 10 November 1914 entry, Riddell diary, Add. Mss., 62974, ff. 239–40, BL. At a dinner party, the wife of Reginald McKenna, the Home Secretary, told Riddell that her husband 'would have had Northcliffe court-martialled if he had his way'. 7 November 1914 entry, Riddell diary, Add. Mss., 62974, ff. 233–4, BL.
39. *Daily Mail*, 28 August 1914.
40. The Bryce Committee findings were published in the United States as the *Report of the Committee on Alleged German Outrages* (New York, 1915).
41. See for example, 'The Glad Eye That Failed', *Daily Mail*, 12 August 1914, an article by F.W. Wile on the Kaiser's twelve-year campaign for American sympathy.
42. Enclosure, Northcliffe to Maxse, 13 October 1914, NADM, 62175, BL.
43. Northcliffe to Willert, 9 August 1917, Willert Papers, Box 6, Sterling Library, Yale University.
44. 26 October 1914, NADM, 62180, BL.
45. Marion Siney, *The Allied Blockade of Germany 1914–1916* (Ann Arbor, Michigan, 1957), p. 12; Armin Rappaport, *The British Press and Wilsonian Neutrality* (Stanford, 1951), p. 14.
46. Willert to Northcliffe, 8 January 1915, NADM, 62255, BL.
47. N.d., NADM, 62328, BL.
48. *Daily Mail*, 18 December 1914.
49. Ibid., 30 December 1914.
50. 14 January 1915, NADM, 62328, BL.
51. *Daily Mail*, 6, 8 February 1915.
52. 21 February 1915, NADM, 62245, BL. The Northcliffe papers were eventually all cut in page count and size.
53. 1 June 1915, NADM, 62255, f. 51, BL. Woodrow Wilson stayed true to his unwavering desire to keep the United States out of the war. Though numerous diplomatic notes were issued in response to the tightening of the British blockade, American sentiment, political philosophy and economic self-interest kept the United States from extreme measures. Any economic losses were more than made up for by the increased Allied orders that inundated American factories and farms. In the end the lives lost to German submarine activity counted more seriously. This economic link, which by late 1915 also included loans, continued to expand until America officially became an Associate of the Allied cause in April 1917.
54. Magnus, *Kitchener*, p. 285.
55. Ibid., p. 310. For Kitchener's strategic considerations of Russia and the Dardanelles operation, see Keith Neilson, *Strategy and Supply: The Anglo-Russian Alliance, 1914–17* (London, 1984), pp. 61–77.
56. Magnus, *Kitchener*, p. 332. Rather than try new channels of ordering and procurement, Kitchener continued to support the unimaginative methods of his Master-General of Ordnance, Sir Stanley Von Donop, R.J.Q. Adams, *Arms and the Wizard* (London, 1978), pp. 12–14, 23. Some attempts have been made to rehabilitate Kitchener's reputation against what has been seen as a bias towards Lloyd George's version of events. For example, see Cassar, *Kitchener*, and Peter Fraser, 'The British "Shell's Scandal" of 1915', *Journal of Canadian History*, 18 (April 1983), 69–86.

57. Northcliffe to French, 3 March 1915, NADM, 62159, BL.
58. 20 March 1915, French Papers, Imperial War Museum.
59. 25 March 1915, NADM, 62159, BL.
60. Magnus, *Kitchener*, p. 334.
61. Some would say he originated them. Lloyd George accused McKenna of inspiring articles against him. Jenkins, *Asquith*, p. 356.
62. Asquith, *Letters to Venetia Stanley*, p. 517. Unfortunately, Asquith told Miss Stanley he could not write down the nature of McKenna's evidence, and it remains unknown; however, Margot Asquith recorded in her diary that McKenna had mistakenly opened a letter to the Treasury, meant for Lloyd George, which outlined the plot. Robert Skidelsky, *John Maynard Keynes: Hopes Betrayed 1883–1920* (London, 1983), p. 306.
63. 5 April 1915, Northcliffe Papers, HA.
64. N.d., NADM, 62234, BL.
65. Northcliffe sent a long memorandum recounting this conference to Brinsley Fitzgerald for Sir John French. It revealed, among other things, Joffre's demands for more English soldiers and the fact that the French commander felt Kitchener 'had not behaved quite straight . . . over the question of troops.' 6 April 1915, Fitzgerald Papers, Imperial War Museum; Memorandum, 6 April 1915, NADM, 62329, BL.
66. V. Williams, *World of Action*, p. 247.
67. 11 April 1915, NADM, 62251, BL.
68. For this controversy, see John Grigg, *Lloyd George: From Peace to War* (London, 1985) pp. 230–8.
69. 15 April 1915, Lloyd George Papers, C/6/82, HLRO.
70. *Daily Mail*, 13 April 1915.
71. Ibid., 15 April 1915.
72. Ibid., 21 April 1915; George Cassar, *Asquith as War Leader* (London, 1994), p. 88.
73. Asquith, *Letters to Venetia Stanley*, p. 562.
74. 1 May 1915, NADM, 62159, BL. The private correspondent mentioned almost certainly refers to Repington, whose army connections allowed him to visit French at General Headquarters as a private citizen, not a war correspondent.
75. Magnus, *Kitchener*, p. 335–6; Richard Holmes, *The Little Field-Marshal, Sir John French* (London, 1981), pp. 287–8.
76. The historian John Grigg found 'credible' Repington's claim to this in his *The First World War 1914–1918* (Boston, 2 vols., 1920), Vol. 1, p. 39. *Lloyd George: From Peace to War, 1912–1916*, p. 248.
77. Pound and Harmsworth, *Northcliffe*, pp. 477–8.
78. *Daily Mail*, 21 May 1915.
79. *Daily News*, 22 May 1915; Michael MacDonagh, *In London During the Great War* (London, 1935), p. 67.
80. Haig to Oswald Fitzgerald (Kitchener's private secretary) 24 May 1915, Kitchener Papers, PRO 30/57/53, PRO; Cassar, *Kitchener*, p. 357.
81. Ian B.M. Hamilton, *The Happy Warrior: A Life of General Sir Ian Hamilton* (London, 1966), p. 322.
82. Wrench, *Geoffrey Dawson*, p. 116.
83. *Daily Mail*, 24 May 1915.
84. N.d. (postmarked 29 May 1915), Lloyd George Papers, D/18/1/4, HLRO.
85. R.F.V. Heuston, *The Lives of the Lord Chancellors 1885–1940* (Oxford, 1964), pp. 221–2.
86. Adams, *Arms and the Wizard*, p. 35; Pound and Harmsworth, *Northcliffe*, p. 480; *History of the Times*, Vol. 4, Pt 1, p. 275.

87. Bentley B. Gilbert, *David Lloyd George: Organizer of Victory* (London, 1992), p. 192.
88. Winston Churchill, *The World Crisis* (New York, 2 vols., 1920), I: 251–2.

CHAPTER 13: STALEMATE, 1915–1916

1. Northcliffe wrote to Thomas Marlowe at the *Daily Mail* that he was 'delighted to accept an invitation to a very simple function on my fiftieth birthday. I am much touched by the fact that my friends have thought of me at this busy time in our history.' 13 July 1915, NADM, 62199, BL.
2. Wrench, *Struggle*, p. 142.
3. General Sir Ian Hamilton, *Gallipoli Diary* (New York, 2 vols., 1920), Vol. 1, p. 340.
4. W. Churchill, *World Crisis*, Vol. 1, pp. 250–1. Other Conservative voices also found a new credence. In a letter to Northcliffe, Leo Maxse, an ally in the call for conscription, commented that, 'after having been regarded as a hopeless lunatic for half a generation it is a curious sensation to be treated as a comparatively sane being, though I do not suppose it will last'. 8 July 1915, NADM, 62175, BL.
5. In August his intelligence resources obtained information which Lloyd George requested about Swedish iron and coal going to Germany. A flow of censored letters from the front continued as well. Northcliffe to Lloyd George, 19 August 1915, Lloyd George Papers, D/18/1/27, HLRO; see extract of a letter of an English officer at the front censored by the Press Bureau dated 15 June 1915, Lloyd George Papers, D/18/1/13, HLRO.
6. Wrench, *Struggle*, p. 143.
7. 29 May 1915, NADM, 62158, BL.
8. Marjoribanks and Colvin, *Lord Carson*, Vol. 3, p. 77.
9. 28 May 1915, Cab. 37/128/25, vols. 110–11, PRO, quoted in Koss, *Political Press*, Vol. 2, p. 281.
10. 11 September 1915, quoted in Marjoribanks and Colvin, *Lord Carson*, Vol. 3, p. 74. When Carson resigned in October 1915, Smith took his place.
11. For the roles of Hamilton and Murdoch in the Gallipoli affair, see Alan Moorehead, *Gallipoli* (New York, 1956), I.B.M. Hamilton, *The Happy Warrior*, and Zwar, *In Search of Keith Murdoch*.
12. Zwar, *In Search of Keith Murdoch*, p. 27.
13. 30 September 1915, NADM, 62179, BL.
14. Moorehead, *Gallipoli*, p. 311.
15. 16 October 1915, Northcliffe Papers, WDM/2/15, TA.
16. *Daily Mail*, 21 December 1915.
17. R.J.Q. Adams and Philip P. Poirier, *The Conscription Controversy in Great Britain, 1900–18* (Basingstoke, 1987), pp. 112–15, 119–20; Randolph S. Churchill, *Lord Derby: King of Lancashire* (New York, 1959), p. 187, 194.
18. The same letter listed several suggestions: stop emigration to the colonies and the escape of men to Ireland and Jersey; shame men into the ranks by requiring an armlet to be worn (under penalty of law) which would identify their status; advertise the scheme, especially in the provinces; have a definite statement made by the Cabinet that, if the scheme failed, compulsion would be inevitable; and, finally, tell 'more truth', so that young men could not say, 'What is the use of all this boresome drilling only to find the war is over.' 20 October 1915, Northcliffe Papers, WDM/2/98, TA.
19. Robert Rhodes James, *Memoirs of a Conservative: J.C.C. Davidson's Memoirs and Papers 1910–1937* (London, 1969), p. 37.
20. 'The Northcliffe Press and Foreign Opinion', marked 'secret' and 'printed for the use of the Cabinet', dated 1 November 1915, Ministry of Information Records,

INF4/1B, PRO. The newspapers cited included the *Kölnische Zeitung*, the *Berliner Tagblatt* and the *Frankfurter Zeitung*.

21. MacDonagh, *In London During the Great War*, p. 86. The *Globe* was soon back in business after delivering an abject apology to the government. Colin Lovelace, 'British press censorship during the First World War', in George Bryce, James Curran and Pauline Wingate, eds., *Newspaper History From the Seventeenth Century to the Present Day* (London, 1978), p. 313. This press incident also may have once again saved Kitchener from dismissal by showing his continued popularity in the country. Robert Blake, *The Unknown Prime Minister: The Life and Times of Andrew Bonar Law, 1858–1923* (London, 1955), p. 276.

22. MacDonagh, *In London During the Great War*, p. 87.

23. *Daily Mail*, 11 December 1915.

24. R.S. Churchill, *Lord Derby*, pp. 201–2.

25. C.P. Scott, *The Political Diaries of C.P. Scott 1911–1928*, ed. Trevor Wilson (Ithaca, New York, 1970), p. 160. Frances Stevenson, Lloyd George's secretary and mistress, and later Countess Lloyd-George, wrote in her diary that the 'chief thing that these Liberals objected to was D.'s [Lloyd George's] association with Lord Northcliffe . . . for Northcliffe is not trusted.' Frances Stevenson, *Lloyd George: A Diary* ed. A.J.P. Taylor (New York, 1971), p. 90.

26. Adams and Poirier, *Conscription Controversy*, pp. 135–8. See also the 27–30 December *Daily Mail*.

27. *Daily Mail*, 6 January 1916.

28. In February 1916 the Navy was responsible for enemy aircraft to the British coast, where the Army took charge. Arthur Marwick, *The Deluge, British Society and the First World War* (Boston, 1965), p. 232.

29. *Daily Mail*, 3, 4, 5, 7, 8, 10 February 1916.

30. Ibid., 16 February 1916.

31. J.M. McEwen, 'Northcliffe and Lloyd George at War 1914–1918', *Historical Journal*, **24**, 3 (1981), p. 655.

32. Riddell, *War Diary*, p. 153. Frances Stevenson, Lloyd George's secretary, feared and distrusted Northcliffe. In her 12 February diary entry, she worried that 'Sir G. says that if Lord N. once gets a footing inside the Government, he will not rest until he is made Dictator. I think there is something in it. Lord N. is unscrupulous, & a dangerous man . . . I do feel that D. [Lloyd George] should not have too much to do with him. N. will use him for his own ends, & throw him over when he has no further use for him.' Stevenson, *Lloyd George: A Diary*, p. 98.

33. *Daily Mail*, 14 February 1916.

34. Gilmour, *Curzon*, p. 450.

35. 24 February 1916, Northcliffe Papers, WDM/2/120, TA. Farnborough was the headquarters of the Air Corps.

36. 25 February 1916, Northcliffe Papers, WDM/2/121, TA.

37. Gilmour, *Curzon*, pp. 450–2.

38. *Parliamentary Debates*, Lords, 5th Series, Vol. 22, 23 May 1916, cols. 124–6.

39. Steed, *Through Thirty Years*, Vol. 2, p. 82.

40. The first dispatch appeared in the 6 March 1916 *Daily Mail*.

41. Pound and Harmsworth, *Northcliffe*, p. 496.

42. *Daily Mail*, 6 April 1916.

43. Norman and Jeanne MacKenzie, *The Life of H.G. Wells* (London, 1987), p. 308.

44. 22 April 1916, NADM, 62161, BL.

45. *Daily Mail*, 29 April 1916.

46. Ibid., 26 May 1916.

47. Riddell, *War Diary*, p. 185.
48. Pound and Harmsworth, *Northcliffe*, p. 500.
49. A.J.P. Taylor, *English History 1914–1945* (London, 1965), p. 58.
50. Riddell diary, 15 June 1916, in Lord Riddell, *The Riddell Diaries 1908–1923*, ed. J.M. McEwen (London, 1986), p. 160. Riddell had recorded on 21 May that he believed Northcliffe and Lloyd George were working to 'dethrone' Asquith.
51. Hankey diary, 8 July 1916, quoted in Stephen Roskill, *Hankey, Man of Secrets* (New York, 3 vols., 1970–4), Vol. 1, p. 283.
52. Gerard De Groot, *Douglas Haig, 1861–1928* (London, 1988), p. 193.
53. 2 June 1916, quoted in Sir William Robertson, *The Military Correspondence of Field-Marshal Sir William Robertson*, ed. David R. Woodward (London, 1989), p. 55.
54. 21 July 1916, entry, Haig diary, Haig Papers, ACCS. 3155/97, NLS.
55. 21 July 1916, 'Lord Northcliffe's Visit to the War', Northcliffe Papers, HA.
56. 23 July 1916, entry, Haig diary, Haig Papers, ACCS. 3155/97, NLS; Robert Blake, *The Private Papers of Douglas Haig 1914–1919* (London, 1952), p. 155.
57. 2 August 1916, 'Lord Northcliffe's Visit to the War', Northcliffe Papers, HA.
58. 6 August 1916, Lloyd George Papers, E/2/21/1, HLRO.
59. 4 August 1916, Northcliffe Papers, WDM/2/129, TA.
60. Steed, *Through Thirty Years*, Vol. 2, p. 122.
61. Ibid. Northcliffe had long since lost the trim figure of his youth. He kept a diary of his continuing battles with his waistline, 'A Fat Man's Gallant Fight Against Fate'. Northcliffe Papers, WDM 4/1, TA.
62. 19 September 1916, NADM, 62160, BL.
63. John Grigg, *Lloyd George: From Peace to War*, p. 384.
64. 14 September 1916, NADM, 62160, BL. Sassoon reported further that Haig's last words to Lloyd George were 'when you have finished your joy riding come and stay two days with me' and that, overall, Lloyd George's visit left Haig 'terribly disappointed in him'. Lloyd George further infuriated the Army by discussing British generalship with the French General Foch. David R. Woodward, *Lloyd George and the Generals* (London, 1983), p. 106.
65. *The Times* and *Daily Mail*, 29 September 1916. See Grigg, *Lloyd George: From Peace to War*, pp. 415–34 for an insightful appraisal of the importance of this interview.
66. Woodward, *Lloyd George and the Generals*, pp. 108–9.
67. 2 October 1916, NADM, 62160, BL.
68. Woodward, *Lloyd George and the Generals*, p. 110; Robertson to Lloyd George, 11 October 1916, Robertson Papers, Liddell Hart Centre for Military Archives, King's College, London.
69. 11 October 1916, quoted in Robertson, *Military Correspondence*, p. 91.
70. 18 October 1916, NADM, 62160, BL. Lord Beaverbrook's more melodramatic version of this story has Northcliffe telling Davies, 'You can tell him that I hear he has been interfering with strategy, and that if he goes on I will break him.' *Politicians and the War*, p. 323. Frances Stevenson's diary entry for October 12 recorded a version closer to Northcliffe's. Stevenson, *Lloyd George: A Diary*, p. 115.
71. Stevenson, *Lloyd George: A Diary*, p. 117; Lloyd George to Robertson, 11 October 1916, quoted in Robertson, *Military Correspondence*, pp. 93–6.
72. 14 October 1916 entry, Riddell, *Diaries*, p. 171.
73. Pound and Harmsworth, *Northcliffe*, p. 512.
74. Although Bonar Law won the vote in this debate over the disposition of captured enemy businesses in Nigeria, many Unionists followed Sir Edward Carson (who since he left the government in October 1915 had been the effective leader of the political opposition) and voted to allow only British interests to bid.

75. Lee, '*A Good Innings*', p. 158. In *Politicians and the War*, p. 360, Beaverbrook claimed that he also tried to bring Northcliffe and Lloyd George together around this time, but with no success.
76. 3 December 1916 entry, in Pound and Harmsworth, *Northcliffe*, p. 513. Apparently on 3 December other matters, including a possible lucrative writing contract for Lloyd George, were discussed as well, although both men later denied this. See McEwen, 'Northcliffe and Lloyd George at War', p. 664.
77. Wrench, *Geoffrey Dawson*, p. 140. Robinson flatly stated that, without Northcliffe's knowledge or advice, he wrote the editorial after talking to Carson, although Lloyd George may well have been Carson's source. Tom Clarke reported in *My Northcliffe Diary*, p. 95, that Northcliffe wrote a two-column article on the political crisis, giving some the impression he had written the *Times* piece. This may refer to a 4 December *Daily Mail* article calling for 'A War Council That Will Act'.
78. McEwen, 'The Press and the Fall of Asquith', p. 881.
79. 4 December 1916, Asquith MS. 31, f. 20, Bodleian Library.
80. 4 December 1916, Asquith MS. 31, f. 21, Bodleian Library.
81. Montagu memo, quoted in Jenkins, *Asquith*, p. 448.
82. Montagu memo, quoted in Jenkins, *Asquith*, p. 448. On 5 December Montagu again pleaded with the Prime Minister not to give a victory to Northcliffe. He listed three factors which had led to Asquith's changed position. First was Northcliffe and the *Times* article; second, the advice of McKenna, Walter Runciman (President of the Board of Trade) and Grey; third, disagreements with Lloyd George as to personnel – particularly Carson. About Northcliffe he wrote, 'It is lamentable to think that you should let him achieve the victory that he has long sought. He wanted to drive you out; he alone is fool enough not to believe in you. His effects were resisted by Lloyd George, by Bonar Law, by Derby, by Carson, by Robertson. Using information that he had no right to obtain, he sees a chance of success, takes it and is successful. He published that article to wreck the arrangement and you have had to let him do it. I do not say that this was avoidable, but I say that his personal victory in this matter is a matter of the deepest possible chagrin to me.' The plea continued, 'Lloyd George sent for me this afternoon and I spent some time with him . . . he wanted to work with you. He did not want a victory for Northcliffe.' 5 December 1916, Asquith MS. 27, f. 186, Bodleian Library.
83. *The Times*, 6 December 1916.
84. 5 December 1916 entry, Dawson diary, Dawson Mss. 66, ff. 181–4, Bodleian Library.
85. Pound and Harmsworth, *Northcliffe*, p. 514.
86. Beaverbrook, *Politicians and the War*, pp. 521, 526.
87. Stanley to Northcliffe, 9 May 1919, NADM, 62158, BL; Isaac Marcosson, *Adventures in Interviewing* (London, 1919), p. 129; Gollin, *Proconsul in Politics*, pp. 373–4.
88. Beaverbrook, *Politicians and the War*, p. 544. Beaverbrook's biographer A.J.P. Taylor casts doubt on this story by questioning whether Beaverbrook was actually with Lloyd George in the first few days of his administration. See A.J.P. Taylor, *Beaverbrook* (London, 1972), pp. 120–7.
89. Hankey's diary, 10 December 1916, quoted in Koss, *Political Press*, Vol. 2, p. 310.
90. T. Clarke, *My Northcliffe Diary*, p. 98.
91. *History of The Times*, Vol. 4, Pt 1, p. 307.
92. This article was reproduced in the next day's *Daily Mail* and *The Times*.
93. Particularly after the recent 'Knock-Out Blow' interview.
94. 3 December 1916, in Woodrow Wilson, *The Papers of Woodrow Wilson*, ed. Arthur Link (Princeton, 69 vols., 1966–82), Vol. 40, p. 133.

95. 22 December 1916, in W. Wilson, *Papers*, Vol. 40, p. 319.
96. 27 December 1916, Lloyd George Papers, F/41/7/2, HLRO.

CHAPTER 14: PEGASUS IN HARNESS, 1917

1. 18, 20 January 1917, NADM, 62335, BL.
2. British propaganda in the Great War, particularly in America, has received recent attention from several scholars. For an overview of this topic, see M.L. Sanders and Philip M. Taylor, *British Propaganda during the First World War* (London, 1982). For a work which considers many of the personalities involved, including Northcliffe, see Gary S. Messinger, *British Propaganda and the State in the First World War* (Manchester, 1992).
3. 23 January 1917, Lloyd George Papers, F/41/7/4, HLRO.
4. N.d., NADM, 63193, BL.
5. The January 1917 reorganization partly followed recommendations made by the journalist Robert Donald in a report prepared at Lloyd George's request. See 'Report on Propaganda Arrangements', INF4/4B, PRO.
6. 1 February 1917, NADM, 62159, BL.
7. Northcliffe to Buchan, 20 February 1917, NADM, 62161, BL.
8. Haig diary, Haig Papers, ACCS. 3155/97, NLS.
9. Neilson, *Strategy and Supply*, pp. 226–9, 251–3.
10. Ibid., p. 262.
11. David French, *The Strategy of the Lloyd George Coalition 1916–1918* (Oxford, 1995), pp. 53–5.
12. 'Message From the Chief', 26 February, Ms. Eng. Hist. d. 303, Bodleian Library. The gardener's cottage still stands, the plainly visible shell hole filled in by a window.
13. Northcliffe to Sir Albert Stanley, 22 February 1917, NADM, 62158, BL.
14. Northcliffe to Higginbottom, 10 March 1917, NADM, 63336, BL; Higginbottom to Northcliffe, 13 March 1917, NADM, 63336, BL.
15. 8 April 1917, NADM, 62336, BL. For Cowdray, see J.A. Spender, *Weetman Pearson, First Viscount Cowdray 1856–1927* (London, 1930).
16. 10 April 1917, NADM, 62336, BL.
17. Speaking to a Birmingham audience in 1918 about his National Service experience, Chamberlain quipped, 'here was a problem big enough to satisfy the most super-eminent of supermen. Why it might even have taxed the energies of Lord Northcliffe himself.' David Dilks, *Neville Chamberlain, Vol. 1: Pioneering and Reform, 1869–1929* (Cambridge, 1984), p. 203.
18. 30 January 1917, NADM, 62335, BL.
19. 27 April 1917, NADM, 62172, BL.
20. 18 March 1917, NADM, 62245, BL.
21. 'The Remaking of Ireland', speech made by Northcliffe to the Irish Club, 17 March 1917, as reported in *The Times*, 19 March 1917, privately printed by Clement Shorter, London, March 1917.
22. 18 March 1917, NADM, 62245, BL.
23. 18 March 1917, NADM, 62199,, BL.
24. *Daily Mail*, 4 April 1917.
25. 4 April 1917, Lloyd George Papers, F/41/7/6, HLRO.
26. 4 April 1917, Lloyd George Papers, F/41/7, HLRO.
27. 5 April 1917, NADM, 62153, BL; 11 April 1917, quoted in Pound and Harmsworth, *Northcliffe*, p. 527.
28. 9 June 1917, Northcliffe Papers, HA. Lord Bertie, the British ambassador to France, also noted in his diary of 11 June that 'Lloyd George wanted to substitute

Northcliffe for Spring-Rice but that was stopped.' Viscount Bertie of Thame, *The Diary of Lord Bertie of Thame, 1914–1918*, ed. Lady Algernon Gordon Lennox (London, 2 vols., 1924), Vol. 2, p. 136.

29. *Daily Mail*, 23, 26 April 1917.
30. 16 May 1917, NADM, 62255, BL.
31. 15 May 1917, NADM, 62158, BL.
32. N.d., NADM, 62153, BL.
33. 17 May 1917, Balfour Add. Mss., 49738, f. 84, BL.
34. 20 May 1917, Balfour Add. Mss., 49738, ff. 90–1, BL.
35. 27 May 1917, NADM, 62253, BL.
36. *Daily Mail*, 28 May 1917.
37. 28 May 1917, NADM, 62336, BL.
38. A copy of this report can be found in the Northcliffe Papers, NOR/3/4/4, TA.
39. Lord Beaverbrook's account in *Men and Power 1917–1918* (London, 1956), pp. 63–4, emphasizes that Lloyd George was considering bringing Winston Churchill back into the government – a move he believed Northcliffe would bitterly oppose.
40. Roskill, *Hankey, Man of Secrets*, Vol. 3, p. 393.
41. 27–28 June 1917 entry, Scott, *Political Diaries*, p. 296.
42. Repington, *The First World War*, Vol. 1, p. 590–1.
43. Robinson to Willert, 4 June 1917, Arthur Willert Papers, Series I, Box 1, Sterling Library, Yale University. In this letter Geoffrey Robinson also told Willert that their chief had 'started for America in a great hurry – too much of a hurry perhaps to give him a chance of grasping the business at this end'.
44. The terms are listed in a confidential Cabinet document dated 31 May 1917 and signed by Lloyd George. See the copy in the NADM, 62157, ff. 76–7, BL.
45. Steed, *Through Thirty Years*, Vol. 2, pp. 140–1.
46. Page 5 of that morning's *Daily Mail* carried a small notice that, at the invitation of the War Cabinet, Northcliffe had accepted the mission to America as 'Successor to Mr. Balfour' and that he had already sailed for the United States. Northcliffe left his business affairs in the hands of George Sutton. He notified Lloyd George that if Sutton was forced into the military he would have to return.
47. Northcliffe to Davies, 1 June 1917, NADM, 62157, BL. Lloyd George read and approved this.
48. 7 June 1917, in W. Wilson, *Papers*, Vol. 42, p. 461.
49. 9 June 1917, Howard Papers, Library of Congress.
50. 9, 11 June 1917 entries, House diaries, House Papers, Series II, Vol. 11, Sterling Library, Yale University. For Wiseman, see W.B. Fowler's *British American Relations 1917–1918, The Role of Sir William Wiseman* (Princeton, 1969).
51. 12 June 1917, House Papers, Series I, Box 83a, Sterling Library, Yale University.
52. 12 June 1917, in W. Wilson, *Papers*, Vol. 42, pp. 487–8. House also told the President that Northcliffe had refused to see a representative of Wilson's critic, Randolph Hearst, telling him that if his employer wished to see him he should come himself. If Hearst did, House continued, Northcliffe planned to tell him 'some home truths which may be good for his soul'.
53. Arthur Willert, *The Road to Safety* (London, 1952), p. 109.
54. Frederic Boyd Stevenson, *Brooklyn Daily Eagle*, 17 June 1917; George Harvey, 'The Man of the War', *North American Review*, Vol. 206, July 1917, pp. 15–23.
55. Lord Hardinge, *Old Diplomacy* (London, 1947), p. 213.
56. 2 June 1917, Northcliffe Papers, HA. The reports apparently came from the department heads who had briefed Northcliffe in London.
57. 14 June 1917, NADM, BL.

58. Daniels diary, 15 June 1917, in Josephus Daniels, *The Cabinet Diaries of Josephus Daniels 1913–1921*, ed. E. David Cronon, (Lincoln, Nebraska, 1963), p. 164.
59. 15 June 1917 entry, House diaries, House Papers, Series II, Vol. 11, Sterling Library, Yale University.
60. Northcliffe to Davies, 20 June 1917, Lloyd George Papers, F/41/7/8, HLRO.
61. 1 July 1917, Northcliffe Papers, HA.
62. W. Wilson, *Papers*, Vol. 42, p. 542.
63. Willert, *Road to Safety*, pp. 104–5.
64. Northcliffe to Davies, 20 June 1917, Lloyd George Papers, F/41/7/8, HLRO. The other Americans Northcliffe included as voicing this argument were Lane, at the Interior Department, Houston, at the Agriculture Department, and Hoover, the Food Administrator.
65. Louis Tracy, 'The British War Mission in the United States: Its Objects and Personnel', in *Who's Who in the British War Mission to the United States 1917* (New York, 1917), pp. x–xi.
66. 28 June 1917, House Papers, Series I, Box 10, Sterling Library, Yale University. House responded the next day that the matter was receiving his 'undivided attention'.
67. William G. McAdoo, *Crowded Years* (Boston 1931), p. 400. McAdoo vividly described Northcliffe. 'I have met few men who had such a quick comprehension as Northcliffe. It was never necessary to explain anything to him twice. He was dynamic, his phrases were vivid, his ideas crisp and clear, and he had a way of getting down at once to the vital thought in any question under discussion . . . His strong point was in determining how to do things – the shortest and surest road to accomplishment. He had a fine political and public sense; he always thought of the effect of actions on public opinion.'
68. Northcliffe to House, 20 July 1917, House Papers, Series I, Box 83a, Sterling Library, Yale University.
69. 14 July 1917, House Papers, Series I, Box 73, Sterling Library, Yale University. By this time, McAdoo also found it impossible to work with Hardman Lever, the British financial expert sent over to deal with the crisis – one of the reasons Northcliffe was so involved. McAdoo, himself not a technical expert, seemed to prefer dealing with Northcliffe. Kathleen Burk, *Britain, America and the Sinews of War 1914–1918* (London, 1985), p. 163.
70 André Tardieu, *France and America: Some Experiences in Cooperation* (Boston, 1927), p. 227. Kathleen Burk has argued, further, that 'supercession of Britain by the United States as the leading financial power can be seen occurring, step-by-step, in the negotiations between the British Treasury mission and the American government during 1917–18; in the daily dealings of the Treasury mission can be seen the passing of hegemony from Britain to the United States'. *Sinews of War*, p. 5.
71. For a detailed organizational chart, see *Who's Who in the British War Mission*.
72. *Public Ledger* (Philadelphia), 11 November 1917.
73. 2 July 1917, FO 800/209, PRO.
74. 25 August 1917, Lloyd George Papers, F/41/7/14, HLRO.
75. 11 August 1917, House Papers, Series I, Box 123, Sterling Library, Yale University.
76. 12 August 1917 entry, House diaries, House Papers, Series II. Vol. 11, Sterling Library, Yale University.
77. 12 August 1917, House Papers, Series I, Box 123, Sterling Library, Yale University. Wiseman opposed this idea and suggested that the ambassador be called home for consultations.
78. 17 August 1917, FO 800/209, PRO.

79. Northcliffe to PM, Balfour, War Cabinet and Shipping Controller, 21 August 1917, Lloyd George Papers, F/41/7/13, HLRO.
80. 25 August 1917, in Edward M. House, *The Intimate Papers of Colonel House*, ed. Charles Seymour (London, 4 vols., 1926–8), Vol. 3, p. 90.
81. 24 September 1917, House Papers, Series I, Box 70a, Sterling Library, Yale University.
82. 10 October 1917, Wiseman Papers, Series I, Box 3, Sterling Library, Yale University.
83. Northcliffe circular letter, 12 August 1917, Northcliffe Papers, HA.
84. Lord Northcliffe, 'What America is Fighting For', *Current Opinion*, 63 (October 1917): 236.
85. 1 October 1917 entry, House diaries, House Papers, Series II, Vol. 12, Sterling Library, Yale University.
86. For example, Amos Pinchot, a confidant of Wilson's, had informed him that Northcliffe was 'making a vigorous campaign to get the American newspapers to stand behind the British program. Doubtless you know all about this.' Pinchot to Wilson, 25 July 1917, in W. Wilson, *Papers*, Vol. 43, pp. 276–8.
87. 13 July 1917, Northcliffe Papers, HA.
88. Pomeroy Burton and others had warned Northcliffe of the special need for publicity in this region for years, and he had heard the same sentiment from American passengers on his voyage over. Burdened with his official duties, Northcliffe dispatched Geoffrey Butler, head of the publicity staff in the New York mission office, to Chicago personally to appraise the situation. Butler to Buchan, 27 June 1917, FO 395/79 News America File, PRO. Butler kept Buchan, whose Department of Information had official responsibility for US propaganda, informed on Northcliffe's varied activities.
89. Arthur Willert, *Washington and Other Memories* (Boston, 1972), p. 105.
90. The editor of *The Times* explained to his chief that S.F. Edge, a former representative of Ford's British competitors (and presently attached to the Ministry of Munitions), had done everything in his power, including the staging of unfair tests, to attack the American machines. As a condition of an inheritance, Geoffrey Robinson changed his name to Dawson in July 1917. Dawson to Northcliffe, 23 August 1917, NADM, 62245, BL.
91. 6 October 1917, Wiseman Papers, Series I, Box 3, Sterling Library, Yale University.
92. *The Press* (Cleveland), 23 October 1917; *Daily Mail*, 24 October 1917.
93. Northcliffe circular letter, 21 October 1917, Northcliffe Papers, HA. Herrick told Northcliffe that he considered it 'little short of criminal that the British Government does not realize the need for propaganda in this country'. In Cleveland, Northcliffe also met Thomas Edison, who he reported was 'doing very good anti-submarine work and hates the Germans like poison . . . they stole all his patents'.
94. 'Lord Northcliffe Scorns Sugar in His Tea', *The Press* (Cleveland), 22 October 1917.
95. *Chicago Herald*, 25 October 1917, quoted in 26 October *Daily Mail*.
96. *St Louis Post-Dispatch*, 26, 27 October 1917.
97. Daniels diary, 29 October 1917, in Daniels, *Cabinet Diaries*, p. 228.
98. For a closer examination of the Midwest tour and Northcliffe's propaganda activities in America, see J. Lee Thompson, '"To Tell the People of America the Truth": Lord Northcliffe in the USA, Unofficial British Propaganda, June–November 1917', *Journal of Contemporary History*, **34**, 2 (April 1999).
99. Northcliffe cabled Rothermere on 7 September requesting him to come in early November. He told his brother that he planned to return to England to give his

views to the government and then return with some 'urgently needed people'. After initial enthusiasm for the idea, Rothermere replied in October that labour problems in Britain would keep him there. Sir Frederick Black became the temporary head of the mission in Northcliffe's absence. Wiseman Papers, Series I, Box 3, Sterling Library, Yale University.

100. C.J. Phillips to Northcliffe, 1 November 1917, NADM, 62157, BL.
101. Willert, *Washington and Other Memories*, p. 106.

CHAPTER 15: AN UNRULY MEMBER, 1917–1918

1. *Daily Mail*, 12 November 1917. The most active campaign carried out by the paper in Northcliffe's absence was the autumn 1917 crusade against air-service incompetence.
2. 12 November 1917, NADM, 62253, BL.
3. 29 October 1917, Daniels diary, in Daniels, *Cabinet Diaries*, p. 228.
4. 14 November 1917 entry, House diary, House Papers, Series II, Vol. 12, Sterling Library, Yale University.
5. 15 November 1917 entry, House diary, House Papers, Series II, Vol. 12, Sterling Library, Yale University.
6. Ibid.
7. *The Times*, 16 November 1917. Lord Cowdray, the head of the Air Board, had led the reconstruction work in the preceding months for the new Air Ministry and had assumed he would be its head. Cowdray soon resigned and never forgave Lloyd George for offering the job to Northcliffe without telling him first, which only inflicted further damage to the already fractured Liberal Party. Spender, *Viscount Cowdray*, pp. 234–5. David Lloyd George, *War Memoirs* (Boston, 6 vols., 1934), Vol. 4, pp. 124–8. Cowdray apparently did not hold Northcliffe responsible, although it must be admitted that the latter did not treat Cowdray, with whom he had been friendly, very well in this affair.
8. 17 November 1917 entry, Riddell diary, Add. Mss., 62980, f. 162, BL. Lloyd George also mentioned that Rothermere was supporting him, not his brother, in this affair because he was angling for the War Office, for which Lloyd George said he was unsuited.
9. 24 November 1917 entry, Riddell diary, Add. Mss., 62980, ff. 174–5, BL.
10. 27 November 1917 entry, House diary, House Papers, Series II, Vol. 12, Sterling Library, Yale University. Honours were distributed to many members of the American mission. Willert and Campbell Stuart both received knighthoods.
11. Ibid. Northcliffe had suggested Rothermere to the Prime Minister in an undated note in NADM, 62157, BL. Rothermere served until April 1918.
12. 11 December 1917 entry, House diary, House Papers, Series II, Vol. 12, Sterling Library, Yale University. House recorded, 'I cannot help dwelling upon the thought that my particular work might have been very much more effective if I had had a different man to deal with than LG. He makes an appealing speech, states his case well, has a charming personality, and there, as far as I can see, his usefulness ends.'
13. 6 December 1917, Northcliffe Papers, HA.
14. Wrench, *Geoffrey Dawson*, pp. 156–7; *History of the Times*, Vol. 4, Pt 1, pp. 336, 342.
15. 3 December 1917 entry, Riddell diary, Add. Mss., 62980, f. 193, BL.
16. 7 December 1917 diary entry, in Brigadier-General John Charteris, *At G.H.Q.* (London, 1931), p. 273.
17. 13 December 1917, in Keith Grieves, *The Politics of Manpower, 1914–1918* (Manchester, 1988), p. 165.

18. 13 December 1917, NADM, 62160, BL.
19. 27 December 1917, NADM, 62156, BL.
20. 3 January 1918, in Pound and Harmsworth, *Northcliffe*, p. 607.
21. Repington, *The First World War*, Vol. 2, p. 149.
22. Repington to Howard Corbett, 16 January 1918, NADM, 62253, BL. The major disagreement was with his editor, Geoffrey Dawson, over revisions of Repington's articles.
23. 26 January 1918, Strachey Papers, S/12/1/2, HLRO.
24. 29 January 1918, Strachey Papers, S/12/1/2, HLRO.
25. Fraser, 'Private Notes for Lord Northcliffe', n.d., NADM, 62251, BL.
26. *Daily Mail*, 24, 28 January 1918; 'Message From the Chief', 22 January 1918.
27. Woodward, *Lloyd George and the Generals*, p. 246.
28. L.S. Amery, *My Political Life* (London, 3 vols., 1953–5), Vol. 2, p. 138.
29. 28 January 1918 entry, Riddell diary, Add. Mss., 62981, ff. 29–30, BL.
30. 26 January 1918 statement, Beaverbrook Papers, C261, HLRO. A further unsigned, undated document in the Beaverbrook Papers, which appears to be in Lloyd George's hand, states that the 'Prime Minister, at the request of the Chancellor of the Duchy of Lancaster, has appointed Lord Northcliffe to undertake the direction of all propaganda in foreign countries'. It was not unreasonable for Northcliffe to report to Lloyd George, with whom he had been in direct contact since June 1917 on War Mission affairs. Those who point to this arrangement as unorthodox, such as A.J.P. Taylor in *Beaverbrook*, p. 138, n. 2, apparently were unaware that Northcliffe continued his duties as head of the British War Mission in London (though these were admittedly nominal after he tackled Enemy Propaganda).
31. Northcliffe to Beaverbrook, 7 February 1918, Beaverbrook Papers, C261, HLRO; Northcliffe to Beaverbrook, 13 February 1918, NADM, 62161, BL; A.J.P. Taylor, *Beaverbrook*, p. 139; Peter Fraser, *Lord Esher: A Political Biography* (London, 1973), p. 382.
32. Haig diary, 17 February 1918, quoted in R.S. Churchill, *Lord Derby*, p. 332. There may be grounds for Haig's fears. Northcliffe told Steed that during the propaganda discussions it was hinted that he might be asked to go to the War Office instead. Steed, *The Fifth Arm*, p. 15.
33. 17 February 1918, NADM, 62154, BL.
34. Brigadier-General John Charteris, *Field-Marshal Earl Haig* (London, 1929), p. 293.
35. *Parliamentary Debates*, Commons, 5th Series, Vol. 103, cols. 633–45.
36. Sir Charles Petrie, *The Life and Letters of the Right Hon. Austen Chamberlain* (London, 2 vols., 1939–40), Vol. 2, p. 107. Chamberlain was disappointed by their lack of response. Milner, who thought Chamberlain was 'barking up the wrong tree', recommended to Lloyd George that, in the face of the strong feeling in Parliament, there was nothing to be done except 'to lie low till the storm blows over . . . The less people hear or see of Northcliffe, Beaverbrook (certainly the most unpopular name of all) . . . the next few weeks the better.'
37. *Parliamentary Debates*, Commons, 5th Series, Vol. 104, cols. 40–2.
38. Lloyd George, *War Memoirs*, Vol. 5, pp. 63–73.
39. Northcliffe to Balfour, 24 February 1918, FO 899/764, PRO.
40. Northcliffe to Balfour, 27 February 1918, FO 899/764, PRO; Steed, *The Fifth Arm*, p. 17.
41. Steed to Northcliffe, 7 March 1918, Northcliffe to Steed, 19 March 1918, NADM, 62246B, BL.
42. 21 March 1918, NADM, 62206, BL.
43. *Daily Mail*, 23 March 1918.

44. 24 March 1918, NADM, 62209, BL.
45. The details of the campaign, including samples of the leaflet messages, can be found in Steed's 30 April 1918 'Report on the British Mission for Propaganda in Austria-Hungary', NADM, 62163, BL; Steed, *The Fifth Arm*, pp. 29–30.
46. Lloyd George sent Northcliffe these reports on 22 April 1918.
47. 4 April 1918, NADM, 62175, BL.
48. 10 April 1918, NADM, 62175, BL.
49. 13 April 1918, Maxse Papers, quoted in Fraser, *Lord Esher*, pp. 391–2.
50. 16 April 1918, answering Maxse's letter of the 15th, Maxse Papers, quoted in Fraser, *Lord Esher*, p. 392.
51. Lord Beaverbrook, 'Death of Lord Northcliffe', *Daily Express*, 15 August 1922.
52. Northcliffe to R.B. Marston, 25 March 1918, in Pound and Harmsworth, *Northcliffe*, p. 629. Marston was editor of *Fishing Gazette*.
53. Pound and Harmsworth, *Northcliffe*, p. 630.
54. Petrie, *Austen Chamberlain*, Vol. 2, p. 118.
55. *Daily Mail*, 19 April 1918.
56. Petrie, *Austen Chamberlain*, Vol. 2, p. 118.
57. Northcliffe to Beaverbrook, 19 April 1918, NADM, 62161, BL.
58. 23 April 1918, Beaverbrook Papers, C/261, HLRO.
59. Lloyd George to Northcliffe, 22 April 1918, Lloyd George Papers, F/41/8/7, HLRO.
60. 28 April 1918, Lloyd George Papers, F/41/8/8, HLRO. The 27 April 1918 *Daily Mail* announced that Northcliffe was recuperating from a nine-week bout of flu and had agreed to stay in his job until the government could find someone to replace him.
61. H.G. Wells, *Experiment in Autobiography* (London, 2 vols., 1934), Vol. 2, p. 697. Wells also thought that Northcliffe 'knew something of what I had in mind and sympathized with it and wanted to forward it. But his undoubtedly big and undoubtedly unco-ordinated brain was like a weather-chart in stormy times; phases of high and low pressure and moral gradients and depressions chased themselves across his mental map. His skull held together, in a delusive unity, a score of flying fragments of purpose.' Ibid., p. 700.
62. An undated synopsis of the 'Great Propaganda' plan is in NADM, 62162, f. 10, BL.
63. 'Minutes of the Third Meeting of the Committee for Propaganda in Enemy Countries', 31 May 1918, Beaverbrook Papers, E/3/9, HLRO.
64. 10 June 1918, FO 899/780, PRO.
65. 14 June 1918, NADM, 62205, BL.
66. Pound and Harmsworth, *Northcliffe*, p. 645.
67. John Turner, *British Politics and the Great War: Coalition and Conflict, 1915–1918* (New Haven, 1992), p. 308. The new law had extended the franchise to almost all men over twenty-one and to women over thirty, as a response to their sacrifice in the war.
68. N.d., NADM, 62161, BL. He added that the former St Paul's boy was 'no doubt full of sinister designs against this country'. Wells could imagine 'nothing more utterly mischievous than this campaign to make every human being of German origin hate us as bitterly as possible & I can see no possibility of conducting a propaganda against the German Government while it goes on'.
69. 16 July 1918, NADM, 62161, BL.
70. 17 July 1918, NADM, 62161, BL.
71. 25 July 1918, NADM, 62161, BL. Wells remained on the Committee and made occasional comments at its meetings.

72. 6 August 1918, in Pound and Harmsworth, *Northcliffe*, p. 650.
73. 'Minutes of the Tenth Meeting of the Committee for Propaganda in Enemy Countries', 3 September 1918, NADM, 62162, BL; Steed, *Through Thirty Years*, Vol. 2, p. 241.
74. 16 August 1918, Lloyd George Papers, F/41/8/21, HLRO. In addition to being director of Propaganda in Enemy Countries, Northcliffe was also chairman of the London headquarters of the British War Mission to the United States and chairman of the committee responsible for British Propaganda in Italy. The new organization would be directly responsible to the War Cabinet and have direct relations with the Treasury, which Propaganda in Enemy Countries did not have.
75. 29 August 1918 General Order; 'A Hindenburg Manifesto to the German People', 2 September 1918, in Ralph H. Lutz, *Fall of the German Empire 1914–1918* (Stanford, 2 vols., 1932), Vol. 1, pp. 162–3.
76. 2 October 1918, NADM, 62160, BL.
77. *Daily Mail*, 20 September 1918.
78. 30 September 1918, NADM, 62251, BL.
79. 27 September 1918 entry, Riddell diary, Add. Mss. 62982, f. 93, BL.
80. 3 October 1918, Riddell diary, Add. Mss. 62982, f. 119, BL.
81. Howard Corbett, 'Why Northcliffe Quarrelled With Lloyd George', *World's Press News*, 5 May 1932.
82. 3 October 1918, in Riddell diary, Add. Mss., 62982, f. 119, BL.
83. Riddell, *War Diary*, p. 366.
84. 'Report on the 4 October 1918 First Meeting of the Policy Committee of the British War Mission', Beaverbrook Papers, E/3/9, HLRO.
85. 'Reports on 8, 9 October Emergency Meetings of the British War Mission Policy Committee', Beaverbrook Papers, E/3/9, HLRO.
86. 'The German Offer. What it Means', *Daily Mail*, 7 October 1918.
87. Steed, *Through Thirty Years*, Vol. 2, pp. 244–5; Sir Peter Chalmers Mitchell, *My Fill of Days* (London, 1937), p. 297. Steed dated this meeting 9 October and Mitchell 15 October 1918.
88. The non-negotiable terms included the restoration of Belgium and France (with Alsace-Lorraine as a reparation to France for the 'wrong done in 1871'), the readjustment of the disputed frontiers of Italy along lines of nationality, an assurance that the nationalities in Austria-Hungary would be allowed to unite, the evacuation of all Russian territory and the annulment of all treaties since the Russian Revolution, the formation of an independent Polish state with access to the sea, the abrogation of the Treaty of Bucharest, the restoration of Serbia, Romania and Montenegro, the removal of Turkish dominion from non-Turkish peoples, a poll of Schleswig to determine its allegiance, reparations for Germany's illegal submarine campaign, the appointment of a tribunal to consider crimes of war and crimes against humanity, and, finally, the loss of the German colonies as a result of Germany's illegal aggression against Belgium. The negotiable conditions included the adjustment of claims for damages of war and the establishment of a 'League of Free Nations' to prevent future wars and improve international relations. The final clause called for the League to be designed 'to create a world in which, when the conditions of the Peace have been carried out, there shall be opportunity and security for the legitimate development of all Peoples'. 'Propaganda Peace Policy', Beaverbrook Papers, E/3/9, HLRO.
89. *Daily Mail*, 23, 25 October 1918.
90. 27 October 1918, House Papers, Series I, Box 83a, Sterling Library, Yale University.

91. 3 November 1918, Lloyd George Papers, F/41/8/26, HLRO.
92. Almost a year after Northcliffe's death, Leo Amery reported in his diary that the King had confided to him at a dinner that he had seen letters from Northcliffe to Lloyd George that confirmed that Northcliffe had suggested he be included in the War Cabinet and demanded to be made a part of the peace commission at Paris and that Lloyd George had civilly turned down the first request and had not responded at all to the second. 17 July 1923 entry in L.S. Amery, *The Leo Amery Diaries, Vol. 1: 1896–1929*, ed. John Barnes and David Nicolson (London, 1980), p. 334.
93. David Lloyd George, *Memoirs of the Peace Conference* (New Haven, 2 vols., 1939), Vol. 1, p. 176.
94. *Parliamentary Debates*, Commons, 5th Series, Vol. 110, cols. 1779–80.
95. Lloyd George, *Memoirs of the Peace Conference*, Vol. 1, p. 176. After receiving these instructions, Bonar Law drily noted, Northcliffe 'promptly came to see me at the Treasury'. Blake, *The Unknown Prime Minister*, p. 391.
96. Geddes to Geoffrey Harmsworth, 9 December, 1953, in Pound and Harmsworth, *Northcliffe*, pp. 682–3.
97. L.S. Amery, *My Political Life*, Vol. 2, p. 180. Perhaps the wily Lloyd George (who knew Carson already to be incensed at the attacks on Milner) incited Carson to attack Northcliffe by conveying his version of the demands.
98. *Parliamentary Debates*, Commons, 5th Series, Vol. 110, cols. 2350–2.
99. Marjoribanks and Colvin, *Lord Carson*, Vol. 3, p. 367.
100. *Daily Mail*, 11 November 1918.
101. Sanders and Taylor, *British Propaganda During the First World War*, p. 238.
102. Northcliffe to Prime Minister, 12 November 1918, Lloyd George Papers, F/41/8/27; Lloyd George to Northcliffe, 12 November 1918, Lloyd George Papers, F/41/8/28, HLRO. Lloyd George asked for Sir Campbell Stuart to remain at Crewe House until the end of the year, to close down the operation. John Buchan performed the same task at the Ministry of Information.
103. 13 November 1918, NADM, 62153, BL.
104. 13 November 1918, NADM, 62153, BL.

CHAPTER 16: THE ROAD TO RUIN, 1918–1919
1. *Daily Mail*, 12 November 1918.
2. 22 November 1918, NADM, 62344, f. 65, BL.
3. J. Turner, *British Politics and the Great War*, p. 318.
4. 27 November 1918, NADM, 62206, f. 193, BL.
5. 'Message From the Chief,' 28 November 1918, MS. Eng. Hist. d. 303, Bodleian Library.
6. 18 December 1918, Northcliffe Papers, HA.
7. For Dawson's view of the struggle, see Wrench, *Geoffrey Dawson*, pp. 170–91, and also *History of The Times*, Vol. 4, Pt 1, pp. 446–86.
8. 30 November 1918, NADM, 62245, f. 149, BL.
9. 1 December 1918, NADM, 622245, f. 142, BL.
10. Thomas Marlowe agreed. He reported that the Prime Minister was 'under suspicion of forgiving the Germans & forgetting the war too quickly. He is acting on the belief that Englishmen like to shake hands after a fight: so they do, but not this time. They don't regard the Hun as a clean fighter and they don't want to shake hands with him. People . . . resent the impertinence of "British Sportsmanship" being exploited by international financiers. I am glad you insist on keeping out the Huns & hope you will ram this "stunt" down the Prime Minister's throat.' Marlowe to Northcliffe, 27 November 1918, NADM, 62199, ff. 142–3, BL.

11. 30 November 1918, NADM, 62245, f. 149, BL.
12. 6 December 1918, Lloyd George Papers, F/41/86/30, HLRO.
13. 7 December 1918, Lloyd George Papers, F/41/8/31, HLRO.
14. *Daily Mail*, 12 December 1918.
15. Ibid., 9 December 1918.
16. Robert Bunselmeyer, *The Cost of the War 1914–1919* (London, 1975), p. 133.
17. 'It really does seem to me that some sort of link should be allowed to exist', argued Tracy, 'between government policy in Great Britain and the people of the United States, who are simply hungering for the right sort of information.' Tracy to Northcliffe, 22 November 1918, NADM, 62164, ff. 102–3, BL.
18. 4 December 1918, NADM, 62164, f. 104, BL.
19. 29 November 1918, NADM, 62344, ff. 103–4, BL.
20. 24 November 1918, NADM, 62344, BL.
21. 18 December 1918, NADM, 62245, BL.
22. Northcliffe to Balfour, 17 December 1918, Balfour to Northcliffe, 18 December 1918, Balfour Add. Miss., 49748, BL.
23. 20 December 1918, NADM, 62156, BL.
24. 25 December 1918, NADM, 62156, BL.
25. *Daily Mail*, 30 December 1918. Fisher, a Conservative MP and president of the Local Government Board since June 1917, had been in charge of organizing the new electoral register after the passing of the Reform Act of 1918. Lloyd George felt Fisher had mismanaged this duty. Fisher was elevated to the peerage as Lord Downham to remove him. Blake, *The Unknown Prime Minister*, pp. 381–3.
26. 31 December 1918, Northcliffe Papers, HA.
27. *Daily Mail*, 3 January 1919.
28. Arthur Mitchell, *Revolutionary Government in Ireland: Dáil Éireann, 1919–1922* (Dublin, 1995), p. 20.
29. 12 January 1918, in Pound and Harmsworth, *Northcliffe*, p. 693.
30. 19 January 1919, NADM, 62203, BL.
31. 12 January 1919, NADM, 62245, BL.
32. 25 January 1919, NADM, 62245, BL.
33. 28 January 1919, NADM, 62240, BL.
34. Steed, *Through Thirty Years*, Vol. 2, pp. 259–60.
35. For an example of this, see Steed to Northcliffe, 12 March 1919, NADM, 62246B, BL.
36. Auchinloss diary, 28 March 1919, in Inga Floto, *Colonel House in Paris, A Study of American Policy at the Paris Peace Conference 1919* (Copenhagen, 1972), p. 197, n. 249.
37. He also suggested that the owner of the *Daily Mail* should take over the ambassadorship in Washington. Steed reported that Auchinloss told him, 'Far and away the best man would be Northcliffe. Pilgrims and sinners would run off his back without hurting him & he knows our people.' Steed to Northcliffe, 15 March 1919, NADM, 62246B, BL.
38. Baker diary, 17 April 1919, in Floto, *Colonel House in Paris*, p. 198.
39. Humphrey Davy to Marlowe, 8 April 1919, NADM, 62199, BL.
40. 5 April 1919 entry in Riddell, *Diaries*, p. 265.
41. 13 April 1919, NADM, 62196, BL.
42. Pound and Harmsworth, *Northcliffe*, pp. 710–11.
43. 10 April 1918, in ibid., p. 712.
44. Stevenson, *Lloyd George: A Diary*, p. 180.
45. Howard Alcock, *Portrait of a Decision: The Council of Four and the Treaty of Versailles*

(London, 1972), p. 206. Bottomley, the owner of *John Bull*, had been elected in December to a seat in the Commons.

46. *Parliamentary Debates*, Commons, 5th Series, Vol. 114, Cols. 2951–3.
47. Alcock, *Portrait of a Decision*, p. 208.
48. 4 May 1919 entry in Riddell, *Diaries*, p. 272.
49. Esher, *Journals and Letters*, Vol. 4, p. 231.
50. Steed, *Through Thirty Years*, Vol. 2, pp. 321–2.
51. 18 April 1919, NADM, 62246B, BL.
52. 19 April 1919, Steed Papers, TA.
53. Pound and Harmsworth, *Northcliffe*, p. 741.
54. 17 July 1919, NADM, 62200, BL.
55. 2, 4, 12–15 July entries, Riddell diary, Add. Mss., 62984, BL.
56. 5 July 1921, NADM, 62247, BL.
57. 10 July 1921, NADM, 62247, BL.
58. 20 July 1921, NADM, 62247, BL.
59. 'An Irish Settlement', *The Times*, 24 July 1919.
60. 24 July 1921, NADM, 62247, BL.
61. 28 July 1919, NADM, 62348, BL.
62. Pound and Harmsworth, *Northcliffe*, p. 741.
63. *Gaelic American*, 3 August 1919.
64. 22 July entry, Riddell diary, Add. Mss., 62984, BL.
65. 3 August entry, Riddell diary, Add. Mss., 62984, BL.
66. 9 August 1919, NADM, 62247, BL.
67. 11 August 1919, NADM, 62247, BL.
68. T. Clarke, *Northcliffe in History*, p. 176.
69. Pound and Harmsworth, *Northcliffe*, p. 749.
70. 16 December 1919, NADM, 62351, BL.
71. 27 November 1919, NADM, 62350, BL.
72. 23 November 1919, Northcliffe Papers, WDM1, TA.
73. 15 December 1919, NADM, 62156, BL.
74. Quoted in Koss, *Political Press*, Vol. 2, pp. 366–7.
75. 28 December entry, Riddell diary, Add. Mss., 62984, BL.

CHAPTER 17: STRIKES AND TROUBLES, 1920–1921

1. 31 January 1920, in Pound and Harmsworth, *Northcliffe*, p. 762.
2. 10 February, 1920, NADM, 62200, BL.
3. 8 January entry, Riddell diary, Add. Mss., 62985, BL.
4. 14, 15 January entries, Riddell diary, Add. Mss., 62985, BL. Later in the same month, Stuart told Riddell that Northcliffe was unhappy with Churchill's aggressive Russian policy and revealed that if there was any dispute over intervention he would support Lloyd George. When Riddell communicated this to the Prime Minister, he recorded that Lloyd George was 'much interested and began to speculate as to the meaning and intention. He surmised that Northcliffe was anxious for a rapprochement and regarded this as the first olive branch. I doubted if so much importance could be attached to the message and suggested that Northcliffe was honestly apprehensive of Winston's policy. LG however would not accept this explanation. The wish is often father to the thought. Evidently he would welcome an arrangement. Such is politics. Your enemy of today is your friend of tomorrow.' 22 January entry, Riddell diary, Add. Mss., 62985, BL.
5. Northcliffe to Haig, 22 April 1920, Haig to Northcliffe, 22 April 1920, NADM, 62354, BL.

6. 18 July 1920, NADM, 62356, BL.
7. 4 March 1920, NADM, 62179, BL.
8. 28 May 1920 entry, in Lord Riddell, *Lord Riddell's Intimate Diary of the Peace Conference and After 1918–1923* (London, 1934), pp 197–8.
9. Pound and Harmsworth, *Northcliffe*, p. 768.
10. T. Clarke, *Northcliffe in History*, p. 182.
11. Ruth Lee diary, 3 June 1920, in Lee, '*A Good Innings*', p. 196.
12. 15 July 1920, NADM, 62356, BL.
13. 26 August 1920, NADM, 62357, BL.
14. 1 September 1920, NADM, 62357, BL.
15. 23 October 1920 entry, Riddell diary, Add. Mss., 62985, BL.
16. 11, 13 November entries, Riddell diary, Add. Mss., 62985, BL.
17. Bullock to Northcliffe, 1 September 1920, NADM, 62209, BL.
18. 25 October 1920, NADM, 62358, BL.
19. 21 November 1920, NADM, 62359, BL.
20. 2 June entry, Riddell diary, Add. Mss., 62985, BL.
21. Pound and Harmsworth, *Northcliffe*, p. 776.
22. 20 January 1921, NADM, 62361, BL.
23. Pound and Harmsworth, *Northcliffe*, p. 775.
24. 1 December 1920, in Koss, *Political Press*, Vol. 2, p. 378.
25. 5 December 1920, in Pound and Harmsworth, *Northcliffe*, p. 777.
26. Pound and Harmsworth, *Northcliffe*, p. 781.
27. Ibid., p. 779.
28. 19 December 1920, NADM, 62360, BL.
29. 18 December entry, Riddell diary, Add. Mss., 62985, BL.
30. 'Statement on Disarmament', n.d., NADM, 62360, BL.
31. AP to Northcliffe, 24 December 1920, NADM, 62360, BL.
32. 20 December 1920, in Koss, *Political Press*, Vol. 2, p. 363, n. 1.
33. 2 January 1921, NADM, 62361, BL.
34. 4 January 1921, NADM, 62361, BL. For Lee's view of this episode, see his '*A Good Innings*', pp. 203–5.
35. 13 January 1921, NADM, 62361, BL.
36. 11 January 1921, NADM, 62361, BL.
37. 17 January 1921, NADM, 62361, BL.
38. 20 January 1921, NADM, 62187, BL.
39. 20 March 1921, NADM, 62209, BL.
40. 9 February 1921, NADM, 62209, BL.
41. 18 February 1921, NADM, 62241, BL.
42. 24 February 1921, NADM, 62200, BL.
43. N.d., NADM, 62361, BL. Sykes, the former chief of the Air Staff, was Controller-General of Civil Aviation.
44. Northcliffe to Kerr, 26 March 1921, NADM, 62362, BL.
45. 22 March 1921, in Koss, *Political Press*, Vol. 2, p. 391.
46. 7 May 1921, NADM, 62364, BL.
47. 11 May 1921, NADM, 62364, BL.
48. 7 May 1921, NADM, 62173, BL.
49. Northcliffe to Greenwood, 21 April 1921; Greenwood to Northcliffe, 27 April 1921, NADM, 62363, BL.
50. 5 April 1921, NADM, 62241, BL.
51. 26 April 1921, NADM, 62363, BL.
52. 9 May 1921, NADM, 62364, BL.
53. 2 March 1921, in *History of the Times*, Vol. 4, Pt 2, p. 590.

54. 5 April 1921, in Koss, *Political Press*, Vol. 2, p. 383.
55. 24 April 1921, NADM, 62248A, BL.
56. 25 April 1921, NADM, 62248A, BL.
57. For this, see *History of the Times*, Vol. 4, Pt 2, pp. 590–8.
58. *The History of The Times* credits his mother and wife for squashing any such plan. Vol. 4, Pt 2, p. 598.
59. 28 June 1921, NADM, 62366, BL.
60. Northcliffe to Employees Committee, n.d., NADM, 62364, BL.
61. 11 May 1921, NADM, 62364, BL.
62. 19 May 1921, NADM, 62364, BL.
63. Northcliffe to Londonderry, 19 May, Londonderry to Northcliffe, 21 May 1921, NADM, 62364, BL.
64. Northcliffe to Steed, n.d., NADM, 62248A, BL.
65. N.d., NADM, 62364, BL.
66. 20 May 1921, NADM, 62364, BL.
67. 7 June 1921, NADM, 62365, BL.
68. 7 June 1921, NADM, 62365, BL; Pound and Harmsworth, *Northcliffe*, p. 798.
69. 8 June 1921, NADM, 62365, BL.
70. Rose, *King George V*, p. 239.

CHAPTER 18: WORLD WHIRL, 1921–1922

1. 5 July 1921, NADM, 62366, BL.
2. 15 July 1921, NADM, 62367, BL.
3. Pound and Harmsworth, *Northcliffe*, p. 798. He sent a similar letter to Rothermere.
4. Ibid., pp. 799–800.
5. 22 July 1921, NADM, 62169, BL.
6. 15 July 1921, NADM, 62367, BL. For Northcliffe's 'revived faith' regarding Steed, in the view of *The Times*'s historian, see *History of The Times*, Vol. 4, Pt 2, pp. 602–6.
7. 18 July 1921, in Martin Gilbert, *Winston S. Churchill*, Vol. 4 Companion, Pt 3 (London, 1977), p. 1558.
8. *The Times*, 13 July 1921.
9. 17 July entry in Riddell, *Diaries*, p. 346.
10. 18 July 1921, NADM, 62367, BL. For Lloyd George's comments in full, see *Parliamentary Debates*, Commons, 5th Series, Vol. 144, cols. 1747–9.
11. 20 July 1921, NADM, 62367, BL.
12. 21 July 1921, NADM, 62187, BL.
13. New York *Herald*, 31 July 1921.
14. *Parliamentary Debates*, Commons, 5th Series, Vol. 145, cols. 915–17.
15. *History of The Times*, Vol. 4 Pt 2, p. 611.
16. Pound and Harmsworth, *Northcliffe*, p. 803.
17. 31 July 1921, NADM, 62367, BL.
18. 5 August 1921, NADM, 62367, BL.
19. 31 July entry in Riddell, *Diaries*, p. 348.
20. 1 August 1921, NADM, 62187, BL.
21. Pound and Harmsworth, *Northcliffe*, p. 805.
22. *Daily Graphic*, 30 July 1921.
23. 3 August 1921, NADM, 62241, BL.
24. Alfred Viscount Northcliffe, *My Journey Round the World* (London, 1923), pp. 4–6. This work is a collection of Northcliffe's circular letters home, lightly edited by his brothers Cecil and St John. The complete letters are in three volumes, 62395–7, of the Northcliffe Additional Manuscripts at the British Library.
25. Pound and Harmsworth, *Northcliffe*, p. 806.

26. 10 August 1921, NADM, 62187, BL.
27. Northcliffe dispatches, 5, 14 August 1921, NADM 62395, BL.
28. Northcliffe, *My Journey*, p. 12.
29. 16 August 1921, NADM, 62187, BL.
30. 17 August 1921, NADM, 62209, BL.
31. Pound and Harmsworth, *Northcliffe*, p. 807.
32. Northcliffe, *My Journey*, p. 30.
33. Ibid, p. 37.
34. The *Herald* (Melbourne), 12 September 1921.
35. The *Herald* (Melbourne), 14 September 1921.
36. Northcliffe, *My Journey*, p. 50.
37. N.d., NADM, 62187, BL.
38. Northcliffe dispatch, 17 October 1921, NADM, 62396, BL.
39. 21 September 1921, NADM, 62368, BL.
40. 10 October 1921, NADM, 62368, BL.
41. *The Times*, 3 October 1921.
42. Northcliffe, *My Journey*, p. 56.
43. 27 October 1921, NADM, 62223, BL.
44. Northcliffe to Price, 16 October 1921, NADM, 62241, BL.
45. 24 October 1921, NADM, 62209, BL.
46. 28 October 1921, NADM, 62200, BL.
47. Northcliffe, *My Journey*, p. 89.
48. N.d., NADM, 62248B, BL.
49. Northcliffe, *My Journey*, p. 103.
50. 'A Gentleman with a Duster' (Harold Begbie), *The Mirrors of Downing Street* (London, 1921), pp. 51–7.
51. Pound and Harmsworth, *Northcliffe*, p. 813.
52. Northcliffe, *My Journey*, p. 124.
53. Pound and Harmsworth, *Northcliffe*, p. 815.
54. 16 November 1921 circular letter, NADM, 62396, BL. This revelation was excised from the published text of Northcliffe's voyage.
55. Northcliffe, *My Journey*, p. 150.
56. 12 November 1921, NADM, 62187, BL.
57. 6 November 1921, NADM, 62200, BL.
58. 10 November 1921, NADM, 62200, BL.
59. 14 November 1921, NADM, 62200, BL.
60. 30 November 1921, NADM, 62169, BL.
61. 22 November 1921, NADM, 62179, BL.
62. Murdoch to Northcliffe, 7 December, Northcliffe to Murdoch, 10 December 1921, NADM, 62179, BL.
63. Pound and Harmsworth, *Northcliffe*, p. 818.
64. 5 January 1922, NADM, 62187, BL.
65. Sutton to Northcliffe, Rothermere to Northcliffe, n.d., NADM, 62368, BL. Campbell Stuart confided in Riddell that it was Rothermere who had drawn his mother's attention to the matter. Beaverbrook was behind it all, Stuart believed, because Birkenhead had claimed to have the Northcliffe press in his pocket. 3 January 1922 entry, Riddell diary, Add. Mss., 62989, BL.
66. 6 December 1921, NADM, 62187, BL.
67. Pound and Harmsworth, *Northcliffe*, p. 819.
68. Northcliffe, *My Journey*, p. 182.
69. Pound and Harmsworth, *Northcliffe*, p. 816. Some have seen this short letter to the

widow of an old colleague as indicative of a noticeable change in Northcliffe; however, the letter seems reasonable, particularly given the irksome claims Kennedy Jones had so recently made.

70. Northcliffe, *My Journey*, p. 197.
71. Northcliffe dispatch, 20 December 1921, NADM, 62397, BL.
72. 5 January 1922, NADM, 62248B, BL.
73. 15 January 1922, NADM, 62248B, BL.
74. G.H. Bennett, *British Foreign Policy during the Curzon Period, 1919–1924* (London, 1995), p. 170; Ruddock Mackay, *Balfour: Intellectual Statesman* (Oxford, 1985), p. 333. The five powers were the USA, Britain, Japan, France and Italy, which, with no Pacific interests, was excluded from the Four Power Treaty.
75. Northcliffe, *My Journey*, p. 211.
76. Ibid., p. 240.
77. Before leaving the country, Northcliffe sent Prince Edward a note through Lord Cromer at his camp at Mysore to express his 'deep admiration of the immense services' the Prince had rendered to the Empire in his travels through Canada, Australia and India. The message went on that he had 'heard countless expressions of pleasure and loyalty at Your Royal Highness's democratic greetings of the peoples, and especially the gracious handshake which has enchained so many to his Majesty's Empire'. 20 January 1922, NADM, 62369, BL.
78. 18 January 1922, in Pound and Harmsworth, *Northcliffe*, p. 821.
79. 26 January 1922, in Hyde, *Lord Reading*, p. 367.
80. 27 January 1922, NADM, 62187, BL.
81. Northcliffe to Sutton, 21 February 1922, NADM, 62187, BL.
82. 28 January 1922, NADM, 62241, BL.
83. 11 January 1922, NADM, 62187, BL.
84. 27 January 1922, NADM, 62169, BL.
85. 28, 29 January entries, Riddell diary, Add. Mss., 62989, BL. Campbell Stuart, Riddell told Lloyd George, had already suggested an earldom, to be given in celebration of the Irish settlement, in which Northcliffe had taken a leading part.
86. Northcliffe, *My Journey*, p. 264.
87. Pound and Harmsworth, *Northcliffe*, p. 823.
88. The 'Declaration' was made in a letter from Balfour, the Foreign Secretary, to Lord Rothschild dated 2 November 1917. For this, see Leonard Stein, *The Balfour Declaration* (New York, 1961), p. 548; Ronald Sanders, *The High Walls of Jerusalem: A History of the Balfour Declaration and the Birth of the British Mandate for Palestine* (New York, 1983), p. xvii.
89. Northcliffe, *My Journey*, p. 270.
90. *The Times*, 8 February 1922.
91. Northcliffe, *My Journey*, p. 273.
92. Ibid., p. 284.

CHAPTER 19: INTO THE DARKNESS, 1922

1. Northcliffe to Steed, 18 February 1922, NADM, 62248B, BL.
2. 14 February 1922, NADM, 62248B, BL.
3. 22 February 1922, NADM, 62187, BL.
4. 21 February 1922, NADM, 62187, BL. While the foreign news situation languished, Northcliffe complained to the editor of the *Daily Mail*, stories by Valentine Williams, the head of the delinquent organization, were appearing in competing publications. 'No man can serve two masters,' he told Marlowe.
5. 25 January 1922, NADM, 62223, BL.

6. 10 February 1922, NADM, 62223, BL.
7. Pound and Harmsworth, *Northcliffe*, p. 831.
8. Pemberton, *Lord Northcliffe*, p. 247.
9. Pound and Harmsworth, *Northcliffe*, pp. 835–6.
10. *The Times*, 18 February 1922.
11. *Daily Mail*, 23 February 1922.
12. 28 February 1922, in Chaim Weizmann, *The Letters and Papers of Chaim Weizmann* (Jerusalem, 23 vols., 1974–), Vol. 11 (ed. Bernard Wasserstein), p. 61. Weizmann felt that Northcliffe had fallen under the evil influence of Colonel Vivian Gabriel, the anti-Zionist financial adviser to the British military administration in Palestine.
13. Pound and Harmsworth, *Northcliffe*, p. 846. For Weizmann's appraisal of the interview, see his memoir, *Trial and Error* (London, 1949), p. 351.
14. *The Times*, 11 April 1922.
15. 1 March 1922, NADM, 62369, BL.
16. 10 March 1922, NADM, 62242, BL.
17. Northcliffe to Stuart, 12 March 1922, NADM, 62242, BL.
18. Pound and Harmsworth, *Northcliffe*, p. 850.
19. *History of The Times*, Vol. 4, Pt 2, p. 627–8; Pound and Harmsworth, *Northcliffe*, p. 830. Pound and Harmsworth place this meeting on 3 March. The 1½d price was only for those who registered with their newsagents; others paid 2d. The lower price was extended to all on 27 March.
20. 7 March entry, Riddell diary, Add. Mss., 62989, BL.
21. *History of The Times*, Vol. 4, Pt 2, p. 629.
22. Pound and Harmsworth, *Northcliffe*, pp. 834–5.
23. 4 March 1922, NADM, 62369, BL.
24. 15 March 1922, NADM, 62221, BL. Northcliffe turned down the many requests from publishers seeking to bring out his 'little review' in book form. He had H.G. Price reply to one such query: 'My fleeting impressions of a flash round the world had best remain where they are – buried deep down in the files of Printing House Square'.
25. T. Clarke, *Northcliffe in History*, p. 158; Pemberton, *Lord Northcliffe*, p. 246.
26. Pound and Harmsworth, *Northcliffe*, pp. 840, 844.
27. Ibid., pp. 837–8. Derby denied to Stuart that he wanted to be Prime Minister, as Northcliffe believed, but revealed that he was prepared to take office as Secretary of State for India, provided the government would agree to his terms. The ambassador did not think Lloyd George would agree, but Stuart told him that 'when a ship is sinking people are not able to scrutinise too closely the composition of life savers'. Stuart to Northcliffe, 15 March 1922, NADM, 62242, BL.
28. 19 March 1922, NADM, 62169, BL.
29. Grigg to Briand, 30 March 1922, in Morgan, *Consensus and Disunity*.
30. *The Times*, 29 March 1922.
31. Stuart to Northcliffe, 21 March 1922, NADM, 62242, BL. After Bonar Law, Stuart ranked the leading Conservative candidates as Balfour, Birkenhead and Derby.
32. *History of The Times*, Vol. 4, Pt 2, p. 661.
33. Steed, *Through Thirty Years*, Vol. 2, p. 383. The editor described the conference as an 'orgy of intrigue and counter-intrigue'.
34. 24 April 1922, in Gilbert, *Churchill*, Vol. 4, Companion, Pt 3, p. 1872.
35. Pound and Harmsworth, *Northcliffe*, p. 851–2.
36. 20 May 1922 entry, Riddell diary, Add. Mss., 62989, BL.
37. 18 April 1922, NADM, 62179, BL.
38. 12 May 1922, in Pound and Harmsworth, *Northcliffe*, p. 854.

39. *History of The Times*, Vol. 4, Pt 2, p. 676.
40. Northcliffe to Price, 28 April 1922, in *Northcliffe*, Pound and Harmsworth, p. 846–7.
41 24 May 1922, NADM, 62373, BL.
42. Pound and Harmsworth, *Northcliffe*, p. 854.
43. Ibid., 860–1.
44. 2 June 1922, in ibid., p. 863.
45. 4 June 1922, NADM, 62187, BL.
46. 5 June 1922, NADM, 62187, BL.
47. 4 June 1922, in S.J. Taylor, *The Great Outsiders*, p. 216.
48. Douglas Reed, *Insanity Fair* (London, 1938), p. 59.
49. *History of The Times*, Vol. 4, Pt 2, p. 646; Pound and Harmsworth, *Northcliffe*, p. 869.
50. Pound and Harmsworth, *Northcliffe*, pp. 865–6.
51. 'Northcliffe's Last Days', statement by Steed to Willert made in Geneva, 1929, Willert Papers, Box 13 Series II, Yale University Library. Another, more detailed and lurid, record by Steed is in his papers at the Archive of *The Times*.
52. Ibid. Steed went on that this system had been in place for years and that Northcliffe insisted on having the telephone girls send him records of conversations. Among the things which caused the press lord to hate Dawson so much at the end, he added, were two intercepted conversations between Dawson and Lady Astor.
53. 13 June 1922, in Pound and Harmsworth, *Northcliffe*, p. 871.
54. S.J. Taylor, *The Great Outsiders*, p. 214.
55. *Daily Mail*, 16 June 1922.
56. 11, 17 June 1922 entries, Riddell diary, Add. Mss., 62989, BL.
57. Whether or not a Wassermann test was ever completed has been brought into question by Paul Ferris. See *The House of Northcliffe*, p. 271. S.J. Taylor has suggested that the streptococcus originated in a septic infection at the roots of Northcliffe's teeth and dismisses the tertiary-syphilis explanation for the press lord's death in a brief appendix. *The Great Outsiders*, pp. 213, 363.
58. 16 July 1922, in Martin Gilbert, *Winston S. Churchill*, Vol. 4 Companion, Pt 2 (London, 1977), p. 1932.
59. 29 July entry, Riddell diary, Add. Mss., 62989, BL.
60. 17 August 1922, NADM, 62153, BL.
61. *British Weekly*, 17 August 1922.
62. *Manchester Guardian*, 18 August 1922.
63. *Daily Express*, 15 August 1922.

Bibliographic Note

In the interest of keeping this study within a reasonable length, a concerted effort was made to limit the number of reference endnotes. In addition to contemporary newspaper accounts, government documents held at the Public Record Office, and published sources shown in the endnotes, a number of manuscript collections, public and private, were consulted for this study, some of which are not listed elsewhere. Archival sources include the papers of:

Herbert H. Asquith, Bodleian Library
Stanley Baldwin, Cambridge University Library
Arthur James Balfour, British Library and Scottish Record Office
Lord Beaverbrook, House of Lords Record Office
Charles Frederic Moberly Bell, Archive of *The Times*
George Earle Buckle, Archive of *The Times*
Lord Burnham, Imperial War Museum
Lord Robert Cecil (Lord Cecil of Chelwood), British Library
Winston S. Churchill (Chartwell Trust Papers), Churchill College, Cambridge
Lord Curzon, Oriental and India Office Collections, British Library
Geoffrey Dawson, Bodleian Library, Oxford, and Archive of *The Times*
Lord Derby, Liverpool City Library
Master of Elibank (Lord Murray), National Library of Scotland
Lord Fisher of Kilverstone, Churchill College, Cambridge
Brinsley Fitzgerald, Imperial War Museum
Lord French, Imperial War Museum
A.G. Gardiner, British Library of Economic and Political Science, London
J.L. Garvin, Harry Ransom Humanities Research Center, The University of Texas, Austin

H.A. Gwynn, Bodleian Library
Lord Haig, National Library of Scotland
Lord Haldane, National Library of Scotland
Lord Hardinge of Penshurst, Cambridge University Library
Lord Harmsworth, Harmsworth Archive
Edward M. House, Sterling Library, Yale University
Lord Jellicoe, British Library
Lord Kitchener, Public Record Office
Lord Lansdowne, British Library
Andrew Bonar Law, House of Lords Record Office
David Lloyd George, House of Lords Record Office
Walter Long, British Library
Reginald McKenna, Churchill College, Cambridge
Lord Milner, Bodleian Library
Lord Northcliffe, British Library, Archive of *The Times* and Harmsworth Archive
Lord Reading, Oriental and India Office Collections, British Library
Lord Riddell, British Library
Lord Rennell of Rodd, Bodleian Library
Charles à Court Repington, Archive of *The Times*
Field Marshal Sir William Robertson, Liddell Hart Centre for Military Archives,
　　King's College, London
Lord Rosebery, National Library of Scotland
Lord Rothermere, Harmsworth Archive
Lord Salisbury, Hatfield
J.S. Sandars, Bodleian Library
Lord Selborne, Bodleian Library
Cecil Spring-Rice, Churchill College, Cambridge
Henry Wickham Steed, Archive of *The Times*
John St Loe Strachey, House of Lords Record Office
Josiah Wedgwood, Imperial War Museum
Arthur Willert, Sterling Library, Yale University
Field Marshal Sir Henry Wilson, Imperial War Museum
William Wiseman, Sterling Library, Yale University

Index

Abercorn, James Hamilton, 2nd Duke of, 45, 52, n. 31
Acland-Hood, Sir Alexander, 126
Aehranthal, Count Lexa von, 160
Agadir crisis (1911), 205, 206, 207
Aitken, William Maxwell *see* Beaverbrook, 1st Baron
Alexandra, Queen, 189, 372
Algeciras Conference (1906), 125, 132
Allenby, General Edward Henry Hynman Allenby, 1st Viscount, 377
Amery, Leo S., 114, n. 41,116, 120; turns down editorship of *Observer*, 121; 203, 218, n. 71, 311, n. 92
Amiens Dispatches affair, 227–9
Answers (magazine), 9; first edition (2 June 1888), 10; 11; puzzle mania, 12; 'Pound A Week For Life' contest, 12–13; 14, 15, 16, 17, 26, 361, 397
Anti-Northcliffe Daily Mail, 269
Arnold-Foster, Hugh Oakley, 106
Ashley, Evelyn, 27, 29, 52, n. 31
Asquith, Herbert Henry 1st Earl of Oxford and Asquith: first meets N, 37; 47; 1900 election as Liberal Imperialist, 77–8; and Liberal League, 90; speaks against Tariff Reform, 101; 105; joins Campbell-Bannerman at Exchequer, 126; becomes PM, 147; 149; stand on Lords and Budget (1909), 163–4; 170, 173; and Jan. 1910 election, 182; 186; and death of Edward

VII, 189; 191, 195, 202; informs Balfour and Lansdowne he will create peers, 204; 207, 208; meets N during July 1914 Irish crisis, 218; 218, n. 71, 219; appoints Kitchener War Secretary, 224; 228, 234; and rumours that Lloyd George intends to topple government, 236; 238, 239, 241; May 1915 coalition, 242; 245, 246, 247, 248; criticizes N press, 249; gives in to conscription (Jan. 1916), 250; 252, 253, 254, 256, 259; Lloyd George pressures to accept small War Committee, 260; refuses and fails to reorganize cabinet, 261, 262, 263; admits role of *Times* in Dec. 1916, 264; 276, 301, 307, 315, 319, 348
Asquith, Margot, Countess of Oxford and Asquith: shares political gossip with N, 47; 236, n. 62, 338
Associated Newspapers Limited, 119
Astor, John Jacob, 1st Baron, 397
Astor, Waldorf, 199
atrocities, charges of German, 231–3
Auchinloss, Gordon, 323

Baden-Powell, Major Baden Fletcher Smyth, 154
Baden-Powell, Robert (*later* 1st Baron), 66, 67; *Daily Mail* helps make create Mafeking myth, 73
Baker, Sir John, 29
Baker, Ray Stannard, 323

Index

Baldwin, Stanley (*later* 1st Earl), 348
Balfour, Arthur James (*later* 1st Earl):
congratulates N on *Daily Mail*, 34; 36, 53, 63, 64, 65; reassures N on South African settlement, 67–8; 70; and 1900 election, 78; defends in 'breach of privilege' debate, 88; becomes PM, 93; 99, 100, 102; proposes retaliatory tariffs, 105, 105, n. 19, 106, 107; delays possible election (1903), 112; 113, 114; turns down J. Chamberlain's colonial conference scheme, 115; 116; moderation over 'Dogger Bank Incident', 117; 121, 122; resigns as PM (1905), 125; 126; congratulates N on peerage, 127; 128, 129, 130; appraisal of 1906 election, 131–2; 133, 143, 147; N complains to about *Manchester Courier*, 148; 152; at Pau for Wright demonstration, 161; 163; condemns 1909 Budget, 164; 166, 173, 176, 181, and Jan. 1910 election, 182, 184, 185; rejects Lloyd George 1910 coalition plan, 193; 194; declares for Tariff Reform referendum, 195; N compliments on 'magnificent lead' in 1910, 196; 201, 202, 204; steps down as party leader (1911), 206; 242; to Admiralty (1915), 260; N papers call for exclusion from 1916 government, 262; mission to USA, 272; tries to block N as successor in USA, 274; 276, 277, 279, 281; caution in stating war aims, 299; 304, 305, 313, 318, 365; and Washington Conference, 373, 374, 380
Balfour, Lady Betty, 202
Balfour Declaration (1917), 377
Balfour, Gerald, 88
Barnes, George, 315
Barrow, Gen. Sir Edmund, 122–4
Beattie, Charles, 320
Beaumont, Alexander Spink, 10
Beaverbrook, William Maxwell Aitken, 1st Baron: *Daily Mail* praises as 'new type' MP (Dec.1910), 195; discusses politics with N, 197–8; 199, 258, n. 70, 259, 260, n. 75, 263, 275, n. 39; heads Ministry of Information, 296–7; 298, 301, 302, 343, 395, 398
Beefsteak Club, 73
Beeton, Mayson, 35, 135, 214–15
Beit, Alfred, 129
Bell, Charles Frederick Moberly, 52, 129; sabotages Pearson bid for *Times* (1908),

141–3; meets N to discuss sale, 144; considers how to keep N 'in order', 145; 146, 147, 150, 151, 169; N criticism of, 177; with N in America, 178–9; 186, 197, 199; death, 200
Bell, Edward Price, 331, 332
Bell, Sir Francis, 362
Bennet, E. Layton, 146
Bernstorff, John Heinrich, Count, 205, 206
Berry, William (*later* 1st Viscount Camrose), 343, 397
Bicycling News, 9, 360
Birkenhead, 1st Earl of *see* Smith, F.E.
Black, Sir Frederick, 288, n. 99
Bland, John, 146
Blatchford, Robert: *Daily Mail* series on German threat (Dec. 1909), 183–4; reprises series (Nov. 1910), 194
Blériot, Louis, 172
Bloemfontein Conference (1899), 63
Blumenfeld, Ralph D., 80, 129, n. 20
Borden, Sir Robert, 271
Botha, Gen. Louis, 78
Bottomley, Horatio, 325, 325, n. 45
Boxer Rebellion (1900), 75, 76
Boyle, John, 22
Boy's Friend (magazine), 18
Braddon, Edward, 44
Brade, Sir Reginald, 269
Briand, Aristide, 252
Brisbane, Arthur, 81, 134; N comments on Admiral Fisher to, 230
British Automobile Club, 73
British Weekly, 251, 353
Brittain, Harry: at Imperial Press Conference, 168, 171–2; and Empire Press Union, 172; 203
Brodrick, William St John (*later* 1st Viscount Midleton), 28; to War Office, 79–80; controversy with N over War Office press leaks, 86–8; 88, n. 16, 92, 98, to India Office, 106; supports Kitchener against Curzon in India, 123–4
Brooklyn Daily Eagle, 278
Brumwell, George, 393
Bryce, James, Viscount, 232
Buchan, John (*later* 1st Baron Tweedsmuir): head of Department of Information, 267–8; 286, n. 88, 313, n. 102
Buckle, George Earle, 110, 121; works against sale of *Times* to Pearson, 141, 143; 144, 145, 146, 150, 151, 151, n. 36, 152,

447

Index

Churchill, Winston S. (*cont.*)
against food taxes, 102; 102, n. 11, 104;
criticizes N for supporting Balfour and
retaliation, 105; joins Liberal party, 114;
115; criticism of N, 118–19; 130, 131; to
Board of Trade under Asquith, 147; anger
at *Manchester Courier* articles, 148–9; 162,
162, n. 8, 163; at Imperial Press
Conference, 170; 177, 182; and Agadir
Crisis, 206; First Lord of Admiralty,
206–7; suggests N take submarine cruise,
211; 214, 216, 217, 224, 224, n. 5; and
Amiens dispatches, 228–9; 229, n. 29;
Antwerp failure, 230; 231; proposes
Dardanelles campaign, 235; 236; leaves
Admiralty, 242; 243; comments on N
1915 influence, 244–5; 254, 258, 263, 275,
n. 39, 286, 320; N supports
demobilization scheme of, 321; 332, 336,
n. 4, 347, 356, 369, 376, 387, 388, 396
Civil Aerial Transport Committee, 270, 275
Clarke, Sir George, 106, n. 21
Clemenceau, Georges, 55, 304, 322, 323
Clough, Walter, 29
Cody, Samuel Franklin: first aeroplane flight
in England (16 Oct. 1908), 155
Coffin, Howard, 272
Colonial Institute, 381
Comic Cuts (magazine), 14, 387
Committee of Imperial Defence (CID), 96;
dismisses invasion possibilities, 122; 147
Connaught, William Patrick Albert, Duke
of, 189, 213
Conscription campaign (1915–16), 245, 246,
248, 250, 252, 253
Continental Daily Mail, 121; Paris office
evacuated (Sept. 1914), 229; 312, 322,
341, 382
Cook, (Sir) Edwin Tyas, 52, n. 31
Cook, Sir Joseph, 363
Corbett, Howard, 215
Coupon Election (1918), 314, 315, 319
Cowans, Sir John, 349
Cowdray, Weetman Dickinson Pearson, 1st
Viscount: persuades N to head Civil
Aerial Transport Committee, 270; 292,
n. 7
Crewe, Robert Offley Ashburton Crewe-
Milnes, 1st Marquess of: at Imperial Press
Conference, 169; at 1910 Constitutional
Conference, 191; 248, 260, 298
Cromer, Evelyn Baring, 1st Earl of : N

meets in Cairo, 49; 50; at Imperial Press
Conference, 170; 208, 373, 377
Curnock, George, 202, 304
Curragh Incident (1914), 216
Current Opinion, 285
Curzon of Kedleston, George Nathaniel
Curzon, Marquess: invites N for weekend
at The Priory, 47; appointed Viceroy of
India, 53; comments to N from India, 95;
116; Kitchener controversy, 122–4; 143,
170; N remarks to on Dec. 1910 election,
196; 203–4, 208, 209; head of Air Board,
251; in War Cabinet, 262; 273, 298; N
press says not qualified to attend
Washington Conference, 357–8; 359, 360
Cyclist (magazine), 7, 16

Dáil Éireann, 319, 330
Daily Chronicle, 115, 145, 262, 308
Daily Express, 106, 141, 358
Daily Herald, 387
Daily Mail: founding of, 33–5; 36, 37, 38, 39;
supports Rhodes in Jameson Raid
investigation, 41–2; 43, 44; E.E. William's
'Made in Germany' campaign, 45; 48–9;
supports USA in Spanish-American War,
51; 53; Omdurman campaign, 54;
Fashoda Crisis, 55–7; 59–60; supports
'Uitlanders' and Rhodes, 62; backs Milner
after Bloemfontein Conference, 63; 64;
reaction to Boer ultimatum, 65; 66;
Mafeking dispatches, 67; praises Roberts
and Kitchener, 68; rails against obsolete
guns sent to Cape, 69; 'Oldest
Government on Record' campaign, 70;
calls for 'A Man' to lead country, 71; fears
'Peace with Dishonour', 72; French
invasion scare, 73; relief of Mafeking, 74;
Boxer Rebellion blunder, 75–6; supports
Liberal Imperialists and Joseph
Chamberlain in 1900 election, 77–8; 79,
accused of bribing War Office clerks, 86;
'Challenge to Mr Brodrick', 87; 88, 89;
praises Rosebery's Chesterfield speech,
90; 91, 92; disappointed at 1902 Imperial
Conference, 94; Edward VII coronation,
95; 96, 98, 99; reaction to J. Chamberlain
call for Tariff Reform,100; publishes
Tariff Reform poll, 102; supports
Balfour's retaliation stand, 105; fiscal
'ABCs' series, 106; N declares own Tariff
Reform policy in, 108; hails

449

Index

Derby, Edward George Villiers Stanley,
  17th Earl of, 88; joins Balfour
  government, 106; 183; recruiting
  campaign, 248–50; attempts to co-
  ordinate air forces, 251; 255, 257; to War
  Office, 268; 296, 297, 302, 340, 343, 386,
  387, 387, n. 27, n. 31
Desborough, William Henry Grenfell, 1st
  Baron, 202, 346
De Valera, Éamon, 374
Devlin, Joseph, 329
Devonport, 251; N aid in entering 1916
  government, 262; 266, 273
Devonshire, Victor Christian William
  Cavendish, 9th Duke of: opposes J.
  Chamberlain's Tariff Reform plan, 99;
  102, n. 11, 105; leaves Balfour
  government, 106; 396
Dewar, G.A.B., 35
Dilke, Sir Charles, 36, 52, 170
Dillon, John: charges that *Daily Mail*
  brought down government (May 1915),
  243; 309, 311
Dilnot, Frank, 176
Disraeli, Benjamin, xii, 25
Dogger Bank Incident (1904), 117
Donald, Robert, 267, n. 5
Doyle, (Sir) Arthur Conan, 16
Dreadnought, HMS, 117, 134
Dreyfus Affair, 55–6

'Easter Rising' (1916), 253
Edinburgh, Prince Alfred, Duke of, 45
Edison, Thomas Alva: N visits, 83; 286, 286,
  n. 93
Edward VII, King, 41; N presented to, 45;
  62, 89, 92; coronation, 95; 98;
  recommends N for baronetcy, 112–13;
  115, 117, n. 51; suggests peerage for N to
  Balfour, 126; 128, 134, 151, 156, 170, 173;
  death, 188; 190, 191, 372
Edward, Prince of Wales (*later* King Edward
  VIII and Duke of Windsor) 332, 366,
  388, 373, 374, 375, 375, n. 77
Elgin, Victor Alexander Bruce, 9th Earl of,
  92, 126
Ellen Terry waltz, 8
Ellerman, Sir John, 343
Elmwood, 15, 32, 33, 52
Empire Press Union, 172, 363
English-Speaking Union, 381
Esher, Reginald Baliol Brett, 2nd Viscount,

85, appraisal of N, 89; 106; discusses
  acquisition of *Times* with N, 151–2; 170,
  326
Evans, W. J., 382, 383, 389
Evening News: purchased by N, 22–5; 24–5;
  attack on Liberals in 1895 election, 30;
  supports Rhodes and Jameson after Raid,
  31–2; mirrors N's hostility to 'stomach
  taxes', 101; 112; Soap Trust campaign,
  137; 241; and fall of Asquith, 260–2, 305,
  309, 330, 370, 382, 396
Evening Standard, 309, 358
Everybody's Magazine, 267

Farman, Henri, 154
Fashoda Incident (1898), 53–7
Ferrier, David, 72
Figaro, Le, 72
Fish, Walter G., 193, 222
Fisher, Adm. Sir John (*later* 1st Baron), 97,
  106, n. 21; policies as First Sea Lord,
  117–18; 117, n. 51; recommends Garvin
  as editor for *Times*; 152–3, 162, 163;
  arranges naval review for Imperial Press
  Conference, 170; made baron, 180;
  recalled to Admiralty as First Sea Lord
  (1914), 230; resigns, 240; 336
Fisher, William Hayes (*later* Baron
  Downham), 319, 319, n. 25
Fitzgerald, Brinsley, 237, n. 65
Foch, Marshal Ferdinand, 306
Ford, Henry: N appeases, 286
Forget-Me-Not (magazine), 15
Foulger, Frederick, 356
Fowler, Sir Henry, 37
Fowler, Herbert, 339
Franz Ferdinand, Archduke of Austria:
  assassinated, 217
Fraser, Lovat, 230, 237, 295, 307, 335, 346
French, F.M. Sir John (*later* 1st Viscount):
  and Boer War, 69–70; 206; leads BEF,
  225; 226; N offers intelligence to, 229; N
  suggests aerial propaganda scheme, 230;
  and Shells Scandal, 235, 236, 237, 237, n.
  65, 238, 239, 240, 248; 250, 320
Fyfe, Henry Hamilton: made editor of *Daily
  Mirror*, 110, 175, 188, 212; dispatched to
  war front for *Daily Mail*, 222; 227, 229,
  288, 300, 315

Galsworthy, John, 164
Galthrop, Guy, 251

Index

452

Index

Harmsworth, Alfred (N's father), 2–4; death, 12
Harmsworth, Cecil Bisshopp (*later* Lord Harmsworth), 4, 13, 25, 52, n. 31; and 1900 election, 77–9; present when N first meets Lloyd George, 174; 189, 216, 254, 260, 261, 302, 320, 321, 330, 331, 335, 348, 360, n. 24, 396
Harmsworth, Charles, 2
Harmsworth, Charles Harmondsworth, 5
Harmsworth, Christabel Rose, 5
Harmsworth, Esmond (*later* 2nd Viscount Rothermere), 306, 324
Harmsworth, Geoffrey, xi
Harmsworth, Geraldine Adelaide Hamilton (N's sister), 3, 13, 213
Harmsworth, Geraldine Mary (Northcliffe's mother), 3–4, 56, 60, 135; refuses to visit Mt Vernon, 157; 188; gets promise from N on flying, 202; 215, 218, N reports to from USA, 279; 286, 351, 359, 361, 362; lectures N on Irish policy of papers, 370–1; 381, 386, 394, 392, 396, 397
Harmsworth, Harold Sydney (*later* 1st Viscount Rothermere), 3–4; joins publishing business, 12; 18, 24, 52, n. 31; 60, 62; scouts Newfoundland, 94; 135, 214, n. 56; made baron, 215; and 1914 Irish crisis, 218; 270, 288; appointed Air Minister, 293; 293, n. 8, 298; proposes 'old gang' coalition, 307; 319, 320, 322, 324, 325, 346, 350, 352, 359, 364, 368, 371, 380, 385, 386, 396, 397, 398
Harmsworth, Harry Stanley Giffard, 5
Harmsworth, Hildebrand Aubrey, 4; joins publishing business, 13; 15; and 1900 election, 77–9
Harmsworth, Robert Leicester, 4, 13, 15, 52; and 1900 election, 78–9; 394
Harmsworth, Vere (*later* 3rd Viscount Rothermere), 259
Harmsworth, Violet Grace, 4
Harmsworth, Vyvyan (N's nephew), 212, 213
Harmsworth, Vyvyan George, 5, 15, 396
Harmsworth, William Albert St John, 5, 15; made a director of businesses, 58; auto accident, 135; 355, 360, n. 4
Harmsworth Magazine, 58
Harper, Harry, 135–6,
Harrison, Austin, 121
Harvey, George, 73, 278–9, 348–9

Hay, Col. John, 50–1, 52, n. 31
Hearst, William Randolph, 51; describes N, 81; 82, 278, n. 52; papers accuse N of leaving army of propagandists in USA, 339; 373
Henderson, Sir Alexander, 141
Henderson, Arthur, 248, 262, 314
Henderson, Gen. Sir David, 250
Henley House School Magazine, 6
Herald (Melbourne), 363, 370
Herald (New York), 341, 344
Herald (Washington), 373
Herrick, Myron, 286
Hicks-Beach, Sir Michael: *Daily Mail* attacks during Boer War, 68, 69; 93
Higginbottom, Frederick, 270
Hindenburg, F.M. Paul von, 306, 307
Hobhouse, Emily, 86
Hobhouse, Henry, 104
Hooper, Horace Everett, 140, 142
Hoover, Herbert, 283
Horder, Sir Thomas, 1, 395, 396
Horne, Sir Robert, 338, 346, 348, 352, 353
House, Col. Edward M., 257, 265; against N leading British mission to USA, 277; efforts to keep N 'straight', 278; 281, 282; comes to respect N, 283; 284, 285; works with N to spur on Lloyd George, 291–3; 308; N gives propaganda peace policy, 310; 318, 322, 323, 331, 393
Howard, Keble, 215
Howard, Roy, 257; applauds N appointment to 1917 USA mission, 277–8; 284
Hozier, Clementine (Mrs Winston Churchill), 148
Hudson, Sir Robert, 328, 345, 356, 361, 376, 387, 392, 394, 395, 397
Hughes, Charles Evans, 346, 360
Hughes, William M. 327
Hulton, Sir Edward, 343
Hutier, Gen. Oskar von, 306

Iliffe, William, 9, n. 16, 17, 22, n. 1
Illustrated London News, 7
Imperial Conferences, 43–5 (1897), 93–4 (1902), 203 (1911)
Imperial Press Conference (1909), 168–71, 176
Inchcape, James Lyle Mackay, 1st Viscount (*later* 1st Earl), 355, 361, 385
Ingram, William, 7, 9

453

Index

Index

Paderewski, Ignace, 44

Page, Walter Hines, 83, 213, 214, 265, 276

Pall Mall Gazette, 23, 209

Pankhurst, Emmeline, 131, 217

Parker, Sir Gilbert, 79, 267

Parliament Bill (1911), 203–5

Paulhan, Louis, 188

Pearson, Sir Cyril Arthur, 17, 112; takes *Standard* over N bid, 116, 118; resigns as Chairman of Tariff Reform League,119; believes he has *Times*, 141; 142, 143, 144, 145, 179, 270; death, 371

Pearson's Weekly, 17

Peel, William Robert Wellesley Peel, 1st Earl of, 251

'Pekin Massacre' (1900), 75–6

Pelican (weekly), 115

Pemberton, Max: describes young N, 6; 7, 10–11, 382, 386

'People's Budget' (1909), 163, 164, 166, 172, 173, 174, 175, 176, 178, 180, 181, 182, 186, 188

Pershing, Gen. John J., 274

Pétain, Gen. Philippe, 252

Poincaré, Raymond, 1, 219, 222, 394

Polk, Frank, 280

Popular Wireless (magazine), 391

Post (Washington), 373

Press (Cleveland), 286

Price, George Ward, 217; to front for *Daily Mail*, 222; 225

Price, H.G., 383, 384, 385, 386, 388, 390, 393

Price, Dr Seymour, 191, 386, 394

Primrose League, 26, 27

Prioleau, John, 217; accompanies N on world tour, 356; 372, 385

Pryor, S.J., 70

Pulitzer, Joseph, 51, 81–2, 165

Pulitzer, Ralph, 333

Punch (magazine), 151, 356

Quarterly Review, 153

Ralph, Julian, 65, 67

Rayleigh, John William Strutt, 3rd Baron, 167

Reading, Stella, Marchioness of, 374, 375

Reading, Rufus Isaacs, 1st Marquess of, 138; thanks N for support in Marconi scandal, 214; N calls for Reading to be financial representative to USA, 282; 284, 288, 289,

292, 293, 295, 318, 331, 333, 346, 374; N supports as Viceroy of India, 375; 384, 387

Redmond, John, 126; *Daily Mail* dubs 'Dollar Dictator', 185; 186, 193,194

Reed, Douglas, 392

Repington, Charles à Court, 147, n. 24, 153, n. 45, 188, 225; Shells Scandal, 240; 254, 257, 258, 268, 274, 291; resigns from *Times*, 295

Reynold's Illustrated News, 174

Rhodes, Cecil: first meets N, 26; 31–3, 41–2, 42, n. 3, 49, 52; rallies support for South Africa policy, 61–2; 66, 73; discusses South Africa with N, 86; death, 90; 145; Wrench credits for Overseas Club idea, 210

Riddell, George, 1st Baron, 231; urges Kitchener to allow correspondents at front, 237; 251, 259, 270, 293, 307, 308, 323, 326, 327, 330, 334, 335, 336, 337, 338, 339, 343, 348, 357, 359, 376, 377, 385, 388, 390, 395, 396

Ripon, Henrietta Anne Theodosia, Marchioness of, 274

Ritchie, Charles Thomas Ritchie, 1st Baron, 93; supports Free Trade; 95, 99; resigns Exchequer (1903), 105

Roberts, Field Marshal Frederick Sleigh Roberts, 1st Earl, 26; and Boer War, 68, 69, 71, 72, 78; 86, 92; calls for national training, 126; and National Service League, 133–4; 134, n. 35, 159, 184, 204, 213, 216

Robertson, Gen. Sir William, 247; made CIGS, 248; calls for manpower (1916), 252; tries to convince Haig to use press, 254; complains to N about Lloyd George interference, 257–8; 268; against Nivelle offensive, 269; 291; N turns on after Cambrai, 294; 295, 296; replaced as CIGS (Feb. 1918), 297; 301

Robinson, Geoffrey, *see* Dawson Geoffrey

Rodd, James Rennell (*later* 1st Baron), 49

Rolls, Harry, 60

Roosevelt, Theodore, 85, 137; gives lunch to N at White House (1908), 157–8; 189; at Sutton Place (1910), 190; 212; sees N in USA (1917), 283

Rosebery, Archibald Primrose, 5th Earl of: and Liberal Imperialism, 25; grants N interview at Dalmeny, 37; 52; begins

Index

Steevens, G.W.: begins to write for *Daily Mail*, 36; 45, 49, 50–1; and Boer War, 65, 67; death, 70

Sterling, Gen. John Barton, 143, 146

Stevenson, Frances (*later* Countess Lloyd George), 250, n. 25, 251, n. 32

Steyn, Marthinus, 75

Strachey, John St Loe, 74, 84; supports Unionist Free Traders, 100–1; 145, 152, 190; fears N aims to be PM, 295

Straight, Sir Douglas, 52, n. 31

Stuart, Sir Campbell, 282, 293, n. 10; Vice-Chairman of War Mission, 302; 303, 305, 311, 313, n. 102; at Paris Peace Conference, 322; 327, 330, 335, 337, 339, 341, 342, 347, 350, 351, 355, 357, 360, 371, 375, 381, 384, 385, 386, 387, 390, 392

Sun, The, 23

Sun, The (New York), 83; N interview forecasts long war (Dec. 1914), 232; 278

Sunday Pictorial: calls for N to take National Service Department (1917), 270

Sutton, George: joins *Answers*, 13; 18; made a director of businesses, 58; 84; and acquisition of *Times*, 141, 142, 144; 161, 187, 188, 193, 199, 207, 214, 277, n. 46, 331, 346, 355, 358, 359, 361, 363, 364, 369, 371, 375, 376, 381, 390, 391, 392, 393, 395

Sutton Place (house), Surrey, 77, 86

Swaffer, Hannen, xi

Swinton, Sir Ernest: official 'Eyewitness' (1914–15), 228

Swope, Herbert, 351

Sylvan Debating Club, 4, 27

Taft, William Howard, 212

Talbot, Lord Edmund, 349

Tardieu, André, 282

Tariff Reform League, 104, 112, 118–19, 176

Tatler, 87

Tennant, Sir Edward, 143

Terry, Ellen, 38

Thomas, Sir William Beach, 381

Thomson, Sandy, 46, 386, 391

Times, The, 52, 65, 69, 80, 82, 83, 91, 110, 114, 116, 120–1, 139, 140; *Sibley v. Walter*, 141; N acquires, 142–3; brings up to date, 144–5; 146, 147, 148, 149, 150, 151, 152, 153, 158, 162, 166; notes change in

opinion on 1909 Budget, 175; 177, 178, 179, 180, 181; criticizes Asquith's 'orgy of promises' in Jan. 1910, 182; correctly predicts Jan. 1910 election result, 185; 186, 187, 188, 189; supports Garvin's call for 'Truce of God', 191; supports federal solution to 1910 constitutional crisis, 193; 196, 199, 200, 206, 208, 210; fears spread of Balkan War (1912), 212, 215, 216; reveals King's role in Irish negotiations (July 1914), 219; calls for Kitchener at War Office, 224; Amiens Dispatches affair, 227–8; 234, 237, 239; Repington Shells Scandal article (May 1915), 240; 241, 244, 245, 246, 247, 249; and Asquith Cabinet reorganization (4 Dec. 1916), 260–1; 264, 271, 272, 276, 280, 284, 291, 292, 293; calls for Cambrai investigation (1917), 294; 295, 299, 304, 305, 307, 310, 311, 316, 318, 319, 320, 321, 322, 326; publishes Irish plan (24 July 1919), 328–9, 330, 332, 334, 338, 340, 341, 342, 343, 346, 347, 348, 349; N threatens to sell, 350–1; 354, 355, 357, 358, 366, 367, 368, 369, 370, 371, 373, 375, 376, 381, 383, 384, 385, 386, 387, 388, 390, 391, 392, 393, 395, 397

Tirpitz, Admiral Alfred von, 72, 159

Tit-Bits (magazine), 8, 9,11, 14, 58

Tracy, Louis, 22, 23, 317

Treves, Sir Frederick, 392, 394

Twain, Mark: N attends New York reading by, 83; 179, n. 64

Tweedmouth, Edward Marjoribanks, 2nd Baron, 147

Tyrrell, William, 150, 157, 331, 332

Ulster Covenant (1912), 210, 216

Union Jack (journal), 18

Vanderbilt, W.K., 76

Vanity Fair (magazine), 27

Verdun, Battle of (1916), 252

Vereeniging, Treaty of (1902), 92

Versailles, Treaty of (1919), 327, 344

Victoria, Queen, xii; Diamond Jubilee, 42–3; death, 83–4

Viviani, René, 219

Von Donop, Sir Stanley, 235, n. 56

Wakefield, Russell, 201

Wallace, Edgar, 65, 133